Public Works History in the United States

A Guide to the Literature

By the

Public Works Historical Society

Compiled and Edited by

Suellen M. Hoy

and

Michael C. Robinson

Rita C. Lynch

Research Associate

The American Association for State and Local History

Nashville, Tennessee

Publication of this book was made possible in part by funds from the National Endowment for the Humanities. The book is a co-operative project of the Public Works Historical Society and the American Association for State and Local History.

Library of Congress Cataloguing-in-Publication Data

Hoy, Suellen M.
Public works history in the United States.

"A co-operative project of the Public Works Historical Society and the American Association for State and Local History"—T.p. verso.
Includes index.
1. United States—Public works—History—Bibliography. I. Robinson, Michael C. II. American Association for State and Local History. III. Public Works Historical Society. IV. Title.
Z7164.P97H68 [HD3885] 016.363'0973 81-19114
ISBN 0-910050-63-5 AACR2

Public Works History in the United States

Contents

Preface

THE preparation of a bibliography is a large and, at times, overwhelming task. Although public works history has been recognized only recently as a field of historical inquiry, its dimensions are broad and deep. In this project, as in others of a similar nature, finite amounts of time and funds necessitated limitations on the kinds of material included, the extent of bibliographical searches, and the degree of annotation. Nevertheless, this publication should serve as an effective instrument in building bridges between scholars, educators, public officials, and private citizens who are concerned about the environmental implications related to the development and management (planning, design, construction, maintenance, and operation) of public works systems.

For the purpose of this bibliography, public works history is broadly defined to include the basic infrastructure upon which modern civilization rests. In general, these subordinate parts and installations are the physical structures and facilities developed or acquired by public agencies to house governmental activities and provide water, waste disposal, power, and transportation services. This study restricts its scope to systems and structures located in the United States.

The principal criterion for listing and annotating a work (except for those the compilers were not able to obtain) in this bibliography is that it is written as history—that it treats a subject that took place in the past. Therefore, the bibliography does not include the published materials that researchers use as primary sources. Nor does the bibliography generally contain the technical literature of the public works/engineering profession, contemporary reports of public works industries, polemical writings on the environmental movement, or "hardware" histories of technology. There are, however, exceptions. A good deal of the literature on public works subjects begins with a historical review or draws upon historical examples. In instances where little research has been conducted by historians, this material was particularly welcome. Some works, such as Rudolph Hering's 1882 report to the National Board of Health on sewage works, are classics and should be included in a bibliography of this kind.

In an attempt to enhance the usefulness of this compilation, it is organized topically into fourteen chapters—planning, engineering, and administration; irrigation; waterways; flood control and drainage; sewers and wastewater treatment; community water supply; solid wastes; roads, streets, and highways; urban mass transportation; airways and airports; public buildings; parks and recreation; energy; and military installations—and alphabetically by author within each chapter. Brief introductions, outlining the range of the material that follows, precede each chapter. Due to the multifaceted and interrelated nature of public works history, some entries appear with full citations in one chapter and are then cross-referenced to other appropriate chapters. Despite an original intent to list only published works, we have included numerous doctoral dissertations and some masters' theses. Because of the unexpected costs and restraints involved in acquiring these studies, however, many remain unannotated. *Dissertation Abstracts International* and Warren F. Kuehl's *Dissertations in History* often provided essential information. Other standard historical and engineering bibliographies were also consulted in the preparation of this guide, most of which are cited in individual chapters.

This bibliography contains books and articles released in late 1980. However, given the time lag between publication and bibliographical listing in standard sources or acquisition by libraries, references to some books and articles published in that year may not appear. The compilers will continue to list or arrange for the review of published works in the quarterly newsletter of the Public Works Historical Society. Since it is not unlikely that a supplement may be prepared at a future date, users are encouraged to inform the staff of the Public Works Historical Society of omissions as well as newly published books and articles and recently completed dissertations and theses.

A grant from the National Endowment for the Humanities (RT-0031-79-1053) and financial assistance from the American Public Works Association (APWA) made this reference work possible.

Special mention is due the directors of APWA and the trustees of the Public Works Historical Society who recognized the significance of the project and who supported it even as it grew.

Robert D. Bugher, APWA's executive director since 1958, deserves our sincerest gratitude for his valuable advice at various stages of the project and his unqualified trust in the compilers.

Rita C. Lynch, a graduate of the Public Historical Studies Program at the University of California at Santa Barbara, exhibited extraordinary discipline and dedication in carrying out assignments that demanded an unusual degree of persistence and precision.

Noel M. Spain, who typed the manuscript, brought to the project a unique ability to type fast and accurately as well as an enthusiasm and joie de vivre that remains unmatched.

This bibliography would remain undone if it had not been for the daily assistance provided by the Charles E. Merriam Center for Public Administration Library (MCL), located in the building housing the society's headquarters. The effort expended by Patricia Coatsworth, head librarian; Sue Lannin and Claudia Michniewicz, assistant librarians; and Betsy Kadanoff and Joyce Maxberry, principal pages, extended far beyond what was initially planned. During the seventeen months from July 1979 through November 1980, they ably handled nearly six thousand requests for material and devoted approximately seventeen hundred hours of MCL staff time to the project. At various times, they received aid from Johnnie Bond, an APWA staff assistant, and other MCL employees Liz Lathrop, Dierdre Fennessy, Vince Webster, and Mike Wilson.

We also appreciate the special services provided by individuals at the University of Chicago libraries, the John Crerar Library, the Center for Research Libraries, and the Library of Congress.

Our fear of omitting a major work has been lessened because numerous historians graciously responded to our requests for specific information or consented to review draft chapters as they were prepared. We thank each and every one: Carl Abbott, Portland State University; Leonard J. Arrington, Brigham Young University; Joseph Barnes, City of Rochester; Gail Casterline, Chicago Historical Society; Jean Christie, Fairleigh Dickinson University; Carl W. Condit, Northwestern University; Jeffrey J. Crow, North Carolina Division of Archives and History; Joan Draper, University of Illinois at Chicago Circle; Frederick J. Dobney, Loyola University; Gordon Dodds, Portland State University; Robert G. Dunbar, Montana State University; Ronald J. Fahl, Forest History Society; Dale E. Floyd, Army Corps of Engineers; Mark S. Foster, University of Colorado; Paul D. Friedman, Science Applications, Inc.; Stuart Galishoff, Georgia State University; John Greenwood, Army Corps of Engineers; Martin Greif, Main Street Press; H. Duane Hampton, University of Montana; Daniel Hurley, Cincinnati Historical Society; Barbara S. Irwin, New Jersey Historical Society; Leland R. Johnson, Army Corps of Engineers; Nancy T. Koupal, South Dakota Historical Society; Nick A. Komons, Federal Aviation Administration; Lawrence B. Lee, San Jose State University; Antoinette J. Lee, National Trust for Historic Preservation; Mary Ellen McElligott, Illinois State Historical Society; Martin V. Melosi, Texas A & M University; Raymond H. Merritt, University of Wisconsin at Milwaukee; Jon A. Peterson, Queens College; Douglas I. Pirus, American Aviation Historical Society; Francis Paul Prucha, Marquette University; William M.E. Rachal, Virginia Historical Society; John B. Rae, Harvey Mudd College; Larry Remele, State Historical Society of North Dakota; John W. Reps, Cornell University; Martin Reuss, Army Corps of Engineers; Mark Rose, Michigan Technological University; Alfred Runte, University of Washington; Alan M. Schroder, State Historical Society of Iowa; Frank N. Schubert, Army Corps of Engineers; Joel A. Tarr, Carnegie-Mellon University; William F. Trimble, Historical Society of Western Pennsylvania; Marilyn Weigold, Pace University; and John H. White, Jr., Smithsonian Institution. For any omissions or errors in this bibliography, however, the compilers alone accept responsibility.

The Public Works Historical Society, established in 1975 and located on the University of Chicago campus, is committed to preserving the heritage of the public works/engineering profession and demonstrating to local, community, and urban historians the importance of public works in their research, teaching, archival collections, preservation work, and museum exhibitions. With the completion of this bibliography, we believe we have advanced one step further—especially since publication of the *History of Public Works in the United States* in 1976—in achieving our goal.

SUELLEN M. HOY and MICHAEL C. ROBINSON

Public Works History in the United States

1

Planning, Engineering, and Administration

For more than two hundred years, public works have provided the physical infrastructure essential to the social and economic development of American civilization. They make human settlements possible and are indispensable to commerce and industry. Effective public works facilities and services are of utmost importance in every community and, in the United States, they account for federal, state, and local expenditures of more than $60 billion annually. Additional billions are also invested in similar privately developed and operated facilities such as schools, utilities, and sports arenas.

It is not money that ultimately determines the effectiveness of public works systems, however—it is people. The planning, design, construction, operation, and maintenance of public works facilities have always demanded a high level of training and proficiency in a variety of disciplines. Skyrocketing costs of government, rapid advances in science and technology, and the pressing need for public works to serve an increasingly urbanized populace have made it imperative that public works practitioners be able to respond to the gamut of social, economic, environmental, and political factors inherent in program planning, policy resolution, and project management.

The history of the public works/engineering profession and its practices is long, rich, and varied. Listed below are books, articles, and dissertations that relate directly or indirectly to the evolution of the public works/engineering profession and its practices. Some general urban, environmental, and political histories have been included, especially if they contain substantive information on the acquisition or development of physical structures and facilities by public agencies to house governmental functions or to provide water, waste disposal, power, or transportation services. Biographies and autobiographies of individuals who have played a part in the nation's public works history are also listed.

Abbott, Henry L. "The Corps of Engineers." *Journal of the Military Service Institution*, XV (March 1894), 413-27. A historical sketch by a brigadier general. The text is complemented by a list of the chiefs of the corps from 1774 to 1893.

Adams, Thomas. *Outline of Town and City Planning: A Review of Past Efforts and Modern Aims*. New York: Russell Sage Foundation, 1935. 368 pp. Illustrations, maps, diagrams, notes, appendix, bibliography, and index. A general review of the history and practice of city planning. The author describes the meaning and scope of city planning, outlines the character of early efforts, summarizes city planning developments in the United States and other countries since 1830, and concludes with a discussion of modern methods and aims. The foreword is by Franklin D. Roosevelt (1932).

Adams, Thomas. *Planning the New York Region: An Outline of the Organization, Scope and Progress of the Regional Plan*. New York: Regional Plan of New York and Its Environs, 1927. 129 pp. Illustrations and maps. A review of all the elements (people and agencies involved, studies and surveys completed, conferences and discussions held, etc.) that went into making New York's regional plan. Part III describes the "origin of the plan."

Agnew, Dwight L. "The Government Land Surveyor as a Pioneer." *Mississippi Valley Historical Review*, XXVIII (Dec. 1941), 369-82.

Aitken, Hugh G. J. *Taylorism at Watertown Arsenal: Scientific Management in Action, 1908-1915*. Cambridge: Harvard University Press, 1960. ix + 269 pp. Tables, chart, notes, bibliographical essay, and index. An excellent analysis of the implementation of scientific management practices at the government-owned arsenal.

Akagi, Roy Hidemichi. *The Town Proprietors of the New England Colonies: A Study of Their Development, Organization, Activities and Controversies, 1620-1770*. Philadelphia: University of Pennsylvania, 1924. xiii + 348 pp. Notes, bibliography, and index. Includes incidental information on the planning of colonial towns.

Akeley, Roger P. "Implementing the 1909 Plan of Chicago: An Historical Account of Planning Salesmanship." Master's thesis, University of Texas, 1973.

Alberts, Robert C. *The Shaping of the Point: Pittsburgh's Renaissance Park*. See chapter on "Parks and Recreation."

Aldrich, Mark. "Earnings of American Civil Engineers, 1820-1859." *Journal of Economic History*, XXXI (June 1971), 407-19. Charts the course of earnings for three distinct grades of antebellum civil engineers from 1820 through 1859.

Alexander, Sally Kennedy. "A Sketch of the Life of Major Andrew Ellicott." *Records of the Columbia Historical Society of Washington, D.C.*, 2 (1899), 158-202. A brief biographical statement on a prominent engineer-surveyor. Numerous pieces of Ellicott's correspondence accompany the sketch.

Alexander, Thomas G. *A Clash of Interests: Interior Department and Mountain West, 1863-96*. Provo: Brigham Young University Press, 1977. xii + 256 pp. Maps, notes, appendix, bibliography, and index. A perceptive and balanced scholarly treatment of the influence of Interior Department activities on the Rocky Mountain West. Included are sections on the land surveys, disposition of the public domain, and reclamation.

Allan, Carlisle. "George W. Whistler, Military Engineer." *Military Engineer*, XXIX (May-June 1937), 177-80. A biographical sketch of a nineteenth-century railroad engineer (1800-1849).

Allen, C. Frank. "An Engineer's Reminiscences of the Southwest." *Civil Engineering*, 10 (June 1940), 355-58. Describes his engineering work with the Santa Fe Railroad at the turn of the century. The author is a professor emeritus at MIT.

Allinson, Edward P., and Boies Penrose. *Philadelphia, 1681-1887: A History of Municipal Development*. Philadelphia: Allen, Lane & Scott, 1887. xi + 392 pp. Tables, notes, appendices, and index. A volume in the Johns Hopkins University Studies in Historical and Political Science Series, this book records "the history of the development of the municipal institutions of Philadelphia." There is a brief introduction explaining the character of "local government in Pennsylvania" and entire sections of the following five chapters are devoted to such subjects as highways, water, markets, public squares, water department, gas works, survey department, and public building.

Altshuler, Alan. *The City Planning Process: A Political Analysis*. See chapter on "Roads, Streets, and Highways."

Ambrose, Stephen E. *Duty, Honor, Country: A History of West Point*. Baltimore: Johns Hopkins Press, 1966. xv + 357 pp. Illustrations, maps, notes, bibliography, and index. A thoroughly researched institutional history that underscores both the timelessness and the change characteristic of the United States Military Academy.

***American City* editors.** "Twenty-five Years of *The American City*—and of American Cities." *American City*, XLIX (Sept. 1934), 53-56. On how the magazine has recorded "a quarter-century of solid municipal and civic progress," particularly in the public works field.

American Consulting Engineers Council. *American Consulting Engineers Council: A History*. Washington, D.C.: American Consulting Engineers Council, 1979. iv + 107 pp. Appendices and index. A brief history of the council (1973) and its immediate predecessors, the American Institute of Consulting Engineers (1905) and the Consulting Engineers Council of the United States (1956).

American Road Builders Association. "History of ARBA, 1902-1977." *American Road Builder*. See chapter on "Roads, Streets, and Highways."

American Society of Civil Engineers. Committee on History and Heritage of American Civil Engineering. *A Biographical Dictionary of American Civil Engineers*. New York: American Society of Civil Engineers, 1972. x + 163 pp. Illustrations and index. Contains about 170 entries of civil engineers born before the Civil War. Those included were "judged to be the most frequently referred to in the historical literature that relates to civil engineering." A useful reference tool.

American Society of Landscape Architects. "Minute on the Life and Services of Charles Mulford Robinson, Associate Member." *Landscape Architecture*, 9 (July 1919), 180-93. Biographical sketch of Robinson (1869-1917) who began his career as a journalist in Rochester, New York, and later became a consultant to numerous American cities on civic improvement and planning. When he died, he was professor of civic design at the University of Illinois.

Andrews, Richard. "Environmental Policy and Administrative Change: The National Environmental Policy Act of 1969-1970-1971." Doctoral dissertation, University of North Carolina, Chapel Hill, 1972. 626 pp.

Archer, John. "Puritan Town Planning in New Haven." *Journal of the Society of Architectural Historians*, XXXIV (May 1975), 140-49. A discussion of the colony's seventeenth-century plan and Pastor John Davenport's role in implementing it.

Armstrong, Ellis L.; Michael C. Robinson; and Suellen M. Hoy, eds. *History of Public Works in the United States, 1776-1976*. Chicago: American Public Works Association, 1976. xv + 736 pp. Illustrations, maps, drawings, tables, graphs, suggested readings, and index. The only one of its kind—a comprehensive reference work on the development of public works in the United States. There are lengthy chapters on the following subjects: waterways, roads, streets, and highways; highway structures and traffic controls; railroads; urban mass transportation; airways and airports; community water supply; flood control and drainage; irrigation; light and power; sewers and wastewater treatment; solid wastes; public buildings; educational facilities; public housing; parks and recreation; military installations; aerospace; and the public works profession. The introductory essay is on "Public Works and Private Rights."

Armytage, W. H. G. *A Social History of Engineering*. London: Faber and Faber, 1961. 378 pp. Illustrations, tables, bibliography, and index. Mainly a history of technological developments in Great Britain, with an indication of "how they have affected and been affected by social life at certain stages." One chapter discusses briefly American engineering expansion during the Civil War and after.

Arnold, Joseph L. *The New Deal in the Suburbs: A History of the Greenbelt Town Program 1935-1954*. Columbus: Ohio State University Press, 1971. xiii + 272 pp. Notes, bibliography, and index. Describes one major city planning project undertaken by the federal government in 1930s.

Arrington, Leonard. "The New Deal in the West: A Preliminary Statistical Inquiry." *Pacific Historical Review*, XXXVIII (Aug. 1969), 311-16. Statistical overview of federal spending in western states during the New Deal.

Babcock, John B. "The Boston Society of Civil Engineers and Its Founder Members." *Journal of the Boston Society of Civil Engineers*, XXIII (July 1936), 151-77. An informative article on the history of the nation's oldest engineering society by its president.

Baber, Adin A. *Lincoln with Compass and Chain: Surveying Career as Seen in His Notes and Maps, and with an Account of the Hanks Family Cousins, Makers of Fine Surveying and Mathematical Instruments*. Kansas, Ill.: privately published by author, 1968. xx + 180 pp. Illustrations, maps, diagrams, notes, and index. A "labor of love" by the author, who provides "ample evidence of Lincoln's skill as a surveyor" in what is now Menard County, Illinois.

Bach, Ira J. "A Reconsideration of the 1909 Plan of Chicago," *Chicago History*, 11 (Spring-Summer 1973), 132-41. David Burnham's plan to beautify Chicago's lakefront.

Bade, William Frederic. *The Life and Letters of John Muir*. See chapter on "Parks and Recreation."

Badger, Reid. *The Great American Fair: The World's Columbian Exposition & American Culture*. Chicago: Nelson-Hall, Inc., 1979. xvi + 177 pp. Illustrations, appendices, notes, bibliography, and index. Analyzes "the extent to which the Columbian Exposition could be said to be a representative cultural event" and the effect of the fair on "the overall psychological or emotional condition of American society in the 1890s." It relates to the beginnings of modern American planning.

Baker, M. N. "Municipal Engineering: Urban Growth and Progress." *Engineering News-Record*, 92 (April 17, 1924), 691-93. Useful, largely statistical overview of the growth of various urban public works services in the late nineteenth and early twentieth centuries.

Baker, M. N. *Municipal Engineering and Sanitation*. New York: Macmillan Company, 1902. viii + 317 pp. Index. A classic overview of municipal transportation, water supply, sewage disposal, refuse collection, parks, and administration.

Baker, Ray Palmer. *A Chapter in American Education: Rensselaer Polytechnic Institute, 1824-1924*. New York: Charles Scribner's Sons, 1924. viii + 170 pp. An anniversary testimonial to the influence of Rensselaer Polytechnic Institute on other educational institutions in the United States. Of special interest may be the chapters on "The Public Services," "Canals and Railroads," and "Engineering Education."

Baker, T. Lindsay. "The Survey of the Santa Fe Trail." *Great Plains Journal*. See chapter on "Roads, Streets, and Highways."

Bannister, Turpin C. "Early Town Planning in New York State." *New York History*, XXIV (April 1943), 185-95. Reviews "the foundation and early growth of a number of New York State communities during the Colonial and Early Republican periods."

Bannister, Turpin C. "Oglethorpe's Sources for the Savannah Plan." *Journal of the Society of Architectural Historians*, XX (May 1961), 47-62.

Barbour, Ian G., ed. *Western Man and Environmental Ethics: Attitudes Toward Nature and Technology*. Reading, Mass.: Addison-Wesley, 1973. 276 pp. Bibliography.

Barde, Robert E. "Arthur E. Morgan, First Chairman of TVA." *Tennessee Historical Quarterly*, XXX (Fall 1971), 299-314. Perspectives on the stormy career of this controversial public servant.

Barsness, Richard W. "The Department of Transportation: Concept and Structure." *Western Political Quarterly*, XXII (Sept. 1970), 500-15. Good overview of efforts to rationalize and unify the federal government's role in transportation.

Bartlett, Richard A. *Great Surveys of the American West*. Norman: University of Oklahoma Press, 1962. xxiii + 408 pp. Illustrations, maps, notes, bibliography, and index. The definitive account of the Hayden, King, Powell, and Wheeler surveys of the American West conducted in the 1870s.

Bassett, Edward M. *Zoning: The Laws, Administration, and Court Decisions During the First Twenty Years*. New York: Russell Sage Foundation, 1940. 275 pp. Notes, bibliography, and indexes. First published in 1936, this book brings together "the court decisions on zoning" and outlines the early development of zoning in this country." In a new introduction, the author restates the principles of zoning for height, area, and use and analyzes planning experiments of the 1930s.

Bates, J. Leonard. "Fulfilling American Democracy: The Conservation Movement, 1907-1921." *Mississippi Valley Historical Review*, XLIV (June 1957), 29-57.

Bates, Ralph S. *Scientific Societies in the United States*. New York: Columbia University Press, 1958. xi + 297 pp. Notes, bibliography, and index. A general but comprehensive history of the growth of scientific (and engineering) societies in the United States from the eighteenth century to the 1940s. The author states that with the "triumph of specialization" between 1866 and 1918, engineers were the first professionals to organize strongly and that the tendency continued into the 1940s.

Bathe, Greville. *An Engineer's Miscellany*. Philadelphia: Press of Patterson & White Company, 1938. xii + 136 pp. Illustrations.

Bathe, Greville, and Dorothy. *Oliver Evans: A Chronicle of Early American Engineering*. Philadelphia: Historical Society of Pennsylvania, 1935. xviii + 362 pp. Illustrations, maps, diagrams, notes, appendices, and index. A well-researched biography of an early American inventor and engineer. Many of Evans' letters, both personal and professional, are presented in full throughout the volume. (Reprinted in 1972 by Arno Press.)

Baum, Alvin, Jr. "Chicago and the City Beautiful, 1890-1910." Honors thesis, Harvard University, 1952.

Baum, Robert J. *Ethics and Engineering Curricula*. Hastings-on-Hudson, N.Y.: Institute of Society, Ethics, and the Life Services, 1980. x + 79 pp. Notes and bibliography. Contains one chapter entitled "A Brief History of the Teaching of Engineering Ethics." This booklet is part of a series which addresses "the states, problems, and possibilities of the teaching of ethics in higher education."

Beard, Mary Ritter. *Woman's Work in Municipalities*. See chapter on "Solid Wastes."

Beckman, Norman. "Federal Long-Range Planning: The Heritage of the National Resources Planning Board." *Journal of the American Institute of Planners*, XXVI (May 1960), 89-97. On the board's accomplishments during its ten-year existence (1933-1943).

Bedini, Silvio A. "Benjamin Banneker and the Survey of the District of Columbia 1791." *Records of the Columbia Historical Society of Washington, D.C.* (1969-1970), 7-30. A precise description of the contribution made by Banneker, the Afro-American self-taught mathematician and almanac-maker, to the survey of Washington City begun in 1791.

Bedini, Silvio A. *The Life of Benjamin Banneker*. New York: Charles Scribner's Sons, 1972. xvii + 434 pp. Illustrations, map, diagrams, notes, bibliography, and index. A full-length biography of a free Negro who "contributed a tangible bit to the fabric of science in America." The author disproves "erroneous exaggerations" that have been perpetuated. Bedini dispels the legend that after Pierre L'Enfant's dismissal and his refusal to make available his plan of the city of Washington that Andrew Ellicott was able to reconstruct it in detail from Banneker's recollection.

Bedini, Silvio A. *Thinkers and Tinkers: Early American Men of Science*. New York: Charles Scribner's Sons, 1975. xix + 520 pp. Illustrations, notes, glossary, bibliography, and index. An overview of "how the practical sciences were required and how they were utilized" in the British colonies of North America and during the early years of the United States. The material on surveying and map making is significant.

Beers, Henry P. "A History of the U.S. Topographical Engineers, 1813-1863." 2 parts. *Military Engineer*, XXXIV (June and July 1942), June: 287-91; July: 348-52. Describes origins and development.

Bell, Laura Palmer. "A New Theory on the Plan of Savannah." *Georgia Historical Quarterly*, XLVIII (June 1964), 147-65. A discussion of the source of the plan for the city.

Bender, A. B. "Opening Routes across West Texas, 1848-1850." *Southwestern Historical Quarterly*. See chapter on "Roads, Streets, and Highways."

Benson, Barbara E., ed. *Benjamin Henry Latrobe & Moncure Robinson: The Engineer as Agent of Technological Transfer*. Greenville, Del.: Eleutherian Mills Historical Library, 1975. 71 pp. Illustrations and notes. On the engineering careers of Latrobe (by Edward C. Carter II) and Robinson (by Darwin H. Stapleton) with a commentary (by John B. Rae). These presentations were given at a Regional Conference in Economic History, sponsored by the Eleutherian Mills Historical Library, on May 17, 1974.

Benson, Barbara E. "The Engineer as an Agent in Technology Transfer." *Technology and Culture*, 16 (Jan. 1975), 67-69. A brief conference (Eleutherian Mills Historical Library, 1974) report which illustrates that in nineteenth-century America individual engineers were mechanisms of technological advance.

Bestor, George C. *City Planning Bibliography: A Basic Bibliography of Sources and Trends*. New York: American Society of Civil Engineers, 1972. xvi + 518 pp. Index. Includes citations on the history of city planning.

Bigger, Richard, and James D. Kitchen. *How the Cities Grew: A Century of Municipal Independence and Expansionism in Metropolitan Los Angeles*. Los Angeles: Bureau of Governmental Research (University of California), 1952. x + 256 pp. Maps, tables, notes, and bibliography. A study of political movements that "participated in the attempts to incorporate communities" in the Los Angeles metropolitan area from 1850 to 1950.

Billington, Ray Allen. "Full Speed Ahead and Damn the Tomorrows: Our Frontier Heritage of Waste." *American Heritage*, 29 (Dec. 1977), 4-13. On the American habit of squandering natural resources.

Birch, Eugene Ladner. "Advancing the Art and Science of Planning: Planners and Their Organizations, 1909-1980." *Journal of the American Planning Association*, 46 (Jan. 1980), 22-49. Identifies and explains five distinct periods in the seventy-year history of planning organizations.

Birch, Eugene Ladner. "Planners—Let's Not Bury Our History." *Planning*, 46 (Sept. 1980), 12-15. Advocates the inclusion of planning history courses in the curriculum of graduate schools of planning.

Bishop, Joseph Bucklin. *Goethals, Genius of the Panama Canal: A Biography*. See chapter on "Waterways."

Bjork, Kenneth. *Saga in Steel and Concrete: Norwegian Engineers in America*. Northfield, Minn.: Norwegian-American Historical Association, 1947. xii + 504 pp. Illustrations, tables, notes, and index. A good history of the significant role played by Norwegian engineers and architects in the development of America. There are specific chapters on bridge building, tunneling, and engineering organizations.

Black, Russell VanNest. *Planning and the Planning Profession: The Past Fifty Years 1917-1967*. Washington, D.C.: American Institute of Planners, 1968. 77 pp. Contains a short essay on the evolution of the planning profession and brief biographical sketches of the organization's founders and award winners.

Bloom, John Porter, ed. *The American Territorial System*. Athens: Ohio University Press, 1973. xvi + 248 pp. Notes and bibliography. Includes an essay by Thomas G. Alexander on the operation of the federal land survey in the West in the late nineteenth century.

Blust, Frank A. "The U.S. Lake Survey, 1841-1974." *Inland Seas*, 32 (Summer 1976), 91-104. A history of the federal agency that, until 1974, conducted surveys and made navigation charts of the Great Lakes.

Bonney, Orrin H., and Lorraine Bonney. *Battle Drums and Geysers: The Life and Journals of Lt. Gustavus Cheyney Doane, Soldier and Explorer of the Yellowstone and Snake River Regions*. See chapter on "Parks and Recreation."

Bowden, J. J. *Surveying the Texas and Pacific Land Grant West of the Pecos River*. El Paso: Texas Western Press, 1975. 89 pp. Illustrations and bibliography.

Bowie, William. "One Hundred Years of Control Surveys." *Civil Engineering*, 3 (Aug. 1933), 467-68. By the U.S. Coast and Geodetic Survey.

Bowman, Waldo G. "A Century of Probing the Future." *Engineering News-Record*, 192 (April 30, 1974), 507-33. "Historical highlights of *Engineering News-Record*'s weekly role in promoting construction progress over the past 100 years."

Boynton, Edward C. *History of West Point, and Its Military Importance during the American Revolution: And the Origin and Progress of the United States Military Academy*. New York: D. Van Nostrand, 1871. xviii + 416 pp. Illustrations, maps, notes, appendix, and index. On early history (first issued in 1863) of West Point, beginning with a discussion of land acquisition for the academy.

Boynton, Robert Paul. "The Council-Manager Plan: An Historical Perspective." *Public Management*, 56 (Oct. 1974), 3-5. How it has contributed to professionalism in city government.

Bradford, Ernest S. *Commission Government in American Cities*. New York: MacMillan Company, 1911. xiv + 339 pp. Illustration, chart, tables, notes, bibliography, and index. Analyzes the advantages and disadvantages of the commission form of city government, first adopted in Galveston, Texas, after the disastrous flood of 1900.

Bradford, E. S. "Twelve Years of Commission Government." *Municipal Engineering*, XLV (Dec. 1913), 502-10. Points out defects in the commission plan and compares it with the city manager plan.

Braeman, John; Robert H. Bremner; and David Brody, eds. *Change and Continuity in Twentieth-Century America: The 1920's*. Athens: Ohio State University Press, 1968. xii + 456 pp. Tables, notes, and index. A collection of essays on the transformation of American society in the 1920s that contains little information on public works. Charles N. Glaab's essay on "Metropolis and Suburb: The Changing American City" discusses the development of regional planning groups during the decade in Chicago, Boston, Los Angeles, and other metropolitan areas.

Bremer, William W. "Along the 'American Way': The New Deal's Work Relief Programs for the Unemployed." *Journal of American History*, LXII (Dec. 1975), 636-52. Examines the importance "that reformers of the 1930s attached to the psychological effects of many federal programs." The author concludes that "New Dealers made a gallant attempt to sustain the unemployed psychologically" but work relief "remained more relief than work, more charity than employment."

Brennan, Roland M. "Brigadier General Richard L. Hoxie, United States Army, 1861-1930." *Records of the Columbia Historical Society of Washington, D.C.* (1957-1959), 87-95. Records Hoxie's "major engineering accomplishments" in the development of Washington, D.C., from 1874 to 1884 when he was chief engineer officer for the district's board of commissioners.

Bridenbaugh, Carl. *Cities in Revolt: Urban Life in America, 1743-1776*. New York: Capricorn Books, 1964. xi + 433 + xxi pp. Bibliographical note and index. A profound study of American cities during the Revolutionary era. Substantial portions of the book are devoted to street paving, sewer construction, surveying, water supply development, and other public works subjects rarely covered in histories of this period. (First published in 1955.)

Bridenbaugh, Carl. *Cities in the Wilderness: The First Century of Urban Life in America 1625-1742*. New York: Capricorn Books, 1964. xii + 500 pp. Tables, notes, bibliography and index. First published in 1938, this excellent book is one of the few that address the development of municipal public works during the Colonial era. The author profiles the evolution of five towns—Boston, Newport, New York, Philadelphia, and Charles Town—from the standpoint of physical, economic, social, and cultural aspects. Virtually every aspect of public works is discussed.

Brittain, James E. *A Brief History of Engineering in Georgia and Guide to 76 Historic Engineering Sites*. Atlanta: Georgia Institute of Technology, 1976. iv + 36 pp. Illustrations, map, and bibliography. Includes short sections on various canals, bridges, power plants, and dams and brief descriptions of seventy-six historic engineering sites in Georgia.

Brittain, James E., and Robert C. McMath, Jr. "Engineers and the New South Creed: The Formation and Early Development of Georgia Tech." *Technology and Culture*, 18 (April 1977), 175-201. The authors demonstrate how two trends, "the development of professional engineering education and the beginning of an industrialized New South," came together in the establishment of the Georgia School of Technology in the 1880s. They also compare instruction at Georgia Tech with experiments in engineering education elsewhere in the Southeast.

Brooks, Robert B. "Robert E. Lee—Civil Engineer." *Civil Engineering*. See chapter on "Waterways."

Brown, A. Theodore. "The Politics of Reform: Kansas City's Municipal Government, 1925-1950." Doctoral dissertation, University of Chicago, 1957. vi + 422 pp. Notes, appendix, and bibliography. Well-researched history that includes in-depth treatments of city planning and the water department.

Brown, A Theodore, and Lyle W. Dorsett. *K.C.: A History of Kansas City, Missouri*. Boulder, Colo.: Pruett Publishing Company, 1978. x + 303 pp. Illustrations, bibliographical essay, and index. A history of Kansas City's growth and development. The study contains more material (excluding the chapter on Pendergast) on the city's public works than found in most urban histories.

Brown, Esther Lucile. *The Professional Engineer*. New York: Russell Sage Foundation, 1936. 86 pp. Tables, diagram, and notes. A brief statement on the education, associations, and salaries of engineers, particularly during the late 1920s and early 1930s. There is also a short discussion of future engineering trends.

Brown, Frederick D. *The Engineers' Club of Philadelphia: A Centennial Address, 1877-1977*. New York: Newcomen Society in North America, 1978. 21 pp. By the club's president.

Brown, Glenn. "The American Institute of Architects—Its Policies and Achievements." *American Architect*. See chapter on "Public Buildings."

Brown, Glenn. "The Plan of L'Enfant for the City of Washington and Its Effect upon the Future Development of the City." *Records of the Columbia Historical Society of Washington, D.C.* 12 (1909), 1-20. Reviews "the remarkable beauties and utilitarian features of the L'Enfant plan" and recommends "reinstating this plan and building future Government structures on the lines originally suggested."

Brownell, Blaine A. "The Commercial-Civic Elite and City Planning in Atlanta, Memphis, and New Orleans in the 1920s." *Journal of Southern History*, XLI (Aug. 1975), 339-68. Shows that the most influential local citizens in three urban southern cities during the 1920s uniformly supported systematic, comprehensive city planning. Leading commercial and civic groups saw in it a way to solve urban ills and direct future development.

Brownell, Blaine A. *The Urban Ethos in the South*. Baton Rouge: Louisiana State University Press, 1975. xxi + 238 pp. Tables, notes, bibliographical essay, and index. Most of this book focuses on social and economic subjects. However, Chapter VI, "The Urban Ethos and Municipal Policy," is a brilliant discussion of the efforts of commercial elites to promote city improvements. Chambers of commerce and other organizations constantly advocated construction of paved streets, waterworks, street lighting, and sewers to attract new business and citizens. The chapter also includes some excellent insights on city planning in the South.

Brownlow, Louis. *A Passion for Politics: The Autobiography of Louis Brownlow*. Vol. I. Chicago: University of Chicago Press, 1955. xii + 606 pp. Illustrations and index. A straightforward account of Brownlow's childhood in a small town in the Missouri Ozarks as well as his experiences as a newspaper reporter in Nashville and Louisville and as a Washington correspondent for the Haskin Syndicate. Volume I ends on January 26, 1915, when the author became commissioner of the District of Columbia.

Brownlow, Louis. *A Passion for Anonymity: The Autobiography of Louis Brownlow*. Vol. II. Chicago: University of Chicago Press, 1958. x + 499 pp. Illustration and index. When Brownlow became commissioner of the District of Columbia, he "foresook forever" the journalism profession and entered the field of public administration. In volume II he describes his experiences as commissioner of the district; city manager of Petersburg, Virginia, and of Knoxville, Tennessee; municipal consultant in the building of Radburn, a housing experiment in Bergen County, New Jersey; and director of the Public Administration Clearing House—now the Charles Merriam Center for Public Administration and the headquarters of the American Planning and American Public Works associations.

Bryan, Wilhelmus Bogart. *A History of the National Capital: From Its Foundation through the Period of the Adoption of the Organic Act*. 2 vols. New York: MacMillan Company, 1914 (Vol. I), 1916 (Vol. II). Vol. I: xv + 669 pp; Vol. II: xvi + 707 pp. Illustrations, maps, notes, and index. A thorough history of the nation's capital. Volume I covers the period from 1790 to 1814; volume II continues the story from 1815 to 1818. There are numerous topics, discussed at varying lengths, that will be of interest to those conducting research on public works topics: the plan of the Capitol Building; street lighting and street improvements; bridges, roads, and canals; sewers and water supply; and Alexander R. Shepherd's term as president of the board of public works.

Budd, Ralph. "Developing the Pacific Northwest." *Civil Engineering*, I (Sept. 1931), 1071-74. Emphasizes the engineers' part in developing the Pacific Northwest.

Buder, Stanley. *Pullman: An Experiment in*

Industrial Order and Community Planning, 1880-1930. New York: Oxford University Press, 1967. xvi + 263 pp. Illustrations, tables, figures, notes, note on sources, and index. A well-documented study that removes Pullman from the confines of labor history by treating it from the perspective of community planning.

Buder, Stanley. "The Model Town of Pullman: Town Planning and Social Control in the Gilded Age." *Journal of the American Institute of Planners*, XXXIII (Jan. 1967), 2-10. Underscores the town's significance to the American planning tradition, particularly its relationship to the Model Tenement and Garden City movements.

Bugbee, Mary F. "The Early Planning of Sites for Federal and Local Use in Washington, D.C." *Records of the Columbia Historical Society of Washington, D.C.*, 51-52 (1951-1952), 19-31. Describes how various sites were selected, L'Enfant's plan, and the surveying work of Andrew Ellicott, James R. Dermott, and Nicholas and Robert King.

"Building a Greater America." *Engineering News-Record*, 143 (Sept. 1, 1949), 119-28. From ENR's seventy-fifth anniversary issue. After reviewing significant changes in the American landscape, the editors conclude: "In the first half of the 20th century, the American construction engineer has made his record. It is a better America than when he started."

Bull, Storm. "Technical Education at the University of Wisconsin." *Wisconsin Engineer*, 3 (Jan. 1899), 1-17. A general history since 1868.

Bunting, Bainbridge. "The Plan of the Back Bay Area in Boston." *Journal of the Society of Architectural Historians*, XIII (May 1954), 19-24. Shows how the plan of Boston's well-known residential area "represents a significant chapter in the history of city planning in nineteenth-century America."

Burg, David. F. *Chicago's White City of 1893*. Lexington: University of Kentucky Press, 1976. xvi + 382 pp. Illustrations, notes, and index. Tells the story of the World's Columbian Exposition and explains its significance in relation to the origins of modern American planning.

Burmeister, W.J. "The Changing Image of the Highway Official." *American Road Builder*. See chapter on "Roads, Streets, and Highways."

Burnham, Daniel H., and Edward H. Bennett. *Plan of Chicago*. New York: Da Capo Press, 1970. xviii + 164 pp. Illustrations, maps, and index. First published in 1909, Burnham and Bennett's *Plan of Chicago* demonstrates that they made "no Little Plans." This volume is the culmination of some thirty-five years of planning and organization by Burnham dating from the start of his partnership with John Wellborn Root. Nearly every chapter will be of special interest to those studying Chicago's development. Note particularly "City Planning in Ancient and Modern Times," "The Chicago Park System," "Transportation," and "Streets Within the City."

Burran, James A. "The WPA in Nashville, 1935-1943." *Tennessee Historical Quarterly*, XXXIV (Fall 1975), 293-308. An assessment of WPA projects (successes and failures) in Nashville specifically and in Tennessee in general.

Burton, Ian, and Robert W. Kates, eds. *Readings in Resource Management and Conservation*. Chicago: University of Chicago Press, 1965. xi + 609 pp. Charts, tables, graphs, notes, and indexes. A good anthology of the writings of scholars and scientists from a number of fields. The focus is on managing natural resources, the conservation ethic, scientific and technological change, and the relationships between resources and economic development. Chapter 3, "The Growth of the Movement," contains selections from the works of Charles R. Van Hise, Grant McConnell, and Samuel P. Hays.

Busching, Herbert W., and Randolph Russell. "American Road Building—Fifty Years of Progress." *Journal of the Construction Division, Proceedings of the American Society of Civil Engineers*, 101 (Sept. 1975), 565-81. On developments and refinements in "automated paving, materials handling, and excavation equipment" as well as in legislation "to assist with highway finance and construction."

Buzzaird, Raleigh B. "America's First Chief Engineer." *Military Engineer*, XXXIX (Dec. 1947), 505-10. A biographical sketch of Colonel Richard Gridley (1710-1796).

Byrne, J. J., ed. "Engineering in the Forest Service: Six Memoirs," *Forest History*. See chapter on "Parks and Recreation."

Caemmerer, H. Paul. *The Life of Pierre Charles L'Enfant*. New York: Da Capo Press,

1970. xxvi + 480 pp. Illustrations, maps, appendices, and index. First published in 1950, this book is a straightforward biography of the architect-engineer commissioned in 1791 by President George Washington to prepare a plan for the capital of the United States. The author, secretary of the National Commission of the Fine Arts, explains how the commission has guided the development of Washington along the lines of the L'Enfant plan since 1910.

Caemmerer, H. Paul. *Washington: The National Capital*. Washington: U.S. Government Printing Office, 1932. xxv + 736 pp. Illustrations, bibliography, and index. A lengthy study which includes an abundance of material on the city plan as well as on the capital's public buildings and parks.

Calhoun, Daniel Hovey. *The American Civil Engineer: Origins and Conflict*. Cambridge: Technology Press of MIT, 1960. xiv + 295 pp. Map, notes, appendices, bibliographical note, and index. A thorough and significant examination of the work experiences of the early nineteenth-century civil engineer. The author concentrates on those engineers who worked on large public works projects, mainly canals and railroads. "Public works," as then used, included government construction as well as the entire range of internal improvements in the transportation field.

Callow, Alexander B., Jr. *The Tweed Ring*. New York: Oxford University Press, 1966. xi + 351 pp. Illustrations, notes, bibliography, and index. An excellent study of the corrupt political machine built by William Marcy Tweed, New York City's commissioner of public works in the late 1860s and early 1870s.

Calvert, Monte A. *The Mechanical Engineer in America, 1830-1910: Professional Cultures in Conflict*. Baltimore: Johns Hopkins Press, 1967. xviii + 296 pp. Illustrations, tables, notes, bibliography, and index. A thorough examination of the professionalization of the field of mechanical engineering and its response to the bureaucratization and industrial rationalization of the period. A major theme is the conflict between two cultures—that of the shop owner and that of the educator. Railroad and naval engineering were both rich sources of professional mechanical engineers.

Calvin, Ross, ed. *Lieutenant Emory Reports: A Reprint of Lieutenant W. H. Emory's Notes of a Military Reconnaissance*. Albuquerque: University of New Mexico Press, 1951. vi + 208 pp. Illustrations, maps, and notes. A young lieutenant's scientific account (1846) of the American Southwest, a vast and mainly unknown track including New Mexico and California. The book contains a helpful introduction by the editor as well as footnotes that identify and explain persons or places of interest.

Campbell, Ballard C. *Representative Democracy: Public Policy and Midwestern Legislatures in the Late Nineteenth Century*. Cambridge: Harvard University Press, 1980. xii + 260 pp. Tables, notes, appendix, and index. Through an analysis of late nineteenth-century state legislatures in Illinois, Iowa, and Wisconsin, the author shows that during this period the preponderance of power lay with state governments rather than with policymakers in Washington, D.C. The author also examines public policy conflicts. Two general inquiries guide his analysis: what issues divided lawmakers and their responses to the controversies.

Campbell, Warren M. "Politics, Procedures, and City Planning: The Master Plan as an Instrument of Policy Formulation and Control." Doctoral dissertation, Stanford University, 1963. 543 pp.

Carlson, Everett E. "The Engineers' Club of St. Louis: A Century of Its History, 1868-1968." *Bulletin of the Missouri Historical Society*, XXV (July 1969), 307-20. A review of its problems and progress as well as a discussion of how the club contributed to the developing professionalization of St. Louis' engineers.

Caro, Robert A. "Robert Moses: Great Builder of the Twentieth Century." *Civil Engineering*, 47 (Oct. 1977), 121-26. An excerpt from Caro's introduction to *The Power Broker: Robert Moses and the Fall of New York*, New York, 1974.

Caro, Robert A. *The Power Broker: Robert Moses and the Fall of New York*. New York: Alfred A. Knopf, 1974. x + 1246 + xxxiv pp. Illustrations, maps, notes and sources, and index. A monumental study of "the single most powerful man" in the city and state of New York by an investigative reporter. According to this fascinating portrait of an extraordinary man, Moses—when denied power within the framework of the democratic process—"stepped outside that framework to grasp power sufficient to shape a great city and to hold sway over the very texture of millions of lives." The author demonstrates a lack of historical perspective by severely criticizing Moses for building the parkways and highways that New Yorkers as well as the nation as a whole were demanding.

Carr, Lois Green. "The Metropolis of Maryland: A Comment on Town Development Along the Tobacco Coast." *Maryland Historical Magazine*, LXIX (Summer 1974), 124-45.

Carroll, Eugene J. "John B. Kendrick's Fight for Western Water Legislation, 1917-1933." *Annals of Wyoming*. See chapter on "Irrigation."

Carter, Edward C. II. "Benjamin Henry Latrobe and Public Works: Professionalism, Private Interest, and Public Policy in the Age of Jefferson." *Essays in Public Works HIstory*, 3 (Dec. 1976), 1-29. On the making of the leading American public works engineer administrator of the early nineteenth century. The appendix contains Latrobe's letter to President James Madison (April 1816) regarding the appointment of a principal engineer for Virginia. Latrobe clearly expresses his thoughts on the state and needs of civil engineering in America.

Carter, Edward C. II. "The Papers of Benjamin Henry Latrobe and the Maryland Historical Society, 1885-1971: Nature, Structure and Means of Acquisition." *Maryland Historical Magazine*, 66 (Winter 1971), 436-54. A description of the Latrobe papers and an outline of plans to publish them with a short explanation of the significance of Latrobe's engineering and architectural career.

Carter, Edward C. II, ed. *The Papers of Benjamin Henry Latrobe: The Virginia Journals of Benjamin Henry Latrobe, 1795-1798*. See chapter on "Public Buildings."

Carter, William Harding. "Claude Crozet." *Journal of the Military Service Institution of the United States*, LIII (July-Aug. 1913), 1-6. A biographical sketch of the French engineer-soldier who subsequently became a professor at West Point (1817) and state engineer of Virginia (1824).

Cassedy, James Higgins. *Charles V. Chapin and the Public Health Movement*. See chapter on "Sewers and Wastewater Treatment."

Cassella, William N., Jr. "City-County Separation: The 'Great Divorce' of 1876." *Missouri Historical Society Bulletin*, XV (Jan. 1959), 85-104. Reviews the events that preceded the City of St. Louis' secession from St. Louis County in 1876.

Chan, Loren Briggs. *Sagebrush Statesman: Tasker L. Oddie of Nevada*. See chapter on "Irrigation."

Chang, Tso-Shuen. *History and Analysis of the Commission and City Manager Plans of Municipal Government in the United States*. Iowa City: University of Iowa, 1918. 290 pp. Notes and index. This book appears as Volume VI in the University of Iowa's *Studies in the Social Sciences* series. The author traces the origin and development of the commission plan and the city manager plan "with a view of ascertaining the defects of the older forms of city government" and demonstrates "the extent to which the alleged advantages of the new plans have been sustained in actual experience."

Channing, J. Parke; Philip N. Moore; and Alfred D. Flinn. *Engineering Council: A Brief History*. n.p.: United Engineering Society, 1921. 28 pp. Appendices. An overview of the purposes and programs of a council, which was formed in June 1917 and discontinued in December 1920. Composed of the American Society of Civil Engineers, American Institute of Mining and Metallurgical Engineers, American Society of Mechanical Engineers, American Institute of Electrical Engineers, American Society for Testing Materials, and American Railway Engineering Association, the council was established to deal cooperatively with public issues affecting all engineers and with inter-society affairs. Failing to increase its resources, it yielded to the Federated American Engineering Societies.

Chapman, Edmund H. "City Planning under Industrialization: The Case of Cleveland." *Journal of the Society of Architectural Historians*, XII (May 1953), 19-24. Shows how the few efforts to control the city's expansion during the second half of the nineteenth century were thwarted.

Chapman Edmund H. "City Planning under Mercantile Expansion: The Case of Cleveland, Ohio." *Journal of the Society of Architectural Historians*, X (Dec. 1951), 10-17. Evaluates the influence of pre-industrial events on the growth of Cleveland.

Chapman, Edmund H. *Cleveland: Village to*

Metropolis, A Case Study of Problems of Urban Development in Nineteenth-century America. Cleveland: Western Reserve Historical Society and the Press of Western Reserve University, 1964. xiv + 166 pp. Illustrations, notes, bibliography, and index. Contains a good deal of information on the planning and buildings (public, commercial, and private) of Cleveland.

Chapman, Edmund Haupt. "The Lessons of History and City Planning." *College Art Journal*, XI (Fall 1951), 75-86. Looks closely at zoning laws, building codes, and city planning commissions in Cleveland—a case study.

Charles, Searle F. "Harry L. Hopkins: New Deal Administrator, 1933-1938." Doctoral dissertation, University of Illinois, Urbana-Champaign, 1953. 369 pp.

Chase, Charles Perry. "A Half Century of Engineering." *Palimpsest*, XXVIII (Sept. 1947), 310-20. Personal reminiscences of engineering in Clinton, Iowa, by its city engineer.

Checkoway, Barry Norman. "Suburbanization and Community: Growth and Planning in Postwar Lower Bucks County, Pennsylvania." Doctoral dissertation, University of Pennsylvania, 1977. 266 pp.

Chicago Department of City Planning. *The Chicago Plan Commission: A Historical Sketch, 1909-1960*. Chicago: Department of City Planning, 1960. 41 pp. Illustrations, maps, and appendix. This booklet describes briefly the commission's major achievements and the personalities associated with them.

Chittenden, Russell H. *History of the Sheffield Scientific School of Yale University, 1846-1922*. 2 vols. New Haven: Yale University Press, 1928. Vol. I: ix + 298; Vol. II x + 299 - 610 pp. Illustrations, appendix, and index. Chapter XII in volume II presents a brief history of the engineering department from 1856. The author was director of the Sheffield Scientific School from 1898 to 1922.

Christensen, Daphne, ed. *Chicago Public Works: A History*. Chicago: Rand McNally & Company, 1973. vii + 238 pp. Illustrations, maps, appendices, and index. A tribute to Chicago's public works. The volume is nicely illustrated and filled with factual information on the city's major public works facilities and services. The volume was sponsored and prepared by Chicago's Department of Public Works.

Christie, Jean. "Morris Llewellyn Cooke: Progressive Engineer." Doctoral dissertation. See chapter on "Energy."

Christie, Jean. "New Deal Resources Planning: The Proposals of Morris L. Cooke." *Agricultural History*, 53 (July 1979), 597-608.

Christie, Jean. "The Mississippi Valley Committee: Conservation and Planning in the Early New Deal." *Historian*, XXXII (May 1970), 449-69. Valuable case study of New Deal water resource planning.

Church, William Conant. "John Ericsson, The Engineer." *Scribner's Magazine*. See chapter on "Military Installations."

Church, William Conant. *The Life of John Ericsson*. 2 vols. London: Sampson, Low, Marston, Searle, & Rivington, 1890. Vol. I: xii + 303 pp.; Vol. II: x + 357 pp. Illustrations, diagrams, and index. A comprehensive biography of a prominent nineteenth-century engineer who is described by the author, a friend and an admirer, as a man possessing "a great intellect and a generous heart." Volume I begins with Ericsson's "Early Years in Sweden" and concludes with a chapter on the "Success of the *Monitor*." Among other subjects pertaining to Ericsson's personal life, volume II underscores the effect of the *Monitor* on his career and discusses at length his plans for harbor defense and his contributions to steam engineering.

Clark, Earl. "John F. Stevens: Pathfinder for Western Railroads." *American West*, VIII (May 1971), 28-33, 62-63. Describes some of Stevens' survey work.

Clark, John Maurice. *Economics of Planning Public Works*. Washington, D.C.: National Planning Board, 1935. vi + 194 pp. Graphs and notes. A short, first chapter is historical in nature and outlines "The Background of the American Problem." In general, the volume presents a portion of the research conducted by the staff serving the National Planning Board set up under the Public Works Administration in 1933.

Clarke, Robert. *Ellen Swallow: The Woman Who Founded Ecology*. See chapter on "Sewers and Wastewater Treatment."

Clawson, Marion; H. Burnell Held; and Charles H. Stoddard. *Land for the Future*. See chapter on "Parks and Recreation."

"Clemens Herschel." *Journal of the Boston Society of Civil Engineers*, XIX (May 1932), 313-17. Good biographical sketch of a famous hydraulic engineer. His achievements include many pioneering hydroelectric projects.

Clement, Priscilla Ferguson. "The Works Progress Administration in Pennsylvania, 1935 to 1940." *Pennsylvania Magazine of History and Biography*, XCL (April 1971), 244-60. Describes how the WPA altered traditional federal-state government relationships in Pennsylvania.

Cleveland Engineering Society. *The Golden Anniversary Book of the Cleveland Engineering Society*. Cleveland: Cleveland Engineering Society, 1930. 129 pp. Illustrations, chart, and appendices. Outlines the contributions of Cleveland's engineers and scientists to the city's development during the past fifty years. Three essays are particularly interesting: "Cleveland's Water Supply—Its Source, Distribution and Treatment" by A.G. Levy; "Cleveland's System of Sewage Collection and Treatment" by William L. Havens; and "A Brief Review of the Cleveland Engineering Society" by Carlton R. Sabin.

Cline, Gloria Griffen. *Exploring the Great Basin*. Norman: University of Oklahoma Press, 1963. xviii + 254 pp. Illustrations, maps, notes, bibliography, and index. A sound account of early explorations of the area between the Sierra Nevada of California and the Wasatch Range in central Utah. The period from 1776 to 1844 is covered.

Colbert, Leo Otis. "Earliest Maps of Washington, D.C." *Military Engineer*, XLI (July-Aug. 1949), 247-50. A description and exploration of the significance (to city planning) of the first four of the early city maps of the District of Columbia.

Colles, Christopher. *A Survey of the Roads of the United States of America, 1789*. Cambridge: Belknap Press of the Harvard University Press, 1961. xii + 227 pp. Illustrations, maps, notes, bibliographies, and indexes. A description of the conditions of roads in most parts of the country in 1789. (Roads of all types probably totaled less than 3,000 miles.) As an introduction to the survey, Walter W. Ristow has written a lengthy biographical sketch entitled "Christopher Colles: Early American Engineer and Cartographer" (pp. 3-116) which includes a bibliography of Colles' writings.

Combs, Lewis B. "Functions of the Civil Engineer Corps in the Naval Establishment." *Civil Engineering*, 12 (June 1942), 320-23. In reviewing the navy's history, the author shows "how the utilization of civilian engineers and consultants developed naturally into a Civil Engineer Corps as an integral part of the commissioned personnel."

Comey, Arthur C. "The Plan of Boston, Massachusetts: A Capital City." *Transactions of the American Society of Civil Engineers*, 99 (Oct. 1934), 777-88. Describes how Boston grew without a plan. The first planning board was not established until the early twentieth century.

Committee on History and Heritage of American Civil Engineering. *The Civil Engineer: His Origins*. New York: American Society of Civil Engineers, 1970. v + 116 pp. Illustrations, diagrams, notes, and indexes. Three essays reprinted from the American Society of Civil Engineers' Transactions. They include: Hunter McDonald's "Origin of the Word 'Engineer'" (1914); J. Elfreth Watkins' "The Beginnings of Engineering" (1890); and H.D. Hoskold's "Historical Notes upon Ancient and Modern Surveying and Surveying Instruments" (1893).

Condit, Carl W. *Chicago, 1910-29: Building, Planning, and Urban Technology*. Chicago: University of Chicago Press, 1973. xiv + 354 pp. Illustrations, maps, tables, notes, bibliography, and index. A description of the continuing evolution of a city (Chicago) accompanied by an evaluation of "how well its building achievements have answered the needs of those who have lived and worked in it." The author devotes whole sections to such public works topics as waterways, streets, mass transit, public buildings, and parks. Meticulously researched and well written, Condit's examination of Chicago's development provides a model for others wishing to study a particular city.

Condit, Carl W. *Chicago, 1930-1970: Building, Planning, and Urban Technology*. Chicago: University of Chicago Press, 1974. xvi + 351 pp. Illustrations, maps, tables, diagrams, notes, bibliography, and index. A conclusion of the biography of an American city begun by Condit in *Chicago, 1910-1929*. In this second volume, the author records "the drastic discontinuity in urban development that came with the long hiatus in building caused by the depression of the thirties and the war that followed it." There are important chapters on public buildings, streets and expressways, and waterways and airports.

Condit, Carl W. "Sullivan's Skyscrapers as the Expression of Nineteenth Century Technology." *Technology and Culture*. See chapter on "Roads, Streets, and Highways."

Conkin, Paul K. *Tomorrow a New World: The New Deal Community Program*. Ithaca: Cornell University Press, 1959. ix + 350 pp. Illustrations, footnotes, appendices, bibliography, and index. Brilliant description and analysis of the planned communities built during the New Deal.

Connery, Robert H., and Richard H. Leach. *The Federal Government and Metropolitan Areas*. Cambridge: Harvard University Press, 1960. xi + 275 pp. Maps, chart, notes, and index. A survey of urban problems facing the federal government in the late 1950s. Chapter 1, "Federal Programs in Metropolitan Areas," traces the evolution of programs for water resources, water pollution control, airports, military installations, highways, and recreation.

Conrad, David E. "The Whipple Expedition on the Great Plains." *Great Plains Journal*, 2 (Spring 1963), 42-67. An examination of army surveyor and explorer Amiel Weeks Whipple's expedition (1853) on the Great Plains.

Cooke, Morris L. *Business Methods in Municipal Works*. Philadelphia: 1913. 64 pp. Illustration and tables. "An informal record of the operations of the Department of Public Works, of the City of Philadelphia, under the Administration of Mayor (Rudolph) Blankenburg" by its most prominent public works director.

Cooke, Morris Llewellyn. *Our Cities Awake: Notes on Municipal Activities and Administration*. Garden City, N.Y.: Doubleday, Page & Company, 1918. xxiii + 351 pp. Illustrations, tables, and appendix. A classic study of the workings of the Philadelphia Department of Public Works (1912-1916) by its director, a protege and close friend of Frederick W. Taylor. Cooke was successful in applying many of the principles of scientific management to government. This volume explains how he replaced "rule-of-thumb" notions and practices, increased the efficiency of the public works department, and developed the professionalism of its employees.

Cooke, Morris Llewellyn. "Public Engineering and Human Progress." *Journal of the Cleveland Engineering Society*, IX (Jan. 1917), 242-63. On the evolution of a profession by a prominent public works engineer-administrator.

Cooley, Mortimer E. "The Development of Engineering Education during the Last Fifty Years." *Journal of Engineering Education*, XVII (Jan. 1926), 514-28. A straightforward account of general trends.

Coontz, John Leo. "L'Enfant's Dream of Washington Coming True." *American City*, XXXVIII (Feb. 1928), 79-81. Argues that L'Enfant's plan became a "factual reality" with Congress' authorization (January 1928) of $25 million for the purchase of land within the Triangle.

Corbetta, Roger H. "Evolution of Concrete Construction." *Journal of the American Concrete Institute*, 25 (Feb. 1954), 501-12. Traces the growth of the concrete construction industry through improvements in materials, techniques, and equipment.

Cortes-Comerer, Nhora. "The Extraordinary Genius of Arthur E. Morgan." *Civil Engineering*. See chapter on "Flood Control and Drainage."

Cotton, Gordon A. *A History of the Waterways Experiment Station, 1929-1979*. Vicksburg, Miss.: U. S. Army Corps of Engineers, 1979. x + 306 pp. Illustrations, notes, appendices, bibliography, and index. Traces the facility from a small hydraulics laboratory into a 700-acre complex that covers a host of fields—earthquake engineering, soil dynamics, concrete, geology, and environmental relationships.

Couper, William. *Claudius Crozet: Soldier-Scholar-Educator-Engineer (1789-1864)*. See chapter on "Roads, Streets, and Highways."

Couper, William. *One Hundred Years at V.M.I.* 4 vols. Richmond, Va: Garrett and Massie, 1939. Vol. I: xi + 360 pp; Vol. II: vii + 343 pp; Vol. III: vii + 409 pp; Vol. IV: viii + 453 pp. Illustrations, notes, bibliography, and index. The Virginia Military Institute's early years (Volume I), with its emphasis on engineering education and under the influence of Colonel Claudius Crozet, are especially important to any study of the evolution of the engineering profession.

Cowdrey, Albert E. *A City for the Nation: The Army Engineers and the Building of Washington, D.C., 1790-1967*. Washington, D.C.: Historical Division, Office of Administrative Services, Office of the Chief of Engineers, 1978. v + 75 pp. Illustrations, maps, notes, appendix, and bibliography. A readable history of the Army Corps of Engineers' role in building the nation's capital. The book begins with L'Enfant's plan and concludes with Washington's Metro subway. In between, there are bridges, aqueducts, public buildings, and monuments.

Cox, Richard J. "Professionalism and Civil Engineering in Early America: The Vicissitudes of James Shriver's Career, 1815-1826." *Maryland Historical Magazine*, 74 (March 1979), 23-28. Examines the development of the civil engineering profession by studying the career of a pioneering practitioner (1794-1826) who was associated with two large public works projects, the National Road and the Chesapeake and Ohio Canal.

Cranford, F.L. "Fifty Years of Contracting." *Engineering News-Record*, 92 (April 17, 1924), 664-66. A review of the method by which most public works construction is carried out by the president of the Associated General Contractors of America.

Crawford, Andrew Wright. "The Development of Park Systems in American Cities." *Annals of the American Academy of Political and Social Science*. See chapter on "Parks and Recreation."

Creighton, Wilbur Foster. *The Life of Major Wilbur Fisk Foster: A Civil Engineer, Confederate Soldier, Builder, Churchman and Free Mason*. Nashville: Tennessee Historical Society, 1961. 58 pp. Illustrations and maps. A short biography of a Massachusetts-born engineer "who came south [Tennessee] . . . and contributed much to the laying out and construction of the mid-south railroad system."

Creighton, Wilbur F., Jr. "Wilbur Fisk Foster, Soldier and Engineer." *Tennessee Historical Quarterly*. See chapter on "Sewers and Wastewater Treatment."

Crimmins, M. L. "Captain John Pope's Route to the Pacific." *Military Engineer*, XXIII (March-April 1931), 154-58. On Pope's surveying (from the Red River to the Rio Grande) in 1854.

Croes, J. James R. "A Century of Civil Engineering." *Transactions of the American Society of Civil Engineers*, XLV (June 1901), 599-616. Thoughts on the evolving and expanding definition of civil engineering.

Crow, Jeffrey J. "People in Public Works: Harriet M. Berry." *APWA Reporter*. See chapter on "Roads, Streets, and Highways."

Cumming, William P. "Wimble's Maps and the Colonial Cartography of the North Carolina Coast." *North Carolina Historical Review*, XLVI (April 1969), 157-70. A description of James Wimble's maps of the North Carolina coast, "the best coastal chart of the region until the end of the eighteenth century."

Cunningham, Frank. *Big Dan: The Story of a Colorful Railroader*. Salt Lake City: Deseret News Press, 1946. 350 pp. Illustrations, bibliography, and index. A biography of Daniel G. Cunningham by his nephew. During his railroad career, "Big Dan"—who began as an apprentice—served as general foreman on the Norfolk and Western, general foreman for the Santa Fe at Needles, superintendent of shops for the Denver & Rio Grande Western at Salt Lake, superintendent of motive power for the Denver & Salt Lake; and master mechanic of the Salt Lake Division of the Rio Grande.

Dahlberg, James S. *The New York Bureau of Municipal Research: Pioneer in Government Administration*. New York: New York University Press, 1966. xiv + 258 pp. Tables, notes, and bibliography. A study of the bureau's many activities and innovations from 1906 to 1921 and how they affected the development of the public administration field.

Dallaire, Gene. "The Birth and Growth of History's Most Exciting Building Material [Prestressed Concrete]." *Civil Engineering*, 47 (Oct. 1977), 118-20. The story of the "most revolutionary of all structural materials"—prestressed concrete. Developed in Europe, its use became widespread in the United States following construction of a prestressed bridge in Philadelphia.

Dallaire, Gene. "The Engineer: What Role in the Development of Civilization?" *Civil Engineering*, 47 (Oct. 1977), 64-70. An associate editor of *Civil Engineering* takes a look at the engineer's "historical role" in an attempt to "rekindle a renewed pride in the noble profession of engineering."

Daniels, George H. *Science in American So-*

ciety: A Social History. See chapter on "Waterways."

Daniels, Roger. *Public Works in the 1930s: A Preliminary Reconnaisance*. Chicago: Public Works Historical Society and Georgetown University, 1975. 26 pp. Illustrations and notes. On the 1930s as "a watershed in public works history." The essay is followed by comments by Wayne F. Anderson, executive director of the Advisory Commission on Intergovernmental Relations, and Paul Simon, Illinois congressman in the U. S. House of Representatives.

Darling, Arthur B., ed. *The Public Papers of Francis G. Newlands*. See chapter on "Energy."

Darrah, William Culp. *Powell of the Colorado*. See chapter on "Irrigation."

Darrah, William Culp. "Powell of the Colorado." *Utah Historical Quarterly*, 28 (July 1960), 222-31. On Powell's explorations of the Colorado River and his subsequent proposals for surveying the Colorado Valley.

Davis, Franklin M., and Thomas T. Jones, eds. *The U.S. Army Engineers–Fighting Elite*. New York: Franklin Watts, 1967. x + 181 pp. Tables. A series of uneven essays on various aspects of the Army Corps of Engineers' civil and military activities. Selections on mapping, surveying, exploring, and military construction are included.

Davis, Grant Miller. *The Department of Transportation*. Lexington, Mass.: D.C. Heath and Company, 1970. xviii + 244 pp. Charts, tables, notes, and bibliography. Explores the legislative and administrative history that led to the creation of the department in 1967. Some background information on the agencies that comprise the department is also included.

Davis, Harvey N. "Engineering and Health." *Journals of the Franklin Institute*, 226 (July-Dec. 1938), 429-40. Cites examples of how the engineering profession has promoted public health, particularly in the field of sanitation.

Davis, Helen W.; Edward M. Hatch; and David G. Wright. "Alexander Parris: Innovation in Naval Facility Architecture." *IA: The Journal of the Society for Industrial Archeology*. See chapter on "Military Installations."

Davis, Lenwood G. *The History of Urban Growth and Development: A Selected Bibliography, 1872-1975*. Monticello, Ill.: Council of Planning Librarians, 1976. 28 pp. Few of the citations in this sketchy bibliography address public works and city planning topics.

Davis, William E. "The Engineering Experiment at Colorado University." *Colorado Magazine*, XLII (Fall 1965), 330-43. On the teaching of engineering which began in 1883, "a scant six years from the time the university had first opened its doors in 1877."

Davison, George S. "A Century and a Half of American Engineering," *Proceedings of the American Society of Civil Engineers*, LII (Dec. 1926), 1956-78. An inventory of achievements in the areas of surveying, waterways, highways, railways, power, shipbuilding, bridges, tunneling, water supply, city planning, sewage disposal, structural engineering, and irrigation.

Derry, T.K., and Trevor I. Williams. *A Short History of Technology: From the Earliest Times to A.D. 1900*. Oxford: Clarendon Press, 1960. xviii + 782 pp. Illustrations, maps, tables, diagrams, bibliography, and indexes. A fact-filled history of technology divided in two parts: "the first telling the story up to 1750—the beginning of the industrial revolution in Britain—and the second continuing it up to 1900." There are important chapters on building construction, transportation, and sources of power. (The history includes the ancient Near East and Western Europe as well as North America.)

Detweiler, Robert; Jon N. Sutherland; and Michael S. Werthman, eds. *Environmental Decay in Its Historical Context*. Glenview, Ill.: Scott, Foresman and Company, 1973. vii + 142 pp. Reprinted portions of essays that provide "an introduction to the historical record of human beings in relation to their environment and identify the historical roots of the present ecological crisis." After describing the roots of environmental decay, how nature has been abused, and the blight of urban life, the editors conclude with a section intended to develop an ethic of environment. Because of the generality of the approach and the brevity of the selections, this objective is not achieved. The essays are only indirectly related to public works.

Diamondstone, Judith M. "Philadelphia's Municipal Corporation, 1701-1776." *Pennsylvania Magazine of History and Biography*, XC (April 1966), 183-201. The corporation's history with some explanation of its inability to provide needed public services and facilities.

Dickinson, Ellen E. "Joshua Forman, the Founder of Syracuse." *Magazine of American History*, VIII (1882), 400-07. A biographical sketch of Judge Forman, a leader in the affairs of New York's Onordaga County for twenty-five years and the "inventor" of the city of Syracuse.

Dickinson, H.W. "The Value of History in Engineering Education." *Rensselaer Polytechnic Institute Bulletin*, No. 55 (Nov. 1938), 1-11. Argues that the knowledge of history is of "personal value" but has "no practical, material, money-making value."

Diner, Steven J. *A City and Its Universities: Public Policy in Chicago, 1892-1919*. Chapel Hill: University of North Carolina, 1980. xi + 263 pp. Illustrations, notes, appendices, bibliography, and index. Shows how activist professors used information networks and local institutions to demand reforms in municipal administration, social welfare, education, and criminal justice. Of special interest is the chapter on "The Fight for City Government" which highlights the political career of University of Chicago professor Charles E. Merriam.

Dober, Richard P. *Environmental Design*. New York: Van Nostrand Reinhold Company, 1969. viii + 278 pp. Illustrations, maps, diagrams, and index. An examination of environmental design as an interdisciplinary art—"larger than architecture, more comprehensive than planning, more sensitive than engineering." Historical references are scattered throughout the volume.

Dodds, Gordon B. *Hiram Martin Chittenden: His Public Career*. See chapter on "Flood Control and Drainage."

Dodge, Grenville M. "The Engineer's Work in the West: At an Early Day and during the Civil War." *Journal of the Western Society of Engineers*, XIV (Feb. 1909), 1-17. The author, a graduate of Norwich University, reviews his career as an army engineer who built railroads during the Civil War and later became chief engineer of the Union Pacific.

Dole, Esther Mohr. "Municipal Improvements in the United States, 1840-1850." Doctoral dissertation, University of Wisconsin, 1926.

Dorsett, Lyle W. *The Pendergast Machine*. New York: Oxford University Press, 1968. xvi + 163 pp. Notes, bibliographical essay, and index. An intriguing study of the "structural and functional side" of machine politics in Kansas City, Missouri. Dorsett chronicles the rise and decline of the Pendergast organization and demonstrates "how the Pendergasts continually searched for ways to serve, and find areas of agreement among the numerous individuals and groups that had interests to protect and grab to attain." The role of municipal public works operations in the Pendergast extension of power is emphasized in the chapter, "The Pendergast Machine and New Deal Politics."

Dorsett, Lyle W. *The Queen City: A History of Denver*. Boulder: Pruett Publishing Company, 1977. 320 pp. Illustrations, bibliographical note, and index. Public works receive scant attention in this otherwise fine urban history. Some material is included on city planning.

Dorsey, Florence L. *Master of the Mississippi: Henry Shreve and the Conquest of the Mississippi*. See chapter on "Waterways."

Dorsey, Florence. *Road to the Sea: The Story of James B. Eads and the Mississippi River*. See chapter on "Roads, Streets, and Highways."

Dougherty, J.P. "Baroque and Picturesque Motifs in L'Enfant's Design for the Federal Capital." *American Quarterly*, XXVI (March 1974), 23-36. A discussion of the apparent incongruity between Washington's "radial avenues and formal landscaping, reminiscent of European autocracies, and the egalitarianism professed by the new republic."

Dubay, Robert W. "The Civilian Conservation Corps: A Study of Opposition, 1933-1935." *Southern Quarterly*, VI (April 1968), 341-58. Challenges the view that the CCC was a uniformly popular New Deal program.

Duis, Perry R., and Glen E. Holt. "One Hundred Years of Smoke." *Chicago* (Sept. 1979), 140-42, 144. A short article describing Chicago's "war on smoke" at the end of the nineteenth century.

Dunne, David M. "The Engineer School—Past and Present." *Military Engineer*, XLI (Nov.-Dec. 1949), 411-16. A review of engineering training and curriculum from the eighteenth century.

Dupree, A. Hunter. *Science in the Federal Government: A History of Policy and Activities to 1940*. Cambridge: Belknap Press of Harvard University Press, 1957. x + 460 pp. Chronology, notes, bibliographical essay, and index. A chronological and comprehensive tracing of the development of United States government policies and activities in science from 1787 to 1940. Whole chapters are devoted to explorations and surveys (1842-61), the decline of science in the military services (1865-90), the Geological Survey (1867-85), conservation, and medicine and public health (1865-1916). The author also discusses the effects of wars and the Great Depression on science and technology as well as the growth of the federal scientific establishment. The study was funded in large part by the National Science Foundation.

Dupuy, R. Ernest. *Men of West Point: The First 150 years of the United States Military Academy*. New York: William Sloane Associates, 1951. xvii + 486 pp. Illustrations, maps, notes, appendix, bibliography, and index. A narrative history (1802-1951) prepared by a retired colonel and published in celebration of the academy's sesquicentennial.

Durand, W.F. "Robert Henry Thurston." *Annual Report of the Board of Regents of the Smithsonian Institution*. See chapter on "Military Installations."

Durand, W.F. "The Engineer and Civilization." *Mechanical Engineering*, 48 (Jan. 1926), 1-5, 66. An essay on the evolution of the engineering profession since "the beginnings of material civilization" by the president of the American Society of Mechanical Engineers.

Duryee, Sacket L. *A Historical Summary of the Work of the Corps of Engineers in Washington, D.C. and Vicinity, 1852-1952*. Washington, D.C.: U. S. Army Corps of Engineers, 1952. 129 pp. Illustrations and map. The volume was prepared by the Washington Engineer District; Duryee served as chairman of the Historical Committee.

East, John Porter. *Council-Manager Government: The Political Thought of Its Founder, Richard S. Childs*. Chapel Hill: University of North Carolina Press, 1965. x + 183 pp. Notes, bibliography, and index. An historical analysis of Childs' efforts on behalf of municipal reform.

Eaton, Leonard K. *Landscape Artist in America: The Life and Work of Jens Jensen*. See chapter on "Parks and Recreation."

Ebner, Michael H. "Passaic, New Jersey, 1855-1912: City-Building in Post-Civil War America." Doctoral dissertation, University of Virginia, 1974. ii + 301 pp. Tables, notes, and bibliography. Study of the influence of industrialization and politics on urban growth.

Ebner, Michael H., and Eugene M. Tobin. *The Age of Urban Reform: New Perspectives on the Progressive Era*. Port Washington, N.Y.: Kennikat Press, 1977. viii + 211 pp. Maps, tables, notes, bibliographical essay, and index. Ten essays by young historians that document the responses of communities to problems such as haphazard growth, impure water supplies, and poor utility service during the Progressive era. The diverse essays are organized around three common themes: the qualitative implications of growth, disparate political leaders and issues, and the varying responses to social and economic problems.

Ehrenberg, Ralph E. "Nicholas King: First Surveyor of the City of Washington, 1803-1812." *Records of the Columbia Historical Society of Washington, D.C.* (1969-1970), 31-65. A biographical account of King and an explanation of how he helped transform Pierre Charles L'Enfant's plan for the city of Washington into a reality. The article is illustrated with King's drawings of a proposed canal at Harpers Ferry.

Eiseman, Harry J. "Origins of Engineering Education in Missouri." *Missouri Historical Review*, LXIII (July 1969), 451-460. Recounts the events leading to the establishment of the Missouri School of Mines and Metallurgy at Rolla in 1871.

Eisenbud, Merril. *Environment, Technology, and Health: Human Ecology in Historical Perspective*. New York: New York University Press, 1978. x + 384 pp. Illustrations, tables, charts, bibliography, and indexes.

Eliot, Charles. *Charles Eliot: Landscape Architect*. See chapter on "Parks and Recreation."

Ellis, Robert R. "Richard Gridley: First Chief Engineer of the Army." 3 parts. *Military Engineer*, 55 (May-June, July-Aug., Sept.-Oct. 1963), May-June: 157-60; July-Aug.: 265-68; Sept.-Oct.: 344-47. A biographical sketch.

Ellis, Roy. *A Civic History of Kansas City, Missouri*. Springfield, Mo.: Elkins-Swyers Company, 1930. viii + 243 pp. Illustration, tables, chart, notes, and index. A chronicle of

Kansas City's growth and development. There are useful chapters on transportation; streets, parks, and playgrounds; street railways and gas and electric companies; water supply; and municipal finance.

Ellis, W.T. *Memories: My Seventy-Two Years in the Romantic County of Yuba, California.* See chapter on "Flood Control and Drainage."

"Engineering Fifty Years Ago." *Engineering News-Record*, 96 (Jan. 14, 1926), 95. A short review of engineering in the United States and abroad for 1875. (Reprinted from *Engineering News*, Jan. 1876.)

"Engineering Today and Yesterday: A Composite View." *Engineering News-Record*, 92 (April 17, 1924), 642-51. Twenty-seven engineers, who have been engaged in engineering or construction work for the major part of the fifty years, respond to the question: "What is the essential difference . . . between engineering of today and engineering when you started practice?"

Ericsson, Henry, and Myers, Lewis E. *Sixty Years a Builder: The Autobiography of Henry Ericsson*. See chapter on "Public Buildings."

Ernst, Joseph W. "With Compass and Chain: Federal Land Surveyors in the Old Northwest, 1785-1816." Doctoral dissertation, Columbia University, 1958. 328 pp.

Eyrick, George J., Jr. "The Development of Specifications for Reinforced Concrete." *Proceedings of the American Concrete Institute*, XXV (1929), 622-31. During previous ten years. A result of the work of the Joint Committee on Standard Specifications for Concrete and Reinforced Concrete.

Fabos, Julius Gy.; Gordon T. Milde, and V. Michael Weinmayr. *Frederick Law Olmsted, Sr.: Founder of Landscape Architecture in America*. See chapter on "Parks and Recreation."

"Fact Book, 1970-1971: The Society of American Military Engineers." *Military Engineer*, 62 (Nov.-Dec. 1970), 427-50. Lists names, places, and events pertaining to the society's origin and growth and includes a copy of the organization's constitution and by-laws.

Fairbanks, Robert B. "Cincinnati and Greenhills: The Response to a Federal Community, 1935-1939." *Cincinnati Historical Society Bulletin*, 36 (Winter 1978), 233-41. Good discussion of one of the New Deal's Greenbelt Towns.

Fairlie, John A. *Municipal Administration*. New York: MacMillan Company, 1901. xiii + 448 pp. Tables, notes, and index. This book begins with an historical survey of cities and their governments. It includes ancient and medieval cities as well as nineteenth-century European and United States cities. The remainder of the study deals with "the active functions of municipal administration" (the majority of which are public works) and "the problems of municipal finance."

Fairweather, Virginia. "Jane Jacobs: Urban Planning Heretic." *Civil Engineering,* 47 (Oct. 1977), 127-30. How Jacobs' book, *The Death and Life of Great American Cities*, affected urban planning. "She peered at the city through a magnifying glass and saw why grand schemes weren't working. What's more, she told what was good about American cities—their diversity, vitality, color and texture."

Falk, Stanley L. "Soldier-Technologist: Major Alfred Mordecai and the Beginnings of Science in the United States Army." 2 vols. Doctoral dissertation, Georgetown University, 1959. Vol. I.: vii + 285 pp.; Vol. II: 286-617 pp. Notes and bibliography. A biographical study of "a leader in technical military research and in the practical application of science to war." The first chapters on "the education of a soldier-technologist" and "the technologist as engineer" are of special interest.

Farquhar, Francis P. "Exploration of the Sierra Nevada." *California Historical Society Quarterly*. See chapter on "Parks and Recreation."

Farquhar, Francis P., ed. *Up and Down California in 1860-1864: The Journal of William H. Brewer, Professor of Agriculture in the Sheffield Scientific School of Agriculture from 1864 to 1903*. Berkeley: University of California Press, 1966. xxiii + 583 pp. Illustrations, notes, and index. First published in 1930, this volume contains "a comprehensive view of the physical structure of the state of California" prepared as part of the California State Geological Survey. This survey produced a wealth of information later used by numerous agencies of state and local government and had widespread influence on the conduct of subsequent surveys throughout the United States.

Fein, Albert. *Frederick Law Olmsted and the American Environmental Tradition*. See chapter on "Parks and Recreation."

Fein, Albert, ed. *Landscape into Cityscape: Frederick Law Olmsted's Plans for a Greater New York City*. Ithaca: Cornell University Press, 1967. x + 490 pp. Illustrations, maps, notes, and indexes. Nine of the twelve reprinted documents in this volume are reports to governmental bodies regarding public works for some part of New York City. An introductory chapter by the editor describes Olmsted's influence on New York City's physical environment.

Feinstein, Estelle F. *Stamford in the Gilded Age: The Political Life of a Connecticut Town, 1868-1893*. Stamford, Conn.: Stamford Historical Society, 1973. xi + 319 pp. Illustrations, maps, charts, notes, bibliography, and index. Of special interest are the chapters on "The Issue of Public Works" (the town hall, a memorial monument, and Shippan Point Park) and "The Protection of the Public Health" (the question of garbage removal and the issue of sewage disposal).

Fellmeth, Robert C. *Politics of Land: Ralph Nader's Study Group Report on Land Use in California*. New York: Grossman Publishers, 1973. xvii + 715 pp. Notes, appendices, and index. This book studies the use and abuse of California land by private and public interests. Subjects treated include water pollution and distribution, zoning, highway networks, and airports.

Ferrell, John R. "Water in the Missouri Valley: The Inter-Agency River Committee Concept at Mid-Century." *Journal of the West*. See chapter on "Flood Control and Drainage."

Field, Cynthia R. "The City Planning of Daniel Hudson Burnham." Doctoral dissertation, Columbia University, 1974. 557 pp.

"Fifty Years Ago, 1920-1970: The Society of American Military Engineers." 5 parts. *Military Engineer*, 62 (Jan.-Feb., March-April, May-June, Sept.-Oct., Nov.-Dec., 1970), Jan.-Feb.: 1-5; March April: 89-90; May-June: 182-83; Sept.-Oct.: 326-27; Nov.-Dec.: 396. A brief history of the society by the editors of *Military Engineer*.

Finch, James Kip. "A Century of Engineering Progress: 1852-1952." *Scientific Monthly*, LXXV (Aug. 1952), 99-108. On "the tremendous influence that engineering has had on Western Civilization."

Finch, James Kip. *A History of the School of Engineering, Columbia University*. New York: Columbia University Press, 1954. xi + 138 pp. Illustrations, notes, and index. A bicentennial history by Columbia's dean emeritus of civil engineering.

Finch, J. K. "A Hundred Years of American Civil Engineering, 1852-1952." *Transactions of the American Society of Civil Engineers*, CT (1953), 28-96. Traces the growth of specialities in civil engineering—bridges, tunnels, highways, water supply, sewage treatment, irrigation, and power.

Finch, J. K. *Early Columbia Engineers: An Appreciation*. New York: Columbia University Press, 1929. x + 41 pp. Illustrations. Biographical sketches of "pioneer American engineers" who were graduates of Columbia University: John Stevens of the class of 1768; James Renwick of 1807; Horatio Allen of 1823; and Alfred Wingate Craven of 1829.

Finch, J. K. *Engineering and Western Civilization*. New York: McGraw-Hill Book Company, 1951. x + 397 pp. Illustrations, diagrams, tables, bibliography, and index. A survey by a professor of civil engineering which describes the role of engineering in the western world from ancient times to the mid-twentieth century. Espousing an "engineering interpretation of history," the author contends that the past and future of western civilization are indissolubly linked to engineering advances.

Finch, J. K. "John Bloomfield Jervis, Civil Engineer." *Transactions of the Newcomen Society (London) for the Study of the History of Engineering and Technology*. See chapter on "Community Water Supply."

Finch, J. K. "Our Indebtedness to the Old Surveyor." *Military Engineer*, XVII (July-Aug. 1925), 320-25. The story of the surveyor, "an essential figure to the progress of civilization, the maintenance of property rights, and the building of engineering works. . . ."

Finch, J. K. "The Engineering Profession in Evolution." *Transactions of the American Society of Civil Engineers*, CT (1953), 112-24. A discussion of the evolution of civil engineering, the oldest branch, and its growth in professional stature.

Finch, James Kip. *The Story of Engineering*. Garden City, N.Y.: Doubleday, 1960. 528 pp. Illustrations.

Finn, Terence T. "Conflict and Compromise: Congress Makes a Law, the Passage of the National Environmental Policy Act." Doctoral dissertation, Georgetown University, 1973. 702 pp.

Fisher, Edwin A. "Engineering and Public Works in the City of Rochester During the Past Century." *Centennial History of Rochester, New York*, III (1934), 157-240. An extraordinary piece of work by "the dean of Rochester engineers"—city engineer (1896-1903) and superintendent of city planning (1917-1923) among other positions held during his long career. Fisher's article includes material on the city's public works officials and boards, surveys, sewers and sewage disposal, bridges, pavements, street lighting, utilities, parks, markets, railroads and railways, harbors and canals, flood protection and water storage, refuse collection and disposal, and waterworks.

Fisher, Jane. *Fabulous Hoosier: A Story of American Achievement*. See chapter on "Roads, Streets, and Highways."

Fitch, James Marston. *Architecture and the Esthetics of Plenty*. New York: Columbia University Press, 1961. xii + 304 pp. Illustrations, notes, and index. A collection of essays of general interest. Public work researchers may find "The Impact of Technology" and "The Engineer: Friend or Foe?" of particular use.

FitzGerald, Desmond. "Address at the Annual Convention at Cape May, N. J., June 27, 1899." *Transactions of the American Society of Civil Engineers*, XLI (June 1899), 596-617. A general history of engineering by the president of the American Society of Civil Engineers.

Fitzgerald, Richard. "Land Use Planning in Southern California: The Matter of Sears, Roebuck and Co. and the City of Riverside." *Southern California Quarterly*, LII (Dec. 1970), 383-403. In this case study, the author demonstrates that in the early 1960s Riverside, like many other local communities, was a victim of its "need to expand." He also shows how difficult it is for planning and/or public works departments to develop public consensus on overall planning goals—the Master Plan—in a growing area.

Fitzpatrick, Edward A., ed. *Experts in City Government*. New York: D. Appleton and Company, 1919. xiv + 363 pp. Charts, appendix, and index. A collection of essays intended to foster expert "city-making"—government administered by trained individuals. The authors, prominent public administrators, share their insights on how American municipal government can be established "on a firm basis of democratic and community efficiency." Philadelphia's former Director of Public Works Morris L. Cooke's "Training in Municipal Service" is particularly interesting as is Seattle's Commissioner of Public Utilities Charles M. Fossett's "Utility Problems and Expert City Government." Historical references are scattered.

FitzSimons, Neal, ed. *The Reminiscences of John B. Jervis: Engineer of the Old Croton*. See chapter on "Community Water Supply."

Flanagan, Vincent J. "Gouverneur Kemble Warren, Explorer of the Nebraska Territory." *Nebraska History*, 51 (Summer), 171-98. A study of Warren's contribution to the exploration of the West (1855-1857). The author believes that the subject of this article, "an inquisitive soldier-explorer," deserves the title, "Explorer of the Nebraska Territory."

Fleming, Thomas J. *West Point: The Men and Times of the United States Military Academy*, New York: William Morrow & Company, 1969. vii + 402 pp. Illustrations, note on sources, bibliography, and index. A full-scale history of the academy by a professional writer who had initially intended to prepare a biography of Sylvanus Thayer. The project was funded by *Reader's Digest*.

Fletcher, Robert. "Schoolmen vs. Practicians—Looking Backward Fifty Years." *Engineering News-Record*, 92 (April 17, 1924), 668-69. A review of engineering education from the days "when practicing engineers in America looked askance at engineering schools and their graduates" by the director-emeritus of the Thayer School of Civil Engineering at Dartmouth College.

Florman, Samuel C. *Engineering and the Liberal Arts: A Technologist's Guide to History, Literature, Philosophy, Art, and Music*. New

York: McGraw-Hill Book Company, 1968. x + 278 pp. Notes and index. The author advocates "the cause of liberal education" for engineers and explores ways in which engineering is related to the liberal arts. The most interesting chapters are the first three: "The Civilized Engineer"; "The Bridge to History: The History of Technology"; and "The World of History."

Florman, Samuel C. *The Existential Pleasures of Engineering*. New York: St. Martin's Press, 1976. xi + 160 pp. Notes. An engaging short book in which the author reappraises the engineer's role in society. He argues against the stereotype of the engineer as "an insensitive materialist whose activities are hostile to humanistic values" and contends that technology, like art, is the result of a "commission"—implicit or explicit—from society.

Fogelson, Robert M. *The Fragmented Metropolis: Los Angeles, 1850-1930*. See chapter on "Community Water Supply."

Folwell, A. Prescott. "American Society of Municipal Improvements." *American City*, III (Oct. 1910), 184-86. Brief historical account of a predecessor organization (1894) of the American Public Works Association.

Forbes, R. J. *Man the Maker: A History of Technology and Engineering*. New York: Henry Schuman, 1950. xii + 355 pp. Illustrations, bibliographical essay, and index. A history of mankind's accomplishments in the field of discovery, invention, and engineering from prehistoric times to the 1950s. Of particular interest to public works researchers are the chapters with sections on improved city services, canal and drainage projects, asphalt and concrete roads, bridges, steam power, and land traffic.

Ford, George B., ed. *City Planning Progress in the United States, 1917*. Washington, D. C.: American Institute of Architects, 1917. viii + 207 pp. Illustrations, maps, diagrams, bibliography, and index. Compiled by the Committee on Town Planning of the American Institute of Architects "to meet the widespread and insistent demand for information" on city planning. The volume is essentially a report on what had been accomplished or was projected in all United States cities of over 25,000 inhabitants; a few cities and towns with smaller populations are included where their work is of special interest. The editor and committee have emphasized the economic and engineering side of city planning.

Foreman, Grant, ed. *A Pathfinder in the Southwest: The Itinerary of Lieutenant A. W. Whipple during His Explorations for a Railway Route from Fort Smith to Los Angeles in the Years 1853 & 1854*. Norman, University of Oklahoma Press, 1941. xv + 298 pp. Illustrations, maps, notes, bibliography, and index. Amiel Weeks Whipple's account of his survey from St. Louis and Fort Smith, through Oklahoma and the country west, to the Pacific Ocean. The road conceived by Whipple (an 1841 graduate of the United States Military Academy and topographical engineer) along the route believed by him to be the most favorable was never built. His work, however, should not go unnoticed.

Foreman, H. E. "The Contract Method for American Construction." *Transactions of the American Society of Civil Engineers*, CT (1953) 231-46. Traces the development of the construction industry and the contract method in the United States. The author is managing director of the Associated General Contractors of America.

Forman, Sidney. "The First School of Engineering." *Military Engineer*, XLIV (March-April 1952), 109-12.

Forman, Sidney. "Why the United States Military Academy was Established in 1802." *Military Affairs*, XXIX (Spring 1965), 16-28. Reviews the reasons leading to the establishment of West Point in 1802.

Foulke, William Dudley. "Coming of Age: Municipal Progress in Twenty-One Years." *National Municipal Review*, V (1916), 12-23. A short history of the National Municipal League presented in an address by its president.

Fowle, Frank F. "Octave Chanute: Pioneer Glider and Father of the Science of Aviation." *Indiana Magazine of History*. See chapter on "Airways and Airports."

Fox, Kenneth. *Better City Government: Innovation in American Urban Politics, 1850-1937*. Philadelphia: Temple University Press, 1977. xxi + 222 pp. Tables, notes, bibliographical essay, and index. A well-crafted study of the transformation of municipal government in the late nineteenth and early twentieth centuries. Unfortunately, the book does not give adequate attention to the public works aspects of municipal reform.

Fox, Kenneth Paul. "The Census Bureau and the Cities: National Development of Urban Government in the Industrial Age, 1870-1930." Doctoral dissertation, University of Pennsylvania, 1972. 371 pp.

Foy, Bernard L., comp. *A Bibliography for the TVA Program*. See chapter on "Flood Control and Drainage."

Frady, Donald S., and Ray A. Vanneman, co-comps. *History of the Virginia-District of Columbia-Maryland Chapter*. Arlington, Va.: Virginia-D.C.-Maryland Chapter, American Public Works Association, 1977. vi + 79 pp. Illustrations. Describes the membership growth and professional development of an individual chapter (1956) of the American Public Works Association.

Frank, Carrolyle M. "Who Governed Middletown? Community Power in Muncie, Indiana, in the 1930s." *Indiana Magazine of History*, LXXV (Dec. 1979), 320-43. An important article which demonstrates the critical role of public works issues, particularly as a result of the New Deal, in local decision making in Muncie, Indiana. The specific incidents examined are the municipal airport affair, Civil Works Administration projects, and sewage treatment.

Franzwa, Gregory M. *Legacy: The Sverdrup Story*. St. Louis: Sverdrup Corporation and Patrice Press, 1978. xiii + 286 pp. Illustrations, maps, and index. An organizational history of a prominent, St. Louis-based consulting engineering firm.

Franzwa, Gregory M., and William J. Ely. *Leif Sverdrup*. Gerald, Mo.: Patrice Press, 1980. xiii + 387 pp. Illustrations, maps, and index. A full-length biography of a prominent twentieth-century soldier who was also the founder of the engineering firm of Sverdrup & Parcel in St. Louis, Missouri.

Fraser, Chelsea. *The Story of Engineering in America*. New York: Thomas Y. Crowell Company, 1928. viii + 471 pp. Illustrations, diagrams, and index. An explanation of the work of engineers in the past as well as the present. The volume was written for young adults and contains numerous historical sketches of famous roads, bridges, tunnels, canals, lighthouses, and buildings.

Fremont, J. C. *Report of the Exploring Expedition to the Rocky Mountains in the Year 1842, and to Oregon and North Carolina in the Years 1843-'44*. Washington, D. C.: Gales and Seaton, 1845. 693 pp. Illustrations, maps, tables, and diagrams. Published versions of the 1843 and 1845 reports submitted by Fremont to Colonel J. J. Abert, chief of the Corps of Topographical Engineers. Fremont presents nothing, "either in the narrative or in the maps, which was not the result of positive observation."

Fries, Sylvia Doughty. *The Urban Idea in Colonial America*. Philadelphia: Temple University Press, 1977. xviii + 218 pp. Illustrations, notes, bibliography, and index. Explains "the idea of the city in American civilization, not from the perspective of what it became, but of whence it came." There is a substantial amount of material on early city plans (Boston, Philadelphia, Williamsburg, and Savannah) but only occasional references to public works.

Friis, Herman Ralph. "Highlights in the First Hundred Years of Surveying and Mapping and Geographical Explorations of the United States by the Federal Government, 1775-1880." *Surveying and Mapping*, 18 (April-June 1958), 186-206.

Friis, Herman R., and Suzanne Pitzer. *Federal Exploration of the American West Before 1880.* Washington, D.C.: National Archives, 1963. 31 pp.

Friis, Herman R., and Ralph E. Ehrenberg. "Nicholas King and His Wharfing Plans of the City of Washington, 1797." *Records of the Columbia Historical Society of Washington, D. C.* (1966-1968), 34-46. Reviews King's major contributions "to the early history of the City of Washington specifically, and to the history of surveying and mapping by the Federal Government generally."

Funigiello, Philip J. "City Planning in World War II: The Experience of the National Resources Planning Board." *Social Science Quarterly*, 53 (June 1972), 91-104. On the board's activities in the area of neighborhood conservation and rehabilitation planning during the period of defense preparations (1940-1941).

Funigiello, Philip J. *The Challenge to Urban Liberalism: Federal-City Relations During World War II*. Knoxville: University of

Tennessee Press, 1978, xx + 273 pp. Notes, bibliographical essay, and index. Includes good discussions on the influence of federal programs on city planning. The author also perceptively identifies the fears and suspicions of cities with respect to the centralizing tendencies of the New Deal.

Fungiello, Philip J. *Toward a National Power Policy: The New Deal and the Electric Utility Industry, 1933-1941*. See chapter on "Energy."

Furman, Franklin De Ronde, ed. *Morton Memorial: A History of the Stevens Institute of Technology . . . and a Record of the Achievements of the Stevens Family of Engineers*. Hoboken, N. J.: Stevens Institute of Technology, 1905. xxii + 641 pp. Illustrations. The book is divided into three parts: "History of the Institute"; "The Stevens Family"; and "Biographies" of institute trustees, faculty, and alumni.

Galbraith, J. K. *The Economic Effects of the Federal Public Works Expenditures, 1933-1938*. Washington, D.C.: U. S. National Resources Planning Board, 1940. vii + 131 pp. Charts, tables, graphs, notes, appendices, glossary, and index. Report prepared under the direction of the National Resource Planning Board's Public Works Committee. The report summarizes and draws "lessons from the experience which the United States Government has had during the past decade in its efforts to use public works construction expenditure as an aid to employment and recovery."

Gallagher, H. M. Pierce. *Robert Mills: Architect of the Washington Monument, 1781-1855*. See chapter on "Public Buildings."

Gallaher, Ruth A. "J. N. Nicollet Map Maker." *Palimpsest*, XXVI (Oct. 1945), 289-302. A biographical sketch of the French mathematician, scientist, and explorer/surveyor who became an authority on Iowa's boundaries.

Galll, Geraldine. "100 Years of Construction News." *Engineering News-Record*, 192 (April 30, 1974), 433-505. A list of milestones in public works construction. The list is divided into sections on airports, bridges, buildings, construction's tools, dams, design theory and specifications, foundations, highways, irrigation, power, public transportation, river control, tunnels, waste treatment, and water supply and purification.

Galloway, John D. "Theodore Dehone Judah—Railroad Pioneer." *Civil Engineering*, 11 (Oct. 1941; Nov. 1941), Oct.: 586-88; Nov.: 648-51. A two-part, biographical sketch of a railroad engineer who was largely responsible for building the Central Pacific line.

Galloway, K. Bruce, and Robert Boure Johnson, Jr. *West Point: America's Power Fraternity*. New York: Simon and Schuster, 1973. 448 pp. Notes, appendices, bibliography, and index. A critical examination of the role of the Army Corps of Engineers in "the tragedy called Vietnam." The early chapters of the book, in particular, discuss the way in which West Point has traditionally trained its cadets.

Gardner, Asa Bird. "Henry Burbeck: Brevet Brigadier-General United States Army—Founder of the United States Military Academy." *Magazine of American History*, IX (April 1883), 251-65. A biographical sketch (1754-1848).

Garny, Patricia M. *The Alaskan Earthquake, 1964*. Charlotteville, N.Y.: Samttar Press, 1973. 29 pp. Bibliography. An overview of the disaster that includes some material on post-earthquake planning, zoning, and the reconstruction of roads as well as other public facilities.

Garr, Daniel. "Hispanic Colonial Settlement in California: Planning and Urban Development on the Frontier, 1769-1850." Doctoral dissertation, Cornell University, 1972.

Garrett, Charles. *The La Guardia Years: Machine and Reform Politics in New York City*. New Brunswick, N. J.: Rutgers University Press, 1961. xii + 423 pp. Illustrations, notes, bibliographical essay, and index. Contains extensive material on public works projects undertaken by Robert Moses.

Garvan, Anthony N. B. *Architecture and Town Planning in Colonial Connecticut*. See chapter on "Public Buildings."

Garvan, Anthony. "The Origin of Colonial Architecture and Town Planning in Connecticut: A Study in American Social History." Doctoral dissertation, Yale University, 1948.

Gayer, Arthur D. *Public Works in Prosperity and Depression*. New York: National Bureau of Economic Research, 1935. xx + 460 pp.

Charts, tables, notes, appendices, and index. Excellent study of the scope, volume, and effect of public works construction in the United States from 1919 to 1934. It was the first attempt to analyze public works as a countercyclical fiscal strategy.

Gelfand, Mark I. *A Nation of Cities: The Federal Government and Urban America, 1933-1965*. New York: Oxford University Press, 1975. xvii + 476 pp. Notes, bibliography, and index. Traces federal involvement in urban (large central cities) affairs from the New Deal. A good deal of the book relates to public works policies and practices.

"George Washington—Engineer." *Engineering News-Record*, 108 (Feb. 18, 1932), 238-39. A review of Washington's early engineering experiences, particularly as a land surveyor.

Gerckens, Laurence C. "Glancing Back." *Planning*, 46 (Oct. 1980), 23-26. Reviews Cincinnati's planning history and highlights the career of Alfred Bettman, a founding member of the American City Planning Institute and a member of the city planning commission of Cincinnati from 1925 to 1945.

Gibb, Hugh R. "Mendes Cohen: Engineer, Scholar and Railroad Executive." *Maryland Historical Magazine*, 74 (March 1979), 1-10. On Cohen's railroad career—as engineer and administrator—and his professional activities.

Giedion, Siegfried. *Space, Time and Architecture: The Growth of a New Tradition*. Cambridge: Harvard University Press, 1954. xxii + 778 pp. Illustrations, maps, diagrams, notes, and index. A general history of architecture with a strong emphasis on city planning. The book, first printed in 1941, began as an outgrowth of the author's lectures and seminars given at Harvard University in 1938-1939.

Gilbert, Bill. *This City, This Man: The Cookingham Era in Kansas City*. Washington, D.C.: International City Management Association, 1978. ix + 267 pp. Illustrations and index. A lively, revealing biography of a twentieth-century urban administrator by the director of public affairs for the Metropolitan Washington Council of Governments. In 1940 L. P. (Perry) Cookingham, already nationally known as the creative manager of Saginaw, Michigan, became city manager of Kansas City, Missouri. The city was infamous for its corruption and violence, especially the scandals associated with the "Boss" Pendergast political machine. Gilbert provides a penetrating, anecdotal account of the challenges faced and met by his subject.

Gilchrist, Agnes Addison. *William Strickland: Architect and Engineer, 1788-1854*. See chapter on "Public Buildings."

Gill, Norman N. *Municipal Research Bureaus: A Study of the Nation's Leading Citizen-Supported Agencies*. Washington, D.C.: American Council on Public Affairs, 1944. 178 pp. Tables, notes, and index. A study of twenty municipal research bureaus—organizations which "have long been in the forefront of the fight for better government." The introductory chapter reviews the "History of the Research Bureau Movement." One section within the chapter on "Research Activities" is devoted to public works; for, as the author notes, "public works planning ranks second only to finance and budgeting in the number of bureau studies."

Glaab, Charles N. *The American City: A Documentary History*. See chapter on "Waterways."

Glaab, Charles N. "Visions of Metropolis: William Gilpin and Theories of City Growth in the American West." *Wisconsin Magazine of History*, XLV (Autumn 1961), 21-31. Explores "some early and often fanciful theories of city growth and planning" by examining the writings of William Gilpin, a strong believer in America's manifest destiny.

Godard, George S. "Washington as an Engineer." *Connecticut Society of Civil Engineers*, 48 (1932), 11-14. A quick look at some of Washington's surveying work.

Goddard, Dwight. *Eminent Engineers: Brief Biographies of Thirty-two of the Inventors and Engineers Who Did Most To Further Mechanical Progress*. New York: Derry-Collard Company, 1906. 280 pp. Illustrations. These short biographical sketches of American and European engineers and inventors were written from 1903 to 1906 and issued monthly by Wyman & Gordon, manufacturers of drop forgings, in Worcester, Massachusetts, and Cleveland, Ohio. The individuals included in this volume contributed to the development and application of power and machinery. The Americans are B. Franklin, J. Fitch, N. Read, O. Evans, R. Fulton, J. Stevens, R. L. Stevens,

E. Whitney, T. Blanchard, E. Howe, J. Ericsson, P. Cooper, G. H. Corliss, A. L. Holley, W. R. Jones, and J. B. Eads.

Goetzmann, William H. *Army Exploration in the American West*. New Haven: Yale University Press, 1959. xx + 509 pp. Illustrations, maps, notes, appendices, bibliographical essay, and index. A thorough examination of "the role played by the U. S. Army in exploring the trans-Mississippi West and in particular the role of the Topographical Engineers between the years 1838 and 1863." Whole chapters are devoted to such subjects as John C. Frémont, particular surveys, and the wagon road program.

Goetzmann, William H. *Exploration and Empire: The Explorer and the Scientist in the Winning of the American West*. New York: Alfred A. Knopf, 1966. xxvi + 656 + xviii pp. Illustrations, maps, notes, bibliographical essay, and index. Perhaps the most comprehensive and insightful book on western exploration and surveying during the nineteenth century. The author does not let his sound research get in the way of telling an exciting story. The third part of the book, "Exploration and the Great Surveys," offers excellent analyses of the Wheeler, Hayden, and Powell surveys. The book is illustrated with three excellent portfolios of photographs.

Goetzmann, William H. "The Grand Reconnaissance." *American Heritage*, XXIII (Oct. 1972), 44-59; 92-95. Describes the Army's 1853 Pacific Railroad Surveys, "the capstone of an American age of exploration in the Far West."

Goff, John S. *George W. P. Hunt and His Arizona*. See chapter on "Irrigation."

Good, H. G. "New Data on Early Engineering Education." *Journal of Educational Research*, 20 (Sept. 1935), 37-46. A brief review of formal engineering education in the early nineteenth century.

Goodwin, Rutherford. *A Brief & True Report Concerning Williamsburg in Virginia: Being an Account of the Most Important Occurrences in the Place From Its First Beginning to the Present Time*. Williamsburg: Colonial Williamsburg, Inc., 1941.

Gordon, Roy. "Engineering for People: 200 Years of Army Public Works." *Military Engineer*. LXVIII (May/June 1976), 180-85. Useful overview of the accomplishments of the Army Corps of Engineers.

Gosnell, Harold F. *Machine Politics: Chicago Model*. Chicago: University of Chicago Press, 1968. xxxii + 247 pp. Illustrations, maps, charts, tables, notes, appendices, bibliography, and index. First published in 1937, the vitriolic book illustrates how political corruption and graft compromise the delivery of public works and other services to the people.

Gottman, Jean. *Megalopolis: The Urbanized Northeastern Seaboard of the United States*. New York: Twentieth Century Fund, 1961. xi + 810 pp. Illustrations, maps, notes, and index. A landmark study of the dynamics of urban growth. Material is included on changing uses of land and the transformation of metropolitan transportation systems.

Gould, Jay M. *The Technical Elite*. New York: Augustus M. Kelley, 1966. 178 pp. Charts, notes, appendix, and index. In testing the thesis set forth in Thornstein Veblen's *The Engineers and the Price System*, the author traces the exponential growth of a technical labor force in the United States and gives some striking information about the role of technology in the country's economic life. Special emphasis is placed on engineers and scientists in private industry with only minor discussions of engineers in government.

Graham, Frank, Jr. *Man's Dominion: The Story of Conservation in America*. New York: M. Evans and Company, distributed by J. B. Lippincott, 1971. xii + 339 pp. Illustrations, notes, bibliographical essay, and index. A popular account of the conservation movement from the middle 1880s. Theodore Roosevelt, Gifford Pinchot, Stephen T. Mather, John Muir, and William T. Hornaday are the subjects of whole chapters. The author also devotes one chapter to a discussion of the Tennessee Valley Authority.

Graham, Otis L., Jr. *Toward a Planned Society. From Roosevelt to Nixon*. New York: Oxford University Press, 1976. xviii + 357 pp. Notes, bibliography, and index.

Grant, Ulysses S., 3rd. "Planning the Nation's Capital." *Records of the Columbia Historical Society of Washington, D.C.*, 30 (1948-1950), 43-58. A review of past and present plans for Washington, D.C., by the chairman of the National Capital Park and Planning Commission.

Grant, Ulysses S., 3rd. "The L'Enfant Plan and Its Evolution." *Records of the Columbia Historical Society of Washington, D.C.*, 33-34 (1932), 1-24. Describes the plan's evolution (from 1790) and its unique characteristics—"its grand scale and the fact that it was laid out so as to utilize to the fullest extent the natural topography."

Graves, Gregory R., and Sally L. Simon, eds. *A History of Environmental Review in Santa Barbara County*. Santa Barbara: Graduate Program in Public Historical Studies, University of California, 1980. xvii + 386 pp. Illustrations, chronology, maps, charts, notes, bibliography, glossary, and appendix. A study of the evolution of the environmental review process in Santa Barbara County. Part one represents a "Historical Overview"; part two contains ten "Case Studies."

Grayson, Lawrence P. "A Brief History of Engineering Education in the United States." *Engineering Education*, 68 (Dec. 1977), 246-64. A chronological discussion of the evolution of engineering education. It includes one and a half pages of "references and bibliographic notes."

Great Plains Committee. *The Future of the Great Plains*. Washington, D.C.: U.S. Government Printing Office, 1936. 194 pp. Illustrations, maps, tables, graphs, appendices, and bibliography. A report on the efficient utilization of resources of the Great Plains area by a special, Roosevelt-appointed committee of which Morris L. Cooke, administrator of the Rural Electrification Administration and former public works director of Philadelphia, served as chairman. Historical data and statistics are scattered throughout the report.

Greeley, M. L. "Land Surveying—Its Foundation and Superstructure." *Civil Engineering*, 3 (Sept. 1933), 508-10. General description since 1784.

Green, Constance McLaughlin. *American Cities in the Growth of the Nation*. London: John De Graff, 1957. xii + 258 pp. Illustrations, bibliography, and index. Surveys the history of some sixteen American cities. Incidental material is included on city planning and government.

Greene, B. Franklin. *Rensselaer Polytechnic Institute*. Troy, N.Y.: Rensselaer Polytechnic Institute, 1931. 26 pp. Extracts from a pamphlet published in 1855 by Greene, who was director of Rensselaer Polytechnic Institute from 1846 to 1858 and who reorganized institute courses in 1849 after studying the curricula of European technical schools.

Greene, Benjamin Franklin. *The True Idea of a Polytechnic Institute: A Facsimile Reprint from the Report of Benjamin Franklin Green, Director of Rensselaer Institute, 1846-1858*. Troy, N.Y.: Rensselaer Polytechnic Institute, 1949. vi + 33-80 + ii pp. Illustration and notes. Greene's entire report to the institute's board of trustees that summarizes the progress of technical education in Europe and sets forth his ideas for the development of a polytechnic institute, was written in 1849 and published in 1855. The second section, considered a classic in the history of engineering education, was reprinted on the one hundred and twenty-fifth anniversary of Rensselaer. In it Green presents his plan for "an educational discipline complete in itself, not narrowly vocational . . . ."

Greene, Lee S.; Malcolm E. Jewell; and Daniel R. Grant. *The States and the Metropolis*. University, Ala.: University of Alabama Press, 1968. 145 pp. Notes and index. A useful series of five essays on changes in the interrelationships between state and city governments.

Gregg, Kate L., ed. *The Road to Sante Fe: The Journal and Diaries of George Champlin Sibley and Others Pertaining to the Surveying and Marking of a Road from the Missouri Frontier to the Settlements of New Mexico, 1825-1827*. See chapter on "Roads, Streets, and Highways."

Gregory, Malcolm S. *History and Development of Engineering*. London: Longman, 1971. x + 190 pp. Illustrations, bibliographies, and index. An attempt to assess the current position of the engineer in society by looking backward. The author provides an overview of some of the forces around the world that have served to define the role of today's engineering designer.

Gressley, Gene M. "Arthur Powell Davis, Reclamation, and the West." *Agricultural History*. See chapter on "Irrigation."

Griffith, Ernest S. *A History of American City Government: The Colonial Period*. New York: Oxford University Press, 1938. 464 pp. Notes, appendices, and index. A history of "the political city," written to demonstrate "the interaction of the political with the economic and cultural." The most useful chapter is that entitled "Emerging Urbanism." It deals with basic public works needs and functions in colonial municipalities.

Griffith, Ernest S. *A History of American City Government: The Conspicuous Failure, 1870-1900*. New York: Praeger Publishers, 1974. xii + 308 pp. Tables, notes, and index. The emphasis in this study of American municipal government in the late nineteenth century is on corruption and the initial impulse for reform. The author identifies new public works responsibilities and functions which cities generally adopted in the areas of public health, transportation, and utilities. (First published in 1938.)

Griffith, Ernest S. *A History of American City Government: The Progressive Years and Their Aftermath, 1900-1920*. New York: Praeger Publishers, 1974. x + 352 pp. Tables, notes, appendix, and index. An upbeat history of American municipal government in the early twentieth century. The author concludes that city government was fairly successful in its search "for integrity, accountability, political democracy, humanitarianism, and even community." Public works engineering and administration are not ignored. The author discusses sanitation (sewage treatment and water supply), mass transportation, parks and recreation, public utilities, and capital improvements in general. (First published in 1938.)

Grossman, Edward. "George Washington, Engineer." *Journal of the Boston Society of Civil Engineers*, XIX (March 1932), 71-97. Chronicles one part of Washington's career which "has been sadly neglected by his biographers"—his aptitude and experiences as an engineer.

Gutermuth, Clinton Raymond. "Origins of the Natural Resources Council of America: A Personal View." *Forest History*, 17 (Jan. 1974), 4-17. Elwood R. Maunder interviews Gutermuth, a founder of the Natural Resources Council of America (1946), on his environmental activities.

Gutheim, Frederick. *Worthy of the Nation: The History of Planning for the National Capital*. Washington, D.C.: Smithsonian Institution Press, 1977. xvii + 415 pp. Illustrations, maps, diagrams, bibliographical essay, and index. A comprehensive and beautifully illustrated study of Washington "as the planned capital city." The National Capital Planning Commission is complimented for choosing to celebrate its fiftieth anniversary and the nation's bicentennial by sponsoring the preparation and publication of such a fine volume.

Gutheim, Frederick, and Wilcomb E. Washburn. *The Federal City: Plans & Realities*. Washington, D.C.: Smithsonian Institution Press, 1976. xiv + 170 pp. Illustrations, maps, bibliographical essay, and index. Published in conjunction with an exhibition of plans and models of the Federal City, co-sponsored by the Smithsonian Institution, the National Capital Planning Commission, and the Commission of Fine Arts. The first part of the book, an historical chronicle, offers a "brief view of the planned capital city;" the second part, which describes the exhibition, includes material on alleys, public buildings, markets, bridges, transportation, and parks.

Gutman, Herbert G. "The Failure of the Movement by the Unemployed for Public Works in 1873." *Political Science Quarterly*, LXXX (June 1965), 254-76. Trenchant analysis of abortive efforts to create public employment for workers put out of jobs as a result of a nationwide Depression.

Guttenberg, Albert Z., comp. *Environmental Reform in the United States: The Populist-Progressive Era and the New Deal: Exchange Bibliography No. 85*. Monticello, Ill.: Council of Planning Librarians, 1969. 15 pp. Not annotated.

Haber, Samuel. *Efficiency and Uplift: Scientific Management in the Progressive Era, 1890-1920*. Chicago: University of Chicago Press, 1964. xii + 181 pp. Notes, bibliographical note, and index. An analysis of America's perceptions of efficiency during the Progressive era. Of particular importance is the author's evaluation of Frederick W. Taylor's program of industrial management.

Haldeman, B. Antrim. "A Review of the Progress of City Planning." *Proceedings of the Engineers' Club of Philadelphia*, XXVIII (July 1911), 215-45. Largely a review of European developments with suggestions that the practice be more widely adopted in the United States.

Haller, William. *The Puritan Frontier: Town-Planting in New England Colonial Development, 1630-1660*. New York: Columbia University Press, 1951. 119 pp. Notes, bibliography, and index. A well-documented history of Puritan efforts to create towns in the wilderness.

Hamlin, Talbot. *Benjamin Henry Latrobe*. See chapter on "Public Buildings."

Hammond, A. J. "History of the Movement." *Civil Engineering*, 8 (March 1938), 155-59. Describes the history of the movement to create a federal department of public works.

Hammond, H. P. "Engineering Education—The Past." *Proceedings of the Society for the Promotion of Engineering Education*, LI (June 1943), 26-33. An overview of developments since the society was founded in 1893 by the dean of engineering at Pennsylvania State College.

Hammond, H. P. "Promotion of Engineering Education in the Past Forty Years." *Proceedings of the Society for the Promotion of Engineering Education*, XLI (June 1933), 44-61. Discusses curriculum, research activities, non-collegiate engineering schools, methods of teaching, employment, and professional involvement.

Hammond, John Hays. *The Engineer*. New York: Charles Scribner's Sons, 1921. 196 pp. Bibliography. Written for a general audience as a guide to a career choice, the volume contains a brief, historical introduction on "the profession of engineering."

Hancock, John L. "John Nolen: The Background of a Pioneer Planner." *Journal of the American Institute of Planners*, XXVI (Nov. 1960), 302-12. A biographical sketch of Nolen "up to the eve of his first major planning efforts."

Hancock, John Loretz. "John Nolen and the American City Planning Movement: A History of Culture, Change and Community Response, 1900-1940." Doctoral dissertation, University of Pennsylvania, 1964.

Hancock, John L. "Planners in the Changing American City, 1900-1940." *Journal of the American Institute of Planners*, XXXIII (Sept. 1967), 290-304. The author contends that "the American planning profession pioneered socially enhancing ideals of comprehensive physical organization" beginning in the early 1900s. By 1940 they had become widely accepted and continued to "inform planning's basic alignment with urban policy" throughout the 1960s.

Handlin, Oscar, and John Burchard, eds. *The Historian and the City*. Cambridge: M. I. T. Press and Harvard University Press, 1963. xii + 299 pp. Notes, bibliography, and index. A publication of the Joint Center for Urban Studies, a cooperative venture of the Massachusetts Institute of Technology and Harvard University. The volume contains twenty-two essays on such subjects as the city in technological innovation and economic development, the city as a factor in intellectual life, an analysis of the city as artifact, and the city and its planners. Very little relates to the city and its publicly owned or developed physical structures and facilities. Of special interest is Philip Dawson and Sam B. Warner, Jr., "A Selection of Works Relating to the History of Cities," a comprehensive bibliography.

Hannah, James Joseph. "Urban Reaction to the Great Depression in the United States, 1929-1933." Doctoral dissertation, University of California, Berkeley, 1957.

Hansen, Harry. *Scarsdale: From Colonial Manor to Modern Community*. See chapter on "Community Water Supply."

Hardy, Bruce Allen. "American Privatism and the Urban Fiscal Crisis of the Interwar Years: A Financial Study of the Cities of New York, Chicago, Philadelphia, Detroit, and Boston, 1915-1945." Doctoral dissertation, Wayne State University, 1977. 531 pp.

Harlow, LeRoy F. *Without Fear or Favor: Odyssey of a City Manager*. Provo: Brigham Young University, 1977. x + 350 pp. Illustrations and index. A fascinating look at "city hall from the inside." This autobiography vividly illustrates the challenges that regularly confront city administrators: developing productivity, combating graft, balancing development and preservation interests, handling refuse collection and disposal, removing snow, hiring and firing key officials, etc.

Hartman, J. Paul. *Civil Engineering Landmarks: State of Florida*. n. p.: Florida Section, American Society of Civil Engineers, 1976. iii + 26 pp. Illustrations and bibliography. Contains brief historical sketches of noteworthy public works (waterways, roads, airports, lighthouses, forts, buildings, and bridges) in Florida.

Hartman, John Paul. "Historic Engineering in Florida." Reprint from the *Journal of the Florida Engineering Society* (Dec. 1973 through April 1974), 1-8. Presents an overview of Florida's engineering history.

Haupt, Herman. *Reminiscences of General Herman Haupt: With Notes and a Personal Sketch by Frank Abial Flower*. See chapter on "Roads, Streets, and Highways."

Hauser, Philip M. "Ecological Aspects of Urban Research" in Leonard D. White, ed., *The State of the Social Sciences: Papers Presented at the 25th Anniversary of the Social Science Research Building, The University of Chicago, November 10-12, 1955*. Chicago: University of Chicago Press, 1956. 229-54. Notes. A statement on the significance of ecological research on the urban community within the framework of sociology as well as a review of important ecological studies already in print.

Haworth, James R. "How the City Manager Idea Got Its Start in America." *American City*, 39 (Sept. 1928), 111-12. Contains a selection from the minutes of the Staunton City Council for August 7, 1906.

Hays, Samuel P. *Conservation and the Gospel of Efficiency: The Progressive Conservation Movement, 1890-1920*. Cambridge: Harvard University Press, 1959. iv + 297 pp. Notes, bibliographical index, and index. This classic study remains the most insightful, comprehensive, and provoking examination of the Progressive conservation crusade. The book chronicles efforts to promote efficient and scientific development of natural resources. Hays presents an especially thorough overview of conflicts between the Army Corps of Engineers and advocates of multiple-use water development. Scholars have yet to explore many questions raised by this brilliant book.

Hays, Samuel P. "The Changing Political Structure of the City in Industrial America." *Journal of Urban History*, 1 (Nov. 1974), 6-38. Most of this article discusses forces that influenced social and political integration. The author rejects the "reform framework" that dominates urban historical analysis and suggests a context in which "urban development is considered a constant tension between forces making for decentralization and forces making for centralization in human relationships and institutions . . . between differentiation and social integration." The role of civil engineers and architects in shaping the "urban physical organization" is briefly treated.

Hazen, Richard. "People in Public Works: Allen Hazen." *APWA Reporter*. See chapter on "Community Water Supply."

Hemple, H. W. "Geodetic Surveying Moves Forward." *Transactions of the American Society of Civil Engineers*, CT (1953), 872-85. Describes the development of geodetic surveying techniques by highlighting the activities of the United States Coast Guard and Geodetic Survey.

Hendrickson, Walter B. "David Dale Owen and Indiana's First Geological Survey." *Indiana Magazine of History*, XXXVI (March 1940), 1-15. In 1837 to guarantee "the successful prosecution of our public works" (*Indiana House Journal*, Session of 1835-1836).

Henline, Henry H. "Engineering Education—Its History and Prospects." *Transactions of the American Institute of Electrical Engineers*, 45 (Sept. 1926), 1147-58. A brief history of United States electrical engineering which illustrates the responses of curricula to changing technologies.

Herlihy, Elisabeth. "Planning for Boston—1630-1930." *City Planning*, 6 (Jan. 1930), 1-13.

Herndon, G. Melvin. "The 1806 Survey of the North Carolina Coast, Cape Hatteras to Cape Fear." *North Carolina Historical Review*, XLIX (July 1972), 242-53. An account of the successful survey and chart of the North Carolina coast. The author concludes that this "success undoubtedly strengthened President Jefferson's request for additional surveys."

Herschel, Clemens. "On the Advancement of the Profession of Civil Engineer." *Journal of the Association of Engineering Societies*, X (March 1891), 132-45. Compares the status of the civil engineer in the United States with that in European countries and looks briefly at major engineering events in the United States and abroad. Herschel was president of the Boston Society of Civil Engineers in 1891.

Heskin, Allan David. "Crisis and Response: A Historical Perspective on Advocacy Planning." *Journal of the American Planning Association*, 46 (Jan. 1980), 50-63. Sees advocacy planning as a response to the urban crisis of the 1960s.

Heusser, Albert H. *George Washington's Map Maker: A Biography of Robert Erskine*. New Brunswick, N. J.: Rutgers University Press, 1966. xix + 268 pp. Illustrations, maps, notes, and index. Largely a collection of letters by the man who served as surveyor-general of the American armies from 1775 to 1780. The volume was first published in 1928.

Hindle, Brooke. *Technology in Early America: Needs and Opportunities for Study*. Chapel Hill: University of North Carolina Press, 1966. xix + 145 pp. Notes, index, and "A Directory of Artifact Collections" by Lucius F. Ellsworth. The fifth publication in the Institute of Early American History and Culture's "Needs and Opportunities for Studies" series. This volume, like the others in the series, is the result of a conference (October 1965) "to explore a special historical field which scholars have neglected or indifferently exploited or in which renewed interest has developed in our own times." Still useful are the bibliographical sections on "Civil Engineering and Transportation"; "Heat, Light, and Electricity"; and "Surveying Instruments."

Hindle, Brooke. *The Pursuit of Science in Revolutionary America, 1735-1789*. Chapel Hill: University of North Carolina Press, 1956. xi + 410 pp. Illustrations, notes, bibliographical essay, and index. The author contends that the most important element inherited from the Revolutionary generation was its faith in science and the belief that it would flourish in America. Hindle notes the lack of engineering skills by Americans during the Revolution and gives some attention to steps taken to overcome this inadequacy.

Hine, Robert V. *Edward Kern and American Expansion*. New Haven: Yale University Press, 1962. xix + 180 pp. Illustrations, notes, bibliographical essay, and index. The biography of an individual who, through the Topographic Corps, made his chief contribution as a scientist and later used his sketch pad to illustrate the Frémont expedition.

Hines, Thomas S. *Burnham of Chicago: Architect and Planner*. See chapter on "Public Buildings."

Hines, Thomas S. "The Paradox of 'Progressive' Architecture: Urban Planning and Public Buildings in Tom Johnson's Cleveland." *American Quarterly*. See chapter on "Public Buildings."

"History Week by Week: Engineering News-Record's Role in Building a Greater America." *Engineering News-Record*, 143 (Sept. 1, 1949), A24-32. A look at *ENR*'s beginnings (1874) and how it reported to the nation's engineers and contractors—Eads Bridge, Johnstown flood, Panama Canal, typhoid fever and water supplies, Chicago drainage canal, early use of concrete, Quebec bridge collapse, construction cost data, St. Francis Dam failure, wartime construction, etc.

Hoffecker, Carol E. *Wilmington, Delaware: Portrait of an Industrial City, 1830-1910*. See chapter on "Sewers and Wastewater Treatment."

Hoffman, Abraham. "People in Public Works: Joseph Barlow Lippincott, an Engineer for His Time." *APWA Reporter*. See chapter on "Community Water Supply."

Holli, Melvin George. "Hazen S. Pingree: Urban and Pre-Progressive Reformer." Doctoral dissertation, University of Michigan, 1966. 376 pp.

Holli, Melvin G. *Reform in Detroit: Hazen S. Pingree and Urban Politics*. See chapter on "Urban Mass Transportation."

Hollister, S. C. "Sixty-Two Years of Concrete Engineering." *Concrete International*, 1 (Oct. 1979), 63-66. A review of memorable American Concrete Institute (ACI) events over the past sixty-two years by an ACI elder statesman who is also professor emeritus of engineering at Cornell University.

Holt, W. Stull. *The Office of the Chief of Engineers of the Army: Its Non-Military History, Activities, and Organization*. Baltimore: Johns Hopkins Press, 1923. xii + 166 pp. Notes, appendices, bibliography, and index. The first sixty pages describe the history of the establishment and development of the service, particularly as it relates to river and harbor improvements, public buildings and bridges in the District of Columbia, roads in national parks and Alaska, and land surveys.

Horowitz, Louis J., and Boyden Sparkes. *The Towers of New York: The Memoirs of a Master Builder*. See chapter on "Military Installations."

Houston, Edwin J. "A Review of the Progress

of the American Institute of Electrical Engineers." *Transactions of the American Institute of Electrical Engineers*, XI (1894), 275-84. A brief summary of the institute's advancement since its founding in 1884.

How, Louis. *James B. Eads*. See chapter on "Roads, Streets, and Highways."

Howard, Donald S. *The WPA and Federal Relief Policy*. New York: Russell Sage Foundation, 1943. 879 pp. Maps, tables, graphs, notes, appendix, and index. An exhaustive, generally laudatory analysis of WPA policies and administration.

Howland, W. E. "The Argument: Engineering Education for Special Leadership." *Technology and Culture*, 10 (Jan. 1969), 1-10. A review of engineering education and recommendations on what is needed to expand and enrich the education of the engineer. John G. Burke, Samuel C. Florman, and James C. Wallace present brief comments (pp. 11-19) on "the argument." All of the above was first presented at a Society for the History of Technology symposium entitled "Technology for Man."

Howland, W. E. "The History of Engineering." *Journal of the Western Society of Engineers*, 43 (April 1938), 62-70. Advocates the study of engineering history by engineering students.

Hoy, Suellen M. "Building Bridges for Professionals." *Public Historian*, 2 (Winter 1980), 60-65. Describes the origins and development of the Public Works Historical Society.

Hoy, Suellen M. "People in Public Works: A. M. Rawn." *APWA Reporter*. See chapter on "Sewers and Wastewater Treatment."

Hoy, Suellen M. "People in Public Works: Admiral Ben Moreell." *APWA Reporter*. See chapter on "Military Installations."

Hoy, Suellen M. "People in Public Works: Ben Franklin." *APWA Reporter*. See chapter on "Roads, Streets, and Highways."

Hoy, Suellen M. "People in Public Works: Caroline Bartlett Crane." *APWA Reporter*. See chapter on "Solid Wastes."

Hoy, Suellen M. "People in Public Works: Charles H. Purcell." *APWA Reporter*. See chapter on "Roads, Streets, and Highways."

Hoy, Suellen M. "People in Public Works: Earl L. Mosley." *APWA Reporter*. See chapter on "Community Water Supply."

Hoy, Suellen M. "People in Public Works: Ellen Swallow Richards." *APWA Reporter*. See chapter on "Sewers and Wastewater Treatment."

Hoy, Suellen M. "People in Public Works: Harry W. Morrison." *APWA Reporter*. See chapter on "Flood Control and Drainage."

Hoy, Suellen M. "People in Public Works: Jack Sverdrup." *APWA Reporter*. See chapter on "Roads, Streets, and Highways."

Hoy, Suellen M. "People in Public Works: Jean Vincenz." *APWA Reporter*. See chapter on "Solid Wastes."

Hoy, Suellen M. "People in Public Works: John H. Gregory." *APWA Reporter*. See chapter on "Community Water Supply."

Hoy, Suellen M. "People in Public Works: Mary McDowell." *APWA Reporter*. See chapter on "Solid Wastes."

Hoy, Suellen M. "People in Public Works: Morris L. Cooke." *APWA Reporter*, 43 (Dec. 1976), 8-9, 10.

Hoy, Suellen M. "People in Public Works: Robert Moses." *APWA Reporter*. See chapter on "Parks and Recreation."

Hoy, Suellen M. "People in Public Works: Washington and Emily Roebling." *APWA Reporter*. See chapter on "Roads, Streets, and Highways."

Hoy, Suellen M. "People in Public Works: William Phelps Eno." *APWA Reporter*. See chapter on "Roads, Streets, and Highways."

Hubbard, Theodora Kimball. "H. W. S. Cleveland: An American Pioneer in Landscape Architecture and City Planning." *Landscape Architecture*. See chapter on "Parks and Recreation."

Hubbard, Theodora Kimball, and Henry Vincent. *Our Cities To-Day and To-Morrow: A Survey of Planning and Zoning Progress in the United States*. Cambridge: Harvard University Press, 1929. xviii + 389 pp. Illustrations, maps, notes, appendices, and index. An early survey and analysis of United States' planning practices. The first chapter contains a brief history of the planning movement. There are useful chapters on streets, mass transportation, and parks and recreation.

Huber, Walter L. "An Engineering Century in

California." *Transactions of the American Society of Civil Engineers*, CT (1953), 97-111. The emphasis is on water—first for mining, then irrigation, and finally power.

Huggins, Kay Haire. "City Planning in North Carolina, 1900-1929." *North Carolina Historical Review*, XLVI (Oct. 1969), 377-97. The author demonstrates that both the "City Beautiful" and "City Useful" movements of the early twentieth century "provided some of the legal and theoretical groundwork and paved the way for public acceptance of planning" in North Carolina. The author also describes the civic activities of the state's women's clubs.

Huggins, Koleen Alice Haire. "The Evolution of City and Regional Planning in North Carolina: 1900-1950." Doctoral dissertation, Duke University, 1967.

Hulchanski, John David, comp. *History of Modern Town Planning, 1800-1940: Exchange Bibliography No. 1239*. Monticello, Ill.: Council of Planning Librarians, 1977. 24 pp. Not annotated.

Hunsberger, George S. "The Architectural Career of George Hadfield." *Records of the Columbia Historical Society of Washington, D.C.* See chapter on "Public Buildings."

Hunt, Charles Warren. *Historical Sketch of the American Society of Civil Engineers*. New York: American Society of Civil Engineers, 1897. 92 + vi pp. Illustrations, diagram, table, notes, and index. A brief account of ASCE's early years by its secretary. The volume contains a rich collection of photographs: twenty-five of past presidents and nine of other officers.

Hunt, Chas. Warren. "The Activities of the American Society of Civil Engineers during the Past Twenty-Five Years." *Transactions of the American Society of Civil Engineers*, LXXXII (Dec. 1918), 1577-652. A description of ASCE's growth, headquarters building, library facilities, local associations of members, amendments to the constitution, annual meetings, publications, and special committees by its executive officer for twenty-three of the twenty-five years reviewed.

Hunt, Chas. Warren. "The First Fifty Years of the American Society of Civil Engineers: 1852-1902." *Transactions of the American Society of Civil Engineers*, XLVIII (Aug. 1902), 220-26. A sketchy summary.

Huntington, W. C. "The Construction Engineer—The Centenarian." *Civil Engineering*, 3 (Aug. 1933), 425-26. On his contributions as the nation's builder.

Hurd, Richard M. *Principles of City Land Values*. New York: Record and Guide, 1905. viii + 159 pp. Illustrations, maps, tables, and diagrams. An interesting, pioneering attempt to define the dynamics of urban growth and planning. The books contains some rare and unusual maps and photographs.

Hutchins, Jere C. *Jere C. Hutchins: A Personal Story*. See chapter on "Urban Mass Transportation."

Huth, Mary Jo. *The Urban Habitat: Past, Present, and Future*. Chicago: Nelson-Hall, 1970. xi + 305 pp. Illustrations, maps, charts, tables, notes, bibliography, and index. Contains a strong chapter on the history of city planning.

Hutton, Frederick Remsen. *A History of the American Society of Mechanical Engineers from 1880 to 1915*. New York: American Society of Mechanical Engineers, 1915. vii + 355 pp. Illustrations, appendix, and index. A complete history of ASME from its founding in 1879-80 to 1914 by the society's former secretary and officer. Founded "to promote the Arts and Sciences connected with Engineering and Mechanical Construction," its members included army and navy, hydraulic, mining, operating, railway, and electrical engineers as well as engineering contractors.

Hutton, F. R. "The Mechanical Engineer and the Function of the Engineering Society." *Proceedings of the American Society of Mechanical Engineers*, XXIX (Dec. 1907), 627-62. Includes a brief discussion of the nature of civil engineering. The author, president of the American Society of Mechanical Engineers, comments on an 1827 definition emanating from a meeting of the Council of the Institution of Civil Engineers of Great Britain.

Ickes, Harold L. *The Autobiography of a Curmudgeon*. New York: Reynal and Hitchcock, 1943. xi + 350 pp. Illustrations and index. This autobiography is disappointing in that it includes very little information on Ickes' career as secretary of the Department of the Interior and administrator of the Public Works Administration during the New Deal. His eccentricity and gargantuan ego show through in this heroic account of his own life.

Ickes, Harold L. *Back to Work: The Story of PWA*. New York: Macmillan Company, 1935. xiii + 276 pp. Illustrations, appendices, and index. Entertaining and hyperbolic overview of the activities of the Public Works Administration by its flamboyant administrator.

Ickes, Harold L. *The Secret Diary of Harold L. Ickes: The First Thousand Days, 1933-1936*. New York: Simon and Schuster, 1954. xi + 738 pp. Index. Entertaining insights on New Deal public works policies and programs. As secretary of the Department of the Interior and head of the Public Works Administration, Ickes directed key New Deal programs.

Illuminating Engineering Society Historical Committee. "Illuminating Engineering Society." *General Electric Review*, 57 (July 1954), 39-41. A short history of the society.

"Illinois Society [of Engineers] Celebrates Its 50th Anniversary." *Engineering News-Record*, 116 (Feb. 13, 1936), 252-53. Reviews general advances in public works engineering (water supply, sewage disposal, flood control and drainage, roads, and surveying) in Illinois since 1886.

Ingram, Robert L. *The Bechtel Story: Seventy Years of Accomplishment in Engineering and Construction*. San Francisco: Bechtel Corporation, 1968. xi + 157 pp. Illustrations and appendix. An organizational history—largely post World War II— of one of the nation's largest construction/engineering firms.

Inkster, Tom. "John Frank Stevens, American Engineer." *Pacific Northwest Quarterly*. See chapter on "Waterways."

Institute for Government Research. *The U. S. Geological Survey: Its History, Activities, and Organization*. New York: D. Appleton and Company, 1918. xi + 163 pp. Maps, appendices, bibliography, and index.

Isakoff, Jack F. *The Public Works Administration*. Urbana: University of Illinois Press, 1938. 166 pp. Tables, notes, bibliography, and Index. A good overview of the Public Works Administration program. Topics covered include administrative problems, finances, allotments, and construction policies.

Issac, Paul E. "Municipal Reform in Beaumont, Texas, 1902-1909." *Southwestern Historical Quarterly*, LXXVIII (April 1975), 409-30. Describes the impetus behind Beaumont's reform movement. Led by well-to-do businessmen, they wanted the city to have greater control in the financing and building of essential public works. There are scattered references to the reformers' desire for improved streets, sewage treatment, parks, etc.

"ITE: A Retrospective." *ITE Journal*, 50 (Aug. 1980), 9-23. A special issue devoted to the history of the Institute of Transportation Engineers.

Jackson, Dugald C., and W. Paul Jones, eds. *The Profession of Engineering*. New York: John Wiley & Sons, 1929. ix + 124 pp. A small collection of essays by engineers about their profession. Published to assist young people in selecting a career, there is only a brief account in one essay (civil engineering) on historical developments.

Jackson, John Brinckerhoff. *American Space: The Centennial Years, 1865-1876*. New York: W. W. Norton, 1972. 254 pp. Illustrations, bibliography, and index. On nineteenth-century efforts to improve the environment through better use of communal space.

Jackson, Joseph. *Early Philadelphia Architects and Engineers*. Philadelphia: n.p., 1923. xii + 285 pp. Illustrations and index.

Jackson, William Turrentine. *Early Planning Efforts at Lake Tahoe: The Role of Joseph F. McDonald, 1956-1963*. Davis, Calif.: Institute of Governmental Affairs, 1974. iii + 131 pp. Illustrations and bibliography.

Jackson, W. Turrentine, and Terry L. Dailey. *Environmental Planning Efforts at Lake Tahoe*. Davis, Calif.: Institute of Governmental Affairs, 1974. iii + 76 pp. Notes and bibliography. Excellent case study of area environmental planning.

Jackson, W. Turrentine. "Governmental Exploration of the Upper Yellowstone, 1871." *Pacific Historical Review*, XI (June 1942), 187-99. Description of the F. V. Hayden survey.

Jacobs, James Ripley. *The Beginning of the U. S. Army, 1783–1812*. Princeton: Princeton University Press, 1947. xi + 419 pp. Illustrations, notes, bibliography, and index. Includes a chapter on the founding of West Point and the early formal training of military engineers.

Jamieson, Ducan R. "Toward a Cleaner New York: John H. Griscom and New York's Public Health, 1830-1870." Doctoral dissertation, Michigan State University, 1972. 322 pp.

Jamison, James Knox. "The Survey of the Public Lands in Michigan." *Michigan History*, 42 (June 1958), 197-214. From 1815 to 1851.

Jarchow, Merrill E. "Charles D. Gilfillan: Builder Behind the Scenes." *Minnesota History*. See chapter on "Community Water Supply."

Jarrett, Henry, ed. *Perspectives on Conservation*. Baltimore: Johns Hopkins Press, 1958. xii + 260 pp. Notes and index. A good compilation of essays on various aspects of conservation planning. Particularly outstanding are the contributions by Samuel P. Hays, "The Mythology of Conservation"; Abel Wolman, "Selective Opportunism, the Surest Way"; and Gilbert F. White, "Broader Bases for Choice: The Next Key Move."

Jennings, J. L. Sibley, Jr. "Artistry as Design: L'Enfant's Extraordinary City." *Quarterly Journal of the Library of Congress*, XXXVI (Summer 1979), 225-78.

Jervey, James Postell. "George W. Goethals—The Man." *Military Engineer*. See chapter on "Waterways."

Jervis, John B. "A Memoir of American Engineering." *Transactions of the American Society of Civil Engineers*, VI (Jan.-Dec. 1877), 39-67. Insightful autobiography by one of the nineteenth-century's outstanding engineers.

Jewett, Henry C. "History of the Corps of Engineers to 1915." *Military Engineer*, XIV (Sept.-Oct; Nov.-Dec., 1922), Sept.-Oct.: 304-06; Nov.-Dec.: 385-88. A broad-brush overview that leaves out much.

"John Ericsson." *Railroad and Engineering Journal*, LXIII (April 1889), 151-56. A biographical sketch of a prominent nineteenth-century engineer-inventor. It includes the introduction to a statement he prepared on his "principal labors during the last third of a century" and submitted in 1876 to the commissioners of the Centennial Exhibition in Philadelphia.

Johnson, Charles W. "The Army and the Civilian Conservation Corps, 1933-42." *Prologue: The Journal of the National Archives*, 4 (Fall 1972), 139-56.

Johnson, Charles William. "The Civilian Conservation Corps: The Role of the Army." Doctoral dissertation, University of Michigan, 1968. 246 pp. Largely an administrative history of the Army's cooperation with the Civilian Conservation Corps.

Johnson, Frederick. "The Dead Horse Cart." *Public Works*, III (July 1980), 72-73. Reviews some early public works construction procedures and equipment.

Johnson, Leland R., ed. "An Army Engineer on the Missouri in 1867." *Nebraska History*. See chapter on "Waterways."

Johnson, Leland R. *Engineers on the Twin Rivers: A History of the Nashville District Corps of Engineers United States Army*. See chapter on "Waterways."

Johnson, Leland R. "Sword, Shovel, and Compass." *Military Engineer*, 68 (May-June 1976), 159-65. Overview of the lives and contributions of military engineers such as Jonathan Williams, Zebulon Pike, Stephen H. Long, and Hiram Martin Chittenden.

Johnson, Mary Elizabeth. *Emergency Employment in Onondaga County*. Syracuse: Onondaga County Citizens, 1933. 99 pp. Illustrations, map, charts, tables, and notes. The most complete chronicle of public works projects (parks, sewers, highways, bridges, sidewalks, etc.) built by the Onondaga County (New York) Emergency Work Bureau from November 1931 to August 1933.

Johnston, Johanna. *Frederick Law Olmsted: Partner with Nature*. See chapter on "Parks and Recreation."

Johnson, Norman J. "The Frederick Law Olmsted Plan for Tacoma." *Pacific Northwest Quarterly*, 66 (July 1975), 97-104. Describes the plan and explains why it was abandoned (1874).

Jones, Charles O. "From Gold to Garbage: A Bibliographical Essay on Politics and the Environment." *American Political Science Review*, LXVI (June 1972), 588-95. A review of fourteen books of several types—collections of conference papers, the "eco-scare" volumes, and general and scientific analyses of environmental issues. Only a few relate directly to public works.

Jordan, E. O.; G. C. Whipple; and C. E. A. Winslow. *A Pioneer of Public Health, William*

Thompson Sedgewick. See chapter on "Sewers and Wastewater Treatment."

Joyce, Davis D. "Before Teapot Dome: Senator Albert B. Fall and Conservation." *Red River Valley Historical Review*, 4 (Fall 1979), 44-51. Describes Hall's opposition to many conservation measures before becoming secretary of the interior in the Harding Administration.

Judd, Dennis R. *The Politics of American Cities: Private Power and Public Policy*. Boston: Little, Brown and Company, 1979. xiv + 402 pp. Charts, tables, graphs, notes, and index. The primary focus of this book is the close relationship between public authority and the private sector. The author traces the interplay between government and the institutions of private investment and analyzes its effect on city politics, particularly during the past twenty years. Public works facilities are discussed only indirectly—as they relate to the growth of suburbs, urban redevelopment, revenue sharing, and the new federalism.

Kahn, Edgar Myron. "Andrew Smith Hallidie." *California Historical Society Quarterly*. See chapter on "Roads, Streets, and Highways."

Kanarek, Harold. "People in Public Works: William P. Craighill." *APWA Reporter*. See chapter on "Military Installations."

Kansas City Section, ASCE. *History of the Kansas City Section, American Society of Civil Engineers*. Kansas City: ASCE Kansas City Section, 1976. vii + 69 pp. Illustrations and appendix. From 1921. The booklet was prepared by the section's Bicentennial Committee.

Kantor, Harvey A. "Charles Dyer Norton and the Origins of the Regional Plan of New York." *Journal of the American Institute of Planners*, 39 (Jan. 1973), 35-42. Good description of Norton's role in the passage of the nation's first comprehensive zoning law in 1916.

Kantor, Harvey. "Modern Urban Planning in New York City: Origins and Evolution, 1890-1933." Doctoral dissertation, New York City University, 1971. 466 pp.

Kantor, Harvey A. "The City Beautiful in New York." *New-York Historical Society Quarterly*, LVII (April 1973), 148-71. On the New York City Improvement Plan of 1907 and the reasons for its failure.

Kaplan, Barry J. "Andrew H. Green and the Creation of a Planning Rationale: The Formation of Greater New York City, 1865-1890." *Urbanism Past & Present*, 8 (Summer 1979), 32-41. The author illustrates the relationship between urban planning and administrative centralization by analyzing Green's career. He was the seminal figure in the consolidation of Greater New York in 1898.

Karl, Barry D. *Charles E. Merriam and the Study of Politics*. Chicago: University of Chicago Press, 1974. xiv + 337 pp. Illustration, notes, and index. Exhaustive biography of the political scientist who had a profound influence on the development of public administration in the United States. During the New Deal, Merriam played a key role in the creation of the National Resources Planning Board and founded the Public Administration Clearing House that served as the center for associations of state and local governmental officials. The latter, since renamed the Charles E. Merriam Center for Public Administration, serves as headquarters for the American Planning Association, the American Public Works Association, and the Public Works Historical Society.

Karl, Barry Dean. *Executive Reorganization and Reform in the New Deal: The Genesis of Administrative Management, 1900-1939.* Cambridge: Harvard University Press, 1963. xv + 292 pp. Notes and index. An analysis of the 1939 reorganization of the presidency through a study "of the backgrounds of the three men whom Franklin Roosevelt appointed to his Committee on Administrate Management in 1936, Louis Brownlow, Charles E. Merriam, and Luther H. Gulick." Merriam and Brownlow founded, and directed the Public Administration Clearing House, now the headquarters of the American Planning and American Public Works associations and the Public Works Historical Society.

Karl, Barry D. "Public Administration and American History: A Century of Professionalism." *Public Administration Review*, 36 (Sept./Oct. 1976), 489-503. A thoughtful essay on the professionalization of public administration from the late nineteenth century.

Karl, Barry Dean. "Twentieth Century Concepts in Public Administration: Merriam, Brownlow and Gulick." Doctoral dissertation, Harvard University, 1961.

Kaufman, Herbert. "Robert Moses: Charismatic Bureaucrat." *Political Science Quarterly*, 90 (Fall 1975), 521-38. A review essay of Robert Caro's *The Power Broker* (1974).

Kaufmann, Edgar, Jr., ed. *The Rise of American Architecture*. See chapter on "Parks and Recreation."

Keeble, Eleanor Louise. "A History of the Tennessee State Planning Commission, 1934-1947." Master's thesis, University of Tennessee, 1948. 167 pp. Tables, notes, appendices, and bibliography. A report on the activities of the Tennesssee State Planning Commission since its establishment in 1935.

Kerekes, Frank, and Harold B. Reid, Jr. "Fifty Years of Development in Building Code Requirements for Reinforced Concrete." *Journal of the American Concrete Institute*, 25 (Feb. 1954), 441-70.

Kershner, Frederick D., Jr. "From Country Town to Industrial City: The Urban Pattern in Indianapolis." *Indiana Magazine of History*, XLV (Dec. 1949), 327-38. A traditional look at the impact of the urbanization process on Indianapolis. Almost no attention is directed to the city's public works development.

Kershner, Frederick D., Jr. "George Chaffey and the Irrigation Frontier." *Agricultural History*. See chapter on "Irrigation."

Kevles, Daniel J. "Federal Legislation for Engineering Experiment Stations: The Episode of World War I." *Technology and Culture*, 12 (April 1971), 182-89. Explains why the movement during World War I to create a federally funded system of engineering experiment stations failed.

Kiely, Edmond Richard. *Surveying Instruments: Their History and Classroom Use*. New York: Columbia University, 1947. xiii + 411 pp. Illustrations, diagrams, and bibliography.

Kingman, Edward Dyer. "Roger Sherman, Colonial Surveyor." *Civil Engineering*, 10 (Aug. 1940), 514-15. Describes Sherman's career as a surveyor in Connecticut from 1743 to 1760 and reports that Sherman possessed a copy of Richard Norwood's *Epitome*, one of the first important books on surveying printed in English, and in it made notes of his own which constitute a comprehensive treatise on land surveying as practiced in his day.

Kinnear, Duncan Lyle. *The First 100 Years: A History of Virginia Polytechnic Institute and State University*. Blacksburg: Virginia Polytechnic Institute Educational Foundation, 1972. xiv + 498 pp. Illustrations, maps, appendices, bibliography, and index. A comprehensive history of Virginia's land-grant institution at Blacksburg in commemoration of its centennial.

Kirby, Richard Shelton. "Engineering Pioneering Since John Smeaton." *Civil Engineering*, 8 (Jan. 1938), 26-30. Traces engineering developments through three generations of nineteenth-century engineers. "The first was responsible for cast-iron arch and wrought-iron suspension bridges, canals, crushed-stone roads, and steam railroads. The second generation produced early water-supply systems, truss bridges, and paved city streets; and the third, machinery and power development, applications of steel and reinforced concrete, and sanitation."

Kirby, Richard Shelton; Sidney Withington; Arthur Burr Darling; and Frederick Gridley Kilgour. *Engineering in History*. New York: McGraw-Hill Book Company, 1956. vii + 530 pp. Illustrations, notes, bibliographies, and index. A general history of civil, mechanical, electrical, and metallurgical engineering from their origins in to the twentieth century. Of special interest are the chapters on "Roads, Canals, Bridges," "Modern Transportation," "Sanitary and Hydraulic Engineering," and "Construction."

Kirby, Richard Shelton. "Some Early American Civil Engineers and Surveyors." *Connecticut Society of Civil Engineers*, 46 (1930), 26-47. There are distinct sections on David Rittenhouse, John Christian Senf, Andrew Ellicott, Robert Fulton, William Weston, Christopher Colles, Thomas Paine, James Finley, Theodore Burr, Benjamin Henry Latrobe, and the Loammi Baldwins.

Kirby, Richard Shelton, and Philip Gustave Laurson. *The Early Years of Modern Civil Engineering*. New Haven: Yale University Press, 1932. viii + 324 pp. Illustrations, notes, selected bibliographies, biographical outlines, and index. A useful survey of the modern beginnings of many public works structures. There are separate and highly informative chapters on surveying, canals, roads and pavements, railroads, bridges, tunnels and subways, waterworks and water power, sewers, and river and harbor improvements.

Kite, Elizabeth S., ed. *L'Enfant and Washington, 1791-1792: Published and Unpublished Documents Now Brought Together for the First Time*. Baltimore: Johns Hopkins Press, 1929. xii + 182 pp. Illustrations, map, notes, and bibliography. An important contribution to the history of urban planning. Through a chronological arrangement of the records, Pierre Charles L'Enfant is placed "in historic relation to the design of the City of Washington." A helpful, thirty-page essay on "Major L'Enfant and the Federal City," by J. J. Jusserand, Ambassador of France to the United States (1902-1925), serves as the introduction.

Klaw, Spencer. "West Point: 1978—What Happened to the Long Gray Line." *American Heritage*, 29 (June/July 1978), 6-15. Describes, in brief, West Point's history and examines its "proper role" and ways to achieve it.

Kliewer, Waldo O. "The Foundations of Billings, Montana." *Pacific Northwest Quarterly*, XXXI (July 1940), 255-83. Contains a brief section describing the community's water system, refuse disposal practices, and care of streets.

Kluger, James Robert. "Elwood Mead: Irrigation Engineer and Social Planner." Doctoral dissertation. See chapter on "Irrigation."

Knowles, Morris. "History of Civil Engineering in Western Pennsylvania." *Proceedings of the Engineers' Society of Western Pennsylvania*, 47 (April 1931), 184-210. Reviews "local engineering events" of the previous fifty years. There are separate sections on "Waterways," "Flood Control and River Terminals," "Rail Transportation," "Bridge Engineering," "Highway Engineering," "Sanitary Engineering," "Comprehensive Planning," and "Engineering Education."

Knowles, Morris. "Western Pennsylvania's Engineering Progress." *Civil Engineering*, I (Feb. 1931), 377-81. Reviews engineering developments in Pittsburgh during the previous fifty years.

Knutson, Robert. "The White City: The World's Columbian Exposition of 1933." Doctoral dissertation, Columbia University, 1956. 295 pp.

Korr, Charles P. "William Hammond Hall: The Failure of Attempts at State Water Planning in California, 1878-1888." *Southern California Quarterly*. See chapter on "Irrigation."

Kramer, Howard D. "The Scientist in the West, 1870-1880." *Pacific Historical Review*, XII (Sept. 1943), 239-51. A general description of the work of scientists, geologists, and engineers who were part of federally funded surveys of the Rocky Mountain region.

Kranz, Marvin W. "Pioneering in Conservation: A History of the Conservation Movement in New York State, 1816-1903." Doctoral dissertation, Syracuse University, 1961. 634 pp.

Kranzberg, Melvin, and Carroll W. Pursell, Jr. *Technology in Western Civilization*. 2 vols. New York: Oxford University Press, 1967. Vol. I: xii + 802 pp.; Vol. II: xii + 772 pp. Illustrations, maps, diagrams, bibliographical essays, indexes. Volume I, "The Emergence of Modern Industrial Society," covers the seventeenth through nineteenth centuries; vol. II deals with "Technology in the Twentieth Century." Planned as a textbook for use in courses of the U. S. Armed Forces Institute, this work is long and the essays vary in quality. However, it remains one of the best collaborative studies in demonstrating the pivotal role of technology in the development of modern society. A number of chapters—particularly those on transportation, energy, land use and planning in the second volume—deserve the attention of public works historians.

Krueckeberg, Donald A. "The Story of the Planners' Journal, 1915-1980." *Journal of the American Planning Association*, 46 (Jan. 1980), 5-21. Reviews "the dynamics of its [*Journal*] content, style, and usefulness" and comments on its value to the planning field.

Kulski, Julian Eugene. *Land of Urban Promise: Continuing the Great Tradition: A Search for Significant Urban Space in the Urbanized Northeast*. Notre Dame: University of Notre Dame Press, 1967. xx + 282 pp. Illustrations, maps, diagrams, notes, bibliography, and index. Portions of this pedestrian book discuss the evolution of city planning and the impact of transportation systems on urban structures.

Kutler, Stanley I. *Privilege and Creative Destruction: The Charles River Bridge Case*. See chapter on "Roads, Streets, and Highways."

Lanford, J. C. "The Story of C. R. Mason: An Early Virginia Contractor." *Virginia Road*

Builder, XXXIV (March-April 1978), 6-10. Mason (1800-1886) built mostly railroads.

Lansburgh, Richard H. "The Management Movement." *Bulletin of the Taylor Society*, VIII (April 1923), 46-52. Credits Frederick W. Taylor for laying the foundations for "the management movement" during the 1880s.

Lapping, Mark B. "Toward a Social Theory of the Built Environment: Frank Lloyd Wright and Broadacre City." *Environmental Review*, III (Spring 1979), 11-23. Describes Wright's image of the perfect environment as expressed in his "Broadacre City" ideas. There is some discussion of the place of highways and public buildings in this "thoroughly decentralized, motorized middle landscape."

Larkin, Daniel F. "The New York Years of John B. Jervis: A Builder of Nineteenth Century America." Doctoral dissertation. See chapter on "Community Water Supply."

Larsen, Lawrence H. *The Urban West at the End of the Frontier*. See chapter on "Solid Wastes."

Larson, Larry Thomas. "Citizen Participation in Public Administration: The City of Los Angeles Department of City Planning Experience." Doctoral dissertation, University of Southern California, 1975.

Larson, Laurence Marcellus. "A Financial and Administrative History of Milwaukee." *Bulletin of the University of Wisconsin: Economics and Political Science Series*, IV (1908), 137-318. A study of municipal financing and administration in Milwaukee from 1834 to 1906. Separate sections of this long essay are devoted to harbors, bridges, and viaducts; streets, street lighting, and sidewalks; sewers and flushing tunnels; water works construction; and the city hall.

Larson. T. A. "The New Deal in Wyoming." *Pacific Historical Review*, XXXVIII (Aug. 1969), 249-73. Influence of New Deal programs on the state's politics and economy.

Layne, J. Gregg. "Edward Otho Cresap Ord: Soldier and Surveyor." *Quarterly Publication of the Historical Society of Southern California*, XVII (Dec. 1935), 139-42. A biographical sketch of the individual who made the first survey and map of the city of Los Angeles.

Layton, Edwin T., Jr. "American Ideologies of Science and Engineering." *Technology and Culture*, 17 (Oct. 1976), 688-701. In the nineteenth and twentieth centuries and how these ideologies interacted.

Layton, Edwin T., Jr. "Frederick Haynes Newell and the Revolt of the Engineers." *Mid-continent American Studies Journal*, 3 (Fall 1962), 17-26. Perceptive account of Newell's unsuccessful attempts to create a comprehensive national federation of American engineers.

Layton, Edwin T., Jr. *The Revolt of the Engineers: Social Responsibility and the American Engineering Profession*. Cleveland: Case Western Reserve University Press, 1971. xiv + 286 pp. Notes, bibliographical essay, and index. A critical survey of the history of the engineering profession in which the author examines the question of why engineers have not demonstrated more concern for or awareness of the problems which their profession helped to create. He attributes a lack of social responsibility to divided loyalties among engineers and ideological problems of identity. Herbert Hoover, Morris L. Cook, scientific management as well as the American Institute of Electrical Engineers, American Institute of Mining Engineers, and the American Society of Civil Engineers are given extended treatment.

Layton, Edwin T., Jr. "Veblen and the Engineers." *American Quarterly*, XIV (Spring 1962), 64-72. An examination of Thorstein Veblen's mistaken prediction that "the engineers would constitute the revolutionary class in America."

Le Bold, William K.; Robert Perrucci; and Warren Howland. "The Engineer in Industry and Government." *Journal of Engineering Education*, 56 (March 1966), 237-73. The results of a National Science Foundation-American Society for Engineering Education survey to determine "the educational needs and goals" of engineers in industry and government. Many of the reported statistics span the period from 1900 to 1964.

Lee, Robert Rue. "Local Government Public Works Decision-Making." Doctoral dissertation. See chapter on "Community Water Supply."

"L'Enfant's Reports to President Washington, Bearing Dates of March 26, June 22, and August 19, 1791." *Records of the Columbia Historical Society of Washington, D.C.*,

2 (1889), 26-48. Previously unpublished documents which "complete, as far as possible, the history of L'Enfant's authorship of the plan of the city of Washington."

Lenney, John J. *Caste System in the American Army: A Study of the Corps of Engineers and Their West Point System*. New York: Greenberg Publisher, 1949. xx + 233 pp. Notes, appendices, and bibliographies. There is one chapter on the "historical background" of the West Point system.

Lenzen, U. F. *Benjamin Peirce and the U.S. Coast Survey*. San Francisco: San Francisco Press, 1968. vii + 51 pp. Illustrations, chart, index, and appendices. A broad-brush biography of the scientist who served as superintendent of the U.S. Coast Survey from 1867 to 1874.

Lepawsky, Albert. *State Planning and Economic Development in the South*. Kingsport, Tenn.: National Planning Association Committee of the South, 1949. xx + 193 pp. Tables and notes. An interesting study of planning authorities and development agencies in the southern states. It originated as a project of the Subcommittee on Public and Private Services of the Committee of the South of the National Planning Association. The first chapter reviews the "History and Background" of planning and development in the South; it is followed by separate chapters on "Highways and Airports," "State Public Works," and "Recreation"; and an entire section is devoted to "Regional, Interstate, and Federal-State Relations."

Leunes, Barbara Laverne Blythe. "The Conservation Philosophy of Stewart L. Udall, 1961-1968." Doctoral dissertation. See chapter on "Parks and Recreation."

Lewis, Eugene. *Public Entrepreneurship: Toward a Theory of Bureaucratic Political Power–The Organizational Lives of Hyman Rickover, J. Edgar Hoover, and Robert Moses*. See chapter on "Parks and Recreation."

Lewis, Gene D. *Charles Ellet, Jr.: The Engineer as Individualist, 1810-1862*. See chapter on "Roads, Streets, and Highways."

Lewis, Nelson P. *The Planning of the Modern City: A Review of the Principles Governing City Planning*. New York: John Wiley & Sons, 1916. xv + 423 pp. Illustrations, maps, tables, diagrams, and index. The first major book on city planning by an American public works engineer-administrator, who in 1902 was appointed New York City's chief engineer of the Board of Estimate and Apportionment. In this position, Lewis became the most influential engineer in the city, since the board had to approve all proposed public improvements. Lewis believed that planning was fundamentally an engineering responsibility and dedicated this volume to "the municipal engineers of the United States, the first men on the ground in city planning as in city building, in the hope that it may help them to realize their responsibilities and opportunities in determining the manner in which our cities will develop."

Lewis, R. A. *Edwin Chadwick and the Public Health Movement, 1832-1854*. See chapter on "Sewers and Wastewater Treatment."

Lieb, John W., Jr. "The Organization and Administration of National Engineering Societies." *Transactions of the American Institute of Electrical Engineers*, XXIV (1905), 283-96. Contains some statistics (number of members, fee schedules, etc.) on the American Society of Civil Engineers, American Institute of Mining Engineers, American Society of Mechanical Engineers, and American Institute of Electrical Engineers.

Lilienthal, David E. *The Journals of David Lilienthal: Volume I: The TVA Years, 1939-1945*. See chapter on "Flood Control and Drainage."

Lilienthal, David E. *The Journals of David E. Lilienthal: Volume II: The Atomic Energy Years*. See chapter on "Energy."

Lillibridge, Robert M. "Pullman: Town Development in the Era of Eclecticism." *Journal of the Society of Architectural Historians*, XII (Oct. 1953), 17-22. Good overview of the structure and architecture of this historic Illinois community.

Lingelbach, William E. "William Penn and City Planning." *Pennsylvania Magazine of History and Biography*, LXVIII (Oct. 1944), 398-418. On Penn as a pioneer in the field of city planning—one who had "vision, courage and wisdom" and saw to it that his plans were carried out according to many of his 1682 "Instructions." In these he outlined the importance of a clean and adequate water supply, proper sewer disposal plants and farms, repaired docks, radiating highways, open spaces, aesthetically placed buildings of limited height and receding fronts, etc.

Liphshitz, I. N. "The Study of Technical History: A Plea for an Organization in This Country Devoted to the Study of Engineering History." *Mechanical Engineering*, 57 (Jan. 1935), 143-47. Advocates the establishment of an organization devoted to "the study of technical history in America."

Lippincott, J. P. "William Mulholland—Engineer, Pioneer, Raconteur." *Civil Engineering*. See chapter on "Community Water Supply."

Lively, Robert A. "The American System: A Review Article." *Business History Review*, XXIX (March 1955), 81-96. An examination of the role of government in the ante-bellum American economy. The author reviews the work of several scholars and concludes that "official vision and public resources have been associated so regularly with private skill and individual desire that the combination may be said to constitute a principal determinant of American economic growth." Lively refers particularly to internal improvements.

Lockmiller, David A. *History of the North Carolina State College of Agriculture and Engineering of the University of North Carolina, 1889-1939*. Raleigh: Edwards & Broughton Company, 1939. xviii + 310 pp. Illustrations, map, notes, appendices, bibliography, and index. A chronicle of the founding and growth of a southern agricultural and engineering college, from the pioneering work of founder, Leonidas L. Polk, through the consolidation program of Alumnus-Governor O. Max Gardner.

Logan, Thomas H. "The Americanization of German Zoning." *Journal of the American Institute of Planners*, 42 (Oct. 1976), 377-85. Discusses "the origins of zoning in the reform era which also gave rise to the planning professions in both Germany and the United States."

Logan, Robert R. "Notes on the First Land Surveys in Arkansas." *Arkansas Historical Quarterly*, 19 (Autumn 1960), 260-70. In 1815-1816.

Lohr, Lenox R., ed. *Centennial of Engineering: History and Proceedings of Symposia, 1852-1952*. Chicago: Museum of Science and Industry, 1953. v + 1079 pp. Illustrations, charts, graphs, tables, notes, and index. Prepared in commemoration of the hundredth anniversary of the founding of the American Society of Civil Engineers. A collection of essays, more or less historical, on subjects related to the broad fields of the engineering profession, transportation, structures and construction, energy, and urbanization.

Loretz, John. "John Nolen and the American City Planning Movement: A History of Culture Change and Community Response, 1900-1940." Doctoral dissertation, University of Pennsylvania, 1964.

Love, John. *Geodaesia: Or the Art of Surveying and Measuring Land Made Easy*. New York: Samuel Campbell, 1796. ix + 189 + lxv pp. Diagrams, tables, and appendix. A classic treatise on surveying techniques.

Love, John Barry. "The Colonial Surveyor in Pennsylvania." Doctoral dissertation, University of Pennsylvania, 1970. 297 pp.

Lowenthal, David. *George Perkins Marsh: Versatile Vermonter*. See chapter on "Irrigation."

Lowitt, Richard. *George W. Norris: The Persistence of a Progressive, 1913-1933*. See chapter on "Irrigation."

Lowry, Goodrich. *Streetcar Man: Tom Lowry and the Twin City Rapid Transit Company*. See chapter on "Urban Mass Transportation."

Lubove, Roy. *Community Planning in the 1920's: The Contribution of the Regional Planning Association of America*. Pittsburgh: University of Pittsburgh Press, 1963. xii + 155 pp. Notes and index. A history of the Regional Planning Association of America (founded in 1923) which highlights (1) RPAA's search for the basic principles underlying an urban structure "best suited to the satisfaction of human biological and social needs"; and (2) RPAA's efforts "to make community planning an integrated discipline."

Lubove, Roy. *The Progressives and the Slums: Tenement House Reform in New York City, 1890-1917*. Pittsburgh: University of Pittsburgh Press, 1962. xviii + 284 pp. Illustrations, notes, appendices, and index. Especially important is Chapter 8 on "Progressivism, Planning and Housing." It underscores the significance of the Columbian Exposition and the City Beautiful Movement to urban planning in the United States.

Lubove, Roy. *Twentieth-Century Pittsburgh: Government, Business and Environmental Change*. New York: John Wiley & Sons, 1969. x + 189 pp. Illustrations, maps, notes, and index. A perceptive history of city planning and environmental change in Pittsburgh, particularly the post World War II "Renaissance." Lubove points out that the business and professional leadership of the city dominated these reforms through voluntary civic organizations. In the 1960s, neighborhood-centered groups challenged the elite hegemony. Material is included on public works, especially zoning, parks, and flood control.

Luckingham, Bradford. "The City in the Westward Movement—A Bibliographical Note." *Western Historical Quarterly*, V (July 1974), 295-306. Good analysis of the historical literature on this subject.

Lyddan, R. H. "A Century of Topographic Surveying and Mapping." *Transactions of the American Society of Civil Engineers*, CT (1953), 836-44. Describes "the progress of surveying and mapping in the West during the past 100 years." The author is chief of the U.S. Geological Survey's Plans and Coordination Branch.

Lynch, Rita C. "People in Public Works: Kansas City's Pioneer Engineers." *APWA Reporter*, 47 (July 1980), 4-5. Briefly reviews the careers of eight prominent Kansas City engineers and the firms they founded.

Lynch, Rita C. "People in Public Works: Louis R. Ash." *APWA Reporter*, 46 (Dec. 1979), 4-5, 24. A biographical sketch of a Kansas City municipal engineer who was also one of the founders of the engineering firm of Howard, Needles, Tammen and Bergendoff.

Lynn, Kenneth S., ed. *The Professions in America*. Boston: Houghton Mifflin Company, 1965. xiv + 273 pp. Notes and appendix. In C. Richard Soderberg's essay on "The American Engineer," he includes a section on the engineer's historical background in Western civilization. There is some historical information in William Alonso's chapter on "Cities and City Planners."

McCarthy, G. Michael. *Hour of Trial: The Conservation Conflict in Colorado and the West, 1891-1907*. Norman: University of Oklahoma Press, 1977. xvi + 327 pp. Illustrations, map, notes, bibliography, and index.

McCarthy, Michael P. "Chicago Businessmen and the Burnham Plan." *Journal of the Illinois State Historical Society*, LXIII (Autumn 1970), 228-56. Bankers, realtors, merchants, manufacturers, and other executives took the initiative in guiding the growth and development of Chicago's lakefront and business district.

McCarty, Richard Justin. *Work and Play: An Autobiography—The Ancestry and Experience of Richard Justin McCarty, 1851-1934*. Kansas City: Empire Printing Company, 1925. 273 pp. Illustrations. Reminiscences of a nineteenth-century railroad engineer.

McClelland, John M., Jr. *R. A. Long's Planned City: The Story of Longview*. Longview, Wash.: Longview Publishing Co., 1976. ix + 288 pp. Illustrations, map, appendix, and index. A history of the planning and building of Longview, Washington (1918), a project of R. A. Long and his Long-Bell Lumber Company which was headquartered in Kansas City. One chapter describes the roads and bridges that were constructed to provide easy access to the city, particularly from the Pacific Highway.

Macaulay, David. *Underground*. Boston: Houghton, Mifflin Company, 1976. 112 pp. Illustrations and glossary. A marvelous explanation of that network of walls, columns, cables, pipes, and tunnels beneath the buildings and streets of modern cities and how it works.

MacColl, E. Kimbark. *The Growth of a City: Power and Politics in Portland, Oregon, 1915 to 1950*. Portland, Ore.: Georgian Press, 1979. xiii + 717 pp. Illustrations, maps, notes, bibliography, and index. One of the few urban biographies that give adequate coverage to the development of the municipal infrastructure. Virtually every field of public works is addressed in this fine book.

McGeary, M. Nelson. *Gifford Pinchot: Forester-Politician*. Princeton: Princeton University Press, 1960. xii + 481 pp. Illustrations, notes, bibliography, and index. A god biography of Pinchot's career as a forester-conservationist. The book places greater emphasis on the subject's political skills than most biographies of his public career.

McGivern, James Gregory. *First Hundred Years of Engineering Education in the United States (1807-1907)*. Spokane: Gonzaga University Press, 1960. vii + 171 pp. Tables and index. A tightly organized, chronological examination of the development of engineering education in the United States. The author emphasizes technical educational philosophies and methodologies, community and national needs, professional societies, and the contributions of educators such as Sylvanus Thayer, Robert H. Gardiner, and Stephen Van Rensselaer.

MacKaye, Benton. *The New Exploration: A Philosophy of Regional Planning*. New York: Harcourt, Brace and Company, 1928. xiv + 235 pp. Maps, notes, and index. A general discussion of regional planning's effect on the environment. The author quotes voluminously from Henry David Thoreau, "the philosopher of environment," and Lewis Mumford, one of "the classic writers on environment."

McKelvey, Blake. "A History of City Planning in Rochester." *Rochester History*, VI (Oct. 1944), 1-24. A study of "patch-work or functional planning and of the successive attempts at more comprehensive city planning" in Rochester from the early 1900s.

McKelvey, Blake. *A Panoramic History of Rochester and Monroe County, New York*. Woodland Hills, Ca.: Windsor Publications, 1979. 264 pp. Illustrations, bibliography, and indexes.

McKelvey, Blake. "American Urban History Today." *American Historical Review*, LVII (July 1952), 919-29. Insightful analysis of the historiography of the American city to the early 1950s. Some references to public works facilities and services are made.

McKelvey, Blake. " 'Canaltown': A Focus of Historical Traditions." *Rochester History*, XXXVII (April 1975), 1-24. A brief history of the South Water Street district and its link to Rochester's urban core (by four successive Main Street bridges and two successive aqueducts).

McKelvey, Blake. "Rochester and Monroe County: An Historic Partnership." *Rochester History*, XXXIII (April 1971), 1-24. Describes the 150-year relationship, including the execution of many public works functions.

McKelvey, Blake. "The Physical Growth of Rochester." *Rochester History*, XIII (Oct. 1951), 1-24. Describes Rochester's phenomenal growth in the nineteenth century and its general effects on public works.

Mackesey, Thomas W., comp. *History of City Planning: Exchange Bibliography No. 19*. Monticello, Ill.: Council of Planning Librarians, 1961. 65 pp. Index. Not annotated.

McLaughlin, Charles Capen, ed., and Charles E. Beveridge, assoc. ed. *The Papers of Frederick Law Olmsted: Volume I–The Formative Years, 1822-1852*. See chapter on "Parks and Recreation."

Maclear, Anne Bush. *Early New England Towns: A Comparative Study of Their Development*. New York: Columbia University—Green & Co. Agents, 1908. 181 pp. Notes. Describes the institutional life of five Massachusetts towns—Salem, Dorchester, Watertown, Roxbury, and Cambridge. The study describes in limited fashion town plans, surveying practices, finances, highways, commons, general regulations, and the duties of public officials.

Macmahon, Arthur W.; John D. Millett; and Gladys Ogden. *The Administration of Federal Work Relief*. Chicago: Public Administration Service, 1941. x + 407 pp. Tables, notes, and index. A classic, insightful analysis of the organization and administration of the Work Progress Administration.

McMath, Robert E. "Engineers, Their Relations and Standing." *Journal of the Association of Engineering Societies*, VI (Jan. 1887), 94-100. After a brief review of the Corps of Engineers' history, the president of the Engineers' Club of St. Louis recommends the creation of a national bureau of public works where civil and military engineers would join "in an effort to better the public service, render it more efficient in work and more honorable in public estimation, and so elevate the profession of engineer."

MacMechen, Edgar C. *Robert W. Speer: A City Builder*. Denver: Smith Brooks Printing Company, 1919. 79 pp. Illustrations and appendix. A testimonial to "a big man," Denver's mayor from 1904-1912. According to the author, this biography is intended "to serve, not alone as a biography, but as a public record of Denver's golden age of development." MacMechen argues that this record of planning and building is "unequalled in the history of American municipalities."

McNair, James B. *With Rod and Transit: The Engineering Career of Thomas S. McNair*

(1824-1901). Los Angeles: James B. McNair, 1951. xv + 267 pp. Illustrations, maps, notes, and bibliography. A biography of a mining and railroad engineer who acquired his training as an apprentice (axman and rodman) on the Pennsylvania Canal and the North Pennsylvania Railroad. In 1860 McNair obtained full professional status when he became a chief engineer on the Maryland and Delaware Railroad. This volume, based largely on correspondence found in twelve of McNair's letterbooks, gives particular attention to his developing "Engineering Career" (pp. 85-215).

McNamara, Katherine. *Bibliography of Planning, 1928-1935*. Cambridge: Harvard University Press, 1936. x + 232 pp. Indexes. A supplement to the *Manual of Planning Information* (1928), this volume lists only material issued subsequent to July 1928. One section of the bibliography is devoted to "History."

McVoy, Arthur D. "A History of City Planning in Portland, Oregon." *Oregon Historical Quarterly*, XLVI (March 1945), 3-21. A history of planning in Portland from 1903 "when the Olmsted Brothers, landscape architects of Brookline, Massachusetts, were invited . . . to prepare a plan for the Lewis and Clark Exposition."

Madden, R. B. "The American Society of Naval Engineers." *General Electric Review*, 57 (May 1954), 35-36. A brief history of the society by one of its staff.

Maher, Marty. *Bringing Up the Brass: My 25 Years at West Point*. New York: David McKay Company, 1951. xii + 234 pp. Illustrations. For a general audience, preferably West Point alumni.

Malone, Michael P. "The New Deal in Idaho." *Pacific Historical Review*, XXXVIII (Aug. 1969), 293-310. Includes some material on CCC, PWA, and WPA programs.

Mandel, Siegfried, and Margaret Shipley. *Proud Past—Bright Future: A History of the College of Engineering at the University of Colorado, 1893-1966*. Boulder: University of Colorado, 1966. xi + 331 pp. Illustrations, bibliography, appendix, and index. Describes some of the early civil engineering sources at this western school.

Mann, C. R. "Report of Progress in the Study of Engineering Education." *Proceedings of the Society for the Promotion of Engineering Education*, XXIV (June 1916), 48-97. An incomplete progress report on engineering education since the eighteenth century.

Mann, Charles Riborg. *A Study of Engineering Education: Prepared for the Joint Committee on Engineering Education of the National Engineering Societies*. New York: Carnegie Foundation for the Advancement of Teaching, 1918. xi + 139 pp. Tables, notes, appendix, bibliography, and index. Of particular interest are the chapters on the "Development of Engineering Schools in the United States," "Aims and Curricula of the Early Schools," "The Struggle for Resources and Recognition," and "Development of the Curriculum into Its Present Form."

Manning, Thomas G. *Government in Science: The U.S. Geological Survey, 1867-1894*. Lexington: University of Kentucky Press, 1967. xiv + 257 pp. Maps, notes, bibliographical essay, and index. Discusses the origins, founding, and activities of this federal agency during the late nineteenth century. The well-researched and lucidly written volume contains chapters on Yellowstone Park and John Wesley Powell's irrigation survey. Throughout the book, emphasis is given to the political context of the survey's work and the changing role of the government in science. Manning also points out how the agency's activities "harmonized with general historical trends of post-Civil War America—westward expansion, the rise of industry, the extension of federal power, and urbanization."

Mansfield, E. D. *Personal Memoirs: Social, Political, and Literary with Sketches of Many Noted People, 1803-1843*. Cincinnati: Robert Clarke & Co., 1879. viii + 348 pp. Contains some reflections on life at West Point, beginning in 1815, and government survey work.

Maples, William A., and Robert E. Wilde. "A Story of Progress: Fifty Years of the American Concrete Institute." *Journal of the American Concrete Institute*, 25 (Feb. 1954), 409-36. A brief account of significant administrative and technical developments.

Marcello, Ronald E. "The Selection of North Carolina's WPA Chief, 1935: A Dispute Over Political Patronage." *North Carolina Historical Review*, LII (Winter 1975), 59-76. Explains that the selection of George W. Coan, Jr., a recently retired mayor of Winston-Salem, as WPA chief represented "a workable compromise to the patronage problems that had plagued the federal relief effort in the Tar Heel State ever since its inception in 1933."

Marine, Gene. *America the Raped: The Engineering Mentality and the Devastation of a Continent*. New York: Simon and Schuster, 1969. 312 pp. Notes and indexes.

Mark, Irving. "The Homestead Ideal and Conservation of the Public Domain." *American Journal of Economics and Sociology*, 22 (April 1963), 262-78. Think piece that illustrates the complimentary aspects of the homestead ideal and desire to conserve the public domain.

Marshall, Douglas W. "The British Engineers in America: 1775-1783." *Journal of the Society for Army Historical Research*, LI (Autumn 1973), 155-63. Gives special attention to John Montresor, "perhaps the most ambitious and enterprising member" of the British Corps of Engineers to serve in America. His engineering record includes twenty-three years of service on the North American continent.

Marshall, Douglas W. *The City in the New World: The Military Contribution*. Ann Arbor: University of Michigan, 1973. 20 pp. Breezy discussion of the contributions of military engineers to early city planning.

Marshall, T. A., Jr. "Engineers Joint Council." *Mechanical Engineering*, 76 (July 1954), 582-84. A short history of the council since its beginning in 1941.

Marston, Anson, and Mark B. Morris. "A Century of Progress in Civil Engineering." *Civil Engineering*, I (July 1931), 929-32. A description of several engineering milestones.

Martin, C. T. (Deac). *From School to Institute: An Informal Story of Case*. Cleveland: World Publishing Co., 1967. 125 pp. Illustrations, map, and chronology. A dull, pointless history of the Case Institute of Technology by an uninspired alumni.

Martin, Roscoe C., et al. *River Basin Administration and the Delaware*. See chapter on "Flood Control and Drainage."

Mason, Alpheus Thomas. *Bureaucracy Convicts Itself: The Ballinger-Pinchot Controversy of 1910*. New York: Viking Press, 1941. 224 pp. Illustrations, notes, appendices, bibliographical essay, and index. A dated, superficial account of this conservation cause célèbre.

Mason, Herbert Molloy. *Death from the Sea: Our Greatest Natural Disaster, the Galveston Hurricane of 1900*. See chapter on "Flood Control and Drainage."

Massouh, Michael. "American Building History: The Need to Teach It." *American Professional Constructor*, 4 (Autumn 1977), 19-22. The author argues that the study of the history of building materials, techniques, and structures has a place in the curriculum of a construction program.

Massouh, Michael. "Tom Loftin Johnson: Engineer-Entrepreneur (1869-1900)." Doctoral dissertation, Case Western Reserve University, 1970. 243 pp.

Mathews, Catharine Van Cortlandt. *Andrew Ellicott: His Life and Letters*. New York: Grafton Press, 1908. x + 256 pp. Illustrations, maps, and index. A biography of the surveyor-general of the United States who redrew L'Enfant's plan of Washington, D.C., incorporating many of Thomas Jefferson's ideas. Numerous Ellicott letters—mainly to his wife—are printed in their entirety.

Matson, Robert William. *William Mulholland: A Forgotten Forefather*. See chapter on "Community Water Supply."

Maury, William M. *Alexander "Boss" Shepherd and the Board of Public Works*. Washington, D.C.: George Washington University, 1975. v + 57 pp. Illustrations, notes, and bibliography. Part of a series of monographs on Washington, D.C. The focus is on the city as a major urban center rather than as the federal capital. The author analyzes the rise and fall of the Territory of the District of Columbia in the early 1870s. Shepherd and his associates undertook costly public programs which bankrupted the territorial government but effected dramatic improvements in the physical appearance of the city. Maury recounts in detail the blend of civic zeal and personal avarice which produced the outburst of grading, paving, planting, and laying of sewers.

Mavis, Frederic T. "Backgrounds of Engineering Education." *Transactions of the American Society of Civil Engineers*, CT (1953), 133-46. A summary of the advancements in engineering education from earliest times.

Mayer, Harold M. *Chicago: City of Decisions*. Chicago: Geographic Society of Chicago,

1955. 40 pp. Illustrations and maps. An overview of the development of city planning in Chicago.

Meigs, Peveril. "John G. Hales, Boston Geographer and Surveyor, 1785-1832." *New England Historical and Genealogical Register*, 129 (Jan. 1975), 23-29. A biographical sketch emphasizing Hales' geographical and surveying work in Boston and surrounding towns from 1814 to 1833.

Melosi, Martin V., ed. *Pollution and Reform in American Cities, 1870-1930*. See chapter on "Solid Wastes."

Mendenhall, Herbert D. "The History of Land Surveying in Florida." *Surveying and Mapping*, 10 (Jan.-March 1950), 278-83. From 1513 to 1931.

Merdinger, Charles J. *Civil Engineering through the Ages*. Washington, D.C.: Society of American Military Engineers, 1963. 159 pp. Illustrations and notes. A collection of historical public works articles first published in *Military Engineer* beginning in 1952. There are separate articles on roads, sewerage systems, water supply, construction materials, canals, bridges, tunnels, irrigation, flood control, harbors and docks, railroads and surveying.

Merino, James Anthony. "A Great City and its Suburbs: Attempts to Integrate Metropolitan Boston, 1865-1920." Doctoral dissertation, University of Texas at Austin, 1968. 167 pp. Insightful exploration of the problems of annexation and metropolitan coordination.

Merriam, Charles E. "The National Resources Planning Board: A Chapter in American Planning Experience." *American Political Science Review*, XXXVIII (Dec. 1944), 1075-88. A review of the purposes and work of the National Resources Planning Board (1939) by one of its members.

Merritt, Raymond H. *Engineering in American Society, 1850-1875*. Lexington: University Press of Kentucky, 1969. xi + 199 pp. Notes, bibliographical essay, and index. Describes the vital role played by engineers in producing a technological society. It also explains in some detail the changes they helped to bring about in American education, industry, professional status, urban existence, cultural values, and world perspectives.

Michie, Peter S. *The Life and Letters of Emory Upton, Colonel of the Fourth Regiment of Artillery, and Brevet Major-General, U.S. Army*. New York: D. Appleton and Company, 1885. xxviii + 511 pp. Illustrations and index. Contains one chapter on Upton's education and training at West Point.

Mikesell, Stephen D. "Historical Analysis and Benefit-Cost Accounting: Planning for the New Melones Dam." *Public Historian*, 1 (Winter 1979), 50-65. An excellent case study of how historians can make use of policy tools derived from basic benefit-cost analysis as conducted by agencies at all levels of government. The author contends that it is possible to integrate historical research and policy decision-making.

"Milestones in U.S. Civil Engineering." *Civil Engineering*, 47 (Oct. 1977), 142-43. A brief list of civil engineering milestones: buildings and bridges; tunnels, roads, and canals; dams, reservoirs, and aqueducts; sanitary engineering; and surveying, mapping, and planning. It dates from the mid-seventeenth century.

Miller, Joseph Arthur. "Congress and the Origins of Conservation: Natural Resource Policies, 1865-1900." Doctoral dissertation, University of Minnesota, 1973. 504 pp.

Miller, Nyle H. "Surveying the Southern Boundary Line of Kansas: From the Private Journal of Col. Joseph E. Johnston." *Kansas Historical Quarterly*, 1 (Nov. 1931), 104-39. Contains a short introduction followed by entries from Johnston's journal from May 16 to October 29, 1857.

Miller, Roberta Balstad. *City and Hinterland: A Case Study of Urban Growth and Regional Development*. Westport, Conn.: Greenwood Press, 1979. xiv + 179 pp. Maps, tables, notes, appendix, bibliographical essay, and index. Outstanding study that places urban growth within a regional context. It shows how the introduction of new transportation systems in Onondaga County, New York, began the gradual transformation of the dominant rural economy into a clearly differentiated urban, village, and agricultural economies.

Miller, William D. *Memphis during the Progressive Era, 1900-1917*. See chapter on "Sewers and Wastewater Treatment."

Miller, Zane. *The Urbanization of Modern America: A Brief History*. New York: Harcourt Brace Jovanovich, 1973. xiv + 241 pp. Illustrations and index. Presents some material on the history of city planning.

Millett, John D. *The Works Progress Administration in New York City*. Chicago: Public Administration Service, 1938. xi + 189 pp. Tables, notes, and index.

Mills, George. "Iowa's Planning Programs of the Past and Present." *Annals of Iowa*, 42 (Spring 1975), 583-96. Includes histories of the four principal Iowa planning organizations prior to the current "Iowa 2000": the Iowa Twenty-Five Year Conservation Plan of 1933; the Iowa State Planning Board of 1934-1939; the Iowa Postwar Rehabilitation Commission of 1944; and the 1958 Governor's Committee of One Hundred on Iowa's Economic and Social Trends.

Mills, John. *The Engineer in Society*. New York: D. Van Nostrand Company, 1946. xix + 196 pp. An interesting essay on the role of the engineer in society. The author frequently looks back to gain insight into the engineer's current (1945-1946) position, particularly in the private sector.

Milton, Ellen Fink. *A Biography of Albert Fink*. Rochester, N.Y.: Commercial Controls Corporation, 1951. xiii + 102 pp. Illustrations and appendix. A short, biographical testimonial to a prominent engineer, who has been called "the father of railway economics and statistics in the United States." By his daughter.

Mitchell, J. Paul. "Progressivism in Denver: The Municipal Reform Movement, 1904-1916." Doctoral dissertation, University of Denver, 1966. 425 pp.

Moehring, Eugene Peter. "Public Works and the Patterns of Urban Real Estate Growth in Manhattan, 1835-1894." Doctoral dissertation, City University of New York, 1976. vi + 280 pp. Notes and bibliography. An original and provoking examination of the impact of public works expenditures on land values and patterns of urban growth.

Moeller, Beverly Bowen. *Phil Swing and Boulder Dam*. See chapter on "Irrigation."

Mohl, Raymond A., and James F. Richardson, eds. *The Urban Experience: Themes in American History*. Belmont, Calif.: Wadsworth Publishing Company, 1973. xi + 265 pp. Illustrations, appendix, bibliographical essay, and index. Students of public works history will be interested in the following essays: Joseph L. Arnold's, "City Planning in America," and Kenneth T. Jackson's, "The Crabgrass Frontier: 150 Years of Suburban Growth in America."

Molloy, Peter Michael. "Technical Education and the Young Republic: West Point as America's École Polytechnique, 1802-1833." 2 vols. Doctoral dissertation, Brown University, 1975. Vol. I: viii + 270 pp.; Vol. II: 271-489. Notes and bibliography. A lengthy examination of the first thirty years of the military academy's history, "from the standpoint of the history of engineering education."

Moniz, James. "Capital Construction Planning and Financing in Maryland and New Jersey, 1946-1966: A Comparative Study." Doctoral dissertation, Clark University, 1968.

Monzione, Joseph. "People in Public Works: William R. Hutton." *APWA Reporter*. See chapter on "Waterways."

Mooney, Booth. *Builders for Progress: The Story of the Associated General Contractors of America*. New York: McGraw-Hill Book Company, 1965. 194 pp. Illustrations and index. A general history of AGC with special mention being made of the individuals who contributed significantly to its development. More descriptive than analytical, the author discusses such topics as the association's founding and early years; problems of the building industry in the late 1920s and 1930s, AGC's role in the war effort; the postwar years of growth; and the highway building programs, missile bases, and defense projects of the 1960s.

Moore, Charles. *Daniel H. Burnham: Architect, Planner of Cities*. 2 vols. Boston: Houghton Mifflin Company, 1921. Vol. I: xviii + 260 pp.; Vol. II: ix + 238 pp. Illustrations, maps, diagrams, appendix, and index. A full-fledged biography of a prominent architect and planner by a contemporary and an admirer. The author includes many long excerpts from speeches and correspondence both to and from Burnham. In the appendix, Moore provides chronological lists of the buildings designed by Burnham and by Burnham and Root.

Moore, Floyd Wayne. "Kalamazoo, Michigan:

The Evolution of a Modern City Free from General Fund Indebtedness." Doctoral dissertation, Northwestern University, 1941. ix + 314 pp. Maps, charts, tables, notes, appendices, and bibliography. Includes a strong chapter on the management of the public works and water departments.

Moran, Daniel E. "Foundation Development during Fifty Years." *Engineering News-Record*, 92 (April 17, 1924), 670-73. In reviewing foundation design, the author concludes that "foundations for buildings have been improved, particularly the spread footing; but in deep foundation work there has been practically no advance, and the methods used today, in general, were old in 1874."

Moreell, Ben. "50 Years of Engineering." *Military Engineer*, 62 (July-Aug. 1970), 228-30. Founder of the Seabees and past president of the Society of American Military Engineers reviews engineering milestones since 1920.

Morgan, Anne Hodges. *Robert S. Kerr: The Senate Years*. See chapter on "Waterways."

Morgan, James Dudley. "Maj. Pierre Charles L'Enfant, the Unhonored and Unrewarded Engineer." *Records of the Columbia Historical Society of Washington, D.C.*, 2 (1899), 116-57. Testimonial to L'Enfant's engineering career. The introductory statement is followed by numerous examples, "exhibits," from L'Enfant's correspondence.

Morison, Elting E. *From Know-How to Nowhere: The Development of American Technology*. New York: Basic Books, 1974. xiii + 199 pp. Illustrations, bibliography, and index. A penetrating examination of how America's "capacity for building and making things developed and grew." Morison begins with inventive and enterprising farmers and artisans and concludes with today's highly skilled scientists and engineers. He studies their purposes and motives and suggests ways "to build an environment that will really fit our *human* nature."

Morison, George S. *The New Epoch as Developed by the Manufacture of Power.* Boston: Houghton, Mifflin and Company, 1903. ix + 134 pp. Illustration. Contains a classic statement of engineering philosophy.

Morrill, John Barstow, and Paul O. Fischer, eds. *Planning the Region of Chicago*. Chicago: Chicago Regional Planning Association, 1956. 191 pp. Illustrations, maps, and index. This study was prepared by Daniel H. Burnham, Jr., and Robert Kingery. Almost every chapter (see especially "The Chicago Regional Planning Association," "Transportation: Highway—Railway—Waterway—Airway," "Water Supply and Sanitation," "Parks, Forests and Recreation") has historical sections that are worth consulting.

Morrison, A. J. "Colonel Tatham and Other Virginia Engineers." *William and Mary College Quarterly*, II (April 1922), 81-84. Brief biographical sketches of William Tatham, John Wood, and Hugh Paul Taylor, nineteenth-century engineers and surveyors.

Morse, Roy W. "People in Public Works: William Chester Morse." *APWA Reporter*, 46 (Aug. 1979), 4-5. Records the career of an individual responsible for the development of several Pacific Northwest cities and who for 11 years served as chairman of Seattle's Board of Public Works.

Morse, Roy W.; Myra L. Phelps; and Leslie Blanchard. *Public Works in Seattle: A Narrative History of the Engineering Department, 1875-1975*. Seattle: Seattle Engineering Department, 1978. xiv + 304 pp. Illustrations, maps, tables, notes, bibliography, and index. A comprehensive chronicle of Seattle's public works growth and development, prepared under the direction of a former city engineer (1957-1971). The book's twenty-one chapters are arranged by subject. Each is an historical survey of an important public works program or administrative function. The selections on bridges, streets, water supply, street lighting, sewers, and refuse disposal are contributions to established areas of public works historiography. And the table of contents lists topics—seawalls, capital improvement financing, annexation, street names and house numbering, and surveying and mapping—that have been either totally ignored or received only cursory treatment from professional historians.

Moses, Robert. *Public Works: A Dangerous Trade*. New York: McGraw-Hill Book Company, 1970. xxxvi + 952 pp. Illustrations, maps, charts, and index. An autobiographical source book "with quotations from reports, talks, writings, and correspondence since 1919, with incidental notations to make them understandable, and with plenty of illustrations." This volume is a chronicle of environmental planning and public works and contains interesting observations on such ambitious projects as Jones Beach State Park and the St. Lawrence Seaway by one of New York's most prominent and controversial public servants.

Mosher, Frederick C., ed. *American Public Administration: Past, Present, Future*. University of Alabama Press, 1975. xiv + 298 pp. Notes, appendix, and index. Good series of essays on the evolution of public administration. Public works historians will be particularly interested in Alice B. and Donald C. Stone "Early Development of Education in Public Administration."

Mosher, Frederick C., et al. *City Manager Government in Seven Cities*. Chicago: Public Administration Office, 1940. viii + 448 pp. Notes and index. Seven essays on the development of city government in Rochester, New York; Berkeley, California; Hamilton, Ohio; Ames, Iowa; Dayton, Ohio; Long Beach, California; and Winnetka, Illinois by political scientists and public administrators. All of the cities analyzed operated under a city manager plan of government. There are discussions of varying lengths throughout the book on how city managers related to municipal public works issues.

Mullins, Lawrence E. "Geographical Survey of the West, 1871-1879." *Military Engineer*, 55 (May-June 1963), 183-84. Summary of the survey conducted by George M. Wheeler.

Mumey, Nolie. *John Williams Gunnison (1812-1853): The Last of the Western Explorers—A History of the Survey through Colorado and Utah with a Biography and Details of His Massacre*. Denver: Artcraft Press, 1955. xvii + 180 pp. Illustrations, maps, notes, appendices, and index. Includes a detailed description of Gunnison's exploratory survey over the Rocky Mountains in 1853.

Mumford, Lewis. *Sticks and Stones: A Study of American Architecture and Civilization*. See chapter on "Public Buildings."

Mumford, Lewis. *The Brown Decades: A Study of Arts in America, 1865-1895*. New York: Harcourt, Brace and Company, 1931. xii + 266 pp. Illustrations and index. A study of engineering, architecture, landscape design, and painting in a formative period in American culture. The author claims that a "hidden renaissance" was present in these decades. Brooklyn Bridge, for example, awakened the age to a "side of engineering which the engineer had least concerned himself with: its human and aesthetic effect."

Mumford, Lewis. "The Heritage of the Cities Movement in America: An Historical Survey." *Journal of the American Institute of Architects*, VII (Aug. 1919), 349-54. Describes the birth of civic consciousness in the United States—"The year was 1892; the place was Chicago."—and subsequent developments during the early twentieth century.

Munro, William Bennett. *Municipal Government and Administration*. 2 vols. New York: MacMillan Company, 1925. Vol. I: xii + 459 pp.; Vol. II: vi + 517 pp. Notes and index. In the first seven chapters on "The Evolution of the City," the author sketches briefly the history of municipal development from "earliest times to the present day." The remainder of the book is devoted to describing the current organization of municipal government, indicating the chief administrative problems, and explaining attempts to solve these problems. One section in the second volume (five chapters) deals with "City Planning and Public Works."

Myhra, David. "Rexford Guy Tugwell: Initiator of America's Greenbelt New Towns, 1935 and 1936." *Journal of the American Institute of Planners*, 40 (May 1974), 176-88.

Myres, S. D., ed. *Pioneer, Surveyor, Frontier Lawyer: The Personal Narrative of O. W. Williams, 1877-1902*. El Paso: Texas Western College Press, 1966. xii + 350 pp. Illustrations, maps, and bibliography.

Nash, Gary B. "City Planning and Political Tension in the Seventeenth Century: The Case of Philadelphia." *Proceedings of the American Philosophical Society*, 112 (Feb. 15, 1968), 54-73. Demonstrates that the founding of Philadelphia—William Penn's "holy experiment"—was a "nettlesome and complex affair, marked by changes of plans, unfulfilled promises, misunderstandings, opportunism . . . ." The author examines in detail "the question of the planting of Philadelphia," the source of a major controversy for decades.

Nash, Roderick, ed. *The American Environment: Readings in the History of Conservation*. Reading, Mass.: Addison-Wesley Publishing Company, 1968. xix + 236 pp. Illustrations, chronology, and bibliographical essay. An excellent classroom reader on conservation as well as environmental topics. The selections tend to deal with preservationist and wilderness values, but there are items on reclamation, Civilian Conservation Corps, Tennessee Valley Authority, and the Echo Park controversy.

Nash, Roderick. "The State of Environmental History." *The State of American History*, ed. by Herbert J. Bass. Chicago: Quadrangle Books, 1970. Pp. 249-60. Identifies achievements in the broad field of "environmental history" and suggests areas for further research.

National Resources Committee. *Urban Government*. Vol. I. Washington, D. C.: Government Printing Office, 1939. 303 pp. Charts, tables, graphs, and notes. On August 9, 1937, the National Resources Committee submitted to the President its report on the role of cities in the national economy. In preparing that report, a large amount of information was collected which could not be included. The committee, therefore, published two supplementary volumes "to make such data and information available to interested persons and organizations." In volume I there are chapters on the "Development of Urban Government" and "Federal Relations to Urban Governments," but the most important chapter is Harold D. Smith's "Associations of Cities and Municipal Officials." It presents brief histories of organizations of which city officials are members: state leagues, American Municipal Association, United States Conference of Majors, and International Union of Local Authorities.

National Resources Planning Board. *Our Public Works Experience*. Washington, D. C.: National Resources Planning Board, 1941. 36 pp. Charts, tables, and bibliography. A summary of a longer study (*The Economic Effects of Federal Public Works Expenditures, 1933-38*) which examines the effects of six years of federal public works expenditures on employment and business activity. The Public Works Committee of the National Resources Planning Board sponsored the study.

Neff, Gene L. "People in Public Works: Pioneer Bridge Builder Wendell Bolman, 1814-1884." *APWA Reporter*. See chapter on "Roads, Streets, and Highways."

Neill, Wilfred T. "Surveyors' Field Notes as a Source of Historical Information." *Florida Historical Quarterly*, XXXIV (April 1956), 329-33. An important historical resource.

Nelson, Daniel. *Managers and Workers: Origins of the New Factory System in the United States, 1880-1920*. Madison: University of Wisconsin Press, 1975. x + 234 pp. Tables, notes, bibliographical note, and index. Includes a chapter on "The Rise of Scientific Management."

Neufeld, Maurice. "The White City: The Beginnings of a Planned Civilization in America." *Journal of the Illinois State Historical Society*, XXVII (April 1934), 71-93. A description of the 1893 World's Columbian Exposition and its influence on planning in the United States.

Nevada Chapter, American Public Works Association. *Chapter Officers, Activities, By-Laws, History, and Members of APWA Nevada Chapter*. Las Vegas: APWA, Nevada Chapter, 1979. 43 pp. Illustrations. Includes a brief review of the Nevada Chapter's growth since 1965 by Calvin J. Dodson, formerly public works director of the city of Sparks.

New York-New Jersey Metropolitan Chapter, American Public Works Association. *Public Works in Metropolitan New York-New Jersey*. New York: APWA New York-New Jersey Metropolitan Chapter, 1978. 126 pp. Illustrations and maps. Contains historical sketches of noteworthy public works projects (public buildings, parks, sewerage and water supply systems, bridges, airports, highways, tunnels, rapid transit systems, and waste disposal facilities) in the New York-New Jersey metropolitan area.

Nixon, Edgar B., ed. *Franklin D. Roosevelt and Conservation, 1911-1945*. 2 vols. Hyde Park: N. Y.: Franklin D. Roosevelt Library, 1957. Vol. I: xiv + 614 pp.; Vol. II: 700 pp. Illustration, notes, and index. A well-edited collection of public papers that reflect Roosevelt's conservationist thinking and actions. The compilation includes material on irrigation, flood control, energy, and other aspects of natural resource development.

Noble, David F. *America by Design: Science, Technology, and the Rise of Corporate Capitalism*. New York: Alfred A. Knopf, 1977. xxvi + 384 pp. Notes and index. Traces the history of "the twin forces which together gave shape to modern America—scientific technology and corporate capitalism—by focusing upon their common medium, modern engineering." Noble argues that between 1880 and 1930 a relatively small cadre of engineers and scientists, devoted to the objectives of large-scale private enterprise, forged a link between the corporation and the university that remains unbroken today.

Noble, David Franklin. "Science and Technology in the Corporate Search for Order: American Engineers and Social Reform, 1900-1929." Doctoral dissertation, University of Rochester, 1974. 567 pp.

Nolen, John, ed. *City Planning: A Series of Papers Presenting the Essential Elements of a City Plan*. New York: D. Appleton and Company, 1929. xxx + 513 pp. Illustrations, maps, tables, diagrams, bibliographies, and index. First published in 1916 in the National Municipal League Series, the second volume deals more fully with "problems that confront practically all towns and cities, and it presents the lines of investigation, planning and control which have been found most sound in theory and most successful in practice." There are essays on "Local and Minor Streets," "Public Buildings and Quasi-Public Buildings," "Park Systems," "Water Supply and the City Plan," "Transportation and Main Thoroughfares and Street Railways," and "The Effect of Rapid Transit on the City plan" as well as several pieces on a variety of city planning dimensions. Frederick Law Olmsted prepared the book's introduction.

Nolen, John. "Twenty Years of City Planning." *National Municipal Review*, XVI (June 1927), 369-73. Describes "the character and extent of twenty years' progress in city planning."

Norris, George W. *Fighting Liberal: The Autobiography of George W. Norris*. See chapter on "Flood Control and Drainage."

"Notable Concrete Structures . . . Old and New." *Journal of the American Concrete Institute*, 25 (Feb. and April 1954), Feb: 437-40, 472-76, 497-500, 522-24; April: 631-32, 643-44, 655-56. A gallery of photographs (with detailed captions) in commemoration of the fiftieth anniversary of the American Concrete Institute.

Nyland, Keith Ryan. "Doctor Thomas Walker (1715-1794): Explorer, Physician, Statesman, Surveyor and Planter of Virginia and Kentucky." Doctoral dissertation, Ohio State University, 1971.

O'Callaghan, Jerry A. "Significance of the United States Public Land Survey." *Western Pennsylvania Historical Magazine*, 50 (Jan. 1967), 51-59. Describes the origins of the public land survey.

O'Connell, James C. "People in Public Works: Ellis S. Chesbrough." *APWA Reporter*. See chapter on "Sewers and Wastewater Treatment."

Oliver, John W. *History of American Technology*. New York: Ronald Press Co., 1956. viii + 676 pp. Notes and index. An early comprehensive, historical account of American technology and invention and their effect on the nation's culture. The survey extends from the seventeenth century to the mid-twentieth century and contains several useful chapters on transportation and building technologies.

Olmsted, Frederick Law. "The Town-Planning Movement in America." *Annals of the American Academy of Political and Social Science*, LI (Jan. 1914), 172-81. An historical review of the importance and purpose of planning—"not merely to meet the temporary circumstances but rather those of the expected future town conceived in the imagination"—by one of the United States' most prominent landscape architects.

O'Mara, Paul. "Chicago: 100 Years of New Towns." *Planning*, 40 (April/May 1974), 22-25. On Riverside, Pullman, and Park Forest South.

Opie, John, ed. *Americans and Environment: The Controversy over Ecology*. Lexington, Mass.: D. C. Heath and Company, 1971. xiv + 203 pp. Bibliography. A collection of writings documenting the rise of environmentalism and challenges to the traditional point of view that "American civilization is . . . defined by its economic growth, industrial progress, and capital development." Selections by Ralph Waldo Emerson, John Muir, Gifford Pinchot, Rachel Carson, Paul Ehrlich, and Herman Kahn are included. Public works subjects receive scant attention.

O'Riordan, Timothy. "Public Interest Environmental Groups in the United States and Britain." *Journal of American Studies*, 13 (Dec. 1979), 409-38. Compares the roles and tactics of American and British public interest environmental groups by reviewing their development.

O'Riordan, Timothy. "The Third American Conservation Movement: New Implications for Public Policy." *Journal of American Studies*, 5 (Aug. 1971), 155-71. Compares and contrasts the environmentalism of the 1960s and 1970s with what the author perceives as the first two conservation movements—1890 to 1920 and 1933 to 1943.

Osborn, Frederick J. *Green-Belt Cities*. New York: Schocken Books, 1969. x + 203 pp. Maps, notes, bibliography, and index. First published in 1946, the book is "a statement of the views, proposals and hopes of an advocate of the new towns policy before any governmental action on it had begun." There is a new preface by the author and a foreward by Lewis Mumford, both of which put what follows in historical perspective. Of special interest are the chapters on town planning, landscaping, and the use of public buildings and open spaces.

Ostrom, Vincent. *Water & Politics: A Study of Water Policies and Administration in the Development of Los Angeles*. See chapter on "Community Water Supply."

Our First Five Decades. Aurora, Ill.: Barber-Greene Company, 1966. 63 pp. Illustrations and diagrams. A short fiftieth-anniversary history of the Barber-Greene Company, equipment manufacturers.

Padover, Saul K., ed. *Thomas Jefferson and the National Capital: Containing Notes and Correspondence Exchanged between Jefferson, Washington, L'Enfant, Ellicott, Hallett, Thornton, Latrobe . . . relating to the Founding, Surveying, Planning, Designing, Constructing, and Administering of the City of Washington, 1783-1818. . . .* Washington, D.C.: U. S. Government Printing Office, 1946. xxxvi + 522 pp. Illustrations, maps, tables, and bibliography.

Parker, Robert D. "Fort Wayne with Might and Main." *Old Fort News*, 37 (1974), 2-13. Various aspects of city planning in Fort Wayne, Indiana, prior to World War I.

Parkhill, Forbes. "Colorado's First Survey." *Colorado Magazine*, XXXIII (July 1956), 177-80. Made in 1858 in the San Luis Valley by A. P. Wilbar, deputy surveyor general of New Mexico.

Parsons, John E. *West on the 49th Parallel: Red River to the Rockies, 1872-1876*. New York: William Morrow and Company, 1963. xiv + 208 pp. Illustrations, maps, appendix, bibliographical essay, and index. A testimonial to the American British and Canadian surveyors who explored and located the northern international boundary between the United States and Canada from the Lake of the Woods to the Rocky Mountains.

Parsons, Mabel, ed. *Memories of Samuel Parsons: Landscape Architect of the Department of Public Parks, New York*. See chapter on "Parks and Recreation."

Patterson, James T. "The New Deal in the West." *Pacific Historical Review*, XXXVIII (Aug. 1969), 317-27. Illustrates the political, economic, social, and other factors that were the basis of the West's unenthusiastic response to the New Deal.

Pattison, William D. "Beginnings of the American Rectangular Land Survey System, 1784-1800." Doctoral dissertation, University of Chicago, 1957. vii + 248 pp. Maps, notes, appendix, and bibliography. Excellent history of the land survey system developed in the nineteenth century.

Pattison, William D. "The Survey of the Seven Ranges." *Ohio Historical Quarterly*, 68 (April 1959), 115-40. By Thomas Hutchins and government surveyors (1785-1788) in southeastern Ohio.

Patton, Clifford W. *The Battle for Municipal Reform: Mobilization and Attack, 1875-1900*. Washington, D. C.: American Council on Public Affairs, 1940. 91 pp. Notes and bibliography. Standard treatment of municipal reform in the Progressive era. The author reviews "the progress attained . . . in better municipal administration, better living conditions for the people, and better governmental machinery."

Paul, Charles L. "Colonial Beaufort." *North Carolina Historical Review*, XLII (April 1965), 139-52. On the laying out of Beaufort, North Carolina (1713), and the town's plan.

Pearson, Ralph L., and Linda Wrigley. "Before Mayor Richard Lee: George Dudley Seymour and the City Planning Movement in New Haven, 1907-1924." *Journal of Urban History*, 6 (May 1980), 297-319. Explains why Seymour, a private citizen, "committed most of his personal and professional resources to arousing concern for the physical environment and to soliciting governmental and business support for community planning."

Peckworth, Howard F. "Fifty Years in the Technical Development of Concrete Pipe." *Journal of the American Concrete Institute*, 25 (Feb. 1954), 513-21. A broad outline of the technical developments in the concrete pipe industry.

Pendergrass, Lee F. "The Formation of a Municipal Reform Movement: The Municipal League of Seattle." *Pacific Northwest Quarterly*, 66 (Jan. 1975), 13-25. Describes the public purposes, objectives, and programs of Seattle's Municipal League, created in 1910.

Penick, James, Jr. *Progressive Politics and Conservation: The Ballinger-Pinchot Affair*. Chicago: University of Chicago Press, 1968. xv + 207 pp. Notes, bibliographical essay, and index. A sound treatment of this noteworthy conservation embroglio. The author presents the contending attitudes on natural resources and political realities that set the context for this episode.

Pennington, John T. *History of U. S. Army Engineer Topographic Laboratories (1920 to 1970)*. Fort Belvoir: U. S. Army Engineer Topographic Laboratories, 1973. xiv + 362 pp. Illustrations, charts, notes, bibliography, and appendices. Overview of the laboratories' role in the research and development of topographic science equipment, procedures, and techniques.

Perkins, Frances. *The Roosevelt I Knew*. New York: Viking Press, 1946. viii + 408 pp. Illustrations and index. Secretary of labor during the 1930s and a friend of the Roosevelt family, Perkins writes about her personal relationship with and her deep admiration for President Franklin D. Roosevelt. She is perceptive in her analysis of his mind and character. Of particular interest is the chapter entitled "Public Works." In it Perkins describes the origins of New Deal public works programs.

Perloff, Harvey S., ed. *Planning and the Urban Community: Essays on Urbanism and City Planning presented before a Seminar Sponsored by the Joint Committee on Planning and Urban Development of Carnegie Institute of Technology and University of Pittsburgh*. Carnegie Institute of Technology, University of Pittsburgh Press, 1961. xvii + 235 pp. Chart. Interesting essays on the role of planning in the urban community. A few of the essays have brief introductions on the history of planning.

Perrucci, Robert, and Joel E. Gerstl. *Profession without Community: Engineers in American Society*. New York: Random House, 1969. viii + 194 pp. Charts, tables, notes, and index. Discusses in general terms the evolution of the engineering profession and its changing values and practices. The data in this book—part of a series on "Occupations and Professions"—were drawn from a national survey of engineering graduates in industry and government.

Perrucci, Robert, and Joel E. Gerstl, eds. *The Engineers and the Social System*. New York: John Wiley & Sons, 1969. xii + 344 pp. Tables, bibliographies, and index. A collection of original essays analyzing the engineering profession in the context of social systems. The volume is organized around four themes: "the historical and occupational setting of the profession, the processes of recruitment and socialization, the nature of work roles and organizations, and the links between careers and society." The editors are sociologists from Purdue and Temple universities.

Peterson, Charles S. "Albert F. Potter's Wasatch Survey, 1902: A Beginning for Public Management of Natural Resources in Utah." *Utah Historical Quarterly*, 39 (Summer 1971), 329-53. The author finds Potter's survey to be "a study in practical ecology"—determining "how the immediate needs of both the people and the lands could best be met." These are outlined.

Peterson, J. L. "History and Development of Precast Concrete in the United States." *Journal of the American Concrete Institute*, 25 (Feb. 1954), 477-96. Discusses the development and structural applications of precast concrete, especially in relation to bridges and buildings.

Peterson, Jon A. "The City Beautiful Movement: Forgotten Origins and Lost Meanings." *Journal of Urban History*, 2 (Aug. 1976), 415-34. Sees the City Beautiful Movement, which began between 1897 and 1902, as the precursor to comprehensive city planning. The article contains a short biographical sketch of Charles Mulford Robinson.

Peterson, Jon A. "The Impact of Sanitary Reform upon American Urban Planning." *Journal of Social History*, 13 (Fall 1929), 83-103. Discusses the ways in which sanitary betterment ideas stimulated interest in water, sewerage, parks, and other physical improvements. The article is lucidly written and deeply researched.

Peterson, Jon A. "The Origins of the Comprehensive City Planning Ideal in the United States, 1840-1911." Doctoral dissertation, Harvard University, 1967.

Petulla, Joseph M. *American Environmentalism: Values, Tactics, Priorities*. College Station: Texas A & M University Press, 1980. xiv + 239 pp. Notes and index. An excellent historical examination of the environmental movement's assumptions, goals, values, politics, and priorities.

Pfiffner, John M. "The City Manager Plan in Iowa." 2 parts. *Iowa Journal of History and Politics*, XXVI and XXVII (Oct. 1928 and Jan. 1929), Oct.: 520-90; Jan.: 3-81. An extensive look at the plan's history and successful operation in numerous Iowa cities—Ames, Bettendorf, Clarinda, Iowa Falls, Manchester, Maquoketa, Mount Pleasant, Red Oak, Villisca, and West Liberty. The author also examines "unsuccessful attempts" in several cities.

Pharo, Elizabeth B., ed. *Reminiscences of William Hasell Wilson (1811-1902)*. Philadelphia: Patterson & White Company, 1937. iii + 68 pp. Illustrations. Memoirs of a railroad engineer (president of the Philadelphia & Erie R. R. Co.), who was born in Charleston, South Carolina, and whose father was chief civil and military engineer of the State of South Carolina and subsequently chief engineer of the Pennsylvania State Railway. These reminiscences were written in 1895-1896 and later edited (and published) by Wilson's granddaughter.

Pike, Donald G. "Four Surveyors Challenge the Rocky Mountain West: Fighting Bureaucracy and Indians in a Wild Land." *American West*, IX (May 1972), 4-13. A description of the obstacles encountered in producing "the four great surveys of the Rockies."

Pike, Donald G. "Reconnoitering the Barrier: Early Spanish and American Exploration in the Rockies." *American West*, IX (Sept. 1927), 28-33, 60.

Pinchot, Gifford. *The Fight for Conservation*. Seattle: University of Washington Press, 1967. xxvii + 152 pp. Notes and index. First published in 1910, this conservationist manifesto outlines the Progressive view of natural resources. The introduction by Gerald Nash is a perceptive analysis of Pinchot's philosophy and career as an environmental activist.

Pinchot, Gifford. *Breaking New Ground*. See chapter on "Irrigation."

Pinkett, Harold T. "Gifford Pinchot and the Early Conservation Movement in the United States." Doctoral dissertation, American University, 1953. 243 pp.

Pinkett, Harold T. *Gifford Pinchot: Private and Public Forester*. Urbana: University of Illinois Press, 1970. xii + 167 pp. Illustrations, notes, bibliography, and index. The best biography of one of the United States' foremost conservationists. In addition to Pinchot's career as a forester, the book profiles his interest in the conservation and careful utilization of all natural resources. Consequently, it is a valuable source of information on Progressive land and water philosophy.

Platt, Harold Lawrence. "Urban Public Services and Private Enterprise: Aspects of the Legal and Economic History of Houston, Texas, 1865-1905." Doctoral dissertation, Rice University, 1974. v + 291 pp. Illustrations, maps, tables, notes, and bibliography. An excellent study of Houston's transformation from a frontier settlement into an urban center. The author investigates "the process of city building, the institutions created to direct development, and the impact of growth on older patterns of social organization." Central attention is given to a comparison of public and private sector responses to community needs for essential public works services and environmental improvements. A good portion of the dissertation examines the economic and legal relationships between municipal government, utility companies, and citizen consumers.

Podufaly, Edward T. "Topographer of the Army." *Military Engineer*, 62 (Sept.-Oct. 1970), 336-39. Traces the army's topographic programs from 1777 to 1969.

Poe, A. David. "The Political Career of John Holmes Overton, 1912-1928." Master's thesis. See chapter on "Flood Control and Drainage."

Pomerantz, Sidney I. *New York: An American City, 1783-1803*. See chapter on "Community Water Supply."

Posadas, Barbara M. "A Home in the Country: Suburbanization in Jefferson Township, 1870-1889." *Chicago History*, VII (Fall 1978), 134-50.

Powell, Allen L. "Surveys for Engineering and

Science." *Military Engineer*, 68 (May-June 1976), 198-201.

Pred, Allan. *City Systems in Advanced Economies: Past Growth, Present Processes, and Future Development Options*. New York: Wiley, c1977. 256 pp. Illustrations, bibliography, and index.

Pred, Allan R. *The Spatial Dynamics of U. S. Urban-Industrial Growth, 1800-1914: Interpretive and Theoretical Essays*. Cambridge: M.I.T. Press, 1966. x + 225 pp. Illustrations, maps, and bibliographical footnotes.

Pred, Allan. *Urban Growth and City-Systems in the United States, 1840-1860*. Cambridge: Harvard University Press, 1980. xv + 282 pp. Maps, tables, notes, appendix, and index. Pioneer study of the growth of urban areas which focuses on communication, transportation, as well as business and economic patterns. The author offers a data collection and analysis mode for other students of this subject to follow.

Prescott, Samuel C. *When M. I. T. Was "Boston Tech," 1861-1916*. Cambridge: Technology Press, 1954. xviii + 350 pp. Illustrations, notes, appendix, and index. An "essay in interpretation and remembrance" on the Massachusetts Institute of Technology's first fifty years by a former dean. There are short descriptions of the public health work of William T. Sedgwick and Ellen Swallow Richards.

Pritchett, C. Herman. *The Tennessee Valley Authority: A Study in Public Administration*. See chapter on "Flood Control and Drainage."

Public Works Administration. *America Builds: The Record of PWA*. Washington, D. C.: Government Printing Office, 1939. vii + 298 pp. Illustrations, graphs, tables, notes, appendix, and index. Harold L. Ickes had this volume prepared "in order to present in a single, comprehensive report, such essential information regarding the history, experience and activities of PWA as may be of interest to citizens generally as well as to students of the theory of public works and its efficacy in helping to bring about economic recovery." It is critical to any study of public works in the 1930s.

Purmont, Jon E. "Environmental History: A New Challenge for the Social Studies." *Social Studies*, LXVII (Jan.-Feb. 1976), 3-6. A brief article suggesting ways (case studies) in which environmental history can be integrated into the social studies course. The same holds true for public works and/or engineering history.

Pursell, Carroll W., Jr., ed. *From Conservation to Ecology: The Development of Environmental Concern*. New York: Thomas Y. Crowell Company, 1973. 148 pp. Selected bibliography. Collection of readings whose purpose is to present a narrative account of the development of American concern for the environment. The emphasis, although cursory, is on public policy.

Pursell, Carroll W., Jr. *Readings in Technology and American Life*. New York: Oxford University Press, 1969. ix + 470 pp. Chart, table, notes, and bibliographical essay. A collection of readings that attempts to assess how Americans have viewed the effects of technology on their lives—as a "means to" or as a "measure of" progress. Several parts of the book indicate the growing professionalism of the engineer.

Pursell, Carroll W., Jr. "The Technical Society of the Pacific Coast, 1884-1914." *Technology and Culture*, 17 (Oct. 1976), 702-17. Demonstrates how one engineering society "played a critical role in linking science and technology in 19th-century America."

Rabbitt, J. C. and M. C. "The U. S. Geological Survey: 75 Years of Service to the Nation, 1879-1954." *Science*, 119 (May 28, 1954), 741-58.

Rabbitt, Mary C. *Minerals, Lands, and Geology for the Common Defense and General Welfare, Volume I: Before 1879*. Washington, D.C.: Government Printing Office, 1979. 331 pp. Illustrations, maps, diagrams, notes, bibliography, and subject index. First in a four-volume series that will trace the history of the U. S. Geological Survey.

Rae, John B. "Engineering Education as Preparation for Management: A Study of M.I.T. Alumni." *Business History Review*, XXIX (March 1955), 64-74. A discussion of "the fitness of the engineer for management" by reviewing the records of M.I.T. alumni (at least one in five were found in some kind of managerial position). The author concludes that "the flow of engineering graduates into management has been persistent, substantial, and steadily increasing in volume."

Rae, John B. "Engineers Are People." *Technology and Culture,* 16 (July 1975), 404-18. Presidential address delivered at the annual meeting of the Society for the History of Technology on December 28, 1974. Rae encourages his audience "to pursue the engineer as an individual through history" since the profession knows "a good deal more about engineering works than . . . about engineers."

Rae, John B. "The 'Know How' Tradition: Technology in American History." *Technology and Culture,* 1 (Spring 1960), 139-50. The author sites numerous examples of how the history of technology can be incorporated into "the total picture of American life."

Rath, Frederick L., and Merrilyn Rodgers O'Connell, eds. *A Bibliography on Historical Organization Practices: Historic Preservation.* See chapter on "Public Buildings."

Randolph, Isham. *Gleanings from a Harvest of Memories.* Columbia, Mo.: E.W. Stephens Company, 1937. 84 pp. Illustrations. The author (1848-1920) recalls his experiences as an axeman on surveys for the Winchester and Strausburg Railroad, consulting engineer for the Chicago Division of the Baltimore and Ohio Railroad, chief engineer of the Chicago Sanitary District, and member of the International Board of Consulting Engineers on the Panama Canal.

Randolph, Jennings. "Robert Moses—Man of Action." *APWA Reporter,* 43 (June 1976), 23-24. A testimonial to Moses by the chairman of the Senate Public Works Committee.

Randall, Robert Henry. "Federal Surveys: Coast and Geodetic, Geological, etc." *Surveying and Mapping,* 18 (April-June 1958), 207-12. Since 1879.

Ratigan, William. *Highways over Broad Waters: Life and Times of David B. Steinman, Bridgebuilder.* See chapter on "Roads, Streets, and Highways."

Rawick, George Philip. "Conservation Corps, the National Youth Administration, and the American Youth Congress." Doctoral dissertation, University of Wisconsin, 1957. 416 pp.

Reading, Don C. "New Deal Activity and the States, 1933 to 1939." *Journal of Economic History,* XXXIII (Dec. 1973), 792-810. The author concludes that "New Deal agencies failed to expand in a pattern that would effect reform, but did expand in a pattern that would contribute to relief and recovery and at the same time improve the utilization of natural resources."

Reeves, William Dale. "The Politics of Public Works: 1933-1935." Doctoral dissertation, Tulane University, 1968. 226 pp. Excellent study of the founding and administration of the Public Works Administration. Reeves explores the role of business and civic organizations in founding the agency.

Reps, John W. *Cities of the American West: A History of Frontier Urban Planning.* Princeton: Princeton University Press, 1979. xiv + 827 pp. Illustrations, maps, table, diagrams, notes, bibliography, and index. A significant contribution to American public works and urban history. In this comprehensive survey, the author examines the history of town planning on the frontier (American and French settlements in the Ohio and Mississippi valleys; Spanish and Mexican towns; mining, religious, and railroad communities in the High Plains and Rocky Mountain areas; and finally Oklahoma's "overnight" cities) and describes the positive influence of public works structures and services on community and settlement life. Reps demonstrates that western cities were the products of planning and design and that they were the *first* phase in the frontier process of growth. The book's illustrations, largely maps, plans, and views, are magnificent.

Reps, John W. "Great Expectations and Hard Times: The Planning of Cairo, Illinois." *Journal of the Society of Architectural Historians,* XVI (Dec. 1957), 14-21.

Reps, John W. *Monumental Washington: The Planning and Development of the Capital Center.* Princeton: Princeton University Press, 1967. xv + 221 pp. Illustrations, maps, notes, bibliography, and index. An analysis of the development of Washington, D.C. The author describes in detail the Senate Park Commission's plan "prepared for the central portion of Washington in 1901 and the fate of its proposals."

Reps, John W. "New Madrid on the Mississippi." *Journal of the Society of Architectural Historians,* XVIII (March 1959), 21-26.

Reps, John W. "Planning in the Wilderness: Detroit, 1805-1830." *Town Planning Review,* XXV (Jan. 1955), 240-50. Shows how the June 1805 fire "provided the opportunity for one of the most unusual attempts at city planning in the nation's history."

Reps, John W. *The Making of Urban America: A History of City Planning in the United States.* Princeton: Princeton University Press, 1965. xv + 574 pp. Illustrations, maps, diagrams, notes, bibliography, and index. A comprehensive assessment of town and city planning from the time of colonial settlement to World War I. Single chapters are devoted to such subjects as "cemeteries, parks, and suburbs"; boulevard and street designs; planning the nation's capital; and the Chicago Fair and early attempts at modern city planning. This volume should not be overlooked by public works and urban historians.

Reps, John W. "Thomas Jefferson's Checkerboard Towns." *Journal of the Society of Architectural Historians,* XX (Oct. 1961), 108-14.

Reps, John W. *Tidewater Towns: City Planning in Colonial Virginia and Maryland.* Williamsburg: Colonial Williamsburg Foundation, 1972. xii + 345 pp. Illustrations, maps, diagrams, notes, bibliography, and index. A complete discussion of "the forms and designs man has used in planning American towns," especially in the tidewater area of Virginia and Maryland around Chesapeake Bay and along its river estuaries. The author demonstrates conclusively that urban planning is not "an invention of the present era"; it too has a history.

Reps, John W. "Town Planning in Colonial Georgia." *Town Planning Review,* XXX (Jan. 1960), 273-85. Emphasizes the role of General James Oglethorpe.

Reps, John W. *Town Planning in Frontier America.* Princeton: Princeton University Press, 1969. xii + 473 pp. Illustrations, maps, diagrams, notes, bibliography, and index. A thorough review of the American urban planning tradition through "an examination of city plans prepared before the middle of the 19th century, beginning with the first permanent European settlement in 1565 at St. Augustine." This book is a condensed version of the first half of *The Making of Urban America,* but it includes some new material and some rearrangement of the old.

Reps, John W. "Urban Redevelopment in the Nineteenth Century: The Squaring of Circleville." *Journal of the Society of Architectural Historians,* XIV (Dec. 1955), 23-26. On the planning and subsequent redevelopment of Circleville, Ohio, from 1810.

Rice, R. Bradley. "The Galveston Plan of City Government by Commission: The Birth of a Progressive Idea." *Southwestern Historical Quarterly,* LXXVII (April 1975), 365-408. Describes in some detail the work and politics of the Deep Water Committee, organized in 1882 to promote needed harbor improvements, as well as the reasons Galveston adopted the commission form of government following the 1900 storm that devastated the Texas port city.

Rice, Robert Bradley. *Progressive Cities: The Commission Government Movement in America, 1901-1920.* Austin, Texas: University of Texas Press, 1977. xix + 160 pp. Notes, appendix, bibliography, and index. A sound historical study of the commission form of government from 1901 to 1920. Rice begins with case studies of Galveston, Texas, and other early commission cities and goes on to document how the plan was modified in other locales. By 1920 some 500 cities were using this form of government.

Richardson, Elmo R. "Western Politics and New Deal Policies: A Study of T.A. Walters of Idaho." *Pacific Historical Quarterly.* See chapter on "Flood Control and Drainage."

Rickard, T. A. *Retrospect: An Autobiography.* New York: Whittlesey House, 1937. xi + 402 pp. Illustrations. The autobiography of mining engineer, T.A. Rickard. He records his engineering activities in Colorado's mines; his travels in Australia, Africa, Italy, and Spain; and his experiences as editor of three mining publications.

Ricketts, Palmer C. *History of Rensselaer Polytechnic Institute, 1824-1914.* New York: John Wiley and Sons, 1914. xiii + 269 pp. Illustrations, appendices, bibliography, and index. In this second edition, the author (a former president and director of Rensselaer) describes in particular the development of curriculum and methods of instruction. One chapter is devoted to Stephen Van Rensselaer and Amos Eaton and another to the establishment of the department of civil engineering.

Ridgway, Robert. *Robert Ridgway.* New York: privately published, 1940. x + 370 pp. Illustration. The fascinating reminiscences of a public works engineer who spent fifty-two years "in the service of my native city of New York" as assistant engineer on the New Croton

Aqueduct, senior assistant engineer for the Rapid Transit Railroad Commission, division engineer of the East River Tunnel, department engineer of the Board of Water Supply, chief engineer of the Board of Transportation, consulting engineer on the Midtown Tunnel, and other positions.

Ristow, Walter W., comp. *Guide to the History of Cartography: An Annotated List of References on the History of Maps and Mapmaking.* Washington, D.C.: Library of Congress, 1973. 96 pp. Index. An exemplary compilation that offers good access to the Library of Congress cartographic collection.

Ritter, Joyce N. "People in Public Works: Thomas H. MacDonald and Charles D. Curtiss." *APWA Reporter.* See chapter on "Roads, Streets, and Highways."

Roach, Hannah Benner. "The Planting of Philadelphia, A Seventeenth-Century Real Estate Development." 2 parts. *Pennsylvania Magazine of History and Biography,* XCII (Jan. and April 1968), Jan.: 3-47; April: 143-94.

Robbins, Peggy. "Galveston's 'Hurricane Hell.'" *American History Illustrated,* X (Nov. 1975), 4-9, 49-52. Describes in detail the results of the September 8, 1900, killer storm that swept over Galveston Island. Only a few paragraphs are devoted to the clean-up work and rebuilding.

Robinson, Charles Mulford. *Better Binghamton: A Report to the Mercantile-Press Club of Binghamton, N.Y.* Binghamton: Mercantile-Press Club, 1911. 140 pp. Illustrations and maps. A report by a professional in "town and city planning." Before "suggesting physical changes which will both better the present city and prepare it for the growth that lies ahead," Robinson reviews the city's early history. In a chapter entitled "Needs and Recommendations," he discusses paving, sidewalks, streets, parks, playgrounds and the public market.

Robinson, Edgar Eugene, and Paul Carroll Edwards, eds. *The Memoirs of Ray Lyman Wilbur, 1875-1949.* See chapter on "Irrigation."

Robinson, Michael C. "People in Public Works: Arthur Powell Davis." *APWA Reporter.* See chapter on "Flood Control and Drainage."

Robinson, Michael C. "People in Public Works: Charles H. Rust." *APWA Reporter,* 46 (Jan. 1979), 4-5. A biographical sketch of the first Canadian president (1903) of the American Society of Municipal Improvements.

Robinson, Michael C. "People in Public Works: Frederick Haynes Newell." *APWA Reporter.* See chapter on "Irrigation."

Robinson, Michael C. "People in Public Works: George E. Waring, Jr." *APWA Reporter.* See chapter on "Sewers and Wastewater Treatment."

Robinson, Michael C. "People in Public Works: George H. Benzenberg." *APWA Reporter.* See chapter on "Community Water Supply."

Robinson, Michael C. "People in Public Works: Henry J. Kaiser." *APWA Reporter.* See chapter on "Flood Control and Drainage."

Robinson, Michael C. "People in Public Works: James B. Eads." *APWA Reporter.* See chapter on "Roads, Streets, and Highways."

Robinson, Michael C. "People in Public Works: John B. Jervis." *APWA Reporter.* See chapter on "Community Water Supply."

Robinson, Michael C. "People in Public Works: Othmar H. Ammann." *APWA Reporter.* See chapter on "Roads, Streets, and Highways."

Robinson, Michael C. "People in Public Works: Peter Kiewit, Jr." *APWA Reporter.* See chapter on "Flood Control and Drainage."

Robinson, Michael C. "People in Public Works: Robert Mills." *APWA Reporter.* See chapter on "Public Buildings."

Robinson, Michael C. "People in Public Works: Samuel Arnold Greeley." *APWA Reporter,* 43 (Nov. 1976), 8-9. Reviews the career of the founder of the engineering firm of Greeley and Hansen—a dynamic individual who spent over a half century developing water, sewer, and refuse systems for cities such as New York, Chicago, and Washington, D.C.

Robinson, Michael C. "People in Public Works: Sydney B. Williamson." *APWA Reporter,* 45 (May 1978), 4-5. Describes the expertise of a talented and versatile public works engineer-administrator who was involved in a variety of public works projects and programs.

Robinson, Michael C. "People in Public

Works: William Mulholland." *APWA Reporter*. See chapter on "Community Water Supply."

Robinson, William M., Jr. "The Corps of Topographical Engineers." *Military Engineer*, XXIII (July-Aug. 1931), 303-06. A short history of the corps since its beginning in 1813.

Rodgers, Cleveland. *American Planning: Past-Present-Future*. New York: Harper & Brothers, 1947. xiv + 290 pp. Notes and index. A thin, breezy discussion of federal planning primarily with respect to natural resources.

Rodgers, Cleveland. *Robert Moses: Builder for Democracy*. New York: Henry Holt and Company, 1952. xxviii + 356 pp. Illustrations, notes, and index. A full-length biography of "the man who gets things done" by a long-time member of the New York City Planning Commission.

Root, Irving C. "A New Plan for Historic Alexandria, Virginia." *City Planning*, 9 (Jan. 1933), 1-9. Reviews the results of several Alexandria planning commissions—the first was appointed in 1748—and ordinances.

Rose, Albert C. *Public Roads of the Past*. See chapter on "Roads, Streets, and Highways."

Rosenberg, Nathan. *Technology and American Economic Growth*. New York: Harper and Row Publishers, 1972. xi + 211 pp. Tables, graphs, notes, and index. An exploration of the relationship between technological change and the growth of the American economy over time. In the concluding chapter, the author considers the effects of this relationship on the environment. The amount of energy consumed as well as the miles of surfaced roads built in the nineteenth and twentieth centuries is compared and discussed in several chapters.

Rosow, Jerome M., ed. *American Men in Government: A Biographical Dictionary and Directory of Federal Officials*. Washington, D.C.: Public Affairs Press, 1949. xxiii + 472 pp. Map, charts, graphs, and indexes. A collection of short biographical sketches of executives occupying the top administrative, diplomatic, military, professional, scientific, and technical positions in the federal government. The one-paragraph biographies are organized alphabetically by last name. To assist a researcher in locating biographical information on an individual (name unknown) heading a federal public works agency, for example, the editor has provided an organizational index to names. There is also an occupational and professional index.

Ross, John R. "Conservation and Economy: The North Carolina Geological Survey, 1891-1920." *Forest History*, 16 (Jan. 1973), 20-27. On the state's survey of natural resources.

Ross, John R. "Man Over Nature: Origins of the Conservation Movement." *American Studies*, XVI (Spring 1975), 49-62. Insightful and well-written essay that identifies how the ideas of George Perkins Marsh, John Wesley Powell, Lester Frank Work, and W.J. McGee provided the theoretical framework for the conservation movement of the early twentieth century.

Ross, John R. " 'Pork Barrels' and the General Welfare: Problems in Conservation, 1900-1920." Doctoral dissertation, Duke University, 1969. 592 pp. Describes the development of multiple-purpose resource management policies and programs, particularly in North Carolina.

Rothstein, William G. "The American Association of Engineers." *Industrial and Labor Relations Review*, 22 (Oct. 1968), 48-72. An historical study of the heydey (1919-1923) of the American Association of Engineers, a professional society which acted in many ways like a labor union. The author demonstrates through AAE's meteoric rise and fall the challenge of organizing engineers for the pursuit of common economic objectives.

Rouse, Hunter. *Hydraulics in the United States, 1776-1976*. Iowa City: University of Iowa, 1976. ix + 238 pp. Illustrations, bibliographies, and index. Includes an especially strong section on nineteenth-century stream investigations.

Roysdon, Christine, and Linda A. Khatri. *American Engineers of the Nineteenth Century: A Biographical Index*. New York: Garland Publishing, 1978. xv + 247 pp. An index of periodicals containing biographical information on engineers and technologists who died during or before 1900. The persons indexed, therefore, were largely engaged in the development of railroads and canals. A good number of manufacturers and mechanical engineers are also included.

Ruebens, Beatrice G. "State Financing of Private Enterprise in Early New York." Doctoral dissertation, Columbia University, 1960. 324 pp.

Ruhloff, F. Carl. "Evolution of Modern Construction Machinery." *Civil Engineering,* 3 (Aug. 1933), 451-54. Particularly for the building of dams, levees, and highways.

Ryan, Garry David. "War Department Topographical Bureau, 1831-1963: An Administrative History." Doctoral dissertation, American University, 1968. 364 pp.

Sackheim, Donald E., comp. *Historic American Engineering Record: Catalog, 1976.* Washington, D.C.: National Park Service, U.S. Department of the Interior, 1976. xi + 193 pp. Illustrations, diagrams, index. Presents "the documentation in the HAER collection, both in the Library of Congress and awaiting transmittal from the HAER office, produced between January 1, 1969, and December 31, 1975." This catalog is the first comprehensive review of industrial and engineering sites HAER has compiled.

Salkowski, Albert S. "Reconstructing a Covered Timber Bridge." *Civil Engineering.* See chapter on "Roads, Streets, and Highways."

Salt, Harriet. *Mighty Engineering Feats: Clear and Concise Descriptions of Ten of the Greatest American Engineering Feats.* Philadelphia: Penn Publishing Company, 1937. 308 pp. Illustrations. A popular treatment of the following "engineering feats": first transcontinental railroad, Panama Canal, New York City's water supply, Wilson Dam, Alaska Railroad, Holland Tunnel, Columbia River Highway, George Washington Bridge, Boulder Dam, and the San Francisco Oakland and Golden Gate bridges.

Saville, Thorndike. "Achievements in Engineering Education." *Transactions of the American Society of Civil Engineers,* CT (1953), 147-62. Reviews the development of engineering schools, their facilities and curricula as well as their relationship to professional societies.

Schalck, Harry G. "Mini-Revisionism in City Planning History: The Planners of Roland Park." *Journal of the Society of Architectural Historians,* XXIX (Dec. 1970). A discussion of the origin of the plans for Roland Park. It was recently discovered in the papers of the defunct Roland Park Company that "Frederick L. Olmsted, Sr., was not at all responsible for any planning in Roland Park. . . ."

Schalck, Harry G. "Planning Roland Park, 1891-1910." *Maryland Historical Magazine,* 67 (Winter 1972), 419-28. An investigation of the central features of this pioneer planning experiment in year-round suburban living for the middle class.

Scharf, Thomas L. "Amiel Weeks Whipple and the Boundary Survey in Southern California." *Journal of San Diego History,* XIX (Summer 1973), 18-31. Following the Mexican-American War and the signing of the Guadalupe-Hidalgo Treaty (1848).

Scheiber, Harry N. "Entrepreneurship and Western Development: The Case of Micajah T. Williams." *Business History Review.* See chapter on "Waterways."

Schiesl, Martin J. *The Politics of Efficiency: Municipal Administration and Reform in America, 1880-1920.* Berkeley: University of California Press, 1977. ix + 259 pp. Notes, bibliography, and index. An examination of urban political reforms in the Progressive era. The author's major theme is the impact of efficiency upon governmental operations and services. He identifies three key concepts in the movement for governmental efficiency—"nonpartisanship, the strong executive, and the separation of politics from administration."

Schmidt, Lewis A. *The Engine-Ear: Fifty Years of Engineering.* New York: Vantage Press, 1977. vii + 166 pp. Illustrations. Reminiscences of a civil engineer who worked on numerous dam and hydroelectric projects in Kentucky, Oklahoma, Wisconsin, Michigan, Tennessee, and Texas beginning in 1923. During the 1930s and 1940s, he held responsible positions with the Tennessee Valley Authority. From 1944 to his retirement in 1973, Schmidt engaged in private practice and participated in the programs of a variety of professional engineering organizations.

Schmidt, Lorraine H., comp. *Washington—The Design of the Federal City.* Washington, D.C.: National Archives, 1972. 80 pp. Illustrations, maps, and notes. This catalog, based on a 1971 exhibit in the National Archives Building, illustrates the city's transformation through photographs, maps, and sketches.

Schott, Richard Lockwood. "Professional

Education and the Public Service: The Education of the Engineer Federal Executive." Doctoral dissertation, Syracuse University, 1972. 257 pp.

Schubert, Frank N. "Legacy of the Topographical Engineers: Textual and Cartographic Records of Western Exploration, 1819-1860." *Government Publications Review,* 7A (1980), 111-16. Identifies and discusses the major guides to the textual and cartographic documents relating to exploring expeditions by the Topographical Engineers.

Schubert, Frank N., ed. *March to South Pass: Lieutenant William B. Franklin's Journal of the Kearny Expedition of 1845.* Washington, D.C.: Historical Division, Office of the Chief of Engineers, 1979. xiv + 41 pp. Illustrations, map, and notes. A masterful editing of a journal virtually ignored by historians of western exploration and discovery. Franklin's journal is the least known of the four diaries written by members of the party. It is an excellent example of the roles pre-Civil War engineers played as explorers, topographers, and cartographers.

Schubert, Frank N. "People in Public Works: G. Kemble Warren." *APWA Reporter,* 45 (Dec. 1978), 4-5. Describes the extensive surveys conducted by this Army Corps of Engineers officer in the western United States before the Civil War.

Schubert, Frank N. *Vanguard of Expansion: Army Engineers in the Trans-Mississippi West, 1819-1879.* Washington, D.C.: Office of the Chief of Engineers, 1980. xii + 160 pp. Illustrations, maps, notes, and index. A compact and elegantly written narrative history of the Corps of Engineers activities in the trans-Mississippi West during the years of expansion and settlement. This brilliant study relies heavily on the journals and reports of surveyors and explorers. It supplements and compliments other in-depth histories of this subject.

Schultz, Stanley K., and Clay McShane. "To Engineer the Metropolis: Sewers, Sanitation, and City Planning in Late-Nineteenth-Century America." *Journal of American History,* LXV (Sept. 1978), 389-411. Municipal engineers played an important role in both the technological and political arenas of late nineteenth-century urban America. They were resourceful in applying technology to the solution of human problems. And, as these authors demonstrate, "their successful demands for political autonomy in solving the physical problems of the cities contributed to the ultimate insistence for efficient government run by skilled professionals."

Schuyler, Hamilton. *The Roeblings: A Century of Engineers, Bridge-Builders and Industrialists.* See chapter on "Roads, Streets, and Highways."

Scofield, Edna. "The Origin of Settlement Patterns in Rural New England." *Geographical Review,* XXVIII (Oct. 1938), 652-63. Shows how "two different types of rural landscape developed."

Scott, Mel. *American City Planning Since 1890.* Berkeley: University of California Press, 1971. xxii + 745 pp. Illustrations, maps, graphs, notes, bibliography and index. A well-written, comprehensive, survey of the beginnings and subsequent growth of the city planning profession. The book includes a wealth of information gleaned from original sources and interviews with pioneers of the profession. It is also a rich source of information on the development of highway and street planning.

Scott, Mel. *The San Francisco Bay Area: A Metropolis in Perspective.* Berkeley: University of California, 1959. Illustrations, maps, notes, bibliography, and index. A study of the growth and development of the Bay Area with an emphasis on planning and regionalism. There are individual chapters on "The Burnham Plan for San Francisco," "The Panama Canal: Stimulus to Planning," "Seeds of Metropolitan Regionalism," "Postwar Planning," and "The Regional Metropolis."

Scully, Arthur, Jr. *James Dakin, Architect: His Career in New York and the South.* See chapter on "Public Buildings."

Scully, Vincent. *American Architecture and Urbanism.* See chapter on "Public Buildings."

Sears, Joan Niles. *The First One Hundred Years of Town Planning in Georgia.* Atlanta: Cherokee Publishing Company, 1979. xiii + 220 pp. Illustrations, maps, diagrams, notes, bibliography, and index. A history of the colonial, courthouse, and state town plans in Georgia from 1733 to 1835. Sears is a landscape architect with a background in art history.

Sears, Joan N. "Town Planning in White and Habersham Counties, Georgia." *Georgia Historical Quarterly,* LIV (Spring 1970), 20-40. Describes and compares the plans used in Clarksville, Cleveland, Cornelia, Helen, Robertstown, and Demorest.

Sears, Louis Martin. "The Engineer and the Historian." *Mechanical Engineering,* 69 (July 1947), 581-84. Advocates a partnership that can be mutually beneficial.

Sellers, Charles L. "Early Mormon Community Planning." *Journal of the American Institute of Planners,* XXVIII (Feb. 1962), 24-30. Highlights "evidences of good design in typical Mormon communities."

Selznick, Philip. *TVA and the Grass Roots: A Study in the Sociology of Formal Organization.* Berkeley: University of California Press, 1949. ix + 274 pp. Tables, notes, bibliography, and index. A solid study of how TVA established a working relationship with local governments and public interest groups.

Sever, William. "Thomas A. Walter and His Works." *Americana.* See chapter on "Public Buildings."

Sewell, Eldon D. "Fifty Years of Aerial Photography—Beginning in 1880." *Photogrammetric Engineer,* XXIII (Dec. 1957), 835-50. Survey of the field's development based on patent research.

Shallat, Todd A. "People in Public Works: Stephen Harriman Long." *APWA Reporter.* See chapter on "Waterways."

Shallat, Todd A. "People in Public Works: Joseph Strauss." *APWA Reporter.* See chapter on "Roads, Streets, and Highways."

Shambaugh, Benjamin F., ed. *Municipal Government and Administration in Iowa.* 2 vols. Iowa City: State Historical Society of Iowa, 1930. Vol. I: xi + 608 pp.; Vol. II: xi + 668 pp. Notes and indexes. An innovative study of government and administration in Iowa by the State Historical Society of Iowa and leading authorities in the field of municipal government. The volumes' planners did not intend them as "a manual of government" but designed them to "suggest the problems of the municipalities and to some degree point to their solution." The volumes, published as part of the Iowa Applied History Series, contain chapters on each of the following: the city engineer as well as the municipal administration of public safety, public works, planning and zoning, and public health.

Shambaugh, Benjamin F. "The Founding of Iowa City." *Palimpsest.* See chapter on "Public Buildings."

Shannon, M.A.S. "Charles Bulfinch, the First American Architect." *Architecture.* See chapter on "Public Buildings."

Shelton, Ronald Lee. "The Environmental Era: A Chronological Guide to Policy and Concepts, 1962-1972." Doctoral dissertation, Cornell University, 1973. A good source for key benchmarks in the development of federal environmental policies.

Sherwood, Morgan B. *Exploration of Alaska, 1965-1900.* New Haven: Yale University Press, 1965. xvi + 207 + xx pp. Illustrations, maps, notes, chronology, and index. A well-written account of exploration in Alaska during the late nineteenth century that was primarily undertaken by the army. The author suggests that these expeditions were a memorable chapter in the history of American science and geographical discovery. Given the area's tiny population, remoteness, and limited economic inducements to development, federal exploration of Alaska was relatively rapid and extensive.

Shurtleff, Flavel. "City and Regional Planning since 1876." *American Architect,* CXXIX (Jan. 5, 1926), 57-60. Emphasizes the role of the city engineer in early planning work as well as the forces that created the city planning movement.

Simpson, Thomas. "The Early Government Land Survey in Minnesota West of the Mississippi River." *Collections of the Minnesota Historical Society,* 10 (Part 1, 1905), 57-67.

Sites, George E., Jr. "The Bradford Map of Nogales, Arizona." *Journal of Arizona History,* 11 (Spring 1970), 1-13. On the first official map of the town, prepared by civil engineer William Bradford, Jr.

Skramstad, Harold K. "The Engineer as Architect in Washington: The Contribution of Montgomery Meigs." *Records of the Columbia Historical Society of Washington, D.C.* See chapter on "Public Buildings."

Skramstad, Harold K. "The Professional Life

of William Rich Hutton, Civil Engineer." Doctoral dissertation. See chapter on "Waterways."

Sloan, Edward William, III. *Benjamin Franklin Isherwood Naval Engineer: The Years as Engineer in Chief, 1861-1869.* See chapter on "Waterways."

Sly, John Fairfield. *Town Government in Massachusetts (1620-1930).* Cambridge: Harvard University Press, 1930. x + 244 pp. Notes and index. The author concentrates on the Massachusetts town meeting; he includes almost no information on Massachusetts' public works.

Smallwood, Johnny B., Jr. "George W. Norris and the Concept of a Planned Region." Doctoral dissertation, University of North Carolina, 1963. 458 pp. Contains some history of the regional planning movement prior to the establishment of the Tennessee Valley Authority.

Smart, Charles E. *The Makers of Surveying Instruments in America since 1700.* 2 vols. Troy, N.Y.: Regal Art Press, 1962 and 1967. Vol. I: 182 pp.; Vol. II: 183-282 pp. Illustrations, bibliography, and index. These small books are essentially lists, with brief annotations, of the makers of surveying instruments.

Smilor, Raymond W. "Confronting the Industrial Environment: The Noise Problem in America, 1893-1932." Doctoral dissertation, University of Texas, Austin, 1978. 294 pp.

Smith, Albert W. *John Edson Sweet: A Story of Achievement in Engineering And of Influence Upon Men.* New York: American Society of Mechanical Engineers, 1925. xiii + 220 pp. Illustrations, notes, appendices, and index. Of value to individuals interested in the professionalization of engineering. Sweet was a founder of the American Society of Mechanical Engineers.

Smith, Dwight L. "The Engineer and the Canyon." *Utah Historical Quarterly,* XXVIII (July 1960), 263-73. Explains the importance of Robert Brewster Stanton's engineering survey "to determine the feasibility and worth of a railroad along the river from Grand Junction, Colorado, to the Gulf of California."

Smith, Frank E., ed. *Conservation in the United States, A Documentary History: Land and Water, 1900-1970.* New York: Chelsea House Publishers, 1971. xxv + 782 pp. Index. An outstanding collection of documents relating to twentieth-century water and land development. The subjects covered include reclamation, land policies, power, forestry, soil conservation, flood control, and development of broad federal conservation policies. The author, a member of the Board of Directors of the Tennessee Valley Authority, does not include examples of preservationist attitudes toward natural resources.

Smith, Henry Nash. "Clarence King, John Wesley Powell, and the Establishment of the United States Geological Survey." *Mississippi Valley Historical Review,* XXXIV (June 1947), 37-58. Points out, in particular, the role of John Wesley Powell in establishing the survey.

Smith, Margaret Supplee. "Between City and Suburb: Architecture and Planning in Boston's South End." Doctoral dissertation, Brown University, 1976.

Smith, Page. *As a City Upon a Hill: The Town in American History.* New York: Alfred A. Knopf, 1966. Contains some information on town plans and settlement but includes no discussion of early public works services or practices.

Smith, Ralph J. *Engineering as a Career.* New York: McGraw-Hill, 1969. xi + 418 pp. Illustrations, tables, graphs, and index. Includes a brief history of the engineering profession.

Snyder, Charles E. "The Eads of Argyle." *Iowa Journal of History and Politics.* See chapter on "Roads, Streets, and Highways."

Sparks, Edwin E. "The School of Engineering at the Pennsylvania State College." *Journal of the Engineers' Society of Pennsylvania,* VII (1915), 318-23. A short history of the school since its beginning in 1862.

Sparling, Samuel Edwin. "The League of Wisconsin Municipalities." *Iowa Journal of History and Politics,* II (April 1904), 199-217. Outlines the reform work of the league in Wisconsin and reviews its accomplishments.

Sprague, Norman S. "Recent History of the American Society for Municipal Improvements." *Proceedings of the American Society for Municipal Improvements,* 25 (1918), 308-13. On the society's amalgamation with the Association for Standardizing Paving Specifications.

Spray, Anne. "People in Public Works: Mark Owen." *APWA Reporter.* See chapter on "Sewers and Wastewater Treatment."

Spray, Anne. "People in Public Works: A. Baldwin Wood." *APWA Reporter*. See chapter on "Flood Control and Drainage."

Spurr, Stephen H. "George Washington, Surveyor and Ecological Observer." *Ecology,* 32 (Oct. 1951), 544-49.

Stanislawski, Dan. "The Origin and Spread of the Grid-Iron Pattern Town." *Geographical Review,* 36 (1946), 105-20.

Stapleton, Darwin Heilman. "The Transfer of Technology to the United States in the Nineteenth Century." Doctoral dissertation, University of Delaware, 1975. 351 pp.

Starr, John T. "Long's Expedition to the West." *Military Engineer,* 53 (March/April 1961), 116-18. A lively written, undocumented account of Major Stephen H. Long's expedition to the Rocky Mountains during 1819-1820. The author discusses the military and scientific aspects of the reconnaissance.

Starrett, Paul. *Changing the Skyline: An Autobiography*. See chapter on "Public Buildings."

Stegner, Wallace. *Beyond the Hundredth Meridian: John Wesley Powell and the Second Opening of the West.* See chapter on "Irrigation."

Stegner, Wallace. "Getting to Know the National Domain." *American Heritage.* See chapter on "Irrigation."

Stellar, Gary A. *CERL: A History of the U.S. Army Construction Engineering Research Laboratory*. Champaign, Ill.: n.p., n.d. 36 pp. Illustrations, charts, and tables.

Sterling, Everett W. "The Powell Irrigation Survey, 1888-1893." *Mississippi Valley Historical Review,* XXVII (Dec. 1940), 421-34. Definitive article on efforts by John Wesley Powell to survey the water resources of the western United States.

Stevens, Herbert W. "The Rebuilding of a City." *Bulletin of the Historical and Philosophical Society of Ohio,* XIV (July 1956), 211-20. Cincinnati's director of planning reviews the impact of history on the development and redevelopment of the city.

Stevens, John Austin. "Christopher Colles: The First Projector of Inland Navigation in America." *Magazine of American History.* See chapter on "Waterways."

Stevens, John F. *An Engineer's Recollections.* See chapter on "Waterways."

Stevenson, Elizabeth. *Park Maker: A Life of Frederick Law Olmsted.* See chapter on "Parks and Recreation."

Stevenson, Frederic R., and Carl Feiss. "Charleston and Savannah." *Journal of the Society of Architectural Historians,* X (Dec. 1951), 3-9. Describes how expansion and congestion influenced two distinctive civic plans.

Stewart, Frank Mann. *A Half Century of Municipal Reform: The History of the National Municipal League.* Berkeley: University of California Press, 1950. xi + 289 pp. Notes, appendices, bibliography, and index. A history of the National Municipal League. The study "outlines the conditions which brought this citizens' organization for better government into existence, describes its program for the improvement of local government, analyzes its methods, techniques, and problems, and attempts to evaluate the contribution of the League to fifty years of municipal reform, 1894-1944." The author relies almost entirely on material found in publications and files of the league.

Stewart, Ian Robert. "Central Park 1851-1871: Urbanization and Environmental Planning in New York City." Doctoral dissertation. See chapter on "Parks and Recreation."

Stewart, John. "Early Maps and Surveyors of the City of Washington, D.C." *Records of the Columbia Historical Society of Washington, D.C.,* 2 (1899), 48-71. A review of the work of various surveyors of Washington, D.C. and a discussion of some early city maps.

Stewart, Lowell O. *Public Lands Surveys: History, Instructions, Methods.* Ames, Iowa: Collegiate Press, 1935. xii + 202 pp. Illustrations, maps, diagrams, bibliography, and index. A rather pedestrian history of eighteenth-century land surveying in the United States. The book's principal value is its material on the evolution of surveying techniques.

Still, Bayrd. "Patterns of Mid-Nineteenth-Century Urbanization in the Middle West." *Mississippi Valley Historical Review,* XXVIII (Sept. 1941), 187-206. The author describes in general terms the new public works services and functions midwestern cities assumed as they advanced "from village to city."

Still, Bayrd. *Urban America: A History with Documents.* Boston: Little, Brown and Company, 1974. xxvi + 566 pp. Notes, bibliography, and index. Few of the documents in this collection deal with public works, but there are some scattered selections on city planning, public transportation, streets, and parks.

Stillman, Richard J., II. *The Rise of the City Manager: A Public Professional in Local Government.* Albuquerque: University of New Mexico Press, 1974. 170 pp. Tables, notes, appendices, bibliographical essay, and index. This study traces the growth of the city management profession. Early managers were, in large part, trained engineers who were most capable of dealing with the major problems of community life during the early twentieth century. City dwellers were in need of such physical structures as water and sewer systems, improved roads, refuse disposal facilities, and lighted streets.

Stine, Jeffrey K. "People in Public Works: M.M. O'Shaughnessy." *APWA Reporter*. See chapter on "Community Water Supply."

Stine, Jeffrey K. "People in Public Works: Nelson P. Lewis." *APWA Reporter*, 46 (June 1979), 4-5. A biographical sketch of New York City's chief engineer of the Board of Estimate and Apportionment (1902) and one of the first American engineers to become actively involved in city planning.

Stone, Alice B., and Donald C. Stone. "Early Development of Education in Public Administration" in Frederick C. Mosher, ed., *American Public Administration: Past, Present, and Future.* University, Ala.: University of Alabama Press, 1976. pp. 11-48. In their examination of education for public service, the authors describe the organization of public officials, including municipal engineers and/or public works practitioners, into professional and public-interest associations. They also explain the origins of the New York Bureau of Municipal Research and show the ways it contributed to any improvements in budgeting, accounting, and purchasing in the fields of public works and public health.

Stone, Harold A.; Don K. Price; and Kathryn H. Stone. *City Manager Government in Nine Cities.* Chicago: Public Administration Service, 1940. viii + 544 pp. Charts, tables, notes, appendices, and index. An analysis of city manager government in operation under varying circumstances during the previous ten to twenty years. Information on the effect of this form of government on municipal public works development is scanty.

Stone, Harold A.; Don K. Price; and Kathryn H. Stone. *City Manager Government in the United States: A Review after Twenty-Five Years.* Chicago: Public Administration Service, 1940. xvi + 279 pp. Map, notes, appendix, and index. Summarizes the principal results of the city manager plan "in forty-eight cities that are operating under it and in two cities that have abandoned it." Most early city managers were trained as civil engineers; and, as this study reports, "experience in engineering was the most common preparation for managership in the cities studied."

Story, Russell McCullouch. *The American Municipal Executive.* Urbana: University of Illinois, 1918. 231 pp. Index. Prepared by a political scientist, this book analyzes the qualifications and functions of the chief municipal executive officer—the mayor, commissioner, and city manager. Chapter 2 discusses "The Historical Development of the Mayoralty."

Stout, Ray L. "Over the Brush and Through the Trees: Surveying 1900-1909." *Oregon Historical Quarterly,* 73 (Dec. 1972), 322-58. Land surveying reminiscences in Oregon and Washington.

Straub, Hans. *A History of Civil Engineering: An Outline from Ancient to Modern Times.* London: Leonard Hill Limited, 1952. xviii + 258 pp. Illustrations, notes, tables, selected bibliography, and indexes. Translated from German, this survey of building and engineering techniques and theories (chiefly outside the United States) explores "the mutual relationship between civil engineering proper and the art of building at large."

Strickland, William; Edward H. Gill; and Henry R. Campbell, eds. *Public Works of the United States of America.* London: John

Weale, Architectural Library, 1841. 40 plates. The American editors "formed an Association for the purpose of selecting, designing, and describing the best examples of their Public Works" in order that they may be submitted to the British nation, "with the hope of inducing a kindred feeling towards the citizens of America, and of affording to the Professional Student numerous splendid examples of the triumph of professional skill, industry, and enterprise." The drawings included in this volume are of structures such as the Philadelphia gas works and water works; twin locks on the Schuylkill Canal at Plymouth, Pennsylvania; and Joshua's Falls Dam, James River and Kanawha Canal, Virginia.

Strong, Douglas H. "Teaching American Environmental History." *Social Studies,* LXV (Oct. 1974), 196-200. Discusses approaches to teaching environmental history. Too few items on public works history are listed in the bibliography.

Stuart, Charles B. *Lives and Works of Civil and Military Engineers of America.* New York: D. Van Nostrand, 1871. 343 pp. Illustrations, appendices, and index. Biographical sketches of twenty prominent engineers of the nineteenth century by an author who values "their virtues and patriotism" as well as their talent. Those included are A. Ellicott, J. Geddes, B. Wright, C. White, D. Bates, N. Roberts, G. Bryant, J. Swift, J. Williams, W. McRee, S. Kneass, J. Childe, F. Harbach, D. Douglas, J. Knight, B. Latrobe, C. Ellet, Jr., S. Forrer, W. Watson, and J. Roebling.

Studer, Jack J. "The First Map of Oakland, California: An Historical Speculation as Solution to an Enigma." *California Historical Society Quarterly,* XLVIII (March 1969), 59-71. On the planning and surveying of present-day downtown Oakland and speculations as to the whereabouts of the city's first map.

Studer, Jack J. "Julius Kellersberger: A Swiss as Surveyor and City Planner in California, 1851-1857." *California Historical Society Quarterly,* XLVII (March 1968), 3-14. Describes his early surveying work in Oakland and his career as a United States deputy surveyor (1855) for California.

Struik, Dirk J. *Yankee Science in the Making.* Boston: Little, Brown and Company, 1948. xiii + 430 pp. Diagram, notes, bibliography, and index. An investigation of science and technology in pre-Civil War New England. In 1780 there were only a few persons in New England interested in science; modern industry and engineering were absent. But by 1860 the situation had entirely changed. The author discusses such public works topics as canal, turnpike, and bridge construction; surveying; early West Point engineering; and Boston's water supply.

Suskind, Charles. *Understanding Technology.* Baltimore: Johns Hopkins University Press, 1973. x + 163 pp. Illustrations, notes, and indexes. A rather superficial attempt "to provide an overview of the development of modern technology and of its main social and political consequences." Little of the subject matter relates to public works, though there are brief historical discussions of transportation, building technology, and engineering education.

Sutherland, Douglas. *Fifty Years on the Civic Front.* See chapter on "Solid Waste."

Swain, Donald C. *Wilderness Defender: Horace M. Albright and Conservation.* See chapter on "Parks and Recreation."

Swain, George F. "The Status of the Engineer." *Proceedings in the Association of Engineering Societies,* XVIII (Feb. 1897), 180-88. A critique of the engineering profession by the president of the Boston Society of Civil Engineers. Following brief references to the origin and evolution of the profession, he charges that "the principal defect among engineers to-day is a lack of breadth and culture."

Swanson, Merwin R. "The New Deal in Pocatello." *Idaho Yesterdays,* 23 (Summer 1979), 53-57.

Sweeney, Stephen B. "Some Aspects of the Profession's History." *Public Management,* 56 (Oct. 1974), 7-9. A general discussion of the development of "the profession of city management."

Swing, H.L., and D.E. Mohler. "Eugene F. Falconnet, Soldier, Engineer, Inventory." *Tennessee Historical Quarterly,* XXI (Sept. 1962), 219-34. A biographical sketch of "a brave and ambitious soldier" in the Confederate Army, "an able and well-trained civil engineer" who planned and supervised the construction of several Tennessee railroads, and "a scientist whose knowledge of metallurgy was far in advance of that of most of his contemporaries."

Talbot, Arthur N. "Origin of the Society for the Promotion of Engineering Education." *Proceedings of the Society for the Promotion of Engineering Education,* XLI (June 1933), 39-43. On the individuals responsible for founding the society (1893) and its first annual meeting (1894).

Tarleton, Lavonne Olson. "John Millington, Civil Engineer and Teacher, 1779-1868." Master's thesis, College of William and Mary, 1966.

Tarr, Joel Arthur. *A Study in Boss Politics: William Lorimer of Chicago.* See chapter on "Waterways."

Tate, Roger D., Jr. "Easing the Burden: The Era of Depression and New Deal in Mississippi." Doctoral dissertation, University of Tennessee, Knoxville, 1978. v + 223 pp. Notes and bibliography. Chapter 5 of this dissertation, "Men Working?", is an excellent overview of the public works jobs created by such agencies as FERA, CWA, CCC, PWA, and WPA. Particular emphasis is placed upon the construction of roads, parks, and public buildings.

Taylor, Ben, and Robert S. Hopson. *Public Works Services to People: A History of the North Carolina Chapter of the American Public Works Association, 1957-1977.* Charlotte, N.C.: APWA, North Carolina Chapter, 1978. 53 pp. Illustrations. An account of the work and professional involvement of North Carolina's municipal public works practitioners.

Taylor, Emerson Gifford. *Gouverneur Kemble Warren: The Life and Letters of An American Soldier, 1830-1882.* Boston: Houghton Mifflin Company, 1932. xii + 256 pp. Illustrations, notes, and index. The sections devoted to the subject's exploration and surveying of "the empire lying beyond the Mississippi" prior to the Civil War will be of interest to public works researchers. A West Point graduate, Warren was a member of the Corps of Topographical Engineers.

Teaford, Jon C. *City and Suburb: The Political Fragmentation of Metropolitan America, 1850-1970.* Baltimore: Johns Hopkins University Press, 1979. vii + 231 pp. Tables, notes, bibliography, and index. Includes material on annexation and the growth of sewer, water supply, and other public works services.

Teaford, Jon C. *The Municipal Revolution in America: Origins of Modern Urban Government, 1650-1825.* Chicago: University of Chicago Press, 1975. viii + 152 pp. Tables, notes, bibliography, and index. A concise and perceptive analysis of the evolution of urban government through the colonial and early national periods. The author describes "the transformation in the political structure, function, and external relationships of the American municipality between 1650 and 1825, the vital years in which Americans discarded the model of urban government inherited from medieval Europe and substituted an ideal which determined the course of municipal development up to the present." The volume includes material on annexation and the growth of sewer, water supply, and other public works services.

Terrell, John Upton. *The Man Who Rediscovered America: A Biography of John Wesley Powell.* See chapter on "Irrigation."

"The Almanac of Significant Events in Building a Greater America, 1874-1949." *Engineering News-Record,* 143 (Sept. 1, 1949), A1-A23. A list of milestones in the fields of sewage disposal, water supply, water purification, foundations, buildings, bridges, concrete dams, earth and rockfill dams, design theory, highways, construction machinery, river control and tunnels.

"The Corps of Engineers, 1775 to 1955." *Military Engineer,* XLVII (July-Aug. 1955), 259-62. A short history of the Army Corps of Engineers' civil and military "service to the nation."

Thernstrom, Stephan. *Poverty, Planning, and Politics in the New Boston: The Origins of ABCD.* New York: Basic Books, 1969. xv + 199 pp. Notes, appendix, and index. A short history of the early years (1961-1964) of Action for Boston Community Development. The author concludes that "the plans and strategies developed by ABCD during the period under scrutiny . . . failed to bring about the basic changes the planners sought." Thernstrom's best example is the Boston school system.

Thomas, Phillip Drennen. "The United States Army as the Early Patron of Naturalists in the Trans-Mississippi West, 1803-1920." *Chronicles of Oklahoma,* LVI (Summer 1978), 171-93. Illustrates how the "Lewis and Clark, Pike and Long expeditions played a crucial role in the initial delineation of the natural history of the west."

Thompson, Paul W. *What the Citizen Should Know About the Army Engineers.* New York: W.W. Norton, 1942. 210 pp. Illustrations.

Thornton, Mary Lindsay. "The Price and Strother: First Actual Survey of North Carolina." *North Carolina Historical Review,* XLI (Oct. 1964), 477-83. Recounts the work of surveyors Jonathan Price and John Strother and their efforts to publish a map of North Carolina "from actual survey."

Tichi, Cecelia. *New World, New Earth: Environmental Reform in American Literature from the Puritans Through Whitman.* New Haven: Yale University Press, 1979. xii + 290 pp. Bibliography and index.

Tichy, Marjorie F. "New Mexico's First Capital." *New Mexico Historical Review,* XXI (April 1946), 140-44. On the first capital's precise location.

Tillson, George W. "The Early History of the American Society for Municipal Improvements." *Proceedings of the American Society for Municipal Improvements,* 25 (1918), 300-07. By the society's past president and second secretary.

Timoshenko, Stephen P. *History of Strength of Materials: With a Brief Account of the History of Theory of Elasticity and Theory of Structures.* New York: McGraw-Hill Book Company, 1953. x + 452 pp. Illustrations, diagrams, notes, and indexes. A general historical review of the principal steps in the development of strength of materials. The author, a professor of engineering mechanics, includes brief biographies of the most prominent individuals in this field and discusses "the relation of the progress in strength of material to the state of engineering education and to the industrial development in various countries."

Tindall, William. *Origin and Government of the District of Columbia.* Washington, D.C.: Government Printing Office, 1907. 224 pp. Appendices and index. A description of "the principal legislative and official measures affecting the origin, establishment, and local government of the permanent seat of government of the United States." There are brief but useful sections on street cleaning, collection and disposal of refuse, street lighting, water supply, sewer system, parks and parking, and public markets.

Tindall, William. *Standard History of the City of Washington from a Study of the Original Sources.* Knoxville, Tenn.: H.W. Crew & Co., 1914. vi + 600 pp. Illustrations.

Tinzmann, Otto J. "The Education of Charles E. Merriam." Master's thesis, De Paul University, 1969. 64 pp. Features the municipal activities in which Merriam was involved while an alderman in the Chicago City Council from 1909 to 1917. Only a few were directly related to public works, but all affected the overall administration of city government.

Todd, Charles Burr. "L'Enfant and the Planning of Washington." *American Architect and Building News,* LIII (Aug. 15, 1896), 53. In praise of L'Enfant's work—"his grandest monument and noblest epitaph."

Toll, Seymour I. *The Zoned American.* New York: Grossman Publishers, 1969. xii + 370 pp. Illustrations and bibliography.

Tolman, William Howe. *Municipal Reform Movements in the United States.* New York: Fleming H. Revell Company, 1895. 219 pp. Following a general introductory chapter, the remainder of the book contains sketches of municipal reform and civic betterment organizations throughout the United States. These sketches give dates of establishment and reasons for organizing. Many of the groups came together to work for paved and lighted streets, better drainage and safer water supplies, cleaner alleys and streets, more public parks and bath houses, etc. One section of the book is devoted to "Women's Work in Municipal Reform."

Trani, Eugene P. "Hubert Work and the Department of the Interior, 1923-28." *Pacific Northwest Quarterly,* 61 (Jan.1970), 31-40. Deals extensively with the programs and policies of the Bureau of Reclamation during this period.

Trombley, Kenneth E. *The Life and Times of a Happy Liberal: A Biography of Morris Llewellyn Cooke.* New York: Harper & Brothers, 1954. xviii + 270 pp. Illustration and index. A partisan biography of a prominent public works engineer-administrator by a contemporary. The book was prepared "in the glow of the subject's irrepressible personality and soul-stirring inspiration."

Truesdell, W. A. "A Talk to Young Engineers." *Wisconsin Engineer,* 3 (Jan. 1899), 18-34. On the changes in engineering education in the late nineteenth century.

Tunnard, Christopher. *The Modern American City.* Princeton: D. Van Nostrand Company, 1968. 191 pp. Illustrations, notes, bibliography, and index. Contains good essays on the dynamics of the American city that are complemented by a selection of readings. The volume includes specific material on planning (1910-1930), the City Beautiful Movement (1880-1910), and municipal parks (1850-1900).

Tunnard, Christopher, and Henry Hope Reed. *American Skyline: The Growth and Form of Our Cities and Towns.* Boston: Houghton Mifflin Company, 1955. xviii + 302 pp. Illustrations, maps, bibliography, and index. An interesting examination of "man-made America" from the seventeenth century to the mid twentieth. The book describes "how this scene was shaped, how it became part of the American heritage, how it affects the lives we lead, and how we may in turn shape it toward the future." Substantial parts of the study are devoted to city planning, public buildings, traffic and highways, and parking.

Turnbull, Archibald Douglas. *John Stevens: An American Record.* See chapter on "Waterways."

Turneaure, F. E. "The Engineering School and the Engineer." *Journal of the Western Society of Engineers,* XXII (Jan. 1917), 1-15. A brief outline of "the development of the engineering school as related to the development of the engineering profession" by the dean of the University of Wisconsin's College of Engineering.

Upton, Neil. *An Illustrated History of Civil Engineering.* New York: Crane Russak, 1975. 192 pp. Illustrations, diagrams, bibliography, and index. An overview of civil engineering achievements in Western societies. The author emphasizes transportation structures—canals, railroads, bridges, tunnels, and roads.

U.S. Department of Commerce. Bureau of the Census. *Historical Statistics of the United States: Colonial Times to 1970.* Washington, D.C.: Government Printing Office, 1975. Part 1: xvi + 609 pp. + A-32 pp; Part 2: xvi + 610-1200 pp. + A-32 pp. Tables, charts, notes, appendices, and indexes. A valuable reference tool and one that should not be overlooked when conducting research on parks and recreation; land and water utilization; highway, water, and air transportation; energy; employment of engineers; and federal, state, and local government revenue, expenditure, and debt. (This is the bicentennial edition and the third in the Historical Statistics series.)

U.S. Department of the Interior. "A Century of Conservation, 1849-1949." *Conservation Bulletin,* 39 (June 1950), 1-37. Broadbrush overview of federal conservation landmarks.

U.S. Geological Survey. *A Brief History of the U.S. Geological Survey.* Washington, D.C.: Government Printing Office, 1975. 36 pp. Illustrations.

U.S. Geological Survey. *Ferdinand Vandiveer Hayden and the Founding of the Yellowstone National Park.* See chaper on "Parks and Recreation."

U.S. National Planning Board. *U.S. National Planning Board: Federal Emergency Administration of Public Works, Final Report, 1933-34.* Washington, D.C.: Government Printing Office, 1934. vii + 123 pp. Maps, graphs, notes, appendix, and index. A report on the board's activities since its members (Frederic A. Delano, Charles E. Merriam, and Wesley C. Mitchell) were appointed on July 20, 1933.

U.S. National Resources Committee. *Public Works Planning.* Washington, D.C.: Government Printing Office, 1936. x + 221 pp. Maps, tables, notes, and appendices. A thought-provoking report prepared by the National Resources Committee on Public Works Planning, chaired by Secretary of the Interior Harold L. Ickes. As a means of organizing long-time public works plans, the committee suggests: a national public works authority; a panel of appraisers (responsible to this authority) for allocation of costs; and a fiscal advisory committee to adjust public works programs to the national needs for economic stabilization.

Urban Planning and Development Division, American Society of Civil Engineers. "Civil Engineers in Urban Planning, Fifty Years of Accomplishment, 1923-1973. *Journal of the Urban Planning and Development Division (ASCE),* 100 (Nov. 1974), 115-54. Presents a brief account of the origin, purpose, and accomplishments of ASCE's planning division.

Uzes, Francois D. *Chaining the Land: A History of Surveying in California.* Sacramento: Landmark Enterprises, 1977. xv + 315 pp. Illustrations, maps, diagrams, notes, appendices, bibliographies, and index. A unique volume on a topic rarely addressed by historians. The book contains a discussion of the field instruments and procedures used in early California land surveys, and it presents a description and analysis of state and federal surveys.

Van Tassel, David D., and Michael G. Hall, eds. *Science and Society in the United States.* Homewood, Ill.: Dorsey Press, 1966. vii + 360 pp. Notes, bibliographical essays, chronology, glossary, and index. A collection of essays which "provide an introduction to the ways in which the modern scientific revolution has become interwoven in the political, economic, and social institutions of the United States." Since the emphasis is on pure science rather than technology, public works/engineering subjects are only referred to in Clarence G. Lasby's "Science and the Military" and Carroll W. Pursell, Jr.'s "Science and Government Agencies."

Verner, Coolie. "Surveying and Mapping the Federal City: The First Printed Maps of Washington, D.C." *Imago Mundi,* XXIII (1969), 59-72. Contains two useful sections on the surveying and then the planning of the city.

Vogel, Donald Barry. "The Origin, Growth, and Development of the International City Managers Association." Doctoral dissertation, University of Iowa, 1967. 321 pp.

Vose, George L. "Loammi Baldwin." *Journal of the Association of Engineering Societies.* See chapter on "Waterways."

Wade, Richard. "Urban Life in Western America, 1790-1830." *American Historical Review,* LXIV (Oct. 1958), 14-30. Argues that "towns were the spearheads of the American frontier" and discusses briefly how urban residents and their governments dealt with "the problems of living together." Many of the solutions to these problems were found in the construction or operation of public works structures or services.

Wager, Paul W., ed. *County Government across the Nation.* Chapel Hill: University of North Carolina Press, 1950. xiii + 819 pp. Illustrations, maps, tables, notes, bibliography, and index. A collection of articles describing the organization and operations of one county in each state. The introductory chapter presents a short historical sketch of the county's English origins and its subsequent development in the United States. The Institute for Research in Social Science at the University of North Carolina sponsored the study.

Wager, Paul Woodford. *County Government and Administration in North Carolina.* Chapel Hill: University of North Carolina Press, 1928. xiii + 447 pp. Illustrations, tables, notes, bibliography, and index. A general work describing "the development, present organization and practice, and the outstanding needs of North Carolina county government." The first chapter is a "History of the North Carolina County."

Wainwright, Nicholas B. "Plan of Philadelphia." *Pennsylvania Magazine of History and Biography,* LXXX (April 1956), 164-226. On a manuscript volume found in the Cadwalader Collection at the Historical Society of Pennsylvania.

Waite, H.M. "Reflections on a Quarter of a Century of Public Works." *Public Works Engineers Yearbook 1935: Proceedings of American Society of Municipal Engineers and International Association of Public Works Officials* (1935), 16-19. By the former deputy administrator of the Federal Emergency Administration of Public Works.

Wakstein, Allen M., ed. *The Urbanization of America: An Historical Anthology,* Boston: Houghton Mifflin Company, 1970. ix + 502 pp. Tables, notes, and bibliography. An excellent reader of previously published material. Students of public works history will be especially interested in the following: Nelson M. Blake, "The Need for an Urban Water Supply"; George Rogers Taylor, "Building an Intra-Urban Transportation System"; Roy Lubove, "The Roots of Urban Planning"; Robert M. Fogelson, "Los Angeles, the Fragmented Metropolis"; and Wilfred Owen, "Problems of a Motor Age."

Walker, Forrest A. *The Civil Works Administration: An Experiment in Federal Work Relief, 1933-1934.* New York: Garland Publishing, 1979. ii + 22 pp. Notes, bibliography, and index. A sound institutional analysis of a short-lived New Deal agency. Though it existed for only five months, it was the Roosevelt Administration's initial attempt to give work directly to the unemployed. It served as a precedent for later federally sponsored work programs.

Walker, William B. "The Health Reform Movement in the United States, 1830-1870." Doctoral dissertation, Johns Hopkins University, 1955. 105 pp.

Wallace, Edward S. *The Great Reconnaissance: Soldiers, Artists and Scientists on the Frontier, 1848-1861.* Boston: Little, Brown and Company, 1955. xviii + 288 pp. Illustrations, notes, bibliography, and index. An informal history of the activities of the U.S. Corps of Topographical Engineers in the American West from 1848 to 1861. The book discusses various surveying and exploration work, including the establishment of a new boundary with Mexico and the mapping of routes for wagon roads and railroads. It also relates the achievements of artists and scientists who sketched and painted views of the landscape as well as collected and classified flora and fauna.

Walter, L. W. "Thirty Years' Field Experience with Concrete." *Proceedings of the American Concrete Institute,* XXV (1929), 47-62. Describes methods and materials used in concrete construction from 1899.

Ward, James Arthur. *That Man Haupt: A Biography of Herman Haupt.* Baton Rouge: Louisiana University Press, 1973. xvi + 278 pp. Bibliography.

Waring, George E., Jr., comp. *Report on the Social Statistics of Cities.* 2 vols. Washington, D.C.: Government Printing Office, 1887. Vol. I: 843 pp.; Vol. II: 915 pp. Maps, tables, and index. An invaluable source of data on late nineteenth-century cities and towns. The volumes offer city-by-city profiles of municipal functions such as drainage, garbage, municipal cleansing, parks, water pollution, public buildings, streets, waterworks, and harbors.

Warken, Philip W. *A History of the National Resources Planning Board, 1933-1943.* New York: Garland Publishing Company, 1979. i + 294 pp. Footnotes, bibliography, and index. Excellent study of this important New Deal public works planning agency.

Warken, Philip W. "A History of the National Resources Planning Board, 1933-1943." Doctoral dissertation, Ohio State University, 1969. 296 pp.

Warner, Sam Bass, Jr. *The Urban Wilderness: A History of the American City.* See chapter on "Urban Mass Transportation."

Wasil, Benjamin A. "An Early History of the Construction and Design of Reinforced Concrete." *Midwest Engineer,* 7 (Nov. 1954), 3-4; 13-15. Since the mid-nineteenth century in the United States and Europe.

Watkins, J. Elfreth. "The Beginnings of Engineering." *Transactions of the American Society of Civil Engineers,* XXIV (May 1891), 309-84. The first sections are devoted to ancient engineering practices; these are followed by eleven pages on the "History of Engineering in the United States" (eighteenth- and nineteenth-century canals, roads, and railroads). The most useful material is contained in "Evolution of Engineering Instruments."

Watson, Sara Ruth and Emily. *Famous Engineers.* New York: Dodd, Mead & Company, 1950. viii + 152 pp. Illustrations and index. Biographical sketches of American and British engineers, including John Roebling, James B. Eads, George W. Goethals, Joseph B. Strauss, and David B. Steinman.

Waugh, E. D. J. *West Point: The Story of the United States Military Academy Which Rising from the Revolutionary Forces Has Taught American Soldiers the Art of Victory.* New York: MacMillan Company, 1944. xii + 246 pp. Appendix and bibliography. A popular history, written during World War II with the cooperation of the academy's public relations officer.

Webb, Lester A. *Captain Alden Partridge and the United States Military Academy.* Northport, Ala.: American Southern, 1965. ix + 224 pp. Illustrations, tables, notes, appendices, bibliography, and index. Attempts to explain Partridge's rise and fall as superintendent of the United States Military Academy and to analyze his contributions to improving the academy's administration, curriculum, and physical plant.

Weber, Gustavus A. *The Coast and Geodetic Survey: Its History, Activities and Organization.* Baltimore: Johns Hopkins Press, 1923. xii + 107 pp. Appendices, bibliography, and index. One of the "Service Monographs" prepared by the Institute for Government Research. The first chapter is a fourteen-page history of the Department of Commerce's Coast and Geodetic Survey.

Weeks, Charles J. "The Eastern Cherokee and the New Deal." *North Carolina Historical Review,* LIII (July 1976), 303-19. The author states that "public works projects of the New Deal introduced a short-term and artificial prosperity" on the reservation of the North Carolina Cherokee.

Weiner, Ronald R. "A History of Civic Land Use Decision Making in the Cleveland Metropolitan Area, 1880-1930." Doctoral dissertation, Kent State University, 1974.

Weinstein, James. "Organized Business and the City Commission and Manager Movements." *Journal of Southern History,* XXVIII (May 1962), 166-82. Explains how the movement for municipal reform became "the adopted child of organized business" and contends that the significance of the commission-manager plan lies "not in its success, but rather in the way this movement to rationalize municipal government illuminates the goals and political ideology of businessmen" at the turn of the twentieth century.

Weiss, Ellen. "Robert Morris Copeland's Plans for Oak Bluffs." *Journal of the Society of Architectural Historians,* XXXIV (March 1975), 60-66. On the 1866 plan for Oak Bluffs, located on the island of Martha's Vineyard.

Wemett, W.M. "Making a Path to the Pacific: The Story of the Stevens' Survey." *North Dakota History,* 29 (Oct. 1962), 302-19. Demonstrates that to Isaac I. Stevens, governor of the newly organized Territory of Washington in 1850, "belongs the credit for working out the most northern of the three great pathways from the Mississippi to the Pacific coast."

Western Society of Engineers. *The Centennial of the Engineer.* Chicago: Western Society of Engineers, 1970. 241 pp. Illustrations, tables, and charts. The Western Society of Engineers' "Centennial Book" includes "100 Years of Progress," a short history of the society, as well as photographs and biographical sketches of its past presidents.

Wheat, Carl I. "Mapping the American West, 1540-1857." *Proceedings of the American Antiquarian Society,* 64 (April 1954), 19-194. A preliminary examination of major groups of western maps, relating to Spanish exploration from the south; French penetration from the east; British efforts to the north and in the northwest; the treks of Lewis and Clark, Pike and Long; the fur trade era; the work of the Army's Topographical Engineers; the trails of gold-seekers and emigrants; and the Pacific Railroad Surveys.

Wheat, Carl Irving. *Mapping the Transmississippi West, 1540-1861.* 5 vols. San Francisco: Institute of Historical Cartography, 1957-1963. Illustrations, notes, and bibliography.

Wheeler, Raymond A. "50 Years of Our Society." *Military Engineer,* 62 (July-Aug. 1970), 225-27. A former Society of American Military Engineers' president discusses the organization's growth and accomplishments since 1920.

Whinery, S. *Municipal Public Works: Their Inception, Construction and Management.* New York: Macmillan Company, 1903. xiv + 241 pp. A classic collection of essays, prepared "for the inexperienced city official and for the urban citizen," on the principles involved in "the carrying out of municipal public works."

Whisenhunt, Donald W. *The Environment and the American Experience: A Historian Looks at the Ecological Crisis.* Port Washington, N.Y.: Kennikat Press, 1974. vi + 136 pp. Notes and index.

White, Josiah. *Josiah Whtie's History Given by Himself.* See chapter on "Waterways."

White, Katherine H. "Spanish and Mexican Surveying Terms and Systems." *Password,* VI (Winter 1961), 24-27.

White, Leonard D. *The City Manager.* Chicago: University of Chicago Press, 1927. xvii + 355 pp. Illustrations, graphs, tables, notes, appendices, and index. An analysis of the council-manager movement in American municipal government during the first quarter of the twentieth century. Most city managers first served their communities as either municipal engineers or businessmen. The author gives special attention to the managers of Cleveland, Cincinnati, Kansas City, Pasadena, and Dayton.

White, Richard. "Land Occupation and

Environmental Change in Island County, Washington, 1780-1940: A Case Study." Doctoral dissertation, University of Washington, 1975. 265 pp.

White, Ruth. *Yankee From Sweden: The Dream and the Reality in the Days of John Ericsson.* New York: Henry Holt and Company, 1960. xix + 299 pp. Illustrations, appendices, bibliography, and index. A full-scale biography of the energetic Swedish immigrant who designed the *Monitor* and who, after 1850, identified himself as both a civil and mechanical engineer.

White, Theo B. *Paul Philippe Cret: Architect and Teacher.* See chapter on "Public Buildings."

Whitman, Willson. *David Lilienthal: Public Servant in a Power Age.* See chapter on "Flood Control and Drainage."

Whitmore, George D. "City Surveys—Past, Present, and Future." *Civil Engineering,* 3 (Aug. 1933), 468-70. Reviews the history of city surveys during the previous century.

Whitnall, Gordon. "History of Zoning." *Annals of the American Academy of Political and Social Science,* 155 (May 1931), 1-14.

Whyte, James H. "The District of Columbia Territorial Government, 1871-1874." *Records of the Columbia Historical Society of Washington, D.C.,* 51-52 (1951-1952), 87-102. Discusses the act which created the Board of Public Works, the public improvements that were undertaken and financed during this period, and Alexander Shepherd's involvement in these activities.

Wickens, James F. "The New Deal in Colorado." *Pacific Historical Review,* XXXVIII (Aug. 1969), 275-91. Summarizes the influence of the PWA, WPA, and other programs on the state's economy.

Wilcox, Delos F. *Municipal Franchises.* 2 vols. Chicago: University of Chicago Press, 1910. Vol. I: xix + 710 pp.; Vol. II: xxi + 885 pp. Indexes.

Wild, Peter. *Pioneer Conservationists of Western America.* Missoula, Mont.: Mountain Press Publishing Company, 1979. xxv + 246 pp. Illustrations, bibliography, and index. A well-written collection of essays on conservationists who sought to preserve the American West. The following are included: John Muir, John Wesley Powell, Gifford Pinchot, Stephen Mather, Enos Mills, Mary Hunter Austin, and Aldo Leopold.

Wilde, Robert E. "75 Years of Progress: The ACI [American Concrete Institute] Saga." *Concrete International,* 1 (Oct. 1979), 8-39. An account of the American Concrete Institute's (ACI) growth over the past seventy-five years. It summarizes and highlights ACI's developments in concrete technology, design, and construction. The article contains numerous illustrations.

Wilkins, Thurman. *Clarence King: A Biography.* New York: Macmillan Company, 1958. ix + 441 pp. Illustrations, notes, bibliography, and index. The definitive biography of one of the nineteenth-century's foremost surveyors. King became head of the U.S. Geological Survey in 1879.

Wilkinson, Norman B. "The Forgotten 'Founder' of West Point." *Military Affairs,* XXIV (Winter 1960), 177-88. Recognizes "the part played by Louis de Tousard who first conceived the idea of a national military school with a comprehensive curriculum and a prescribed training program."

Williams, James C., ed. *Old Town, Santa Barbara: A Narrative History of a State Street from Gutierrez to Ortega, 1850-1975.* Santa Barbara: Graduate Program in Public Historical Studies, University of California, 1977. xiii + 314 pp. Illustrations, tables, charts, notes, bibliography, and appendices. A history of a Santa Barbara street which touches on a few public works developments.

Williams, J. Kerwin. *Grants-in-Aid Under the Public Works Administration: A Study in Federal-State-Local Relations.* New York: Columbia University Press, 1939. 292 pp. Tables, notes, and index. An excellent analysis of how the Public Works Administration program influenced the relationships between federal, state, and local governments.

Williams, Samuel C. *William Tatham Watuagan.* Johnson City, Tenn.: Watauga Press, 1947. 109 pp. Illustration, notes, and appendices. A short biography of an individual who the author believes is "the father of the United States topographical and coast surveys." This is the second revised edition; the first appeared in 1922.

Williamson, Harold F., and Kenneth M.

Meyers. *Designed for Digging: The First 75 Years of Bucyrus-Erie Company.* Evanston: Northwestern University Press, 1955. 384 pp. Illustrations, bibliography, appendices, and index. Excellent company history.

Wilson, Howard E. *Mary McDowell, Neighbor.* See chapter on "Solid Wastes."

Wilson, Richard Guy. "Idealism and the Origin of the First American Suburb: Llewellyn Park, New Jersey." *American Art Journal,* XI (Oct. 1979), 79-90. On the United States' first planned garden suburb, which was laid out between 1853 and 1857.

Wilson, W. Hasell, and Solomon W. Roberts. *Notes on the Internal Improvements of Pennsylvania, by W. Hasell Wilson, C.E. and Reminiscences of the First Railroad over the Allegheny Mountain, by Solomon W. Roberts, C.E.* Philadelphia: Railway World, 1879. 83 pp. Illustration, diagrams, and tables. The "Introductory Notice" provides biographical sketches of two nineteenth-century railroad engineers, Wilson and Roberts. The remainder of the book deals with railroad construction.

Wilson, William Edgar. "Environment as a Cross National Problem: Great Lakes Water Pollution, 1948-1972." Doctoral dissertation, Fletcher School of Law and Diplomacy, 1974. 427 pp. Tables, charts, notes, appendices, and bibliography. Turgid legal and administrative history of intergovernmental efforts to control water pollution under the auspices of the International Joint Commission.

Wilson, William H. "Harrisburg's Successful City Beautiful Movement, 1900-1915." *Pennsylvania History,* XLVII (July 1980), 213-33.

Wilson, William H. "'More Almost Than the Men': Mira Lloyd Dock and the Beautification of Harrisburg." *Pennsylvania Magazine of History and Biography,* XCIX (Oct. 1975), 490-99. Shows the diverse aspects of the City Beautiful Movement in Harrisburg through the efforts of Mira Lloyd Dock.

Wilson, William H. *The City Beautiful Movement in Kansas City.* Columbia: University of Missouri Press, 1964. xvii + 171 pp. Illustrations, maps, notes, bibliography, and index. An historical examination of the problems and benefits of city planning by looking at "one movement and the group of men who led it in a single city."

Wilson, William H. "The Founding of Anchorage: Federal Town Building on the Last Frontier." *Pacific Northwest Quarterly,* 58 (July 1967), 130-31. Excellent description of the planning problems of carving a city out of the wilderness.

Winkley, John W. *John Muir: A Concise Biography of the Great Naturalist.* See chapter on "Parks and Recreation."

Winpenny, Thomas R. "The Nefarious Philadelphia Plan and Urban America: A Reconsideration." *Pennsylvania Magazine of History and Biography,* CI (Jan. 1977), 103-13. The author challenges the view of many historians that gridiron street patterns have "not been responsive to human needs." The article, however, deals primarily with social and aesthetic questions rather than transportation.

Wisconsin Chapter, American Public Works Association. *APWA: 25 Years.* Milwaukee: APWA, Wisconsin Chapter, 1979. 35 pp. Illustrations. An anniversary (25th) yearbook that chronicles the chapter's growth.

Wisely, William H. *The American Civil Engineer, 1852-1974: The History, Traditions, and Development of the American Society of Civil Engineers.* New York: American Society of Civil Engineers, 1974. vii + 464 pp. Illustrations, charts, appendices, and index. This volume is a history of the American Society of Civil Engineers by a former executive director. While documenting the society's many activities since its founding in 1852, it lacks a broad perspective and fails to explain, for example, how the accelerated urbanization of the United States at the turn of the century affected engineers.

Wisely, William H. "Professional Turning Points in ASCE History." *Civil Engineering,* 47 (Oct. 1977), 137-40. Former executive director of ASCE describes "the hallmarks of a profession" and how ASCE has been a leader "among U.S. engineering specialities in encouraging this evolution to professional status."

Wodehouse, Lawrence. "Frank Pierce Milburn (1868-1926), A Major Southern Architect." *North Carolina Historical Review.* See chapter on "Public Buildings."

Wolfe, Linnie Marsh. *Son of the Wilderness: The Life of John Muir.* See chapter on "Parks and Recreation."

Wolman, Abel. "George Warren Fuller: A Reminiscence." *Essays in Public Works History.* See chapter on "Community Water Supply."

Wolman, Abel. "The Trend of Civil Engineering Since Franklin." *Journal of the Franklin Institute,* 226 (July-Dec. 1938), 413-28. Paean to the engineering profession.

Wolman, Abel. "Values in the Control of Environment." *American Journal of Public Health.* See chapter on "Sewers and Wastewater Treatment."

Wolner, Edward Wallace. "Daniel Burnham and the Tradition of the City Builder in Chicago: Technique, Ambition and City Planning." Doctoral dissertation, New York University, 1977.

Wood, Richard G. *Stephen Harriman Long, 1784-1864: Army Engineer, Explorer, Inventor.* Glendale, Calif.: Arthur H. Clark Company, 1966. 292 pp. Illustrations, map, notes, bibliography, and index.

Woodard, C.S. "The Public Domain: Its Surveys and Surveyors." *Michigan Pioneer and Historical Collections,* 27 (1896), 306-23.

Woodman, Lyman L. "Captain Raymond Explores the Yukon." *Water Spectrum,* 7 (Summer 1975), 1-10. Recounts the first American military exploration of Alaska's interior (1869) by an expedition led by a young U.S. Army Engineer Corps officer, Charles Walker Raymond.

Woodruff, Clinton Rogers, ed. *City Government by Commission.* New York: D. Appleton and Company, 1911. x + 381 pp. Tables, notes, bibliography, and index. Includes one essay entitled "History of the Commission Government Idea."

Woods, James R. "The Legend and the Legacy of Franklin D. Roosevelt and the Civilian Conservation Corps (CCC)." Doctoral dissertation, Syracuse University, 1964. 453 pp.

Wright, Aflred J. "Joel Wright, City Planner." *Ohio State Archaeological and Historical Quarterly,* LVI (July 1947), 287-94. Biographical sketch of the individual who prepared the original plan for Columbus.

Wright, John D. "Robert Peter and the First Kentucky Geological Survey." *Register of the Kentucky Historical Society,* 52 (July 1954), 201-12.

Yonce, Frederick J. "The Public Land Surveys in Washington." *Pacific Northwest Quarterly,* 63 (Oct. 1972), 129-41. Of the General Land Office (1850s to 1920s).

Yost, Edna. *Modern American Engineers.* Philadelphia: J.B. Lippincott Company, 1952. ix + 182 pp. Contains biographical sketches on twelve "modern" engineers. Of particular interest to public works practitioners and researchers are those chapters on Arthur Morgan, former chairman of the Tennessee Valley Authority, and Ole Singstad, designer of the Holland Tunnel and its ventilating system.

Young, Hugh E. "The Value of Planned City Development: A Record of 24 Years of Progress Under the Chicago Plan." *Civil Engineering,* 3 (Sept. 1933), 503-05. Reviews major public improvements, especially parks and streets, in Chicago since adoption of the Burnham Plan (1909).

Young, James Sterling. *The Washington Community, 1800-1828.* New York: Columbia University Press, 1966. xviii + 307 pp. Maps, charts, tables, notes, bibliography, and index. Chapter 1, "The Community Plan," is particularly interesting. The author shows that the plan for Washington—a city built specifically for the national government—was "a statement of the kind of governmental establishment the politicians *intended* to create."

Zucker, Paul. *Town and Square: From the Agora to the Village Green.* Cambridge: M.I.T. Press, 1970. xxiii + 287 pp. Illustrations, figures, bibliography, and index. A fascinating study on "the artistically shaped *void,*" the square or plaza. Only the last chapter deals with "Early American Public Squares," and it is by another author, Carl Feiss. The book was first printed in 1959.

Zueblin, Charles. *American Municipal Progress: Chapters in Municipal Sociology.* New York: Macmillan Company, 1903. 380 pp. Tables, notes, appendices, and index. A classic look at the relationship of public works to municipal progress. There are individual chapters on public works in general, transportation, sanitation, public buildings, parks and boulevards, and public recreation.

2
Irrigation

Human survival in arid regions has always depended upon cooperative conservation and sharing of scarce water supplies. Indians in the Southwest first established settlements near irrigated fields that provided food and fiber. They were followed by Spanish missionaries and colonists who introduced water conservation techniques practiced for centuries in their homeland. Mormon pioneers, who settled the Salt Lake Valley in the late 1840s, diverted mountain streams to irrigate thousands of acres. Others tried to emulate that success, but in many areas streams flooded in spring, dried up in summer, and homesteaders often lacked the skills and financial resources to construct dams that could store water for the dry growing season.

During the twentieth century, large federal and state water projects evolved from a desire to expand western settlement as well as manage development of all natural resources. The activities of the Bureau of Reclamation and other entities entailed construction of vast systems of dams, canals, and attendant facilities. The irrigation projects eventually evolved into multiple-purpose water resource systems spanning entire river basins. Since World War II, however, large water projects have been assailed by environmentalists as threats to interdependent ecological systems and pristine areas of natural beauty. Therefore, water agencies now face the challenge of serving water and power users while preserving and augmenting environmental quality.

Scholarship on this subject is far more extensive and advanced than in many other public works fields, since water management has always been of central importance to the arid West. The books, articles, and dissertations that follow offer a vast panorama of the environmental, institutional, legal, and technical aspects of the subject. Publications on irrigation and related water uses are weighted heavily in the evolution of western water laws and policies as well as the creation of cooperative and semipublic entities to govern the development and allocation of the resource. Questions raised by organized opponents of water projects are offering new lines of historical inquiry: disruption of ecological systems, safety hazards, economic feasibility, impacts on historic sites, effects on fish and wildlife, and Indian water rights. The technical side is less well represented, but there are some key sources that discuss the design, construction, and operation of structures that store, divert, and transmit water.

Alexander, Thomas G. *A Clash of Interests: Interior Department and Mountain West, 1863-96.* See chapter on "Planning, Engineering, and Administration."

Alexander, Thomas G. "An Investment in Progress: Utah's First Federal Reclamation Project, The Strawberry Valley Project." *Utah Historical Quarterly,* 39 (Summer 1971), 286-304. Presents the history of this successful project—"the first large scale diversion of water from the Colorado River Basin into the Great Basin."

Alexander, Thomas G. "John Wesley Powell, the Irrigation Survey, and the Inauguration of the Second Phase of Irrigation Development in Utah." *Utah Historical Quarterly,* 37 (Spring 1969), 190-206. Shows how the Powell Irrigation Survey "marks the transfer of interest in the reclamation of arid lands from the local level to the national level."

Alexander, Thomas G. "The Powell Irrigation Survey and the People of the Mountain West." *Journal of the West,* VII (Jan. 1968), 48-54. Explores in a comprehensive manner the causes of western opposition to the Powell survey.

Allen, Richard Cardell. "Governor George H. Dern and Utah's Participation in the Colorado River Compact, 1922-1933." Master's thesis, University of Utah, 1958. vi + 107 pp. Maps, tables, notes, appendices, and bibliography. Utah's role in the development of the Colorado River Compact is discussed in the thesis. Dern was a staunch defender of what he perceived as his state's vital interests.

Alston, Richard Moss. *Commercial Irrigation Enterprise, the Fear of Water Monopoly, and the Genesis of Market Distortion in the Nineteenth Century American West.* New York: Arno Press, 1978. viii + 241 pp. Graphs, notes, and bibliography. A perceptive and challenging analysis of the development of western water laws, policies, and institutions. The author contends that the growth of cooperative, semi-public enterprises for the allocation of water resources resulted from an unjustified fear of monopolistic control. He further argues that legal reforms should be encouraged "which would take from the hands of bureaucratic agencies a considerable amount of discretionary power which is subject to strong political pressure." The book contains a great deal of historical information on the development of federal and state water policies.

Armstrong, Ellis L.; Michael C. Robinson; and Suellen M. Hoy, eds. *History of Public Works in the United States, 1776-1976.* See chapter on "Planning, Engineering, and Administration."

Arneson, Edwin P. "Early Irrigation in Texas." *Southwestern Historical Quarterly,* XXV (Oct. 1921), 121-30. A good discussion of Spanish irrigation, principally in the area of El Paso. Descriptions are given of the works that were built to divert and transmit water for agricultural and domestic use.

Arrington, Leonard J. *Great Basin Kingdom: An Economic History of the Latter-Day Saints, 1830-1900.* Cambridge: Harvard University Press, 1958. xix + 534 pp. Illustrations, notes, bibliographical essay, and index. Seminal work on Mormon settlement during the nineteenth century. Arrington includes a host of information on Mormon irrigation systems and other public works.

Arrington, Leonard J. "Taming the Turbulent Sevier: A Story of Mormon Desert Conquest." *Western Humanities Review,* V (Autumn 1951) 393-406. Well-written account of the human struggle required to transform the west-central Utah desert to a productive agricultural settlement.

Arrington, Leonard J., and Thomas C. Anderson. "The 'First' Irrigation Reservoir in the United States: The Newton, Utah Project." *Utah Historical Quarterly,* 39 (Summer 1971), 207-23. Built in 1871 by a Mormon community "to store water for purposes of irrigation."

Arrington, Leonard J., and Davis Bitton. *The Mormon Experience: A History of the Latter-Day Saints.* New York: Alfred A. Knopf, 1979. xx + 404 pp. Illustrations, maps, notes, appendix, bibliographical essay, and index. Includes an extensive discussion of Mormon contributions to western irrigation.

Arrington, Leonard J., and Lowell Dittmer. "Reclamation in Three Layers: The Ogden River Project, 1934-1965." *Pacific Historical Review,* 35 (1966), 15-34. Solid account of a project designed to meet the needs of domestic and irrigation water users.

Arrington, Leonard J., and Dean May. "'A Different Mode of Life': Irrigation and Society in Nineteenth-Century Utah." *Agricultural History,* XLIX (Jan. 1975), 3-20. By far the most insightful treatment of the origins of irrigation practices and institutions in the West. Arrington and May thoroughly analyze economic and social aspects of the irrigation-based civilization created by the Mormons.

Aston, Rollah E. "Boulder Dam and the Public Utilities." Master's thesis, University of Arizona, 1936. iv + 298 pp. Notes and bibliography. An often overlooked and challenging analysis of organized private utility opposition to the Boulder Canyon Project Act. The thesis describes the interest groups that supported each side of the public versus private power issue.

August, Stephen M. "Resolution of Water Regulation Conflict in the Colorado River Basin: The Interstate Compact." Master's thesis, University of Colorado, 1972.

Bailey, Reed W. "Watershed Management: Key to Resource Conservation." *Journal of Forestry,* 48 (Sept. 1950), 393-96. Includes some historical information on watershed management in the twentieth century.

Baird, Richard E. "The Politics of Echo Park and Other Water Development Projects in the Upper Colorado River Basin, 1945-1956." Doctoral dissertation, University of Illinois, Urbana-Champaign, 1960. 580 pp.

Baker, Riley E. "Water Development as an Important Factor in the Utilization of the High Plains of Texas." *Southwestern Social Science Quarterly,* 34 (Sept. 1953), 21-34. Discusses the evolution of well drilling, pumps, and sources of power for water-lifting devices in this semiarid region.

Baker, Thomas Lindsay. "Building the Roosevelt Dam." *Arizona Professional Engineer,* XXVII (Aug. 1975), 6-7. Summary of the construction of the first large storage dam built by the Reclamation Service.

Baker, T. Lindsay. "Some Unusual Water Pipelines of the Southwest." *Cast Iron Pipe News.* See chapter on "Community Water Supply."

Baker, T. Lindsay, et al. *Water for the Southwest: Historical Survey and Guide to Historic Sites.* New York: American Society of Civil Engineers, 1973. xii + 204 pp. Illustrations, maps, diagrams, notes, bibliography, and index. A documentary and pictorial summary of early water supply systems in the Southwest. Sixty sites, which represent locations of historical and technological significance, are presented. The book includes an excellent brief narrative history of efforts by Indians, Spanish, and Anglo-Americans to secure and maintain water supplies in the arid region prior to 1900.

Baldridge, Kenneth W. "Nine Years of Achievement: The Civilian Conservation Corps in Utah." Doctoral dissertation, Brigham Young University, 1971. vi + 389 pp. Map, tables, notes, appendices, and bibliography. One of the best case studies of this key New Deal agency. Projects undertaken in Utah included rehabilitation and construction work on roads, wildlife refuges, parks, recreational areas, and irrigation facilities. The dissertation also has especially strong chapters on administration, life in camps, and community relations.

Baldridge, Kenneth W. "Reclamation Work of the Civilian Conservation Corps, 1933-1942." *Utah Historical Quarterly.* See chapter on "Flood Control and Drainage."

Bancroft, George J. "Diversion of Water from the Western Slope." *Colorado Magazine,* XXI (Sept. 1944), 178-80. Thin discussion of efforts to divert water from the west slope of Rockies prior to the Colorado-Big Thompson Project.

Barrett, Glen. "Reclamation's New Deal for Heavy Construction: M-K in the Great Depression." *Idaho Yesterdays,* 22 (Fall 1978), 21-27. Excellent discussion of the dramatic growth of the Morrison-Knudsen Company in the 1930s due to its major role in the construction of Hoover Dam and other key water projects. It is one of the few good case studies of a construction firm.

Batman, Richard Dale. "Gospel Swamp . . . The Land of Hog and Hominy." *Journal of the West,* IV (April 1965), 231-57. Comprehensive article on the development of irrigation and flood control in Orange County, California.

Beidleman, Richard G. "The Gunnison River Diversion Project, Part I; Part II." *Colorado Magazine,* XXXVI (July and Oct. 1959), Part I. 187-201; Part II: 266-286. Excellent construction history of the Gunnison Tunnel, one of the first major projects of the Reclamation Service.

Bercaw, Louise O.; A.M. Hannay; and Esther M. Colvin. *Bibliography on Land Settlement with Particular Reference to Small Holdings and Subsistence Homesteads.* Washington, D.C: United States Department of

Agriculture, 1934. iv + 492 pp. Index. A good bibliographical tool for sources on irrigation development in the western United States and the attendant problems of settlers.

Berkman, Richard L., and W. Kip Viscusi. *Damming the West: Ralph Nader's Study Group Report on the Bureau of Reclamation.* New York: Grossman Publishers, 1973. xiv + 272 pp. Maps, notes, appendix, and index. A diatribe against the agency's activities which the authors feel should be stopped, curtailed, or redirected. The book charges that the reclamation program adversely affects the environment, runs roughshod over Indian water rights, lines the pockets of corporation farmers, and is based upon specious cost-benefit and technical criteria. It is the quintessence of anti-reclamation literature.

Billington, Monroe. "W.C. Austin Irrigation Project." *Chronicles of Oklahoma, XXX* (Summer 1952), 207-15. A superficial description of the first Bureau of Reclamation project built in Oklahoma.

Bingham, Jay R. "Reclamation and the Colorado." *Utah Historical Quarterly,* XXVIII (July 1960), 233-49. Presents a general history of the Colorado River, the last undeveloped "Water Hole," and argues that the Colorado River Storage Project "will provide the water needed to conquer this last great frontier." The author is executive director of the Utah Water and Power Board.

Bird, John W. "A History of Water Rights in Nevada." 2 parts. *Nevada Historical Society Quarterly,* XVIII and XIX (Spring 1975; Spring 1976), 27-32 and 27-34. A good legal discussion.

Black, Archibald. *The Story of Tunnels.* See chapter on "Roads, Streets, and Highways."

Blackorby, E.C. "Theodore Roosevelt's Conservation Policies and Their Impact upon America and the American West." *North Dakota History.* See chapter on "Waterways."

Blake, Nelson M. *Land into Water—Water into Land.* Tallahassee: University Presses of Florida, 1980. viii + 344 pp. Illustrations, maps, notes, and index. Outstanding history of successive efforts to manipulate and control the natural water flow of South Florida by the construction of elaborate engineering works. Blake is especially critical of the Cross-Florida ship canal and the persistent dream of draining the Everglades to develop arable land.

Blanchard, C.J. "Winning the West: An Account of the Marvelous Progress of Our Reclamation Service in Reclaiming the Desert." *National Geographic Magazine,* XVII (Feb. 1906), 82-100. Paean to the agency's activities by one of its engineers.

Blouet, Brian W., and Frederick C. Luebke. *The Great Plains: Environment and Culture.* Lincoln: University of Nebraska Press, 1979. xxviii + 246 pp. Illustrations, map, charts, graphs, tables, and notes. A collection of essays which "illustrate changing and contrasting interpretations of the interaction of environment and culture on the Great Plains." Of particular interest are "Agricultural Adjustments to Great Plains Drought: The Republican Valley, 1870-1900" by Bradley H. Baltensperger; "Nebraska Populism as a Response to Environmental and Political Problems," by David S. Trask; "The Great Plains as Part of an Irrigated Western Empire, 1890-1914," by Timothy J. Rickard; and "The Great Plains: Promises, Problems, and Prospects" by Gilbert C. Fite.

Boening, Rose M. "History of Irrigation in the State of Washington." 2 parts. *Washington Historical Quarterly,* IX and X (Oct. 1918 and Jan. 1919), Part I: 259-76; Part II: 21-45. Emphasizes irrigation's part in the state's economic development.

Bolton, Herbert E. "The Founding of the Missions of the San Gabriel River, 1745-1749." *Southwestern Historical Quarterly,* XVII (April 1914), 323-78. Deals extensively with the missions' irrigation systems.

Boslaugh, Paul E. "The Great North Platte Dam, Power and Irrigation Project." *Nebraska History,* XXIII (July-Sept. 1942), 170-87. Discusses the Tri-County Project in western Nebraska that includes dams on the Platte River for irrigation and hydroelectric power generation.

Boyd, David. "Irrigation Near Greeley, Colorado." *Water Supply and Irrigation Papers of the United States Geological Survey,* 9 (1897), 1-90. Describes the growth and development of irrigation in the valley of the Cache la Poudre, in the northern part of Colorado. The article includes excellent illustrations as well as an introduction by F.N. Newell.

Boyle, Robert H.; John Graves; and T.H. Watkins. *The Water Hustlers.* San Francisco: Sierra Club, 1971. 253 pp. Maps, notes, and bibliography. A highly critical examination of "water resources manipulation" and its impact on the environments of Texas, California, and New York. The authors state that the nation does not face "a shortage of water but a prodigious shortage of human foresight." The book is especially vitriolic in its denunciation of the Army Corps of Engineers, Bureau of Reclamation, and plans to augment New York City's water supply.

Brandhorst, L. Carl. "The Panacea of Irrigation: Fact or Fancy." *Journal of the West,* VII (Oct. 1968), 491-509. The author contends that although irrigation produces higher yields, it does not stabilize crop production. The historical analysis of two Nebraska counties suggests that hazards such as hail, disease, and insects account for wide variations in crop production.

Brough, Charles Hillman. "Irrigation in Utah." *Johns Hopkins Studies in Historical & Political Science,* XIX (1898), 1-212. Classic study of irrigation in the state that focuses on legislation and institutions.

Brown, Leahmae. "The Development of National Policy with Respect to Water Resources." Doctoral dissertation. See chapter on "Waterways."

Bruce, William James. "Administrative Problems in the Preliminary Phases of the Planning and Construction of the Hoover Dam." Doctoral dissertation, Stanford University, 1942. x + 256 pp. Charts, notes, and bibliography. Weak discussion of the intergovernmental and administrative problems that arose in implementing the provisions of the Boulder Canyon Project Act.

Brykit, James W. "A Log of the Verde: The 'Taming' of an Arizona River." *Journal of Arizona History,* 19 (Spring 1978), 31-54. Competent discussion of water development and settlement within the Verde River Basin.

Carlson, Martin Evald. "The Development of Irrigation in Nebraska, 1854-1910: A Descriptive Survey." Doctoral dissertation, University of Nebraska-Lincoln, 1963. 376 pp.

Carlson, Martin E. "William E. Smythe: Irrigation Crusader." *Journal of the West,* VII (Jan. 1968), 41-47. Describes the philosophy and activities of the foremost irrigation crusader of the early 1890s.

Carr, Ralph. "Delph Carpenter and River Compacts Between Western States." *Colorado Magazine,* XXI (Jan. 1944), 5-14. A salute to the "father of interstate river treaties."

Carroll, Eugene T. "John B. Kendrick's Fight for Western Water Legislation, 1917-1933." *Annals of Wyoming,* 50 (Fall 1978), 319-33. Describes the Wyoming senator's efforts to obtain support for federal reclamation projects in his state.

Carroll, John Alexander. "Broader Approaches to the History of the West: A Descriptive Bibliography." *Arizona and the West,* I (Autumn 1959), 217-31. Evaluates forty-four works "that may be considered 'general'—both in chronological span and geographical compass—in treatment of the American West."

Chan, Loren Briggs. *Sagebrush Statesman: Tasker L. Oddie of Nevada.* Reno: University of Nevada Press, 1973. 189 pp. Illustrations, map, notes, bibliography, and index. A solid biography of this politician who served as governor of Nevada (1911-1914) and represented the state in the United States Senate (1921-1933). One chapter discusses his role in the authorization and subsequent development of the Boulder Canyon Project.

Chase, Stuart. *Rich Land, Poor Land: A Study of Waste in the Natural Resources of America.* See chapter on "Flood Control and Drainage."

Chatterton, Fenimore. "History of the Inspection of Riverton and Riverton Irrigation Project in Fremont County, Wyoming." *Annals of Wyoming,* 25 (Jan. 1953), 83-89. Records the work of the Wyoming Central Irrigation Company.

Clark, Alfred. "The San Gabriel River: A Century of Dividing the Waters." *Southern California Quarterly,* LII (June 1970), 155-69. Discusses compromises that were reached to resolve disputes among farmers, cities, and power companies for the flow of the San Gabriel River. It is a good case study of competitive water demands in the western United States.

Clark, Earl. "Rufus Woods: Grand Coulee Promoter." *Montana: The Magazine of Western History,* XXIX (Oct. 1979), 38-51. Shows that the dam might never have been built "had it not been for the catalyst provided by a feisty small town newspaper publisher named Rufus Woods."

Clark, Ira G. "The Elephant Butte Controversy: A Chapter in the Emergence of Federal Water Law." *Journal of American History,* LXI (March 1975), 1006-33. One of the best case studies of conflicts over water rights.

Cleaveland, Frederic Neill. "Federal Reclamation Policy and Administration: A Case Study in the Development of Natural Resources." Doctoral dissertation, Princeton University, 1951. 316 pp. Excellent study of the evolution of the Bureau of Reclamation's policies, organization, and administration from 1902 to 1950. Material is included on how power programs shaped the course of the agency's development.

Clements, Roger V. "British-Controlled Enterprise in the West between 1870 and 1900, and Some Agrarian Reactions." *Agricultural History,* 27 (Oct. 1953), 132-41. Describes western irrigation problems between 1870 and 1900 and shows how British investment in the trans-Mississippi West consisted "much more of enterprises that made western development bend to British purposes and interests."

Cleworth, Marc M. "Artesian-Well Irrigation: Its History in Brown County, South Dakota, 1899-1900." *Agricultural History,* 15 (1941), 194-201. One of the few articles written on the attempt to use artesian water for irrigation in the nineteenth century. Cleworth describes unsuccessful efforts to obtain federal subsidies for the plan and environmental factors that made the scheme impractical.

Clyde, George D. "History of Irrigation in Utah." *Utah Historical Quarterly,* XXVII (Jan. 1959), 26-36. Utah's governor reflects on the positive effects of irrigation on the state and argues that "water developed for irrigation purposes is 'water in the bank!'"

Clyde, George D. "Irrigation in the United States." *Transactions of the American Society of Civil Engineers,* CT (1953), 311-42. A detailed summary of irrigation development in the western United States by the chief of the Soil Conservation Service's Division of Irrigation, Engineering, and Water Conservation.

Coate, Charles Eugene. "Water Power and Politics in the Central Valley Project, 1933-1967." Doctoral dissertation. See chapter on "Energy."

Cole, Donald Barnard. "Transmountain Water Diversion in Colorado." *Colorado Magazine,* XXV (March and May 1948), March: 49-65; May: 118-35. Fine study of the Colorado-Big Thompson Project that includes general information on the history of irrigation in Colorado.

Collins, Kay. "The Transmountain Diversion of Water from the Colorado River: A Legal-Historical Study." Master's thesis, University of New Mexico, 1965.

Colorado Water Conservation Board. *A Hundred Years of Irrigation in Colorado: 100 Years of Organized and Continuous Irrigation, 1852-1952.* Denver: Colorado Water Conservation Board and Colorado Agricultural and Mechanical College, 1952. 111 pp. Illustrations and graphs. A series of short essays on various aspects of Colorado's irrigation history. Subjects covered include irrigation practices, administering water allocations, groundwater, return flows, 160-acre limitation, and water law.

Coman, Katherine. "Some Unsettled Problems of Irrigation." *American Economic Review,* I (March 1911), 1-19. A competent summary of the evolution of western irrigation and problems encountered during the first decade of the federal reclamation program.

Conkin, Paul K. "The Vision of Elwood Mead." *Agricultural History,* 34 (April 1960), 88-97. An exemplary historical analysis of the career of an engineer-social philosopher. Mead played a significant role in western reclamation and served for eleven years as commissioner of the Bureau of Reclamation. Conkin lauds Mead for going "beyond his recognized pre-eminence in engineering to formulate a humanitarian vision of an improved rural society."

Cooke, W. Henry. "The Controversy Over Water Rights in the Santa Margarita River." *Pacific Historical Review,* XXV (1956), 1-28. Important case that set predecents for adjudication between state and federal governments concerning water rights.

Cooper, Erwin. *Aqueduct Empire: A Guide to Water in California, Its Turbulent History and Its Management Today.* Glendale, Calif.: Arthur H. Clark Company, 1968. 439 pp. Illustrations, map, notes, appendix, bibliography, and index. The author provides sound historical discussions to give perspective to water-related issues facing California in the late 1960s. Coverage is given to all aspects of the state's water history, including the Los Angeles

Aqueduct, St. Francis Dam failure, Boulder Canyon Project, and California Water Project. Though the book has a journalistic character, it is a noteworthy attempt to survey a complex subject.

Cooper, Margaret. "Land, Water and Settlement in Kern County, California, 1850-1890." Master's thesis, University of California, Berkeley, 1953.

Cory, H.T. *The Imperial Valley and the Salton Sink.* San Francisco: John J. Newbegin, 1915. xiv + 437 pp. Illustrations, maps, tables, diagrams, and notes. An outstanding early study of irrigation and flood control in California's Imperial Valley. Thorough coverage is given of the California Development Company, the Reclamation Service's Yuma Project, and flood fights on the Colorado River. The book also includes some fine drawings of various engineering works.

Coulter, Calvin Brewster. "Building the Tieton Irrigation Canal." *Pacific Northwest Quarterly,* 49 (Jan. 1958), 11-18. Outstanding article on a key project built by the Reclamation Service in the Yakima Valley from 1906 to 1911. It offers good insights into labor problems, difficulties within contractors, and other setbacks the agency faced.

Coulter, C. Brewster. "The New Settlers on the Yakima Project, 1880-1910." *Pacific Northwest Quarterly,* 61 (Jan. 1970), 10-21. Good social history of a Reclamation Service project built in the state of Washington. The article illustrates the tension that often existed between the settlers and the federal agency.

Coulter, Calvin B. "The Victory of National Irrigation in the Yakima Valley, 1902-1906." *Pacific Northwest Quarterly,* 42 (April 1951), 99-122. Perceptive and well-written study of one of the Reclamation Service's largest and most successful early projects.

Coyle, David Cushman. *Conservation: An American Story of Conflict and Accomplishment.* See chapter on "Flood Control and Drainage."

Cruz, Gilbert Ralph. "Spanish Town Patterns in the Borderlands: Municipal Origins in Texas and the Southwest, 1618-1810." Doctoral dissertation, Saint Louis University, 1974. 342 pp.

Cullen, Allan H. *Rivers in Harness: The Story of Dams.* Philadelphia and New York: Chilton Books, 1962. 175 pp. Illustrations and index. A competent historical overview of high-dam building in the United States. It largely focuses on federal projects such as Hoover Dam, TVA, and the St. Lawrence Seaway.

Cummings, Larry G. "Arizona's Stand in the Colorado River Controversy." Master's thesis, University of Southern California, 1963.

Cunnea, Patricia Edgeworth. "Water Resources Policy Formation in the Appropriations Process: Congress and the Bureau of Reclamation." Doctoral dissertation, University of Chicago, 1963. xviii + 349 pp. Notes and bibliography. A thoroughly researched analysis of changes in reclamation policy and administration from the late 1920s to the early 1950s. The author demonstrates how the agency promoted changes in the appropriations process that enhanced the economic feasibility of its projects.

Dana, Marshall N. "Reclamation, Its Influence and Impact on the History of the West." *Utah Historical Quarterly,* XXVII (Jan. 1959), 38-49. Positive account of the impact of reclamation on western growth by the first president of the National Reclamation Association.

Dangberg, Grace Melissa. *Conflict on the Carson.* Minden, Nev.: Carson Valley Historical Society, 1975. xv + 467 pp. Illustrations, table, bibliography, and index.

Darling, Arthur B., ed. *The Public Papers of Francis G. Newlands.* See chapter on "Energy."

Darrah, William C. "John Wesley Powell and an Understanding of the West." *Utah Historical Quarterly,* 37 (Spring 1969), 146-51. A reflective essay on Powell's legacy: the United States Geological Survey, the Bureau of American Ethnology, and the Bureau of Reclamation. Among the proposals executed following his death: "withdrawal of public lands for the public good, harnessing of the waters of the Colorado River, a bureau of forestry, and a federal department or agency of the encouragement of science."

Darrah, William Culp. *Powell of the Colorado.* Princeton: Princeton University Press, 1951. xii + 426 pp. Illustrations, notes, bibliography, and index. The definitive biography of the famous explorer, surveyor, scientist, ethnographer, and social philosopher. Powell explored the Colorado River, founded the U.S.

Geological Survey, and supported reclamation of western desert lands by the construction of dams and other public works.

Darrah, William Culp. "Powell of the Colorado." *Utah Historical Quarterly.* See chapter on "Planning, Engineering, and Administration."

Davis, Arthur Powell. *Irrigation Works Constructed by the United States Government.* New York: John Wiley & Sons, 1917. xvi + 413 pp. Illustrations, tables, diagrams, and index. A classic survey of the first irrigation projects undertaken by the Reclamation Service. The project-by-project summaries provide information on the design, construction, and operation of dams, canals, and hydroelectric power plants.

Davis, Arthur P. "Reclamation of Arid West by Federal Government." *Annals of the American Academy of Political and Social Science,* XXI (Jan.-June 1908), 203-18.

Davis, Arthur P. "The Colorado River Surveys." *Community Builder* (March 1928), 13-19. Reviews engineering studies of the river by the Reclamation Service and the U.S. Geological Survey.

Davis, E. H. "Oregon—First in 'Portable' Irrigation." *Oregon Historical Quarterly,* LXXXVIII (Dec. 1977), 351-54. Argues that "Oregon led the nation in the early development of portable sprinkler irrigation."

Davison, George S. "A Century and a Half of American Engineering." *Proceedings of the American Society of Civil Engineers.* See chapter on "Planning, Engineering, and Administration."

Davison, Stanley R. "The Leadership of the Reclamation Movement, 1875-1902." Doctoral dissertation, University of California-Berkeley, 1952.

Davisson, Lori. "Arizona's White River—A Working Watercourse." *Journal of Arizona History,* 19 (Spring 1978), 55-72. Outstanding article on the development of the river for the irrigation needs of the White Mountain Apache tribe. The study includes an interesting description of a water supply system constructed for Fort Apache in 1882.

de Roos, Robert. *The Thirsty Land: The Story of the Central Valley Project.* Palo Alto: Stanford University Press, 1948. xii + 265 pp. Maps, notes, and index. A popular, subjective history of the project that transformed California's water resources. The book traces the project's background and staunchly defends the Bureau of Reclamation's water development philosophy and program. The author strongly opposes construction of power dams by the Army Corps of Engineers as well as attempts by private utilities to market electricity generated by federally owned power plants.

Dick, Everett. *Conquering the Great American Desert: Nebraska.* Lincoln: Nebraska State Historical Society, 1975. xiii + 456 pp. Illustrations, notes, bibliography, and index. A brilliant study of the environmental adaptation of western settlers. It includes an especially strong chapter on irrigation.

Dick, Everett. *The Lure of the Land: A Social History of the Public Lands from the Articles of Confederation to the New Deal.* Lincoln: University of Nebraska Press, 1970. xii + 413 pp. Illustrations, bibliography, and index. A lucid and substantive volume based upon prodigious research and keen insights into the evolution of federal land policies. Several excellent chapters discuss the uses of land grants to foster internal improvements, the evolution of western irrigation, and the conservation movement of the early twentieth century.

Dickerman, Alan R. *Foundations of Federal Reclamation Policies: An Historical Review of Changing Goals and Objectives.* Fort Collins: Colorado State University, 1970.

Dobkins, Betty Brooke Eakle. "The Spanish Element in Texas Water Law." Doctoral dissertation, University of Texas-Austin, 1958. 236 pp.

Dodds, Gordon B. "Conservation & Reclamation in the Trans-Mississippi West: A Critical Bibliography." *Arizona and the West,* 13 (Summer 1971), 143-71. A still useful annotated bibliography that covers the entire conservation field. It includes citations on irrigation, flood control, and parks.

Dodds, Gordon B. *Hiram Martin Chittenden: His Public Career.* See chapter on "Flood Control and Drainage."

Dodds, Gordon B. "The Historiography of American Conservation: Past and Prospects." *Pacific Northwest Quarterly,* 56 (April 1965),

75-81. A somewhat dated but still useful discussion of sources on the history of conservation. Dodd's insights into the literature of this field are challenging and sound. Numerous sources are listed on irrigation, flood control, and parks.

Doerksen, Harvey Ray. "The Columbia Interstate Compact: Politics of Water Resources in the Pacific Northwest." Doctoral dissertation. See chapter on "Energy."

Dunbar, Robert G. "Pioneering Groundwater Legislation in the United States: Mortgages, Land Banks, and Institution-Building in New Mexico." *Pacific Historical Review,* XLVII (Nov. 1978), 565-84. How efforts by citizens of the Roswell Artesian Basin to obtain federal land bank loans prompted New Mexicans to create groundwater management institutions that influenced other states.

Dunbar, Robert G. "The Arizona Groundwater Controversy at Mid-Century." *Arizona and the West,* 19 (Spring 1977), 5-24. Excellent case study of a subject that should receive greater attention from historians.

Dunbar, Robert G. "The Origins of the Colorado System of Water-Right Control." *Colorado Magazine,* XXVII (Oct. 1950), 241-62. Outstanding article on the legal and administrative framework developed to control water rights in Colorado. Dunbar points out that the Colorado system was adopted in many other western states as well as Canada and Australia.

Dunbar, Robert G. "The Search for a Stable Water Right in Montana." *Agricultural History,* XXVIII (Oct. 1954), 138-49.

Dunbar, Robert G. "The Significance of the Colorado Agricultural Frontier." *Agricultural History,* XXXIV (July 1960), 119-25. Excellent discussion of how pioneer Colorado farmers "borrowed a water right from the mining frontier, made it the exclusive water right of their state, and then invented institutions for the regulation of that right which have in some measure been copied by the other Western states."

Dunbar, Robert G. "Water Conflicts and Controls in Colorado." *Agricultural History,* 22 (1948), 180-86. A thoughtful discussion of Colorado irrigation development in the 1870s and 1880s.

East, Lewis R. "Parallel Irrigation Development—United States and Australia." *Transactions of the American Society of Civil Engineers,* CT (1953), 400-11. A comparative historical review.

Eaton, E. Courtland, and Frank Adams. "Irrigation Development Through Irrigation Districts." *Proceedings of the American Society of Civil Engineers,* LII (March 1926), 423-33. Superficial discussion of the evolution and significance of irrigation districts.

Eaves, Charles Dudley. "Post City: A Study in Colonization on the Texas Plains." Doctoral dissertation. See chapter on "Community Water Supply."

Farris, Martin Theodore. "The Economic Significance of the Preference Clause in Public Water Policy on the Development of the Pacific Northwest." Doctoral dissertation, Ohio State University, 1957. 366 pp.

Ferrell, John Robert. "Water Resource Development in the Arkansas Valley: A History of Public Policy to 1950." Doctoral dissertation, University of Oklahoma, 1968. 238 pp.

Finch, J.K. "A Hundred Years of American Civil Engineering, 1852-1952." *Transactions of the American Society of Civil Engineers.* See chapter on "Planning, Engineering, and Administration."

Fisher, Edwin A. "Engineering and Public Works in The City of Rochester During the Past Century." *Centennial History of Rochester, New York.* See chapter on "Planning, Engineering, and Administration."

Fite, Gilbert C. *The Farmer's Frontier, 1865-1900.* New York: Holt, Rinehart and Winston, 1966. Illustrations, maps, notes, bibliographical essay, and index. A strong treatment of the growth of irrigation is included in this excellent study of the "true harbingers of advancing civilization."

Flores, Dan L. "Islands in the Desert: An Environmental Interpretation of the Rocky Mountain Frontier." 2 vols. Doctoral dissertation, Texas A&M University, 1978. Vol. I: xii + 231 pp; Vol. II: 232-486 pp. Maps, notes, and bibliography. Rather superficial effort to illustrate how ecological factors shaped the development of culture and social institutions in the Rocky Mountain West. It includes a chapter on the evolution of irrigation practices.

Forbes, R.H. "History of Irrigation Development in Arizona." *Reclamation Era,* 26 (Oct. 1936), 226-27. A brief overview by the former director of an agricultural experiment station.

Force, Edwin T. "The Use of the Colorado River in the United States, 1850-1933." Doctoral dissertation, University of California, Berkeley, 1937. 74 pp.

Fowler, Lloyd Charles. "A History of the Dams and Water Supply of Western San Diego County." Master's thesis, University of California, 1953.

Frank, Bernard, and Anthony Netboy. *Water, Land, and People.* See chapter on "Flood Control and Drainage."

Frazer, Robert W. "Army Agriculture in New Mexico, 1852-53." *New Mexico Historical Review,* L (Oct. 1975), 313-34.

Frome, Michael. *Whose Woods These Are: The Story of the National Forests.* Garden City, N.Y.: Doubleday & Company, 1962. iii + 360 pp. Illustrations, maps, bibliography, and index. Chronicles the movement to establish the national forests and describes the physical characteristics of specific forests. Of interest to public works researchers is the chapter entitled "Watering the Great Desert (Arizona)."

Fuhriman, Walter U. "Federal Aid to Irrigation Development." *Journal of Farm Economics,* XXXI (Nov. 1949), 965-75. Thin, broad-brush historical overview of the Bureau of Reclamation program.

Galli, Geraldine. "100 Years of Construction News." *Engineering News-Record.* See chapter on "Planning, Engineering, and Administration."

Ganoe, John Tilson. "Federal Reclamation Policies." Doctoral dissertation, University of Wisconsin, 1929.

Ganoe, John T. "The Beginnings of Irrigation in the United States." *Mississippi Valley Historical Review,* XXV (June 1938), 59-78. Discussion of western irrigation from the 1840s to the 1880s.

Ganoe, John T. "The Desert Land Act in Operation, 1877-1891." *Agricultural History,* 11 (April 1937), 142-57. Excellent overview of the act's lack of success in promoting settlement of the arid West. Emphasis is placed on the use of the law by stock growers and entrepreneurs to gain control of water rights.

Ganoe, John T. "The Desert Land Act Since 1891." *Agricultural History,* 11 (Oct. 1937), 266-77. Deals extensively with western opposition to this act.

Ganoe, John T. "The Origin of a National Reclamation Policy." *Mississippi Valley Historical Review,* XVIII (June 1931), 34-52. Definitive, although dated, study of the evolution of federal efforts to promote the reclamation of arid western lands.

Gardiner, Dorothy. *Snow-Water.* New York: Doubleday, Doran & Company, 1939. 360 pp. Entertaining novel about the trials of irrigators in the arid west.

Gates, Paul, and Robert W. Swenson. *History of Public Land Law Development.* Washington, D.C.: Government Printing Office, 1968. xv + 828 pp. Notes, bibliography, appendices, and index. Comprehensive and authoritative history written for the Public Land Law Review Commission. The book contains major discussions on the disposition of the public domain in the West and the evolution of the federal reclamation program.

Gates, William H. *Hoover Dam: Including the Story of the Turbulent Colorado River.* Los Angeles: Wetzel Publishing Company, 1932. 88 pp. Illustrations and maps. A simplistic, heavily illustrated study of the construction of Hoover Dam.

Gertsch, William Darrell. "The Upper Snake River Project: A Historical Study of Reclamation and Regional Development, 1890-1930." Doctoral dissertation, University of Washington, 1974. iii + 262 pp. Map, notes, and bibliography. A significant contribution to the study of western reclamation. The case study of the only generally successful large-scale private irrigation enterprise undertaken in response to the 1894 Carey Act offers comparisons of public and private reclamation projects.

Gertsch, W. Darrell. "Water Use, Energy, and Economic Development in the Snake River Basin." *Idaho Yesterdays,* 23 (Summer 1979), 58-72.

Gies, Joseph. *Wonders of the Modern World.* See chapter on "Sewers and Wastewater Treatment."

Glass, Mary Ellen. "Hot Summer in the Sierra: An Early Contest for Resource Rights at Lake Tahoe." *California Historical Quarterly,* LI (Winter 1972), 306-14. Interesting case studies of competition among irrigators, recreationists, and power companies for the lake's water supply.

Glass, Mary Ellen. "The First Nationally Sponsored Arid Land Reclamation Project: The Newlands Act in Churchill County, Nevada." *Nevada Historical Society Quarterly,* XIV (Spring 1971), 2-12. Good discussion of the problems associated with the first federal reclamation project.

Glass, Mary Ellen. "The Newlands Reclamation Project: Years of Innocence, 1903-1907." *Journal of the West,* VII (Jan. 1968), 55-63. A good brief article about the early years of the first irrigation project authorized under the 1902 Reclamation Act. Glass discusses the hopeful optimism of settlers and their subsequent loss of "innocence" as the project became plagued with floods, poor soil conditions, and other problems.

Glass, Mary Ellen. *Water for Nevada: The Reclamation Controversy, 1885-1902.* Carson City: University of Nevada Press, 1964. 62 pp. Notes, appendix, bibliography, and index. A perceptive, well-written account of Nevada's efforts to obtain federal support for construction of dams, canals, and other irrigation facilities. The short book contains the best treatment of Congressman Francis G. Newlands' role in the reclamation crusade of the 1890s.

Glick, Thomas F. *The Old World Background of the Irrigation System of San Antonio, Texas.* El Paso: Texas Western Press, 1972. 67 pp. Maps and notes. A generally overlooked and highly significant case study of the adoption of Spanish irrigation practices in the Americas. Glick explores the technological and institutional aspects of his topic in a highly sophisticated manner.

Goff, John S. *George W.P. Hunt and His Arizona.* Pasadena: Socio Technical Publications, 1973. 286 pp. Illustrations, notes, bibliographical and biographical notes, and index. A biography of the "Old Roman," which contains a full account of the controversy over the waters of the Colorado river during Hunt's lifetime.

Golzé, Alfred R. *Reclamation in the United States.* Caldwell, Idaho: Caxton Printers, 1961. xiii + 486 pp. Illustrations, maps, tables, charts, graphs, bibliographies, and index. This uncritical book remains one of the best introductions to the federal reclamation program. Its principal purposes are to provide instructional material for college courses in engineering and economics and to present a profile of the agency's various multiple-purpose programs. A great deal of historical material is included.

Gopalakrishnan, Chennat. "The Doctrine of Prior Appropriation and Its Impact on Water Development." *American Journal of Economics and Sociology,* 32 (Jan. 1973), 61-72. A good critical study of the legal framework for water resource development in the western United States.

Gordon, Alexander. "Irrigation in the Arid Section of the United States." Doctoral dissertation, Cornell University, 1927.

Gramlich, Samuel V., Jr. "Salinity: Mexico Versus the United States on Colorado River Water." Master's thesis, Pacific Union College, 1964. v + 112 pp. Notes, appendix, and bibliography. Dated but useful overview of the disputes between the United States and Mexico regarding salinity levels in the Colorado River.

Great Plains Committee. *The Future of the Great Plains.* See chapter on "Planning, Engineering, and Administration."

Green, Donald E. *Land of the Underground Rain: Irrigation on the Texas High Plains,1910-1970.* Austin: University of Texas Press, 1973. xvii + 293 pp. Illustrations, maps, figure, notes, appendix, bibliography, and index. A finely crafted volume on the history of pump irrigation in the Texas Panhandle. Irrigation began from 1910 to 1920 with large-scale pumping plants built by land speculators. By 1959 more than 5 million acres were watered by "underground rain." Green discusses the problem of falling water tables and explores other aspects of the myth of "inexhaustible supply." He also compares and contrasts his subject with other western history themes such as the mining frontier. In addition, the role of the federal government in the area's water resource development is traced.

Green, Donald Edward. "The Irrigation Frontier on the Texas High Plains, 1910-1960." Doctoral dissertation, University of Oklahoma, 1969. 351 pp.

Greenleaf, Richard E. "Land and Water in Mexico and New Mexico, 1700-1821." *New Mexico Historical Review,* XLVII (April 1972), 85-112. Discussion of Spanish colonial water and land law.

Gressley, Gene M. "Arthur Powell Davis, Reclamation, and the West." *Agricultural History,* XLII (July 1968), 241-57. Brilliant analysis of the head of the Reclamation Service. Gressley contends that Davis was a perceptive conservationist-engineer, despite charges during his career that he was a narrow-thinking engineer and a questionable administrator.

Gressley, Gene M., ed. *The American West: A Reorientation.* Laramie: University of Wyoming, 1966. xiv + 172 pp. Notes. Outstanding collection of essays on various topics. Students of public works history will find the following to be excellent: William Lilley II and Lewis L. Gould, "The Western Irrigation Movement, 1878-1902: A Reappraisal; and Gerald Nash, "Government Enterprise in the West: The San Francisco Harbor, 1863-1963."

Grody, Harvey P. "From North to South: The Feather River Project and Other Legislative Water Struggles in the 1950s." *Southern California Quarterly,* LX (Fall 1978), 287-326. The author attempts "to illustrate the significance to statewide water policy development of the process and mechanics of legislative politics." He attributes passage in 1959 of major water legislation to the political skill of Governor Edmund G. Brown. Excellent insights are provided on executive-legislative relationships with respect to water policy development.

Grody, Harvey P. "The California Legislature and Comprehensive Water Resources Development, 1941-1959." Doctoral dissertation, University of California, Los Angeles, 1971. 518 pp.

Gustafson, A.F., et al. *Conservation in the United States.* See chapter on "Parks and Recreation."

Hamaker, Gene Edward. "Irrigation Pioneers: A History of the Tri-County Project to 1935." Doctoral dissertation, University of Nebraska-Lincoln, 1958. 977 pp.

Hanks, Eva H. "Federal-State Conflicts Over Western Waters." Doctoral dissertation, Columbia University, 1970.

Hart, Henry C. *The Dark Missouri.* See chapter on "Flood Control."

Haury, Emil W. "Arizona's Ancient Irrigation Builders." *Natural History,* LIV (Sept. 1945), 300-10. Includes an excellent map of the Hohokam irrigation system.

Haury, Emil W. "The Hohokam: First Masters of the American Desert." *National Geographic Magazine,* 131 (May 1967), 670-95. Discusses the irrigation systems developed by the Indians near present-day Phoenix.

Havemeyer, Loomis, ed., et al. *Conservation of Our Natural Resources,* New York: Macmillan Company, 1930. xvii + 551 pp. Illustrations, maps, tables, notes, appendices, and index. This update of Van Hise's *The Conservation of Natural Resources in the United States* (1910) offers a good perspective of American conservationist thought in 1930. The book contains chapters on mineral resources, water, forests, land, and wild life. Frederick Haynes Newell's chapter on water is a brilliant, comprehensive treatment of the subject.

Hawley, John Arthur. "The Decision to Irrigate: Irrigation Practices and Water Supply on the South Plains of Texas." Doctoral dissertation, Texas Technical College, 1961.

Heim, Peggy. "Financing the Federal Reclamation Program, 1902-1919: The Development of Repayment Policy." Doctoral dissertation, Columbia University, 1953. 386 pp. Exhaustive analysis of changes made in the repayment policies for Reclamation Service projects. It illustrates the economic shortsightedness of the 1902 Reclamation Act.

Hendricks, William O. "Developing San Diego's Desert Empire." *Journal of San Diego History,* XVII (Summer 1971), 1-11.

Hendrickson, Gordon Olaf. "Water Rights on the North Platte River: A Case Study of the Resolution of an Interstate Water Conflict." Doctoral dissertation, University of Wyoming, 1975. 315 pp.

Hess, Ralph H. "The Beginnings of Irrigation in the United States." *Journal of Political Economy,* 20 (Oct. 1912), 807-33. Provides information on Indian, Spanish, and Mormon irrigation institutions.

Hibbard, Benjamin Horace. *A History of the Public Land Policies.* Madison: University of Wisconsin Press, 1965. xxvii + 579 pp. Maps, charts, tables, notes, and index. The first historical survey of federal legislation and policies on the disposition of the public domain (originally published in 1924). It includes chapters on the desert land acts, such as the 1902 Reclamation Act, and Theodore Roosevelt's conservation accomplishments.

Hill, Raymond A. "Development of the Rio Grande Compact of 1938." *Natural Resources Journal,* 14 (April 1974), 163-99. Thorough overview of a compact between the states of Colorado, New Mexico, and Texas to divide the waters of the Rio Grande.

Hinds, Julian. "Continuous Development of Dams Since 1850." *Transactions of the American Society of Civil Engineers,* CT (1953), 489-520. Technical discussion of the development of dam design and construction.

History and Heritage Committee, Los Angeles Section of the American Society of Civil Engineers. *Historic Civil Engineering Landmarks of Southern California.* Los Angeles: Southern California Edison Company, 1974. 43 pp. Illustrations and map. Brief sketches of historic public works structures in southern California. The booklet contains a good deal of material on the area's water resource projects. There is also information on public buildings and roads.

Hixson, Wilma. "The Influence of Water Upon the Settlement of the Llano Estacado." Master's thesis, West Texas State Teachers College, 1940. vii + 101 pp. Map, notes, and bibliography. A competent chronicle of groundwater development for livestock and agriculture in the Texas Panhandle and parts of eastern New Mexico.

Hodge, Carle, and Peter C. Duisberg, eds. *Aridity and Man: The Challenge of the Arid Lands in the United States.* Washington, D.C.: American Association for the Advancement of Science, 1963. xx + 584 pp. Illustrations, maps, tables, bibliographies, and index. Contributors to this volume explore various aspects of the problem of arid areas. Most of the essays tend to be critical of mankind's use of the environment. Students of western water history will find the following selections especially useful: Richard B. Woodbury, "Indian Adaptations to Arid Environments"; John Hay, "Upper Rio Grande: Embattled Empire"; and Warren A. Hall, "Los Angeles: Growing Pains of a Metropolis."

Holbrook, Stewart H. *The Columbia.* See chapter on "Waterways."

Hollon, W. Eugene. "The Great American Desert. New York: Oxford University Press, 1966. ix + 284 pp. Illustrations, maps, bibliography, and index. Outstanding historical overview of the settlement and development of the American West. Chapter 9, "Blossom Like the Rose," is an excellent summary of the establishment and expansion of irrigated agriculture.

Hollon, W. Eugene. *The Southwest: Old and New.* New York: Alfred A. Knopf, 1961. xvii + 486 + xix pp. Illustrations, maps, notes, bibliographical essay, and index. A brilliant book that treats "various aspects of the social, political, and cultural history of the American Southwest from the early cliff dwellers to the present." The publication includes brief discussions of urban and agricultural water supply development.

Holmes, Beatrice Hort. *A History of Federal Water Resources Programs, 1800-1960.* Washington, D.C.: U.S. Department of Agriculture, 1972. iv + 51 pp. Illustrations and notes. A useful introduction to the evolution of federal water laws and programs.

Holmes, Beatric Hort. *History of Federal Water Resources Programs and Policies, 1961-70.* Washington, D.C.: Government Printing Office, 1979. x + 331 pp. Notes, tables, appendix, and index. A comprehensive account of major federal water and related land programs. It discusses most relevant federal legislation and the functioning of programs involving research, planning, construction, and regulations. The activities of the Army Corps of Engineers, Bureau of Reclamation, Soil Conservation Service, Tennessee Valley Authority, Environmental Protection Agency, and other federal agencies are covered.

Hornig, Edgar Albert. "Reclamation of Arizona's Arid Lands." Master's thesis, University of Oklahoma, 1942. iv + 107 pp. Map, tables, notes, and bibliography. A competent survey of the private, state, and federal irrigation projects undertaken in Arizona. The author makes good use of primary materials.

Houghton, N.D. "Problems of the Colorado River as Reflected in Arizona Politics." *Western Political Quarterly,* IV (Dec. 1951), 634-43. An interesting study of water and politics that contains some accurate prognostications on difficulties the state would encounter in obtaining support for the Central Arizona Project.

Houghton, Samuel G. *A Trace of Desert Waters: The Great Basin Story.* Glendale, Calif.: Arthur H. Clark Company, 1976. 287 pp. Illustrations, maps, bibliography, and index. Good description of the water resources of the arid intermountain West.

Howe, Charles W., and K. William Easter. *Interbasin Transfers of Water: Economic Issues and Impacts.* Baltimore: Johns Hopkins University Press, 1971. xiv + 196 pp. Maps, charts, tables, graphs, notes, bibliography, and index. A perceptive analysis of the costs, benefits, prospects, and problems of large-scale transfers of water from one river basin to another. The West receives the greatest emphasis because it is the area where interbasin transfers have been most frequently undertaken or proposed. Historical discussions of some major water projects are included.

Hoy, Suellen M. "People in Public Works: Harry W. Morrison." *APWA Reporter.* See chapter on "Flood Control and Drainage."

Huber, Walter L. "An Engineering Century in California." *Transactions of the American Society of Civil Engineers.* See chapter on "Planning, Engineering, and Administration."

Hudson, James. "Irrigation Water Use in the Utah Valley, Utah." Doctoral dissertation, University of Chicago, 1962. xiii + 249 pp. Maps, tables, graphs, notes, appendix, and bibliography. This study of agricultural water use contains some historical information on the development of irrigation practices and institutions.

Huffman, Roy E. *Irrigation Development and Public Water Policy.* New York: Ronald Press Company, 1953. xi + 336 pp. Map, charts, tables, notes, bibliography, and indexes. The volume reviews the past development of irrigated agriculture and how this experience has become institutionalized in the nation's economic, social, and legal structure. Huffman concludes that past policies have been haphazard and based on short-term goals. He postulates twenty planning principles that should govern future irrigation development.

Humlum, J. *Water Development and Water Planning in the Southwestern United States.* See chapter on "Community Water Supply."

Hundertmark, C.A. "Reclamation in Chaves and Eddy Counties, 1887-1912." *New Mexico Historical Review,* XLVII (Oct. 1972), 301-16. History of private and federal efforts to control floods and develop irrigation in the Pecos Valley of New Mexico. The article includes a discussion of the Reclamation Service's Carlsbad and Hondo projects.

Hundley, Norris, Jr. "Clio Nods: Arizona v. California and the Boulder Canyon Act—A Reassessment." *Western Historical Quarterly,* III (1972), 17-51. In-depth critique of the 1963 landmark Supreme Court decision regarding apportionment of Colorado River water. Hundley believes the decision was "grounded on a faulty reading of the Boulder Canyon Project Act" with respect to Congress' power to allocate water.

Hundley, Norris, Jr. *Dividing the Waters: A Century of Controversy Between the United States and Mexico.* Berkeley: University of California Press, 1966. xii + 266 pp. Illustrations, maps, notes, bibliography, and index. An objective, comprehensive book on a subject that is both convoluted and controversial. Hundley traces the bitter feud between the United States and Mexico over apportionment of the flow of the Rio Grande and Colorado River. The flaws in the resultant 1944 treaty "restricted its effectiveness and . . . revived sources of international friction" in the following two decades.

Hundley, Norris, Jr. "The Colorado Waters Dispute." *Foreign Affairs,* 42 (April 1964), 495-500. Reviews relations between the United States and Mexico over the waters of the Colorado River since 1944.

Hundley, Norris, Jr. "The Dark and Bloody Ground of Indian Water Rights: Confusion Elevated to Principle." *Western Historical Quarterly,* IX (Oct. 1978), 455-82. Excellent legislative overview of a complex subject.

Hundley, Norris. "The Politics of Reclamation: California, the Federal Government, and the Origins of the Boulder Canyon Act—A Second Look." *California Historical Quarterly,* LII (Winter 1973), 292-325. The most comprehensive analysis of the background of the passage of the Boulder Canyon Act. Hundley's exemplary research enables him to identify many new aspects of this subject.

Hundley, Norris. "The Politics of Water and Geography: California and the Mexican-American Treaty of 1944." *Pacific Historical Review,* XXXVI (May 1967), 209-26. Excellent discussion of the convoluted history of international disputes between the United States and Mexico over appropriation of Colorado River water.

Hundley, Norris, Jr. *Water and the West: The Colorado River Compact and the Politics of Water in the American West.* Berkeley: University of California Press, 1975. xxii + 395 pp. Maps, tables, notes, bibliography, and index. Perhaps the most important book on western water resource development published in the past two decades. The author's prodigious research is evident throughout this multidimensional analysis of the Colorado River's development. No other study offers a comparable view of the complexity of water-related issues in the West.

Hutchins, Wells A., and Harry A. Steele. "Basic Water Rights Doctrines and Their Implications for River Basin Development." *Journal of Law and Contemporary Problems,* 22 (1957), 276-300. A rather turgid essay that nevertheless offers a good summary of basic water law, especially in the West.

Hutchins, Wells A. "The Community Acequia: Its Origin and Development." *Southwestern Historical Quarterly,* XXXI (Jan. 1928), 261-84. Excellent article on the development of community-maintained irrigation ditches. Hutchins explores the Spanish and Indian origins of the system and its adaptation by later settlers.

Ickes, Harold L. *The Secret Diary of Harold L. Ickes: The First Thousand Days, 1933-1936.* See chapter on "Planning, Engineering, and Administration."

Ingram, Helen M. *Patterns of Politics in Water Resource Development: A Case Study of New Mexico's Role in the Colorado River Basin Bill.* See chapter on "Flood Control and Drainage."

Institute for Government Research (Brookings). *The U.S. Reclamation Service: Its History, Activities and Organization.* New York: D. Appleton and Company, 1919. xi + 177 pp. Appendices, bibliography, and index. The first thirty-two pages are an account of the agency's history.

Israelsen, O.W. "The History of Irrigation in Utah." *Civil Engineering,* 8 (Oct. 1938), 672-74. Emphasizes the long-range influence of the Mormon's experiments in irrigation.

Jackson, W. Turrentine, and Donald J. Pisani. *A Case Study in Interstate Resource Management: The California-Nevada Water Controversy, 1865-1955.* Davis, Calif.: University of California, Water Resources Center, 1973. ii + 51 pp. Maps and notes. An excellent analysis of an interstate water controversy heretofore virtually ignored by historians. The study focuses on the formal interstate efforts to satisfy competing interests and determine an equitable way of dividing "surplus" water between the states. The authors skillfully describe the geographical basis of the dispute as well as the contending parties that battled for the runoff of the Sierra Nevadas.

Jackson, W. Turrentine, and Alan M. Paterson. *The Sacramento-San Joaquin Delta: The Evolution and Implementation of Water Policy on Historical Perspective.* Davis, Calif.: California Water Resources Center, 1977. iii + 192 pp. Illustrations, maps, and notes. Excellent history of the attempts to control the encroachment of salinity from San Francisco Bay into the delta of the Sacramento and San Joaquin rivers.

Jacobsen, J. Myron, and Roy M. Mersky. *Water Law Bibliography, 1847-1965: Source Book on U.S. Water and Irrigation Studies: Legal, Economic and Political.* Silver Spring, Md.: Jefferson Law Book Company, 1966. xvi + 249 pp. Indexes. Although this finding aid misses some essential sources, it is a good introduction to the literature on irrigation. The book offers a state-by-state compilation of sources that is especially useful.

James, George Whaton. *Reclaiming the Arid West: The Story of the United States Reclamation Service.* New York: Dodd, Mead and Company, 1917. xxii + 411 pp. Illustrations and index. Despite the author's obvious subjectivity, the highly laudatory account of the Reclamation Service's early years offers unique information on irrigation development. The project-by-project survey includes discussions of engineering features as well as the activities of the first homesteaders.

Jarrett, Henry, ed. *Perspectives on Conservation.* See chapter on "Planning, Engineering, and Administration."

Johnson, J.W. "Early Engineering Centers in California." *California Historical Society Quarterly,* XXIX (June 1950), 193-209. Fine history of nineteenth-century engineering projects in Nevada County, California, and adjoining areas. Most of the examples cited are dams and canals.

Jones, Paul. "Reclamation and the Indian." *Utah Historical Quarterly,* XXVII (Jan. 1959), 50-56. Description of the need and plans for the Navajo Indian Irrigation Project by the chairman of the Navajo Tribal Council.

Kahrl, William L., ed. *The California Water Atlas.* Sacramento: State of California, 1977. vi + 118 pp. Illustrations, maps, charts, graphs, diagrams, and bibliography. A visual and narrative feast. The finely crafted, masterful volume covers every aspect of water supply, delivery, and use in the state. Splendid historical essays are included by scholars such as Robert Kelley, Lawrence B. Lee, Norris Hundley, and the editor.

Kathka, David Arlin. "The Bureau of Reclamation in the Truman Administration: Personnel, Politics, and Policy." Doctoral dissertation, University of Missouri-Columbia, 1976. 975 pp. Excellent study of the bureau during an important transitional era. The major strength of the dissertation is its discussion of the agency's opposition to attempts to weaken the 160-acre provision.

Keener, B.K. "Dams, Then and Now." *Transactions of the American Society of Civil Engineers,* CT (1953), 521-35. The Bureau of Reclamation's chief designing engineer looks at the evolution of larger dams.

Kelley, Robert L. *Gold vs. Grain: The Mining Debris Controversy.* Glendale, Calif.: Arthur H. Clark Company, 1959. 327 pp. Illustrations, map, notes, bibliography, and index. This finely crafted volume recounts "one of the first successful attempts in modern American history to use the concept of general welfare to limit free capitalism." The well-organized, lucid book traces the efforts of California farmers and communities to stop the effects of hydraulic mining. Debris, dislodged by gold mining, washed downstream and caused floods, buried farms, and halted river navigation. Kelly discusses the legislative battles to end this degradation that led to the creation of the California Debris Commission. He regards the lessons learned by the government engineers during this period as the foundation of elaborate river control systems that were subsequently built.

Kelley, Robert L. "The Mining Debris Controversy in the Sacramento Valley." *Pacific Historical Review,* XXV (1956), 331-46. Excellent study of efforts to end the environmental degradation caused by hydraulic mining in the late nineteenth century.

Kelly, William R. "Colorado-Big Thompson Initiation, 1933-1938." *Colorado Magazine,* XXXIV (Jan. 1957), 66-77. Presents some of the little-known history of one of the larger irrigation projects constructed by the Bureau of Reclamation.

Kelly, William R. "Rationing the Rivers: A Decade of Interstate Waters and Interstate Commerce in the Supreme Court." *Rocky Mountain Law Review,* 14 (Dec. 1941), 1-20. Outlines judicial principles declared by the Supreme Court in resolving interstate water disputes.

Kennan, George. *The Salton Sea: An Account of Harriman's Fight with the Colorado River.* New York: MacMillan Company, 1917. vii + 106 pp. Illustrations and maps. In 1906 the Colorado River broke from its banks and ran unchecked into the Imperial Valley, creating the large body of water called the Salton Sea. This book recounts efforts to control the flood and foster irrigated agriculture in the valley.

Kershner, Frederick D., Jr. "George Chaffey and the Irrigation Frontier." *Agricultural History,* 27 (Oct. 1953), 115-22. Comprehensive biography of the entrepreneur and irrigation engineer who promoted and managed projects in California and Australia.

King, Judson. *The Conservation Fight: From Theodore Roosevelt to the Tennessee Valley Authority.* See chapter on "Flood Control and Drainage."

Kleinsorge, Paul. *The Boulder Canyon Project: Historical and Economic Aspects.* Stanford University, Stanford Press, 1941. xiv + 330 pp. Illustrations, map, tables, notes, bibliography, and index. Although somewhat dated, this book remains one of the most comprehensive treatments of the building of Hoover Dam and other aspects of the Boulder

Canyon Project. Kleinsorge covers the early history of the Lower Colorado River, the Colorado River Compact, the Boulder Canyon Project Act, construction problems, and the economic effect of the project's water and power systems.

Kluger, James Robert. "Elwood Mead: Irrigation Engineer and Social Planner." Doctoral dissertation, University of Arizona, 1970. 249 pp.

Knight, Oliver. "Correcting Nature's Error: The Colorado-Big Thompson Project." *Agricultural History,* 30 (Oct. 1956), 157-69. The Bureau of Reclamation project that diverts water from the west to the east slope of the Rockies is thoroughly examined in this essay. The hydroelectric power dimension of the undertaking is also comprehensively discussed.

Koppes, Clayton R. "Public Water, Private Land: Origins of the Acreage Limitation Controversy, 1933-1953." *Pacific Historical Review,* XLVII (Nov. 1978), 607-36. Good summary of controversies surrounding enforcement of the 160-acre limitation provision of federal reclamation law.

Korr, Charles P. "William Hammond Hall: The Failure of Attempts at State Water Planning in California, 1878-1888." *Southern California Quarterly,* XLV (March 1963), 305-22. A good biography of California's first state engineer. Hall fought tirelessly against powerful interests to create a unified water program for the state.

Krenkel, John H. "The Founding of the Salt River Water Users Association." *Journal of the West,* XVII (Jan. 1978), 82-89. Good discussion of the early development of the Salt River Project, which "demonstrated the feasibility and desirability of federally supported reclamation projects."

Krutilla, John V. *The Columbia River Treaty: The Economics of an International River Basin Development.* See chapter on "Waterways."

Lacy, Leslie Alexander, *The Soil Soldiers: The Civilian Conservation Corps in the Great Depression.* See chapter on "Parks and Recreation."

Lampen, Dorothy. *Economic and Social Aspects of Federal Reclamation.* Baltimore: Johns Hopkins Press, 1930. 125 pp. Tables, notes, and index. An insightful, comprehensive anaysis of the economic problems encountered by the federal reclamation program from 1902 to the late 1920s. The author also surveys social conditions on the projects and suggests various legislative and administrative reforms that could improve the conditions of settlers.

Landstrom, Karl S. "Reclamation Under the Desert Land Act." *Journal of Farm Economics,* XXVI (Aug. 1954), 500-08.

Larson, Olaf Frederick. "Man-Land Adjustment Processes in Weld County, Colorado—Colonized in Answer to the 'Go West' Call." Doctoral dissertation, University of Wisconsin, 1941. xiii + 386 pp. Illustrations, maps, tables, notes, appendices, and bibliography. Broad environmental study that includes considerable historical data on irrigation.

Larson, T.A. *History of Wyoming.* Lincoln: University of Nebraska Press, 1965. xi + 619 pp. Illustrations, maps, notes, appendices, bibliography, and index. An exemplary state history. Larson provides extensive treatments of Wyoming's reclamation and highway developments.

Lasky, Moses. "From Prior Appropriation to Economic Distribution of Water by the State—Via Irrigation Administration." 8 parts. *Rocky Mountain Law Review,* I and II (April 1929 and Nov. 1929), April: 161-216; Nov.: 35-58. Somewhat turgid, but useful, overview of the evolution of western water law with respect to irrigation.

Laurent, Francis W., comp. *A Compilation of the More Important Congressional Acts, Treaties, Presidential Messages, Judicial Decisions and Official Reports and Documents having to do with the Control, Conservation, and Utilitization of Water Resources.* See chapter on "Flood Control and Drainage."

Lee, Lawrence B. "American Influences in the Development of Irrigation in British Columbia" in Richard A. Preston, ed., *The Influence of the United States on Canadian Development: Eleven Cases Studies.* Durham, N.C.: Duke University Press, 1972, 144-63. Notes. Perceptive and well-researched study of the American influence on the British Columbia water code, the engineering of dams and canals, as well as the perfecting of irrigation practices.

Lee, Lawrence B. "California Water Politics: Opposition to the CVP, 1944-1980." *Agricul-*

tural History, 54 (July 1980), 402-23. Outstanding article that narrates the conflict between various groups to further their own interests by manipulating state and federal water and power policies.

Lee, Lawrence B. "Dominion Ditches and British Columbia Canals: A History of the Western Canada Irrigation Association." *Journal of the West,* VII (Jan. 1968), 31-40. An excellent article that describes how "Canadians borrowed the institutional trappings of the American promotional organization, its purposes and philosophy in order to insure the success of the Dominion and British Columbia irrigation institutions. . . ." Most of the piece discusses the association's campaigns during the early twentieth century.

Lee, Lawrence B. "Environmental Implications of Governmental Reclamation in California." *Agricultural History,* XLIX (Jan. 1975), 223-29. Excellent overview of changing public attitudes toward water projects and the negative environmental impacts of the California Water Plan and other endeavors.

Lee, Lawrence B. "100 Years of Reclamation Historiography." *Pacific Historical Review,* XLVII (Nov. 1978), 507-64. A meticulous, exhaustive compilation and analysis of water resource development in the West. Lee's brilliant appraisal of the field's literature helps to establish it as an important dimension of the literature on conservation, environmentalism, and civil engineering.

Lee, Lawrence B. *Reclaiming the American West: An Historiography and Guide.* Santa Barbara, Calif.: ABC-Clio, 1980. xix + 131 pp. Notes, appendices, bibliography, glossary, and index. Brilliant, comprehensive historiographical essay on the literature of western reclamation. Biographical profiles of key scholars and historical figures are included.

Lee, Lawrence B. "The Canadian-American Irrigation Frontier, 1884-1914." *Agricultural History,* 40 (1965), 271-83. A perceptive comparative study of the evolution of irrigation practices and institutions.

Lee, Lawrence B. "The Mormons Come to Canada, 1887-1902." *Pacific Northwest Quarterly,* 59 (Jan. 1968), 11-22. Excellent article that focuses primarily on the role of the Canadian government in encouraging Mormon settlement in Alberta.

Lee, Lawrence B. "William E. Smythe and San Diego, 1901-1908." *Journal of San Diego History,* 19 (1973), 10-24. Important chapter in the career of this irrigation crusader.

Lee, Lawrence B. "William Ellsworth Smythe and the Irrigation Movement: A Reconsideration." *Pacific Historical Review,* XLI (Aug. 1972), 289-311. A stellar article on one of the principal nineteenth-century irrigation crusaders. Lee convincingly demonstrates that Smythe should be accorded greater recognition for his role in organizing advocates of western water development. The essay is one of the best sources for perspectives on the origins of the 1902 Reclamation Act.

Lee, Robert Rue. "Local Government Public Works Decision-Making." Doctoral dissertation. See chapter on "Community Water Supply."

Leonard, Ernest E. "The Imperial Irrigation District: Agency Behavior in a Political Environment." Doctoral dissertation, Claremont Graduate School, 1972. vi + 271 pp. Maps, tables, notes, appendix, and bibliography. Insightful analysis of the district's history, administration, organization, and goals. The author concludes that the social and economic stratification in the area is maintained by long-established patterns of ownership, production, and class.

Lepawsky, Albert. "Water Resources and American Federalism." *American Political Science Review.* See chapter on "Waterways."

Leunes, Barbara Laverne Blythe. "The Conservation Philosophy of Stewart L. Udall, 1961-1968." Doctoral dissertation. See chapter on "Parks and Recreation."

Lewis, Christine. "The Early History of the Tempe Canal Company." *Arizona and the West,* 7 (Autumn 1965), 227-38. History of the early American irrigation canal that drew water from the Salt River.

Lillard, Richard G. *Desert Challenge: An Interpretation of Nevada.* Westport, Conn.: Greenwood Press, 1979. vii + 388 pp. Illustrations, bibliography, and index. This state history includes some material on Nevada's irrigation and road systems.

Lingenfelter, Richard E. *Steamboats on the*

Colorado River, 1852-1916. See chapter on "Waterways."

Lockmann, Ronald F. "Forests and Watersheds in the Environmental Philosophy of Theodore P. Lukens." *Journal of Forest History,* 23 (April 1979), 82-91. Illustrates the support forestry received from conservationists who sought to preserve irrigation and municipal water supplies.

Lorwin, Lewis L. *Youth Works Programs: Problems and Policies.* See chapter on "Public Buildings."

Lovin, Hugh T. "A 'New West' Reclamation Tragedy: The Twin Falls-Oakley Project in Idaho, 1908-1931." *Arizona and the West,* 20 (Spring 1978), 5-24. Fine summary of the difficulties encountered by irrigators on this project planned under the auspices of the Carey Act.

Lovin, Hugh. "Footnote to History: 'The Reservoir . . . Would Not Hold Water.'" *Idaho Yesterdays,* 24 (Spring 1980), 12-19. Summary of an engineer's analysis of the history of problems facing a Carey Act irrigation project in 1914.

Lowenthal, David. *George Perkins Marsh: Versatile Vermonter.* New York: Columbia University Press, 1958. xii + 442 pp. Illustrations, notes, bibliography, and index. An excellent biography of a versatile nineteenth-century American. Marsh's life spanned careers as a lawyer, editor, farmer, manufacturer, congressman, scholar, and diplomat. However, he is best remembered for his book, *Man and Nature,* that was published in 1864. It is a seminal work on the complexity of ecological relationships, humankind's transformation of the environment, and the need to protect and conserve natural resources. In 1874 Marsh published a report on European irrigation that was a source of inspiration and support for John Wesley Powell and other conservation crusaders.

Lowitt, Richard. *George W. Norris: The Persistence of a Progressive, 1913-1933.* Urbana: University of Illinois Press, 1971. xv + 590 pp. Illustrations, notes, bibliographical essay, and index. A good bibliography of the public career of the Nebraska senator who maintained his commitment to progressive causes during the Wilson, Harding, Coolidge, and Hoover administrations. The book discusses his support of river-basin planning and public power as well as Norris' decisive role in the Muscle Shoals controversy.

Lyons, Barrow. *Tomorrow's Birthright: A Political and Economic Interpretation of Our Natural Resources.* New York: Funk & Wagnalls Company, 1955. viii + 424 pp. Notes, appendices, and index. A plea for better government management of all natural resources that includes perceptive sections on irrigation as well as public versus private power production and distribution.

Lythgoe, Eliza R. "Colonization of the Big Horn Basin by the Mormons." *Annals of Wyoming,* 14 (Jan. 1942), 39-50. Includes some information on irrigation canals.

Maass, Arthur, and Raymond L. Anderson. *. . . and the Desert Shall Rejoice: Conflict, Growth, and Justice in Arid Environments.* Cambridge: MIT Press, 1978. 447 pp. Illustrations, maps, charts, tables, graphs, notes, and index. One of the most important books on the history of irrigation. The authors analyze the development of irrigation institutions in Spain as well as parts of California, Utah, and Colorado.

McBride, Conread L. "Federal State Relations in the Development of the Water Resources of the Colorado River Basin." Doctoral dissertation, University of California, Los Angeles, 1962.

McClellan, L.N. "Forward Steps in Irrigation Engineering." *Transactions of the American Society of Civil Engineers,* CT (1953), 388-99. Highlights improvements in irrigation practices.

McConnell, Grant. "The Conservation Movement—Past and Present." *Western Political Quarterly,* VII (Sept. 1954), 463-78. A good discussion of the ideological and political origins of the conservation movement. The author notes that there has always been a cleavage in the conservation movement "between humanism and something more mystical." A sound analysis is offered of how these contending points of view manifested themselves in controversies such as the Echo Park Dam embroglio.

McGeary, M. Nelson. *Gifford Pinchot: Forester-Politician.* See chapter on "Planning, Engineering, and Administration."

McHendrie, A.W. "The Hatcher Ditch (1846-1928): The Oldest Colorado Irrigation Ditch

Now in Use." *Colorado Magazine,* V (June 1928), 81-95. Discusses founding of an irrigation canal near present-day Trinidad, Colorado.

MacKendrick, Donald A. "Before the Newlands Act: State-sponsored Reclamation Projects in Colorado, 1888-1903." *Colorado Magazine.* See chapter on "Flood Control and Drainage."

McKinley, Charles. *Uncle Sam in the Pacific Northwest: Federal Management of Natural Resources in the Columbia River Valley.* Berkeley: University of California Press, 1952. xx + 673 pp. Maps, charts, tables, notes, and index. An exhaustive public administration and policy study that discusses the activities of some twenty-five federal agencies. The book was prompted by post-World War II debates over whether a regional authority should be created for the Columbia River Basin similar to the Tennessee Valley Authority. Chapters are included on the Army Corps of Engineers, Bureau of Reclamation, Bonneville Power Administration, and Soil Conservation Service. The book is particularly good at revealing the client groups served by each agency.

McKinley, John Lawrence. "The Influence of the Platte River Upon the History of the Valley." Doctoral dissertation, University of Nebraska, 1938. iii + 138 pp. Maps, charts, notes, and bibliography. Outstanding, comprehensive analysis of the development of the Platte River in Colorado, Nebraska, and Wyoming. Short sections on hydroelectric production and Denver's municipal water supply are included.

McLaird, James D. "Building the Town of Cody: George T. Beck, 1894-1943." *Annals of Wyoming,* 40 (April 1968), 73-105. Describes the birth and growth of Cody as part of entrepreneur Beck's irrigation scheme.

Malone, Thomas Edward. "The California Irrigation Crisis of 1886: Origins of the Wright Act." Doctoral dissertation, Stanford University, 1964. ix + 238 pp. Maps, tables, notes, appendices, and bibliography. Excellent study of nineteenth-century institutions in California that were created to govern the appropriation of irrigation water. The dissertation is particularly perceptive in its treatment of water law.

Mann, Dean E. *The Politics of Water in Arizona.* Tucson: University of Arizona Press, 1963. 317 pp. Illustrations, maps, notes, and bibliography. Includes some history of irrigation and land management.

Manning, Thomas G. *Government in Science: The U.S. Geological Survey, 1867-1894.* See chapter on "Planning, Engineering, and Administration."

Martin, David L. "California Water Politics: The Search for Local Control." Doctoral dissertation, Claremont Graduate School, 1973. 249 pp. Exhaustive analysis of the role of special districts in the regulation and distribution of water in California.

Matthews, William Kenneth. "A History of Irrigation in the Lower Rio Grande Valley." Master's thesis, University of Texas, Austin, 1938. viii + 128 pp. Illustrations, maps, tables, notes, and bibliography. An excellent case study that covers the geographical, institutional, legal, and technical aspects of the subject.

Mayo, Dwight E. "Arizona and the Colorado River Compact." Master's thesis, Arizona State University, 1964.

Mead, Elwood. *Irrigation Institutions.* New York: Macmillan Company, 1903. ix + 392 pp. Graphs and index. A discussion of the economic and legal questions raised by the growth of irrigated agriculture in the West. This classic work established Mead as one of the foremost authorities on irrigation and settlement. It is one of the best overviews of nineteenth-century irrigation.

Mead, Elwood. "Modern Methods Used on Reclamation Projects." *Civil Engineering,* 3 (Aug. 1933), 448-51. Illustrates the progress made in reclamation methods since the late nineteenth century.

Merdinger, Charles J. *Civil Engineering through the Ages.* See chapter on "Planning, Engineering, and Administration."

Meredith, H. L. "Reclamation in the Salt River Valley, 1902-1917." *Journal of the West,* VII (Jan. 1968), 76-83. A narrative account of the Salt River Project, which was built to deliver irrigation water to desert areas near Phoenix, Arizona. It discusses negotiations between the water users and the Reclamation Service, construction of Roosevelt Dam, and development of water delivery systems.

Merrill, Stephen A. "Reclamation and the Economic Development of Northern Utah: The

Weber River Project." *Utah Historical Quarterly*, 39 (Summer 1971), 254-64. Describes how the Mormon settlers in the northern portion of the valley of the Ogden and Weber rivers expanded their irrigation facilities and obtained sufficient water to meet their economic needs for nearly a century.

Meyer, Roy W. "Fort Berthold and the Garrison Dam." *North Dakota History*, 35 (Summer/Fall 1968), 217-355. Examines the disruption of the lives of people on the Fort Berthold Indian Reservation caused by the construction of the Garrison Dam.

"Milestones in U.S. Civil Engineering." *Civil Engineering*. See chapter on "Planning, Engineering, and Administration."

Miller, Gordon R. "Shaping California Water Law, 1781 to 1928." *Southern California Quarterly*, LV (Spring 1973), 9-42. A perceptive and well-organized treatment of a difficult, convoluted subject. The author illustrates how the legal framework evolved in response to competing water demands and use.

Mitchell, Bruce. "Rufus Woods and Columbia River Development." *Pacific Northwest Quarterly*, 52 (Oct. 1961), 139-44. Biographical profile of the newspaper editor who played a key role in promoting the Columbia Basin Project and Grand Coulee Dam.

Moberly, Alan Lee. "Fences and Neighbors: El Chamizal and the Colorado Salinity Disputes in United States-Mexican Relations." Doctoral dissertation, University of California, Santa Barbara, 1974. x + 291 pp. Illustrations, notes, glossary, and bibliography. Details the negotiations between the United States and Mexico regarding salinity levels of Colorado River water.

Moeller, Beverley Bowen. *Phil Swing and Boulder Dam*. Berkeley: University of California Press, 1971. xiii + 199 pp. Illustrations, map, notes, bibliography, and index. A history of the Boulder Canyon Project Act from the standpoint of the California congressman most responsible for its passage. Moeller skillfully presents the individuals and interest groups that opposed and supported harnessing the Colorado River. The book's most challenging argument is that Herbert Hoover obstructed and delayed construction of the dam that bears his name.

Moreel, Ben. *Our Nation's Water Resources—Policies and Politics*. See chapter on "Flood Control and Drainage."

Morgan, Murray. *The Dam*. New York: Viking Press, 1954. xviii + 162 pp. Illustrations, map, and diagram. A well-written, popular history of the construction of Grand Coulee Dam and its impact on the economy and ecology of the Northwest.

Morrison, Margaret Darsie. "Charles Robinson Rockwood: Developer of the Imperial Valley." *Southern California Quarterly*, XLIV (Dec. 1962), 307-30. A sound account of early irrigation development in California's Imperial Valley. Rockwood is lauded by the author for his persistence, self-denial, and integrity. The article contains an outstanding account of flood fights on the Colorado River at the turn of the century.

Murphy, Paul L. "Early Irrigation in the Boise Valley." *Pacific Northwest Quarterly*, 44 (Oct. 1953), 177-84. Perceptive analysis of the legal, economic, and environmental problems faced by irrigators in the 1880s and 1890s.

Nadeau, Remi A. *The Water Seekers*. Garden City, N.Y.: Doubleday and Company, 1950. 309 pp. Illustrations, bibliographical essay, and index. A well-informed historical narrative on those chiefly responsible for water resource development in the West. The author gives special attention to William Mulholland, William B. Mathews, and the Los Angeles Aqueduct.

Neil, J. Meredith. "A Forgotten Alternative: Reclamation by the States." *Idaho Yesterdays*, 9 (Winter 1965-66), 18-21. Describes early Idaho proposals for state reclamation projects.

Nelson, Robert. "The National Reclamation Association: A Study of a Pressure Group." Master's thesis, University of Chicago, 1955. Survey of lobbying organization that sought greater support for federal water projects in the West.

Newcomb, Rexford. *The Old Mission Churches and Historic Houses of California*. See chapter on "Public Buildings."

Newell, F.H. "Forty Years of Research Into Water Resources." *Engineering News-Record*, 104 (Jan. 23, 1930), 132-36. Salute to the research activities of the U.S. Geological Survey.

Newell, F.H. "Irrigation Developments in the

United States." *Engineering Record,* (Dec. 16, 1911, and Dec. 23, 1911), 711-14; 745-47. Review of the activities of the Reclamation Service by its director.

Newell, Frederick Haynes. *Irrigation in the United States.* New York: Thomas Y. Crowell & Company, 1902. xix + 417 pp. Illustrations, maps, graphs, diagrams, and index. Perhaps the best source on nineteenth-century irrigation techniques and practices. The book includes chapters on dam and canal construction, irrigation methods, groundwater, pumping, sewage irrigation, and water law. The material is presented in a non-technical manner and is easily understood. Clearly, the volume was written to promote passage of a national reclamation law.

Newell, F.H. "Reclamation and Home-making: I.-Review of General Conditions in the Reclamation Service." *Scientific American,* CV (Aug. 12, 1911), 144-48, 156-57. Overview of the Shoshone, Payette-Boise, Belle Fourche, Yuma, Salt River, and other early federal reclamation projects.

Newell, Frederick Haynes. *Water Resources: Present and Future Uses.* New Haven: Yale University Press, 1920. 310 pp. Illustrations, notes, and index. The book is based on a series of lectures given by Newell at Yale University in 1913. Newell, one of the leading Progressive conservationists, presents a multi-dimensional portrait of hydrological engineering. Following a discussion of precipitation and run off, the author surveys irrigation, dams, flood control, municipal supplies, power production, navigation, and water law. The volume is one of the best early statements of Progressive water philosophy.

Nixon, Edgar B., ed. Franklin D. Roosevelt and Conservation, 1911-1945. See chapter on "Planning, Engineering, and Administration."

Norcross, Fred N. "The Genesis of the Colorado-Big Thompson Project." *Colorado Magazine,* XXX (1953), 29-37. Former Colorado state senator describes his efforts to promote construction of the project that diverts water from the west to the east slope of the Colorado Rockies. The article is especially valuable for its insights into negotiations between the water users and the Bureau of Reclamation.

Papageorge, Nan Taylor. "The Role of the San Diego River in the Development of Mission Valley." *Journal of San Diego History,* XVII (Spring 1971), 14-27. Excellent article on the river's influence from the first irrigation system built by Spanish priests to the development of water supply and flood control projects. The narrative and research are first rate.

Parkins, A.E., and J.R. Whitaker, eds. *Our Natural Resources and Their Conservation.* See chapter on "Flood Control and Drainage."

Parsons, Malcolm B. "Origins of the Colorado River Controversy in Arizona Politics, 1922-1923." *Arizona and the West,* 4 (Spring 1962), 27-44. Perceptive article that contends that Arizona's opposition to the Colorado River Compact for more than twenty years was the result of political attitudes and arguments spawned in the early 1920s.

Parsons, Malcolm B. "Party and Pressure Politics in Arizona's Opposition to Colorado River Development." *Pacific Historical Review,* XIX (Feb. 1950), 47-58. Explores the political details of Arizona's opposition to a division of Colorado River water by various western states.

Paterson, Alan Murray. "Rivers and Tides: The Story of Water Policy and Management in California's Sacramento San Joaquin Delta, 1920-1977." Doctoral dissertation, University of California, Davis, 1978. 403 pp.

Paulson, George W. "The Congressional Career of Joseph Maull Carey." *Annals of Wyoming,* 35 (April 1963), 21-81. Covers the period from 1885 to 1895 and features the events surrounding passage of the Carey Act, that was important to the development of arid states such as Wyoming.

Peffer, E. Louise. *The Closing of the Public Domain: Disposal and Reservation Policies, 1900-50.* Stanford: Stanford University Press, 1951. xi + 372 pp. Tables, notes, appendix, and index. A definitive book on twentieth-century land policies. Strong chapters discuss the 1902 Reclamation Act and the Conservation Movement of the early 1900s.

Penick, James, Jr. *Progressive Politics and Conservation: The Ballinger-Pinchot Affair.* See chapter on "Planning, Engineering, and Administration."

Peterson, Elmer T. *Big Dam Foolishness: The Problem of Modern Flood Control and Water*

Storage. See chapter on "Flood Control and Drainage."

Peterson, Ottis. "The Story of a Bureau." *Journal of the West,* VII (Jan. 1968), 84-95. A paean to the reclamation program.

Pinchot, Gifford. *Breaking New Ground.* New York: Harcourt, Brace and Company, 1947. xvii + 522 pp. Illustrations and index. An excellent autobiography by one of the nation's foremost Progressive conservationists. Although the book is primarily a "personal story of how Forestry and Conservation came to America," it contains valuable information on the evolution of federal water and power policies in the early twentieth century.

Pinkett, Harold T. *Gifford Pinchot: Private and Public Forester.* See chapter on "Planning, Engineering, and Administration."

Pisani, Donald Joseph. "Conflict Over Conservation: The Reclamation Service and the Tahoe Contract." *Western Historical Quarterly,* X (April 1979), 167-90. Suggests that the Reclamation Service was not in tune with the broad conservation ideals of the Progressive Era. The well-researched article is an insightful analysis of how the agency operated in the field.

Pisani, Donald J. "Federal Reclamation and Water Rights in Nevada." *Agricultural History,* LI (July 1977), 548-58.

Pisani, Donald J. "Storm Over the Sierra: A Study in Western Water Use." Doctoral dissertation, University of California, Davis, 1975. Deals extensively with California's and Nevada's disputes regarding the use of water from the Northern Sierra Nevada. The author concludes that water has been subject to the same carelessness and lack of planning as other basic natural resources.

Pisani, Donald J. "The Strange Death of the California-Nevada Compact: A Study in Interstate Water Negotiations." *Pacific Historical Review,* XLVII (Nov. 1978), 637-58. Skillful analysis of the intricate history of this water controversy. Pisani concludes that the "death of the California-Nevada compact suggests that interstate treaties may have outlived their usefulness in settling water disputes."

Pisani, Donald J. "Water Law Reform in California, 1900-1913." *Agricultural History,* 54 (April 1980), 295-317.

Pisani, Donald J. "Western Nevada's Water Crisis, 1915-1935." *Nevada Historical Society Quarterly,* XXII (Spring 1979), 3-20.

Pisani, Donald J. "'Why Shouldn't California Have the Grandest Aqueduct in the World?': Alexis Von Schmidt's Lake Tahoe Scheme." *California Historical Quarterly,* LIII (Winter 1974), 347-60. Well-written account of a bold scheme first proposed in the 1860s to divert water from Lake Tahoe to northern California.

Pomeroy, Earl. *The Pacific Slope: A History of California, Oregon, Washington, Idaho, Utah, and Nevada.* See chapter on "Community Water Supply."

Powell, John Wesley. *Report on the Lands of the Arid Region of the United States: With a More Detailed Account of the Lands of Utah.* Cambridge: Belknap Press of Harvard University Press, 1962. xxvii + 202 pp. Maps, charts, tables, notes, and index. One of the most significant and seminal books ever written about the West. First published in 1878, the volume outlines Powell's vision of water and land development beyond the hundredth meridian. Powell is generally regarded as the father of the irrigation crusade that led to the founding of the Reclamation Service in 1902. He also forecasted with accuracy the consequences of trying to transplant eastern habits and institutions in the West: droughts, floods, crop failures, land and water monopolies, and jurisdictional quarrels.

Rait, Mary. "Development of Grand Junction and the Colorado River Valley to Palisade from 1881 to 1931." Master's thesis, University of Colorado, 1931. iv + 156 pp. Maps, notes, and bibliography. A good source for information on the development of irrigation in the vicinity of Grand Junction, Colorado.

Reid, Bill G. "Franklin K. Lane's Idea for Veteran's Colonization, 1918-1921." *Pacific Historical Review,* XXXIII (Nov. 1964), 447-61. Largely deals with attempts by the secretary of the interior to encourage veteran settlement on federal reclamation projects.

Relander, Click. "The Battleground of National Irrigation." *Pacific Northwest Quarterly,* 52 (Oct. 1961), 144-49. Excellent article on the origins of the Columbia Basin Project.

Ressler, John Q. "Indian and Spanish Water Control on New Spain's Northwest Frontier." *Journal of the West,* VII (Jan. 1968), 10-17.

One of the best articles on Indian and mission irrigation. It describes the systems that were created and the uses to which water was put.

Rhodes, Benjamin Franklin, Jr. "Thirsty Land: The Modesto Irrigation District, A Case Study of Irrigation Under the Wright Law." Doctoral dissertation, University of California, Berkeley, 1943. iv + 170 pp. Maps, notes, and bibliography. A comprehensive history of irrigation near Modesto from the 1860s to the 1920s. The dissertation offers especially good insights on the evolution, operation, and administration of irrigation districts.

Richard, John Betram. "State Administration and Water Resources in Wyoming." Doctoral dissertation, University of Illinois, 1965. 322 pp.

Richardson, Elmo R. *Dams, Parks & Politics: Resource Development & Preservation in the Truman-Eisenhower Era.* Lexington: University of Kentucky Press, 1973. vi + 247 pp. Illustrations, notes, bibliographical essay, and index. The definitive study of water, land, power, and park policies during the Truman and Eisenhower administrations. The study is based on an extraordinary investigation of federal and state primary sources. Particularly thorough coverage is given to controversies surrounding the attempt to create a Columbia Valley Authority, impound water within Dinosaur National Monument, and public versus private hydroelectric power development.

Richardson, Elmo R. "The Interior Secretary as Conservation Villain: The Notorious Case of Douglas 'Giveaway' McKay." *Pacific Historical Review,* XLI (Aug. 1972), 333-45. A sound analysis of the first secretary of the interior appointed by President Dwight D. Eisenhower. The article offers interesting insights into the Bureau of Reclamation's controversial Hells Canyon and Echo Park projects that were not built due to private sector and environmental opposition.

Richardson, Elmo R. *The Politics of Conservation: Crusades and Controversies, 1897-1913.* See chapter on "Waterways."

Richardson, Elmo R. "Western Politics and New Deal Policies: A Study of T.A. Walters of Idaho." *Pacific Northwest Quarterly.* See chapter on "Flood Control and Drainage."

Ridgeway, Marian E. *The Missouri Basin's Pick-Sloan Plan: A Case Study in Congressional Policy Determination.* See chapter on "Flood Control and Drainage."

Riesch, Anna. "Conservation Under Franklin D. Roosevelt." Doctoral dissertation, University of Wisconsin, 1952. 165 pp.

Robbins, Roy M. *Our Landed Heritage: The Public Domain, 1776-1970.* Lincoln: University of Nebraska Press, 1976. xii + 503 pp. Illustrations, maps, notes, bibliography, and index. First published in 1942, this book is regarded as the definitive account of the administration and settlement of public lands. This revised edition extends the coverage to 1970. National policies with respect to parks and reclamation receive particularly good treatment.

Robinson, Edgar Eugene, and Paul Carroll Edwards, eds. *The Memoirs of Ray Lyman Wilbur, 1875-1949.* Stanford: Stanford University Press, 1960. xiv + 687 pp. Illustrations, notes, bibliography and index. Autobiography of the former secretary of the Department of the Interior that includes an insightful chapter on the Boulder Canyon Project.

Robinson, Michael C. "People in Public Works: Arthur Powell Davis." *APWA Reporter.* See chapter on "Flood Control and Drainage."

Robinson, Michael C. "People in Public Works: Frederick Haynes Newell." *APWA Reporter,* 47 (March 1980), 6-7. A biographical sketch highlighting Newell's work as head of the United States Reclamation Service.

Robinson, Michael C. "People in Public Works: Peter Kiewit, Jr." *APWA Reporter.* See chapter on "Flood Control and Drainage."

Robinson, Michael C. "Water for the West: The Bureau of Reclamation, 1902-1977." *Reclamation Era,* 63 (1978), 1-13. Overview of the evolution of the federal reclamation program. This seventy-fifth anniversary issue of the *Reclamation Era* contains additional historical articles dealing with the agency's development.

Robinson, Michael C. *Water for the West: The Bureau of Reclamation, 1902-1977.* Chicago: Public Works Historical Society, 1979. iv + 117 pp. Illustrations, maps, bibliography, and index. First comprehensive book-length treatment of the agency's history. Landmark statutes, policies, projects, and programs are discussed and set within the context of major themes of water resource and public works history. It is designed to stimulate further exploration of this subject.

Rockwood, Charles Robinson. *Born of the Desert.* Calexico, Calif.: Calexico Chronicle, 1930. 44 pp. Illustration. First published in 1909, the autobiography recounts the author's leading role in the reclamation and settlement of the Imperial Valley.

Rohn, Arthur H. "Prehistoric Soil and Water Conservation on Chapin Mesa, Southwestern Colorado." *American Antiquity,* XXVIII (April 1963), 441-55. Results of an archeological survey on Chapin Mesa in Mesa Verde National Park. The findings describe stone masonry check-dams, farming terraces, and other soil- and water-conservation devices built by the Indians.

Ross, John R. "Man Over Nature: Origins of the Conservation Movement." *American Studies.* See chapter on "Planning, Engineering, and Administration."

Ross, John Ray. "'Pork Barrels' and the General Welfare: Problems in Conservation, 1900-1920." Doctoral dissertation. See chapter on "Flood Control and Drainage."

Rowe, Robert S., comp. *Bibliography of Rivers and Harbors and Related Fields in Hydraulic Engineering.* See chapter on "Waterways."

Rutherford, John. "Interplay of American and Australian Ideas for Development of Water Projects in Northern Victoria." *Annals of the Association of American Geographers,* 54 (March 1964), 88-106. This article will be of interest to students of water history and technology transfer. Furthermore, it chronicles the contributions of Elwood Mead, who later served as commissioner of the United States Bureau of Reclamation, to Australian irrigation development.

Sageser, A. Bower. "Attempted Economic Adjustments in Holt County During the 1890's." *Nebraska History,* 40 (June 1959), 105-18. Includes some material on irrigation districts created in the 1880s and 1890s.

Sageser, A. Bower. "Editor Bristow and the Great Plains Revival of the 1890's." *Journal of the West,* III (Jan. 1964), 75-89. Description of the Kansas editor-politician's involvement in the irrigation crusade of the 1890's.

Sageser, A. Bower. *Joseph L. Bristow: Kansas Progressive.* Lawrence: University Press of Kansas, 1968. x + 197 pp. Illustrations, notes, bibliography, and index. A fine biography of the Kansas politician who served in the United States Senate from 1909 to 1915. During the 1890s, Bristow was editor of the *Irrigation Farmer* and became heavily involved in the movement to reclaim arid lands.

Sageser, A. Bower. "Joseph L. Bristow: The Editor's Road to Politics." *Kansas Historical Quarterly,* XXX (Summer 1964), 153-62. Includes a discussion of Bristow's active role in the irrigation crusade of the 1890s.

Sageser, A. Bower. "Los Angeles Hosts an International Irrigation Congress." *Journal of the West,* (July 1965), 411-24. A good description of the personalities and ideas that were discussed at this landmark irrigation congress. It offers insight into the status of the reclamation crusade in 1893.

Sageser, A. Bower. "Windmill and Pump Irrigation on the Great Plains, 1890-1910." *Nebraska History,* 48 (Summer 1967), 107-18. Comprehensive discussion of early attempts to overcome the limits of aridity through windmill and pump irrigation. It includes unusual photographs of the windmill systems that were used.

Sandström, Gösta E. *Man the Builder.* See chapter on "Roads, Streets, and Highways."

Sayles, Stephen Paul. "Clair Engle and the Politics of California Reclamation, 1943-1960." Doctoral dissertation, University of New Mexico, 1978. viii + 326 pp. Notes and bibliography. Outstanding dissertation on the flamboyant California congressman who played a key role in the water and power battles of the 1950s. The study offers a great deal of insight into the expansion of the Central Valley Project after World War II.

Scheel, Paul Edmund. "Resource Development Politics in the Missouri Basin: Federal Power, Navigation, and Reservoir Operation Policies, 1944-1948." Doctoral dissertation, University of Nebraska, 1969. 419 pp.

Schmalz, Bruce L. "Headgates and Headaches: The Powell Tract." *Idaho Yesterdays,* 9 (Winter 1965-66), 22-25. On the failure of the Big Lost River Project, known as the Powell Tract and located in Butte County.

Schnitter, N.J. "The Evolution of the Arch Dam: Part One, Part Two." *International Water Power and Dam Construction,* 28 (Oct. 1976 and Nov. 1976), Oct.: 34-40; Nov.: 19-21.

Landmarks in arch dam construction from antiquity to the present.

Schonfeld, Robert G. "The Early Development of California's Imperial Valley." 2 parts. *Southern California Quarterly,* L (Sept. and Dec. 1968), Sept.: 279-308; Dec.: 395-426. History of late nineteenth- and early twentieth-century irrigation in the valley by private enterprise and the Reclamation Service.

Seckler, David, ed. *California Water: A Study in Resource Management.* Berkeley: University of California Press, 1971. xiv + 348 pp. Maps, charts, tables, graphs, notes, and index. A series of thoughtful, individually authored essays on virtually every aspect of water regulation and use in California. The book's four sections discuss the California Water Plan, water use, the technology of water supply, and the political economy of water resources. Together the essays illustrate how "the range of choices in water management has expanded as the difficulties of choice have become more profound."

Sewell, William M. "Studies in the Development of Irrigation and Hydro-Electric Power in California." Master's thesis, Occidental College, 1928. 163 pp. Notes, chart, and bibliography. Competent summary of the growth of irrigation in California as well as the beginnings of hydroelectric production.

Shallat, Todd A. "Fresno's Water Rivalry: Competition for a Scarce Resource, 1887-1970." *Essays in Public Works History,* 8 (Sept. 1979), 1-37. A landmark in the fields of public and applied history. It is perhaps the best case study ever written on a regional water resource system, and provides a useful contribution to the future management of Fresno's water resources program. Basically, the study chronicles the lengthy history of the fierce competition between urban and rural water agencies for San Joaquin water.

Sheldon, Addison E. *Land Systems and Land Policies in Nebraska.* Lincoln: Nebraska State Historical Society, 1936. xvi + 383 pp. Illustrations, maps, charts, tables, graphs, notes, appendices, and index. Some historical information on early irrigation systems is included in this study of the effects of national land policies on Nebraska.

Simmonds, A.J. "Water for the Big Range." *Utah Historical Quarterly,* 39 (Summer 1971), 224-37. Explains how the Bear River was diverted to the Big Range.

Simmons, Marc. "Spanish Irrigation Practices in New Mexico." *New Mexico Historical Review,* XLVII (April 1972), 135-50. One of the best case studies of Spanish irrigation institutions. The article discusses community acequias and other irrigation systems used by settlers in the Upper Rio Grande Basin.

Smith, Courtland L. *The Salt River Project: A Case Study in Cultural Adaptation to an Urbanizing Community.* Tucson: University of Arizona Press, 1972. viii + 151 pp. Illustrations, tables, graphs, appendix, bibliography, and index. An excellent study of institutional adaptation. The Salt River Project was created in 1903 to serve the irrigation and power needs of farmers in the Phoenix area. The book discusses the changes the entity underwent as urbanization made increasing demands for water, land, and electricity. Much historical information on the evolution of the project's facilities and administration is included.

Smith, Frank E., ed. *Conservation in the United States, a Documentary History: Land and Water, 1900-1970.* New York: Chelsea House Publishers, 1971. xxv + 782 pp. Notes and index. A good collection of documents that illustrate the evolution of federal policies with respect to land, water, and hydroelectric energy. The preservationist side of American conservation is not incorporated. Subjects covered include: reclamation, the Inland Waterways Commission, federal forestry, flood control on the Mississippi River, soil conservation, and the Tennessee Valley Authority.

Smith, Frank E. *The Politics of Conservation.* New York: Pantheon Books, 1966. xii + 338 pp. Bibliography and index. A very readable, comprehensive survey of the politics of conservation in the nineteenth and twentieth centuries. The book tends to focus on water resource development, but it also touches on parks and efforts to create wilderness areas. Smith is critical of the "pork barrel conservation system" but believes "it has often succeeded in spite of itself." The author, however, takes issue with the "preservationist-conservationist doctrine and its 'special elite' concept which suggests that the wilderness values are to be preserved for only that small fragment of the population considered capable of proper appreciation." In the conclusion, he argues for a better coordinated, comprehensive approach to natural resources planning.

Smith, Guy-Harold. *Conservation of Natural Resources.* New York: John Wiley & Sons, 1971. xiii + 685 pp. Illustrations, maps, charts, tables, graphs, notes, bibliographies, and index. One of the better conservation readers. The essays are concise, well-written, and include the entire spectrum of national, state, and local programs. Examples include water pollution, irrigation, waterways, flood control, water power, and recreation.

Smith, Norman. *A History of Dams.* (London: Peter Davies, 1971. xv + 279 pp. Illustrations, diagrams, notes, bibliography, glossary, and index. The major strength of this book is the discussion of Roman, Byzantine, Persian, and early Spanish dams. The chapters describing nineteenth- and twentieth-century dam technology are somewhat superficial. Many noteworthy United States structures are not included.

Smith, Stephen C. "Legal and Institutional Controls in Water Allocation." *Journal of Farm Economics,* XLII (Dec. 1960), 1345-58. A good discussion of laws and institutions established to moderate competing demands for western water resources.

Smythe, William E. *The Conquest of Arid America.* New York: Macmillan Company, 1911. xxvi + 360 pp. Illustrations, appendices, and index. A classic piece of promotional literature by one of the oracles of the irrigation crusade. First published in 1899, the book is a paean to the agrarian myth. A great deal of useful historical information is included in Mormon irrigation, the Greeley Colony, and other "real utopias of the arid west."

Soffar, Allan Jarrell. "Differing Views on the Gospel of Efficiency: Conservation and Controversies between Agriculture and Interior, 1898-1938." Doctoral dissertation, Texas Tech University, 1974. 423 pp.

Sorensen, Corner. "Federal Reclamation on the High Plains: The Garden City Project." *Great Plains Journal,* 15 (Spring 1976), 115-33. Description of "the failure of federal reclamation on the High Plains" near Garden City in western Kansas.

Stamp, L. Dudley, ed. *A History of Land Use in Arid Regions.* Paris: United Nations Educational, Scientific and Cultural Organization, 1965. 388 pp. Maps, notes, and bibliographies. A worldwide overview of aridity that includes a discussion of the development of irrigation institutions in the American West.

Stegner, Wallace. *Beyond the Hundredth Meridian: John Wesley Powell and the Second Opening of the West.* Cambridge: Riverside Press, 1962. x + 438 pp. Maps, notes, and index. By far the most competent and perceptive biography of Powell's public career. Chapter 3, "Blueprint for a Dryland Democracy," outlines his vision for the settlement of western lands through the creation of irrigation districts and other locally autonomous institutions. Powell's activities as an explorer, conservationist, and head of the U.S. Geological Survey are comprehensively covered.

Stegner, Wallace. "Getting to Know the National Domain." *American Heritage,* 30 (Feb.-March 1979), 60-62. A tribute to John Wesley Powell's role in the founding of the U.S. Geological Survey and Bureau of Ethnology. Both, according to the author, have since "given direction, form, and stimulation to the science of the earth and science of man, and in so doing have touched millions of lives." For example, the Bureau of Reclamation and the Bureau of Land Management evolved from the U.S. Geological Survey.

Steinel, Alvin T. *History of Agriculture in Colorado: A Chronological Record of Progress in the Development of General Farming, Livestock Production and Agricultural Education and Investigation, on the Western Border of the Great Plains and in the Mountains of Colorado.* Fort Collins, Col.: Colorado State Agricultural College, 1926. 659 pp. Illustrations, map, notes, and index. A comprehensive history of the beginnings of agriculture in Colorado. Large sections are devoted to irrigation colonies and the major projects undertaken by the Bureau of Reclamation.

Sterling, Everett W. "The Powell Irrigation Survey, 1888-1893." *Mississippi Valley Historical Review.* See chapter on "Planning, Engineering, and Administration."

Strebel, George Lofstrom. "Irrigation as a Factor in Western History: 1847-1890." Doctoral dissertation, University of California, Berkeley, 1965. 527 pp.

Strong, Douglas H. "The Sierra Forest Reserve: The Movement to Preserve the San Joaquin Watershed." *California Historical So-*

ciety Quarterly, XLVI (March 1967), 3-17. Discusses the joint efforts by irrigators and preservationists to stop lumbering that would degradate water supplies and destroy scenic areas.

Sundborg, George. *Hail Columbia: The Thirty-Year Struggle for Grand Coulee Dam.* New York: Macmillan Company, 1954. xviii + 467 pp. Index. The first major attempt to survey the history of water resource development in the Columbia River Basin. The undocumented book places heavy emphasis on the politicians, government officials, and engineers who promoted and built Grand Coulee Dam and other projects. It is a very laudatory treatment of the subject.

Sunseri, Alvin R. "Agricultural Techniques in New Mexico at the Time of the Anglo-American Conquest." *Agricultural History,* 47 (Jan. 1973), 329-37. Excellent overview of Spanish and Indian water-control practices.

Sutton, Imre. "A Comparative Analysis of Environmental Factors in the Planning and Construction of Multi-Purpose Dams in the United States." Master's thesis, University of California, Los Angeles, 1958.

Sutton, Imre. "Geographical Aspects of Construction Planning: Hoover Dam Revisited." *Journal of the West,* VII (July 1968), 301-44. A brilliant account of the planning and construction of Hoover Dam. Sutton has a firm grasp of the broad spectrum of the engineering and environmental factors the dam builders had to address. Few historians have mastered the technical aspects of water resource development as well as this author.

Swain, Donald C. *Federal Conservation Policy, 1921-1933.* Berkeley: University of California Press, 1963. 221 pp. Illustrations, notes, bibliographical essay, and index. One of the best conservation monographs. Swain examines every contour of federal conservation policy and notes that the appeal of this issue remained strong despite a general retreat from Progressivism during the 1920s. The book contains a strong discussion of the Boulder Canyon Project as well as the Muscle Shoals controversy.

Swain, Donald C. "The Bureau of Reclamation and the New Deal, 1933-1940." *Pacific Northwest Quarterly,* 61 (July 1970), 137-46. Outstanding study of the evolution of Bureau of Reclamation administration, policies, and programs during the New Deal. Swain illustrates how the agency was transformed from a single- to a multiple-purpose water agency.

Taylor, Paul Schuster. *Essays on Land, Water, and the Law in California.* New York: Arno Press, 1979. 400 pp. Bibliography.

Taylor, Paul S. "Reclamation: The Rise and Fall of an American Idea." *American West,* 7 (July 1970), 27-33, 63. Discusses irrigation congresses held in the 1890s.

Taylor, Paul S. "The Excess Land Law: Legislative Erosion of Public Policy." *Rocky Mountain Law Review,* 30 (June 1958), 480-516. Excellent historical overview of the 160-acre limitation provision of federal reclamation law.

Taylor, Paul S. "The Excess Land Law: Pressure vs. Principle." *California Law Review,* 47 (Aug. 1959), 499-541. Outstanding, deeply researched discussion of the history of efforts to circumvent acreage limitations for federal reclamation projects.

Taylor, Paul S. "Water, Land, and People in the Great Valley—Is It True That What We Learn from History Is That We Learn Nothing From History?" *American West,* V (March 1968), 24-29, 68-71. Thoughtful overview of the growth of western irrigation, particularly in California's Central Valley. Taylor is highly critical of corporate ownership of land and water and favors strict enforcement of the 160-acre limitation for Bureau of Reclamation projects.

Taylor, William B. "Land and Water Rights in the Viceroyalty of New Spain." *New Mexico Historical Review.* See chapter on "Community Water Supply."

Teele, Ray Palmer. *Irrigation in the United States: A Discussion of Its Legal, Economic and Financial Aspects.* New York: D. Appleton and Company, 1915. xiii + 253 pp. Map, tables, graph, and index. A perceptive analysis of climate, water supply, crops, laws, distribution systems, and organizations as they relate to western irrigation. The author concludes that the Reclamation Service failed to achieve its social and economic goals. He suggests various legal and organizational reforms that would improve the attempt to reclaim arid western lands.

Teele, R.P. "The Financing of Non-Governmental Irrigation Enterprises." *Journal of Land and Public Utility Economics,* 2 (Oct. 1926), 427-40. Still-useful historical treatment of public and private methods of financing irrigation projects.

Teilmann, Henrik. "The Role of Irrigation Districts in California's Water Development." *American Journal of Economics and Sociology,* 22 (April 1963), 409-15. A sketchy overview of the origins of California's irrigation districts.

Terral, Rufus. *The Missouri Valley: Land of Drouth, Flood, and Promise.* New Haven: Yale University Press, 1947. ix + 274 pp. Maps, notes, bibliography, and index. A perceptive, balanced study of water resource development in the Missouri River Basin. The book traces the valley's history with respect to droughts as well as floods and describes the formulation of the Pick-Sloan Plan. The author recommends the formation of a Missouri Valley Authority to direct the region's development of water and related power resources.

Terrell, John Upton. *The Man Who Rediscovered America: A Biography of John Wesley Powell.* New York: Weybright and Talley, 1969. 281 pp. Maps, bibliography, and index. A rather superficial biography that offers nothing new or unique on the career of the explorer-scientist.

Terrell, John Upton. *War for the Colorado River.* 2 vols. Glendale, Calif.: Arthur H. Clark Company, 1965. Vol. I: 324 pp.; Vol. II: 323 pp. Maps, notes, appendices, and indexes. Two poorly crafted volumes on post-World War II interstate controversies surrounding the storage, appropriation, and use of Colorado River water. The first volume discusses the battles between California and Arizona engendered by the Central Arizona Project. The second covers the legislative conflicts over the Colorado River Storage Project that authorized dams for irrigation, power, and other uses in the river's upper basin. The books are based almost entirely on government documents and congressional testimony.

"The Almanac of Significant Events in Building a Greater America, 1874-1949." *Engineering News-Record.* See chapter on "Planning, Engineering, and Administration."

"The Story of Hoover Dam." *U.S. Department of the Interior. Conservation Bulletin,* 9 (1961), vii + 78 pp. A good popular discussion of the history of the Boulder Canyon Project.

Thoburn, Joseph B. "Ancient Irrigation Ditches on the Plains." *Chronicles of Oklahoma,* IX (March 1931), 56-62. An interesting, generally ignored article on the remains of ancient Indian irrigation works in the Oklahoma Panhandle and adjacent portions of southwestern Kansas and the Texas Panhandle. These people developed a remarkably sophisticated system that emulated practices of the puebloan Indians.

Thomas, Franklin. "Value of Water in Southern California: A Historical Resume of the Cost of Its Development for Irrigation and Domestic Use." *Civil Engineering,* 3 (Oct. 1933), 555-59. Reviews the history of irrigation and domestic water pricing in the Los Angeles area.

Thomas, George. *Early Irrigation in the Western States.* n.p.: University of Utah, 1948. viii + 63 pp. Bibliographies and index. Perhaps the best introduction to the first irrigation institutions and practices established in the West. The volume chronicles water resource development by the pre-Columbian Indians, the Spanish, and the Mormons prior to the Civil War.

Thomas, George. *The Development of Institutions Under Irrigation.* New York: Macmillan Company, 1920. xi + 291 pp. Illustrations and index. An essential book for students of western water history. Thomas describes the development of early Mormon community canals and the subsequent growth of institutions that governed the ownership and allocation of water. The author's chapters on irrigation districts, county water commissioners, and drainage remain the best treatments of these subjects.

Thompson, Carl D. *Public Ownership: A Survey of Public Enterprises, Municipal, State, and Federal, in the United States and Elsewhere.* See chapter on "Energy."

Thompson, John T. "Governmental Responses to the Challenges of Water Resources in Texas." *Southwestern Historical Quarterly.* See chapter on "Waterways."

Tininenko, Robert D. "Middle Snake River Development: The Controversy over Hells Canyon, 1947-1955." Master's thesis. See chapter on "Energy."

Townley, John Mark. "Reclamation in Nevada, 1850-1904." Doctoral dissertation, University of Nevada, Reno, 1976. 346 pp.

Trani, Eugene P. "Hubert Work and the Department of the Interior, 1923-28." *Pacific Northwest Quarterly.* See chapter on "Planning, Engineering and Administration."

Turney, Omar A. "Prehistoric Irrigation." 4 parts. *Arizona Historical Review,* 2 (April; July; Oct. 1929; and Jan. 1930), April: 12-52; July: 11-52; Oct.: 9-45; Jan.: 33-73. Still-useful description of the prehistoric irrigation works near Phoenix, Arizona.

Udall, Stewart L. *The Quiet Crisis.* See chapter on "Parks and Recreation."

Uhl, W.F. "Water Power over a Century." *Transactions of the American Society of Civil Engineers.* See chapter on "Waterways."

U.S. Department of Commerce, Bureau of the Census. *Historical Statistics of the United States: Colonial Times to 1970.* See chapter on "Planning, Engineering, and Administration."

Van Brocklin, Ralph Merton. "The Movement for the Conservation of Natural Resources in the United States Before 1901." Doctoral dissertation, University of Michigan, 1953. 269 pp.

Vandevere, Emmett Kaiser. "History of Irrigation in Washington." Doctoral dissertation, University of Washington, 1948. vi + 263 pp. Illustrations, maps, notes, and bibliography. A good descriptive overview of the evolution of irrigation in Washington State. The coverage of federal reclamation projects is especially thorough.

Van Dusen, George. "Politics of 'Partnership': The Eisenhower Administration and Conservation, 1952-1960." Doctoral dissertation. See chapter on "Energy."

Van Petten, Donald R. "Arizona's Stand on the Santa Fe Compact and the Boulder Dam Project." *New Mexico Historical Review,* XVII (Jan. 1942), 1-20. Discusses Arizona's refusal to join with other western states to apportion the waters of the Colorado River. The article also analyzes the state's opposition to the Boulder Canyon Project Act.

Van Hook, Joseph O. "Development of Irrigation in the Arkansas Valley." *Colorado Magazine,* X (Jan. 1933), 3-11. Surveys irrigation on the Arkansas River in Colorado from 1839 to 1890

Warne, William E. *The Bureau of Reclamation.* New York: Praeger Publishers, 1973. 270 pp. Illustrations, maps, charts, bibliography, and index. Uneven historical discussion of the agency since its founding in 1902. It traces the evolution of reclamation projects and programs and assesses its relations with other natural resource agencies.

Waters, Frank. *The Colorado.* New York: Rinehart & Company, 1946. xvi + 400 pp. Illustrations, maps, bibliography, and index. One of the best volumes in the "Rivers of America" series. The third and final portion of the book is a good popular discussion of pioneer irrigation in the Imperial Valley, development of the Boulder Canyon Project, and negotiations with Mexico over the appropriation of the river's water.

Watkins, T.H. "Conquest of the Colorado: Earth-Movers, Dam-Builders, and the End of a Free River." *American West,* VI (July 1969), 5-9. Good overview of the history of Hoover Dam that questions the assumptions and values that support large water projects.

Webb, Walter Prescott. *The Great Plains.* Boston: Ginn and Company, 1931. xiv + 525 pp. Illustrations, maps, tables, notes, bibliographies, and index. A great, classic study on the "relation between environment and institutions." According to Webb, "the Plains destroyed the old formula of living and demanded a new one. . . ." Among the innovations required by the western environment were windmills, irrigation, and dryland farming.

Weil, Samuel C. "Fifty Years of Water Law." *Harvard Law Review,* L (Dec. 1936), 252-304. Focuses on the development of water law in the West and the principles of correlative rights and reasonable use.

Whitaker, J. Russel, and Edward A. Ackerman. *American Resources: Their Management and Conservation.* See chapter on "Sewers and Wastewater Treatment."

White, Gilbert F. "A Perspective of River Basin Development." *Journal of Law and Contemporary Problems.* See chapter on "Flood Control and Drainage."

White, Gilbert F. *Strategies of American Water Management.* See chapter on "Community Water Supply."

Widstoe, John A. "History and Problems of Irrigation Development in the West." *Proceedings of the American Society of Civil En-*

gineers, LII (March 1926), 396-402. Strong appeal to continue the reclamation of western arid lands.

Widstoe, John A. *The Principles of Irrigation Practice.* New York: Macmillan Company, 1920. xxvi + 496 pp. Illustrations, charts, tables, graphs, appendix, bibliographies, and index. A good primer on irrigation practices that includes a great deal of information on the evolution of water utilization in the American West.

Willard, James F., ed. *The Union Colony at Greeley, Colorado, 1869-1871.* Boulder: University of Colorado, 1918. xxxii + 412 pp. Notes and index. Excellent source on the historic irrigation settlement. The strong introduction is followed by collections of minutes, financial records, private correspondence, and other records.

Williams, Albert N. *The Water and the Power: Development of the Five Great Rivers of the West.* New York: Duell, Sloan and Pearce, 1951. xiv + 378 pp. Illustrations, maps, charts, bibliography, and index. A popular, thinly researched account of western water development. The organization is disjointed and the narrative uninspired.

Wilson, Herbert M. "American Irrigation Engineering." *Transactions of the American Society of Civil Engineers,* XXV (July-Dec. 1891), 161-222. Excellent source on the design of early dams, weirs, canals, and other irrigation facilities.

Wood, Richard Coke. *The Owens Valley and the Los Angeles Water Controversy: Owens Valley as I Knew It.* See chapter on "Community Water Supply."

Woodbury, David O. *The Colorado Conquest.* New York: Dodd, Mead, & Company, 1941. xiii + 367 pp. Illustrations, maps, and index. A history of water development on the Lower Colorado River from Spanish settlement to the completion of Hoover Dam. Nearly 200 pages are devoted to irrigation and flooding in the Imperial Valley.

Woodbury, Richard B. "The Hohokam at Pueblo Grande, Arizona. *American Antiquity,* XXVI (Oct. 1960), 267-70. Description of two large irrigation canals built by the Hohokam Indians near present-day Phoenix in the twelfth and thirteenth centuries.

Wright, Harold Bell. *The Winning of Barbara Worth.* Chicago: Book Supply Company Publishers, 1911. 511 pp. Illustrations. Students of western water history will enjoy this historical novel that uses California's Imperial Valley for its setting.

Wright, Jim. *The Coming Water Famine.* New York: Coward-McCann, 1966. 255 pp. Index. A forecast of water shortages induced by over appropriation and pollution. The author is a United States congressman from Texas.

Zucker, Paul. *American Bridges and Dams.* See chapter on "Roads, Streets, and Highways."

3

Waterways

Waterway development for navigation has been an integral part of America's founding and development. Since the colonial era, harbors, lakes, and rivers have provided an extensive water transportation network. Natural streams and estuaries offered the first access to the interior, and these same waterways have been refashioned, maintained, and linked together by canals.

The first navigation improvements consisted of removing snags and other obstructions, extending piers to the navigable depths, and marking channels. From the 1820s to the 1850s, the nation was swept by a canal-building craze that aided the growth of a national market economy before succumbing to depression and railroad competition. For the past century and a half, federal activity in the waterway field has been conducted primarily by the Army Corps of Engineers. The nation's rivers and harbors have been the setting for a vast array of projects that improve navigation. The corps also maintains fleets of dredges, barges, and other equipment to support maintenance and operational activities.

The following books, articles, and dissertations fall into several general categories: pre-Civil War river travel and canal building; the evolution of lighthouses and other aids to navigation; the development of major harbor and port facilities; and the historical evolution of the corps' policies, programs, and projects.

Abbott, Frederick Kendall. "The Role of the Civil Engineer in Internal Improvements: The Contributions of the Two Loammi Baldwins, Father & Son, 1776-1838." Doctoral dissertation, Columbia University, 1952.

Aitken, Hugh G.J. "Financing the Welland Canal: An Episode in the History of the St. Lawrence Waterway." *Bulletin of the Business Historical Society,* XXVI (Sept. 1952), 135-64. Compares and contrasts the relative strengths and weaknesses of the Welland and Erie canals.

Albion, Robert Greenhalgh, and Jennie Barnes Pope. *The Rise of New York Port: [1815-1860]*. New York: Charles Scribner's Sons, 1939. xiv + 485 pp. Illustrations, appendices, bibliography, and index. A comprehensive history of the port of New York during its "significant middle period, when New York definitely drew ahead of its rivals and established itself as the chief American seaport and metropolis." This volume will be useful to individuals conducting research on nineteenth-century internal improvements. Some information on port facilities is included.

Albjerg, Victor J. "Federal Practice Toward Internal Improvements, 1789-1860." Doctoral dissertation, University of Wisconsin, 1927.

Albjerg, Victor J. "Internal Improvements without a Policy (1789-1861)." *Indiana Magazine of History,* XXVIII (Sept. 1932), 168-79. Although a dated overview of early federal internal improvements, the article contains a useful table on the relative distribution of appropriations for rivers and harbors, canals, and roads from 1802 to 1859.

Alperin, Lynn M. *Custodians of the Coast: History of the United States Army Engineers at Galveston.* Galveston, Texas: United States Army Corps of Engineers, Galveston District, 1977. xi + 318 pp. Illustrations, notes, appendices, bibliography, and index. A skillful discussion of the corps' rivers and harbors work along the Texas Gulf Coast since the mid-nineteenth century. The book's strongest chapters discuss the evolution of the Houston Ship Channel and development of deep-water ports at Freeport, Corpus Christi, Brownsville, and other coastal cities. Also included are discussions of flood control, military installations, hydroelectric power production, flood control, and disaster assistance.

Ambler, Charles Henry. *A History of Transportation in the Ohio Valley.* Glendale, Calif.: Arthur H. Clark, 1932. 465 pp. Illustrations, maps, notes, and index. A dull and dated water transportation history.

American Dredging Company. *Four Times Panama: A Century of Dredging the American Way, 1867-1967.* n.p.: American Dredging Company, 1967. 87 pp. Illustrations. Although a company paean, the book is one of the few sources available on a subject that should receive greater attention from scholars. Excellent illustrations on the origins of dredging are included.

American Waterways Operators. *Big Load Afloat: U.S. Inland Water Transportation Resources.* Washington, D.C.: American Waterways Operators, Inc., 1965. vii + 100 pp. Illustrations, maps, and tables. A practical guide to the river and coastal transportation industry in the United States. Historical information on towboats and barges is included, and the publication's maps and statistical summaries are useful.

Applewhite, Joseph David. "Early Trade and Navigation on the Cumberland River." Master's thesis, Vanderbilt University, 1940.

Armroyd, George. *A Connected View of the Whole Internal Navigation of the United States, Natural and Artificial; Present and Prospective.* Philadelphia: H.C. Carye & J. Lea, 1826. 192 pp. Maps. A classic survey of 103 canals built in the United States before 1825. Each sketch describes the canal's length, route, cost, dimensions, and major engineering features such as locks, aqueducts, and reservoirs. It is an excellent source of information on the origins of inland navigation.

Armstrong, Ellis L.; Michael C. Robinson; and Suellen M. Hoy, eds. *History of Public Works in the United States, 1776-1976.* See chapter on "Planning, Engineering, and Administration."

Artingstall, William. "Chicago River Tunnels—Their History and Method of Construction." *Journal of the Western Society of Engineers.* See chapter on "Roads, Streets, and Highways."

Axelrod, Donald. "Government Covers the Waterfront: An Administrative Study of the Background, Origin, Development, and Effectiveness of the Bistate Waterfront Commission of New York Harbor, 1953-1966." Doctoral dissertation, Syracuse University, 1967. 542 pp.

Bailey, Thomas A. "Interest in a Nicaragua Canal, 1903-1931." *Hispanic American Historical Review,* XVI (Feb. 1936), 2-28. Overview of the persistence of this alternative canal route in American foreign policy even after the completion of the Panama Canal.

Bakenhus, Reuben Edwin, ed. *The Panama Canal.* n.p.: U.S. Navy Board of Control, n.d. xi + 257 pp. Illustrations, maps, charts, tables, diagrams, notes, appendix, and index. A collection of articles by various authors originally published in the *Proceedings of the United States Naval Institute*. Most of the essays discuss the engineering and construction aspects of the canal's development. Others cover the waterway's history, role in national defense, and position in international law.

Baldwin, Leland D. *The Keelboat on Western Waters.* Pittsburgh: University of Pittsburgh Press, 1941. xiv + 268 pp. Illustrations, notes, bibliography, and index. A good summary of river navigation to about 1850.

Barbee, John D. "Navigation and River Improvement in Middle Tennessee, 1807-1834." Master's thesis, Vanderbilt University, 1934.

Barber, Henry Eugene. "The History of The Florida Cross-State Canal." Doctoral dissertation, University of Georgia, 1969.

Bard, Edwin W. "The Port of New York Authority." Doctoral dissertation, Columbia University, 1940. 177 pp.

Barnes, Joseph W. "Historic Broad Street Bridge and the Erie Canal Sesquicentennial, 1825-1975." *Rochester History.* See chapter on "Roads, Streets, and Highways."

Barsness, Richard W. "Iron Horses and an Inner Harbor at San Pedro Bay, 1867-1890." *Pacific Historical Review,* XXXIV (Aug. 1965), 289-303. Well-researched study of attempts by the Southern Pacific Railroad to gain access to a deep-water port.

Barsness, Richard W. "Los Angeles' Quest for Improved Transportation, 1846-1861." *California Historical Society Quarterly,* XLVI (Dec. 1967), 291-306. Chronicles efforts by the city to develop a deep-water port that would expand the economy.

Barsness, Richard W. "Maritime Activity and Port Development in the United States since 1900: A Survey." *Journal of Transport History,* II (Feb. 1974), 167-84. Pathbreaking article on the historical development of ports in the United States. It is an excellent source of research ideas on this topic.

Barsness, Richard W. "Railroads and Los Angeles: The Quest for a Deep-Water Port." *Southern California Quarterly,* XLVII (1965), 379-94. Discusses efforts to obtain a deep-water port at San Pedro Bay.

Barsness, Richard W. "The Maritime Development of San Pedro Bay, California, 1821-1921." Doctoral dissertation, University of Minnesota, 1963. 621 pp.

Baughman, James P. "The Evolution of Rail-Water Systems of Transportation in the Gulf Southwest, 1836-1890." *Journal of Southern History,* XXXIV (Aug. 1968), 357-81. Excellent treatment of early efforts to coordinate and integrate transportation systems.

Baumhoff, Richard G. *The Dammed Missouri Valley: One Sixth of our Nation.* See chapter on "Flood Control and Drainage."

Beaver, Patrick. *A History of Lighthouses.* London: Peter Davies, 1971. xii + 158 pp. Illustrations, diagrams, appendices, bibliography, and index. History of British and American lighthouses that offers extensive coverage of construction methods.

Benincasa, Frederick Albert. "The Tennessee Valley Authority from 1933 to 1961." Doctoral dissertation. See chapter on "Flood Control and Drainage."

Bennett, Charles E. "Early History of the Cross-Florida Barge Canal." *Florida Historical Quarterly,* XLV (Oct. 1966), 134-44. A 400-year survey history of attempts to build the controversial waterway. The article begins with plans formulated by sixteenth-century Spanish settlers and closes with the first project appropriations granted by Congress in 1963.

Bennett, Ira E., ed. *History of the Panama Canal, Its Construction and Builders.* Washington, D.C.: Historical Publishing Company, 1915. xi + 543 pp. Illustrations, maps, appendices, and index. The principal value of this popular history is its collection of excellent construction photographs.

Beyer, Barry K. *The Chenango Canal.* n.p.: Chenango County Historical Society, 1968. Illustrations and map. A thin factual summary of the canal's history.

Binns, Archie. *Northwest Gateway: The Story of the Port of Seattle.* Garden City: Doubleday, Doran & Company, 1941. ix + 313 pp. Illustrations and index. Contains little on the history of the port's facilities.

Bishop, Avard Longley. "The State Works of Pennsylvania." *Transactions of the Connecticut Academy of Arts and Sciences,* XIII (1907-1908), 149-297. A dry, uninspired survey of canals and railroads built by the State of Pennsylvania from 1826 to 1859.

Bishop, Joseph Bucklin. *Goethals, Genius of the Panama Canal: A Biography.* New York: Harper & Brothers Publishers, 1930. xiv + 493 pp. Illustrations, appendix, and index. Romantic biography of the builder of the Panama Canal.

Black, W.M. "Advances in Waterways Engineering during a Half Century." *Transactions of the American Society of Civil Engineers,* 93 (1929), 191-217. Good review on progress in the design and construction of river improvements.

Black, W. M. *The United States Public Works.* See chapter on "Flood Control and Drainage."

Blackorby, E. C. "Theodore Roosevelt's Conservation Policies and Their Impact upon America and the American West." *North Dakota History,* 25 (Oct. 1958), 107-17. Describes origins as well as impact.

Blee, C. E. "Development of the Tennessee River Waterway." *Transactions of the American Society of Civil Engineers,* CT (1953), 1132-46. Describes the structures built to facilitate navigation, flood control, and power production.

Bloor, Ralph L. "System of Waterways at Chicago, Ill." *Transactions of the American Society of Civil Engineers,* CT (1953), 1205-14. A brief look at the development of Chicago's nearby inland waterways and their influence on the city's growth.

Bluestone, Daniel M., ed. *Cleveland: An Inventory of Historic Engineering and Industrial Sites.* See chapter on "Community Water Supply."

Bogart, Ernest Ludlow. *Internal Improvements and State Debt in Ohio: An Essay in Economic History.* New York: Langmans, Green and Company, 1924. x + 235 pp. Tables, notes, bibliography, and index. A largely economic history of canal development in Ohio. Little information is included on engineering aspects.

Borger, Henry Charles, Jr. "The Role of the Army Engineers in the Westward Movement in the Lake Huron-Lake Michigan Basin Before the Civil War." Doctoral dissertation, Columbia University, 1954. 287 pp.

Boughter, I. F. "Internal Improvements in Northwestern Virginia: A Study of State Policy prior to the Civil War." Doctoral dissertation. See chapter on "Roads, Streets, and Highways."

Bowman, James S. "Multipurpose River Developments." *Transactions of the American Society of Civil Engineers,* CT (1953), 1125-31. Reviews general trends.

Brandt, Francis Burke. *The Majestic Delaware: The Nation's Foremost Historic River.* Philadelphia: Brandt and Gummere Company, 1929. 191 pp. Illustrations and index. Largely a shipbuilding history of the Philadelphia area that includes a host of information on port facilities and aids to navigation.

Branyan, Robert L. *Taming the Mighty Missouri: A History of the Kansas City District, Army Corps of Engineers, 1907-1971.* See chapter on "Flood Control."

Bray, Oscar S. "Restoring Historic Wharf at Salem, Mass." *Civil Engineering,* 10 (Feb. 1940), 105-07. Gives a brief history of Derby Wharf (the whole waterfront area is a national historic landmark) and describes the role of engineers in the National Park Service's restoration project.

Bridenbaugh, Carl. *Cities in Revolt: Urban Life in America, 1743-1776.* See chapter on "Planning, Engineering, and Administration."

Bridenbaugh, Carl. *Cities in the Wilderness: The First Century of Urban Life in America, 1625-1742.* See chapter on "Planning, Engineering, and Administration.

Brittain, James E. *A Brief History of Engineering in Georgia and Guide to 76 Historic Engineering Sites.* See chapter on "Planning, Engineering, and Administration."

Brooks, Robert B. "Robert E. Lee—Civil Engineer." *Civil Engineering,* 10 (March 1940), 167-69. The author contends that Lee was "a great civil engineer" and shows how his regulating works preserved St. Louis as a river port.

Brown, Alexander Crosby. "Colonial Williamsburg's Canal Scheme." *Virginia Magazine of History and Biography,* 86 (Jan. 1978), 26-32. Interesting canal scheme authorized by the Virginia House of Burgesses in 1772 but never built.

Brown, Alexander Crosby. *The Dismal Swamp Canal.* Chesapeake, Va.: Norfolk County Historical Society, 1967. 143 pp. Illustrations, map, notes, and appendices. A competent history of the oldest artificial waterway in the United States still in use.

Brown, C. M. *Aids to Navigation in Alaska History.* n.p.: Alaska Office of Statewide Cultural Programs, 1974. 57 pp. Illustrations and bibliography. A competent inventory that is preceded by a historical summary of Alaskan aids to navigation.

Brown, D. Clayton. *Rivers, Rockets and Readiness: Army Engineers in the Sunbelt: A*

History of the Fort Worth District U.S. Army Corps of Engineers, 1950-1975. See chapter on "Flood Control."

Brown, Douglas Stewart. "The Iberville Canal Project: Its Relation to Anglo-French Commercial Rivalry in the Mississippi Valley, 1763-1775." *Mississippi Valley Historical Review,* XXXII (March 1946), 491-516.

Brown, Earl I. "The Chesapeake and Delaware Canal." *Transactions of the American Society of Civil Engineers,* 95 (1931), 716-65. Historical synopsis of various phases of the canal's development from 1764 to 1927.

Brown, G.P. *Drainage Channel and Waterway: A History of the Effort to Secure an Effective and Harmless Method for the Disposal of the Sewage of the City of Chicago, and to Create a Navigable Channel between Lake Michigan and the Mississippi River.* See chapter on "Sewers and Wastewater Treatment."

Brown, George W. "The First St. Lawrence Deepening Scheme." *Michigan History Magazine,* X (Oct. 1926), 593-605. Efforts to improve navigation on the St. Lawrence in the 1840s and 1850s.

Brown, George W. "The Opening of the St. Lawrence to American Shipping." *Canadian Historical Review,* VII (March 1926), 4-12.

Brown, George W. "The St. Lawrence Waterway in the Nineteenth Century." *Queen's Quarterly,* XXXV (Autumn 1928), 628-42. An historical account of its development. The author emphasizes the enthusiasm aroused by the waterway's potential since the seventeenth century.

Brown, George Williams. "The St. Lawrence Waterway as a Factor in International Trade and Politics, 1783-1854." Doctoral dissertation, University of Chicago, 1924. 227 pp. Illustrations, maps, notes, and bibliography. Useful discussion of the St. Lawrence as a transportation artery.

Brown, Leahmae. "The Development of National Policy with Respect to Water Resources." Doctoral dissertation, University of Illinois, 1937. An excellent source on the development of federal water policies from the Progressive era to the New Deal. General discussions of navigation, irrigation, flood control, and hydroelectric power are included in the first major portion of the study. Subsequent chapters cover multiple-purpose endeavors such as the Boulder Canyon Project, Tennessee Valley Authority, and the Great Lakes-St. Lawrence Seaway. The dissertation is largely an endorsement of strong national and regional planning.

Buckmaster, Jeanne Arwilda. "Internal Improvements in Illinois from 1818 to 1850." Master's thesis, University of Chicago, 1910. 120 pp. A dated, descriptive overview of the Illinois Michigan Canal, Cumberland Road, Chicago Harbor, and other early internal improvements.

Bunker, John G. *Harbor & Haven: An Illustrated History of the Port of New York.* Woodland Hills, Calif.: Windsor Publications, 1979. iii + 302 pp. Illustrations, bibliography, and index. A well-illustrated, popular account of the Port of New York's development. Research for and publication of the volume were sponsored by the Maritime Association of the Port of New York.

Bunting, W.H., comp. *Portrait of a Port: Boston, 1852-1914.* Cambridge: Belknap Press of Harvard University Press, 1971. xviii + 519 pp. Illustrations, notes, appendices, and index. A book of photographs accompanied by excellent narrative commentary.

Burke, Padraic. *A History of the Port of Seattle.* Seattle: Port of Seattle, 1976. xiv + 134 pp. Illustrations, notes, bibliography, and index. Excellent case study of the port from the 1850s to the present. The book offers an especially insightful chapter on the movement to obtain municipal ownership of ports in the early twentieth century, a subject more historians should investigate.

Burke, Padraic. "The Struggle for Public Ownership: The Early History of the Port of Seattle." *Pacific Northwest Quarterly,* 68 (April 1977), 60-71. The author skillfully analyzes the creation of the Port of Seattle in 1911, which has since become one of the most powerful political and social forces in the city.

Cabell, Branch, and A.J. Hanna. *The St. Johns: A Parade of Diversities.* New York: Farrar & Rinehart, 1943. xii + 324 pp. Illustrations, bibliography, and index. A volume in the "Rivers of America Series" that focuses on the social and economic history of northeastern Florida from the first Spanish settlements to about 1880. Some material is included on river transportation.

Cahill, Walter J. "Water Terminals of Yesterday and Today." *Civil Engineering,* 3 (Aug. 1933), 432-34. An overview of dock and harbor engineering since the mid-nineteenth century.

Cameron, Ian. *The Impossible Dream: The Building of the Panama Canal.* London: Hodden and Stoughton, 1971. 284 pp. Illustrations, diagrams, bibliography, and index. A pedestrian and uninspired history of the canal that offers little that is unique.

Carey, Mathew. *Brief View of the System of Internal Improvement of the State of Pennsylvania: Containing a Glance at Its Rise, Progress, Retardation. . . .* Philadelphia: Society for the Promotion of Internal Improvement, 1831. vii + 36 pp.

Carter, Edward C., II, ed. *The Papers of Benjamin Henry Latrobe: The Virginia Journals of Benjamin Henry Latrobe, 1795-1798.* See chapter on "Public Buildings."

Catlin, George B. *The Story of Detroit.* See chapter on "Community Water Supply."

Chalmers, Harvey, II. *The Birth of the Erie Canal.* New York: Bookman Associates, 1960. 195 pp. Illustrations, map, and bibliography. A rather weak, undocumented account of the efforts of De Witt Clinton and other individuals who promoted the canal's development.

Chaney, Donald E. "Constitutional Validity of a Federal Reforestation Program for Upper Tributaries of Navigable Rivers." *Missouri Law Review,* 25 (June 1960), 317-23.

Chappell, Gordon. *Historic Resource Study—East and West Potomac Parks: A History.* See chapter on "Parks and Recreation."

Chase, Stuart. *Rich Land, Poor Land: A Study of Waste in the Natural Resources of America.* See chapter on "Flood Control and Drainage."

Chevrier, Lionel. *The St. Lawrence Seaway.* Toronto: Macmillan Company of Canada, 1959. x + 174 pp. Illustrations, maps, and index. A fine personal account of the seaway's development by Canada's former minister of transport. The book covers the hydroelectric dimensions of the project as well as cooperation between the United States and Canada in planning and constructing the seaway.

Chorpening, C.H. "Waterway Growth in the United States." *Transactions of the American Society of Civil Engineers,* CT (1953), 976-1041. A general history of waterway development by the Corps of Engineers' assistant chief of engineers for civil works.

Cipra, David L. *Lighthouses & Lightships of the Northern Gulf of Mexico.* n.p.: United States Coast Guard, 1974. 62 pp. Illustrations, maps, and diagrams. The illustrative materials are virtually the only useful dimension of this short book.

Clapp, Gordon R. *The TVA: Approach to the Development of a Region.* See chapter on "Flood Control."

Clark, Thomas D. *The Kentucky.* New York: Farrar & Rinehart, 1942. x + 431 pp. Illustrations, bibliography, and index. One of the better contributions to the "Rivers of America" series. Although some material is included on river transportation and floods, the major portion of the book is devoted to the social history of eastern Kentucky.

Clay, Floyd M. *A Century on the Mississippi: A History of the Memphis District, U.S. Army Corps of Engineers, 1876-1976.* See chapter on "Flood Control and Drainage."

Clay, Floyd M. *A History of the Little Rock District, U.S. Army Corps of Engineers, 1881-1979.* See chapter on "Flood Control and Drainage."

Clement, Thomas M., Jr., and Glenn Lopez. *Engineering a Victory for Our Environment: A Citizen's Guide to the U.S. Army Corps of Engineers.* See chapter on "Flood Control and Drainage."

Clonts, F.W. "Travel and Transportation in Colonial North Carolina." *North Carolina Historical Review,* III (Jan. 1926), 16-35. A discussion of waterways and roads in the northeastern part of North Carolina during the proprietary period.

Cobb, W.C. "The Passes of the Mississippi River." *Transactions of the American Society of Civil Engineers,* CT (1953), 1147-62. Gives special attention to the methods, modifications, and repairs initiated first by James B. Eads, and then by the Corps of Engineers.

Cochran, Thomas C. *The New American State Papers: Transportation.* See chapter on "Roads, Streets, and Highways."

Coffey, Lorraine Mildred. "The Rise and Decline of the Port of Newburyport, 1783-1820." Doctoral dissertation, Boston University, 1975.

Coleman, Peter J. *The Transformation of Rhode Island, 1790-1860.* Providence: Brown University Press, 1965. xiv + 314 pp. Maps, tables, notes, and index. A largely business history of Rhode Island that includes a discussion of early nineteenth-century canal projects.

Colles, Christopher. *Proposal of a Design for the Promotion of the Interests of the United States of America. . . . by Means of Inland Navigable Communications. . . .* New York: By author, 1808. 22 pp. Map.

Comeaux, Malcolm L. "The Atchafalaya River Raft." *Louisiana Studies,* IX (Winter 1970), 217-27. A history of the removal of a 30-mile log jam which blocked the Atchafalaya in the nineteenth century.

Comstock, Howard Payne. "History of Canals in Indiana." *Indiana Magazine of History,* VII (March 1911), 1-15. An undocumented, cursory survey of Indiana canals.

Condit, Carl W. *Chicago, 1930-1970: Building, Planning, and Urban Technology.* See chapter on "Planning, Engineering, and Administration."

Condon, George E. *Stars in the Water: The Story of the Erie Canal.* Garden City, N.Y.: Doubleday & Company, 1974. xv + 338 pp. Illustrations, bibliography, and index. A popular synthesis of the canal's history that offers little unique material.

Corthell, E. L. *A History of the Jetties at the Mouth of the Mississippi River.* New York: John Wiley & Sons, 1881. xvi + 383 pp. Illustrations, maps, charts, diagrams, appendices, and index. A classic treatise on James B. Eads' successful efforts to create a navigable passage at the mouth of the Mississippi River through the construction of jetties.

Cottman, George S. "The Internal Improvement System of Indiana." *Indiana Magazine of History,* III (Sept. 1907), 117-24. An "outline" of Indiana's great plan for internal improvement "which went into active operation with the famous internal improvement law of 1836."

Cowdrey, Albert E. *A City for the Nation: The Army Engineers and the Building of Washington, D.C., 1790-1967.* See chapter on "Planning, Engineering, and Administration."

Cowdrey, Albert E. *Land's End: A History of the New Orleans District, U.S. Army Corps of Engineers, and Its Lifelong Battle with the Lower Mississippi and Other Rivers Wending Their Way to the Sea.* Washington, D.C.: Government Printing Office, 1977. xv + 118 pp. Illustrations, maps, notes, appendices, bibliography, and index. A lucid chronicle that focuses on the flood control and navigation activities of the corps on the Lower Mississippi and its tributaries.

Cowdrey, Albert E. "Pioneering Environmental Law: The Army Corps of Engineers and the Refuse Act." *Pacific Historical Review,* XLIV (Aug. 1975), 331-49. Traces the role of the Army Corps of Engineers in transforming the Refuse Act from navigational to environmental law. The article does much to dispel stereotypes of the corps as an environmental villain.

Cowdrey, Albert E. *The Delta Engineers: A History of the United States Army Corps of Engineers in the New Orleans District.* See chapter on "Flood Control and Drainage."

Cowdrey, Albert Edward. "The Delta Engineers." Doctoral dissertation. See chapter on "Flood Control and Drainage."

Cox, Richard J. "Professionalism and Civil Engineering in Early America: The Vicissitudes of James Shriver's Career, 1815-1826." *Maryland Historical Magazine.* See chapter on "Planning, Engineering, and Administration."

Coyle, David Cushman. *Conservation: An American Story of Conflict and Accomplishment.* See chapter on "Flood Control and Drainage."

Cranmer, H. Jerome. "Internal Improvements in New Jersey: Planning the Morris Canal." *Proceedings of the New Jersey Historical Society,* 69 (1951), 324-41. Good discussion of the state government's role in planning and promoting the project.

Cranmer, H. Jerome. "The New Jersey Canals: A Study of the Role of Government in Economic Development." Doctoral dissertation, Columbia University, 1956. 382 pp.

Creighton, Wilbur Foster. *Building of Nashville.* See chapter on "Public Buildings."

Crittenden, Charles Christopher. "Inland Navigation in North Carolina, 1763-1789." *North Carolina Historical Review,* VIII (April

1931), 145-54. Good case study of colonial inland navigation.

Cross, Whitney R. "Ideas in Politics: The Conservation Policies of the Two Roosevelts." *Journal of the History of Ideas,* 14 (June 1953), 421-38.

Cullen, Allan H. *Rivers in Harness: The Story of Dams.* See chapter on "Irrigation."

Curtis, Gregory G. "Connecticut Historic Riverway: A Case Study of Acceptance and Rejection of a National Recreation Area." Doctoral dissertation. See chapter on "Parks and Recreation."

Cuthbertson, George A. *Freshwater: A History and Narrative of the Great Lakes.* New York: Macmillan Company, 1931. xiv + 315 pp. Illustrations, notes, appendices, bibliography, and index. Contains some information on canals, ports, and aids to navigation.

Daniels, George H. *Science in American Society: A Social History.* New York: Alfred A. Knopf, 1971. xii + 390 pp. + x. Notes, bibliography, and index. Chapter 8 of this fine book, "Geophysics and Politics," discusses the surveying and exploration of army engineers before the Civil War and their contribution to the development of canals, roads, and railroads.

Danker, Donald. "The Influence of Transportation upon Nebraska Territory." *Nebraska History,* 47 (June 1966), 187-208. Largely a breezy discussion of river transportation, railroads, ferries, and wagon roads in the 1850s and 1860s.

Darling, Arthur B., ed. *The Public Papers of Francis G. Newlands.* See chapter on "Energy."

David, Grant Miller. *The Department of Transportation.* See chapter on "Planning, Engineering, and Administration."

Davis, Virgil S. *A History of the Mobile District, 1815 to 1971.* See chapter on "Military Installations."

Dearing, Charles L., and Wilfred Owen. *National Transportation Policy.* See chapter on "Airways and Airports."

Decker, Edwin R. "Replacement—Lock and Dam No. 26: History, Objectives, and Scope." *Journal of the Waterways and Harbors Division, Proceedings of the American Society of Civil Engineers,* 96 (Feb. 1970), 1-8. Historical overview of the facility that attempts to justify a proposed replacement.

de Gast, Robert. *The Lighthouses of the Chesapeake.* Baltimore: Johns Hopkins University Press, 1973. ix + 174 pp. Illustrations, maps, bibliography, and index. A picture album of Chesapeake lighthouses.

Derby, William Edward. "A History of the Port of Milwaukee, 1835-1910." Doctoral dissertation, University of Wisconsin, 1963. 459 pp.

Derry, T.K., and Trevor I. Williams. *A Short History of Technology: From the Earliest Times to A.D. 1900.* See chapter on "Planning, Engineering, and Administration."

Dick, Everett. *The Lure of the Land: A Social History of the Public Lands from the Articles of Confederation to the New Deal.* See chapter on "Irrigation."

Dickie, A. W. "Alviso—A New Old Port." *Pacific Marine Review,* 27 (March 1930), 106-09. Port at the southern end of San Francisco Bay.

Dickinson, John Newton. "The Canal at Sault Ste. Marie, Michigan: Inception, Construction, Early Operation and the Canal Grant Lands." Doctoral dissertation, University of Wisconsin, 1968. 350 pp.

Dimock, Marshall E. *Developing America's Waterways: Administration of the Inland Waterways Corporation.* Chicago: University of Chicago Press, 1935. xv + 123 pp. Charts, tables, notes, bibliography, and index. A good economic and administrative analysis of the federally owned barge company that was founded in 1924. The author discusses the corporation's legislative background as well as its success in promoting river transportation on the Mississippi and other rivers.

Dobney, Frederick J. *River Engineers on the Middle Mississippi: A History of the St. Louis District, U.S. Army Corps of Engineers.* Washington, D.C.: Government Printing Office, 1978. viii + 177 pp. Illustrations, maps, notes, appendices, bibliography, and index. One of the best corps district histories. In addition to describing river improvements and other endeavors, Dobney discusses the economic, environmental, and sociological changes that resulted.

Dodds, Gordon B. *Hiram Martin Chittenden:*

His Public Career. See chapter on "Flood Control and Drainage."

Dorsey, Florence L. *Master of the Mississippi: Henry Shreve and the Conquest of the Mississippi.* New York: Literary Classics, 1941. iii + 301 pp. Illustrations, notes, bibliography, and index. A biography of a steamboat pioneer on the Mississippi River. The last half of the book contains accounts of snagboat operations and river improvements by the Army Corps of Engineers prior to the Civil War.

Douglas, Byrd. *Steamboatin on the Cumberland.* Nashville: Tennessee Book Company, 161. xv + 407 pp. Illustrations, bibliography, and index. A tedious history of navigation on the Cumberland River in Kentucky and Tennessee.

Drago, Harry Sinclair. *Canal Days in America: The History and Romance of Old Towpaths and Waterways.* New York: Clarkson N. Potter, 1972. ii + 311 pp. Illustrations, notes, bibliography, and index. One of the best popular accounts of the pre-Civil War canal era. The author uses a host of rare photographs to supplement the narrative.

Droze, Wilmon Henry. *High Dams and Slack Waters: TVA Rebuilds a River.* Baton Rouge: Louisiana State University Press, 1965. vii + 174 pp. Graph, notes, bibliography, and index. One of the best books on TVA. The study seeks to determine how well TVA developed navigation on the river and the role this use played in the comprehensive basin-management plan. It also assesses the influence of the commercial artery on economic life in the valley.

Droze, Wilmon Henry. "Tennessee River Navigation: Government and Private Enterprise Since 1932." Doctoral dissertation, Vanderbilt University, 1960. ii + 434 pp. Tables, graph, notes, and bibliography. Deals extensively with the construction of dams, locks, and other navigation improvements.

Drumm, Stella M. "Robert E. Lee and the Improvement of the Mississippi River." *Missouri Historical Society Collections,* VI (Feb. 1929), 157-71. A description of river improvements supervised by Robert E. Lee in 1837-1838 that guaranteed an adequate harbor for St. Louis, Missouri.

Dunaway, Wayland Fuller. "History of the James River and Kanawha Company." Doctoral dissertation, Columbia University, 1922. 254 pp. A largely economic history of Virginia's attempt to tap the commerce of the hinterland.

Dunbar, Seymour. *A History of Travel in America: Showing the Development of Travel and Transportation. . . .* See chapter on "Roads, Streets, and Highways."

Durrenberger, Joseph Austin. *Turnpikes: A Study of the Toll Road Movement in the Middle Atlantic States and Maryland.* See chapter on "Roads, Streets, and Highways."

DuVal, Miles P., Jr. *And the Mountains Will Move: The Story of the Building of the Panama Canal.* Stanford University: Stanford University Press, 1947. xvi + 374 pp. Illustrations, maps, notes, appendices, and index. The story of the building of the Panama Canal from 1849 (construction of the Panama Railroad) through 1914 by a United States navy captain who served at the Port of the Pacific Terminal from 1941 to 1944.

DuVal, Miles P., Jr. *Cadiz to Cathay: The Story of the Long Diplomatic Struggle for the Panama Canal.* Stanford: Stanford University Press, 1947. xiv + 548 pp. Illustrations, map, notes, appendices, bibliography, and index. A lengthy, historical account of America's interoceanic canals and an explanation of "the dramatic events that led to the grant of the Canal Zone to the United States in 1903."

"Early American Canal Tunnel Restored for Historic Value." *Engineering News Record,* 113 (Nov. 22, 1934), 657. Description of a restoration project undertaken to preserve a canal tunnel built near Lebanon, Pennsylvania, in 1828. The endeavor was a joint project of the Civil Works Administration and local citizens.

Ehrenberg, Ralph E. "Nicholas King: First Surveyor of the City of Washington, 1803-1812." *Records of the Columbia Historical Society of Washington, D.C.* See chapter on "Planning, Engineering, and Administration."

Elazar, Daniel J. "Gubernatorial Power and the Illinois and Michigan Canal: A Study of Political Development in the Nineteenth Century." *Journal of the Illinois State Historical Society,* LVIII (Winter 1965), 396-423. Case study of the exercise of executive power. The article includes little on the canal's history.

Elliot, D.O. *The Improvement of the Lower*

Mississippi River for Flood Control and Navigation. See chapter on "Flood Control and Drainage."

Ellis, David M., ed. *The Frontier in American Development: Essays in Honor of Paul Wallace Gates.* Ithaca: Cornell University Press, 1969. xxx + 425 pp. Notes, bibliography, and index. A fine collection of essays. The following will be of particular interest to public works historians: Harry N. Scheiber, "The Ohio-Mississippi Flatboat Trade: Some Reconsiderations," and Irene D. Neu, "The Mineral Lands of the St. Mary's Falls Ship Canal Company.

Esarey, Logan. "Internal Improvements in Early Indiana." *Indiana Historical Society Publications,* V (1915), 40-158. An insipid but factual survey of road, railroad, and waterway development in Indiana prior to the Civil War.

Evans, Paul E. "The Magnificent Obsession of TVA." *Civil Engineering.* See chapter on "Flood Control and Drainage."

Ewen, John M. "The Chicago Harbor." *Journal of the Western Society of Engineers,* XIV. (Dec. 1909), 745-83.

Farrell, Richard T. "Internal-Improvement Projects in Southwestern Ohio, 1815-1834." *Ohio History,* 80 (Winter 1971), 4-23. Well-written and heavily documented history of canal and road construction.

Fatout, Paul. "Canalling in the Whitewater Valley." *Indiana Magazine of History,* LX (March 1964), 37-78. An in-depth survey of canal advocacy and construction in southeastern Indiana from the 1820s to the 1860s.

Fatout, Paul. *Indiana Canals.* West Lafayette, Ind.: Purdue University Studies, 1972. ix + 216 pp. Illustrations, maps, notes, bibliography, and index. A well-written popular account of nineteenth-century canal development in Indiana. The author examines the political background of waterway construction as well as the causes of the decline of this transportation system

Federal Writers' Project. *Boston Looks Seaward: The Story of the Port, 1630-1940.* Boston: Writers' Program of the Works Progress Administration in the State of Massachusetts, 1941. 316 pp. Illustrations.

Ferejohn, John A. *Pork Barrel Politics: Rivers and Harbors Legislation, 1947-1968.* See chapter on "Flood Control and Drainage."

Ferguson, H. B. *History of the Improvement of the Lower Mississippi River for Flood Control and Navigation, 1932-1939.* See chapter on "Flood Control and Drainage."

Feringa, P.A., and Charles W. Schweizer. "One Hundred Years of Improvement on Lower Mississippi River." *Transactions of the American Society of Civil Engineers,* CT (1953), 1100-24. The story of the improvement and development of the Mississippi River for navigation and flood control.

Finch, J.K. "John Bloomfield Jervis, Civil Engineer." *Transactions of the Newcomen Society (London) for the Study of the History of Engineering and Technology.* See chapter on "Community Water Supply."

Finer, Herman. *The T.V.A.: Lessons for International Application.* See chapter on "Flood Control and Drainage."

Fisher, Edwin A. "Engineering and Public Works in the City of Rochester During the Past Century." *Centennial History of Rochester, New York.* See chapter on "Planning, Engineering, and Administration."

FitzGerald, Gerald C. "The Port of Los Angeles." *Civil Engineering,* (Sept. 1935), 519-23. Good historical summary of the port's development by the city.

FitzSimons, Neal, ed. *The Reminiscences of John B. Jervis: Engineer of the Old Croton.* See chapter on "Community Water Supply."

Flagler, C.A.F. "Engineering Features of Chesapeake and Delaware, and Norfolk-Beaufort Waterways." *Annals of the American Academy of Political and Social Science,* XXXI (Jan.-June 1908), 73-80.

Flaxman, Edward. *Great Feats of Modern Engineering.* See chapter on "Roads, Streets, and Highways."

Fleming, George Joseph, Jr. "Canal at Chicago: A Study in Political and Social History." Doctoral dissertation, Catholic University of America, 1950. xi + 374 pp. Notes and bibliographical essay. By far the best study of the Illinois and Michigan Canal. The author skillfully handles the waterways' history with respect to finance, land policy, and politics.

Folmsbee, Stanley John. "Sectionalism and Internal Improvements in Tennessee, 1796-1845." Doctoral dissertation, University of

Pennsylvania, 1939. vi + 293 pp. A good history of state-aided efforts to build railroads, navigation improvements, and turnpikes in Tennessee. The author traces the sectional rivalries in the state fostered by internal improvements and the burden of debt imposed by the public works projects.

Forkes, John D. "The Port of Boston, 1783-1815." Doctoral dissertation, Harvard University, 1937.

Foreman, Grant. *A History of Oklahoma.* See chapter on "Roads, Streets, and Highways."

Formwalt, Lee William. "Benjamin Henry Latrobe and the Development of Internal Improvements in the New Republic, 1796-1820." Doctoral dissertation, Catholic University, 1977. 330 pp.

Forness, Norman Olaf. "The Origins and Early History of the United States Department of the Interior." Doctoral dissertation. See chapter on "Public Buildings."

Foy, Bernard L., comp. *A Bibliography for the TVA Program.* See chapter on "Flood Control and Drainage."

Fraser, Chelsea. *The Story of Engineering in America.* See chapter on "Planning, Engineering, and Administration."

Fries, Amos A. "Los Angeles Harbor." *Professional Memoirs,* IV (Jan.-Feb. 1913), 1-35.

Friis, Herman R., and Ralph E. Ehrenberg. "Nicholas King and His Wharfing Plans for the City of Washington, 1797." *Records of the Columbia Historical Society of Washington, D.C.* (1966-1968), 34-46. Illustrates that King played a significant role in laying out the city of Washington.

Gaum, Carl H. "History and Future of Ohio River Navigation." *Journal of the Waterways and Harbors Division, Proceedings of the American Society of Civil Engineers,* 96 (May 1970), 483-95. Largely discusses the evolution of locks and dams on the river.

Geik, George W. "The Restoration of the Port of Philadelphia, 1783-1789." *American Neptune,* XXXII (Oct. 1972), 247-56. Excellent discussion of state and city government efforts to restore and expand port facilities and aids to navigation after the Revolutionary War.

Gibbs, James A. *Sentinels of the North Pacific: The Story of Pacific Coast Lighthouses and Lightships.* Portland: Binfords & Mort, 1955. 232 pp. Illustrations, bibliography, and index. A pedestrian lighthouse history.

Gibbs, Jim. *West Coast Lighthouses: A Pictorial History of the Guiding Lights of the Sea.* Seattle: Superior Publishing Company, 1974. 207 pp. Illustrations, maps, and index. A heavily illustrated state-by-state encyclopedia of west coast lighthouses.

Gilchrist, David T., ed. *The Growth of Seaport Cities, 1790-1825: Proceedings of a Conference Sponsored by the Eleutherian Mills-Hagley Foundation, March 17-19, 1966.* Charlottesville: University Press of Virginia, 1967. xvi + 227 pp. Map, charts, tables, notes, appendices, bibliography, and index. A series of essays largely devoted to economic and demographic topics that include fragmentary information on canals, turnpikes, and horsecar lines.

Gilmore, Harlan. *Transportation and the Growth of Cities.* See chapter on "Roads, Streets, and Highways."

Glaab, Charles N. *The American City: A Documentary History.* Homewood, Ill.: Dorsey Press, 1963. xiv + 478 pp. Notes and suggested readings. Good collection of documents that includes selections on ports, parks, and city planning.

Glasgow, James. "Muskegon, Michigan: The Evolution of a Lake Port." Doctoral dissertation, University of Chicago, 1939. x + 102 pp. Illustrations, maps, tables, notes, and bibliography. Although basically an economic study, considerable information on the port's facilities are included in this solid dissertation.

Glass, Brent D., ed. *North Carolina: An Inventory of Historic Engineering and Industrial Sites.* See chapter on "Roads, Streets, and Highways."

Glunt, Ruth R. *Lighthouses and Legends of the Hudson.* Monroe, N.Y.: Library Research Associates, 1975. xiv + 154 pp. Illustrations and index. A popular account of aids to navigation in the Hudson Valley.

Goldenberg, Joseph. "A Forgotten Dry Dock in Colonial Charlestown." *American Neptune,* XXX (Jan. 1970), 56-61. Description of the nation's first dry dock built in Charleston, Massachusetts, in the late 1670s.

Goodrich, Carter. *Government Promotion of*

American Canals and Railroads, 1800-1890. New York: Columbia University Press, 1965. x + 382 pp. Map, table, notes, bibliography, and index. An excellent study of the role of American governments—federal, state, and local—in the creation of inland transportation facilities. Goodrich points out that planning and operating internal improvements often put an unbearable strain on state and local governments that lacked financial resources as well as engineering and administrative expertise. A primary purpose of the book is to help determine what roles government and private enterprise should play in strengthening the economies of developing nations.

Goodrich, Carter. "The Gallatin Plan After One Hundred and Fifty Years." *Proceedings of the American Philosophical Society,* 102 (1958), 436-41. An excellent analysis of the plan for canal and road improvements published by the secretary of the treasury, Albert Gallatin, in 1808. Goodrich presents the pros and cons of using the plan as a model for building internal improvements in developing nations.

Goodrich, Carter, et al. *Canals and American Economic Development.* New York: Columbia University Press, 1961. viii + 303 pp. Map, tables, graphs, notes, and index. The finest book on the role of public funds in promoting canals and railroads prior to the Civil War. The authors suggest that internal improvements were publicly supported due to the scarcity of capital or lack of private institutions capable of undertaking such projects. Appeals for government support were reinforced by considerations of defense, national unity, and the fear that important transportation systems would be controlled by private monopolies. The book also discusses the influence of canals and railroads on early American economic development.

Gordon, Roy. "Engineering for People: 200 Years of Army Public Works." *Military Engineer,* 68 (May-June 1976), 180-85.

Granger, M.L. *Savannah Harbor: Its Origin and Development, 1733-1890.* Savannah: U.S. Army Engineer District, Savannah, 1968. 53 pp. Maps and notes. History of the harbor that quotes extensively from government documents and other source materials. It is a companion document for the author's history of the Savannah District.

Graves, Herbert C. "The United States Coast and Geodetic Survey." *Marine Review,* XX (Oct. 5, 1899), 12-14. A brief account of the agency's origins and work.

Gray, Ralph Dale. "A History of the Chesapeake and Delaware Canal, 1760-1960." Doctoral dissertation, University of Illinois at Urbana-Champaign, 1962.

Gray, Ralph D. *The National Waterway: A History of the Chesapeake and Delaware Canal, 1769-1965.* Urbana: University of Illinois Press, 1967. xiii + 279 pp. Illustrations, tables, notes, bibliographical essay, and index. One of the best canal histories. The planning, engineering, legislative, and economic aspects are insightfully discussed. Particularly noteworthy is the section on improvements undertaken after the canal was purchased by the federal government in 1919.

Greb, G. Allen. "Opening a New Frontier: San Francisco, Los Angeles, and the Panama Canal." *Pacific Historical Review,* XLVII (Aug. 1978), 405-24. How aggressive businessmen in the two cities formulated special strategies to maximize the benefits expected from the canal's completion. Much of the article deals with the harbor improvements they promoted.

Green, Constance McLaughlin. *Holyoke, Massachusetts: A Case History of the Industrial Revolution in America.* New Haven: Yale University Press, 1939. xiii + 425 pp. Illustrations, map, notes, blbiographical essay, and index. Although the focus of this book is industrial development, it gives ample coverage to this small city's public works as well as the canals and water power systems that served its factories.

Green, Sherman. *History of the Seattle District, 1896-1968.* Seattle: U.S. Army Corps of Engineers, Seattle District, 1969. vi + 125 pp. Illustrations, maps, and appendices. A rather disjointed study that deals with river and harbor improvements as well as military construction.

Gressley, Gene M., ed. *The American West: A Reorientation.* See chapter on "Irrigation."

Grimes, Gordon F. "The Winnipiseogie Canal." *Historical New Hampshire,* 29 (Spring 1974), 1-19. Good canal history based on primary sources that describes the creation of a commercial artery for Dover, New Hampshire.

Gutheim, Frederick. *The Potomac.* New York:

Rinehart & Company, 1949. 436 pp. Illustrations, maps, bibliographical essay, and index. Perhaps the best volume in the "Rivers of America" series. The book contains good discussions of canal and water commerce development in the region. It also includes a description of the growth of public works facilities in Washington, D.C., following the Civil War.

Hadfield, Charles. *The Canal Age.* New York: Frederick A. Praeger, 1968. 233 pp. Illustrations, maps, appendices, bibliography, and index. A sound, popular history of canal development in Great Britain and Europe. The concluding chapter is a broad survey of the United States' canal era. Chapter 5, "Engineering and Construction," is an especially comprehensive treatment of an often-neglected subject.

Hager, Anna Marie. "A Salute to the Port of Los Angeles: From Mud Flats to Modern Day Miracle." *California Historical Society Quarterly,* XLIX (Dec. 1970), 329-35. Some highlights of the port's history.

Hagwood, Joseph J., Jr. *Commitment to Excellence: A History of the Sacramento District, U.S. Army Corps of Engineers, 1929-1973.* See chapter on "Flood Control and Drainage."

Haites, E., and J. Mak. "Ohio and Mississippi River Transportation, 1810-1860." *Explorations in Economic History,* 8 (Winter 1970-71), 153-80. Basically examines the market for river transportation services from 1810 to 1860. It is a study of the comparative economics of keelboating, flatboating, and steamboating.

Haites, Erik F., James Mak; and Gary M. Walton. *Western River Transportation: The Era of Early Internal Development, 1810-1860.* Baltimore: Johns Hopkins University Press, 1975. xi + 209 pp. Charts, tables, notes, appendices, bibliography, and index. Main purpose of this history is to provide a systematic quantitative analysis of early western river transportation.

Hall, Clayton Colman, ed. *Baltimore: Its History and Its People.* See chapter on "Community Water Supply."

Hamming, Edward. "The Port of Milwaukee." Doctoral dissertation, University of Chicago, 1952. x + 162 pp. Illustrations, maps, charts, tables, notes, and bibliography. Very little historical information is included in this otherwise excellent discussion of the port's facilities and operations.

Hanes, J.C., and J.M. Morgan, Jr. *The History and Heritage of Civil Engineering in Virginia.* See chapter on "Roads, Streets, and Highways."

Hanna, Alfred Jackson, and Kathryn Abbey. *Lake Okeechobee: Wellspring of the Everglades.* See chapter on "Flood Control and Drainage."

Hansen, Harry. *The Chicago.* New York: Farrar & Rinehart, 1942. xi + 362 pp. Illustrations, map, bibliography, and index. A weak, poorly written contribution to the "Rivers of America" series. The romantic and turgid volume includes some interesting material on the Illinois and Michigan Canal and the development of bridges across the river.

Hanson, Kenneth R. "An Aerial Survey of the Remains of the Morris Canal." *Proceedings of the New Jersey Historical Society,* 81 (1963), 10-16. Discusses the organization of the survey and how it revealed the encroachment of civilization on the canal.

Harlow, Alvin F. *Old Towpaths: The Story of the American Canal Era.* New York: D. Appleton and Company, 1926. xiv + 403 pp. Illustrations and bibliography. A dated account of the United States' canal era. It still serves as a useful introduction to the subject.

Harris, F.R. "Evolution of Tremie-Placed Concrete Dry Docks." *Civil Engineering,* 12 (June 1942), 308-12. Notes on the development of the design procedures for the two large graving docks at the Philadelphia Navy Yard.

Harris, Robert. *Canals and Their Architecture.* New York: Frederick A. Praeger, 1969. 223 pp. Illustrations, maps, appendices, bibliography, and index. Although most examples in this book are from Great Britain, students of American waterways can profit from its comprehensive analysis of early canal construction.

Harrison, Joseph Hobson, Jr. "The Internal Improvement Issue in the Politics of the Union, 1783-1825." Doctoral dissertation. See chapter on "Roads, Streets, and Highways."

Hart, Henry C. *The Dark Missouri.* See chapter on "Flood Control and Drainage."

Hart, Laurence H. "New York State and Her

Barge Canal." *Journal of the Cleveland Engineering Society,* IX (May 1917), 331-51.

Harte, Charles Rufus. "Some Engineering Features of the Old Northampton Canal." *Connecticut Society of Civil Engineers,* 49 (1933), 21-53. Provides a good deal of historical and engineering information on a little-known canal. Benjamin Wright served as consulting engineer to the project and David Hurd as chief engineer.

Hartman, J. Paul. *Civil Engineering Landmarks: State of Florida.* See chapter on "Planning, Engineering, and Administration."

Hartsough, Mildred L. *From Canoe to Steel Barge on the Upper Mississippi.* University of Minnesota Press for the Upper Mississippi Waterway Association, 1934. xxiv + 308 pp. Illustrations, maps, notes, bibliography, and index. Offers especially good coverage of the rebirth of commercial traffic on the Upper Mississippi after World War I.

Hartsough, Mildred. "Transportation as a Factor in the Development of the Twin Cities." *Minnesota History,* 7 (Sept. 1926), 218-32. A general discussion of transportation developments—waterways, railroads, and roads—in and around the Twin Cities.

Haskin, Frederic J. *The Panama Canal.* Garden City, N.Y.: Doubleday, Page & Company, 1914. x + 386 pp. Illustrations, maps, diagrams, and index. A rather simplistic discussion of the canal's construction intended for the lay reader.

Hatcher, Harlan. *Lake Erie.* Indianapolis: Bobbs-Merrill Company, 1945. 416 pp. Illustrations, maps, bibliographical essay, and index. One of eight volumes in the "American Lakes Series." The book includes scattered discussions of canal and port development as well as a great deal of information on shipping.

Havemeyer, Loomis, ed., et al. *Conservation of Our Natural Resources.* See chapter on "Irrigation."

Havighurst, Walter. *River to the West: Three Centuries of the Ohio.* New York: G.P. Putnam's Sons, 1970. 318 pp. Illustrations, maps, bibliographies, and index. A broadbush, popular history of transportation and settlement on the Ohio River. Material is included on navigation, flood control, and attempts to abate pollution.

Hays, Samuel P. *Conservation and the Gospel of Efficiency: The Progressive Conservation Movement, 1890-1920.* See chapter on "Planning, Engineering, and Administration."

Heap, D.P. *Ancient and Modern Light-Houses.* Boston: Ticknor and Company, 1889. Illustrations and appendix.

Heath, Milton Sydney. *The Role of the State in Economic Development in Georgia to 1860.* Cambridge: Harvard University Press, 1954. xiv + 448 pp. Maps, charts, tables, notes, and index. Includes a superficial chapter on pre-Civil War waterways and roadways.

Heine, Cornelius W. "The Chesapeake and Ohio Canal: Testimony to an Age Yet to Come." *Records of the Columbia Historical Society of Washington, D.C.* (1966-1968), 57-70. Sketchy overview of the canal's development and an appeal to launch a new canal age.

Hepburn, A. Barton. *Artificial Waterways and Commercial Development (With a History of the Erie Canal.)* New York: Macmillan Company, 1909. ix + 115 pp. Appendix and index. Thin, dated overview of the Erie and Panama canals.

Herndon, G. Melvin. "A Grandiose Scheme to Navigate and Harness Niagara Falls." *New-York Historical Society Quarterly,* LVIII (Jan. 1974), 7-17. Interesting proposal that included the use of an inclined plane. The article includes excellent copies of engravings.

Herndon, G. Melvin. "A 1796 Proposal for a Tennessee-Tombigbee Waterway." *Alabama Historical Quarterly,* XXXVII (Fall 1975), 176-82. Proposal formulated in 1796 by William Taltam.

Heuvelmans, Martin. *The River Killers.* See chapter on "Flood Control and Drainage."

High, Jeffrey P. "Coast Guard Public Works." *Military Engineer,* 68 (May-June 1976), 194-97.

Hill, Forest G. *Roads, Rails & Waterways: The Army Engineers and Early Transportation.* Norman: University of Oklahoma Press, 1957. xi + 248 pp. Illustrations, notes, bibliography, and index. Definitive study of the role of the army engineers in developing transportation facilities prior to the Civil War. Hill's writing and research are exemplary.

Hill, Henry Wayland. *A Historical Review of Waterways and Canal Construction in New York State.* Buffalo: Buffalo Historical Society, 1908. xiv + 549 pp. Illustration, map, notes, and index. An exhaustive summary of the growth and decline of the Erie Canal and other waterways. The most valuable portion of the book is its treatment of the revival of interest in waterways during the late nineteenth and early twentieth centuries.

Hindle, Brooke. *Technology in Early America: Needs and Opportunities for Study.* See chapter on "Planning, Engineering, and Administration."

"Historical Sketch of the Port of Chicago." *World Ports,* XIX (Feb. 1931), 371-75.

Hockett, Leola. "The Wabash and Erie Canal in Wabash County." *Indiana Magazine of History,* XXIV (Dec. 1928), 295-305.

Holbrook, Stewart H. *The Columbia.* New York: Rinehart and Company, 1956. 393 pp. Illustrations, maps, bibiography, and index. Largely a social history of the Columbia River Basin. Several chapters discuss the construction of locks, dams, and hydroelectric plants on the river during the twentieth century.

Holland, F. Ross. *The Old Point Loma Lighthouse.* n.p.: Cabrillo Historical Association, 1978. 51 pp. Illustrations and appendix. Well-illustrated history of one of the oldest lighthouses on the West Coast.

Holmes, Beatrice Hort. *History of Federal Water Resources Programs, 1800-1960.* See chapter on "Irrigation."

Holmes, Beatrice Hort. *History of Federal Water Resources Programs and Policies, 1961-70.* See chapter on "Irrigation."

Holmes, William F. "Canal Versus Railroad." *Delaware History,* 10 (Oct. 1962), 152-80. Successful challenge by railroads mounted against the Chesapeake and Delaware Canal.

Holt, W. Stull. *The Office of the Chief of Engineers of the Army: Its Non-Military History, Activities, and Organization.* See chapter on "Planning, Engineering, and Administration."

Howard, W.V. *Authority in TVA Land.* See chapter on "Flood Control and Drainage."

Howe, Walter A., comp. *Documentary History of the Illinois and Michigan Canal.* Springfield: State of Illinois Department of Public Works and Buildings, 1956. 174 pp. Maps. Dull collection of documents interspersed with uninspired narrative.

Hoyt, Franklin. "Influence of the Railroads in the Development of Los Angeles Harbor." *Southern California Quarterly,* XXXV (Sept. 1953), 195-212. Competent overview of some fifty years of effort to create a deep-water harbor for Los Angeles, which was achieved in 1899. Much of the article deals with efforts by the city and railroads to obtain support for the project in Congress.

Hoyt, John C. "Development of the Science of River Measurement Hydrology." *Civil Engineering,* 12 (June 1942), 324-26. A brief historical account in which the author identifies John Wesley Powell, Frederick H. Newell, and Clemens Herschel as pioneers in hydrology in the United States.

Hulbert, Archer Butler. *The Great American Canals: Volume I, The Chesepeake and Ohio Canal and the Pennsylvania Canal.* Cleveland: Arthur H. Clark Company, 1904. 231 pp. Illustrations, maps, notes, and appendices. An early, popular history of these two canals that has been superseded by subsequent studies.

Hulbert, Archer Butler. *The Great American Canals: Volume II, The Erie Canal.* Cleveland: Arthur H. Clark Company, 1904. 234 pp. Illustration, map, notes, and appendix. An unexceptional treatment of the Erie Canal.

Hulbert, Archer Butler. *Waterways of Westward Expansion: The Ohio River and Its Tributaries.* Cleveland: Arthur H. Clark Company, 1903. 220 pp. Maps and notes. The ninth volume in the "Historic Highways of America" series in which the author examines the prominent part played by this waterway as a road to the West.

Hull, William J., and Robert W. *The Origin and Development of the Waterways Policy of the United States.* Washington, D.C.: National Waterways Conference, 1967. vii + 79 pp. Map, notes, appendix, and index. Although the book is basically a justification of the navigation industry's economic viewpoint, it is a good overview of the subject. The authors' notes are a rich source of references.

Hungerford, Edward. *The Story of Public Utilities.* See chapter on "Urban Mass Transportation."

Hunter, Louis C. *Steamboats on the Western Rivers: An Economic and Technological History*. Cambridge: Harvard University Press, 1949. xv + 684 pp. Illustrations, tables, notes, appendices, and index. A splendid, prodigiously researched study of riverine commerce during the nineteenth and early twentieth centuries.

Huston, John. *Hydraulic Dredging: Theoretical and Applied.* Cambridge, Md.: Cornell Maritime Press, 1970. xviii + 332 pp. Illustrations, charts, tables, diagrams, appendix, bibliography, and index. The first chapter of this book briefly surveys the history of dredging.

Hynding, Alan A. "Eugene Semple's Seattle Canal Scheme." *Pacific Northwest Quarterly,* 59 (April 1968), 77-87. Well-documented discussion of attempt in the 1890s and early 1900s to dig a ship canal from Elliot Bay into Lake Washington.

Ickes, Harold L. *The Secret Diary of Harold L. Ickes: The First Thousand Days, 1933-1936.* See chapter on "Planning, Engineering, and Administration."

Inkster, Tom H. "John Frank Stevens, American Engineer." *Pacific Northwest Quarterly,* 56 (April 1965), 82-85. Deals with Stevens' role in the construction of the Panama Canal and western railroads.

Jackson,Carlton. "The Internal Improvement Vetoes of Andrew Jackson." *Tennessee Historical Quarterly,* XXV (Fall 1966), 261-79. Through his internal improvement vetoes, Jackson attained "a power that had been denied all previous presidents" and established "a pattern that was freely used by future veto presidents." There is a lengthy discussion of the Maysville Bill.

Jacobs, David, and Anthony E. Neville. *Bridges, Canals & Tunnels.* See chapter on "Roads, Streets, and Highways."

Jacobs, W.A., and Lyman L. Woodman. *The Alaska District, United States Army Corps of Engineers, 1946-1974.* See chapter on "Military Installations."

Jeffrey, Thomas E. "Internal Improvements and Political Parties in Antebellum North Carolina, 1836-1860." *North Carolina Historical Review,* LV (April 1978), 111-56. Well-researched article on the improvement of rivers, dredging of harbors, and construction of turnpikes and railroads in antebellum North Carolina.

Jensen, Merrill, ed. *Regionalism in America.* See chapter on "Public Buildings."

Jervey, James Postell. "George W. Goethals—The Man." *Military Engineer,* XX (March-April 1928), 161-62. A highly respected biographical sketch.

Johnson, Emory R. "River and Harbor Bills." *Annals of the American Academy of Political and Social Science,* 2 (1892), 782-807.

Johnson, Emory R; Grover G. Huebner; and Arnold K. Henry. *Transportation by Water.* New York: Appleton-Century Company, 1935. xxii + 585 pp. Illustrations, maps, charts, tables, notes, bibliographies, and index. Some historical information on ports, canals, and navigation laws can be found in this survey of the inland and ocean-going shipping industry.

Johnson, Leland Ross. "A History of the Operations of the Corps of Engineers, United States Army in the Cumberland and Tennessee River Valleys." Doctoral dissertation, Vanderbilt University, 1972. xi + 351 pp. Map, notes, appendices, and bibliography. Traces the history of the operations of the Corps of Engineers in the Cumberland and Tennessee valleys from early navigation projects to vast multiple-purpose undertakings. It is one of the strongest case studies of corps activities.

Johnson, Leland R., ed. "An Army Engineer on the Missouri in 1867." *Nebraska History,* 53 (Summer 1972), 253-91. Well-edited journal of Brevet Major Charles W. Howell.

Johnson, Leland R. "Army Engineers on the Cumberland and Tennessee, 1824-1854." *Tennessee Historical Quarterly,* XXXI (Summer 1972), 149-69. Well-written and extensively researched overview of river improvements undertaken by the Army Corps of Engineers.

Johnson, Leland R. *Engineers on the Twin Rivers: A History of the Nashville District, Corps of Engineers, United States Army.* Nashville: U.S. Army Engineer District, 1978. x + 330 pp. Illustrations, maps, notes, appendices, bibliography, and index. Well-written, and deeply researched historical review of the activities of the Army Corps of Engineers on the Cumberland and Tennessee rivers. The undertakings range from frontier mapping and exploration to military construction, canals, canalization, flood control, and multipurpose projects.

Johnson, Leland. *Men, Mountains, and Rivers: An Illustrated History of the Huntington District U.S. Army Corps of Engineers, 1754-1974.* Washington, D.C.: Government Printing Office, 1977. iv + 322 pp. Illustrations, maps, chronology, notes, bibliography, and index. Outstanding corps district history that chronicles the evolution of navigation and flood control projects. The book contains a comprehensive bibliography and footnotes that reflect a mastery of the source material.

Johnson, Leland R. "19th-Century Engineering: The Davis Island Lock and Dam." *Military Engineer,* 71 (July-Aug. 1979; Sept.-Oct. 1979), July-Aug.: 256-58; Sept.-Oct.: 338-40. Lucid discussion of the Army Corps of Engineers' project near Pittsburgh that included a wicket dam and other unique engineering features.

Johnson, Leland R. "19th-Century Engineering: The Muscle Shoals Canal." *Military Engineer,* 63 (July-Aug. 1971), 260-65. Comprehensive and well-illustrated case study of a navigation improvement project built by the Army Corps of Engineers in the 1870s and 1880s.

Johnson, Leland R. *The Falls City Engineers: A History of the Louisville District, Corps of Engineers, United States Army.* Louisville: Army Corps of Engineers, 1974. viii + 347 pp. Illustrations, maps, chronologies, footnotes, appendices, and index. One of the strongest contributions to the corps' district history program. The deeply researched and well-written book focuses on improvements on the Ohio River and its tributaries for navigation and flood control. The book also discusses the district's military mission.

Johnson, Leland R. "The Conquest and Contract of 1824." *Military Engineer,* LXV (May-June and July-Aug. 1973), May-June: 166-71; July-Aug.: 252-56. An account of the political and engineering features of the first federal navigation project on inland rivers.

Johnson, Leland R. *The Headquarters District: A History of the Pittsburgh District, U.S. Army Corps of Engineers.* Pittsburgh: Pittsburgh District, Corps of Engineers, 1979. vii + 380 pp. Illustrations, maps, diagrams, appendices, bibliographical essay, and index. An exemplary corps district history. His study of the corps' work on the Upper Ohio and its tributaries supports his conclusion that this area was the "cradle of American inland commerce." Johnson shows that many innovative waterways engineering methods were first practiced in this district. He also discusses the corps' military activities and role in abating water pollution.

Johnson, Leland R. "Waterways: The Fourth Pillar of Defense." *Military Engineer,* LXXII (Nov.-Dec. 1980), 404-08.

Jonah, F. G. "A Hundred Years of Transportation." *Civil Engineering,* 3 (Aug. 1933), 426-28. Gives some attention to waterways and railway equipment.

Jones, Chester Lloyd. "The Anthracite-Tidewater Canals." *Annals of the American Academy of Political and Social Science,* XXXI (Jan.-June 1908), 102-16.

Jones, Chester Lloyd. *The Economic History of the Anthracite-Tidewater Canals.* Philadelphia: University of Pennsylvania, 1908. v + 181 pp. Map, tabes, notes, bibliography, and index. A sound factual survey of the Lehigh, Delaware and Hudson, Morris, and Schuylkill canals. The book advocates a rebirth of waterway transportation.

Kaiser, William Martin. "Interest Groups and the St. Lawrence Deep Waterway." Master's thesis, University of Chicago, 1950. iv + 111 pp. Notes and bibliography. An excellent study of the interest groups that supported and opposed the seaway project. Midwestern business interests and public power advocates were in favor. Opponents included private power advocates, railroads, and certain labor groups. This thesis offers good perspectives on the role of interest groups in shaping public works policies.

Kahrl, William L., ed. *The California Water Atlas.* See chapter on "Irrigation."

Kanarek, Harold K. *A Monument to an Engineer's Skill: William P. Craighill and the Baltimore Harbor.* Baltimore: Baltimore District, Corps of Engineers, n.d. 31 pp. Illustrations, maps, and notes. An excellent essay on improvements made at Baltimore Harbor from the Civil War to World War I. The focus of the book is William P. Craighill, the army engineer who directed improvement work in the harbor for some thirty years.

Kanarek, Harold. "People in Public Works: William P. Craighill." *AWPA Reporter.* See chapter on "Military Installations."

Kanarek, Harold K. *The Mid-Atlantic Engineers: A History of the Baltimore District, U.S. Army Corps of Engineers, 1774-1974.* Washington, D.C.: Government Printing Office, 1976. vi + 196 pp. Illustrations, maps, notes, appendices, bibliography, and index. An outstanding corps district history. It traces the army engineers' role in the construction of early transportation networks as well as flood control, military construction, and providing domestic water for Washington, D.C.

Kanarek, Harold. "The U.S. Army Corps of Engineers and Early Internal Improvements in Maryland." *Maryland Historical Magazine,* 72 (Spring 1977) 99-109. Early involvement of corps engineers in canal and road work.

Kelley, Robert L. *Gold vs. Grain: The Mining Debris Controversy.* See chapter on "Irrigation."

Kelso, Harold. "Inland Waterways Policy in the United States." Doctoral dissertation, University of Wisconsin-Madison, 1942. vii + 183 + 74 pp. Charts, tables, graphs, notes, appendix, and bibliography. An economic analysis of the costs and benefits of water projects that enhance inland navigation. The study's two principal conclusions are that (1) systematic procedures should be introduced for allocating costs on multiple-purpose river projects; and (2) techniques should be devised for more effective reconsideration of authorized channel improvements.

Kimball, Francis P. *New York—The Canal State: The Story of America's Great Water Route from the Lakes to the Sea, Builder of East and West.* Albany: Argus Press, 1937. xvi + 105 pp. Illustrations, maps, bibliography, appendices, and index. An enthusiastic account of the contributions of the Erie Canal, and later the New York Barge Canal, to the state's development. The last chapter contains a discussion of "the St. Lawrence issue"—against passage of the treaty. (The New York State Waterways Association's president prepared the book's introduction.)

King, Judson. *The Conservation Fight: From Theodore Roosevelt to the Tennessee Valley Authority.* See chapter on "Flood Control and Drainage."

Kinsella, Thomas. "The Development of Albany as a Modern World Port." Doctoral dissertation, Clark University, 1938. vi + 191 pp. Illustration, tables, notes, appendices, and bibliography. A history of the Port of Albany from the completion of the Erie Canal to the early 1930s.

Kirkland, Edward C. *Industry Comes of Age: Business, Labor, and Public Policy, 1860-1897.* New York: Holt, Rinehart and Winston, 1961. xiv + 445 pp. Illustrations, notes, bibliographical essay, and index. Includes a smattering of information on waterways, street paving, municipal water supplies, and street railways.

Kirkland, Edward Chase. *Men, Cities, and Transportation: A Study in New England History, 1820-1900.* 2 vols. Cambridge: Harvard University Press, 1948. Vol. I: xv + 528 pp.; Vol. II: ix + 499 pp. Illustrations, maps, notes, appendix, and index. Although most of these thoroughly documented volumes are devoted to railroads, several excellent chapters on highways, canals, and shipping are included.

Klawonn, Marion J. *Cradle of the Corps: A History of the New York District, U.S. Army Corps of Engineers, 1775-1975.* New York: U.S. Army Engineer Corps, New York District, 1977. xiv + 310 pp. Illustrations, maps, bibliography, and index. Especially strong in its treatment of the development of West Point, New York Harbor, and the corps' flood control and shore protection activities.

Knowles, Morris. "History of Civil Engineering in Western Pennsylvania." *Proceedings of the Engineers' Society of Western Pennsylvania.* See chapter on "Planning, Engineering, and Administration."

Kogan, Bernard P. "Chicago's Pier." *Chicago History.* See chapter on "Parks and Recreation."

Krenkel, John. "Development of the Port of Los Angeles." *American Neptune,* XXV (Oct. 1965), 262-72. Beginning in 1871.

Krenkel, John Henry. "Internal Improvements in Illinois, 1818-1848." Doctoral dissertation, University of Illinois, 1937. v + 259 pp. Notes and bibliography. A well-organized and thoroughly researched history of early road, canal, and railroad improvements in Illinois. The dissertation includes a unique chapter on the administration and construction of the projects.

Krenkel, John H. "The Port of Los Angeles as a Municipal Enterprise." *Pacific Historical Review,* XVI (Aug. 1947), 285-97. Fine administrative history of how the City of Los Angeles developed and managed its deep-water harbor during the early twentieth century. Krenkel concludes that "with municipal ownership and administration, probably greater development has resulted than would have been achieved under either private or state control."

Krutilla, John V. *The Columbia River Treaty: The Economics of an International River Basin-Development.* Baltimore: Johns Hopkins Press, 1967. xv + 211 pp. Principally an economic history of the subject.

Kuentz, Oscar O. "Cape Fear River Channel and Bar." *Military Engineer,* XVII (Jan.-Feb. 1925), 27-30.

Kulik, Gary, and Julia C. Bonham. *Rhode Island: An Inventory of Historic Engineering and Industrial Sites.* See chapter on "Roads, Streets, and Highways."

Kutz, C.W. "Ohio River Canalization—Its History and Possibilities." *Engineering News-Record,* 104 (March 13, 1930), 432-41. A good technical overview of locks, dams, and other navigation improvements.

Kyle, John H. *The Building of TVA.* See chapter on "Flood Control and Drainage."

LaFeber, Walter. *The Panama Canal: The Crisis in Historical Perspective.* New York: Oxford University Press, 1978. xii + 248 pp. Map, notes, bibliography, and index.

Lamb, John M. "Early Days on the Illinois & Michigan Canal." *Chicago History,* III (Winter 1974-75), 168-76. Superficial view of the canal's social and economic impact from 1848 to about 1870.

Landon, Charles E. *The North Carolina State Ports Authority.* Durham: Duke University, Press, 1963. x + 111 pp. Illustrations, maps, tables, notes, and index. Created in 1945, the North Carolina Ports Authority was assigned the task of constructing and operating modern ocean terminals to aid the state's economic development. The book describes the administrative, political, and economic activities and problems of the authority. The facilities and services provided by the ports are discussed.

Landon, Fred. *Lake Huron.* Indianapolis: Bobbs-Merrill Company, 1944. 398 pp. Illustrations, notes, bibliographical essay, and index. Public works facilities and navigation receive sparse attention in this contribution to the "Rivers of America" series.

Landreth, William B. "New York State Barge Canal." *Journal of the Association of Engineering Societies,* XLVII (Sept. 1911), 85-100. Illustrated discussion of the enlargement of the Erie Canal and some of its branches.

Lane, Wheaton J. *From Indian Trail to Iron Horse: Travel and Transportation in New Jersey, 1620-1860.* Princeton: Princeton University Press, 1939. xviii + 437 pp. Illustrations, notes, bibliography, and index. Entertaining, well-written study that includes vivid accounts of travel on early roads and canals.

Lane, Wheaton J. *From Indian Trail to Iron Horse: Travel and Transportation in New Jersey, 1620-1860.* Princeton: Princeton University Press, 1939. xviii + 437 pp. Illustrations, notes, bibliography, and index. Entertaining, well-written study that includes vivid accounts of travel on early roads and canals.

Langbein, W.B. "Hydrology and Environmental Aspects of Erie Canal (1817-99)." *Geological Survey Water-Supply Paper,* 2038 (1976), vi + 92 pp. Brilliant analysis of the canal's planning, design, hydrology, and environmental impact.

Langbein, Walter B. "Our Grand Erie Canal: 'A Splendid Project, a Little Short of Madness.'" *Civil Engineering,* 47 (Oct. 1977), 75-81. A concise, well-written account of the canal's development. It is one of the few treatments that focuses on its design and hydrology.

Larkin, Daniel F. "The New York Years of John B. Jervis: A Builder of Nineteenth Century America." Doctoral dissertation. See chapter on "Community Water Supply."

Larned, J.N. *A History of Buffalo: Delineating the Evolution of the City.* See chapter on "Sewers and Wastewater Treatment."

Larsen, Lawrence H. "Chicago's Midwest Rivals: Cincinnati, St. Louis, Milwaukee." *Chicago History,* V (Fall 1976), 141-51. How Chicago businessmen won the battle for midwestern economic supremacy through the construction of port, canal, and railroad systems.

Larson, Gustave E. "Notes on Rock River Navigation." *Journal of the Illinois State Historical Society,* XXXIII (Sept. 1940), 341-58. Includes some information on efforts to promote navigation improvements from the 1840s to the 1860s.

Larson, John W. *Those Army Engineers: A History of the Chicago District, U.S. Army Corps of Engineers.* n.p., n.p., 1980. xiv + 307 pp. Illustrations, maps, notes, and index. An outstanding corps district history that focuses principally on Chicago and other Lake Michigan harbors. Comprehensive discussions are also included on the Illinois waterway and flood control.

Larson, Laurence Mercellus. "A Financial and Administrative History of Milwaukee." *Bulletin of the University of Wisconsin: Economics and Political Science Series.* See chapter on "Planning, Engineering, and Administration."

Larson, Suzanne B. *"Dig the Ditch!" The History of the Lake Washington Ship Canal.* Boulder, Colo.: Western Interstate Commission for Higher Education, 1975. x + 48 pp. Maps and bibliography. Comprehensive history of a ship canal from Puget Sound to Lake Washington. Much material on Seattle's urban development is included.

Lass, William E. *A History of Steamboating on the Upper Missouri River.* Lincoln: University of Nebraska Press, 1962. xiv + 215 pp. Illustrations, maps, tables, notes, bibliography, and essay. This study traces the development of commercial navigation on the Upper Missouri River from 1819 until 1936, when the last commercial navigation company on this section of the river went out of existence. The author notes in the concluding chapter that since the 1930s river improvements on the Upper Missouri have been for flood control, irrigation, and power production rather than navigation.

Law Department, Sanitary District of Chicago. *Laws of and in Reference to The Sanitary District of Chicago, with annotations and references.* Chicago: Sanitary District of Chicago, 1922. vii + 366 pp. Maps and index. Updates the 1906 *Laws in Reference to The Sanitary District of Chicago* and presents all of the acts of the General Assembly of Illinois passed prior to October 1922.

Leavitt, Francis Hale. "Steam Navigation on the Colorado River: Experimentation and Development, 1850-1864." *California Historical Society Quarterly,* XXII (March 1943), 1-25. Discusses early steam navigation on the Colorado River prompted by the discovery of gold in California and the Mormon settlement of Utah.

Leavitt, Francis Hale. "Steam Navigation on the Colorado River: The Peak of the Colorado River Trade." *California Historical Society Quarterly,* XXII (June 1943), 151-74. Describes waterway transportation on the Colorado River in the 1860s and 1870s and its influence on the growth of the Southwest.

Leavitt, H. Walter. "Some Interesting Phases of the Development of Transportation in Maine." *Journal of the Maine Association of Engineers.* See chapter on "Roads, Streets, and Highways."

Lee, Guy A., ed. "A Diary of the Illinois-Michigan Canal Investigation, 1843-1844." *Transactions of the Illinois State Historical Society* (1943), 38-72. Insightful journal of William Swift, an army engineer, who analyzed the cost of completing the canal for English investors.

Lee, James. *The Morris Canal: A Photographic History.* Easton, Pa.: Delaware Press, 1979. 136 pp. Illustrations, maps, and bibliography. An excellent historical photo album.

Lee, Judson Fiske. "Transportation—a Factor in the Development of Northern Illinois Previous to 1860." *Journal of the Illinois State Historical Society.* See chapter on "Roads, Streets, and Highways."

Lee, W. Storrs. *The Strength to Move a Mountain.* New York: G. P. Putnam's Sons, 1958. 318 pp. Illustrations, notes, chronology, and index. A breezy, error-filled history of the canal's construction based largely on secondary sources.

Leland, Edwin Albert, Jr. "An Administrative History of the Inland Waterways Corporation." Doctoral dissertation, Tulane University, 1960. 338 pp.

Lemly, James H. "The Mississippi River: Friend or Foe?" *Business History Review,* XXXIX (Spring 1965), 7-15. Insightful discussion of how St. Louis' initial reliance on river transportation retarded its adoption of the railroad as an acceptable transportation system. The article explores subsequent efforts by the city to make the most of both river and rails.

Lemon, James T. "Urbanization and the Development of Eighteenth-Century Southeastern Pennsylvania and Adjacent Delaware."

William and Mary Quarterly, XXIV (Oct. 1967), 501-33. Gives only scant attention to transportation development.

Lenik, Edward J. "The Tuxedo-Ringwood Canal." *Proceedings of the New Jersey Historical Society,* 84 (1966), 271-73. Sketchy summary of a 3-mile-long canal built in Orange County, New York, about 1765.

Lepawsky, Albert. "Water Resources and American Federalism." *American Political Science Review,* XLIV (Sept. 1950), 631-49. An examination of state involvement in the field of water resource management beginning in the early nineteenth century. There are separate sections on "Canal, Navigation and Flood Control"; "Irrigation, Drainage and Rural Water Control"; "Urban Water Supply"; "Industrial Waste Disposal, Sewage Control, and Water Pollution"; "Hydro-Electric Power and Multi-Purpose Water Programs"; "The Interstate Commission As a Water Agency"; and "The American Theory of Federalism in Relation to Water Resources."

Le Roy, Bruce, ed. *H. M. Chittenden: A Western Epic.* See chapter on "Flood Control and Drainage."

Le Roy, Edwin D. *The Delaware and Hudson Canal: A History.* Honesdale, Pa.: Wayne County Historical Society, 1950. 95 pp. Illustrations and maps.

Leuba, Clarence J. *A Road to Creativity: Arthur Morgan—Engineer, Educator, Administrator.* See chapter on "Flood Control and Drainage."

Lewis, Gene D. *Charles Ellet, Jr.: The Engineer as Individualist, 1810-1862.* See chapter on "Roads, Streets, and Highways."

Lighthouse Service, Department of Commerce. *The United States Lighthouse Service.* Washington, D.C.: Government Printing Office, 1916. 94 pp. Illustrations, map, and tables. Furnishes general information on the organization and operation of the United States Lighthouse Service. The booklet contains one chapter on the history and growth of the service.

Lilienthal, David E. *TVA: Democracy on the March.* See chapter on "Flood Control and Drainage."

Lingenfelter, Richard E. *Steamboats on the Colorado River, 1852-1916.* Tucson: University of Arizona Press, 1978. xv + 195 pp. Illustrations, notes, appendices, bibliography, and index. An excellent description of a part of America's navigation history generally ignored by scholars. The book includes nonpareil photographs and descriptions of early steamboating, flood fights, dredging, and the settlement of California's Imperial Valley.

Lippincott, Isaac. "A History of River Improvement." *Journal of Political Economy,* XXII (July 1914), 630-60. A still-useful overview of state and federal efforts to improve navigation on the nation's rivers.

Lively, Robert A. "The American System: A Review Article." *Business History Review.* See chapter on "Planning, Engineering, and Administration."

Livingood, James W. "The Canalization of the Lower Susquehanna." *Pennsylvania History,* VIII (April 1941), 131-47. A well-researched canal history based on primary sources.

Lokken, Roscoe L. *Iowa Public Land Disposal.* Iowa City: State Historical Society of Iowa, 1942. 318 pp. Maps, notes, and index. Describes the policies and programs of the federal government in disposing of the public domain in Iowa. The book incorporates unique discussions on the disposition of swamp lands and attempts to make the Des Moines River a navigable waterway.

Lowrey, Walter M. "Navigational Problems at the Mouth of the Mississippi River, 1698-1880." Doctoral dissertation, Vanderbilt University, 1956. 494 pp. Maps, notes, and bibliography. Good description of efforts to create a stable ship channel at the mouth of the Mississippi from French and Spanish attempts to the famous jetties built by James B. Eads.

Lowrey, Walter M. "The Engineers and the Mississippi." *Louisiana History,* V (Summer 1964), 233-55. Excellent historical overview of efforts during the nineteenth century to improve navigation at the mouth of the Mississippi River.

Lowrie, Walter Edward. "France, the United States, and the Lesseps Panama Canal: Renewed Rivalry in the Western Hemisphere, 1879-1889." Doctoral dissertation, Syracuse University, 1975.

Lowry, Charles B. "The PWA in Tampa: A Case Study." *Florida Historical Quarterly,* LII

(April 1974), 363-80. Financing and construction of a drydock.

Ludwig, Ella A. *History of the Harbor District of Los Angeles, Dating from Its Earliest History.* n.p.: Historic Record Company, n.d. 938 pp. Illustrations, maps, and index. A largely social history of San Pedro Bay and the surrounding community. Little information is provided on the harbor facilities.

Luke, Myron H. "The Port of New York, 1800-1810." Doctoral dissertation, New York University, 1950.

Maass, Arthur. "Congress and Water Resources." *American Political Science Review,* 44 (Sept. 1950), 576-93.

McCampbell, Coleman. *Saga of a Frontier Seaport.* Dallas: South-West Press, 1934. viii + 167 pp. Appendices and index. Offers some material on the growth of port facilities at Corpus Christi, Texas.

McCartney, Kenneth H. "Government Enterprise: A Study of the Inland Waterways Corporation." Doctoral dissertation, University of Minnesota, 1958. 262 pp. Tables, notes, bibliography, and appendix. Excellent discussion of the federally owned barge line's legislative, economic, and administrative history.

McClellan, Robert J. *The Delaware Canal: A Picture History.* New Brunswick, N.J.: Rutgers University Press, 1967. xv + 111 pp. Illustrations, maps, diagrams, glossary, and appendix. A good popular account of the canal's history that offers excellent information on its design, construction, and operation.

McCluggage, Robert W. "The Fox-Wisconsin Waterway, 1836-1872: Land Speculation and Regional Rivalries, Politics and Private Enterprise." Doctoral dissertation, University of Wisconsin, 1954. vii + 425 pp. Maps, notes, and bibliography. A fine waterway history that makes judicious use of primary materials.

MacColl, E. Kimbark. *The Growth of a City: Power and Politics in Portland, Oregon, 1915 to 1950.* See chapter on "Planning, Engineering, and Administration."

MacColl, E. Kimbark. *The Shaping of a City: Business and Politics in Portland, Oregon, 1885-1915.* Portland: Georgian Press Company, 1976. xi + 535 pp. Illustrations, maps, charts, bibliography, and index. Interspersed throughout the book are references to the city's harbor, public transportation, streets, and garbage collection.

McCullough, David G. "A Man, a Plan, a Canal, Panama!" *American Heritage,* XXII (June 1971), 64-71; 100-03. A discussion of President Theodore Roosevelt's selection of John Frank Stevens to direct development of the Panama Canal. The author contends that more than any other individual Stevens made "the decisions that would bring the Panama Canal to completion."

McCullough, David. *The Path Between the Seas: The Creation of the Panama Canal, 1870-1914.* New York: Simon and Schuster, 1977. 698 pp. Illustrations, maps, notes, bibliography, and index. A magnificent history of the canal's construction far exceeding the quality of other books on this subject. The fact-filled account of the engineering feat is embellished with vivid detail and biographical insight.

McGee, W. J. "Our Inland Waterways." *Popular Science Monthly,* LXXI (April 1908), 289-303.

MacGill, Caroline E. *History of Transportation in the United States before 1860.* Washington, D.C.: Carnegie Institution of Washington, 1917. xi + 678 pp. Maps, tables, notes, bibliography, and index. A general history of roads, canals, waterways, and railroads in various states and regions of the United States prior to 1860.

McGraw, Thomas K. *Morgan vs. Lilienthal: The Feud within the TVA.* See chapter on "Flood Control and Drainage."

McGraw, Thomas K. *TVA and the Power Fight, 1933-1939.* See chapter on "Energy."

McGroarty, John Steven. *Los Angeles: From the Mountains to the Sea.* Chicago and New York: American Historical Society, 1921. xxix + 414 pp. Illustrations and index. This breezy book includes chapters on the city's port facilities, parks and recreational areas, as well as the Owens Valley Aqueduct.

McIlwraith, Thomas F. "Freight Capacity and Utilization of the Erie and Great Lakes Canals before 1850." *Journal of Economic History,* XXVI (Dec. 1976), 852-75. Comparative economic analysis of United States and Canadian canals that largely focuses on the latter.

McKelvey, Blake. *Rochester: The Water Power City, 1812-1854.* Cambridge: Harvard University Press, 1945. xvi + 383 pp. Illustrations, maps, notes, and index. Fine urban history that discusses the influence of the Erie Canal on the city's development. The various public works systems (water supply, sewers, and streets) are also given some attention.

McKelvey, Blake. The Erie Canal: Mother of Cities." *New York Historical Society Quarterly,* XXXV (Jan. 1951), 54-71. A thoughtful article on the influence of the canal on Albany, Schenectady, Rochester, and other New York cities.

McKelvey, Blake. "Rochetser and the Erie Canal." *Rochester History,* XI (July 1949), 1-24. A study of the canal's "specific contributions to the growth of Rochester."

McKelvey, Blake. "The Port of Rochester: A History of Its Lake Trade." *Rochester History,* XVI (Oct. 1954), 1-24. A study of the "complexities of the port's history" and its "fluctuating fortunes."

McKelvey, William J., Jr. *The Delaware & Raritan Canal: A Pictorial History.* York, Pa.: Canal Press, 1975. 128 pp. Illustrations and bibliography.

McKinley, Charles. *Uncle Sam in the Pacific Northwest: Federal Management of Natural Resources in the Columbia River Valley.* See chapter on "Irrigation."

Maass, Arthur. *Muddy Waters: The Army Engineers and the Nation's Rivers.* See chapter on "Flood Control and Drainage."

Mabee, Carleton. *The Seaway Story.* New York: Macmillan Company, 1961. xii + 301 pp. Illustrations, maps, notes, and index. An excellent history of the century-long struggle to build the St. Lawrence Seaway. The book is written "not so much in terms of engineering calculations, impersonal economic forces, or diplomacy, as in terms of people." Unlike some histories of the seaway, the power dimension of the project is thoroughly treated.

Mack, Gerstle. *The Land Divided: A History of the Panama Canal and Other Isthmian Canal Projects.* New York: Alfred A. Knopf, 1944. xv + 650 + xxxiv pp. Illustrations, maps, diagrams, notes, bibliography, and index. A good account of efforts spanning four centuries to cut a passage through the isthmus. The book covers the international disputes spawned by plans to build the canal and vividly describes construction of the waterway.

Maldonado, Erwin. "Urban Growth during the Canal Era: The Case of Indiana." *Indiana Social Studies Quarterly,* XXXI (Winter 1978-79), 20-37. Good analysis of the influence of canals on the development of Indiana cities.

Malone, Patrick M. *The Lowell Canal System.* Lowell, Mass.: Lowell Museum, 1976. 27 pp. Illustrations. This brief study is a product of the Lowell canal survey conducted by the Historic American Engineering Program.

Maltby, Frank B. "In at the Start of Panama." *Civil Engineering,* 15 (June, July, Aug. and Sept. 1945), June: 260-62; July: 322-24; Aug.: 359-62; Sept.: 421-24. Vivid recollections by an engineer who worked on the historic project.

Martin, Alfred Simpson. "The Port of Philadelphia, 1763-1776: A Biography." Doctoral dissertation, State University of Iowa, 1941. vi + 275 pp. Notes, appendices, and bibliography. An intimate picture of the great colonial seaport during the years immediately prior to the American Revolution.

Martin, Roscoe C. "The Tennessee Valley Authority: A Study of Federal Control." *Law and Contemporary Problems.* See chaper on "Flood Control and Drainage."

Martin, Roscoe C., ed. *TVA: The First Twenty Years, a Staff Report.* See chapter on "Flood Control and Drainage."

Martin, William Elejius. "Early History of Internal Improvements in Alabama." *Johns Hopkins University Studies in Historical and Political Science,* XX (April 1902), 127-205. Simplistic analysis of the construction of railroads, highways, as well as river and harbor improvements.

Martin, William Elejius. "Internal Improvements in Alabama." Doctoral dissertation, Johns Hopkins University, 1901.

Mason, Philip P., ed. "The Operation of the Sault Canal, 1857." *Michigan History,* XXXIX (March 1955), 69-80. Annual report by the superintendent of the state-owned canal.

Masterson, Thomas Robert. "The Milwaukee Board of Harbor Commissioners: A Study in Public Administration." Doctoral dissertation, University of Chicago, 1956. vi + 311 pp.

Illustrations, notes, appendices, and bibliography. A good case study of port development and administration.

Mayer, Harold M. *The Port of Chicago and the St. Lawrence Seaway.* Chicago: University of Chicago Press, 1957. xvii + 283 pp. Illustrations, maps, charts, tables, notes, and bibiography. Analyzes the growth of the Port of Chicago, St. Lawrence Seaway, and Calumet Sag Project. The book offers good descriptions of the facilities.

Mazmainian, Daniel A., and Jeanne Nienaber. *Can Organizations Change?: Environmental Protection, Citizen Participation, and the Corps of Engineers.* Washington, D.C.: Brookings Institution, 1979. x + 220 pp. Appendices and index. The authors compliment the Army Corps of Engineers' efforts to translate environmental concerns into policy and practice.

Mead, Elwood; W.W. Schlecht; and C.E. Grunsky. *The All-American Canal: Report of the All-American Canal Board.* Washington, D.C.: Government Printing Office, 1920. 99 pp. + Exhibits A-D. Tables. Provides for "surveys and studies of the problems of constructing a canal, located entirely within the United States, from Colorado River, at the Laguna Dam, into the Imperial Valley, Calif."

Merdinger, Charles J. *Civil Engineering through the Ages.* See chapter on "Planning, Engineering, and Administration."

Merritt, Raymond H. *Creativity, Conflict & Controversy: A History of the St. Paul District U.S. Army Corps of Engineers.* Washington, D.C.: U.S. Government Printing Office, 1980. 461 pp. Illustrations, maps, tables, notes, appendix, bibliographical essay, and index. A highly sophisticated corps district history that transcends the narrow institutional boundaries of many agency studies. The book discusses the various interest groups that tried to influence the agency's activities and describes its impact on the urban and technological growth of Minneapolis and St. Paul. Few corps district histories offer this breadth of coverage.

Meyer, Balthasar Meyer. *History of Transportation in the United States Before 1860.* Washington, D.C.: Carnegie Institute of Washington, 1917. xi + 678 pp. Maps, tables, notes, bibliography, and index. Still-useful introduction to the history of early canals, roads, and railroads.

Mikesell, Marvin W. "The Changing Role of the Port of Santa Barbara." *Historical Society of Southern California Quarterly,* XXXVI (Sept. 1954), 238-44.

"Milestones in U.S. Civil Engineering." *Civil Engineering.* See chapter on "Planning, Engineering, and Administration."

"Milestones in U.S. Public Works: Chesapeake & Ohio Canal." *APWA Reporter,* 41 (Nov. 1974), 22-23. Records in summary from the important events surrounding the building of the C & O Canal.

"Milestones in U.S. Public Works: The Cape Henry Lighthouse." *AWPA Reporter,* 41 (June 1974), 12-13. Story of the first public works structure built by the federal government.

Miller, Keith Linus. "Building Towns on the Southeastern Illinois Frontier, 1810-1830." Doctoral dissertation, Miami University, 1975. viii + 193 pp. Maps, notes, and bibliography. A good study of frontier town building that includes discussions of roads, bridges, canals, river improvements, and public hearings.

Miller, Nathan. "Private Enterprise in Inland Navigation: The Mohawk Route Prior to the Erie Canal." *New York History,* XXXI (Oct. 1950), 398-413. History of a pioneering canal project built during the 1790s.

Miller, Nathan. "The Enterprise of a Free People: The Erie Canal and the Erie Canal Fund in the Economy of New York State, 1815-1837." Doctoral dissertation, Columbia University, 1959. 392 pp.

Miller, Nathan. *The Enterprise of a Free People: Aspects of Economic Development in New York State during the Canal Period, 1792-1838.* Ithaca: Cornell University Press, 1962. xv + 293 pp. Maps, footnotes, bibliography, appendices, and index. Deeply researched and well-written analysis of the Erie Canal's influence on the state's economy. It is an excellent case study of early public attitudes towards and expectations of public works investments.

Miller, Roberta Balstad. *City and Hinterland: A Case Study of Urban Growth and Regional Development.* See chapter on "Planning, Engineering, and Administration."

Miller, Roberta Gay Balstad. "City and Hinterland: The Relationship between Urban Growth and Regional Development in Nineteenth Century New York." Doctoral dissertation, University of Minnesota, 1973. Insightful and challenging analysis of the influence of the Erie Canal on the economic and social development of Onondaga County, New York.

Mills, Gary B. *Of Men & Rivers: The Story of the Vicksburg District.* See chapter on "Flood Control and Drainage."

Mills, Randall V. "A History of Transportation in the Pacific Northwest." *Oregon Historical Quarterly,* XLVII (Sept. 1946), 281-312. An overview of the development of waterways, railroads, and roads in the Northwest. In the concluding section, the author encourages historians to produce a "complete general history of transportation in the region."

Mills, Randall V. *Stern-Wheelers Up Columbia: A Century of Steamboating in the Oregon Country.* Palo Alto, Calif.: Pacific Books, 1947. ix + 212 pp. Illustrations, maps, appendix, and index. A romantic survey of river commerce on the Columbia from the 1830s to the 1940s. Some material is included on river improvements.

Monzione, Joseph. "People in Public Works: William R. Hutton." *AWPA Reporter,* 44 (Sept. 1977), 6-7. Features Hutton's success as chief engineer for the Chesapeake and Ohio Canal Company and describes his design of the Washington Bridge over Harlem River in New York City.

Moore, Charles. *The Saint Mary's Falls Canal: Exercises at the Semi-Centennial Celebration at Sault St. Marie, Michigan, August 2 and 3, 1903; together with a History of the Canal by John H. Goff, and Papers Relating.* Detroit: Semi-Centennial Commission, 1907. xx + 285 pp. Illustrations, maps, notes, appendices, and index. A good, heavily illustrated introduction to the historic canal.

Moore, Norman. *Improvement of the Lower Mississippi River and Tributaries, 1931-1972.* Vicksburg: Mississippi River Commission, 1972. xii + 241 pp. Illustrations, maps, tables, appendix and index. A good legislative history of the Mississippi River and Tributaries Project, which began in 1928. Moore also addresses some of the technological problems and developments which accompanied the project.

Morgan, Anne Hodges. *Robert S. Kerr: The Senate Years.* Norman: University of Oklahoma Press, 1977. xiv + 337 pp. Bibliography and index. Contains much information on Kerr's role in developing the McClellan-Kerr Waterway and other water resources in Oklahoma and nearby states.

Morgan, Arthur E. *Dams and Other Disasters: A Century of the Army Corps of Engineers in Civil Works.* See chapter on "Flood Control and Drainage."

Morgan, Arthur E. *The Making of the TVA.* See chapter on "Flood Control and Drainage."

Morgan, J. Allen. "State Aid to Transportation in North America." *North Carolina Booklet.* See chapter on "Roads, Streets, and Highways."

Moreell, Ben. *Our Nation's Water Resources—Policies and Politics.* See chapter on "Flood Control and Drainage."

Morrill, John Barstow, and Paul O. Fischer, eds. *Planning the Region of Chicago.* See chapter on "Planning, Engineering, and Administration."

Morris, Charles N. "Internal Improvements in Ohio, 1825-1850." *Papers of the American Historical Association,* III (1889), 105-36. Dull, dated overview of the economic aspects of Ohio internal improvements.

Morris, James. *The Great Port: A Passage through New York.* New York: Harcourt, Brace & World, 1969. xiv + 75 pp. Illustrations and map. Contains a smattering of historical information.

Moss, Frank E. *The Water Crisis.* New York: Frederick A. Praeger, 1967. xiii + 305 pp. Illustrations, maps, charts, bibliography, appendix, and index. A good summary of the competing uses and conflicts that arise in the water resources field. The author, a former United States senator from Utah, uses incisive historical summaries of water-resource development in the nation's major river basins to support his views on policy questions.

Moulton, Harold Glenn. "Waterways Versus Railways." Doctoral dissertation, University of Chicago, 1914.

Moulton, Harold G.; Charles S. Morgan; and Adah L. Lee. *The St. Lawrence Navigation and Power Project.* See chapter on "Energy."

Mueller, Zita A. "The Ohio River: America's

Busy Waterway." *Bulletin of the Historical and Philosophical Society of Ohio,* 10 (July 1952), 177-96. Good description of the evolution of navigation on the river.

Nadeau, Remi A. *City Makers: The Men Who Transformed Los Angeles from Village to Metropolis During the First Great Boom, 1868-76.* Garden City, N.Y.: Doubleday & Company, 1948. xiv + 270 pp. Bibliography and index. Most of this volume deals with the influence of railroad competition on the early growth of Los Angeles. There is some sketchy material on horsecars, wagon roads, and port development.

Nash, Roderick, ed. *The American Environment: Readings in the History of Conservation.* See chapter on "Planning, Engineering, and Administration."

National Automobile Dealers Association. *The History of Transportation.* See chapter on "Roads, Streets, and Highways."

Nelson, E.C. "Presidential Influence on the Policy of Internal Improvements." *Iowa Journal of History and Politics,* IV (Jan. 1906), 3-69. A rather dated and shallow survey of presidential attitudes toward internal improvements prior to 1860. The most useful part of the article is the appendix which lists the road, waterway, and railway improvements undertaken by each administration.

Nettels, Curtis. "The Mississippi Valley and the Constitution, 1815-1829." *Mississippi Valley Historical Review,* XI (Dec. 1924), 332-57. An overview of early internal improvements in the Mississippi Valley. It is especially insightful on federal and state relations.

Neu, Irene D. "The Building of the Sault Canal, 1852-55." *Mississippi Valley Historical Review,* XL (June 1953), 25-46.

Newcomer, Lee. "A History of The Indiana Internal Improvement Bonds." *Indiana Magazine of History,* XXXII (June 1936), 106-15. An explanation of why Indiana's program of internal improvements collapsed in 1839 and what was done to insure that work on the Wabash and Erie Canal continued.

Newell, Frederick Haynes. *Water Resources: Present and Future Uses.* See chapter on "Irrigation."

Newton, John. "The Improvement of East River and Hell Gate." *Popular Science Monthly,* XXVIII (Feb. 1886), 1133-48.

Nicholas, Roger L. "Army Contributions to River Transportation, 1818-1825." *Military Affairs,* XXXIII (April 1969), 242-49. Principally discusses army exploration on the Missouri River.

Nixon, Edgar B., ed. *Franklin D. Roosevelt and Conservation, 1911-1945.* See chapter on "Planning, Engineering, and Administration."

Norris, George W. *Fighting Liberal: The Autobiography of George W. Norris.* See chapter on "Flood Control and Drainage."

Norton, Clark F. "Early Movement for the St. Mary's Falls Ship Canal." *Michigan History,* XXXIX (Sept. 1955), 257-80. History of public agitation for the canal that was opened in 1855.

Olcott, Edward S. "Port Decay and Port Development." *Traffic Quarterly,* 33 (Oct. 1979), 489-500. An exploration of the technological and economic factors that cause ports to decline.

Oliver, James Parker. "A History of the Canal Projects at the Falls of the Ohio River." Master's thesis, University of Kentucky, 1937. xii + 127 pp. Map, tables, notes, and bibliography. Discusses efforts to bypass the falls of the Ohio River opposite Louisville, Kentucky.

Padelford, Norman J. *The Panama Canal in Peace and War.* New York: Macmillan Company, 1942. xii + 327 pp. Maps, chart, notes, and index. A history of the canal that deals principally with its foreign policy and economic significance. Virtually no information is included on the construction and operation of the waterway.

Palmer, William R. "The Whaling Port of Sag Harbor." Doctoral dissertation, Columbia University, 1959.

Parkins, A.E., and J.R. Whitaker, eds. *Our Natural Resources and Their Conservation.* See chapter on "Flood Control and Drainage."

Parkman, Aubrey. *Army Engineers in New England: The Military and Civil Work of the Corps of Engineers in New England, 1775-1975.* Waltham, Mass.: U.S. Army Corps of Engineers, New England Division, 1978. xi + 319 pp. Illustrations, maps, notes, appendix, bibliography, and index. A well-balanced and lucidly written 200-year history of corps' activities in New England. Here the agency's military mission began in 1775 and the area's civil works were among the first undertaken when the corps received its civil mission in 1824. Subjects covered include navigation and harbor projects, the Cape Cod Canal, military construction, flood control, and hydro-electric power.

Parsons, William Barclay. "Cape Cod Canal." *Annals of the American Academy of Political and Social Science,* XXXI (Jan.-June, 1908), 81-101.

Payne, Robert. *The Canal Builders: The Story of Canal Engineers Through the Ages.* New York: Macmillan Company, 1959. ix + 278 pp. Illustrations, maps, bibliography, and index. A romantic treatment of canal building. The publication includes chapters on pre-Civil War canal development in the United States, construction of the Panama Canal, and the building of the St. Lawrence Seaway.

Pellett, M.E. *Water Transportation: A Bibliography, Guide, and Union Catalogue.* New York: H.W. Wilson Company, 1931. lv + 685 pp. Indexes.

Peterson, Arthur Everett, and George William Edwards. *New York as an Eighteenth Century Municipality.* See chapter on "Solid Wastes."

Peterson, William J. "A Century of River Traffic." *Palimpsest,* XXVII (Oct. 1946), 289-316. Breezy sketch that stresses pre-Civil War navigation.

Peyronnin, Chester A. "Evolution of Tidewater Port." *Journal of the Waterways and Harbors Division.* Proceedings of the American Society of Civil Engineers, 96 (May 1970), 387-94. Useful history of the Port of New Orleans.

Phillips, Ulrich Bonnell. *A History of Transportation in the Eastern Cotton Belt to 1860.* New York: Columbia University Press, 1908. xvii + 405 pp. Illustration, maps, notes, bibliography, and index. A history of ante-bellum transportation principally in South Carolina and Georgia. Although the emphasis of the book is on railroads, there is some material on roads, canals, and river navigation.

Pickins, William Hickman. "A Marvel of Nature: The Harbor of Harbors: Public Policy and the Development of the San Francisco Bay, 1846-1926." Doctoral dissertation, University of California, 1976.

Platt, Hermann K. "The Jersey City Water Rights Controversy, 1845-1850." *New Jersey History,* 94 (1976), 141-54. Interesting discussion of a city versus private enterprise struggle to control the waterfront.

Plumb, R.G. "Early Harbor History of Wisconsin." *Transactions of the Wisconsin Academy of Sciences, Arts, and Letters.* XVII (1914), 187-94.

Plumb, R.G. "Early Harbor History of Wisconsin." *Proceedings of the Mississippi Valley Historical Association,* IV (1910-1911), 189-98. Sketchy overview of pre-Civil War harbor improvements.

Poinsatte, Charles R. *Fort Wayne During the Canal Era, 1828-1855: A Study of a Western Community in the Middle Period of American History.* Indianapolis: Indiana Historical Bureau, 1969. viii + 284 pp. Illustrations, maps, notes, appendix, and index.

Poinsatte, Charles Robert. "Fort Wayne, Indiana During the Canal Era, 1828-1855: A Study of a Western Community During the Middle Period of American History." Doctoral dissertation, University of Notre Dame, 1964.

Pomerantz, Sidney I. *New York, an American City, 1783-1803: A Study of Urban Life.* See chapter on "Solid Wastes."

Poor, Henry V. *History of the Railroads and Canals of the United States of America.* New York: Augustus M. Kelley, 1970. 632 pp. Map, tables, and index. A pioneering attempt to survey the development, cost, revenues, expenditures, and financial condition of railroads and canals in the United States. The book offers a remarkably thorough state-by-state profile of these internal improvements. It was first published in 1860.

Porcher, F.A. *The History of the Santee Canal.* Moncks Corner, S.C.: South Carolina Public Service Authority, 1950. 13 pp. Map and appendix. Reminiscence written in 1875.

Porter, David. "Representative Lindsay Warren, the Water Bloc and the Transportation Act of 1940." *North Carolina Historical Review,* L (July 1973), 273-88. Describes efforts by a North Carolina politician to prevent federal control of inland shipping, which almost dealt a serious blow to the development of a national transportation policy.

Pound, Arthur. *Lake Ontario.* Indianapolis:

Bobbs-Merrill Company, 1945. 384 pp. Illustrations, map, notes, bibliographical essay, and index. A contribution to the "American Lakes Series" that contains some sketchy information on port development.

Pred, Allan R. *The Spatial Dynamics of U.S. Urban-Industrial Growth, 1800-1914.* See chapter on "Urban Mass Transportation."

Preston, Howard. *A History of the Walla Walla District, 1948-1970.* See chapter on "Flood Control and Drainage."

Pritchett, C. Herman. *The Tennessee Valley Authority: A Study in Public Administration.* See chapter on "Flood Control and Drainage."

Pross, Edward L. "A History of Rivers and Harbors Appropriation Bills, 1866-1933." Doctoral dissertation, Ohio State University, 1938.

Public Works Administration. *America Builds: The Record of PWA.* See chapter on "Planning, Engineering, and Administration."

Purvis, Neil H. "History of the Lake Washington Canal." *Washington Historical Quarterly,* XXV (April and July 1934), April : 114-27; July: 210-13. Superficial history of an important canal in the Seattle region.

Putnam, George R. *Sentinels of the Coasts: The Log of a Lighthouse Engineer.* New York: W.W. Norton & Company, 1937. x + 368 pp. Illustrations, appendix, and index. A good autobiography by a career Lighthouse Service employee. The book touches upon various aspects of lighthouse design, construction, and operation.

Putnam, James William. *The Illinois and Michigan Canal: A Study in Economic History.* Chicago: University of Chicago, 1918. xiii + 213 pp. Illustrations, maps, notes, appendices, bibliography, and index. A good history of the canal that provided the first commercial route between the Great Lakes and the Mississippi Valley. The author discusses the project's influence on the economic development of the region and devastating effect on the financial stability of the Illinois state government. The early growth of Chicago as a commercial center is also treated.

Quaife, Milo Milton. *Chicago and the Old Northwest, 1673-1835.* Chicago: University of Chicago Press, 1913. vii + 480 pp. Illustrations, notes, appendices, bibliography, and index. Discusses the development of Fort Dearborn and the site's key role in waterborne commerce.

Quaife, Milo M. *Lake Michigan.* Indianapolis: Bobbs-Merrill Company, 1944. 384 pp. Illustrations, maps, notes, bibliographical essay, and index. A volume in the "American Lakes Series" written by the series' editor. The book gives considerable attention to shipping, port development, and the influence of waterborne commerce on the growth of Chicago and other cities that border the lake.

Rae, John Bell. "Federal Land Grants in Aid of Canals." *Journal of Economic History,* IV (Nov. 1944), 167-77. Shallow survey of the reasons why some 4.5 million acres were donated to assist the construction of canal projects.

Randall, Duncan P. "Wilmington, North Carolina: The Historical Development of a Port City." *Annals of the Association of American Geographers,* 58 (Sept. 1968), 441-51.

Randall, Laura Rosenbaum. "The Effect of the Erie Canal on the Economic Growth of New York State, 1820-1850: A Study in Location Theory." Master's thesis, University of Massachusetts, Amherst, 1959. v + 122 pp. Maps, tables, notes, appendix, and bibliography. A good study of the impact of the canal on population shifts, agriculture, commerce, and manufacturing within the state of New York.

Randolph, Robert Isham. "Review of the Development of Chicago Waterways." *Journal of the Western Society of Engineers,* XXVIII (Sept. 1922), 395-401.

Rankin, Ernest H., Sr. "The Founding of the Port of Marquette." *Inland Seas,* 32 (Spring 1976), 3-16. Michigan port founded on the south shore of Lake Superior in the 1840s.

Ransmeier, Joseph Sirera. *The Tennessee Valley Authority: A Case Study in the Economics of Multiple Purpose Stream Planning.* See chapter on "Flood Control and Drainage."

Ransom, Roger L. "Canals and Development: A Discussion of the Issues." *American Economic Review,* LIV (May 1964), 365-89.

Ransom, Roger Leslie. "Government Investment in Canals: A Study of the Ohio Canal, 1825-1860." Doctoral dissertation, University of Washington, 1963. vii + 141 pp. Charts, tables, notes, appendices, and bibliography. A pioneering study of the "external economics" that accrued to producers and consumers in the canal's region. The author concludes that the Ohio Canal was a marginal investment and challenges the importance of government aid for transportation as an important part of the state's growth.

Rapp, Marvin A. "The Port of Buffalo, 1825-1880." Doctoral dissertation, Duke University, 1948.

Reed, Nathaniel. "The Role of the Connecticut State Government in the Development and Operation of Inland Transportation Facilities from 1784 to 1821." Doctoral dissertation, Yale University, 1964.

Reid, William James. *The Building of the Cape Cod Canal, 1627-1914.* Privately printed: 1961. xv + 130 pp. Illustrations and index. Although undocumented, the book offers a comprehensive overview of the canal's development. Of particular interest, are the abortive efforts or private entrepreneurs to build the waterway.

Reid, William J. "The Cape Cod Canal." Doctoral dissertation, Boston University, 1958.

Reinders, Robert C. *End of an Era: New Orleans, 1850-1860.* See chapter on "Public Buildings."

Reiser, Catherine Elizabeth. *Pittsburgh's Commercial Development, 1800-1850.* Harrisburg: Pennsylvania Historical and Museum Commission, 1951. viii + 247 pp. Illustrations, map, tables, notes, appendices, bibliography, and index. A good commercial history that devotes a great deal of attention to the influence of turnpikes, canals, and river transportation on the city's growth.

Reps, John W. *Cities of the American West: A History of Frontier Urban Planning.* See chapter on "Planning, Engineering, and Administration."

Reser, William M. "The Wabash and Erie Canal at Lafayette." *Indiana Magazine of History,* XXX (Dec. 1934), 312-24.

Rice, Bradley R. "The Galveston Plan of City Government by Commission: The Birth of a Progressive Idea." *Southwestern Historical Quarterly.* See chapter on "Planning, Engineering, and Administration."

Rice, Philip Morrison. "Internal Improvements in Virginia, 1775-1860." Doctoral dissertation, University of North Carolina, 1948. ii + 503 pp. Tables, notes, and bibliography. A history of internal improvements in the first commonwealth in the United States to establish a definitive program of public works. Large parts of the dissertation are devoted to river improvements and the road system, including turnpikes and plank roads.

Rice, Philip M. "The Early Development of the Roanoke Waterway—A Study in Interstate Relations." *North Carolina Historical Review,* XXXI (Jan. 1954), 50-74. One of the strongest case studies of an early nineteenth-century canal. The article is extensively researched and explores the trade rivalries that existed between Virginia and North Carolina.

Richard, Alfred Charles, Jr. "The Panama Canal in American National Consciousness, 1870-1922." Doctoral dissertation, Boston University, 1969.

Richardson, Elmo R. *The Politics of Conservation: Crusades and Controversies, 1897-1913.* Berkeley: University of California Press, 1962. xi + 207 pp. Notes, bibliography, and index. Much of this book focuses on the Ballinger-Pinchot affair and efforts by Progressive conservationists to halt exploitation of natural resources by monopolies. The author suggests that conservation was a technically complex issue but had an emotional appeal as well.

Richmond, Henry R., III. *The History of the Portland District, Corps of Engineers, 1871-1969.* Portland: U.S. Army Engineer District, 1970. viii + 274 pp. Maps and illustrations. Traces the corps' activities in the region from earliest exploration to the development of vast multiple-purpose projects. Though most of the book focuses on navigation improvements, sections are devoted to military work, fish conservation, and recreation.

Ridgeway, Marian E. *The Missouri Basin's Pick-Sloan Plan: A Case Study in Congressional Policy Determination.* See chapter on "Flood Control and Drainage."

Ringwalt, J. L. *Development of Transportation Systems in the United States.* Philadelphia: J.L. Ringwalt, 1888. 398 pp. Illustrations, maps, tables, diagrams, and index. A classic tome on the growth of canals, roads, and railroads from the Colonial era to the 1880s. The book is a treasure trove of drawings of early transportation facilities.

Roberts, S. G. "Canalization of the Upper Mississippi River." *Scientific American,* 152 (Feb. 1935), 72-74.

Rogers, Benjamin F. "The Florida Ship Canal Project." *Florida Historical Quarterly,* XXXVI (July 1957), 14-23. Good "story of a ditch that was never dug."

Rogers, Elizabeth, comp. *A Nation in Motion: Historic American Transportation Sites.* Washington, D.C.: U.S. Department of Commerce, 1976. 133 pp. Illustrations. Useful survey of highway water transportation, railroad, and aeronautic sites. The book includes an overview of federal legislation in these fields.

Ross, John P. "'Pork Barrels' and the General Welfare: Problems in Conservation, 1900-1920." Doctoral dissertation. See chapter on "Flood Control and Drainage."

Roth, Lawrence V. "The Growth of American Cities." *Geographical Review,* V (May 1918), 284-98. Interesting discussion of the response of city populations to the opening of transportation routes to the hinterland.

Rowe, Robert S., comp. *Bibliography of Rivers and Harbors and Related Fields in Hydraulic Engineering.* Princeton, N.J.: By author, 1953. 407 pp. Indexes. An annotated bibliography of general works on hydraulic engineering, rivers, harbors, canals and inland navigation, inter-oceanic canals, reclamation, flood dams and reservoirs, water power, and water supply engineering. There are introductory comments of an historical nature preceding each chapter.

Rubin, Julius. *Canal or Railroad?: Imitation and Innovation in the Response to the Erie Canal in Philadelphia, Baltimore, and Boston.* Philadelphia: American Philosophical Society, 1961. 106 pp. Map, diagrams, notes, appendix, bibliography, and index. A thoroughly researched and well-written account of the "desperate urgency" of promoters in Boston, Philadelphia, and Baltimore to develop transportation links to the West. The opening of the Erie Canal in the early 1820s made New York the principal port for western agricultural goods, which threatened the other major seaboard cities with economic stagnation. Rubin exhaustively examines the factors which determined the type of transportation strategy each city adopted. The book is published as volume 51 of the *Transactions of the American Philosophical Society.*

Ruhloff, F. Carl. "Evolution of Modern Construction Machinery." *Civil Engineering.* See chapter on "Planning, Engineering, and Administration."

Russ, William A., Jr. "The Partnership between Public and Private Initiative in the History of Pennsylvania." *Pennsylvania History.* See chapter on "Roads, Streets, and Highways."

Salt, Harriet. *Mighty Engineering Feats: Clear and Concise Descriptions of Ten of the Greatest American Engineering Feats.* See chapter on "Planning, Engineering, and Administration."

Sanderlin, Walter S. "The Expanding Horizons of the Schuykill Navigation Company, 1815-1870." *Pennsylvania History,* XXXVI (April 1969), 174-91. Solid economic history of the waterway based upon company records.

Sanderlin, Walter S. *The Great National Project: A History of the Chesapeake and Ohio Canal.* Baltimore: Johns Hopkins Press, 1946. 331 pp. Notes, appendix, bibliographical essay, and index. The first major scholarly treatment of this historic canal, which attempted to provide an all-water route to the West via the Potomac Valley. The author explores the origins, planning, construction, and decline of the waterway, which is an important chapter in the history of commerce and transportation in the eastern United States.

Sanderson, Dorothy Hurlbut. *The Delaware and Hudson Canalway: Carrying Coals to Rondout.* Ellenville, N.Y.: Rondout Valley Publishing Company, 1974. vi + 278 pp. Illustrations, maps, notes, bibliography, and index. A well-written history of this important waterway.

Sandström, Gösta E. *Man the Builder.* See chapter on "Roads, Streets, and Highways."

Scanlon, Ann Edward. "The Rise of Duluth as an Ore Port, 1890-1901." Master's thesis, University of Chicago, 1941. vi + 101 pp. Illustrations, tables, notes, appendices, and bibliography. Good historical overview of a key Great Lakes port.

Scheel, Paul Edmond. "Resource Development Politics in the Missouri Basin: Federal Power, Navigation, and Reservoir Operation Policies, 1944-1968." Doctoral dissertation. See chapter on "Irrigation."

Scheffauer, Frederick C. *The Hopper*

Dredge: Its History, Development, and Operation. Washington, D.C.: U.S. Government Printing Office, 1954. x + 399 pp. Illustrations, figures, tables, appendices, and indexes.

Scheiber, Harry N. Entrepreneurship and Western Development: The Case of Micajah T. Williams." *Business History Review,* XXXVII (Winter 1963), 345-68. Outstanding discussion of the career of an important "politician-promoter" who played a key role in canal development and banking from 1820 to 1943. He directed state construction of the Miami Canal.

Scheiber, Harry Noel. "Internal Improvements and Economic Change on Ohio, 1820-1860." Doctoral dissertation, Cornell University, 1962.

Scheiber, Harry N. "Land Reform, Speculation, and Governmental Failure: The Administration of Ohio's State Canal Lands, 1836-60." *Prologue,* 7 (Summer 1975), 85-98. Outstanding case study of an effort to promote canal construction through disposition of public domain.

Scheiber, Harry N. *Ohio Canal Era: A Case Study of Government and the Economy, 1820-1861.* Athens: Ohio University Press, 1969. xviii + 430 pp. Maps, tables, notes, appendices, bibliographical essay, and index. One of the best case studies of an American state government's role in transportation and economic development prior to the Civil War. The author suggests that state investment in canals made a crucial contribution to American economic growth. The book also contains a unique treatment of how the day-to-day functioning of the agencies responsible for canal construction and operation touched every important economic interest in the state.

Scheiber, Harry N. "State Policy and the Public Domain: The Ohio Canal Lands." *Journal of Economic History,* XXV (March 1965), 86-113.

Scheiber, Harry N. "The Ohio Canal Movement, 1820-1825." *Ohio Historical Quarterly,* 69 (July 1960), 231-56. Exemplary case study of the activities of able business and political leaders to promote a visionary canal system.

Schenfele, Roy W. *The History of the North Pacific Division, U.S. Army Corps of Engineers, 1888 to 1965.* Portland: North Pacific Division, 1969. iii + 76 pp. Bibliography and appendix. A disjointed and superficial district history.

Schermerhorn, I. Y. "The Rise and Progress of Rivers and Harbor Improvement in the United States." *Journal of the Franklin Institute,* CXXXIX (April 1895), 252-71. Dated and superficial treatment of the subject.

Schlichter, Elmer. "History of Wharf Developments by the Department of Wharves, Docks, and Ferries." *World Ports,* XIX (Sept. 1931), 1175-80. Sketch of Philadelphia's harbor.

Schmid, A. Allan. "Water and the Law in Wisconsin." *Wisconsin Magazine of History,* XLV (Spring 1962), 203-15. A review of the laws regulating Wisconsin's use of its water resources from the mid-nineteenth to the mid-twentieth century.

Schneider, Norris F. *Y Bridge City: The Story of Zanesville and Muskingum County, Ohio.* See chapter on "Roads, Streets, and Highways."

Scriven, George B. "The Susquehanna and Tidewater Canal." *Maryland Historical Magazine,* 71 (Winter 1976), 522-26. Largely deals with the canal's operations shortly before it closed in the 1890s.

Segal, Harvey H. "Canal Cycles, 1834-1861: Public Construction Experience in New York, Pennsylvania, and Ohio." Doctoral dissertation, Columbia University, 1956. 329 pp.

Selznick, Philip. *TVA and the Grass Roots: A Study in the Sociology of Formal Organization.* See chapter on "Planning, Engineering, and Administration."

Settle, William A., Jr. *The Dawning: A New Day for the Southwest: A History of the Tulsa District Corps of Engineers, 1939-1971.* Tulsa, Okla.: U.S. Army Corps of Engineers, Tulsa District, 1973. ix + 179 pp. Illustrations, maps, tables, notes, and index. History of the corps' activities in the Arkansas and Red River basins from the 1930s to the 1970s. The administrative history of the district is discussed as well as the projects that provide navigation, flood control, water supply, and energy benefits.

Shallat, Todd A. "People in Public Works: Stephen Harriman Long." *APWA Reporter,* 46 (Nov. 1979), 4-5. A biographical sketch of one of the nation's leading exponents of river and harbor development of the Mississippi and Ohio valleys in an era when federally financed public works seldom reached west of the Appalachians.

Shank, William H. *The Amazing Pennsylvania Canals.* York, Pa.: Historical Society of York County, 1965. 81 pp. Illustrations, maps, and bibliography. A popular history of the state's canal era that includes excellent illustrations of canal design and operation.

Shaughnessy, Jim. *Delaware & Hudson: The History of an Important Railroad Whose Antecedent Was a Canal Network to Transport Coal.* Berkeley: Howell-North Books, 1967. xi + 476 pp. Illustrations, maps, appendix, bibliography, and index. The first chapter of this heavily illustrated book is a well-written short history of the Delaware and Hudson Canal. The waterway included aqueducts that featured John Roebling's pioneer cable suspension system.

Shaw, Ronald E. "A History of the Erie Canal, 1807-1850, With Particular Reference to Western New York." Doctoral dissertation, University of Rochester, 1954. x + 448 pp. Illustrations, maps, notes, and bibliography. A sound history of the canal's development that focuses on the social and economic influence of the waterway.

Shaw, Ronald E. *Erie Water West: A History of the Erie Canal 1792-1854.* Lexington: University of Kentucky Press, 1966. xiii + 449 pp. Illustrations, map, notes, bibliographical essay, and index. A well-researched, balanced account of the Erie Canal that brings together such varied aspects as political sponsorship and opposition, construction and operation, travel and commerce, and social and cultural significance.

Shelling, Richard I. "Philadelphia and the Agitation in 1825 for the Pennsylvania Canal." *Pennsylvania Magazine for History and Biography,* LXII (April 1938), 175-204. Good summary of the activities of community groups and individuals who promoted the canal's construction.

Shotliff, Don A. "San Pedro Harbor, or Los Angeles Harbor?: Senate W.H. Savage and the Home Rule Advocates Fail to Stem the Tide of Consolidationism, 1906-1909." *Southern California Quarterly,* LIV (Summer 1972), 127-54. Good discussion of the political aspects of harbor development.

Sibley, Marilyn McAdams. *The Port of Houston: A History.* Austin and London: University of Texas Press, 1968. xvi + 246 pp. Illustrations, maps, footnotes, bibliography, and index. One of the finest port histories. The author offers extensive coverage of the subject, including the political aspects of port development.

Siddall, William R. "The Yukon Waterway in the Development of Interior Alaska." *Pacific Historical Review,* XXVIII (Nov. 1959), 361-76. Evolution of shipping on the Yukon River.

Skramstad, Harold. "The Georgetown Canal Incline." *Technology and Culture,* 10 (Oct. 1969), 549-60.

Skramstad, Harold Kenneth. "The Professional Life of William Rich Hutton, Civil Engineer." Doctoral dissertation, George Washington University, 1971. 313 pp. Biographical study of a civil engineer whose career from the 1850s to the 1890s spanned the entire spectrum of the field—canals, ports, bridges, railroads, and municipal water supplies.

Sloan, Edward William III. *Benjamin Franklin Isherwood, Naval Engineer: The Years as Engineer in Chief, 1861-1869.* Annapolis: United States Naval Institute, 1965. xiii + 299 pp. Illustrations, notes, bibliography, and index. A good, well-researched biography of Isherwood's public career. Considerable material is included on advancements made in shore installations during his tenure as engineer-in-chief.

Smith, Darrell Hevenor. *The Panama Canal: Its History, Activities, and Organization.* Baltimore: Johns Hopkins Press, 1927. xviii + 413 pp. Tables, notes, appendices, bibliography, and index. A pedestrian history of the canal's construction and administration is included in a volume that describes the activities of the Panama Canal Company's major divisions.

Smith, Esther Ruth. "The First Crescent City Lighthouse." *California Historical Society Quarterly,* XXXV (Dec. 1956), 325-34. Dull chronology of a lighthouse built on California's northwest coast.

Smith, Frank E., ed. *Conservation in the United States, A Documentary History: Land and Water, 1900-1970.* See chapter on "Planning, Engineering, and Administration."

Smith, Frank E. *The Politics of Conservation.* See chapter on "Irrigation."

Smith, Guy-Harold. *Conservation of Natural Resources.* See chapter on "Irrigation."

Smith, J. Spencer, et al. *Ports of the*

Americas: History and Development. n.p.: American Association of Port Authorities, 1961. iii + 174 pp. Illustrations and chronology. Thumbnail sketches of ports throughout North and South America.

Smith, Melvin T. "The Colorado River: Its History in the Lower Canyon Area." Doctoral dissertation, Brigham Young University, 1972. x + 511 pp. Illustrations, maps, notes, appendix, and bibliography. Summarizes the history of the river until the 1870s. Material is included on the river's role as a transportation route and the development of ferry crossings for wagon roads.

Sneddon, Leonard J. "Maryland and Sectional Politics: Canal Building in the Federal Period." *Maryland Historian,* VI (Fall 1975), 79-84. Good article on the agitation for canals in the 1790s.

Snow, Edward Rowe. *Famous Lighthouses of America: Illustrated with Photographs and Drawings.* New York: Dodd, Mead & Company, 1955. xiv + 314 pp. Illustrations and index. A popular account of America's most famous lighthouses.

Snow, Edward Rowe. *Famous New England Lighthouses.* Boston: Yankee Publishing Company, 1945. 457 pp. Illustrations, map, bibliography, and index. One of the better "buff" books on lighthouses. The narrative is well-written and the illustrations outstanding.

Snow, Edward Rowe. *The Story of Minot's Light.* Boston: Yankee Publishing Company, 1940. 139 pp. Illustrations, notes, and index. A popular history of the facility from the 1850s to the 1940s.

Snyder, Frank E., and Brian H. Guss. *The District: A History of the Philadelphia District, U.S. Army Corps of Engineers, 1866-1971.* Philadelphia: U.S. Army Engineer District, 1974. vi + 263 pp. Illustrations, maps, glossary, notes, bibliography, appendices, and index. Excellent case study of the corps' civil and military missions from 1775. The book offers especially strong treatments of dredging and pre-Civil War river and harbor work.

Sprague, Stuart Seely. "The Canal and the Falls of the Ohio and the Three Cornered Rivalry." *Register of the Kentucky Historical Society,* 72 (Jan. 1974), 38-54. Discusses the roles of land speculation and urban rivalry in delaying the canal's completion until 1830.

Stapleton, Darwin H., ed. *The Engineering Drawings of Benjamin Henry Latrobe.* New Haven: Yale University Press, 1980. xx + 256 pp. Illustrations, notes, appendix, bibliography, and index. A masterful collection of Latrobe's engineering drawings set in perspective by a lucid introductory essay. The drawings include canals, locks, river improvements, the National Road, and waterworks.

Stapleton, Darwin H., and Thomas C. Guider. "The Transfer and Diffusion of British Technology: Benjamin Henry Latrobe and the Chesapeake and Delaware Canal." *Delaware History Journal,* 17 (Spring 1976), 127-38. Lucid article based on original source materials.

Starr, John T. "The Army Engineers . . . Pioneers in American Transportation." *Highway Magazine.* See chapter on "Roads, Streets, and Highways."

Stay, Clarence Reuben. "Theodore E. Burton on Navigation and Conservation: His Role as Chairman of the Committee on Rivers and Harbors, 1898-1909." Doctoral dissertation, Case Western Reserve University, 1975.

Steinbach, John Joseph. "History of the Illinois and Mississippi Canal." Master's thesis, Illinois State University, 1964. v + 141 pp. Illustrations, map, tables, notes, and bibliography. An excellent canal history largely based on original sources. Built from 1892 to 1907, the canal was never of great commercial value and closed in 1951. The thesis discusses state efforts to have the waterway converted to a recreational area.

Stevens, John Austin. "Christopher Colles: The First Projector of Inland Navigation in America." *Magazine of American History,* II (June 1878), 340-48. A biographical sketch of the individual who is credited with being the first to propose and to bring before the public "the feasibility and vast national advantage of a system of water communication" to unite the Great Lakes and the Atlantic Ocean. Colles also published a survey of roads in the United States (1789).

Stevens, John F. *An Engineer's Recollections.* New York: Engineering News-Record, 1936. ix + 70 pp. Illustrations. This booklet is an autobiographical account of the career of Stevens who "rose through achievement to greater achievement until in the prime of his powers he was called to organize the Panama Canal undertaking."

Stevenson, David. *Sketch of the Civil Engineering of North America; Comprising Remarks on the Harbours, River and Lake Navigation, Lighthouses, Steam-Navigation, Water-Works, Canals, Roads, Railways, Bridges, and Other Works in that Country.* London: John Weale, Architectural Library, 1838. xv + 318 pp. Map, illustrations, and table. A fascinating personal report on the state of public works in the United States by an English engineer following a three-month "engineering tour."

Stewart, William H., Jr. "The Tennessee-Tombigbee Waterway: A Case Study in the Politics of Water Transportation." Doctoral dissertation, University of Alabama, 1968. 552 pp.

Stick, David. *North Carolina Lighthouses.* Raleigh: North Carolina Department of Cultural Resources, Division of Archives and History, 1980. xi + 85 pp. Illustrations, maps, bibliographic note, and index. Clearly written, well-illustrated history based in large part on primary sources.

Stickel, Fred G., Jr. "Through the Morris Canal." *New Jersey History,* 89 (1971), 93-114. Travelogue of a state official who explored the 102-mile-long canal after it became the property of New Jersey in 1913.

Still, John S. "Ethan Allen Brown and Ohio's Canal System." *Ohio Historical Quarterly,* 66 (Jan. 1957), 22-56. Good biographical profile of Ohio's foremost canal promoter.

Strickland, William; Edward H. Gill; and Henry R. Campbell, eds. *Public Works of the United States of America.* See chapter on "Planning, Engineering, and Administration."

Stoessel, John. "The Port of Alexandria, Virginia, in the Eighteenth Century." Master's thesis, Catholic University, 1969.

Strobridge, Truman R. *Chronology of Aids to Navigation and the Old Lighthouse Service, 1716-1939.* Washington, D.C.: United States Coast Guard, 1974. 39 pp. A useful chronology.

Stuve, Bernard. "The State's Internal Improvement Venture of 1837-38." *Transactions of the Illinois State Historical Society* (1902), 114-25.

Sundborg, George. *Hail Columbia: The Thirty Year Struggle for Grand Coulee Dam.* See chapter on "Irrigation."

Susskind, Charles. *Understanding Technology.* See chapter on "Planning, Engineering, and Administration."

Swain, Donald C. *Federal Conservation Policy, 1921-1933.* See chapter on "Irrigation."

Tanner, H. S. *A Description of the Canals and Rail-Roads of the United States, Comprehending Notices of all the Works of Internal Improvement Throughout the Several States.* New York: T.R. Tanner & J. Disturnell, 1840. 272 pp. Charts, glossary, and index. An early state-by-state survey of internal improvements in the United States.

Tarr, Joel Arthur. *A Study in Boss Politics: William Lorimer of Chicago.* Urbana: University of Illinois Press, 1971. xi + 376 pp. Illustrations, notes, bibliography, appendices, and index. Excellent study of the Cook County Republican boss and the political system in which he functioned. Scattered throughout the book are treatments of the political ramifications of various public works endeavors such as water transportation, sanitation, and transit.

Tarr, Joel A., ed. *Retrospective Technology Assessment—1976.* See chapter on "Sewers and Wastewater Treatment."

Taylor, George Rogers. *The Transportation Revolution, 1815-1860.* New York: Harper and Row, 1951. xvi + 490 pp. Illustrations, notes, bibliography, appendices, and index. The definitive book on ante-bellum transportation development. It remains a good source for gaining an overview of the evolution of roads, canals, railroads, and river transportation and their influence on the nation's economic development.

Terral, Rufus. *The Missouri Valley: Land of Drought, Flood and Promise.* See chapter on "Irrigation."

"The Old Lighthouse at the Bend of the Harbor." *Indiana History Bulletin,* 51 (April 1974), 44-46. Competent sketch of the facility.

Thompson, Carl D. *Public Ownership: A Survey of Public Enterprises, Municipal, State, and Federal, in the United States and Elsewhere.* See chapter on "Energy."

Thompson, John T. "Governmental Responses to the Challenges of Water Resources in Texas." *Southwestern Historical Quarterly,* LXX (July 1966), 44-64. A well-written, compact history of water problems with respect to port development, river navigation, irrigation, flood control, and pollution abatement. The author points out that increases in consumption, changes in technology, and water competition have resulted in greater roles for the state and federal governments in water management.

Thurston, William N. "Transportation in Florida before the Civil War." Master's thesis. See chapter on "Roads, Streets, and Highways."

Trindell, Roger T. "The Ports of Salem and Greenwich in the Eighteenth Century." *New Jersey History,* LXXXVI (Winter 1968), 199-214. Essentially an economic history of these colonial ports.

Turnbull, Archibald Douglas. *John Stevens: An American Record.* New York: Century Company, 1928. xvii + 545 pp. Illustrations, drawings, and index. Records with pride the varied career of this accomplished engineer (1749-1838) and highlights his accomplishments, particularly in the transportation field.

Turhollow, Anthony F. *A History of the Los Angeles District, U.S. Army Corps of Engineers, 1898-1965.* Los Angeles: U.S. Army Engineer District, 1975. xi + 440 pp. Illustrations, maps, appendix, bibliography, and index. History of the district from its establishment in 1898 to 1965. The topics covered include harbor development, shore protection, flood control, and the district's military role.

Tuttle, E.D. "The River Colorado." *Arizona Historical Review,* 1 (July 1928), 50-68. Sketch of the river's history prior to the Civil War that includes a brief discussion of steamboats and other forms of transportation.

Tweet, Roald. *A History of the Rock Island District Corps of Engineers.* Rock Island, Ill.: U.S. Army Engineer District, Rock Island, 1975. ix + 171 pp. Illustrations, maps, notes, appendices, and bibliography. A useful history of the corps' navigation improvements, military construction, and flood control endeavors on part of the Upper Mississippi.

Tyson, Carl Newton. "The Red River in Southwestern History." Doctoral dissertation, Oklahoma State University, 1975.

Uhl, W.F. "Water Power over a Century." *Transactions of the American Society of Civil Engineers,* CT (1953), 451-60. Records historical data on water power use and resources in the United States from the mid-nineteenth to the mid-twentieth century.

United States Coast Guard. *Historically Famous Lighthouses.* Washington, D.C.: U.S. Coast Guard, 1972. vi + 88 pp. Illustrations and bibliography. A state-by-state picture book of American lighthouses. Short historical summaries are provided for each facility.

U.S. Department of Commerce. Bureau of the Census. *Historical Statistics of the United States: Colonial Times to 1970.* See chapter on "Planning, Engineering, and Administration."

Updike, Richard W. "Winslow Lewis and the Lighthouses." *American Neptune* (Jan. 1968), 31-48.

Veit, Richard F. *The Old Canals of New Jersey: A Historical Geography.* Little Falls: New Jersey Geographical Press, 1963. xi + 106 pp. Illustrations, maps, tables, glossary, bibliography, and index. A brief description of New Jersey's old canals. Special attention is given to the Morris Canal and the Delaware and Raritan Canal.

Vermeule, Cornelius C. "Early Transportation in and about New Jersey." *Proceedings of the New Jersey Historical Society.* See chapter on "Roads, Streets, and Highways."

Vermeule, Cornelius C., Jr. "The Morris Canal and Its Abandonment." *Military Engineer,* XXII (March-April 1930), 114-118. Useful sketch of a canal that was opened between Newark and Easton, New Jersey, in 1831.

Vitz, Carl. "The Cincinnati Waterfront—1848." *Bulletin of the Historical and Philosophical Society of Ohio,* 6 (April 1948), 28-39.

Vogel, Herbert D. "Origins of the Waterways Experiment Station." *Military Engineer,* 53 (March/April 1961), 132-35. An excellent discussion of the Army Corps of Engineers' facility that has significantly advanced the design of hydraulic structures. The station, founded in 1930 near Vicksburg, Mississippi, uses models to conduct its experimental work on river regulation and other water resource problems.

Vogel, Robert M., ed. *Mohawk-Hudson Area Survey*. Washington, D.C.: Smithsonian Institution Press, 1973. x + 210 pp. Illustrations. Includes outstanding examples of aqueducts, locks, and other water transportation facilities.

Vogel, Robert M. *Roebling's Delaware & Hudson Canal Aqueducts.* Washington, D.C.: Smithsonian Institution Press, 1971. 45 pp. Illustrations, maps, diagrams, notes, and bibliography. A handsome, well-written account of the oldest existing American suspension bridge. It is the sole survivor and largest of four suspension aqueducts erected by John A. Roebling from 1847 and 1850 to carry the Delaware and Hudson Canal over rivers.

Voget, Lamberta Margarette. "The Waterfront of San Francisco, 1863-1930: A History of Its Administration by the State of California." Doctoral dissertation, University of California, Berkeley, 1943. ii + 241 pp. Maps, tables, notes, and bibliography. One of the few outstanding port histories. A great deal of material is included on the evolution of the port's physical facilities and administration.

Vose, George L. "Loammi Baldwin." *Journal of the Association of Engineering Societies,* V (Nov. 1885), 10-25. A detailed biographical sketch of a prominent early engineer (1780-1838) who is particularly remembered for his drydocks at Charlestown and at Norfolk.

Wade, Richard C. *The Urban Frontier: The Rise of Western Cities, 1790-1830.* See chapter on "Community Water Supply."

Walker, Barbara K., and Warren S. *The Erie Canal, Gateway to Empire: Selected Source Materials for College Research Papers.* Boston: D.C. Heath and Company, 1963. xiv + 112 pp. Map. A collection of readings.

Walker, Herbert P. "Louisville and Portland Canal." *Indiana Magazine of History,* XXVIII (1932), 21-30. Pedestrian study of a canal completed in 1830 to bypass falls on the Ohio River.

Walker, Paul K. "Building American Canals: Part I—The Federal Period." *Water Spectrum,* 12 (Winter 1979-1980), 18-25. Extremely competent overview of early canal construction in the United States from the late eighteenth century to the 1820s.

Walker, Paul K. "Building American Canals: Part II—From Erie to the Present." *Water Spectrum,* 12 (Summer 1980), 12-23. An excellent overview of the development of American waterways since the 1820s. The beautifully illustrated article is well organized and lucidly written.

Wall, John Furman. "The Civil Works of the United States Army Corps of Engineers: Program Modernization." Doctoral dissertation, Cornell University, 1973. 1018 pp.

Waller, Robert A. "The Illinois Waterway from Conception to Completion, 1908-1933." *Journal of the Illinois Historical Society,* LXV (Summer 1972), 125-41. A well-documented case study of this important commercial artery.

Wallner, Peter A. "Politics and Public Works: A Study of the Pennsylvania Canal System, 1825-1857." Doctoral dissertation, Pennsylvania State University, 1973. viii + 304 pp. Maps, tables, notes, and bibliography. Interesting discussion of the influence of political ideology on public works construction.

Ward, G.W. "Early Development of the Chesapeake and Ohio Canal Project." *Johns Hopkins University Studies in History and Political Science,* XVII (1899), 425-537. A thin and dated discussion of this historic canal.

Waring, George E., Jr. *Report on the Social Statistics of Cities.* See chapter on "Planning, Engineering, and Administration."

Waterman, W.R. "Locks and Canals at the White River Falls." *Historical New Hampshire,* XXII (Autumn 1967), 23-54. Excellent case study of navigation improvements in Connecticut during the 1830s.

Watson, Alan D. "The Ferry in Colonial North Carolina: A Vital Link in Transportation." *North Carolina Historical Review,* LI (July 1974), 247-60. Outstanding article on an important colonial public improvement for transportation. The author makes prodigious use of primary sources.

Watson, Elkanah. *History of the Rise, Progress, and Existing Condition of the Western Canals in the State of New York.* Albany: D. Steele, 1820. iv + 210 pp. Maps.

Watson, Harry L. "Squire Oldway and His Friends: Opposition to Internal Improvements in Antebellum North Carolina." *North Carolina Historical Review,* LIV (April 1977), 105-19. Describes and evaluates individual arguments both for and especially against internal improvements (canals, roads, and railroads) in North Carolina during the first half of the nineteenth century.

Watt, David A. "The Barge Canal of the State of New York." *Engineering* (London), LXXXVI (Sept. 11, 1908), 334-36. Overview of the enlarging of the Erie Canal that offers historical material on the waterway's development.

Wattenberg, Ben. *Busy Waterways: The Story of America's Inland Water Transportation*. New York: John Day Company, 1964. 127 pp. Illustrations, map, and index. Includes one chapter entitled "A Short History of Waterways in America."

Waugh, Richard G., Jr., and Judith M. Hourigan. *A History of the Board of Engineers for Rivers and Harbors*. Fort Belvoir: U. S. Army Corps of Engineers, 1980. vi + 168 pp. Illustrations, notes, and index.

Way, Royal Brunson. "Internal Improvements in the United States (1817-1829)." Doctoral dissertation, University of Wisconsin, 1907.

Way, R. B. "The Mississippi Valley and Internal Improvements, 1825-1840." *Proceedings of the Mississippi Valley Historical Association*, IV (1910-1911), 153-80. Dull, dated discussion of canal and railroad endeavors.

Weaver, Charles Clinton. "Internal Improvements in North Carolina Previous to 1860." Doctoral dissertation, Johns Hopkins University, 1900

Weaver, Charles Clinton. "Internal Improvements in North Carolina Previous to 1860." *Johns Hopkins University Studies in Historical and Political Science*, XXI (March-April 1903), 113-207. Discusses the evolution of rivers, canals, and railroads. The study illustrates how the state initially encouraged private companies and eventually assumed control of the projects.

Weinstein, Robert A. "The Million-Dollar Mud Flat." *American West*, VI (Jan. 1969), 33-43. Popular, heavily illustrated history of early port development at San Pedro Bay.

Weiss, George. *The Lighthouse Service: Its History, Activities and Organization*. Baltimore: Johns Hopkins Press, 1926. xii + 158 pp. Tables, notes, appendix, bibliography, and index. This book, which focuses on the activities and organization of the Lighthouse Service, contains a twenty-four page history of the agency's evolution.

Wells, W. H. "Early Development of the Port of Philadelphia." *World Ports* (Sept. 1931), 1186-91.

Wengert, Norman. "Antecedents of TVA: The Legislative History of Muscle Shoals." *Agricultural History*. See chapter on "Flood Control and Drainage."

Wertenbaker, Thomas J. *Norfolk: Historic Southern Port*. See chapter on "Sewers and Wastewater Treatment."

White, Edward J. "A Century of Transportation in Missouri." *Missouri Historical Review*, 15 (Oct. 1920), 126-62.

White, Josiah. *Josiah White's History Given by Himself*. n.p.: Lehigh Coal and Navigation Company, 1938. 75 pp.

White, M. Maurice. "History of the Illinois Waterway System from 1822 to 1956." Master's thesis, De Paul University, 1957. Maps, tables, notes, and bibliography. Thin, romantic history of the canal and river system.

White, Richard D., and Truman R. Strobridge. "Nineteenth-Century Lighthouse Tenders on the Great Lakes." *Inland Seas*, 31 (Summer 1975), 87-96. Uninspired review of the contributions and lifestyles of lighthouse tenders.

Whitford, Noble E. *History of the Canal System of the State of New York together with Brief Histories of the Canals of the United States and Canada, Volume I*. Albany: Brandow Printing Company, 1906. viii + 1025 pp. Illustrations, maps, table, diagrams, notes, and appendices. An exhaustive, descriptive history of canal development in New York. In addition to the Erie Canal, the study discusses the development of other less well-known waterways. A concluding chronology of important laws and events is especially valuable.

Wilcox, Frank. *The Ohio Canals*. n.p.: Kent State University Press, 1969. xi + 106 pp. Illustrations and bibliography. A pictorial survey of nineteenth-century Ohio canals. Considerable information is included on canal excavation, lock building, and other engineering topics.

Williams, Archibald. *The Romance of Modern Engineering*. See chapter on "Roads, Streets, and Highways."

Williams, C. Arch. *The Sanitary District of Chicago: History of Its Growth and Development As Shown By Decisions Of The Courts and Work Of Its Law Department*. Chicago: Sanitary District of Chicago, 1919. ix + 256 pp. Tables and index. An important history for anyone interested in the development and work of Chicago's Sanitary District. The first part of this study includes portions of court opinions "arranged in logical and chronological order, describing the origin, purpose, powers and achievements of the Sanitary District. The second part sets forth the same history as shown by the records of the Law Department."

Williams, Garnett P. *Washington, D.C.'s Vanishing Springs and Waterways*. Washington, D.C.: U.S. Geological Survey, 1977. iii + 18 pp. Illustrations and references. Traces the disappearance and reduction of springs and waterways due to urbanization.

Williams, Max Harrison. "San Juan River-Lake Nicaragua Waterway, 1502-1921." Doctoral dissertation, Louisiana State University & Agricultural and Mechanical College, 1971.

Williams, Mentor L. "The Chicago River and Harbor Convention, 1847." *Mississippi Valley Historical Review*, XXXV (March 1949), 607-26. Sketches the story of the convention, evaluates the political and economic consequences of its decisions, and demonstrates "its role in the historic melodrama of pre-Civil War economic sectionalism."

Williams, Mentor L. "The Background of the Chicago Harbor and River Convention, 1847." *Mid-America*, XXX (Oct. 1948), 219-32. Companion article to that in *MVHR* (above).

Willoughby, Malcolm F. *Lighthouses of New England*. Boston: T. O. Metcalf Company, 1929. 253 pp. Illustrations, maps, appendices, and index. A standard lighthouse inventory that offers descriptions and photographs of the facilities.

Willoughby, William R. "Early American Interest in Waterway Connections Between the East and the West." *Indiana Magazine of History*, LII (Dec.1956), 321-42. Interesting overview of internal improvement proposals by George Washington, Albert Gallatin, and other national leaders prior to 1830.

Willoughby, William R. *The St. Lawrence Waterway: A Study in Politics and Diplomacy*. Madison: University of Wisconsin Press, 1961. xvi + 381 pp. Illustrations, map, notes, bibliography, and index. A sound, scholarly account of the plans and proposals brought forth to improve navigation on the St. Lawrence River system. Engineering and economic aspects are discussed only when they bear directly on political and diplomatic developments.

Willson, Beckles. *The Story of Rapid Transit*. See chapter on "Urban Mass Transportation."

Winther, Oscar Osburn. "The Place of Transportation in the Early History of the Pacific Northwest." *Pacific Historical Review*. See chapter on "Roads, Streets, and Highways."

Winther, Oscar Osburn. *The Transportation Frontier: Trans-Mississippi West, 1865-1900*. See chapter on "Roads, Streets, and Highways."

Wisner, George Y. "The Brazos River Harbor Improvement." *Transactions of the American Society of Civil Engineers*, XXV (July-Dec. 1891), 519-62. Offers a short history of navigation improvements undertaken on the river.

Witney, Dudley. *The Lighthouse*. Toronto: McClelland and Stewart, 1975. 256 pp. Illustrations, diagrams, and bibliography. A beautifully illustrated survey of lighthouses in Canada and the United States.

Wolfe, Richard W. "The Straightening of the Chicago River." *World Ports*, XIX (Feb. 1931), 391-96.

Woodworth, R. B. "Tunnels, Particularly Subaqueous." *Official Proceedings of the Railway Club of Pittsburgh*. See chapter on "Roads, Streets, and Highways."

Wright, Muriel H. "Early Navigation and Commerce Along the Arkansas and Red Rivers in Oklahoma." *Chronicles of Oklahoma*, VIII (March 1930), 65-88. Sketchy chronicle of navigation on the rivers prior to the Civil War.

Writers Program of the Works Progress Administration for the City of New York. *A Maritime History of New York*. Garden City, N. Y.: Doubleday, Doran and Company, 1941. xvii + 341 pp. Illustrations, bibliography, and index. Useful historical discussion of the Port of New York.

Wyld, Lionel D. *Low Bridge!: Folklore and the Erie Canal*. Syracuse: Syracuse University Press, 1962. x + 212 pp. Illustrations, maps, notes, and index. An entertaining collection and discussion of art, songs, literature, and social customs spawned by the Erie Canal.

Yager, Rosemary. *James Buchanan Eads: Master of the Great River*. Princeton: D. Van Nostrand, 1968. 126 pp. Illustrations, bibliography, and index. Popular biography that focuses on Eads' St. Louis bridge and jetties at the mouth of the Mississippi River.

Yoder, C. P. "Bill." *Delaware Canal Journal: A Definitive History of the Canal and the River Valley Through which it Flows*. Bethlehem, Pa.: Canal Press, Incorporated, 1972. iv + 287 pp. Illustrations, maps, tables, bibliography, and index. An antiquarian history of the canal.

Young, Jeffrie. "The Development of Transportation in Missouri to 1860." Master's thesis. See chapter on "Roads, Streets, and Highways."

Zercher, Frederick K. "The Economic Development of the Port of Oswego." Doctoral dissertation, Syracuse University, 1935. x + 287 pp. Illustrations, maps, charts, notes, appendices, and bibliography. A simple and direct business history of the oldest freshwater port in the United States.

Zimmer, Donald Thomas. "Madison, Indiana, 1811-1860: A Study in the Process of City Building." Doctoral dissertation, Indiana University, 1974. xvii + 270 pp. Maps, tables, notes, and bibliographical essay. This dissertation contains a good discussion of how Ohio River commercial traffic influenced the community's growth and development.

4

Flood Control and Drainage

The expansion of American civilization has been accompanied by the development of public works facilities that provide drainage and protect cities, farms, and industries from flood damage. Flooding occurs when storm runoffs exceed the capacities of normal stream channels. Heavy, widespread storms or the rapid melting of snow can cause floods along major rivers. More localized flooding occurs when sudden torrents inundate the watersheds of smaller streams. Effective flood control has traditionally involved the construction of control measures (dams, levees, and revetments) as well as the development of watershed conservation and erosion abatement programs. Urban areas are protected by storm sewers and other public works that regulate runoff. More recently, federal and state policies have shifted to greater emphasis on mitigating hazards by controlling development in flood-prone areas.

The books, articles, and dissertations cited below tend to focus on the programs of the Army Corps of Engineers, Soil Conservation Service, Bureau of Reclamation, Tennessee Valley Authority, and other governmental agencies involved in multiple-purpose water programs. Urban drainage is a subject rarely addressed by scholars as are the vast land drainage efforts undertaken to reclaim agricultural lands. Therefore, the field's literature is largely limited to the political, economic, and engineering aspects of river control.

Alberts, Don E. "The Corps of Engineers and New Mexico's Water." *New Mexico Historical Review*, LI (April 1976), 93-108. Outstanding case study of the corps' role in developing the state's water resources from 1925 to the 1970s. The author takes a pejorative view of many of the agency's activities.

Alexander, Thomas G. "An Investment in Progress: Utah's First Federal Reclamation Project, the Strawberry Valley Project." *Utah Historical Quarterly*. See chapter on "Irrigation."

Alperin, Lynn M. *Custodians of the Coast: History of the United States Army Engineers at Galveston*. See chapter on "Waterways."

American National Red Cross. *The Mississippi Valley Flood Disaster of 1927: Official Report of the Relief Operations*. Washington, D. C.: American National Red Cross, 1929. vii + 152 pp. Illustrations, maps, charts, appendices, and bibliography. The heroic story of the Red Cross relief campaign following the disastrous Mississippi Valley floods of 1927. Particularly noteworthy is a chapter that discusses the organization's efforts to aid the long-range economic recovery of the victims.

Anderson, Henry W. "Flood Control and Sedimentation from Forest Watersheds." *Transactions of the American Geophysical Union*, 30 (Aug. 1949), 567-86. Flooding in southern California since 1860.

Antrei, Albert. "A Western Phenomenon: The Origins of Watershed Research: Manti, Utah, 1889." *American West*, VIII (March 1971), 42-46. Early case of the use of watershed management to abate flooding.

Armstrong, Ellis L.; Michael C. Robinson; and Suellen M. Hoy, eds. *History of Public Works in the United States, 1776-1976*. See chapter on "Planning, Engineering, and Administration."

Baldridge, Kenneth W. "Reclamation Work of the Civilian Conservation Corps, 1933-42." *Utah Historical Quarterly*, 39 (Summer 1971), 265-85. The author shows how the CCC gave the cause of reclamation in Utah a major boost: 423 dams constructed; 792 springs, waterholes, and small reservoirs developed; and the 5,231 miles of terracing excavated.

Batman, Richard Dale. "Gospel Swamp . . . The Land of Hog and Hominy." *Journal of the West*. See chapter on "Irrigation."

Baumhoff, Richard G. *The Dammed Missouri Valley: One Sixth of our Nation*. New York: Alfred A. Knopf, 1951. xi + 291 + v pp. Illustrations, map, and index. A good description of the inter-agency public works program to control floods, improve navigation, and generate hydroelectric power on the Missouri River and its tributaries. This "journalistic report" surveys the political battles related to the basin's water resource development and presents the social and economic influences of the projects. The second and third chapters offer excellent descriptions of the area's environment.

Belt, Charles. "The 1973 Flood and Man's Construction of the Missisippi River." *Science*, 189 (Aug. 29, 1975), 681-84.

Benincasa, Frederick Albert. "The Tennessee Valley Authority from 1933 to 1961." Doctoral dissertation, St. John's University, 1961. 117 pp.

Bennett, Hugh Hammond. *Elements of Soil Conservation*. New York: McGraw-Hill Book Company, 1947. viii + 406 pp. Illustrations, tables, bibliography, and index. Although basically a "how to" book on controlling soil erosion, it contains historical information on federal and state soil conservation programs.

Benson, Manuel A. "Use of Historical Data in Flood-Frequency Analysis." *Transactions of the American Geophysical Union*, 31 (June 1950), 419-24. Reviews uses of historical data since 1786.

Berberet, William Gerald. "The Evolution of a New Deal Agricultural Program: Soil Conservation Districts and Comprehensive Land and Water Development in Nebraska." Doctoral dissertation, University of Nebraska, Lincoln, 1970. 576 pp.

Bigger, William Richard. "Flood Control in Metropolitan Los Angeles." Doctoral dissertation, University of California, Los Angeles, 1954. ix + 406 pp. Maps, charts, tables, notes, and bibliography. An excellent study of the flood control and water conservation program of the Los Angeles Flood Control District, its development and management, and the complex intergovernmental relationships involved in its administration.

Bingham, Jay R. "Reclamation and the Colorado." *Utah Historical Quarterly*. See chapter on "Irrigation."

Bishopberger, Thomas E. "Early Flood Control in the California Central Valley." *Journal of the West*, XIV (July 1975), 85-94. Good overview of flood control measures undertaken on the lower Sacramento and San Joaquin rivers from the 1850s to the 1870s.

Black, W. M. *The United States Public Works*. New York: John Wiley & Sons, 1895. viii + 276 pp. Illustrations, tables, diagrams, and index. A survey and showcase of public works construction under the charge of the Army Corps of Engineers and the Treasury Department. Examples include public buildings, river and harbor improvements, military posts, and lighthouses. The richly illustrated volume is a valuable source of information on late nineteenth-century public works.

Blackorby, E. C. "Theodore Roosevelt's Conservation Policies and Their Impact upon America and the American West." *North Dakota History*. See chapter on "Waterways."

Blee, C. E. "Development of the Tennessee

River Waterway." *Transactions of the American Society of Civil Engineers*. See chapter on "Waterways."

Bogue, Margaret Beattie. "The Swamp Land Act and Wet Land Utilization in Illinois, 1850-1890." *Agricultural History*, 25 (Oct. 1951), 169-80. Overview of land reclamation in Illinois.

Bowman, James S. "Multipurpose River Developments." *Transactions of the American Society of Civil Engineers*. See chapter on "Waterways."

Branscome, James. "The TVA: It Ain't What It Used to Be." *American Heritage*, XXVIII (Feb. 1977), 68-78. Describes the environmental controversies in which the agency is currently involved. The article suggests that the authority has retreated from the social and environmental ideals it once espoused.

Branyan, Robert L. *Taming the Mighty Missouri: A History of the Kansas City District, Corps of Engineers, 1907-1971*. Kansas City: U. S. Army Corps of Engineers, Kansas City District, 1974. 128 pp. Illustrations and maps.

Bridenbaugh, Carl. *Cities in Revolt: Urban Life in America, 1743-1776*. See chapter on "Planning, Engineering, and Administration."

Bridenbaugh, Carl. *Cities in the Wilderness: The First Century of Urban Life in America, 1625-1742*. See chapter on "Planning, Engineering, and Administration."

Brienes, Marvin. "Sacramento Defies the Rivers, 1850-1878." *California History*, LVIII (Spring 1979), 2-19.

Brittain, James E. *A Brief History of Engineering in Georgia and Guide to 76 Historic Engineering Sites*. See chapter on "Planning, Engineering, and Administration."

Brown, D. Clayton. *Rivers, Rockets and Readiness: Army Engineers in the Sunbelt: A History of the Fort Worth District, U. S. Army Corps of Engineers, 1950-1975*. Washington, D. C.: Government Printing Office, 1979. xv + 193 pp. Illustrations, maps, graph, notes, bibliography, and index. Excellent history of the corps district founded in 1950. The study covers flood control, military construction, and the protests evoked by the proposed Trinity project.

Brown, Leahmae. "The Development of National Policy with Respect to Water Resources." Doctoral dissertation. See chapter on "Waterways."

Brown, Lytle. "Mississippi Flood Control." *Engineering News-Record*, 104 (Feb. 6, 1930), 227-31. Good description of the flood control project for the Lower Mississippi that was adopted by Congress in 1928.

Brown, Lytle. "Waterways Improvements in the United States." *Civil Engineering*, 5 (Oct. 1935), 613-17. Paean to improvements on the nation's rivers, particularly with respect to flood control.

Bybee, Hal P., and Clyde A. Malott. "The Flood of 1913 in the Lower White River Region of Indiana." *Indiana University Bulletin*, XII (Oct. 1914), 105-223. Interesting case study of the impact of a flood on a region's topography, people, and public facilities.

Bybee, Halbert Pleasant. "The Flood of 1913 in the Lower White River Region of Indiana." Doctoral dissertation, Indiana University, 1915.

Call, George R. "The Missouri River Improvement Program." *Annals of Iowa*, 40 (Summer 1969), 62-67. Brief overview of the Pick-Sloan Plan.

Carroll, John Alexander. "Broader Approaches to the History of the West: A Descriptive Bibliography." *Arizona and the West*. See chapter on "Irrigation."

Cassidy, William F. "Twenty-Five Years of National Flood Control." *Military Engineer*, 53 (Sept.-Oct. 1961), 343-45. Praises the Army Corps of Engineers' flood control activities from 1936 to 1961.

Chambers, C. C. "History of the Muskingum Project." *Civil Engineering*, 6 (Jan. 1936), 3-7. Adequate sketch of the pioneering conservancy district.

Chase, Stuart. *Rich Land, Poor Land: A Study of Waste in the Natural Resources of America*. New York: Whittlesey House, 1936. x + 361 pp. Illustrations, maps, tables, diagrams, notes, bibliography, and index. A classic treatise on the need for wise management of forests, water, land, wildlife, and other natural resources. Excellent material is included on TVA, flood control, irrigation, and watershed management.

Christie, Jean. "The Mississippi Valley Committee: Conservation and Planning in the Early New Deal." *Historian*. See chapter on "Planning, Engineering, and Administration."

Clapp, Gordon R. *The TVA: An Approach to the Development of a Region*. Chicago: University of Chicago Press, 1955. xiii + 206 pp. Maps, notes, and bibliography. TVA policy formation since 1933 by a former chairman of the agency.

Clark, Earl. "Rufus Woods: Grand Coulee Promoter." *Montana: The Magazine of Western History*. See chapter on "Irrigation."

Clark, Thomas D. *The Kentucky*. See chapter on "Waterways."

Clay, Floyd M. *A Century of the Mississippi: A History of the Memphis District, U. S. Army Corps of Engineers, 1876-1976*. Memphis: U. S. Army Corps of Engineers, 1976. x + 294 pp. Illustrations, maps, notes, bibliography, appendix, and index. Excellent study of flood control and navigation on this reach of the Mississippi.

Clay, Floyd M. *A History of the Little Rock District, U. S. Army Corps of Engineers, 1881-1979*. Washington, D. C.: U. S. Government Printing Office, 1979. 113 pp. Illustrations and maps. Largely a history of flood control and navigation projects built by the Army Corps of Engineers on the Arkansas River and its tributaries since the 1930s.

Clement, Thomas M., Jr., and Glenn Lopez. *Engineering A Victory for Our Environment: A Citizen's Guide to the U. S. Army Corps of Engineers*. Washington, D. C.: Environmental Protection Agency, Institute for the Study of Health and Society, 1972. Unpaginated. Appendices. An incredible document that lays out a strategy for greater citizen participation in the authorization and planning of corps projects. Some historical information can be found in this criticism of virtually every aspect of corps water programs.

Clepper, Henry. *Origins of American Conservation*. New York: Ronald Press Company, 1966. x + 193 pp. Illustrations, appendix, bibliographies, and index. A fine collection of essays that cover various conservation issues accurately, informatively, and readably. Due to its sponsorship by the Natural Resources Council of America, the book stresses preservationist topics and themes. Subject areas include soil conservation, water supply, pollution control, and parks.

Condit, Carl W. *American Building: Materials and Techniques from the First Colonial Settlements to the Present*. See chapter on "Public Buildings."

Cooper, Erwin. *Aqueduct Empire: A Guide to Water in California, Its Turbulent History and Its Management Today*. See chapter on "Irrigation."

Cortes-Comerer, Nhora. "The Extraordinary Genius of Arthur E. Morgan." *Civil Engineering*, 47 (Oct. 1977), 114-17. A useful sketch of an outstanding engineer-conservationist. Morgan engineered the Miami Conservancy District and was the first chairman of TVA.

Cory, H. T. *The Imperial Valley and the Salton Sink*. See chapter on "Irrigation."

Cowdrey, Albert E. *The Delta Engineers: A History of the United States Army Corps of Engineers in the New Orleans District*. New Orleans: n. p., 1971. iii + 41 pp. Illustrations, maps, and appendices. A well-written, brief overview of the corps' civil works mission that stresses flood control and navigation.

Cowdrey, Albert E. *Lands End: A History of the New Orleans District, U. S. Army Corps of Engineers, and Its Lifelong Battle with the Lower Mississippi and Other Rivers Winding Their Way to the Sea*. See chapter on "Waterways."

Cowdrey, Albert Edward. "The Delta Engineers." Doctoral dissertation, Tulane University, 1971. 232 pp.

Coyle, David Cushman. *Conservation: An American Story of Conflict and Accomplishment*. New Brunswick, N. J.: Rutgers University Press, 1957. xii + 284 pp. Illustrations and index. A competent, undocumented history of conservation from the Progressive era to the 1950s. The strongest sections discuss the water and power programs of the New Deal, including the Tennessee Valley Authority and Rural Electrification Administration.

Craddock, George Washington. "Floods Controlled on Davis County Watersheds." *Journal of Forestry*, 58 (April 1960), 291-93. Efforts to prevent floods in the Utah county from 1923 to 1958 through watershed management techniques.

Craig, James B. "Muskingum Revisited." *American Forests*, 60 (June 1954), 7-13, 36-39. On the conservancy district since 1933.

Craine, Lyle E. "Muskingum Watershed Conservancy District: A Study of Local Control." *Law and Contemporary Problems*, 22 (Summer 1957), 378-404. Sophisticated discussion of an Ohio conservancy district that served as a model for TVA. It demonstrated that multiple-purpose watershed management could be accomplished by local initiative, planning, and organization.

Craine, Lyle E. "The Muskingum Watershed Conservancy District: An Appraisal of a Watershed Management Agency." Doctoral dissertation, University of Michigan, 1956. 345 pp.

Cullen, Allan H. *Rivers in Harness: The Story of Dams*. See chapter on "Irrigation."

Daniel, Pete. *deep'n as it come: The 1927 Mississippi River Flood*. New York: Oxford University Press, 1977. 162 pp. Illustrations, notes, and index. By far the premier human account of this historic flood and the related disaster-relief efforts.

Darling, Arthur B., ed. *The Public Papers of Francis G. Newlands*. See chapter on "Energy."

Davey, Norman. *A History of Building Materials*. See chapter on "Public Buildings."

De Grove, John M. "The Central and Southern Florida Flood Control Project: A Study in Inter-Governmental Cooperation and Administration." Doctoral dissertation, University of North Carolina, 1958. 489 pp.

Detwyler, Thomas R., and Melvin G. Marcus, eds. *Urbanization and Environment: The Physical Geography of the City*. See chapter on "Community Water Supply."

Dobney, Frederick J. *River Engineers on the Middle Mississippi: A History of the St. Louis District, U. S. Army Corps of Engineers*. See chapter on "Waterways."

Dodds, Gordon B. "Conservation & Reclamation in the Trans-Mississippi West: A Critical Bibliography." *Arizona and the West*. See chapter on "Irrigation."

Dodds, Gordon B. *Hiram Martin Chittenden: His Public Career*. Lexington: University Press of Kentucky, 1973. xi + 220 pp. Illustrations, notes, bibliographical essay, and index. An outstanding biography of this Army Corps of Engineer officer who "published the first definitive report advocating the federal construction of irrigation projects, built the tourist roads in Yellowstone Park, made the survey of the boundaries of Yosemite Park, and planned the Lake Washington Canal." It is a perceptive treatment of Chittenden's public career, which spanned the period between the age of exploration and controversies over multiple-purpose resource development during the Progressive era.

Dodds, Gordon B. "The Historiography of American Conservation: Past and Prospects." *Pacific Northwest Quarterly*. See chapter on "Irrigation."

Dodds, Gordon B. "The Stream-Flow Controversy: A Conservation Turning Point." *Journal of American History*, LVI (June 1969), 59-69. Good study of the debate over relative merits of reforestation and reservoirs in promoting flood control. Dodds argues the Army Corps of Engineers deserves greater credit as a promoter of sound conservation practices.

Douglas, Marjory Stoneman. *The Everglades: River of Grass*. New York: Rinehart & Company, 1947. 406 pp. Maps, bibliography, and index. A well-written history of the Everglades that contains one chapter on efforts to reclaim agricultural lands by drainage at the turn of the century.

Duffus, R. L. *The Valley and Its People: A Portrait of TVA*. New York: Alfred A. Knopf, 1946. 167 pp. Illustrations, map, and index. A laudatory, popular account of the economic and social changes wrought by the Tennessee Valley Authority.

Durisch, Lawrence L., and Robert E. Lowry. "State Watershed Policy and Administration in Tennessee." *Public Administration Review*, 15 (Winter 1955), 17-20. Pilot cooperative program between TVA and the state.

Edstrand, John P. "Missouri River Main Stem Reservoirs." *Military Engineer*, XLVII (Jan.-Feb. 1956), 25-29. Useful summary of the six major multiple-purpose dams built by the Army Corps of Engineers on the Missouri River.

Elam, W. E. *Speeding Floods to the Sea: Or the Evolution of Flood Control Engineering on the Mississippi River*. New York: Hobson Book

Press, 1946. viii + 173 pp. Illustrations, maps, and appendix. A disjointed, undocumented account of flood control measures on the Lower Mississippi River in the 1920s and 1930s. The author, an engineer who worked on many of the projects he describes, strongly advocates cutoffs as a means of river regulation.

Ellis, W. T. *Memories: My Seventy-Two Years in the Romantic County of Yuba, California*. Eugene: John Henry Nash, 1939. xv + 308 pp. Illustrations. An extremely entertaining and insightful autobiography. The author, who served as mayor of Marysville, California, was heavily involved in flood control and irrigation activities in the late nineteenth and early twentieth centuries. Few books offer such a highly personal, microcosmic examination of local water institutions. Ellis also recounts the community's efforts to stop the degradation of water resources caused by hydraulic mining.

Evans, Paul E. "The Magnificent Obsession of TVA." *Civil Engineering*, 47 (Oct. 1977), 107-13. A useful historical overview of the Tennessee Valley Authority.

Ferejohn, John A. *Pork Barrel Politics: Rivers and Harbors Legislation, 1947-1968*. Stanford: Stanford University Press, 1974. xiv + 288 pp. Graphs, notes, appendices, bibliography, and index. Examines the extent to which a pork barrel system exists and illuminates the procedures and influences involved in all federal funding of public works.

Ferguson, H. B. *History of the Improvement of the Lower Mississippi River for Flood Control and Navigation, 1932-1939*. Vicksburg: Mississippi River Commission, 1940. 194 pp. Index. A comprehensive history of navigation and flood control improvements on the Mississippi River during the New Deal.

Feringa, P. A., and Charles W. Schweizer. "One Hundred Years of Improvement on Lower Mississippi River." *Transactions of the American Society of Civil Engineers*. See chapter on "Waterways."

Ferrell, John R. "Water in the Missouri Valley: The Inter-Agency River Committee Concept at Mid-Century." *Journal of the West*, VII (Jan. 1968), 96-104. A perceptive article on the founding and first years of the Missouri Inter-Agency Committee. The author discusses the complex problems of coordinating the participating federal, state, and local entities within a huge area of diverse climate and natural resources. He concludes that the committee was the best available alternative to the creation of a federal regional authority such as the Tennessee Valley Authority.

Finer, Herman. *The T. V. A.: Lessons for International Application*. Montreal: International Labour Office, 1944. viii + 289 pp. Map, tables, notes, and appendices. An interesting analysis of how TVA's flood control, navigation, power, and watershed programs could be duplicated in other countries. The book contains especially thorough discussions of the agency's organization and administration.

Fisher, Edwin A. "Engineering and Public Works in the City of Rochester during the Past Century." *Centennial History of Rochester, New York*. See chapter on "Planning, Engineering, and Administration."

Forshey, Caleb. "The Levees of the Mississippi River." *Transactions of the American Society of Civil Engineers*, III (1875), 267-84. Includes an outline history of the Mississippi River's levee system.

Foy, Bernard L., comp. *A Bibliography for the TVA Program*. Knoxville, Tenn.: Tennessee Valley Authority, 1966. iii + 73 pp. Appendix. A sketchy bibliography that covers subjects such as flood control, engineering, navigation, administration, power, forestry, recreation, and the agency's historical background.

Frank, Arthur DeWitt. *The Development of the Federal Program of Flood Control on the Mississippi River*. New York: Columbia University Press, 1930. 269 pp. Notes, bibliography, and index. A comprehensive survey of systematic efforts by federal, state, and local governments to control floods on the Mississippi. The book describes the activities of the Mississippi River Commission, demands for federal control of flood abatement, the historic 1927 flood, and passage of the Jones-Reid Act.

Frank, Bernard, and Anthony Netboy. *Water, Land, and People*. New York: Alfred A. Knopf, 1950. xviii + 331 + xi pp. Illustrations, map, notes, bibliography, and index. A highly critical account of national water and land policies. The book presents the drawbacks of seeking engineering solutions to water resource needs. Included are discussions of public works development in the Tennessee, Missouri, and Columbia river basins.

Galli, Geraldine. "100 Years of Construction News." *Engineering News-Record*. See chapter on "Planning, Engineering, and Administration."

Gies, Joseph. *Wonders of the Modern World*. See chapter on "Sewers and Wastewater Treatment."

Goff, John S. *George W. P. Hunt and His Arizona*. See chapter on "Irrigation."

Golze, Alfred R. *Reclamation in the United States*. See chapter on "Irrigation."

Gordon, Roy. "Engineering for People: 200 Years of Army Public Works." *Military Engineer*. See chapter on "Waterways."

Graham, Frank, Jr. *Man's Dominion: The Story of Conservation in America*. See chapter on "Planning, Engineering, and Administration."

Green, Constance McLaughlin. *Washington: Village and Capital, 1800-1878*. See chapter on "Urban Mass Transportation."

Hagwood, Joseph J., Jr. *Commitment to Excellence: A History of the Sacramento District, U. S. Army Corps of Engineers, 1929-1973*. Sacramento: U. S. Army Engineer District, 1976. xii + 289 pp. Illustrations, maps, bibliography, and index. Solid overview of the corps' military and civil construction activities.

Hagwood, Joseph Jeremiah, Jr. "From North Bloomfield to North Fork: Attempts to Comply with the Sawyer Decision." Master's thesis, Sacramento State College, 1970. ix + 201 pp. Illustrations, notes, appendices, and bibliography. A competent discussion of the impact of hydraulic mining on agriculture and the construction of dams to control debris in California.

Hanna, Alfred Jackson, and Kathryn Abbey. *Lake Okeechobee: Wellspring of the Everglades*. Indianapolis: Bobbs-Merrill Company, 1948. 379 pp. Illustrations, maps, notes, bibliography, and index. One of the better volumes in the "American Lakes Series." The book includes discussions of drainage, canal, and levee projects near Lake Okeechobee and its tributary area.

Hanson, Howard A. "More Land for Industry: The Story of Flood Control in the Green River Valley." *Pacific Northwest Quarterly*, 48 (Jan. 1957), 1-7. Good history of measures undertaken to protect the Port of Seattle and related industrial areas.

Hardin, John R. "Evolution of the Mississippi Valley Flood Control Plan." *Transactions of the American Society of Civil Engineers*, 129 (1959), 207-23. Largely deals with flood control planning on the Lower Mississippi River after 1928.

Harrison, Robert W. *Alluvial Empire: A Study of State and Local Efforts Toward Land Development in the Alluvial Valley of the Lower Mississippi River*. Little Rock, Ark.: Pioneer Press, 1961, xviii + 344 pp. Maps, tables, notes, bibliography, and index. An excellent introduction to land and river improvements on the Lower Mississippi. The chapter on "Flood Control in the Mississippi" is a concise, comprehensive survey of federal, state, and local efforts to battle flooding from the mid-nineteenth to the mid-twentieth century. The following chapter on land drainage offers similarly thorough and well-organized coverage of this subject.

Hart, Henry C. *The Dark Missouri*. Madison: University of Wisconsin Press, 1957. xvii + 260 pp. Illustrations, maps, tables, notes, and index. A well-written history of river improvements in the Missouri Basin. Most of the book focuses on projects built under the Pick-Sloan Plan.

Havemen, Robert H. *Water Resource Investment and the Public Interest: An Analysis of Federal Expenditures in Ten Southern States*. Nashville: Vanderbilt University Press, 1965. xiii + 199 pp. Tables, charts, graphs, notes, appendices, bibliography, and index. A strong polemic against the water resources activities of the Army Corps of Engineers. The author marshalls extensive evidence to illustrate that the system of computing benefit-cost ratios is inaccurate and misleading.

Havemeyer, Loomis, ed., et al. *Conservation of Our Natural Resources*. See chapter on "Irrigation."

Havinghurst, Walter. *River to the West: Three Centuries of the Ohio*. See chapter on "Waterways."

Herget, James E. "Taming the Environment: The Drainage District in Illinois." *Journal of the Illinois State Historical Society*, LXXI (May 1978), 107-18. A unique article on a subject that deserves greater scholarly attention. It focuses on litigation and legislation from 1835 to 1885 and suggests why drainage institutions conformed to prevailing attitudes with respect to taxation, democratic representation, corporate enterprise, and the environment. The Illinois acts were a model for legislation in at least three other states.

Heuvelmans, Martin. *The River Killers*. Harrisburg, Pa.: Stackpole Books, 1974. 224 pp. Illustrations, maps, appendices, bibliography, and index. A vitriolic condemnation of the effects of Army Corps of Engineers projects on the environment. Most of the book focuses on navigation and flood control projects in the state of Florida.

Hinds, Julian. "Continuous Development of Dams since 1850." *Transactions of the American Society of Civil Engineers*. See chapter on "Irrigation."

Hodge, Clarence Lewis. *The Tennessee Valley Authority: A National Experiment in Regionalism*. Washington, D. C.: American University Press, 1938. xii + 272 pp. Charts, notes, bibliography, and index. Although primarily an appeal for regional planning, this book contains summaries of the legislative antecedents of the Tennessee Valley Authority, a survey of the region's environmental characteristics, and a composite picture of the authority's institutional structure.

Holbrook, Stewart H. *The Columbia*. See chapter on "Waterways."

Holmes, Beatrice Hort. *History of Federal Water Resources Programs, 1800-1960*. See chapter on "Irrigation."

Holmes, Beatrice Hort. *History of Federal Water Resources Programs and Policies, 1961-70*. See chapter on "Irrigation."

Howard, W. V. *Authority in TVA Land*. Kansas City, Mo.: Frank Glenn Publishing Company, 1948. vii + 187 pp. Map, notes, and appendices.

Hoy, Suellen M. "People in Public Works: Harry W. Morrison." *APWA Reporter*, 44 (Dec. 1977), 4-5. Describes the early public works career of Morrison as well as the work of the major construction firm (Morrison-Knudsen) he founded. The article emphasizes M-K's involvement in the building of Hoover Dam.

Hoyt, Wiliam G., and Walter B. Langbein. *Floods*. Princeton: Princeton University Press, 1955. x + 469 pp. Illustrations, maps, charts, tables, graphs, notes, bibliography, and index. A fine overview of the hydrologic and geologic aspects of flooding and humankinds attempts to adapt to and control rivers. The book discusses specific river basins and concludes with a chapter on the history of floods.

Hubbard, Preston J. *Origins of the TVA: The Muscle Shoals Controversy, 1920-1932*. Nashville: Vanderbilt University Press, 1961. ix + 340 pp. Illustrations, notes, bibliography, and index. The study comprehensively explores the origins of the Tennessee Valley Authority by examining the struggle to control the Tennessee River system from 1920 to 1932. The focal point of the conflict was the hydroelectric power facilities built by the federal government at Muscle Shoals, Alabama. Much of the book deals with the attempt of Henry Ford to obtain the facilities and efforts by Senator George W. Norris to stop him.

Humphreys, Benjamin G. *Floods and Levees of the Mississippi River*. Washington, D. C.: Mississippi River Levee Association, 1914. viii + 349 pp. Appendices and index. A mishmash of historical narrative, documents, testimony, and other materials assembled to support federal funding for a levee system on the Mississippi River. The author was a member of the U. S. House of Representatives from Mississippi.

Humphreys, Hubert. "In a Sense Experimental: The Civilian Conservation Corps in Louisiana." See chapter on "Parks and Recreation."

Ickes, Harold L. *The Secret Diary of Harold L. Ickes: The First Thousand Days, 1933-1936*. See chapter on "Planning, Engineering, and Administration."

"Illinois Society [of Engineers] Celebrates Its 50th Anniversary." *Engineering News-Record*. See chapter on "Planning, Engineering, and Administration."

Ingram, Helen M. *Patterns of Politics in Water Resource Development: A Case Study of New Mexico's Role in the Colorado River Basin Bill*. Albuquerque: University of New Mexico, 1969. 96 pp. Illustrations and notes. Presents the politics of the 1968 Colorado River Basin Act and gives special attention to New Mexico's role in shaping this policy.

Institute for Government Research (Brook-

ings). *The U. S. Reclamation Service: Its History, Activities and Organization*. See chapter on "Irrigation."

Jacobs, W. A., and Lyman L. Woodman. *The Alaska District, United States Army Corps of Engineers, 1946-1974*. See chapter on "Military Installations."

Jarrett, Henry, ed. *Perspectives on Conservation*. See chapter on "Planning, Engineering, and Administration."

Jenkins, Hal. *A Valley Renewed: The History of the Muskingum Watershed Conservancy District*. n.p.: Kent State University Press, 1976. 206 pp. Illustrations, maps, chronology, appendices, and index. Solid study of a pioneering multiple-purpose water project in Ohio. The book presents a strong portrayal of the roles of Bryce C. Browning and Arthur P. Morgan. Jenkins also illustrates how the locally envisioned project was usurped and modified by the Army Corps of Engineers.

Jennings, Jesse D., and Floyd W. Sharrock. "The Glen Canyon: A Multi-Discipline Project." *Utah Historical Quarterly*, 33 (Winter 1965), 35-50. Describes the University of Utah's project (1957) "to salvage scientific data from areas to be inundated by several large reservoirs."

Jensen, Merrill, ed. *Regionalism in America*. See chapter on "Public Buildings."

Johnson, Leland Ross. "A History of the Operations of the Corps of Engineers, United States Army, in the Cumberland and Tennessee River Valleys." Doctoral dissertation. See chapter on "Waterways."

Johnson, Leland R. *Engineers on the Twin Rivers: A History of the Nashville District, Corps of Engineers, United States Army*. See chapter on "Waterways."

Johnson, Leland R. *Men, Mountains and Rivers: An Illustrated History of the Huntington District, U.S. Army Corps of Engineers, 1754-1974*. See chapter on "Waterways."

Johnson, Leland R. "19th-Century Engineering: The Johnstown Disaster." *Military Engineer*, LXVI (Jan./Feb. 1974), 42-45. Describes the corps' disaster assistance activities, particularly debris removal and bridge construction, following the tragic 1889 dam failure.

Johnson, Leland R. *The Falls City Engineers: A History of the Louisville District, Corps of Engineers, United States Army*. See chapter on "Waterways."

Johnson, Leland R. *The Headwaters District: A History of the Pittsburgh District, U. S. Army Corps of Engineers*. See chapter on "Waterways."

Johnson, Louis George. "Floods and Flood Control in the Missouri River Basin." Doctoral dissertation, University of Missouri, Columbia, 1959. 366 pp.

Kahrl, William L., ed. *The California Water Atlas*. See chapter on "Irrigation."

Kanarek, Harold K. *The Mid-Atlantic Engineers: A History of the Baltimore District, U. S. Army Corps of Engineers, 1774-1974*. See chapter on "Waterways."

Kathka, David Arlin. "The Bureau of Reclamation in the Truman Administration: Personnel, Politics, and Policy." See chapter on "Irrigation."

Keener, K. B. "Dams, Then and Now." *Transactions of the American Society of Civil Engineers*. See chapter on "Irrigation."

Kelley, Robert L. *Gold vs. Grain: The Mining Debris Controversy*. See chapter on "Irrigation."

Kelley, Robert. "Taming the Sacramento: Hamiltonianism in Action." *Pacific Historical Review*, XXXIV (Feb. 1965), 21-49. Brilliant description of river improvements on the Sacramento in the late nineteenth and early twentieth centuries and their influence on the society and economy of the region.

Kelly, William R. "Colorado-Big Thompson Initiation, 1933-1938." *Colorado Magazine*. See chapter on "Irrigation."

Kemper, J. P. *Rebellious River*. Boston: Bruce Humphries, 1949. 279 pp. Map, charts, and appendix. A poorly written, disjointed history of flood control on the Red, Arkansas, Atchafalaya, and Lower Mississippi rivers to 1946.

Kennan, George. *The Salton Sea: An Account of Harriman's Fight with the Colorado River*. See chapter on "Irrigation."

Kettleborough, Charles. *Drainage and Reclamation of Swamp and Overflowed Lands*. Indianapolis: Indiana Bureau of Legislative Information, 1914. 68 pp. Excellent source for material on legislation and the evolution of drainage techniques in Illinois and other states.

King, Judson. *The Conservation Fight: From Theodore Roosevelt to the Tennessee Valley Authority*. Washington, D.C.: Public Affairs Press, 1959. xx + 316 pp. Notes and index. A good survey of the conservation crusade during the early twentieth century by one of the movement's leaders. King focuses on the "birth pains of TVA," but also provides thorough coverage of "the long struggle, stretching over nearly two generations, to secure our country's precious navigable water resources."

Klawonn, Marion J. *Cradle of the Corps: A History of the New York District, U. S. Army Corps of Engineers, 1775-1975*. See chapter on "Waterways."

Kleinsorge, Paul L. *The Boulder Canyon Project: Historical and Economic Aspects*. See chapter on "Irrigation."

Knowles, Morris. "History of Civil Engineering in Western Pennsylvania." *Proceedings of the Engineer's Society of Western Pennsylvania*. See chapter on "Planning, Engineering, and Administration."

Koch, Herbert F. "The Flood of 1913." *Bulletin of the Cincinnati Historical Society*, 25 (April 1967), 136-49. A personal reminiscence.

Koehler, G. "Lottery Authorized in 1819 by the State of Illinois to Raise Funds for Improving the Public Health by Draining the Ponds in the American Bottoms." *Transactions of the Illinois State Historical Society*, 35 (1928), 195-202. Discusses a unique method for funding a drainage project for the American Bottoms, an area across the Mississippi River from St. Louis. Its purpose was to improve public health by reducing outbreaks of malaria.

Krutilla, John V. *The Columbia River Treaty: The Economics of an International River Basin Development*. See chapter on "Waterways."

Kyle, John H. *The Building of TVA*. Baton Rouge: Louisiana State University Press, 1958. xiii + 162 pp. Illustrations, maps, diagrams, and index. A good descriptive inventory of TVA's "physical plant"—dams, buildings, bridges, and steam plants. The book is heavily illustrated with excellent photographs.

Lacy, Leslie Alexander. *The Soil Soldiers: The Civilian Conservation Corps in the Great Depression*. See chapter on "Parks and Recreation."

Lane, E. W. "History of Flood Control on the Mississippi." *Civil Engineering*, 4 (Feb. 1934), 63-67. An historical summary of various theories and plans proposed to control flooding on the Mississippi River.

Langevin, Thomas H. "Development of Multiple-Purpose Water Planning by the Federal Government in the Missouri Basin." *Nebraska History*, XXXIV (March 1953), 1-21. Overview of the Pick-Sloan Plan.

Langevin, Thomas H. "The Missouri Basin: A Study in Multiple-Purpose Water Development." Doctoral dissertation, University of Nebraska, 1951. iii + 384 pp. Notes, appendices, and bibliography. Legislative and institutional study of state and federal programs that provide for flood control, irrigation, navigation, power, and municipal water supply in the Missouri River Basin.

Larson, John W. *Those Army Engineers: A History of the Chicago District, U. S. Army Corps of Engineers*. See chapter on "Waterways."

Laurent, Francis W., comp. *A Compilation of the More Important Congressional Acts, Treaties, Presidential Messages, Judicial Decisions and Official Reports and Documents having to do with the Control, Conservation, and Utilization of Water Resources*. n.p.: Tennessee Valley Authority, 1938. 117 pp. + lvi. Appendices. A rare and useful bibliographical tool. The annotated listings are arranged by chapters on navigation, flood control, irrigation, water power, and multiple-purpose planning.

Lawson, Michael Lee. "Reservoir and Reservation: The Oahe Dam and the Cheyenne River Sioux." *South Dakota Historical Collections*, 37 (1975), 103-233. An assessment of how the dam project disrupted the tribe's way of life. The author concludes that "the damages that the Cheyenne River Sioux suffered as a result of the Oahe project far outweigh the benefits provided to them by the Pick-Sloan Plan."

League of Women Voters (Education Foundation). *The Big Water Fight: Trials and Triumphs in Citizen Action on Problems of Supply, Pollution, Floods, and Planning across* *the U.S.A.* See chapter on "Community Water Supply."

Lee, Robert Rue. "Local Government Public Works Decision-Making." Doctoral dissertation. See chapter on "Community Water Supply."

Leopold, Luna B., and Thomas Maddock, Jr. *The Flood Control Controversy: Big Dams, Little Dams, and Land Management*. New York: Ronald Press Company, 1954. xiii + 278 pp. Maps, tables, graphs, glossary, bibliography, and index. A good summary of the differing flood control philosophies of the Soil Conservation Service and Army Corps of Engineers. The book explores the relative merits of mainstem and upstream dams.

Lepawsky, Albert. "Water Resources and American Federalism." *American Political Science Review*. See chapter on "Waterways."

Le Roy, Bruce, ed. *H. M. Chittenden: A Western Epic*. Tacoma. Washington State Historical Society, 1961. viii + 136 pp. Illustrations, map, notes, bibliography, and index. Selections from the historic engineer's journals, diaries, and reports. His achievements include surveys of Yellowstone National Park, pioneer flood control in the Missouri Valley, and development of the Port of Seattle.

Leuba, Clarence J. *A Road to Creativity: Arthur Morgan–Engineer, Educator, Administrator*. North Quincy, Mass.: Christopher Publishing House, 1971. 323 pp. Illustration, notes, and appendix. A rather thin, largely undocumented biography of the first chairman of the Tennessee Valley Authority. Morgan was a leading spokesman for development of vast water projects encompassing entire river basins that included flood control, navigation, and public power.

Leuchtenburg, William Edward. *Flood Control Politics: The Connecticut River Valley Problem, 1927-1950*. Cambridge: Harvard University Press, 1953. viii + 339 pp. Illustrations, map, notes, bibliography, and index. One of the best books on the economic and political factors that often underlay conflicts over flood control and power policies. Leuchtenburg is particularly adept at demonstrating that once flood control became enmeshed with the power issue, it became involved in an ideological warfare that frequently ignored the best interests of the valley's inhabitants. Private power interests raised the states rights issue to fend off federal power development and received support from political conservatives. Thus, the state attempted to develop the valley by ignoring sound regional principles of river basin management.

Leuchtenburg, William E. "Roosevelt, Norris and the 'Seven Little TVAs.' " *Journal of Politics*, 14 (Aug. 1952), 418-41. Examines the political forces that together "proved to be the death blow for the proposal to make the TVA the pattern for national resources development."

Ligenfelter, Richard E. *Steamboats on the Colorado River, 1852-1916*. See chapter on "Waterways."

Lilienthal, David E. *The Journals of David E. Lilienthal: The TVA Years, 1939-1945*. New York: Harper & Row, 1964. xxxi + 734 pp. Illustrations, appendix, and index. This comprehensive journal provides insights into the development of the Tennessee Valley Authority and New Deal conservation policies.

Lilienthal, David E. *TVA: Democracy on the March*. New York: Harper & Brothers, 1944. xiv + 248 pp. Illustrations, appendix, and index. A laudatory overview of the development and impact of TVA on the area's standard of living. Written by the authority's administrator, the book gives cursory coverage of engineering, construction, and power.

Lohoff, Bruce Alan. "Hoover and the Mississippi Valley Flood of 1927: A Case Study of the Political Thought of Herbert Hoover." Doctoral dissertation, Syracuse University, 1968. viii + 285 pp. Includes an overview of the evolution of competing plans for the prevention of flooding in the Lower Mississippi Basin.

Lord, Russell. *Behold Our Land*. Boston: Houghton Mifflin Press, 1938. x + 310 pp. Illustrations and bibliography. A vivid, journalistic view of land degradation and efforts by the Soil Conservation Service to abate erosion and preserve watersheds.

Lowenthal, David. *George Perkins Marsh: Versatile Vermonter*. See chapter on "Irrigation."

Lowitt, Richard. *George W. Norris: The Persistence of a Progressive, 1913-1933*. See chapter on "Irrigation."

Lubove, Roy. *Twentieth-Century Pittsburgh:*

Government, Business, and Environmental Change. See chapter on "Planning, Engineering, and Administration."

Maass, Arthur. *Muddy Waters: The Army Engineers and the Nation's Rivers.* Cambridge: Harvard University Press, 1951. xiv + 306 pp. Maps, notes, and indexes. A highly critical analysis of the Army Corps of Engineers' flood control, navigation, and allied activities. Maass concludes that "the Engineer Department fails to live up to a great many of the accepted standards of professional responsibility" in regard to its relationships with Congress, the White House, the public, and the engineering proession. The Kings River in central Califonia is used as a case study to support the author's conclusions.

MacColl, E. Kimbark. *The Growth of a City: Power and Politics in Portland, Oregon, 1915-1950.* See chapter on "Planning, Engineering, and Administration."

McCrory, S. H. "Historical Notes on Land Drainage in the United States." *Proceedings of the American Society of Civil Engineers,* LIII (Sept. 1927), 1628-36.

McCullough, David G. *The Johnstown Flood.* New York: Simon and Schuster, 1968. 302 pp. Illustrations, map, appendix, bibliography, and index. A brilliant recreation of the holocaust. The author's prodigious research and extraordinary writing talents are manifest throughout the volume.

McGraw, Thomas K. *Morgan vs. Lilienthal: The Feud within the TVA.* Chicago: Loyola University Press, 1970. xiv + 152 pp. Notes, bibliography, and index. A good analysis of this famous personal controversy over the direction of the Tennessee Valley Authority. McGraw does much to redeem Morgan's reputation.

McGraw, Thomas K. *TVA and the Power Fight, 1933-1939.* See chapter on "Energy."

MacKendrick, Donald A. "Before the Newlands Act: State-Sponsored Reclamation Projects in Colorado, 1888-1903." *Colorado Magazine,* LII (Winter 1975), 1-21. Chronicles Colorado's "brief and disappointing career" in reclaiming arid lands.

McKinley, Charles. "The Valley Authority and Its Alternatives." *American Political Science Review,* XLIV (Sept. 1950), 607-31. This examination of the Tennessee Valley Authority "as an administrative device for Federal water resource management" includes a short section on the agency's development.

McKinley, Charles. *Uncle Sam in the Pacific Northwest: Federal Management of Natural Resources in the Columbia River Valley.* See chapter on "Irrigation."

Magnusson, C. Edward. "Hydro-Electric Power in Washington." *Washington Historical Quarterly.* See chapter on "Energy."

Martin, Roscoe C., et al. *River Basin Administration and the Delaware.* Syracuse: Syracuse University Press, 1960. xii + 390 pp. Maps, charts, tables, notes, and index. An excellent survey of the institutional problems of administering the Delaware River Basin that includes some historical information on the area's development. Part IV of the book is a perceptive overview of the "American Experience in River Basin Administration."

Martin, Roscoe C. "The Tennessee Valley Authority: A Study of Federal Control." *Law and Contemporary Problems,* 22 (Summer 1957), 351-77. One of the best summaries of TVA's evolution and organization. It contains excellent overviews of the agency's various programs.

Martin, Roscoe C., ed. *TVA: The First Twenty Years, a Staff Report.* University, Ala.: University of Alabama and University of Tennessee, 1956. xiv + 282 pp. Charts, tables, notes, and index. A series of essays given by TVA staff members at Florida State University in 1953. The volume offers a comprehensive retrospective analysis of TVA's multiple-purpose programs from the agency's point of view.

Mason, Herbert Molloy, Jr. *Death from the Sea: Our Greatest Natural Disaster, the Galveston Hurricane of 1900.* New York: Dial Press,1972. 260 pp. Illustrations and bibliography. Vivid account of Galveston's devastation and subsequent recovery.

Mazmainian, Daniel A., and Jeanne Neinaber. *Can Organizations Change?: Environmental Protection, Citizen Participation, and the Corps of Engineers.* See chapter on "Waterways."

Mead, Elwood. "Modern Methods Used on Reclamation Projects." *Civil Engineering.* See chapter on "Irrigation."

Merdinger, Charles J. *Civil Engineering*

through the Ages. See chapter on "Planning, Engineering, and Administration."

Meredith, Howard L. "Small Dam Politics: The Sandstone Creek Project." *Great Plains Journal,* 6 (Spring 1967), 97-107. The author contends that the conflict over soil and water conservation in the Sandstone Creek watershed in western Oklahoma "presented a microcosm of the political struggles at each level of government between 1938 and 1952." He stresses the interplay of "contesting ideologies" regarding flood control.

Merritt, Raymond H. *Creativity, Conflict & Controversy: A History of the St. Paul District U. S. Army Corps of Engineers.* See chapter on "Waterways."

"Milestones in U. S. Civil Engineering." *Civil Engineering.* See chapter on "Planning, Engineering, and Administration."

"Milestones in U. S. Public Works: New Orleans—The Leveed City." *APWA Reporter,* 42 (Sept. 1975), 29. A description of the 121 miles of levee that surround New Orleans and protect it from flooding by the Mississippi River.

Mills, Gary B. *Of Men & Rivers: The Story of the Vicksburg District.* Vicksburg: U. S. Army Engineer District, Vicksburg, 1978. xiii + 244 pp. Illustrations, maps, diagrams, and index. Focuses on the revetments, levees, and other flood control works built by the corps and other entities. The navigation, energy, and recreational benefits of corps projects are also discussed.

Mitchell, Broadus. *Depression Decade: From New Era through New Deal, 1929-1941.* New York: Rinehart & Company, 1947. xviii + 462 pp. Illustrations, tables, graphs, notes, appendix, bibliographical essay, and index. This book, Volume IX of the "Economic History of the United States" series, focuses on the "intervention of the federal government in the economic life of the country." General discussions of the Public Works Administration, Works Progress Administration, and Tennessee Valley Authority are included.

Moeller, Beverley Bowen. *Phil Swing and Boulder Dam.* See chapter on "Irrigation."

Moore, Norman R. *Improvement of the Lower Mississippi River and Tributaries, 1931-1972.* See chapter on "Waterways."

Moreell, Ben. *Our Nation's Water Resources–Policies and Politics.* Chicago: University of Chicago Law School, 1956. v + 266 pp. Index. A series of lectures given by the admiral who founded the Seabees during World War II. Moreell, chairman of the Water and Power Committee of the Second Hoover Commission, is highly critical of the federal government's dominion over water and power resources. The book includes a chapter on the evolution of federal water policies.

Morgan, Anne Hodges. *Robert S. Kerr: The Senate Years.* See chapter on "Waterways."

Morgan, Arthur E. *Dams and Other Disasters: A Century of the Army Corps of Engineers in Civil Works.* Boston: Porter Sargent Publisher, 1971. xv + 422 pp. Illustrations, notes, and index. A vitriolic attack on the corps by a leading conservationist. The stated purposes of the book are to show that army engineers are "unsuited for civil engineering needs" and "that there have been over the past 100 years consistent and disastrous failures by the corps in public works areas." The book is the ultimate anti-corps polemic.

Morgan, Arthur E. *The Making of TVA.* Buffalo: Prometheus Books, 1974. xiv + 205 pp. Illustrations, map, and index. An autobiographical account of the author's activities in the establishment and subsequent development of the Tennessee Valley Authority. Morgan relates his views concerning the ideals, objectives, and patterns of operation of this monumental project. He discusses his conflicts with other TVA board members which ultimately resulted in his separation from the authority. The volume also contains an excellent, though self-serving, chapter on Morgan's pre-TVA career.

Morgan, Arthur E. *The Miami Conservancy District.* New York: McGraw-Hill Book Company, 1951. xiii + 504 pp. Illustrations, bibliography, and index. A laudatory account of efforts to control floods in Ohio's Miami Valley by the conservationist-engineer who planned the undertaking. Morgan carefully outlines the multiple-purpose philosophy that underpined the project. The creation of the conservancy district was an important test for water- and land-use principles applied by the Tennessee Valley Authority.

Morgan, Arthur E., and C. A. Bock. "A History of Flood Control in Ohio." *Ohio Archeological* *and Historical Publications,* XXXIV (1923), 474-503. Summary of the flood control measures undertaken by the Miami Conservancy District.

Morgan, Robert J. "The Small Watershed Program." *Law and Contemporary Problems,* 22 (Summer 1957), 405-32. Includes a good discussion of the legislative history of this federal program administered by the Department of Agriculture.

Morrison, Margaret Dorsie. "Charles Robinson Rockwood: Developer of the Imperial Valley." *Southern California Quarterly.* See chapter on "Irrigation."

Mussari, Anthony Joseph. "The Agnes Flood Disaster as an Agent of Community Change in Wilkes-Barre, Pennsylvania, 1972-1976." Doctoral dissertation, University of Iowa, 1978. 385 pp.

Nash, Roderick, ed. *The American Environment: Readings in the History of Conservation.* See chapter on "Planning, Engineering, and Administration."

Neil, J. Meredith. "A Forgotten Alternative: Reclamation by the States." *Idaho Yesterdays.* See chapter on "Irrigation."

Newell, Frederick Haynes. *Water Resources: Present and Future Uses.* See chapter on "Irrigation."

Nixon, Edgar B., ed. *Franklin D. Roosevelt and Conservation, 1911-1945.* See chapter on "Planning, Engineering, and Administration."

Norris, George W. *Fighting Liberal: The Autobiography of George W. Norris.* New York: Macmillan Company, 1945. xv + 419 pp. Illustrations and index. An autobiographical account of the stormy career of this Nebraska senator. The book contains several chapters on Norris' pivotal role in the Muscle Shoals embroglio and the creation of the Tennessee Valley Authority.

Norwood, Alice M., comp. *Congressional Hearings, Reports, and Documents Relating to TVA, 1933-1946.* Knoxville: n. p., 1946. 53 pp. An outstanding source for students of the Tennessee Valley Authority.

Ogilvie, Leon Parker. "Governmental Efforts at Reclamation in the Southeast Missouri Lowlands." *Missouri Historical Review,* LXIV (Jan. 1970), 150-76. Early efforts to reclaim swamplands.

O'Neill, Richard W. *High Steel, Hard Rock, and Deep Water: The Exciting World of Construction.* See chapter on "Roads, Streets, and Highways."

Outland, Charles F. *Man-Made Disaster: The Story of St. Francis Dam.* Glendale, Calif.: Arthur H. Clark Company, 1963. 249 pp. Illustrations, map, notes, bibliography, and index. An account of the place of the St. Francis Dam in Southern California's water system and the tragedy that occurred in March 1928 when the dam failed. The author has excluded sources and material that he judged "sensational and sinister" or "based upon prejudice and emotionalism and not upon facts"; yet he doubts that the definitive study of this subject has been written.

Papageorge, Nan Taylor. "The Role of the San Diego River in the Development of Mission Valley." *Journal of San Diego History.* See chapter on "Irrigation."

Parkins, A. E., and J. R. Whitaker, eds. *Our Natural Resources and Their Conservation.* New York: John Wiley & Sons, 1936. xii + 648 pp. Illustrations, maps, tables, notes, bibliography, and index. An excellent collection of essays on a host of conservation subjects. Each of the following subjects are included and incorporate historical material: soil erosion, irrigation, domestic water supplies, water power, waterways, flood control, and recreational resources.

Parkman, Aubrey. *Army Engineers in New England: The Military and Civil Work of the Corps of Engineers in New England, 1775-1975.* See chapter on "Waterways."

Paterson, Alan Murray. "Rivers and Tides: The Story of Water Policy and Management in California's Sacramento-San Joaquin Delta, 1920-1977." Doctoral dissertation. See chapter on "Irrigation."

Paulsen, David F. *Natural Resources in the Governmental Process: A Bibliography Selected and Annotated.* See chapter on "Parks and Recreation."

Percy, William Alexander. *Lanterns on the Levee: Recollections of a Planter's Son.* New York: Alfred A. Knopf, 1941. 348 pp. Contains a chapter on the 1927 Mississippi flood.

Petersen, William J. "Mississippi River Floods." *Palimpsest,* XLVI (July 1965), 305-69. Sketchy survey of floods on the Mississippi in Iowa from the 1850s to the 1960s.

Peterson, Elmer T. *Big Dam Foolishness: The Problem of Modern Flood Contol and Water Storage.* New York: Devin-Adair Company, 1954. xvi + 224 pp. Illustrations. A compilation of the author's own articles, editorials, and speeches. Peterson is a journalist who for many years advocated "upstream flood control as opposed to big dams." This book tells why.

Peterson, Richard H. "The Failure to Reclaim: California State Swamp Land Policy and the Sacramento Valley, 1850-1866." *Southern California Quarterly,* LVI (Spring 1974), 45-60. Failure of state effort to implement a drainage and reclamation program for the Sacramento Valley.

Pinkett, Harold T. *Gifford Pinchot: Private and Public Forester.* See chapter on "Planning, Engineering, and Administration."

Poe, A. David. "The Political Career of John Holmes Overton, 1912-1948." Master's thesis, Northwestern State College of Louisiana, 1968. iv + 134 pp. Contains a long chapter on Overton's activity in the flood control field during the 1930s.

Preston, Howard. *A History of the Walla Walla District, 1948-1970.* Walla Walla: U. S. Army Corps of Engineers, n. d. x + 351 pp. Illustrations, maps, tables, and bibliography. Largely a project-by-project history of the corps' flood control and navigation activities in the Snake River Basin.

Pritchett, C. Herman. *The Tennessee Valley Authority: A Study in Public Administration.* Chapel Hill: University of North Carolina Press, 1943. xiii + 333 pp. Maps, charts, tables, notes, and index. This book remains one of the best overviews of the Tennessee Valley Authority's (TVA) organization and management. The TVA is regarded as an exemplary experiment in regional development to promote conservation and wise utilization of natural resources within the Tennessee River's 40,000-square-mile watershed. Pritchett views the organization as "a public corporation" that blends "the administrative autonomy and financial freedom of the private business corporation with public accountability and control."

Quinn, Mary-Louise. *The History of the Beach Erosion Board, U. S. Army, Corps of Engineers, 1930-63.* Fort Belvoir: Coastal Engineering Research Center, 1977. 181 pp. Illustrations, charts, notes, bibliography, and appendices.

Ransmeier, Joseph Sirera. *The Tennessee Valley Authority: A Case Study in the Economics of Multiple Purpose Stream Planning.* Nashville: Vanderbilt University Press, 1942. xx + 486 pp. Tables, notes, appendices, bibliography, and index. The book's rather tedious discussion of the theories and problems of cost allocation is preceded by a useful historical overview of federal water policy on the Tennessee River from 1824 to the late 1930s.

Richardson, Elmo R. *Dams, Parks, & Politics: Resource Development & Preservation in the Truman-Eisenhower Era.* See chapter on "Irrigation."

Richardson, Elmo R. *The Politics of Conservation: Crusades and Controversies, 1897-1913.* See chapter on "Waterways."

Richardson, Elmo R. "Western Politics and New Deal Policies: A Study of T. A. Walters of Idaho." *Pacific Northwest Quarterly,* 54 (Jan. 1963), 9-18. From 1933 to 1937, Walters served as first assistant secretary in the Department of the Interior. He was equally involved in making conservation policy and in solving the problems of his Idaho friends and supporters. The author describes an Idaho road-building controversy between Walters and Secretary of the Interior Harold L. Ickes.

Richmond, Henry R., III. *The History of the Portland District, Corps of Engineers, 1871-1969.* See chapter on "Waterways."

Ridgeway, Marian E. *The Missouri Basin's Pick-Sloan Plan: A Case Study in Congressional Policy Determination.* Urbana: University of Illinois Press, 1955. xi + 402 pp. Map, tables, notes, appendix, bibliography, and index. The definitive legislative history of federal water resource development in the Missouri River Basin. The book focuses on the rivalry between the Army Corps of Engineers and Bureau of Reclamation; the resolution of the conflict by the Pick-Sloan Plan; the role of state governments; and plans for navigation, flood control, irrigation, and power generation.

Riesch, Anna. "Conservation under Franklin

D. Roosevelt." Doctoral dissertation, See chapter on "Irrigation."

Robbins, William G. "The Willamette Valley Project of Oregon: A Study in the Political Economy of Water Resource Development." *Pacific Historical Review,* XLVII (Nov. 1978), 585-605. Excellent case study of the influence of politics and economics on water resource development. The article focuses on the close ties that developed among business leaders, the Army Corps of Engineers, as well as state and federal politicians in promoting the multiple-purpose project.

Robertson, Robert R. "Problems of the Sacramento River." *Military Engineer,* XXXIV (Aug. 1942), 392-96.

Robinson, Michael C. "People in Public Works: Henry J. Kaiser." *APWA Reporter,* 44 (Jan. 1977), 8-9. Biographical sketch of a public works contractor who became one of the United States' leading industrialists. The article highlights the role of Kaiser's firm in constructing the Hoover, Bonneville, and Grand Coulee dams.

Robinson, Michael C. "People in Public Works: Arthur Powell Davis." *APWA Reporter, 45 (Oct. 1978), 4-5. A biographical sketch of the individual who may be rightfully considered the "father" of Hoover Dam. From 1914 to 1923, Davis served as director of the United States Reclamation Service.*

Robinson, Michael C. "People in Public Works: Peter Kiewit, Jr." *APWA Reporter,* 47 (Jan. 1980), 6-7. A biographical sketch of a giant of the construction industry whose firm built interstate highways, large dams, and award-winning bridges and tunnels.

Robinson, Michael C. *Water for the West: The Bureau of Reclamation, 1902-1977.* See chapter on "Irrigation."

Ross, John Ray. "'Pork Barrels' and the General Welfare: Problems in Conservation, 1900-1920." Doctoral dissertation, Duke University, 1969. xv + 576 pp. Notes, appendices, and bibliography. A good discussion of efforts by conservationists to gain congressional approval for a comprehensive approach to waterway development. Much of the dissertation describes the conservation movement in North Carolina, particularly the clash of the federal and state governments for control of water and other natural resources. The study contains some unique material on state drainage districts.

Rowe, Robert S., comp. *Bibliography of Rivers and Harbors and Related Fields in Hydraulic Engineering.* See chapter on "Waterways."

Ruhloff, F. Carl. "Evolution of Modern Construction Machinery." *Civil Engineering.* See chapter on "Planning, Engineering, and Administration."

Saindon, Bob, and Bunky Sullivan. "Taming the Missouri and Treating the Depression: Fort Peck Dam." *Montana: The Magazine of Western History,* XXVII (July 1977), 34-57. Lively, heavily illustrated account of the construction of Fort Peck Dam and its role in alleviating unemployment.

Salt, Harriet. *Mighty Engineering Feats: Clear and Concise Descriptions of Ten of the Greatest American Engineering Feats.* See chapter on "Planning, Engineering, and Administration."

Scheel, Paul Edmund. "Resource Development Politics in the Missouri Basin: Federal Power, Navigation, and Reservoir Operation Policies, 1944-1968." Doctoral dissertation. See chapter on "Irrigation."

Schenfele, Roy W. *The History of the North Pacific Division, U. S. Army Corps of Engineers, 1888 to 1965.* See chapter on "Waterways."

Schmidt, Lewis A. *The Engine-Ear: Fifty Years in Engineering.* See chapter on "Planning, Engineering, and Administration."

Schneider, George R. "History and Future of Flood Control." *Transactions of the American Society of Civil Engineers,* CT (1953), 1042-99. Describes in detail the role of the federal government in developing a national flood-control program administered by the Corps of Engineers.

Schneider, Norris F. *Y Bridge City: The Story of Zanesville and Muskingum County, Ohio.* See chapter on "Roads, Streets, and Highways."

Seckler, David, ed. *California Water: A Study in Resource Management.* See chapter on "Irrigation."

Selznick, Philip. *TVA and the Grass Roots: A Study in the Sociology of Formal Organization.*

See chapter on "Planning, Engineering, and Administration."

Settle, William A., Jr. *The Dawning, a New Day for the Southwest: A History of the Tulsa District, Corps of Engineers, 1939-1971.* See chapter on "Waterways."

Short, C. W., and R. Stanley-Brown. *Public Buildings: A Survey of Architecture of Projects Constructed by Federal and Other Governmental Bodies between the Years 1933 and 1939 with the Assistance of the Public Works Administration.* See chapter on "Public Buildings."

Smith, Frank E., ed. *Conservation in the United States, a Documentary History: Land and Water, 1900-1970.* See chapter on "Irrigation."

Smith, Guy-Harold. *Conservation of Natural Resources.* See chapter on "Irrigation."

Smith, Roland M. "The Politics of Pittsburgh Flood Control, 1908-1936."*Pennsylvania History,* XLII (Jan. 1975), 5-24. Outstanding case study of local efforts to enhance flood control. The article stresses the role of committees appointed by Pittsburgh's Chamber of Commerce and illustrates how the leaders' values and socio-economic background influenced the actions that were taken.

Smith, Stephen C. "Legal and Institutional Controls in Water Allocation." *Journal of Farm Economics.* See chapter on "Irrigation."

Snyder, Frank E., and Brian H. Guss. *The District: A History of the Philadelphia District, U. S. Army Corps of Engineers, 1886-1971.* See chapter on "Waterways."

Spray, Anne. "People in Public Works: A. Baldwin Wood." *APWA Reporter,* 45 (April 1978), 4-5. A biographical sketch of the individual who in the early 1900s designed the largest pumps in the world to drain water from New Orleans into Lake Pontchartrain.

Spritzer, Donald E. *Waters of Wealth: The Story of the Kootenai River and Libby Dam.* Boulder, Col.: Pruett Publishing Company, 1979. 167 pp. Bibliography and index. Contains chapters on how succeeding generations have exploited the Kootenai's resources. The concluding chapter deals with the construction of Libby Dam.

St. Francis Levee District. *History of the Organization and Operations of the Board of Directors, St. Francis Levee District of Arkansas, 1893-1945.* West Memphis, Ark.: n. p., n. d. 364 pp. Appendices. A useful history of the development of flood control activities in the St. Francis River Basin.

Steele, Annie Laurie. "A History of the Sandstone Creek Area Up-Stream Flood Prevention Project." *Chronicles of Oklahoma,* XLIII (Winter 1965-1966), 432-42. Overview of a Soil Conservation Service project on the watershed of the Washita River.

Stevens, Walter B. *The Story of the Galveston Disaster.* Galveston: San Luis Press, 1975. 22 pp. Illustrations. A reprint of Stevens' article originally published in *Munsey's Magazine* in 1900. The accompanying illustrations offer a graphic overview of the disaster.

Stimson, George P. "River on a Rampage: An Account of the Ohio River Flood of 1937." *Bulletin of the Cincinnati Historical Society,* 22 (April 1964), 91-109. Good description of how the city tried to cope with the disaster.

Strickland, William; Edward H. Gill; and Henry R. Campbell, eds. *Public Works of the United States of America.* See chapter on "Planning, Engineering, and Administration."

Sundborg, George. *Hail Columbia: The Thirty-Year Struggle for Grand Coulee Dam.* See chapter on "Irrigation."

Sutton, Imre. "Geographical Aspects of Construction Planning: Hoover Dam Revisited."*Journal of the West.* See chapter on "Irrigation."

Swain, Donald C. *Federal Conservation Policy, 1921-1933.* See chapter on "Irrigation."

Swisher, Jacob A. "Floods in Iowa." *Iowa Journal of History and Politics,* XLV (Oct. 1947), 347-79. A descriptive survey of major Iowa floods. The last eight pages of the article are devoted to a superficial discussion of flood prevention and control.

Terral, Rufus. *The Missouri Valley: Land of Drouth, Flood, and Promise.* See chapter on "Irrigation."

Terrell, John Upton. *War for the Colorado River.* See chapter on "Irrigation."

Thompson, John T. "Governmental Responses to the Challenges of Water Resources in Texas."*Southwestern Historical Quarterly.*See chapter on "Waterways."

Tilly, Bette B. "Memphis and the Mississippi Valley Flood of 1927." *West Tennessee Historical Society Papers,* XXIV (1970), 4-56. Role of the city in relief and rescue activities. The article is an interesting case study of how federal, state, and local agencies were coordinated in response to the disaster.

Timmins, William M. "The Failure of the Hatchtown Dam, 1914." *Utah Historical Quarterly,* 36 (Summer 1968), 263-73. Describes the dam's construction, the "history of trouble with the dam site," the aftermath of the dam's failure, and the probable causes of the latter.

Tulga, Louis C. *The First Thirty-Six Years: A History of the Albuquerque District, 1935-1971.* Albuquerque: Corps of Engineers, 1973. 73 pp. Illustrations.

Turhollow, Anthony F. *A History of the Los Angeles District, U. S. Army Corps of Engineers, 1898-1965.* See chapter on "Waterways."

Tweet, Roald. *A History of the Rock Island District, Corps of Engineers.* See chapter on "Waterways."

Uhl, W. F. "Water Power over a Century." *Transactions of the American Society of Civil Engineers.* See chapter on "Waterways."

Wagner, Frederick W., and Edwin J. Durabb. "The Sinking City." *Environment,* 18 (May 1976), 32-39. Useful summary of the historical development of New Orleans' levee system and drainage works. The author discusses the probable environmental consequences of expanding the network.

Walker, Paul K. *The Corps Responds: A History of the Susquehanna Engineer District and Tropical Storm Agnes.* Baltimore: U. S. Army Engineer District, Baltimore Corps of Engineers, 1976. iii + 52 pp. Illustrations, notes, and bibliography. Excellent study of the corps' role in disaster relief and response efforts following the 1972 storm.

Wall, John Furman. "The Civil Works of the United States Army Corps of Engineers: Program Modernization." Doctoral dissertation, Cornell University, 1973. 1018 pp.

Ware, James. "Soldiers, Disasters, and Dams: The Army Corps of Engineers and Flood Control in the Red River Valley, 1936-1946." *Chronicles of Oklahoma,* LVII (Spring 1979), 26-33. Summary of dam and reservoir projects built during the decade.

Waring, George E., Jr. *Report on the Social Statistics of Cities.* See chapter on "Planning, Engineering, and Administration."

Waters, Frank. *The Colorado.* See chapter on "Irrigation."

Wells, Donald T. *The TVA Tributary Development Program.* University: University of Alabama, Bureau of Public Administration, 1964. ix + 153 pp. Illustrations. Insights into TVA's small watershed program and conflicts with the Soil Conservation Service.

Wengert, Norman. "Antecedents of TVA: The Legislative History of Muscle Shoals." *Agricultural History,* 26 (Oct. 1952), 141-47. Excellent overview of the legislative history of this important precursor for TVA.

Wengert, Norman I. *Valley of Tomorrow: The TVA and Agriculture.* Knoxville: University of Tennessee, 1952. xv + 151 pp. Footnotes and index. One of the few good sources that discusses the influence of TVA on the region's agricultural economy.

Whitaker, J. Russell, and Edward A. Ackerman. *American Resources: Their Management and Conservation.* See chapter on "Sewers and Wastewater Treatment."

White, Gilbert F. "A Perspective of River Basin Development." *Journal of Law and Contemporary Problems,* 22 (1957), 157-87. A brilliant, landmark discussion of the limits to which humankind can regulate rivers and still serve basic social and cultural needs. More attention, according to White, needs to be given to "the effects of river works upon economic growth and community stability or change."

White, Gilbert F. *Strategies of American Water Management.* See chapter on "Community Water Supply."

Whitman, Willson. *David Lilienthal: Public Servant in Power Age.* New York: Henry Holt and Company, 1948. vi + 245 pp. A laudatory, undocumented account of Lilienthal's career as chairman of the Tennessee Valley Authority. Much of the book is devoted to political affairs and his disputes with Arthur Morgan.

Whitman, Willson, *God's Valley: People and Power Along the Tennessee River.* New York: Viking Press, 1939. vi + 320 pp. Illustrations, appendix, and index. A highly subjective look at the impact of the Tennessee Valley Authority on the social life and customs of the valley's people.

Williams, Archibald. *The Romance of Modern Engineering.* See chapter on "Roads, Streets, and Highways."

Woodbury, David O. *The Colorado Conquest.* See chapter on "Irrigation."

Yost, Edna. *Modern American Engineers.* See chapter on "Planning, Engineering, and Administration."

5

Sewers and Wastewater Treatment

Concern for water pollution began long before the environmental movement of the 1960s and 1970s. The extensive nationwide effort to improve water quality is an intensification of efforts to control and neutralize wastes that reach back to the beginning of the eighteenth century. Since the colonial era, American cities have built sewers to control and dispose of urban wastewater. After the discovery of the bacterial origin of disease in the nineteenth century, pioneer environmental engineers and scientists developed wastewater treatment systems that municipalities adopted for processing sewage flows. Thus, the current surge of attention to pollution abatement and the skyrocketing expenditures for sewage system construction are rooted in past efforts to protect public health by controlling and treating wastewater.

Few areas of public works history have received less attention from scholars than urban wastewater systems. Students of public health institutions and practices have traditionally neglected this dimension of the subject. Consequently, many of the sources cited in this chapter are dated books and articles largely intended for engineering audiences. During the past decade, case studies have fortunately appeared that trace and analyze the sanitation strategies of specific urban areas. Major landmarks in wastewater control and treatment are being identified that illustrate how public officials, engineers, and scientists sought to protect the public against municipal and industrial wastes. Studies have also been prepared on the evolution of state and federal antipollution legislation and the creation of governmental agencies to enforce the attendant laws and regulations.

To date, the engineering, technological, economic, legal, and institutional dimensions have been outlined. Furthermore, several major studies have defined the critical turning points that shaped the present character of modern wastewater practices. The following annotated citations, therefore, offer an introduction to a complex subject that needs even greater examination.

Abbott, Samuel W. *The Past and Present Condition of Public Hygiene and State Medicine in the United States.* Boston: Massachusetts State Board of Health, 1900. 102 pp. Maps, tables, notes, and appendices. The principal value of this volume is its maps and statistical compilations indicating the percent and location of communities served by sewers and public water supplies.

"Allen Hazen." *Journal of the Boston Society of Civil Engineers,* XIX (May 1932), 319-22. Comprehensive biographical sketch of a sanitary engineer who conducted pioneering work in the purification of water and sewage.

Allen, Kenneth. "The Development of Sewage Treatment." *Municipal Engineering,* LV (June 1918), 244-49. Good summary that identifies most of the milestones.

Andryszak, Nancy. "People in Public Works: Calvin W. Hendrick." *APWA Reporter,* 47 (Nov. 1980), 4-5. A short biographical sketch which highlights Hendrick's work as chief engineer of Baltimore's Sewerage Commission (1899).

Armstrong, Ellis L.; Michael C. Robinson; and Suellen M. Hoy, eds. *History of Public Works in the United States, 1776-1976.* See chapter on "Planning, Engineering, and Administration."

Atkins, Gordon. *Health, Housing, and Poverty in New York City, 1865-1898.* See chapter on "Roads, Streets, and Highways."

Baker, M. N. *Municipal Engineering and Sanitation.* See chapter on "Planning, Engineering, and Administration."

Baker, T. Lindsay. "The Grand Canyon Water Reuse System: Pioneer in Western Effluent Reclamation." *Arizona Professional Engineer,* XXIX (Dec. 1977), 21. Interesting sketch of a sewage treatment system built on the South Rim of Grand Canyon by the National Park Service and Santa Fe Railroad.

Ballard, Robert M. "Pollution in Lake Erie, 1872-1965." *Special Libraries,* 66 (Aug. 1975), 378-82. An analysis of the literature on this topic that includes several sources on the effects of sewage and industrial pollution on municipal water supplies.

Bassett, Carroll. "Inland Sewage Disposal with Special Reference to the East Orange, N.J. Works." *Transactions of the American Society of Civil Engineers,* XXV (July-Dec. 1891), 125-60. Good overview of pioneering wastewater treatment systems.

Beard, Mary Ritter. *Woman's Work in Municipalities.* See chapter on "Solid Wastes."

Bell, A. T. "Early History of Sewers of Memphis, Tenn." *Municipal Engineering,* XXXVII (Oct. 1909), 232-35. Sketch of the evolution of the city's sewer system from 1880 to 1900. The article includes a chronological table indicating the annual mileage and cost of sewers built.

Blake, John B. *Public Health in the Town of Boston, 1630-1822.* See chapter on "Community Water Supply."

Blake, John B. "The Origins of Public Health in the United States." *American Journal of Public Health,* 38 (Nov. 1948), 1539-50. An excellent, concise survey of the growth of the public health movement from 1860 to 1900. Good coverage is given to the development of water and wastewater systems in response to the ravages of diseases.

Bowditch, Henry I. *Public Health Hygiene in America: Being the Centennial Discourse Delivered Before the International Medical Congress, Philadelphia, September 1876.* Boston: Little, Brown, and Company, 1877. ix + 498 pp. Tables, notes, appendices, and index. One of the first attempts to develop an overview of public health organizations and activities. The publication provides a state-by-state survey of public health legislation and pollution control methods. The inclusion of a "Digest of American Sanitary Law" makes the book a useful research tool for public works historians.

Bridenbaugh, Carl. *Cities in Revolt: Urban Life in America, 1743-1776.* See chapter on "Planning, Engineering, and Administration."

Bridenbaugh, Carl. *Cities in the Wilderness: The First Century of Urban Life in America, 1625-1742.* See chapter on "Planning, Engineering, and Administration."

Brown, G. P. *Drainage Channel and Waterway: A History of the Effort to Secure an Effective and Harmless Method for the Disposal of the Sewage of the City of Chicago, and to Create a Navigable Channel between Lake Michigan and the Mississippi River.* Chicago: R. R. Donnelley & Sons Company, 1894. x + 480 pp. Illustrations, maps, charts, tables, diagrams, chronology, bibliography, and index. A useful official history of the Chicago Sanitary and Ship Canal. The volume contains an outstanding collection of construction photographs.

Brownell, Blaine A. *The Urban Ethos in the South.* See chapter on "Planning, Engineering, and Administration."

Bryan, Wilhelmus Bogart. *A History of the National Capital: From Its Foundation through the Period of the Adoption of the Organic Act.* See chapter on "Planning, Engineering, and Administration."

Bureau of the Census (Department of Commerce and Labor). *Statistics of Cities Having a Population of over 30,000: 1904.* See chapter on "Roads, Streets, and Highways."

Bureau of the Census (Department of Commerce and Labor). *Statistics of Cities Having a Population of 8,000 to 25,000: 1903.* See chapter on "Roads, Streets, and Highways."

Busey, Samuel C. "History and Progress of Sanitation of the City of Washington, and the Efforts of the Medical Profession in Relation Thereto." *Sanitarian,* 42 (March 1899), 205-16. Deals with the development of the city's sewer and drainage systems.

Busfield, J. L. "The Chicago Drainage Canal." *Engineering Journal* (Montreal), IX (May 1926), 237-57. A well-done historical review of the canal's technical and financial features. The article also touches upon the international dimensions of Chicago's sanitation strategy.

Cain, Louis P. "Raising and Watering a City: Ellis Sylvester Chesbrough and Chicago's First Sanitation System." *Technology and Culture.* See chapter on "Community Water Supply."

Cain, Louis P. *Sanitation Strategy for a Lakefront Metropolis: The Case of Chicago.* DeKalb: Northern Illinois University Press, 1978. xv + 173 pp. Illustrations, maps, tables, notes, appendices, bibliography, and index. Traces and analyzes the evolution of Chicago's sanitation strategy with respect to water supply, sewage disposal, and drainage. Emphasis is placed on the legal, economic, and technical aspects of the topic.

Cain, Louis P. "The Creation of Chicago's Sanitary District and Construction of the Sanitary and Ship Canal." *Chicago History,* III (Summer 1979), 98-110. Well-written and deeply researched article concerning the canal built by the city to divert sewage away from its water supply—Lake Michigan. The canal was one of the most outstanding public works projects of the nineteenth century.

Cain, Louis Perkins. "The Sanitary District of Chicago: A Case Study of Water Use and Conservation." Doctoral dissertation, Northwestern University, 1969. 618 pp.

Cain, Louis P. "The Search for an Optimum Sanitation Jurisdiction: The Metropolitan Sanitary District of Greater Chicago, a Case Study." *Essays in Public Works History,* 10 (July 1980), 1-35. An excellent case-study analysis of the strengths and weaknesses of single- and multi-purpose special districts. The essay considers reasons for creating special districts for sanitation services; the historical development of the Chicago sanitary district; the sanitation strategies adopted by other cities; and the influence of environmental legislation on institutional arrangements for disposing of wastewater and protecting water supplies.

Cain, Louis P. "Unfouling the Public's Nest: Chicago's Sanitary Diversion of Lake Michigan Water." *Technology and Culture,* 15 (Oct. 1974), 594-613. Examines the history, intergovernmental, economic, geographical, and technological aspects of efforts to resolve the problem of sewage pollution control in the Chicago metropolitan area. The article focuses on the years from 1889 to 1930.

Capers, Gerald M., Jr. *The Biography of a River Town, Memphis: Its Heroic Age.* Chapel Hill: University of North Carolina, 1939. xiv + 292 pp. Illustrations, maps, tables, notes, bibliographical essay, and index. A good urban history that includes an account of public health improvements made following a series of yellow fever epidemics in the early 1880s. The most celebrated reform was the adoption of the first separate sewer system in the United States, which was designed by George E. Waring, Jr.

Carmichael, Donald M. "Forty Years of Water Pollution Control in Wisconsin: A Case Study." *Wisconsin Law Review* (Spring 1967), 350-419. Brilliant, comprehensive discussion of the administration of wastewater pollution control laws in Wisconsin since the late 1920s. The problems of enforcement are dealt with as well as pollution-control efforts of municipalities and major industries.

Cassedy, James Higgins. *Charles V. Chapin and the Public Health Movement.* Cambridge: Harvard University Press, 1962. vii + 310 pp. Notes, appendices, bibliography, and index. A comprehensive biography of a pioneer in the American public health movement. His career spanned the entire half-century after 1876; and from his position as superintendent of health in Providence, Rhode Island, he made numerous contributions to improving the quality of life in the United States. Following extensive research, he formulated a new body of principles which were used to destroy ancient theories about communicable diseases. Chapin then transferred these principles into a workable system of standards for health practitioners.

Cassedy, James H. "Hygeia: A Mid-Victorian Dream of a City of Health." *Journal of the History of Medicine and Allied Sciences,* 17 (April 1967), 217-28. Following passage of the 1875 Public Health Act, British sanitarians formulated a plan of action which remained largely intact until World War II and which did not go unnoticed by their American counterparts. Famous physician Benjamin Ward Richardson shared his vision in a memorable address "Hygeia: A City of Health." Cassedy discusses Richardson's career and his blueprint for a sanitary utopia.

Cassedy, James H. "The Flamboyant Colonel Waring: An Anti-Contagionist Holds the American Stage in the Age of Pasteur and Koch." *Bulletin of the History of Medicine.* See chapter on "Solid Wastes."

Cassedy, James H. "The Roots of American Sanitary Reform, 1843-47: Seven Letters from John H. Griscom to Lemuel Shattuck." *Journal of the History of Medicine and Allied Sciences,* 30 (April 1975), 136-47. The letters confirm Griscom and Shattuck as visionary public health pioneers. Many of their recommendations went unheeded for decades.

Cavins, Harold M. "The National Quarantine and Sanitary Conventions of 1857 to 1860 and the Beginnings of the American Public Health Association." *Bulletin of the History of Medicine,* XIII (1943), 404-26. A fine article on the first attempts to form an organization to fight disease.

Chambers, J. S. *The Conquest of Cholera: America's Greatest Scourge.* See chapter on "Community Water Supply."

Champion, Merrill E. "Seventy-Five Years of Public Health in Massachusetts." *New England Journal of Medicine,* 232 (March 1, 1945), 241-47. Traces Lemuel Shattuck's career and the research conducted at the Lawrence Experiment Station.

Chapin, Charles V. *Municipal Sanitation in the United States.* See chapter on "Solid Wastes."

Chase, E. Sherman. "Progress in Sanitary Engineering in the United States." *Transactions of the American Society of Civil Engineers,* CT (1953), 556-73. A general review of the development of sanitary engineering.

Clarke, Robert. *Ellen Swallow: The Woman Who Founded Ecology.* Chicago: Follett Publishing Company, 1973. xii + 276 pp. Illustrations, bibliography, and index. An engaging biography of a woman who was an active environmentalist a century ago. The first woman graduate of the Massachusetts Institute of Technology, Ellen Swallow Richards (1842-1911) was appointed to the MIT faculty in 1884 as a full-fledged instructor of sanitary chemistry. In that capacity, she taught the analysis of food, water, sewage, and air to pioneer sanitary engineers who later initiated experimental laboratories modeled after hers.

Clayton, John. "How They Tinkered with a River." *Chicago History,* 1 (Spring 1970), 32-46. Deals with early navigation as well as the Sanitary and Ship Canal.

Cleary, Edward J. *The ORSANCO Story: Water Quality Management in the Ohio Valley under an Interstate Compact.* Baltimore: Johns Hopkins Press, 1967. xvi + 335 pp. Illustrations, maps, charts, tables, notes, appendices, and index. A landmark study in the water pollution field by the man who served as executive director and chief engineer of the Ohio River Valley Water Sanitation Commission. Cleary chronicles the evolution, successes, and failures of the interstate compact agency with keen insight, wit, and surprising objectivity. The author concludes that the eight states comprising the compact succeeded "in converting aspirations into realities by uniting the leadership of many and inspiring the participation of all in restoring some measure of wholesomeness to the waters in the Ohio Valley."

Cleveland Engineering Society. *The Golden Anniversary of the Cleveland Engineering Society.* See chapter on "Planning, Engineering, and Administration."

Cohn, Morris M. *Sewers for Growing America.* Ambler, Penn.: Certain-teed Productions Corporation, 1966. 224 pp. Illustrations, maps, tables, and graphs. Includes one chapter on the history of sewers which the author refers to as "conduits of civilization."

Cohn, Morris M., and Dwight F. Metzler. *The Pollution Fighters: A History of Environmental Engineering in New York State.* Albany: New York State Department of Health, 1973. ix + 245 pp. Illustrations and tables. A rambling and somewhat disjointed history of environmental engineering in the state of New York that places emphasis on the origins and activities of the State Board of Health. The book contains useful and unique information on the evolution of water pollution control and solid waste management.

Connery, Robert H., and Richard H. Leach. *The Federal Government and Metropolitan Areas.* See chapter on "Planning, Engineering, and Administration."

Corn, Jacqueline Karnell. "Community Responsibility for Public Health." *Western Pennsylvania Historical Magazine,* 59 (July 1976), 319–39. Reviews public health practices in Pittsburgh from 1851 to 1888.

Corn, Jacqueline Karnell. "Municipal Organization for Public Health in Pittsburgh, 1851-1895." Doctoral dissertation. See chapter on "Community Water Supply."

Cosgrove, J. J. *History of Sanitation.* Pittsburgh: Standard Sanitary Manufacturing Company, 1909. viii + 124 pp. Illustrations.

Craig, W. Allan. "The Development of the Digestion Tank." *Journal of the Boston Society of Civil Engineers,* XXVII (Jan. 1940), 36-41. Technical sketch of this sewage treatment system.

Creighton, Wilbur F., Jr. "Wilbur Fisk Foster, Soldier and Engineer." *Tennessee Historical Quarterly,* XXXI (Fall 1972), 261-75. Describes the career of a confederate army engineer and Nashville's city engineer (1865). The author gives special attention to the modern sewerage system installed during Foster's tenure of office and to the bridges and buildings he designed and built.

Crooks, James B. *Politics & Progress: The Rise of Urban Progressivism in Baltimore, 1895 to 1911.* Baton Rouge: Louisiana State University Press, 1968. xiii + 259 pp. Illustrations, map, tables, notes, and index. Despite being generally neglectful of public works, the book contains some material on Baltimore's sewer system.

Davenport, F. Garvin. "The Sanitation Revolution in Illinois, 1870-1900." *Journal of the Illinois State Historical Society,* LXVI (Autumn 1973), 306-26. An interesting, though shallowly researched, historical overview of sewage treatment and disposal as well as related public health issues in Illinois during the late nineteenth century. The article contains a description of the Sanitary and Ship Canal.

Davies, J. Clarence, III. *The Politics of Pollution.* New York: Pegasus, 1970. xiii + 231 pp. Tables, notes, and index. The best single source on the evolution of federal air and water pollution legislation and the resultant programs. Chapter 2, "Federal Pollution Control Legislation," is a concise, well-written historical summary of the subject.

Davison, George S. "A Century and a Half of American Engineering." *Proceedings of the American Society of Civil Engineers.* See chapter on "Planning, Engineering, and Administration."

DeNevers, Noel, ed. *Technology and Society.* See chapter on "Roads, Streets, and Highways."

Detwyler, Thomas R., and Melvin G. Marcus, eds. *Urbanization and Environment: The Physical Geography of the City.* See chapter on "Community Water Supply."

Dietzler, John Patrick. "Sewage and Drainage in St. Louis, 1764-1954." Master's thesis, St. Louis University, 1954.

Dietzler, John P. "The Mill Creek Sewer Explosion of July 26, 1892." *Missouri Historical Society Bulletin,* XV (Jan. 1959), 125-29. Interesting account of a tragedy in 1892 caused by flammable liquids entering the city's combined sewer system.

Doty, Duane (Mrs.). *The Town of Pullman: Its Growth with Brief Accounts of Its Industries.* Chicago: Pullman Civic Organization, 1974. 263 pp. Illustrations, map, tables, appendix, and index. First published in 1893, this book contains a good deal of information on the water and sewage system of Pullman, the first planned community in the United States.

Draffin, Jasper, Owen. *The Story of Man's Quest for Water.* See chapter on "Community Water Supply."

Duffy, John. *A History of Public Health in New York City, 1625-1866.* See chapter on "Solid Wastes."

Duffy, John. *A History of Public Works in New York City, 1866-1966.* See chapter on "Solid Wastes."

Duffy, John. *Epidemics in Colonial America.* See chapter on "Community Water Supply."

Dworsky, Leonard B., ed. *Conservation in the United States, A Documentary History: Pollution.* New York: Chelsea House Publishers, 1971. xi + 911 pp. Charts, tables, graphs, notes, and index. A good collection of articles and documents on water and air pollution. Most of the selections deal with the development of federal anti-pollution legislation and the growth of federal public health agencies.

Easby, William, Jr. "The Beginnings of Sanitary Science and the Development of Sewerage and Sewage Disposal." *Proceedings of the Engineers' Club of Philadelphia,* XXVIII (April 1911), 89-108. Insightful presidential address covering the evolution of sewerage since ancient times.

Eddy, Harrison P. "Sewerage and Drainage of Towns." *Proceedings of the American Society of Civil Engineers,* LIII (Sept. 1927), 1603-17. Outline history of sewerage and wastewater treatment that identifies many historical benchmarks.

Eddy, Harrison P. "Sewerage and Sewage Disposal." *Engineering News-Record,* 92 (April 17, 1924), 693-95. An uncritical, brief overview of landmarks in wastewater control and treatment from the Civil War to the early 1920s.

Ellis, John H. "Businessmen and Public Health in the Urban South During the Nineteenth Century: New Orleans, Memphis, and Atlanta." *Bulletin of the History of Medicine,* XLIV (May-June; July-Aug. 1970), May-June: 197-212; July-Aug.: 346-71. Includes an interesting discussion of business support of public works to insure their cities would remain viable centers of business enterprise.

Ellis, John H. "Memphis' Sanitary Revolution, 1880-1890." *Tennessee Historical Quarterly,* XXIII (March 1964), 59-72. Deeply researched article on municipal health improvements in Memphis following outbreaks of cholera and yellow fever. The article deals extensively with George E. Waring, Jr.'s separate sewer system, the first built in the United States.

Fair, Gordon M. "The Genius of Sanitation." *Journal of the Boston Society of Civil Engineers,* XXVII (April 1940), 67-78. Vapid presidential address on the history of sanitation.

Fellmeth, Robert C. *Politics of Land: Ralph Nader's Study Group Report on Land Use in California.* See chapter on "Planning, Engineering, and Administration."

Feinstein, Estelle F. *Stamford in the Gilded Age: The Political Life of a Connecticut Town, 1868-1893.* See chapter on "Planning, Engineering, and Administration."

Finch, J. K. "A Hundred Years of American Civil Engineering, 1852-1952." *Transactions of the American Society of Civil Engineers.* See chapter on "Planning, Engineering, and Administration."

Fisher, Edwin A. "Engineering and Public Works in the City of Rochester During the Past Century." *Centennial History of Rochester, New York.* See chapter on "Planning, Engineering, and Administration."

Flannery, James Joseph. "Water Pollution Control: Development of State and National Policy." Doctoral dissertation, University of Wisconsin, 1956. 511 pp.

Folwell, A. Prescott. *Sewerage: The Designing, Construction, and Maintenance of Sewerage Systems.* New York: John Wiley & Sons, 1916. x + 540 pp. Illustrations, graphs, tables, appendix, and index.

Foulkes, Ernest C., and Edward J. Cleary, eds. *Man and His Environment: Aspirations for Improvement and Prospects for Their Realization.* Cincinnati: University of Cincinnati, 1969. iv + 76 pp. An excellent collection of essays on various aspects of the urban environment. The selection by Abel Wolman, "A Delineation of Environmental Deterioration," is an especially perceptive analysis of the rise of environmental consciousness in the 1960s. He identifies a great deal of "pseudoscientific nonsense" that appeared as part of debates over environmental protection.

Frank, Carrolyle M. "Who Governed Middletown?: Community Power in Muncie, Indiana, in the 1930s." *Indiana Magazine of History*. See chapter on "Planning, Engineering, and Administration."

Fuller, George W. "Current Tendencies in Sewage Disposal Practice." *Journal of the Western Society of Engineers*, XXVI (Aug. 1921), 273–88. Interesting perspectives on the field's needs and potentials. It is an excellent overview of the state-of-the-art of sanitary engineering in the early 1920s.

Fuller, George W. "Sewage Disposal Trends in the New York City Region." *Sewage Works Journal*, IV (July 1932), 637–46.

Fuller, George W. "The Place of Sanitary Engineering in Public Health Activities." *American Journal of Public Health*, XV (Dec. 1925), 1069–73. An excellent survey of the role engineers were playing in eradicating disease by the mid-1920s. The fields of sewage treatment, public water supply, and refuse disposal are covered.

Galishoff, Stuart. "Drainage, Disease, Comfort, and Class: A History of Newark's Sewers." *Societas—A Review of Social History*, VI (Winter 1976), 121-38. One of the few solid case studies of municipal sewer development. Galishoff notes "the social forces that shaped the development of sewerage" from 1854 to 1918—disease and indoor plumbing. The study also points out since property owners were required to pay for laterals and hookups many of the poor were without adequate sanitary facilities.

Galishoff, Stuart. "Public Health in Newark, 1832-1918." Doctoral dissertation, New York University, 1969. 541 pp.

Galishoff, Stuart. *Safeguarding the Public Health: Newark, 1895-1918*. Westport, Conn.: Greenwood Press, 1975. xv + 191 pp. Illustrations, tables, charts, notes, appendix, bibliographical essay, and index. A thoroughly researched history of one community's efforts to combat contagious diseases. Two themes run through the book: "(1) increasing government assumption of responsibility for public health; and (2) the interaction of medicine and society." Galishoff has a good grasp of the problems the city faced with respect to water supply and waste disposal. Public works historians will be particularly interested in Chapter 5, "The Passaic Valley Trunk Sewer."

Galishoff, Stuart. "The Passaic Valley Trunk Sewer." *New Jersey History*, LXXXVIII (Winter 1970), 197-214. One of the best case studies of sewer system development. The article discusses the construction of the sewer system in response to the public health needs of a large area of northern New Jersey.

Galli, Geraldine. "100 Years of Construction News." *Engineering News-Record*. See chapter on "Planning, Engineering, and Administration."

Gerhard, William Paul. "A Half Century of Sanitation." *American Architect and Building News*, LXIII (Feb. 25, 1899; March 4, 1899; March 11, 1899), Feb. 25, 1899: 61-62; March 4, 1899: 67-69; March 11, 1899: 75-76. Highlights major sanitation developments in the United States, Great Britain, and Europe.

Gerhard, William Paul. *The Disposal of Household Wastes*. See chapter on "Solid Wastes."

Gies, Joseph. *Wonders of the Modern World*. New York: Thomas Y. Crowell Company, 1966. xii + 241 pp. Illustrations, diagrams, appendices, and index. Contains whole chapters on the Verrazano-Narrows Bridge, the Empire State Building, the Chicago Sewage System, the California Water Plan, and the Interstate Highway System.

Giglierano, Geoffrey. "The City and the System: Developing a Municipal Service, 1800-1915." *Cincinnati Historical Society Bulletin*, 35 (Winter 1977), 223-47. An excellent case study that focuses on how the city's government changed its perceptions of public sanitation needs and the roles of officials in meeting them.

Gillespie, C. G. "Developments in Methods of Sewage Disposal." *Municipal and County Engineering*, LXXI (Sept. 1926), 169-78. Solid article on early sewage treatment methods, particularly digestion tanks.

Glaab, Charles N., and A. Theodore Brown. *A History of Urban America*. See chapter on "Community Water Supply."

Gorgas, William Crawford. *Sanitation in Panama*. New York: D. Appleton and Company, 1915. x + 298 pp. Illustrations and index. Although this book primarily deals with mosquito control, it contains material on sewers, drainage, and the development of wholesome water supplies.

Graff, Maurice O. "The Lake Michigan Water Diversion Controversy: A Summary Statement." *Journal of the Illinois State Historical Society,* XXXIV (Dec. 1941), 453-71. Outlines Chicago's conflicts with Canada and various American cities over the diversion of the city's sewage away from Lake Michigan.

Graham, Frank, Jr. *Disaster by Default: Politics and Water Pollution.* New York: M. Evans and Company, 1966. 256 pp. Appendices and index. An environmental polemic on damage to water resources caused by municipal and industrial wastes. The author uses historical examples of pollution to support his appeal for the expansion of wastewater treatment.

Greeley, Samuel A. "Municipal Facilities for Public Health." *Civil Engineering,* 3 (Aug. 1933), 439-41. On general improvements in waterworks, sewerage systems, and refuse disposal facilities over the past century.

Greeley, Samuel A. "Testing Stations for Sanitary Engineering—An Outstanding Achievement." *Transactions of the American Society of Civil Engineers,* CT (1953), 574-78. Briefly reviews the role and development of sewage and water testing stations since 1887.

Green, Constance McLaughlin. *History of Naugatuck, Connecticut.* New Haven: Yale University Press, 1949. vi + 283 pp. Illustration, maps, bibliographical essay, appendices, and index. An outstanding biography of a small New England city. The breadth of the author's research is extraordinary. Woven throughout the book are discussions of the town's sewers, water supply, streets, street lighting, public transit, and recreational facilities.

Green, Constance McLaughlin. *Holyoke, Massachusetts: A Case History of the Industrial Revolution in America.* See chapter on "Waterways."

Green, Constance McLaughlin. *Washington: Capital City, 1879-1950.* See chapter on "Community Water Supply."

Green, Constance McLaughlin. *Washington: Village and Capital, 1800-1878.* See chapter on "Urban Mass Transportation."

Gregory, George Peter. "A Study in Local Decision Making: Pittsburgh and Sewage Treatment." *Western Pennsylvania Historical Magazine,* 57 (Jan. 1974), 25-42. Solidly researched and thoughtful examination of Pittsburgh's first major attempt at sewage treatment in the 1910s. The study focuses on the proposed sanitation alternatives and the rationale which supported the final policy—treat the water supply instead of adopting a comprehensive sewage treatment system.

Griffith, Ernest S. *A History of American City Government: The Conspicuous Failure, 1870-1900.* See chapter on "Planning, Engineering, and Administration."

Griffith, Ernest S. *A History of American City Government: The Progressive Years and Their Aftermath, 1900-1920.* See chapter on "Planning, Engineering, and Administration."

Haley, F. W. "Recent Additions to the Sewerage System and Disposal Works of Framingham, Mass." *Journal of the Boston Society of Civil Engineers,* XII (June 1925), 253-75. Includes a short historical discussion of the Framingham Sewerage Works that was founded in the late 1880s.

Hall, Clayton Colman, ed. *Baltimore: Its History and Its People.* See chapter on "Community Water Supply."

Harkins, Michael J. "Public Health Nuisances in Omaha, 1870-1900." *Nebraska History,* 56 (Winter 1975), 471-92. A general overview of the city's public health improvements that includes discussions of garbage disposal, sewer construction, and water supply.

Hatch, James N. "Results at the Pasadena Activated Sludge Plant." *Public Works,* 60 (April 1929), 129-33. Describes one of the oldest and largest plants, its methods of operation, and the results obtained during four years (beginning in 1924).

Hatton, T. Chalkley. "Brief History of Sludge Dewatering Investigations at the Milwaukee Testing Station." *Proceedings of the American Society for Municipal Improvements,* 29 (1922), 96-107. Since 1910.

Havinghurst, Walter. *River to the West: Three Centuries of the Ohio.* See chapter on "Waterways."

Hill, C. D. "The Sewerage System of Chicago." *Journal of the Western Society of Engineers,* XVI (Sept. 1911), 545-64. Pedestrian historical overview of Chicago's sewer system from 1855 to the early twentieth century.

"Historic Review of the Development of Sanitary Engineering in the United States during the Past Hundred and Fifty Years." *Proceedings of the American Society of Civil Engineers,* LIII (Sept. 1927), 1585-1645. Collection of articles on the evolution of water supplies, sewerage, refuse collection, and drainage by leading sanitary engineers such as Harrison P. Eddy, George W. Fuller, and Samuel A. Greeley.

Hoffecker, Carol E. *Wilmington, Delaware: Portrait of an Industrial City, 1830-1910.* n.p.: University of Virginia Press, 1974. xvi + 187 pp. Illustrations, maps, tables, notes, appendix, bibliography, and index. Chapter II of this exemplary urban history, "The Dynamics of Physical Growth: Politics and Utilities," includes excellent discussions of wastewater treatment, water, transit, and gas utility systems. This section also illustrates how the structure of municipal government changed in response to demands for greater city services.

Holmes, Beatrice Hort. *History of Federal Water Resources Programs and Policies, 1961-70.* See chapter on "Irrigation."

Hommon, H. B. "History of Sewage and Trade Wastes Treatment and Disposal." *Western Construction News,* 3 (Aug. 25, 1928), 535-36. A shallow overview.

Horner, W. W. "History and Design of the Mill Creek Sewer." *Journal of the Engineers' Club of St. Louis,* 1 (Jan.-Feb. 1916), 59-82. Highly technical history of the development of a major feature of St. Louis' sewer system which originated in 1849.

Howard, William Travis. *Public Health Administration and the Natural History of Disease in Baltimore, Maryland, 1797-1920.* Washington, D.C.: Carnegie Institute of Washington, 1924. vi + 565 pp. Map, tables, charts, and bibliography. Records the development of laws and practices of public health in Baltimore. The section on nuisance prevention and abatement in Chapter VI is the only part of the book directly related to public works.

Hoy, Suellen M. "People in Public Works: A.M. Rawn." *APWA Reporter,* 45 (Aug. 1978), 4-5. A biographical sketch of the chief engineer and general manager of the sanitation districts of Los Angeles County from 1941 to 1958.

Hoy, Suellen M. "People in Public Works: Ellen Swallow Richards." *APWA Reporter,* 44 (July 1977), 6-7. Emphasizes Richard's sanitary engineering work at the Massachusetts Institute of Technology and for the state of Massachusetts at the Lawrence Experiment Station.

Hoy, Suellen M. "People in Public Works: John H. Gregory." *APWA Reporter.* See chapter on "Community Water Supply."

Hubbell, Clarence W. "Background and Development of Detroit's Sewage Disposal Project." *Civil Engineering,* 8 (July 1938), 466-68. Reports on conditions which led to the inception of the project three decades earlier and on subsequent events that have influenced its development.

Hungerford, Edward. *The Story of Public Utilities.* See chapter on "Urban Mass Transportation."

Hunt, Caroline L. *The Life of Ellen H. Richards.* Washington, D.C.: American Home Economics Association, 1958. xix + 202 pp. Illustration and appendices. Biography of one of the founders of the sanitary engineering profession. Richards' analyses of water quality in Massachusetts during the late nineteenth century predated her more generally known role as a principal founder of the home economics movement.

Huse, Charles Phillips. *The Financial History of Boston from May 1, 1822 to January 31, 1909.* See chapter on "Community Water Supply."

"Illinois Society [of Engineers] Celebrates Its 50th Anniversary." *Engineering News-Record.* See chapter on "Planning, Engineering, and Administration."

Isaac, Paul E. "Municipal Reform in Beaumont, Texas, 1902-1909." *Southwestern Historical Quarterly.* See chapter on "Planning, Engineering, and Administration."

Jewell, William J., and Belford L. Seabrook. *A History of Land Application as a Treatment Alternative.* Washington, D.C.: U.S. Environmental Protection Agency, Office of Water Program Operations, 1979. vii + 83 pp. Charts, tables, graphs, appendices, and bibliography. Overview of sewage irrigation in the United States and some other countries.

Johnson, Mary Elizabeth. *Emergency Employment in Onondaga County.* See chapter on "Planning, Engineering, and Administration."

Jones, Alexander J. "The Chicago Drainage Canal and Its Forebear, the Illinois and Michigan Canal." *Transactions of the Illinois State Historical Society* (1906), 153-61. Insipid overview of Chicago's sanitation strategy.

Jordan, E. O.; G. C. Whipple; and C. E. A. Winslow. *A Pioneer of Public Health, William* Thompson Sedgwick. New Haven: Yale University Press, 1924. xvi + 193 pp. Illustrations and appendices. A paean to one of the pioneers in the development of water filtration and wastewater treatment, Sedgwick, who headed the Department of Biology and Public Health at the Massachusetts Institute of Technology, was among the small group of scientists and engineers who founded the historic Lawrence (Massachusetts) Experiment Station. During the 1890s, the station undertook research on sanitation problems that enabled cities to combat waterborne diseases.

Jordan, Philip D. *The People's Health: A History of Public Health in Minnesota to 1948.* See chapter on "Community Water Supply."

Judd, Jacob. "Brooklyn's Health and Sanitation, 1834-1855." *Journal of Long Island History*, VII (Winter-Spring 1967), 40-51. Offers a well-researched account of the city's efforts to provide sewers and street cleaning in the 1840s and 1850s.

Kinnicutt, Leonard P.; C. E. A. Winslow; and R. Winthrop Pratt. *Sewage Disposal.* New York: John Wiley & Sons, 1913. xxvi + 436 pp. Illustrations, charts, tables, diagrams, bibliography, and indexes. One of the best early texts on sanitary engineering. Each chapter is prefaced by a historical summary of the subject under discussion.

Klein, Maury, and Harvey A. Kantor. *Prisoners of Progress: American Industrial Cities, 1850-1920.* See chapter on "Solid Wastes."

Kleinschmidt, Earl E. "The Sanitary Reform Movement in Michigan." *Michigan History Magazine,* XXVI (Summer 1942), 373-401. A descriptive survey of the public health movement in Michigan from the Civil War to the late 1880s. The article contains some interesting information on the sponsoring of "sanitary conventions" throughout the state to promote construction of water and sewer systems and other improvements.

Larned, J. N. *A History of Buffalo: Delineating the Evolution of the City.* 2 vols. New York: Progress of the Empire State Company, 1911. Vol. I: 286 pp.; Vol. II: 321 pp. Volume I of this history offers a chapter on "Constructive Evolution" that discusses the history of the city's sewers, water supply, harbor, parks, streets, street railways, and electric power system.

Larsen, Lawrence H. *The Urban West at the End of the Frontier.* See chapter on "Solid Wastes."

Larson, Laurence Marcellus. "A Financial and Administrative History of Milwaukee." *Bulletin of the University of Wisconsin: Economics and Political Science Series.* See chapter on "Planning, Engineering, and Administration."

"Lawrence Experiment Station." *Municipal Journal and Engineer,* XXIV (Jan. 15, 1908), 71-74. Includes excellent illustrations of the historic facility.

League of Women Voters (Education Foundation). *The Big Water Fight: Trials and Triumphs in Citizen Action on Problems of Supply, Pollution, Floods, and Planning across the U.S.A.* See chapter on "Community Water Supply."

Leavitt, Judith Walzer. "Public Health in Milwaukee, 1867-1910." Doctoral dissertation, University of Chicago, 1975.

Leavitt, Judith Walzer, and Ronald L. Numbers, eds. *Sickness and Health in America: Readings in the History of Medicine and Public Health.* Madison: University of Wisconsin Press, 1978. ix + 454 pp. Illustrations, notes, and index. A good collection of previously published material on the social history of medicine. The following essays are included: Louis P. Cain, "Raising and Watering a City: Ellis Sylvester Chesbrough and Chicago's First Sanitation System"; James H. Cassedy, "The Flamboyant Colonel Waring: An Anticontagionist Holds the American Stage in the Age of Pasteur and Koch."

Le Gacy, Arthur Evans. "Improvers and Preservers: A History of Oak Park, Illinois, 1833-1940." Doctoral dissertation, University of Chicago, 1967. v + 248 pp. Maps, tables, notes, and bibliography. Includes short sections on such public improvements as streets and sewers.

Lemmon, Sarah McCulloch. "Raleigh—An

Example of the 'New South'?" *North Carolina Historical Review.* See chapter on "Community Water Supply."

Lepawsky, Albert. "Water Resources and American Federalism." *American Political Science Review.* See chapter on "Waterways."

Lewis, R. A. *Edwin Chadwick and the Public Health Movement, 1832-1854.* London: Longmans, Green and Company, 1952. viii + 411 pp. Notes, appendix, bibliography, and index. A turgidly written biography of the English civil servant who advocated the construction of sewers and other public health reforms in the 1840s and 1850s. Chadwick was a great influence on American sanitary engineers who developed urban wastewater systems in the last half of the nineteenth century.

Lieber, Harvey. "The Politics of Air and Water Pollution Control in the New York Metropolitan Area." Doctoral dissertation, Columbia University, 1968. 545 pp.

Linton, Ron M. *Terracide: America's Destruction of Her Living Environment.* Boston: Little, Brown and Company, 1970. viii + 376 pp. Bibliography and index. A strong condemnation of environmental degradation caused by modern urban and industrial societies. References are made to the need for improving wastewater and solid waste disposal programs.

Loud, Ralph W. "The Metropolitan Sewerage Works." *Journal of the Boston Society of Civil Engineers,* X (Oct. 1923), 325-74. Summary of the Boston area's sewer system from the 1870s to the 1920s.

Macaulay, David. *Underground.* See chapter on "Planning, Engineering, and Administration."

MacColl, E. Kimbark. *The Growth of a City: Power and Politics in Portland, Oregon, 1915 to 1950.* See chapter on "Planning, Engineering, and Administration."

McKelvey, Blake. *Rochester: An Emerging Metropolis, 1925-1961.* See chapter on "Roads, Streets, and Highways."

McKelvey, Blake. *Rochester on the Genesee: The Growth of a City.* See chapter on "Parks and Recreation."

McKelvey, Blake. *Rochester: The Flower City, 1855-1890.* Cambridge: Harvard University Press, 1949. xviii + 407 pp. Illustrations, charts, notes, and index. Includes particularly strong sections on the city's water supply and sewer systems. Other public works activities are covered less thoroughly.

McKelvey, Blake. *Rochester: The Quest for Quality, 1890-1925.* See chapter on "Urban Mass Transportation."

McKelvey, Blake. *Rochester: The Water-Power City, 1812-1854.* See chapter on "Waterways."

McKelvey, Blake. "The History of Public Health in Rochester, New York." *Rochester History,* XVIII (July 1956), 1-28. Discusses the upgrading of water supply, sewers, and garbage collection to improve public health.

McKelvey, Blake. *The Urbanization of America, 1860-1915.* See chapter on "Community Water Supply."

McLear, Patrick E. "The St. Louis Cholera Epidemic." *Missouri Historical Review,* LXIII (Jan. 1969), 171-81. Good article on sewer planning in St. Louis during the 1840s and 1850s in response to a serious cholera epidemic.

Marcus, Alan I. "The Strange Career of Municipal Health Initiatives: Cincinnati and City Government in the Early Nineteenth Century." *Journal of Urban History,* 7 (Nov. 1980), 3-30.

Massachusetts. Sanitary Commission. *Report of a General Plan for the Promotion of Public and Personal Health.* Boston: Dutton & Wentworth, State Printers, 1850. vii + 544 pp. Tables, notes, appendices, and index. A classic report on public health conditions and measures undertaken to abate diseases. It contains reports on sanitary surveys of various Massachusetts communities as well as recommendations for the disposal of sewage, collection of refuse, and abatement of smoke.

Melnick, Mimi and Robert. "Manhole Covers: Artifacts in the Streets." *California Historical Quarterly.* See chapter on "Roads, Streets, and Highways."

Melosi, Martin V., ed. *Pollution and Reform in American Cities, 1870-1930.* See chapter on "Solid Wastes."

Melosi, Martin V. "Pragmatic Environmentalist: Sanitary Engineer George E. Waring, Jr." *Essays in Public Works History.* See chapter on "Solid Wastes."

Melosi, Martin V. "Urban Pollution: Historical Perspective Needed." *Environmental Review.* See chapter on "Solid Wastes."

Merdinger, Charles J. *Civil Engineering through the Ages.* See chapter on "Planning, Engineering, and Administration."

Metcalf, Leonard. "The Antecedents of the Septic Tank." *Transactions of the American Society of Civil Engineers,* XLVI (Dec. 1901), 456-81. Interesting historical sketch of this sewage disposal method.

Metcalf, Leonard, and Harrison P. Eddy. *American Sewerage Practice.* 2 vols. New York: McGraw-Hill Book Company, 1914. Vol. I: x + 747 pp.; Vol. II: x + 564 pp. Illustrations, charts, tables, graphs, diagrams, and indexes. Classic sanitary engineering text that includes an introductory chapter on "The Lessons Taught by Early Sewerage Works."

Miller, William D. *Memphis during the Progressive Era, 1900-1917.* Memphis: Memphis State University Press, 1957. xiv + 242 pp. Illustrations, notes, and index. Chapter 4 of this excellent book, "Expanding City Services," is one of the few attempts to survey comprehensively the growth of public works during a specific era of a city's history. The author effectively identifies the role of municipal engineering in Progressive reform movements. The discussion covers annexation, sewers, water supply, street paving, street lighting, parks, electric transit, and efforts to form a publicly owned power utility.

Miller, Zane L. *Boss Cox's Cincinnati: Urban Politics in the Progressive Era.* See chapter on "Urban Mass Transportation."

Morehouse, W. W. "Development of the Ground Water Supply of the City of Dayton, Ohio." *New England Water Works Association,* LI (June 1937), 219-26. Includes some historical information from 1870 to the 1930s.

Morrill, John Barstow, and Paul O. Fischer, eds. *Planning the Region of Chicago.* See chapter on "Planning, Engineering, and Administration."

Morris, Margaret Francine, ed. *Essays on the Gilded Age.* See chapter on "Solid Wastes."

Muench, Hugo. "Lemuel Shattuck—Still a Prophet: The Vitality of Vital Statistics." *American Journal of Public Health,* 39 (Feb. 1949), 151-55. A tribute to Shattuck's pathbreaking use of vital statistics in formulating the recommendations set forth in his classic *Report of the Sanitary Commission of Massachusetts* (1850).

Mumford, Lewis. *The City in History: Its Origins, Its Transformations, and Its Prospects.* See chapter on "Solid Wastes."

Murphy, Earl Finbar. *Water Purity: A Study in Legal Control of Natural Resources.* Madison: University of Wisconsin Press, 1961. xi + 212 pp. Notes, bibliography, and index. An outstanding legal and administrative history of water pollution control in Wisconsin. It presents concrete and vivid discussions of how biological and medical knowledge was translated into workable regulation and public works programs.

New York-New Jersey Metropolitan Chapter of the American Public Works Association. *Public Works in Metropolitan New York-New Jersey.* See chapter on "Planning, Engineering, and Administration."

O'Connell, James C. "Chicago's Quest for Pure Water." *Essays in Public Works History,* 1 (June 1976), 1-19. Excellent study of the promotion and planning of Chicago's Sanitary and Ship Canal and other public improvements. The essay outlines the efforts of municipal engineers, public health officials, and businessmen who "were responding effectively to the needs of a new urban society before the Progressive reformers of the early twentieth century popularized the cause."

O'Connell, James C. "People in Public Works: Ellis S. Chesbrough." *APWA Reporter,* 44 (Feb. 1977), 8-9. A biographical sketch of Chicago's first city engineer, who became famous for solving the city's sewage disposal problems and for providing Chicago residents with an ample supply of pure water.

O'Connell, James C. "Technology and Pollution: Chicago's Water Policy, 1833-1930." Doctoral dissertation, University of Chicago, 1980. iii + 214 pp. Notes, bibliographical essay, and selected bibliography. Outstanding study of the evolution of Chicago's wastewater and water supply systems. The author gives close attention to the political and cultural influences that shaped development of the city's public works.

Odell, Frederick S. "The Sewerage of Memphis." *Transactions of the American Society of*

Civil Engineers, X (Feb. 1881), 23-52. Comments by engineers following Odell's paper offer a classic overview of the relative merits and disadvantages of "separate" and "combined" sewer systems.

Olton, Charles S. "Philadelphia's First Environmental Crisis." *Pennsylvania Magazine of History.* See chapter on "Solid Wastes."

Osterweis, Rollin G. *Three Centuries of New Haven, 1638-1938.* See chapter on "Community Water Supply."

Pearse, Langdon. "A Quarter Century of Progress in Sewage Treatment." *Sewage Works Journal,* IV (July 1932), 647-54.

Pearse, Langdon, ed. *Modern Sewage Disposal: Anniversary Book of the Federation of Sewage Works Associations.* New York: Federation of Sewage Works Associations, 1938. x + 371 pp. Illustrations, maps, charts, tables, and bibliographies. A useful introduction to the first half-century of sewage treatment in the United States. The individually authored chapters on various aspects of sewage treatment technology contain a great deal of historical information.

Perrigo, Lynn I. "Municipal Beginnings at Boulder, Colorado, 1871-1900." *Colorado Magazine.* See chapter on "Roads, Streets, and Highways."

Peterson, Jon A. "The Impact of Sanitary Reform upon American Urban Planning." *Journal of Social History.* See chapter on "Planning, Engineering, and Administration."

Phaneuf, Margaret M. "Sanitation and Cholera: Springfield and the 1866 Epidemic." *Historical Journal of Western Massachusetts,* VIII (Jan. 1980), 26-36.

Piehl, Frank J. "Chicago's Early Fight to 'Save Our Lake.'" *Chicago History* (Winter 1976-1977), 223-32. Excellent perspectives on efforts by the city to stop the pollution of Lake Michigan through the construction of sewer and water supply systems. The article covers the period from the 1850s to completion of the Sanitary and Ship Canal in 1900.

Pierce, Bessie Louise. *A History of Chicago.* See chapter on "Community Water Supply."

Pikarsky, Milton. "Sixty Years of Rock Tunneling in Chicago." *Journal of the Construction Division of the American Society of Civil Engineers.* See chapter on "Community Water Supply."

Pisani, Donald J. "The Polluted Truckee: A Study in Interstate Water Quality, 1870-1934." *Nevada Historical Society Quarterly,* 20 (Spring 1970), 150-66. Excellent legislative history of attempts to abate pollution from sawmills and other sources.

Pomerantz, Sidney I. *New York: An American City, 1783-1803.* See chapter on "Community Water Supply."

Powell, J. H. *Bring Out Your Dead: The Great Plague of Yellow Fever in Philadelphia in 1793.* Philadelphia: University of Pennsylvania Press, 1949. xvi + 304 pp. Illustration, map, notes, and index.

Public Works Administration. *America Builds: The Record of PWA.* See chapter on "Planning, Engineering, and Administration."

Rafter George W. "Sewage Irrigation." *Water Supply and Irrigation Papers of the United States Geological Survey,* 3 (1897), 1-100. Remains the most comprehensive survey of sewage irrigation practices before 1900. It presents the methods and justifications for implementing wastewater farming and describes systems in the United States, England, Germany, and France. The study is of great value to current students of this practice, which is gaining increasing attention and support.

Randolph, Robert Isham. "The History of Sanitation in Chicago." *Journal of the Western Society of Engineers,* 44 (Oct. 1939), 227-40. Good summary of Chicago's major wastewater and water supply projects to about 1920.

Ravenel, Mazyck P., ed. *A Half Century of Public Health: Jubilee Historical Volume of the American Public Health Association.* New York: American Public Health Association, 1921. xi + 461 pp. Illustrations, charts, tables, and index. An ambitious undertaking by the American Public Health Association in commemoration of the fiftieth anniversary of its founding. The volume contains nineteen essays on public health-related topics by experts in their respective fields. The most significant of a public works nature are: George C. Whipple's "Fifty Years of Water Purification"; Rudolph Hering's "Sewage and Solid Refuse Removal"; and Earle B. Phelps' "Stream Pollution by Industrial Wastes and Its Control."

Rawn, A. M. *Narrative—C.S.D.* Los Angeles: County Sanitation Districts of Los Angeles County, 1965. xi + 176 pp. Illustrations, maps, graphs, and appendices. Account of the development of the sewage system for Los Angeles County. The book places heavy emphasis on facilities, planning, and administration.

Reinders, Robert C. *End of an Era: New Orleans, 1850-1860.* See chapter on "Public Buildings."

Rinehart, Raymond G. *Clow Corporation: 100 Years of Service to the Water and Wastewater Industries.* New York: Newcomen Society of North America, 1979. 24 pp. Illustrations. History of a firm that manufactures clay, cast iron, and other types of pipe.

Robinson, Michael C. "People in Public Works: George E. Waring, Jr." *APWA Reporter,* 43 (Aug. 1976), 12-13. Summarizes Waring's early career and describes the separate sewer system he designed for Memphis in the wake of outbreaks of yellow fever in 1878 and 1879.

Rose, William Ganson. *Cleveland: The Making of a City.* Cleveland: World Publishing Company, 1950. 1272 pp. Illustrations, maps, appendices, and index. This book's excellent index offers access to a host of information on the city's public works. Unfortunately, the volume's strictly chronological format hinders the readers' ability to follow the evolution of the facilities.

Rosenberg, Charles E. *The Cholera Years: The United States in 1832, 1849, and 1866.* Chicago: University of Chicago Press, 1962. x + 257 pp. Notes, bibliography, and index. A vivid account of epidemics that swept American cities in the nineteenth century. It includes a great deal of information on the creation of boards of health and the adoption of better sanitary practices. But little attention is given to the construction of water supply and sewer systems.

Rosenkrantz, Barbara Gutmann. *Public Health and the State: Changing Views in Massachusetts, 1842-1936.* Cambridge: Harvard University Press, 1972. vii + 259 pp. Notes, bibliography essay, appendices, and index. A brilliant scholarly account that covers much of the state's seminal role in forging the public health and sanitary engineering professions. The book explores the process of transforming moral and scientific knowledge into public policy.

Rosenkrantz, Barbara Gutmann, ed. *Sewering the Cities.* New York: Arno Press 1977. 186 pp. Tables, diagrams, notes, and bibliography. A well-edited sampler of writings by founders of the environmental engineering field. Selections from the works of George E. Waring, Jr., Frederick S. Odell, Rudolph Hering, Hiram F. Mills, Leonard Metcalf, and Harrison P. Eddy are included.

Schultz, Stanley K., and Clay McShane. "To Engineer the Metropolis: Sewers, Sanitation, and City Planning in Late-Nineteenth-Century America." *Journal of American History.* See chapter on "Planning, Engineering, and Administration."

Schwartz, Joel. "Community Building on the Bronx Frontier: Morrisania, 1848-1875." Doctoral dissertation, University of Chicago, 1972. vi + 356 pp. Notes, appendices, and bibliography. Chapter 7 of this dissertation, "Gentlemen Disinfectors," recounts the efforts of the mid-nineteenth-century suburban community to build drainage and water systems.

Sedgwick, William T. "Water Supply Sanitation in the Nineteenth Century and in the Twentieth." *Journal of the New England Water Works Association,* XXX (June 1916), 183-94. Evolution of sanitary engineering by one of the founders of the profession.

Seidel, Harry F., ed. *Iowa's Heritage in Water Pollution Control, Including a History of the Iowa Water Pollution Control Association.* Clear Lake, Iowa: Iowa Water Pollution Control Association, 1974. ix + 613 pp. Illustrations, tables, and indexes. Good history of the Iowa Water Pollution Control Association as well as the evolution of wastewater practices in the state. The book includes chapters on pioneer engineers, the state health department, and waste treatment technology.

Seney, Donald Bradley. "The Development of Water, Sewer and Fire Service in Seattle and King County, Washington: 1851-1966." Doctoral dissertation, University of Washington, 1975. x + 206 pp. Tables, notes, appendices, and bibliography. Describes the evolution of special districts and their role in providing water, sewer, and fire services. The author contends that special districts were a natural adaptation due to the unwillingness or inability of other units of local government to provide these services.

Shedd, J. Herbert. *Report on Sewerage in the City of Providence.* Providence: Hammond, Angell, & Co., 1874. 96 pp. Map, tables, and plates. The chief engineer's (of the Providence Water Works) report on the city's "present system of sewerage." A brief historical introduction is included.

Short, C. W., and R. Stanley-Brown. *Public Buildings: A Survey of Architecture of Projects Constructed by Federal and Other Governmental Bodies between the Years 1933 and 1939 with the Assistance of the Public Works Administration.* See chapter on "Public Buildings."

Simon, Roger D. "Housing and Services in an Immigrant Neighborhood: Milwaukee's Ward 14." *Journal of Urban History,* 2 (Aug. 1976), 435-58. Includes some information on sewers and water mains.

Smillie, W. G. "Lemuel Shattuck—Still a Prophet: Lemuel Shattuck—America's Great Public Health Pioneer." *American Journal of Public Health,* 39 (Feb. 1949), 135-44. Excellent summary of the sanitation pioneer from Massachusetts.

Smillie, Wilson G. *Public Health: Its Promise for the Future.* New York: MacMillan Company, 1955. x + 501 pp. Illustrations, charts, appendix, and indexes. A chronicle of the development of public health in the United States, 1607-1914. There are informative chapters on epidemics, environmental sanitation and sanitary surveys, the 1850 Shattuck report, city and state health departments, and the American Public Health and American Medical associations.

Smillie, W. G. "The National Board of Health, 1879-1883." *American Journal of Public Health,* 33 (Aug. 1943), 925-30. Concise discussion of a short-lived national health program. The author concludes that the board was "good sanitarians but poor politicians." It made the mistake of trying to encroach upon state prerogatives.

Smith, Duane A. *Rocky Mountain Mining Camps: The Urban Frontier.* See chapter on "Roads, Streets, and Highways."

Speer, James Brooks, Jr. "Contagion and the Constitution: Public Health in the Texas Coastal Region, 1836-1909." Doctoral dissertation. See chapter on "Community Water Supply."

Spray, Anne. "People in Public Works: Mark Owen." *APWA Reporter,* 45 (Sept. 1978), 4-5. A detailed discussion of Owen's major accomplishment—solving Dearborn, Michigan's sewage disposal problems.

Stern, Madeleine B. *We the Women: Career Firsts of Nineteenth-Century America.* New York: Schulte Publishing Company, 1963. xi + 403 pp. Illustrations, notes, and index. Short biographical sketches of nineteenth-century women and their accomplishments. Of particular interest is the chapter on Ellen Richards, the first woman graduate of the Massachusetts Institute of Technology who became well known among sanitary engineers for her work with Thomas Messinger Drown in examining Massachusetts' water resources for the State Board of Health.

Stewart, George R. *Not So Rich As You Think.* See chapter on "Solid Wastes."

Still, Bayrd. "Milwaukee, 1870-1900: The Emergence of a Metropolis." *Wisconsin Magazine of History.* See chapter on "Solid Wastes."

Still, Bayrd. *Milwaukee: The History of a City.* Madison: State Historical Society of Wisconsin, 1948. xvi + 638 pp. An excellent city history that gives coverage to the development of the public works infrastructure at various periods of Milwaukee's growth. The discussions of street paving and sewage and garbage disposal are particularly noteworthy.

Stoner, Carol, ed. *Goodbye to the Flush Toilet.* Emmaus, Pa.: Rodale Press, 1977. 296 pp. Illustrations, bibliography, and appendix.

Sutherland, Douglas. *Fifty Years on the Civic Front.* See chapter on "Solid Wastes."

Tannian, Francis Xavier. "Water and Sewer Supply Decisions: A Case Study of the Washington Suburban Sanitary Commission." Doctoral dissertation. See chapter on "Community Water Supply."

Tarr, Joel Arthur. *A Study in Boss Politics: William Lorimer of Chicago.* See chapter on "Waterways."

Tarr, Joel A. "From City to Farm: Urban Wastes and the American Farmer." *Agricultural History,* XLIX (Oct. 1975), 598-612. Definitive historical study of the use of sewage farming to dispose of municipal wastes. Tarr notes that many practices proposed by contemporary environmentalists were widely used in the past.

Tarr, Joel A. "Disputes Over Water Quality Policy: Professional Cultures in Conflict, 1900-1917." *American Journal of Public Health,* 70 (April 1980), 427-35.

Tarr, Joel A., and Francis Clay McMichael. "Decisions About Wastewater Technology: 1850-1932." *Journal of the Water Resources Planning and Management Division, A.S.C.E.,* 103 (May 1977), 47-61. Exemplary study of the evolution of environmental decision-making. The study is divided into three well-defined periods that involved key technological controversies: (1) 1850-1880, whether to build sewers for domestic wastes; (2) 1880-1900, whether to build separate or combined sewers; and (3) 1900-1932, whether to treat domestic sewage before its discharge into natural waterways.

Tarr, Joel A., and Francis Clay McMichael. "Historic Turning Points in Municipal Water Supply and Wastewater Disposal, 1850-1932." *Civil Engineering,* 47 (Oct. 1977), 82-6. Excellent overview of wastewater management practices. The key "turning points" according to the authors were: the replacement of cesspools and privy vaults by sewers; the debate over whether to construct separate or combined sewers; and the decision to discharge untreated sewage into surface waters, relying on natural purification and filtration of community water supplies to safeguard public health.

Tarr, Joel A. "Out of Sight, Out of Mind." *American History Illustrated,* 10 (Jan. 1976), 40-7. Describes how municipalities attempted to secure sound and economical methods of sewage disposal as America's burgeoning population moved into towns and cities at the turn of the century.

Tarr, Joel A., and Francis Clay McMichael. *Retrospective Assessment of Wastewater Technology in the United States, 1800-1972.* Washington, D.C.: National Science Foundation (Grant ERP-08870), 1977. xvi + 333 pp. Notes and bibliography. A seminal and definitive study on the evolution of wastewater treatment systems. The study focuses upon the areas of technology development and implementation; impacts on the health, governmental, economic, and values areas; and the development of policy to deal with the regulation of water quality.

Tarr, Joel A., ed. *Retrospective Technology Assessment—1976.* San Francisco: San Francisco Press, 1977. x + 326 pp. Charts, graphs, notes, and bibliographies. Pathbreaking collection of papers delivered at a 1976 Conference on Retrospective Technology Assessment that attempt to illustrate the value of historical analysis in strengthening technology assessment and policy analysis. Case studies are included on the Erie Canal, BART, evolution of wastewater technology, planning for electrical power supply, and the evolution of airports.

Tarr, Joel A. "The Separate vs. Combined Sewer Problem: A Case Study in Urban Technology Design Choice." *Journal of Urban History,* 5 (May 1979), 309-39. This definitive article "focuses upon the elements in decisions about sewerage system design choice in the later nineteenth and early twentieth centuries." Following a discussion of the replacement of privies and cesspools with water carriage facilities, Tarr relates the struggle of engineers to develop a model, economically feasible wastewater system. Combined sewers were more widely adopted, but they created public health problems for downstream communities. However, urban areas resisted conversion to separate sewers and wastewater treatment plants because of the costs involved. Tarr uses the controversy to provide useful insights into the relationships between scientific theories, engineering practice, technological design, and economics.

Tarr, Joel A., and Francis C. McMichael. "Water & Wastes: A History." *Water Spectrum,* 10 (Fall 1978), 18-25. Solid overview of the evolution of wastewater systems. The authors point out that sewerage solved the immediate problems of waste disposal, but caused pollution of community water supplies.

Teaford, Jon C. *City and Suburb: The Political Fragmentation of Metropolitan America, 1850-1970.* See chapter on "Planning, Engineering, and Administration."

"The Almanac of Significant Events in Building a Greater America, 1874-1949." *Engineering News-Record.* See chapter on "Planning, Engineering, and Administration."

"The Bacterial Purification of Sewage." *En-*

gineering Record, XL (July 22, and July 29, 1899), July 22: 167-69; July 29: 195-98. Identifies important landmarks in the field's development.

Thelen, David P. *The New Citizenship: Origins of Progressivism in Wisconsin, 1885-1900.* See chapter on "Urban Mass Transportation."

Thompson, Carl D. *Public Ownership: A Survey of Public Enterprises, Municipal, State, and Federal, in the United States and Elsewhere.* See chapter on "Energy."

Thompson, John T. "Governmental Responses to the Challenges of Water Resources in Texas." *Southwestern Historical Quarterly.* See chapter on "Waterways."

Tillson, Geo. W. "The Sewerage System of Omaha." *Proceedings of the Nebraska Association of Engineers and Surveyors,* I (1884-1885), 56-64. Reports on the role of George E. Waring (1881).

Tindall, William. *Origin and Government of the District of Columbia.* See chapter on "Planning, Engineering, and Administration."

United States Public Health Service. "Municipal Health Department Practice for the Year 1923: Based upon Surveys of the 100 Largest Cities in the United States." *Public Health Bulletin.* See chapter on "Community Water Supply."

Van Tassel, Alfred J., ed. *Our Environment: The Outlook for 1980.* See chapter on "Community Water Supply."

Wade, Richard C. *The Urban Frontier: The Rise of Western Cities, 1790-1830.* See chapter on "Community Water Supply."

Waring, George E., Jr. *Modern Methods of Sewage Disposal for Towns, Public Institutions, and Isolated Houses.* New York: D. Van Nostrand Company, 1896. vi + 253 pp. Diagrams and index. A classic treatise by a pioneering environmental engineer. The book includes chapters on sewage irrigation, filtration, aeration, chemical treatment, and antipollution laws.

Waring, George E., Jr. *Report on the Social Statistics of Cities.* 2 vols. See chapter on "Planning, Engineering, and Administration."

Waring, George E., Jr. *The Sanitary Drainage of Houses and Towns.* Boston: Houghton, Mifflin and Company, 1898. 366 pp. Maps, tables, diagrams, and index. A classic sanitary treatise by one of the United States' pioneer environmental engineers. Waring describes various methods of handling sewage and storm-water runoff. He advocates the development of separate sewer systems as opposed to more common combined sewers.

Warner, Sam B., Jr. "Public Health Reform and the Depression of 1873-1878." *Bulletin of the History of Medicine,* XXIX (1955), 503-16. Concludes that the depression had only a "slight retarding effect on the public health movement in the United States." Most notably, the article discusses water and sewer projects undertaken by various cities.

Welch, William Henry. *Public Health in Theory and Practice: An Historical Review.* New Haven: Yale University Press, 1925. 51 pp. A breezy, shallow review of public health that contains some historical references to sewers and wastewater treatment.

Wertenbaker, Thomas J. *Norfolk: Historic Southern Port.* Durham: Duke University Press, 1931. xi + 378 pp. Illustrations, map, notes, and index. An exemplary piece of public history. Written under contract with the city of Norfolk, the major portion of the book covers the town's history to about 1880. A great deal of unique material is included on eighteenth- and nineteenth-century public works.

Whatley, Larry. "The Works Progress Administration in Mississippi." *Journal of Mississippi History.* See chapter on "Public Buildings."

Wheeler, Cyrenus, Jr. "Sewers Ancient and Modern." *Collections of the Cayuga County Historical Society,* 5 (1887), 15-108. Rare and insightful case study of sewers built in the county. The article is embellished by numerous drawings of sewerage systems that are an important historical source.

Whipple, George Chandler. *State Sanitation: A Review of the Work of the Massachusetts State Board of Health.* 3 vols. Cambridge: Harvard University Press, 1917.

Whitaker, J. Russell, and Edward A. Ackerman. *American Resources: Their Management and Conservation.* New York: Harcourt, Brace and Company, 1951. xi + 497 pp. Maps, charts, graphs, notes, and indexes. A good conservation text that includes discussions of water pollution, municipal supplies, flood control, irrigation, and hydroelectric power.

White, Gilbert F., ed. *Water, Health and Society: Selected Papers by Abel Wolman.* Bloomington: Indiana University Press, 1969. xii + 400 pp. Outstanding collection of papers, many historical, by one of the nation's foremost engineer-philosophers.

Wilcox, Delos F. *Municipal Franchises.* See chapter on "Urban Mass Transportation."

Williams, Benezette. "The Pullman Sewerage." *Association of Engineering Societies,* I (June 1882), 311-19. Important classic article that describes one of the separate sewer systems built in the United States.

Williams, C. Arch. *The Sanitary District of Chicago: History of Its Growth and Development As Shown By Decisions of the Courts and Work Of Its Law Department.* See chapter on "Waterways."

Williams, Huntington. "The Influence of Edwin Chadwick on American Public Health." *Baltimore Health News,* XXXIII (Dec. 1956), 97-112. Rare and useful source on the origins of environmental engineering and public health. The author provides extensive quotes from the writings of nineteenth century public health pioneers in which they pay homage to Chadwick.

Williams, Ralph Chester. *The United States Public Health Service, 1798-1950.* Washington, D.C.: United States Public Health Service, 1951. 890 pp. Illustrations, map, chart, bibliography, and index. A straightforward account of "the origin, evolution, organization, and activities of the Public Health Service since its establishment" by the assistant surgeon general of the service. Portions of several chapters describe the engineering and sanitation work of the service and deserve attention.

Wilson, William Edgar. "Environment as a Cross National Problem: Great Lakes Water Pollution, 1948-1972." Doctoral dissertation. See chapter on "Planning, Engineering, and Administration."

Winslow, C. E. A. "Lemuel Shattuck—Still a Prophet: The Message of Lemuel Shattuck for 1948." *American Journal of Public Health,* 39 (Feb. 1949), 156-62. A paean to Shattuck's pioneering public health work, especially his *Report of the Sanitary Commission of Massachusetts* (1850).

Winslow, C. E. A. "The Scientific Disposal of City Sewage: Historical Development and Present Status of the Problem." *Technology Quarterly,* XVIII (1905), 317-32.

Wolman, Abel. "Contributions of Engineering to Health Advancement." *Transactions of the American Society of Civil Engineers,* CT (1953), 579-87. Describes the role of the sanitary engineer "in the successful fight against disease in the United States."

Wolman, Abel. "George Warren Fuller: A Reminiscence." *Essays in Public Works History.* See chapter on "Community Water Supply."

Wolman, Abel. "Lemuel Shattuck—Still a Prophet: Sanitation of Yesterday—But What of Tomorrow?" *American Journal of Public Health,* 39 (Feb. 1949), 145-50. Interesting analysis of Shattuck's famous 1850 report on public health conditions in Massachusetts. Wolman contends that many of the unsanitary conditions he documented still exist.

Wolman, Abel. "Values in the Control of Environment." *American Journal of Public Health,* XV (March 1925), 189-94. A classic plea for greater communication and cooperation between engineers and public health officials. Wolman argues that sound principles of engineering and city planning should be implemented to create a healthier environment for citizens.

Wright, Jim. *The Coming Water Famine.* See chapter on "Irrigation."

Wright, Lawrence. *Clean and Decent: The Fascinating History of the Bathroom & the Water Closet.* London: Routledge & Kegan Paul, 1960. xii + 282 pp. Illustrations, bibliography, and index. Although most of the examples in this book are British, it offers a good overview of the evolution of bathroom fixtures.

Zimmerman, Jane. "The Formative Years of the North Carolina Board of Health, 1877-1893." *North Carolina Historical Review.* See chapter on "Community Water Supply."

Zueblin, Charles. *American Municipal Progress: Chapters in Municipal Sociology.* See chapter on "Planning, Engineering, and Administration."

6

Community Water Supply

The development of clean, plentiful water supplies played an important role in America's urbanization. Today, some 80 percent of the United States' population receives its supplies from water systems managed by city and town governments. The public well and the oaken bucket have evolved into sophisticated public works systems comprising collection facilities that tap surface and groundwater supplies, treatment plants that treat and purify raw water, conduits that convey it to cities, and networks of distribution mains that carry the resource to domestic and industrial consumers.

The books, articles, and dissertations cited in this chapter trace the evolution of community water supplies from reliance on nearby streams, wells, and springs in the colonial era to the construction of huge aqueducts that draw upon sources scores of miles from urban centers. As local sources became overtaxed and contaminated, water was sought from outlying rivers and lakes as well as impounded in reservoirs. The burgeoning growth of cities since the Civil War forced governments to make large expenditures for monumental public water systems. The quest for supplies required the creation of large governmental agencies, a rapid expansion of water technology, and cooperative efforts by cities, states, and the federal government. Water treatment systems were also developed to render the supplies safe for public consumption and free from turbidity, color, odor, and bad taste.

Historians are stepping up their efforts to explore the political, engineering, legal, and economic aspects of this subject. Long a relatively neglected corner of urban history, public water supplies are now an important concern of students of the urban environment.

Abbott, Carl. "Civic Pride in Chicago, 1844-1860." *Journal of the Illinois State Historical Society.* See chapter on "Roads, Streets, and Highways."

Abbott, Samuel W. *The Past and Present Conditions of Public Hygiene and State Medicine in the United States.* See chapter on "Sewers and Wastewater Treatment."

Allinson, Edward P., and Boise Penrose. *Philadelphia, 1681-1887: A History of Municipal Development.* See chapter on "Planning, Engineering, and Administration."

Alvord, John W. "Recent Progress and Tendencies in Municipal Water Supply in the United States." *Journal of the American Water Works Association,* 4 (Sept. 1917), 278-99.

Substantive overview of the evolution of municipal water supplies from 1900 to 1916. The article includes interesting tables on the implementation of water filtration, adoption of chlorination, and use of water meters.

"An Outline History of New York's Water Supply." *New York Historical Society Bulletin,* 1 (Oct. 1917), 63-70. Good illustrations but a vapid narrative.

Anderson, Glenn F. "The Social Effects of the Construction of the Wachusett Reservoir on Boylston and West Boylston." *Historical Journal of Western Massachusetts,* III (Spring 1974), 51-58. Amateurish attempt to analyze the reservoir's influence on the growth of two Massachusetts communities.

Andrews, George C. "The Buffalo Water Works." *Journal of the American Water Works Association,* 17 (March 1927), 279-90. Records the facility's history from 1831.

Armstrong, Ellis L.; Michael C. Robinson; and Suellen M. Hoy, eds. *History of Public Works in the United States, 1776-1976.* See chapter on "Planning, Engineering, and Administration."

Armstrong, James W. "History of Water Supply with Local Reference to Baltimore." *Journal of the American Water Works Association,* 24 (1932), 529-44.

Armstrong, Roger W. "The Delaware Water Supply System of the City of New York." *Civil Engineering,* 8 (Sept. 1938), 581-84. Reviews the general history of the project and reports on its present status.

Arpee, Edward. *Lake Forest Illinois: History and Reminiscences, 1861-1961.* Lake Forest: Rotary Club of Lake Forest, 1963. xv + 277 pp. Illustrations, bibliography, and index. Touches briefly upon the history of the community's water supply, streets, and public buildings.

Arrington, Leonard J., and Lowell Dittmer. "Reclamation in Three Layers: The Ogden River Project, 1934-1965." *Pacific Historical Review,* XXXV (Feb. 1966), 15-34. Interesting discussion of a project in northern Utah that provides both domestic and irrigation water.

Arrington, Leonard J., and Thomas G. Alexander. *Water for Urban Reclamation: The Provo River Project.* Logan: Utah State University Press, 1966.

Arthur, J. D., Jr. "The History of Washington's Water Supply System." *Journal of the American Water Works Association,* 25 (Aug. 1933), 1081-83. A thin technical sketch.

Atkins, Gordon. *Health, Housing, and Poverty in New York City, 1865-1898.* See chapter on "Roads, Streets, and Highways."

Baker, M. N. *Municipal Engineering and Sanitation.* See chapter on "Planning, Engineering, and Administration."

Baker, M. N. "New Jersey—Birthplace of the Filter." *Engineering News-Record,* 122 (June 8, 1939), 777-78. Origins of the mechanical filter.

Baker, M. N. "Sketch of the History of Water Treatment." *Journal of the American Water Works Association,* 26 (July 1934), 902-38. Major landmarks of efforts to control disease, odor, and taste through water treatment.

Baker, M. N. "Story of the Boston Broadside." *Engineering News-Record,* 123 (Aug. 31, 1939), 70. Antecedents of Boston's vast Metropolitan Water District.

Baker, M. N. *The Quest for Pure Water: The History of Water Purification From the Earliest Records to the Twentieth Century.* New York: American Water Works Association, 1948. xiv + 527 pp. Illustrations, notes, and index. Dated but still remains the only attempt to comprehensively survey the subject. Baker stresses technological benchmarks and deals little with the institutional development of water systems. The bibliography is an excellent research tool.

Baker, M. N. "The Three Jewells—Pioneers in Mechanical Filtration." *Engineering News-Record,* 126 (Jan. 31, 1941), 51. Tribute to the family that pioneered the rapid filtration of municipal water supplies in the late nineteenth century.

Baker, T. Lindsay. "Ballinger's Early Waterwork System." *Southwest Water Works Journal,* LVI (Nov. 1974), 24. System for a West Texas city.

Baker, T. Lindsay. "Cleburn: A Case Study for Small City Water Systems." *Southwest Water Works Journal,* LVI (Sept. 1974), 34, 36.

Baker, T. Lindsay. "Houston Waterworks: Its Early Development." *Southwest Water Works*

Journal, LVI (July 1974), 37. Short essay on the first Houston waterworks built in 1879.

Baker, T. Lindsay. "Some Unusual Water Pipelines of the Southwest." *Cast Iron Pipe News,* XLII (Spring-Summer 1975), 9-12. In Tombstone, Prescott, and Jerome, Arizona; in Galveston, Texas; and the water pipeline system constructed by the El Paso and Southwestern Railway in central New Mexico.

Baker, T. Lindsay. "The Buffalo Gap Waterworks." *Southwest Water Works Journal,* LVII (Jan. 1976), 6-8.

Baker, T. Lindsay. "The Calvert Water, Ice and Electric Plant." *Southwest Water Works Journal,* LVI (Dec. 1974), 7-8.

Baker, T. Lindsay. "The Fort Davis Military Waterworks." *Southwest Water Works Journal,* LVI (April 1974), 14, 16. Description of a waterworks constructed for the post in the 1880s.

Baker, T. Lindsay. "The 1904 Abilene Water Tower Failure." *Southwest Water Works Journal,* LVI (Aug. 1974), 6-7. Sketch of the failure of a public works facility.

Baker, T. Lindsay. "The Remarkable Cast Iron of the Galveston Ironworks." *Cast Iron Pipe News,* XLII (Winter 1974-1975), 4-8. Describes the nineteenth-century structures in Galveston's waterworks system.

Baker, T. Lindsay. "The Rise of Waterworks in the Southwest." *Southwest Water Works Journal,* LV (Feb. 1974), 4-5, 7. Brief discussions of several early waterworks in small southwestern communities.

Baker, T. Lindsay. "The Windmill Waterworks of Post City." *Southwest Water Works Journal,* LV (March 1974), 4-6. Interesting discussion of an unusual waterworks built for Post City, Texas.

Baldwin, Bert L. "Development of Cincinnati's Water Supply." *Military Engineer,* XXII (July-Aug.), 320-24. Excellent sketch of the city's water supply history that includes rare illustrations of wooden pipes and an 1821 horse-driven pumping station.

Ballard, Robert M. "Pollution in Lake Erie, 1872-1965." *Special Libraries.* See chapter on "Sewers and Wastewater Treatment."

Barnes, Joseph W. "Water Works History: A Comparison of Albany, Utica, Syracuse, and Rochester." *Rochester History,* XXIX (July 1977), 1-24. A sound comparative analysis of water supply development in four upstate New York cities. The author notes that obtaining a dependable supply was often preceded by agonizing delays, trials, and errors. Private water companies eventually gave way to public ownership in the four cities. The essay also recounts the engineering achievements that are the basis of these public works systems.

Barney, Percy C. "Catskill Water System of New York City." *Brooklyn Engineers' Club Proceedings* (Jan. 1911), 51-75. Offers a good overview on the technical planning and legislative aspects of the system.

Bean, Walton. *Boss Reuf's San Francisco: The Story of the Union Labor Party, Big Business, and the Graft Prosecution.* Berkeley: University of California Press, 1967. xii + 345 pp. Illustrations, notes, bibliography, and index. Some information on the history of San Francisco's street railway and water supply systems is included in this fine study of turn-of-the-century machine politics and reform.

Beard, Mary Ritter. *Woman's Work in Municipalities.* See chapter on "Solid Wastes."

Bebout, John E., and Ronald J. Grele. *Where Cities Meet: The Urbanization of New Jersey.* See chapter on "Urban Mass Transportation."

Becker, Elmer W. *A Century of Milwaukee Water: A Historical Account of the Origin and Development of the Milwaukee Water Works.* Milwaukee: Privately printed, 1974. vi + 330 pp. Illustrations, maps, tables, charts, diagrams, and bibliography. This obscure volume is a valuable case study of municipal water supply development. The author, a forty-seven-year veteran of the Milwaukee Water Works, meticulously chronicles the evolution of the system's facilities—intake cribs, reservoirs, water towers, pumping plants, pipes, water treatment, and meters. In addition, the book contains information on maintenance, water rates, department organization, financing, and other subjects rarely addressed by historians.

Bemis, Edward W., ed. *Municipal Monopolies.* See chapter on "Urban Mass Transportation."

Bettmann, Otto L. *The Good Old Days—They Were Terrible!* See chapter on "Solid Wastes."

Black, Gordon G. "The Construction and Reconstruction of Compton Hill Reservoir." *Journal of the Engineers' Club of St. Louis,* 2 (Jan.-Feb. 1917), 4-42. Presents a summary history of St. Louis' water system.

Blake, John B. "Lemuel Shattuck and the Boston Water Supply." *Bulletin of the History of Medicine,* XXIX (1955), 554-62. Outlines Shattuck's role in the development of Boston's water supply in 1840s. The author is critical of the pioneer public health advocate's opposition to municipal ownership of the system.

Blake, John B. "The Origins of Public Health in the United States." *American Journal of Public Health.* See chapter on "Sewers and Wastewater Treatment."

Blake, John B. *Public Health in the Town of Boston, 1630-1822.* Cambridge: Harvard University Press, 1959. x + 278 pp. Maps, notes, appendices, bibliography, and index. Although primarily concerned with the founding and implementation of basic health policies and the prevention and control of yellow fever and small pox, there is a brief discussion of the relationship of the town's sanitary conditions, especially of public water supplies and thoroughfares, to endemic disease.

Blake, Nelson Manfred. *Water for the Cities: A History of the Urban Water Supply Problem in the United States.* Syracuse: Syracuse University Press, 1956. x + 341 pp. Illustrations, maps, notes, and index. The most important book published thus far on urban water supply systems. Blake examines municipal supply problems of New York, Philadelphia, Baltimore, and Boston from 1790 to 1860. The definitive account covers all aspects of his topic—planning, financing, engineering, administration, public health, and politics. The book was written "in the conviction that municipal statesmen and engineers who preserve and enrich life through providing an essential service deserve to have their names and deeds recorded in the history of the nation no less than do presidents, generals, and philosophers. . . ."

Bluestone, Daniel M., ed. *Cleveland: An Inventory of Historic Engineering and Industrial Sites.* Washington, D.C.: Historic American Engineering Record, 1978. vi + 118 pp. Illustrations and index. Includes short, descriptive sketches of waterworks, bridges, and water transportation facilities.

Bridenbaugh, Carl. *Cities in Revolt: Urban Life in America, 1743-1776.* See chapter on "Planning, Engineering, and Administration."

Bridenbaugh, Carl. *Cities in the Wilderness: The First Century of Urban Life in America, 1625-1742.* See chapter on "Planning, Engineering, and Administration."

Brooklyn Water Committee. *Documents and Plans Submitted by the Water Committee, to the Common Council of the City of Brooklyn, For the Year 1854.* Brooklyn: John W. Heighway and Company, 1954. 145 pp. + 27 plates. Illustrations, drawings, maps, and tables. The water committee's report is "a plan to supply the city with water for the determination of the Common Council. . . ."

Brooklyn Water Supply Division. *History and Description of the Water Supply of the City of Brooklyn.* Brooklyn: Department of City Works, Division of Water Supply, 1896. xxiv + 306 pp. Illustrations, diagrams, maps, and bibliography. Contains a beautiful collection of project features, some hand-colored.

Brown, A. Theodore. "The Politics of Reform: Kansas City Municipal Government, 1925-1950." Doctoral dissertation. See chapter on "Planning, Engineering, and Administration."

Brownell, Blaine A. *The Urban Ethos in the South.* See chapter on "Planning, Engineering, and Administration."

Brush, William W. "City Aqueduct to Deliver Catskill Water Supply to the Five Boroughs of Greater New York." *Brooklyn Engineers' Club Proceedings* (Jan. 1911), 76-114. Good source of background and technical information on the Catskill Aqueduct.

Bryan, Wilhelmus Bogart. *A History of the National Capital: From Its Foundation through the Period of the Adoption of the Organic Act.* See chapter on "Planning, Engineering, and Administration."

Bureau of the Census (Department of Commerce and Labor). *Statistics of Cities Having a Population of 8,000 to 25,000: 1903.* See chapter on "Roads, Streets, and Highways."

Bureau of the Census (Department of Commerce and Labor). *Statistics of Cities Having a Population of 30,000: 1904.* See chapter on "Roads, Streets, and Highways."

Burlingame, Roger. *Engines of Democracy: Inventions and Society in Mature America.* See chapter on "Energy."

Cain, Louis P. "Raising and Watering a City: Ellis Sylvester Chesbrough and Chicago's First Sanitation System." *Technology and Culture,* 13 (July 1972), 353-72. Excellent discussion of the sewerage and water supply systems Chesbrough designed and built for Chicago in the 1850s and 1860s.

Cain, Louis P. "The Search for an Optimum Sanitation Jurisdiction: The Metropolitan Sanitary District of Greater Chicago, a Case Study." *Essays in Public Works History.* See chapter on "Sewers and Wastewater Treatment."

Caird, James M. "The Operation of an American or Rapid Water Filtration Plant for Twenty Years at Elmira, New York." *Journal of the American Water Works Association,* 6 (Sept. 1919), 409-21. Illustrates influence of the facility on the city's public health.

Calhoun, Richard Boyd. "From Community to Metropolis: Fire Protection in New York City, 1790-1875." Doctoral dissertation, Columbia University, 1973. 374 pp.

Capen, Charles H., Jr. "History of the Development of the Use of Water in Northeastern New Jersey." *Journal of the American Water Works Association,* 28 (Aug. 1936), 973-82.

Carr, Donald E. *Death of Sweet Waters.* New York: W. W. Norton & Company, 1966. 257 pp. Illustrations, bibliography, and index. An environmental manifesto and survey of various forms of water pollution. In addition to firing broadsides at industrial pollution, the author is critical of the programs of the Army Corps of Engineers, Bureau of Reclamation, and other water resource agencies.

Carrott, Richard G. *The Egyptian Revival: Its Sources, Monuments, and Meaning, 1808–1858.* See chapter on "Public Buildings."

Cassedy, James H. "Hygeia: A Mid-Victorian Dream of a City of Health." *Journal of the History of Medicine and Allied Sciences.* See chapter on "Sewers and Wastewater Treatment."

Catlin, George B. *The Story of Detroit.* Detroit: The Detroit News, 1923. xix + 764 pp. Illustrations, appendix, and index. An informative urban biography that contains insightful vignettes on water supply, streets and bridges, parks, street lighting, mass transit, and harbor improvements.

Caufield, John. "St. Paul Water Works." *Fire and Water,* XXII (May 29, 1897), 182-83. Overview of the city's water works with excellent illustrations.

Chambers, J. S. *The Conquest of Cholera: America's Greatest Scourge.* New York: Macmillan Company, 1938. xiv + 366 pp. Illustrations, maps, notes, bibliography, and index. Although most of the book deals with descriptions of epidemics and the work of microbe hunters, it contains some examples of early water purification and sewage disposal practices.

Chapin, Charles V. *Municipal Sanitation in the United States.* See chapter on "Solid Wastes."

Chase, E. Sherman. "Progress in Sanitary Engineering in the United States." *Transactions of the American Society of Civil Engineers.* See chapter on "Sewers and Wastewater Treatment."

Chase, E. Sherman. "75 Years of Progress in Water Supply Engineering." *Journal of the American Water Works Association,* 48 (Aug. 1956), 915-24. A sketchy survey that discusses some important landmarks.

Chicago Bureau of Public Efficiency. *The Water Works System of the City of Chicago.* Chicago: Chicago Bureau of Public Efficiency, 1917. 207 pp. Maps, charts, tables, graphs, and notes. A good descriptive summary of Chicago's pre-1920 water supply and distribution system.

"Chicago's Water Works a Half-Century Ago." *Public Works,* 62 (June 1931), 30-31, 60.

Civic Club of Allegheny County, Pittsburgh, Pennsylvania. *Fifty Years of Civic History, 1895-1945.* See chapter on "Solid Wastes."

Clark, Alfred. "The San Gabriel River: A Century of Dividing the Waters." *Southern California Quarterly.* See chapter on "Irrigation."

Clarke, T. Wood. *Utica for a Century and a Half.* Utica, N.Y.: Widtman Press, 1952. xiii + 332 pp. Illustrations, bibliography, and index. A pedestrian urban history that includes some sketchy information on water supply, street railways, parks, and electric utilities.

Cleary, Edward J. "Perspective on River-Quality Diagnosis." *Journal of the American Water Works Association,* 69 (Oct. 1977), 522-27. Insightful discussion of past assessments of river-quality conditions. Cleary stresses "the elusiveness of the task and magnitude of effort required to cope with this basic component of water-resources management."

Cleary, Edward J. *The ORSANCO Story: Water Quality Management in the Ohio Valley under an Interstate Compact.* See chapter on "Sewers and Wastewater Treatment."

Clements, Kendrick A. "Engineers and Conservationists in the Progressive Era." *California History,* LVIII (Winter 1979/1980), 282-303. Focuses on the Hetch Hetchy controversy, particularly the role of city engineer Marsden Manson in spearheading the campaign to dam the Tuolumne River to provide San Francisco a dependable water supply.

Clepper, Henry. *Origins of American Conservation.* See chapter on "Flood Control and Drainage."

Cleveland Engineering Society. *The Golden Anniversary Book of the Cleveland Engineering Society.* See chapter on "Planning, Engineering, and Administration."

Conant, E. R. "History of the Artesian Water Supply at Savannah, Georgia." *Journal of the American Water Works Association,* 5 (Sept. 1918), 252-62. Sketch of an unusual municipal water supply system begun in 1882.

Connery, Robert H., and Richard H. Leach. *The Federal Government and Metropolitan Areas.* See chapter on "Planning, Engineering, and Administration."

Cooke, Morris Llewellyn, ed. *Public Utility Regulation.* See chapter on "Energy."

Cooper, Erwin. *Aqueduct Empire: A Guide to Water in California, Its Turbulent History and Its Management Today.* See chapter on "Irrigation."

Corbin, Harry F. "The Politics of Water: Wichita to Washington." Doctoral dissertation, University of Chicago, 1972. v + 251 pp. Notes, appendix, and bibliography. A history of attempts to develop a dependable water supply for Wichita, Kansas, through construction of Cheney Dam on the Ninnescah River.

Corn, Jacqueline Karnell. "Municipal Organization for Public Health in Pittsburgh, 1851-1895." Doctoral dissertation, Carnegie-Mellon University, 1972. 141 pp. Tables, notes, and bibliography. Describes general nineteenth-century public health issues, specific public health conditions in Pittsburgh, how and why residents organized to promote community health, the institutions that evolved, and medical advances which changed policies and practices. The author contends that "when environmental conditions and epidemics of disease in Pittsburgh could no longer be satisfactorily dealt with on an individual basis, the municipality assumed responsibility, albeit limited responsibility, in these matters." The Board of Health's activities are characterized as inadequate and crisis-oriented.

Corn, Jacqueline Karnell. "Social Response to Epidemic Disease in Pittsburgh, 1872–1895." *Western Pennsylvania Historical Magazine,* 56 (Jan. 1973), 59–70. Briefly discusses the public's perception of the need for water systems and other public works to combat disease.

Cowdrey, Albert E. *A City for the Nation: The Army Engineers and the Building of Washington, D.C., 1790-1967.* See chapter on "Planning, Engineering, and Administration."

Cox, James Lee. "The Development and Administration of Water Supply Problems in the Denver Metropolitan Area." Doctoral dissertation, University of Colorado, 1966. 404 pp.

Creighton, Wilbur Foster. *Building of Nashville.* See chapter on "Public Buildings."

Cullen, Allan H. *Rivers in Harness: The Story of Dams.* See chapter on "Irrigation."

Dale, Edward Everett. "Wood and Water: Twin Problems of the Prairie Plains." *Nebraska History,* XXIX (June 1948), 87-104. Relates the difficulties of securing these two necessities.

Darwin, A. Gilbert. "Seattle's Water Supply System." *Western Construction News,* 5 (Feb. 10, 1930), 62-71. Includes a history of the system's operating features.

Davey, Norman. *A History of Building Materials.* See chapter on "Public Buildings."

Davies, J. Clarence III. *The Politics of Pollution.* See chapter on "Sewers and Wastewater Treatment."

Davison, George S. "A Century and a Half of American Engineering." *Proceedings of the American Society of Civil Engineers.* See chapter on "Planning, Engineering, and Administration."

Davisson, William I. "Public Utilities in a Frontier City: The Early History of the Tacoma Light and Water Company." *Pacific Northwest Quarterly,* 46 (April 1965), 40-45. Good case study of a nineteenth-century public utility.

DeBerard, W. W. "Expansion of the Chicago, Ill., Water Supply." *Transactions of the American Society of Civil Engineers,* CT (1953), 588-603. A history of Chicago's water system by the city's deputy commissioner for water.

Derry, T. K., and Trevor I. Williams. *A Short History of Technology: From the Earliest Times to A.D. 1900.* See chapter on "Planning, Engineering, and Administration."

Detwyler, Thomas R., and Melvin G. Marcus, eds. *Urbanization and Environment: The Physical Geography of the City.* Belmont, Calif.: Duxbury Press, 1972. viii + 287 pp. Illustrations, charts, bibliographies, and index. A good physical geography that demonstrates how humankind changed the natural environment by urbanization and how physical features have influenced the growth and function of cities. John C. Schaake, Jr.'s essay on "Water and the City" surveys urban drainage, wastewater treatment, and water supplies. Some historical information is included in this and other essays.

Dick, Everett. "Water: A Frontier Problem." *Nebraska History,* 59 (Autumn 1968), 215-45. Entertaining and deeply researched study of well-digging on the High Plains.

Doerksen, Harvey Ray. "The Columbia Interstate Compact: Politics of Water Resources in the Pacific Northwest." Doctoral dissertation. See chapter on "Energy."

Donaldson, Wellington. "Water Purification—A Retrospect." *Journal of the American Water Works Association,* 26 (Aug. 1934), 1053-63. Focuses on filtration system developed at Knoxville, Tennessee, in 1894.

Dornberger, Suzette. "The Struggle for Hetch Hetchy, 1900-1913." Master's thesis, University of California, Berkeley, 1935.

Doty, Duane (Mrs.) *The Town of Pullman: Its Growth with Brief Accounts of Its Industries.* See chapter on "Sewers and Wastewater Treatment."

Draffin, Jasper Owen. *The Story of Man's Quest for Water.* Champaign, Ill.: Garrad Press, 1939. viii + 232 pp. Illustrations, maps, bibliography, and index. Discusses ways in which communities have obtained pure water supplies in the past. The discussions are quite simple and free from heavy emphasis on engineering and technology. Specific chapters cover early American water works and the development of abundant supplies for Chicago, New York, and Los Angeles.

Dubie, Carol. "The Architecture and Engineering of Elevated Water Storage Structures, 1870-1940." Master's thesis, George Washington University, 1980. 161 pp. Illustrations and notes. A discussion of the evolution of elevated water storage structures focusing on the introduction of the all-metal elevated tank in the United States in the 1890s. Masonry wall towers, metal and concrete standpipes, and wooden and steel elevated tanks are illustrated and placed in the context of late nineteenth and early twentieth century civil engineering and architectural history.

Duffy, John. *A History of Public Health in New York City, 1866-1966.* See chapter on "Solid Wastes."

Duffy, John. *Epidemics in Colonial America.* Baton Rouge: Louisiana State University Press, 1953. xi + 274 pp. Illustrations, maps, notes, bibliographical essay, and index. A comprehensive study of the epidemic sicknesses that plagued colonial life. The author has determined the diseases involved, clarified them "in order of importance," and demonstrated "both collectively and singly their effect upon colonial development." This is an important volume in understanding and appreciating the later work of sanitary engineers and public health officials.

Eaves, Charles Dudley. "Post City: A Study in Colonization on the Texas Plains." Doctoral dissertation, University of Texas, 1943. vii + 340 pp. Illustrations, maps, notes, and bibliography. A study of the building and colonization of Post City during the early twentieth century. A good portion of the dissertation discusses the quest for water—for both city and farm residents.

Eddy, Harrison P. "Water Purification—A Century of Progress." *Civil Engineering,* 2

(Feb. 1932) 82-84. Key landmarks in the history of water infiltration and treatment.

Ellis, John, and Stuart Galishoff. "Atlanta's Water Supply, 1865-1918." *Maryland Historian,* VIII (Spring 1977), 5-22. Well-researched essay on efforts of Atlanta businessmen and water officials to keep the city's water supply abreast of rapid population growth. Fear of illness and threat of fire were used to gain support from taxpayers and politicians.

Ericson, John. *Report on the Water Supply System of Chicago, Its Past, Present and Future.* Chicago: Bureau of Engineering, 1905. 68 pp. Illustrations, charts, tables, and graphs. The principal value of this book is its rare collection of illustrations.

Finch, J. K. "A Hundred Years of American Civil Engineering, 1852-1952." *Transactions of the American Society of Civil Engineers.* See chapter on "Planning, Engineering, and Administration."

Finch, J. K. "John Bloomfield Jervis, Civil Engineer." *Transactions of the Newcomen Society (London) for the Study of the History of Engineering and Technology,* 11 (1930-1931), 109-20. Highlights of the career of the individual who, the author contends, "did more than any other man to make engineering in America a profession." Jervis' public works career included the Erie Canal, Chenango Canal, New York City's Old Croton Aqueduct, and many railroad projects.

Fisher, Edwin A. "Engineering and Public Works in the City of Rochester during the Past Century." *Centennial History of Rochester, New York.* See chapter on "Planning, Engineering, and Administration."

Fisk, Harvey E. "The Introduction of Public Rain Baths in America: A Historical Sketch." *Sanitarian,* XXXVI (June 1896), 481-501. Interesting discussion of efforts to create public baths during the 1890s. Illustrations of the facilities are included.

FitzSimons, Neal, ed. *The Reminiscences of John B. Jervis: Engineer of the Old Croton.* Syracuse, N.Y.: Syracuse University Press, 1971. x + 196 pp. Illustrations, notes, and index. A welcome addition to the limited number of autobiographical works about American engineers. Jervis, an outstanding mid-nineteenth-century engineer, was involved in a wide range of canal, railroad, and water supply projects. His most famous undertaking was New York City's Old Croton Aqueduct which was opened in 1842. The editor notes in the preface that the volume "should be of interest not only to historians of technology and Jervis' professional legatees in engineering, but also to others who would wonder about how our great public works . . . were constructed, and to those who want to gain a greater appreciation for the men who literally built our country."

Flannery, Toni. "The Water Towers of St. Louis." *Missouri Historical Society Bulletin,* XXIX (July 1973), 236-42. Descriptions of the city's five historic water towers, each an outstanding example of a different type of architecture. The article's illustrative materials are excellent.

Flaxman, Edward. *Great Feats of Modern Engineering.* See chapter on "Roads, Streets, and Highways."

Fogelson, Robert M. *The Fragmented Metropolis: Los Angeles, 1850-1930.* Cambridge: Harvard University Press, 1967. xv + 362 pp. Illustrations, maps, charts, tables, notes, bibliography, and index. A masterpiece in the literature of urban history. The book is lucidly written, soundly researched, and offers a brilliant discussion of the evolution of Los Angeles' urban form. Thoughtful coverage is given to city planning, urban water supply, mass transit, and highways. The volume also contains excellent chapters on the municipal-ownership movement during the Progressive era.

Force, Edwin T. "The Use of the Colorado River in the United States, 1850-1933." Doctoral dissertation. See chapter on "Irrigation."

Foster, Laura. "Honeymoon in Hetch Hetchy." *American West.* See chapter on "Parks and Recreation."

Fuller, George W. "Experimental Methods as Applied to Water and Sewerage Works for Large Communities." *Engineering Record,* 54 (July 21, 1906), 80-83. A very useful summary of experiments in water infiltration and purification.

Fuller, George W. "Progress in Water Purification." *Journal of the American Water Works Association,* 25 (Nov. 1933), 1566-76. Comprehensive sketch of the subject.

Fuller, George W. "The Place of Sanitary Engineering in Public Health Activities." *American Journal of Public Health.* See chapter on "Sewers and Wastewater Treatment."

Galli, Geraldine. "100 Years of Construction News." *Engineering News-Record.* See chapter on "Planning, Engineering, and Administration."

Gargan, John Joseph. "The Politics of Water Pollution in New York State: The Development and Adoption of the 1965 Pure Waters Program." Doctoral dissertation, Syracuse University, 1969.

Gilpin, Thomas. "Fairmount Dam and Waterworks, Philadelphia." *Pennsylvania Magazine of History and Biography,* XXXVII (1913), 471-79. Insightful history of the waterworks first published in 1852.

Ginsberg, Stephen F. "The History of Fire Protection in New York City, 1800-1842." Doctoral dissertation, New York University, 1968. 396 pp. Illustrates the influence of the development of the Croton water system upon growth of fire facilities.

Glaab, Charles N., and A. Theodore Brown. *A History of Urban America.* New York: Macmillan Publishing Company, 1976. xi + 350 pp. Bibliographical essay and index. Unfortunately this standard urban history survey includes very little information on the growth of public works services.

Golze, Alfred R. *Reclamation in the United States.* See chapter on "Irrigation."

Gorgas, William Crawford. *Sanitation in Panama.* See chapter on "Sewers and Wastewater Treatment."

Greeley, Samuel A. "Municipal Facilities for Public Health." *Civil Engineering.* See chapter on "Sewers and Wastewater Treatment."

Greeley, Samuel A. "Testing Stations for Sanitary Engineering—An Outstanding Achievement." *Transactions of the American Society of Civil Engineers.* See chapter on "Sewers and Wastewater Treatment."

Green, Constance McLaughlin. *History of Naugatuck, Connecticut.* See chapter on "Sewers and Wastewater Treatment."

Green, Constance McLaughlin. *Holyoke, Massachusetts: A Case History of the Industrial Revolution in America.* See chapter on "Waterways."

Green, Constance McLaughlin. *Washington: Capital City, 1879-1950.* Princeton: Princeton University Press, 1963. xvii + 558 pp. Illustrations, tables, notes, glossary, bibliographical essay, and index. One of the best urban biographies. Students of public works history will be especially interested in a chapter on "Municipal Housekeeping, 1879-1901" that includes excellent descriptions of the various facilities and services. Scattered throughout the volume are discussions of water supply, sewers, parks, highways, street lighting, and mass transportation.

Green, Constance McLaughlin. *Washington: Village and Capital, 1800-1878.* See chapter on "Urban Mass Transportation."

Greenberg, Michael R. "The Implication of Urbanization for Public Water Supply Systems in the New York Metropolitan Region." Doctoral dissertation, Columbia University, 1969. 198 pp.

Griffith, Ernest S. *A History of American City Government: The Conspicuous Failure, 1870-1900.* See chapter on "Planning, Engineering, and Administration."

Griffith, Ernest S. *A History of American City Government: The Progressive Years and Their Aftermath, 1900-1920.* See chapter on "Planning, Engineering, and Administration."

Grody, Harvey P. "From North to South: The Feather River Project and Other Legislative Water Struggles in the 1950s." *Southern California Quarterly.* See chapter on "Irrigation."

Gustafson, A. F., et al. *Conservation in the United States.* See chapter on "Parks and Recreation."

Hall, Clayton Colman, ed. *Baltimore: Its History and Its People.* 3 vols. New York: Lewis Historical Publishing Company, 1912. Vol. I: 721 pp.; Vol. II: 488 pp.; and Vol. III: 936 pp. Illustrations, maps, notes, and indexes. The first volume of this history contains considerable material on Baltimore's water supply, sewerage, streets, parks, street railways, and harbor improvements.

Hamlin, Talbot. *Benjamin Henry Latrobe.* See chapter on "Public Buildings."

Hannum, Warren T. "Water Supply of the District of Columbia." *Professional Memoirs,* IV (March-April 1912), 224-52.

Hansen, Harry. *Scarsdale: From Colonial Manor to Modern Community.* New York: Harper & Brothers, 1954. xii + 340 pp. Illustrations, maps, appendix, and index. A fine urban history that offers a great deal of information on the community's public works. Chapter XII, "The Village Manager and the Essential Services," includes discussions of the water department, street lighting, and public transportation. Subsequent chapters chronicle the growth of parks, zoning, the public library, and construction of the Bronx River Parkway.

Harkins, Michael J. "Public Health Nuisances in Omaha, 1870-1900." *Nebraska History.* See chapter on "Sewers and Wastewater Treatment."

Harris, Fisher Sanford. *100 Years of Water Development.* Salt Lake City: Metropolitan Water District of Salt Lake City, 1942. iii + 129 pp. Illustrations, maps, charts, graphs, and index. An excellent case study prepared under the auspices of the Metropolitan Water District of Salt Lake City. The book explores the city's century-long quest for a dependable water supply which culminated with the Bureau of Reclamation's Provo River Project. It offers good insight into how demands of various user groups were met.

Havemeyer, Loomis, ed., et. al. *Conservation of Our Natural Resources.* See chapter on "Irrigation."

Hazen, Allen. "Public Water Supplies." *Engineering News-Record,* 92 (April 17, 1924), 695-97. A rather sketchy discussion of major water supply and treatment developments from about 1875 to the early 1920s.

Hazen, Allen. *The Filtration of Public Water-Supplies.* New York: John Wiley & Sons, 1900. xii + 321 pp. Illustrations, charts, tables, diagrams, appendices, and index. Classic text on the design and operation of early water filtration systems.

Hazen, Richard. "People in Public Works: Allen Hazen." *APWA Reporter,* 47 (Aug. 1980), 4-6. An unusual biographical sketch which gives insights into Allen Hazen's personality and his long and productive career in sanitary engineering. The piece is by his son.

Heinly, Burt A. "An Aqueduct Two Hundred and Forty Miles Long: How Steel and Concrete will Supply Los Angeles with Water." *Scientific American,* CVL (May 25, 1912), 476. Good overview of the construction of the Owens Valley Aqueduct.

Hennessey, Gregg R. "The Politics of Water in San Diego, 1895-1897." *Journal of San Diego History,* XXIV (Summer 1978), 367-83. Perceptive, well-researched article on the battle between two private companies to control San Diego's water supply.

Hering, Rudolph; Joseph M. Wilson; and Samuel M. Gray. *Report to the Hon. Samuel H. Ashbridge, Mayor of the City of Philadelphia on the Extension and Improvement of the Water Supply of the City of Philadelphia.* Philadelphia: n.p., 1899. 124 pp. + XIV plates. Maps, charts, tables, and appendices. In accordance with "a resolution of the Select and Common Councils of the City of Philadelphia, adopted April 20th, 1899," the mayor chose three experts "as a commission to consider and report upon the question of the improvement and extension "of the city's water supply, acting in conjunction with the director of public works and chiefs of the bureaus of water and surveys. This volume contains their complete report with a brief "Resume and Conclusions."

Hill, John W. "The Cincinnati Water Works." *Journal of the American Water Works Association,* II (1915), 42-60. Excellent survey of the city's water system from 1808 to about 1900. It describes early pumping machinery and water filtration.

Hill, William R. "City Ownership of Water Supply." *Municipal Affairs,* VI (1902), 730-37. Useful information on municipal ownership and the introduction of meters to curb water consumption.

Historic American Engineering Record. *Rehabilitation: Fairmount Waterworks, 1978: Conservation and Recreation in a National Historic Landmark.* Washington, D.C.: Government Printing Office, 1979. vi + 35 pp. Illustrations and appendix. Good overview of the historic system's surviving structures and their potential adaptive uses.

History and Heritage Committee (San Francisco Section/ASCE). *Historic Civil Engineering Landmarks of San Francisco and Northern California.* See chapter on "Public Buildings."

"History of the Buffalo Water Works." *Engineering Record,* XXXVIII (Sept. 24, 1898), 362-64. Technical history of the system's evolution.

Hoffecker, Carol E. *Wilmington, Delaware: Portrait of an Industrial City, 1830-1910.* See chapter on "Sewers and Wastewater Treatment."

Hoffman, Abraham. "Joseph Barlow Lippincott and the Owens Valley Controversy: Time for Revision." *Southern California Quarterly,* LIV (Fall 1972), 239-54. Adds important new perspective to the historiography of the Owens Valley debate.

Hoffman, Abraham. "Origins of a Controversy: The U.S. Reclamation Service and the Owens Valley Los Angeles Water Dispute." *Arizona and the West,* 19 (Winter 1977), 333-46. Excellent, deeply researched article that explores the relationship between the city and the Reclamation Service during the controversy.

Hoffman, Abraham. "People in Public Works: Joseph Barlow Lippincott, an Engineer for His Time." *APWA Reporter,* 47 (May 1980), 6-7. A biographical sketch which gives special attention to Lippincott's involvement in the dispute between Los Angeles and the Owens Valley over the use of the waters of the Owens River.

Hollon, W. Eugene. *The Southwest: Old and New.* See chapter on "Irrigation."

Holmes, Beatrice Hort. *A History of Federal Water Resources Programs, 1800-1960.* See chapter on "Irrigation."

Hopkins, Harry C. *History of San Diego: Its Pueblo Lands & Water.* San Diego: City Printing Company, 1929. 361 pp. Illustrations, maps, and index. Undocumented history of the evolution of San Diego's water supply system.

Hopper, Thomas. "The Utica Water Works." *Transactions of the Oneida Historical Society* (1885-1886), 47-65. Factual overview of the system's historical evolution.

Howard, William Travis. *Public Health Administration and the Natural History of Disease in Baltimore, Maryland, 1797-1920.* See chapter on "Sewers and Wastewater Treatment."

Howe, Charles W., and K. William Easter. *Interbasin Transfers of Water: Economic Issues and Impacts.* See chapter on "Irrigation."

Hoy, Suellen M. "People in Public Works: Earl L. Mosley." *APWA Reporter,* 47 (Feb. 1980), 4-5. A biographical sketch of an individual whose career was devoted in large part to supplying an ample amount of water to several cities in his native state, Colorado.

Hoy, Suellen M. "People in Public Works: Ellen Swallow Richards." *APWA Reporter.* See chapter on "Sewers and Wastewater Treatment."

Hoy, Suellen M. "People in Public Works: John H. Gregory." *APWA Reporter,* 44 (May 1977), 14-15. Reviews the career of one of the most widely known authorities on municipal water supplies in the early twentieth century.

Hudgins, Bert. "Historical Geography of the Detroit Water Supply." *Michigan History Magazine,* XX (Autumn 1936), 351-81.

Humlum, J. *Water Development and Water Planning in the Southwestern United States.* Aarhus, Denmark: Kulturgeografisk Institute, 1969. 240 pp. Illustrations, tables, maps, graphs, bibliography, and index.

Hungerford, Edward. *The Story of Public Utilities.* See chapter on "Urban Mass Transportation."

Hunt, Caroline L. *The Life of Ellen H. Richards.* See chapter on "Sewers and Wastewater Treatment."

Huse, Charles Phillips. *The Financial History of Boston from May 1, 1822 to January 31, 1909.* Cambridge: Harvard University Press, 1916. ix + 395 pp. Notes, appendices, and index. A treasure of information on the financing of municipal public works improvements. The book incorporates extensive, well-researched summaries of the development of waterworks, streets, parks, sewers, and rapid transit.

Hutton, William R. "The Washington Aqueduct, 1853-1898." *Engineering Record,* XL (July 29, 1899), 190-95. Useful technical overview of the project's principal features, such as the Cabin John Bridge.

Hyde, Charles H. *The Lower Peninsula of Michigan: An Inventory of Historic Engineering and Industrial Sites.* Washington, D.C.: Historic American Engineering Record, 1976. xiii + 322 pp. Illustrations, bibliography, and index. Includes descriptions of bridges, waterworks, and hydroelectric power plants.

"Illinois Society [of Engineers] Celebrates Its 50th Anniversary." *Engineering News-*

Record. See chapter on "Planning, Engineering, and Administration."

Jackson, Donald S. "John S. Eastwood and the Mountain Dell Dam." *IA: The Journal of the Society for Industrial Archeology,* 5 (1979), 33-48. Well-written case study of a pioneering multiple-arch, concrete dam completed in 1924 near Salt Lake City.

Jacobson, Daniel. "The Pollution Problem of the Passaic River." *Proceedings of the New Jersey Historical Society,* 76 (1958), 186-98. Overview of the public and governmental response to the polluting of the Passaic River by sewage and industrial wastes during the late nineteenth century.

Jarchow, Merrill E. "Charles D. Gilfillan: Builder Behind the Scenes." *Minnesota History,* 40 (Spring 1967), 221-32. An interesting, biographical article about an individual (1831-1902) whose greatest legacy to St. Paul was "an adequate supply of good water."

Jewell, Ira H. "Reminiscing on the Installation of Mechanical Filtration: Three Decades Ago at Cincinnati." *Water Works and Sewerage,* LXXXII (April 1935), 112-14. Includes good illustrations of the experiments on water filtration conducted in the late 1890s.

Johnson, Joseph French. "The Recent History of Municipal Ownership in the United States." *Municipal Affairs,* VI (1902), 524-38. Extremely valuable overview of the status of municipal ownership of water, transportation, gas, and electrical utilities at the turn of the century. The article contains rare statistical information and trends in legislation.

Johnson, Rich. *The Central Arizona Project, 1918-1968.* Tucson: University of Arizona Press, 1977. 242 pp. Illustrations, map, chronology, bibliography, and index.

Johnson, W. E. "Hartford Water Works, Past and Present." *Journal of the New England Water Works Association,* XXXI (Dec. 1917), 575-80. Brief sketch of the waterworks from 1853 to 1917.

Johnson, William S. "The Water Supply of Salem, Mass." *Journal of the Boston Society of Civil Engineers,* III (Jan. 1916), 1-22. Includes historical sketch of the city's water supply from 1797.

Jordan, E. O.; G. C. Whipple; and C.E.A. Winslow. *A Pioneer of Public Health, William Thompson Sedgwick.* See chapter on "Sewers and Wastewater Treatment."

Jordan, Philip D. *The People's Health: A History of Public Health in Minnesota to 1948.* St. Paul: Minnesota Historical Society, 1953. xii + 524 pp. Illustrations, notes, and index. This volume is "the story of the beginnings and unfolding of public health with emphasis upon social aspects and upon the roles that persons, as well as organizations, have played." It does not contain extended discussions of administration, finances, or intergovernmental relations in public health. Of interest to public works historians and practitioners are the chapters on "The Fight for Pure Water," "With Pump and Pipe," and "Streams That Run Filth."

Judd, Jacob. "Water for Brooklyn." *New York History,* XLVII (Oct. 1966), 362-71. Discusses the city's efforts to develop municipal wells in the 1840s and 1850s.

Kahrl, William L., ed. *The California Water Atlas.* See chapter on "Irrigation."

Kahrl, William L. "The Politics of California Water: Owens Valley and the Los Angeles Aqueduct, 1900-1927." 2 parts. *California Historical Quarterly,* LV (Spring and Summer 1976), Spring: 2-25; Summer: 98-102. The most comprehensive treatment of the creation of the Los Angeles Aqueduct and the controversies it spawned. The research and writing are exemplary.

Kanarek, Harold K. *The Mid-Atlantic Engineers: A History of the Baltimore District, U.S. Army Corps of Engineers, 1774-1974.* See chapter on "Waterways."

King, W. F. "One Hundred Years in Public Heath in Indiana." *Indiana Historical Society Publications,* 7 (1921), 271-91.

Kinnersley, Thomas Harold. "Virginia, Nevada, 1859-1890: A Study of Police, Water, and Fire Problems." Doctoral dissertation, University of California, Los Angeles, 1974. 338 pp.

Kirkland, Edward C. *Industry Comes of Age: Business, Labor, and Public Policy, 1860-1897.* See chapter on "Waterways."

Klein, Maury, and Harvey A. Kantor. *Prisoners of Progress: American Industrial Cities, 1850-1920.* See chapter on "Solid Wastes."

Kleinschmidt, Earl E. "The Sanitary Reform Movement in Michigan." *Michigan History Magazine*. See chapter on "Sewers and Wastewater Treatment."

Kleinsorge, Paul L. *The Boulder Canyon Project: Historical and Economic Aspects*. See chapter on "Irrigation."

Kliewer, Waldo O. The Foundations of Billings, Montana." *Pacific Northwest Quarterly*. See chapter on "Planning, Engineering, and Administration."

Knight, Oliver. *Fort Worth: Outpost on the Trinity*. See chapter on "Urban Mass Transportation."

Knowles, Morris. "History of Civil Engineering in Western Pennsylvania." *Proceedings of the Engineers' Society of Western Pennsylvania*. See chapter on "Planning, Engineering, and Administration."

Knowles, Morris, and Charles Gillman Hyde. "The Lawrence, Mass., City Filter: A History of Its Installation and Maintenance." *Transactions of the American Society of Civil Engineers*, XLVI (Dec. 1901), 258-378. Classic, comprehensive discussion of one of the first and most famous water treatment systems.

Knowles, Morris; Myron Mansfield; and Patrick Nugent. "Lawrence Water Supply—Investigations and Construction." *Journal of the New England Water Works Association*, XXXIX (Dec. 1925), 345-69. Excellent source on the evolution of the Massachusetts town's historic waterworks.

Kulik, Gary, and Julia C. Bonham. *Rhode Island: An Inventory of Historic Engineering and Industrial Sites*. See chapter on "Roads, Streets, and Highways."

Laboon, John F. "The Wheeling (West Virginia) Filtration Plant and Some Operating Results." *Journal of the New England Water Works Association*, XXXIX (Dec. 1925), 291-319. Includes some historical material on the town's waterworks.

LaNier, J. Michael. "Historical Development of Municipal Water Systems in the United States, 1776-1976." *Journal of the American Water Works Association* (April 1976), 173-80. Useful sketch of the evolution of urban water supply and treatment. Many important benchmarks are identified.

Lankton, Larry D. "1842: Old Croton Aqueduct Brings Water, Rescues Manhattan from Fire, Disease." *Civil Engineering*, 47 (Oct. 1977), 92-6. An incisive and well-written historical overview of the 41-mile-long masonry conduit that brought water from the Croton River to Manhattan.

Lankton, Larry D. "The 'Practicable' Engineer: John B. Jervis and the Old Croton Aqueduct." *Essays in Public Works History*, 5 (Sept. 1977), 1-30. One of the few outstanding historical treatments of the basic elements of public works management. Lankton lucidly analyzes Jervis' engineering expertise, dealings with contractors and laborers, as well as his relationships with political leaders.

Lankton, Larry D. "Valley Crossings on the Old Croton Aqueduct." *IA: The Journal of the Society for Industrial Archeology*, 4 (1978), 27-42. Excellent narrative and illustrations describing culverts and bridges along the aqueduct's route.

Lanpher, E. E. "A Century of the Pittsburgh Waterworks." *Proceedings of the Engineers' Society of Western Pennsylvania*, 44 (Jan. 1929), 331-46. Good introductory source on the evolution of the city's water supply system. The article includes a series of responses to the presentation by engineers.

Larkin, Daniel F. "The New York Years of John B. Jervis: A Builder of Nineteenth Century America." Doctoral dissertation, State University of New York at Albany, 1976. An excellent professional biography of one of the United States' pioneering civil engineers. The dissertation offers a comprehensive account of the construction of New York City's Croton water supply system.

Larned, J. N. *A History of Buffalo: Delineating the Evolution of the City*. See chapter on "Sewers and Wastewater Treatment."

Larsen, Lawrence H. *The Urban West at the End of the Frontier*. See chapter on "Solid Wastes."

Larson, Laurence Marcellus. "A Financial and Administrative History of Milwaukee." *Bulletin of the University of Wisconsin: Economics and Political Science Series*. See chapter on "Planning, Engineering, and Administration."

Latrobe, Benjamin Henry. *View of the Practicability and Means of Supplying the City of*

Philadelphia with Wholesome Water. Philadelphia: Corporation of Philadelphia, 1799. 20 pp.

"Lawrence Experiment Station." *Municipal Journal and Engineer.* See chapter on "Sewers and Wastewater Treatment."

League of Women Voters. *The Big Water Fight: Trials and Triumphs in Citizen Action on Problems of Supply, Pollution, Floods, and Planning across the U.S.A.* Brattleboro, Vt: Stephen Greene Press, 1966. ix + 246 pp. Illustrations, appendices, bibliography, and index. The purpose of this volume is to broaden public awareness of the nation's water requirements and to stimulate greater public participation in environmental planning. It includes many examples of citizen involvement in water resource debates. Many historical examples are included of successful campaigns to clean up municipal water supplies.

Lee, Robert Rue. "Local Government Public Works Decision-Making." Doctoral dissertation, Stanford University, 1964. xiii + 369 pp. Maps, tables, notes, appendices, and bibliography. Although this dissertation focuses on public works planning, it contains some interesting material on the evolution of Santa Clara County, California's flood control and water supply problems.

Leiby, Adrian C. *The Hackensack Water Company, 1869-1969.* River Edge, N.J.: Bergen County Historical Society, 1969. xii + 231 pp. Illustrations, maps, and index. A delightful and substantive history of the evolution of a private water company that serves a larger area of New Jersey. The book contains an especially strong chapter concerning water filtration in the early twentieth century.

Lemieux, Linda. "The Salem Waterworks." *Chronicle of the Early American Industries Association,* 34 (Sept. 1981), 41–45. Interesting discussion of a water supply system built in Salem, North Carolina, in the late eighteenth century.

Lemmon, Sarah McCullough. "Raleigh—An Example of the 'New South'?" *North Carolina Historical Review,* XLIII (July 1966), 261-85. Includes a discussion of the development of the city's water supply, sewers, streets, parks, and public transportation in the late nineteenth century.

Lepawsky, Albert. "Water Resources and American Federalism." *American Political Science Review.* See chapter on "Waterways."

Lippincott, J. P. "William Mulholland—Engineer, Pioneer, Raconteur." *Civil Engineering,* 11 (Feb. 1941; March 1941), 105-07; 161-64. A two-part, biographical sketch of Mulholland's career with the city of Los Angeles.

Lohr, Lenox R., ed. *Centennial of Engineering: History and Proceedings of Symposia, 1852-1952.* See chapter on "Planning, Engineering, and Administration."

Loop, Anne. *History and Development of Sewage Treatment in New York City.* New York: n.p., 1954. 102 pp.

Los Angeles. Board of Public Service Commissioners. *Complete Report on Construction of the Los Angeles Aqueduct.* City of Los Angeles: Department of Public Service, 1916. 331 pp. Illustrations, maps, graphs, diagrams, and appendices. An official, heavily illustrated history of the project.

Lotchin, Roger W. *San Francisco, 1846-1856: From Hamlet to City.* See chapter on "Roads, Streets, and Highways."

McAfee, L. T. "How the Hetch Hetchy Aqueduct Was Planned and Built." *Engineering News-Record,* 113 (Aug. 2, 1934), 134-41. Discusses the project's major engineering features.

MacColl, E. Kimbark. *The Growth of a City: Power and Politics in Portland, Oregon, 1915 to 1950.* See chapter on "Planning, Engineering, and Administration."

McGroarty, John Steven. *Los Angeles: From the Mountains to the Sea.* See chapter on "Waterways."

McKelvey, Blake. *Rochester: An Emerging Metropolis, 1925-1961.* See chapter on "Roads, Streets, and Highways."

McKelvey, Blake. *Rochester on the Genesee: The Growth of a City.* See chapter on "Parks and Recreation."

McKelvey, Blake. *Rochester: The Flower City, 1855-1890.* See chapter on "Sewers and Wastewater Treatment."

McKelvey, Blake. *Rochester: The Quest for*

Quality, 1890-1925. See chapter on "Urban Mass Transportation."

McKelvey, Blake. *Rochester: The Water Power City, 1812-1854.* See chapter on "Waterways."

McKelvey, Blake. "The History of Public Health in Rochester, New York." *Rochester History.* See chapter on "Sewers and Wastewater Treatment."

McKelvey, Blake. *The Urbanization of America, 1860-1915.* New Brunswick, N.J.: Rutgers University Press, 1963. ix + 370 pp. Illustrations, notes, bibliography, and index. An exemplary history of urban development that explores the relationship of city growth and other broad historical themes during this period. The author describes economic and demographic forces, political and administrative evolution, social and cultural development, and the emergence of metropolitan regionalism. Scattered throughout the book are discussions of water supply, wastewater, and mass transit systems.

McKelvey, Blake. "Water for Rochester." *Rochester History,* XXI (July 1972), 1-23. Reviews Rochester's attempts to provide its residents with a safe and adequate water supply.

McMahon, Michael. "Fairmount." *American Heritage,* 30 (April/May 1979), 100-07. A useful short article on Philadelphia's Fairmount Waterworks which were designed by Benjamin Latrobe. Outstanding illustrations accompany the text.

MacQueen, Philip O. *History of the Washington Aqueduct, 1852-1952.* Washington, D.C.: Washington District, U.S. Army Corps of Engineers, 1953. 65 pp. Illustrations. Broad-brush history of the water supply system for the nation's capital.

Manson, Marsden. "The Struggle for Water in the Great Cities of the United States." *Journal of the Association of Engineering Societies,* XXXVIII (March 1907), 103-24. Shallow sketch that focuses on New York and San Francisco.

Martin, Robert L. *The City Moves West: Economic and Industrial Growth in Central West Texas.* Austin: University of Texas Press, 1969. ix + 190 pp. Notes, appendices, bibliography, and index. An excellent economic analysis of six Texas communities: Midland, Odessa, Big Spring, Sweetwater, Snyder, and Lamesa. Material is included on the development of some of their respective water supplies.

Martin, Roscoe C., et al. *River Basin Administration and the Delaware.* See chapter on "Flood Control and Drainage."

Martin, Roscoe C. *Water for New York: A Study in State Administration of Water Resources.* Syracuse: Syracuse University Press, 1960. vii + 264 pp. Maps, tables, notes, and index. It is the first study of the manner in which New York State administers its water resources. The functioning of the state's twenty-five water agencies is preceded by several general chapters that contain some historical information. The sections on hydroelectric power development and New York City's supply are particularly illuminating. The author recommends the creation of a state water commission to improve the effectiveness of water resource management.

Massachusetts. Sanitary Commission. *Report of a General Plan for the Promotion of Public and Personal Health.* See chapter on "Sewers and Wastewater Treatment."

Matson, Robert William. *William Mulholland: A Forgotten Forefather.* Stockton, Calif.: Pacific Center for Western Studies, 1976. 89 pp. Maps, notes, bibliography, and index. The first comprehensive biography of the engineer who directed Los Angeles' water department from 1886 to 1928. Good discussions are included on the Owens Valley Aqueduct, failure of St. Francis Dam, and Mulholland's role in planning the Colorado River Aqueduct.

Medeiros, James A. "The Politics of Water Resources Development: The Potomac Experience." Doctoral dissertation, University of Maryland, 1969. 443 pp.

Melosi, Martin V., ed. *Pollution and Reform in American Cities, 1870-1930.* See chapter on "Solid Wastes."

Melosi, Martin V. "Urban Pollution: Historical Perspective Needed." *Environmental Review.* See chapter on "Solid Wastes."

Merdinger, Charles J. *Civil Engineering through the Ages.* See chapter on "Planning, Engineering, and Administration."

Merrill, George F. "The Greenfield Water Works." *Journal of the New England Water*

Works Association, XXIX (June 1915), 149-59. Discusses the original works built in 1872.

Metropolitan Water District of Southern California. *The Great Aqueduct: The Story of the Planning and Building of the Colorado River Aqueduct.* Los Angeles: Metropolitan Water District of Southern California, 1941. 69 pp. Illustrations and maps.

"Milestones in U.S. Civil Engineering." *Civil Engineering.* See chapter on "Planning, Engineering, and Administration."

"Milestones in U.S. Public Works: Chicago's Sanitary and Ship Canal." *APWA Reporter,* 43 (March 1976), 20-29. A brief history of the "eighth wonder of the world," which reversed the flow of the Chicago River and helped protect the city's water supply and beaches from pollution.

"Milestones in U.S. Public Works: Milwaukee's North Point Tower." *APWA Reporter,* 42 (May 1975), 15. Describes the significance and exterior design of one of the original structures of Milwaukee's water system.

"Milestones in U.S. Public Works: Penn Square—Three Centuries of Public Works." *APWA Reporter.* See chapter on "Public Buildings."

"Milestones in U.S. Public Works: Water for New York—the Croton Aqueduct." *APWA Reporter,* 41 (July 1974), 16. Reviews the problems involved in constructing this aqueduct, one of the most notable public works projects of the pre-Civil War era.

Miller, Gordon R. "Los Angeles and the Owens River Aqueduct." Doctoral dissertation, Claremont Graduate School, 1977. xii + 289 pp. Notes and bibliography. Solid history of the aqueduct embellished by chapters on the evolution of California water law as well as the historiography of the topic.

Miller, William D. *Memphis during the Progressive Era,* 1900-1917. See chapter on "Sewers and Wastewater Treatment."

Miller, Zane L. *Boss Cox's Cincinnati: Urban Politics in the Progressive Era.* See chapter on "Urban Mass Transportation."

Milliman, Jerome W. "The History, Organization and Economic Problems of the Metropolitan Water District of Southern California." Doctoral dissertation, University of California, Los Angeles, 1956. xiv + 536 pp. Maps, charts, tables, notes, and bibliography. An exhaustive history of the district's efforts to import water from the Colorado River to southern California. The author comprehensively covers all aspects of construction, operating costs, and water demand.

Mitchell, Karl M. "Water Works Plant of River Forest, Illinois." *Municipal Engineering,* XLVIII (Feb. 1975), 101-104. Interesting account of the development of the waterworks system for a small city.

Monroe, Robert Grier. "The Gas, Electric Light, Water and Street Railway Services in New York City." *Annals of the American Academy of Political and Social Science,* XXVII (Jan.-June 1906), 111-19. Useful historical sketches of the development of these municipal services.

Morgan, Arthur E. *The Miami Conservancy District.* See chapter on "Flood Control and Drainage."

Morrill, John Barstow, and Paul O. Fischer, eds. *Planning the Region of Chica .* See chapter on "Planning, Engineering, and Administration."

Morris, Margaret Francine, ed. *Essays on the Gilded Age.* See chapter on "Solid Wastes."

Morse, Roy, and Mary McWilliams. *Seattle Water Department History, 1854-1954.* Seattle: City of Seattle: 1955. xviii + 262 pp. Illustrations, maps, appendix, bibliography, and index. A highly significant, pioneering case study. The volume comprehensively traces the evolution of the department's facilities and administration.

Moulton, David E. "The Water Supply of Portland, Maine." *Journal of the New England Water Works Association,* XXXI (June 1917), 199-206. Thin but interesting historical overview of a city water supply system.

Mumford, Lewis. *The City in History: Its Origins, Its Transformations, and Its Prospects.* See chapter on "Solid Wastes."

Murdoch, John H., Jr. "75 Years of Too Cheap Water." *Journal of the American Water Works Association,* 48 (Aug. 1956), 925-30. Interesting perspectives on water pricing.

Murphy, Earl Finbar. *Water Purity: A Study in*

Legal Control of Natural Resources. "See chapter on "Sewers and Wastewater Treatment."

Nadeau, Remi. *Los Angeles: From Mission to Modern City.* New York: Longmans, Green and Co., 1960. xvi + 302 pp. Illustrations, bibliography, and index. Includes a discussion of the development of Los Angeles' water system.

Nadeau, Remi. "The Water War." *American Heritage,* XIII (Dec. 1961), 30-35, 103-07. Good description of the opposition of Owens Valley farmers to the diversion of water to meet Los Angeles' needs.

Naglack, James. "Quabbin Reservoir: The Elimination of Four Small New England Towns." *Historical Journal of Western Massachusetts,* IV (Spring 1975), 51-59. Discusses opposition to the construction of a reservoir to supplement Boston's water supply.

Nash, Roderick. "John Muir, William Kent, and the Conservation Schism." *Pacific Historical Review,* XXVI (Nov. 1967), 423-33. Chronicles a break that occurred between the two conservation leaders over the Hetch Hetchy controversy.

New York-New Jersey Metropolitan Chapter of the American Public Works Association. *Public Works in Metropolitan New York-New Jersey.* See chapter on "Planning, Engineering, and Administration."

Newell, Frederick Haynes. *Water Resources: Present and Future Uses.* See chapter on "Irrigation."

O'Connell, James C. "Chicago's Quest for Pure Water." *Essays in Public Works History.* See chapter on "Sewers and Wastewater Treatment."

O'Connell, James C. "People in Public Works: Ellis S. Chesbrough." *APWA Reporter.* See chapter on "Sewers and Wastewater Treatment."

O'Connell, James C. "Technology and Pollution: Chicago's Water Policy, 1833-1930." Doctoral dissertation. See chapter on "Sewers and Wastewater Treatment."

O'Shaughnessy, M. M. *Hetch Hetchy: Its Origin and History.* San Francisco: Recorder Printing and Publishing Company, 1934. 134 pp. Map. On the valley and reservoir in California's Yosemite National Park, the focus of an early twentieth-century environmental controversy.

O'Shaugnessy, M. M. "San Francisco's Hetch Hetchy Water Supply and Power Development." *General Electric Review,* XXVII (Feb. 1924), 78-84. Lucid project description, particularly its power features.

Osterweis, Rollin G. *Three Centuries of New Haven, 1638-1938.* New Haven: Yale University Press, 1953. xv + 541 pp. Illustrations, map, chronology, bibliography, and index. Sketchy material on the city's water, sewer, and street systems are included in this volume.

Ostrom, Vincent. *Water & Politics: A Study of Water Politics and Administration in the Development of Los Angeles.* Los Angeles: Haynes Foundation, 1953. xviii + 297 pp. Maps, tables, notes, bibliography, and index. A brilliant, comprehensive case study of municipal water supply. The book traces Spanish developments, chronicles the City of Los Angeles' struggle to obtain water from the Owens Valley, and the formation of a federation of municipalities and water districts to bring water from the Colorado River to southern California. All engineering, economic, political, legislative, and administrative aspects of this complex subject are analyzed.

Palmer, Marshall B. "A Brief Description of the Water Supply of the City of Syracuse." *Cornell Civil Engineer,* 20 (Jan. 1912), 203-10. Summary of water supply facilities built after 1888.

Papageorge, Nan Taylor. "The Role of the San Diego River in the Development of Mission Valley." *Journal of San Diego History.* See chapter on "Irrigation."

Parkins, A. E., and J. R. Whitaker, eds. *Our Natural Resources and Their Conservation.* See chapter on "Flood Control and Drainage."

Perrigo, Lynn I. "Municipal Beginnings at Boulder, Colorado, 1871-1900." *Colorado Magazine,* XXXIII (April 1956), 112-25. Several pages tell of attempts to secure improved streets and an adequate water supply.

Peterson, Jon A. "The Impact of Sanitary Reform upon American Urban Planning." *Journal of Social History.* See chapter on "Planning, Engineering, and Administration."

Philadelphia Bureau of Municipal Research. *The Water Supply Problem of Philadelphia.* Philadelphia: Bureau of Municipal Research, 1922. 53 pp. Illustrations, maps, and graphs. This analysis of the city's water needs includes a historical review of Philadelphia's waterworks.

Piehl, Frank J. "Chicago's Early Fight to 'Save Our Lake.'" *Chicago History.* See chapter on "Sewers and Wastewater Treatment."

Pierce, Bessie Louise. *A History of Chicago.* 3 vols. New York: Alfred A. Knopf, 1937; 1940; 1957. Vol. I: xxii + 455 pp.; Vol. II: xvi + 576 pp.; Vol. III: xviii + 548 + xxxiii pp. Illustrations, maps, notes, appendices, bibliographies, and indexes. Aside from a smattering of information on the growth of water systems, mass transportation, and sewers, parks, and paved streets in the 1870s and 1890s, the volumes contain little information on Chicago's vast public works system.

Pikarsky, Milton. "Sixty Years of Rock Tunneling in Chicago." *Journal of the Construction Division of the American Society of Civil Engineers* (Nov. 1971), 189-210. The author, a former commissioner of public works in Chicago, discusses water and sewer tunnels. There are numerous photographs of both.

Platt, Harold Lawrence. "Urban Public Services and Private Enterprise: Aspects of the Legal and Economic History of Houston, Texas, 1865-1905." Doctoral dissertation. See chapter on "Planning, Engineering, and Administration."

Pomerantz, Sidney I. *New York, An American City, 1783-1803: A Study of Urban Life.* New York: Columbia University Press, 1938. 531 pp. Illustration, map, notes, appendix, bibliography, and index. A brilliant discussion of municipal change in late eighteenth-century New York. Chapter V, "The Increasing Complexities of Municipal Functions," chronicles an astounding growth of public works during this period. The subjects covered include public buildings, street improvements, dock construction, street cleaning, water supply, sewage disposal, and parks.

Pomeroy, Earl. *The Pacific Slope: A History of California, Oregon, Washington, Idaho, Utah, and Nevada.* New York: Alfred A. Knopf, 1965. xiii + 404 pp. + xvii. Illustrations, map, notes, bibliographical essay, and index. A fine book that includes some sketchy material on the origins of irrigation and development of municipal water supplies.

Prescott, Samuel C. *When M.I.T. Was "Boston Tech," 1861-1916.* See chapter on "Planning, Engineering, and Administration."

Pritchard, John C. "The Saint Louis Water Works—A Century of Operation." *American Society of Municipal Engineers: Official Proceedings of the Thirty-Seventh Annual Convention,* 37 (1931-1932), 253-67. Traces "the developments in the art of water supply, particularly since 1870, as illustrated by the St. Louis water works."

Public Works Administration. *America Builds: The Record of PWA.* See chapter on "Planning, Engineering, and Administration."

Purcell, James M. "Richmond's Development of a Historic Water-Power." *Electrical World,* 63 (April 18, 1914), 867-69. Discussion of steam-hydroelectric pumping station on the James River that offers a brief overview of the city's water supply system since 1840.

Randolph, Robert Isham. "The History of Sanitation in Chicago." *Journal of the Western Society of Engineers.* See chapter on "Sewers and Wastewater Treatment."

Rappole, George H. "The Old Croton Aqueduct." *IA: The Journal for the Society for Industrial Archeology,* 4 (1978), 15-25. Competent summary of the aqueduct's planning, design, and construction.

Ravenel, Mazyck P., ed. *A Half Century of Public Health: Jubilee Historical Volume of the American Public Health Association.* See chapter on "Sewers and Wastewater Treatment."

"Recent Progress and Tendencies in Municipal Water Supply." *Canadian Engineer,* 30 (Jan. 1916), 104-06. Thumbnail sketches of water supply projects and developments in water filtration.

Reinders, Robert C. *End of an Era: New Orleans, 1850-1860.* See chapter on "Public Buildings."

"Removal of a Famous Engineering Landmark." *Scientific American,* LXXXI (Sept. 2, 1899), 152-53. Records the history of the Murray Hill (or Forty-second Street) Reservoir in New York City and describes plans for its removal.

Reps, John W. *Cities of the American West: A History of Frontier Urban Planning.* See chapter on "Planning, Engineering, and Administration."

Richardson, Elmo R. "The Fight for the Valley: California's Hetch Hetchy Controversy, 1905-1913." *California Historical Society Quarterly,* XXXVIII (Sept. 1959), 249-58. Focuses on the political aspects of the classic environmental controversy surrounding San Francisco's efforts to create a reservoir in the Hetch Hetchy Valley.

Ridgway, Robert. *Robert Ridgway.* See chapter on "Planning, Engineering, and Administration."

Rinehart, Raymond G. *Clow Corporation: 100 Years of Service to the Water and Wastewater Industries.* See chapter on "Sewers and Wastewater Treatment."

Robinson, Michael C. "People in Public Works: George H. Benzenberg." *APWA Reporter,* 45 (July 1978), 4-5. A biographical sketch of a Milwaukee city engineer (1882) who led the development of the city's water system. He was also a leading figure in organizing the American Society for Municipal Improvements.

Robinson, Michael C. "People in Public Works: John B. Jervis." *APWA Reporter,* 44 (April 1977), 8-9. A biographical sketch of a nineteenth-century giant in public works engineering and administration. The article emphasizes Jervis' role in building the 40-mile-long Croton Aqueduct, which provided an outside water supply for New York City.

Robinson, Michael C. "People in Public Works: Jose Antonio Canals." *APWA Reporter,* 45 (Jan. 1978), 4-5. Reviews the career of one of the foremost figures of Puerto Rican public works history. His principal accomplishment may well have been the water conservation program he initiated in San Juan at the beginning of the twentieth century.

Robinson, Michael C. "People in Public Works: William Mulholland." *APWA Reporter,* 43 (Sept. 1976), 12-13. Emphasizes his role in the design and construction of the famous Los Angeles Aqueduct.

Robinson, Michael C. *Water for the West: The Bureau of Reclamation, 1902-1977.* See chapter on "Irrigation."

Rose, William Ganson. *Cleveland: The Making of a City.* See chapter on "Sewers and Wastewater Treatment."

Rosenberg, Charles E. *The Cholera Years: The United States in 1832, 1849, and 1866.* See chapter on "Sewers and Wastewater Treatment."

Rosenberg, Roy. *History of Inglewood: Narrative and Biographical.* See chapter on "Airways and Airports."

Rowe, Robert S., comp. *Bibliography of Rivers and Harbors and Related Fields in Hydraulic Engineering.* See chapter on "Waterways."

Ryan, Marian L. "Los Angeles Newspapers Fight the Water War, 1924-1927." *Southern California Quarterly,* L (June 1968), 177-90. A thoughtful article on conflicts that flared when the City of Los Angeles attempted to divert greater amounts of water from the Owens Valley.

Salt, Harriet. *Mighty Engineering Feats: Clear and Concise Descriptions of Ten of the Greatest American Engineering Feats.* See chapter on "Planning, Engineering, and Administration."

"San Francisco Water Supply: An Historical Review." *Engineering News-Record,* 113 (Aug. 1934), 131-33. Concise historical review of the Hetch Hetchy Project with a foreward by M. M. O'Shaughnessy, the city engineer who directed the project. The article includes an excellent chronology of the project.

Saville, Caleb Mills. "A Review of Water Works Progress." *Water Works Engineering,* 85 (Jan. 27, 1932), 85–88. An encyclopedic sketch.

Sawyer, Albert L. "An Old Aqueduct and Its Development." *Journal of the New England Water Works Association,* XXII (Dec. 1908), 442-61. History of an aqueduct built for Haverhill, Massachusetts, during the first decade of the nineteenth century.

Schmid, A. Allan. "Water and the Law in Wisconsin." *Wisconsin Magazine of History.* See chapter on "Waterways."

Schulz, C. F. "The Development of the Water System of Cleveland." *Journal of the Cleveland Engineering Society,* IX (July 1916-May 1917), 125-49. Poorly organized but still useful overview of Cleveland's water system from 1854 to 1916.

Schultz, Stanley K., and Clay McShane. "To Engineer the Metropolis: Sewers, Sanitation, and City Planning in Late-Nineteenth-Century

America." *Journal of American History.* See chapter on "Planning, Engineering, and Administration."

Schwartz, Joel. "Community Building on the Bronx Frontier: Morrisania, 1848-1875." Doctoral dissertation. See chapter on "Sewers and Wastewater Treatment."

Seckler, David, ed. *California Water: A Study in Resource Management.* See chapter on "Irrigation."

Sedgwick, William T. "Water Supply Sanitation in the Nineteenth Century and in the Twentieth." *Journal of the New England Water Works Association,* XXX (June 1916), 183-94.

Seney, Donald Bradley. "The Development of Water, Sewer and Fire Service in Seattle and King County, Washington, 1851-1966." Doctoral dissertation. See chapter on "Sewers and Wastewater Treatment."

Settle, William A., Jr. *The Dawning, A New Day for the Southwest: A History of the Tulsa District, Corps of Engineers, 1939-1971.* See chapter on "Waterways."

Shallat, Todd A. "Fresno's Water Rivalry: Competition for a Scarce Resource, 1887-1970." *Essays in Public Works History.* See chapter on "Irrigation."

Sherman, Charles W. "Great Hydraulic Engineers of New England's Classic Period." *Engineering News-Record,* 107 (Sept. 24, 1931), 475-79. Thumbnail biographical sketches of some twenty engineers "who laid the foundation of the water supply and power arts in America."

Shipler, Guy. "The Impossible Dream—Water for Virginia City." *Nevada: The Magazine of the West,* 38 (Fall 1978), 34-35. Good description of a pioneering water system completed in 1873 that included a nine-mile-long inverted siphon and other engineering landmarks. The siphon, which diverted water from the eastern slope of the Sierra Nevada, was designed by Hermann Schussler.

Short, C. W., and R. Stanley-Brown. *Public Buildings: A Survey of Architecture of Projects Constructed by Federal and Other Governmental Bodies between the Years 1933 and 1939 with the Assistance of the Public Works Administration.* See chapter on "Public Buildings."

Shull, J. W. "Historical Sketch of Wheeling Water Works." *Journal of the American Water Works Association,* XIII (1925), 280-83. Weak overview of the system's engineering features.

Simon, Roger D. "Housing and Services in an Immigrant Neighborhood: Milwaukee's Ward 14." *Journal of Urban Housing.* See chapter on "Sewers and Wastewater Treatment."

Smillie, Wilson G. *Public Health: Its Promise for the Future.* See chapter on "Sewers and Wastewater Treatment."

Smith, Courtland L. *The Salt River Project: A Case Study in Cultural Adaptation to an Urbanizing Community.* See chapter on "Irrigation."

Smith, J. Waldo. "The Catskill Water Supply System." *Journal of the American Water Works Association,* 5 (June 1918), 91-99. Sketchy overview of the major engineering features of the project designed to supplement New York City's water supply.

"Some Notes on the History of Water Purification." *Engineering Record,* 62 (Nov. 12, 1910), 539-42. Comparative discussion of developments in Europe and the United States.

Sorrels, William Wright. *Memphis' Greatest Debate: A Question of Water.* Memphis: Memphis State University Press, 1970. xi + 139 pp. Illustrations, notes, appendices, bibliography, and index. Good case study of the evolution of Memphis' water supply system. The writing and organization of this book are very strong.

Speer, James Brooks, Jr. "Contagion and the Constitution: Public Health in the Texas Coastal Region, 1836-1909." Doctoral dissertation, Rice University, 1974. 168 pp. Notes and bibliography. Examines how cities like Galveston and Houston responded to threats of epidemic disease. Of particular interest to public works historians and practitioners are the author's discussions of the response of municipal authorities to public health crises.

Spriggs, Elisabeth. "History of the Domestic Water Supply of Los Angeles." Master's thesis, University of Southern California, 1931.

Stapleton, Darwin H., ed. *The Engineering Drawings of Benjamin Henry Latrobe.* See chapter on "Waterways."

Stearns, Frederic P. "The Development of Water Supplies and Water-Supply Engineering." *Transactions of the American Society of*

Civil Engineers, LVI (June 1906), 451-63. Breezey address on the development of municipal water supplies.

Stetler, Gilbert A. "The Birth of a Frontier Boom Town: Cheyenne in 1867." *Annals of Wyoming*, 39 (April 1967), 5-34. Discusses briefly the problems of finding an adequate source of water, removing refuse from public thoroughfares, paving streets, etc.

Stevenson, David. *Sketch of the Civil Engineering of North America* . . . . See chapter on "Waterways."

Stewart, George R. *Not So Rich As You Think*. See chapter on "Solid Wastes."

Still, Bayrd. *Milwaukee: The History of a City*. See chapter on "Sewers and Wastewater Treatment."

Stine, Jeffrey K. "People in Public Works: M. M. O'Shaughnessy." *APWA Reporter*, 46 (March 1979), 4-5. A biographical sketch of San Francisco's city engineer (1912). O'Shaughnessy spearheaded the Hetch Hetchy project, which was a response to San Francisco's growing need for additional municipal water supplies.

Stratton, Owen, and Phillip Sirotkin. *The Echo Park Controversy*. See chapter on "Parks and Recreation."

Strickland, William; Edward Gill; and Henry R. Campbell, eds. *Public Works of the United States of America*. See chapter on "Planning, Engineering, and Administration."

Sutton, Imre. "Geographical Aspects of Construction Planning: Hoover Dam Revisited." *Journal of the West*. See chapter on "Irrigation."

Symons, George E. "History of Water Supply 1850 to Present." *Water & Sewage Works*, 100 (May 1953), 191-94. Sketchy outline of landmarks in the history of water supply and treatment.

Tannian, Frances Xavier. "Water and Sewer Supply Decisions: A Case Study of the Washington Suburban Sanitary Commission." Doctoral dissertation, University of Virginia, 1965. 216 pp.

Tarr, Joel A., and Francis Clay McMichael. "Historic Turning Points in Municipal Water Supply and Wastewater Disposal, 1850-1932." *Civil Engineering*. See chapter on "Sewers and Wastewater Treatment."

Tatum, George B. "The Origins of Fairmont Park." *Antiques*. See chapter on "Parks and Recreation."

Taylor, Ray H. *Hetch Hetchy: The Story of San Francisco's Struggle to Provide a Water Supply for Her Future Needs*. San Francisco: R. J. Orozco, 1926. xii + 199 pp. The Hetch Hetchy conflict from the city's point of view.

Taylor, William B. "Land and Water Rights in the Viceroyalty of New Spain." *New Mexico Historical Review*, L (July 1975), 189-212. A thorough discussion of "sedentary Indian (*pueblo*) rights in principle and practice as they applied to the use of water and land in the viceroyalty of New Spain (1535-1810)."

"The Almanac of Significant Events in Building a Greater America, 1874-1949." *Engineering News-Record*. See chapter on "Planning, Engineering, and Administration."

Thelen, David P. *The New Citizenship: Origins of Progressivism in Wisconsin, 1885-1900*. See chapter on "Urban Mass Transportation."

The Tunnels and Water System of Chicago: Under the Lake and Under the River. Chicago: J. M. Wing & Co., 1874. 112 pp. Illustrations. Classic history of Chicago's first major water system accompanied by an outstanding collection of illustrations.

Thompson, Carl D. *Public Ownership: A Survey of Public Enterprises, Municipal, State, and Federal, in the United States and Elsewhere*. See chapter on "Energy."

Thompson, John T. "Governmental Responses to the Challenges of Water Resources in Texas." *Southwestern Historical Quarterly*. See chapter on "Waterways."

Thomson, John. "A Memoir on Water Meters." *Transactions of the American Society of Civil Engineers*, XXV (July-Dec. 1891), 40-69. Useful article on the technology of the first water meters.

Tierno, Mark J. "The Search for Pure Water in Pittsburgh: The Urban Response to Water Pollution, 1893-1914." *Western Pennsylvania Historical Magazine*, 60 (Jan. 1977), 23-36. Examines Pittsburgh's efforts to secure clean water and discusses the way in which the city coped with an early water quality crisis.

Tilden, J. A. "Water Meters." *Journal of the Association of Engineering Societies,* VI (Nov. 1886), 17-22. Sketch of "the water meter as a mechanical device."

Tindall, William. *Origin and Government of the District of Columbia.* See chapter on "Planning, Engineering, and Administration."

Tolman, William Howe. *Municipal Reform Movements in the United States.* See chapter on "Planning, Engineering, and Administration."

Toussaint, Willard I. "'The Fire Fiend Doffs His Hat': Burlington's First Water Works." *Annals of Iowa,* 38 (Winter 1967), 510-25. Case study of a system built in the 1870s.

Tower, D. N. "A Description of the Water Supply System of Cohasset, Mass." *Journal of the New England Water Works Association,* XXIX (June 1915), 160-68. Highly technical overview of the system.

Trautwine, John C., Jr. "A Glance at the Water Supply of Philadelphia." *Journal of the New England Water Works Association,* XXII (Dec. 1908), 419-41. Includes a historical sketch of the system's evolution. Rare drawings are included of the waterworks built by Benjamin Henry Latrobe from 1799 to 1801.

United States Public Health Service. "Municipal Health Department Practice for the Year 1923: Based upon Surveys of the 100 Largest Cities in the United States." *Public Health Bulletin,* 164 (July 1926). xxiii + 782 pp. Provides statistical overview of municipal practices with respect to sewage and water supply.

Van Norman, H. A. "Fifteen Years of Progress in Western Water Works." *Western Construction News,* X (Oct. 1935), 273-81. Reviews advances made in water supply and treatment.

Van Ornum, J. L. "Water Supplies in Southern California." *Proceedings of the Association of Engineering Societies,* XVIII (Feb. 1897), 128-40. A good survey of municipal water supply development in southern California prior to 1900.

Van Tassel, Alfred J., ed. *Our Environment: The Outlook for 1980.* Lexington, Mass.: Lexington Books, 1973. vii + 589 pp. Maps, tables, diagrams, notes, and index. An assessment of conditions affecting the environment—water, air, and solid waste disposal—in 1980. The authors look at different locales and attempt to gauge the state and outlook for the environment in quantitative terms whenever possible. Most of their statistics date from the 1950s.

Wade, Richard C. *The Urban Frontier: The Rise of Western Cities, 1790-1830. Cambridge: Harvard University Press, 1959. vii +* 360 pp. Maps, notes, bibliographical essay, and index. A brilliant discussion of the urbanization of the West that focuses on five major cities: Pittsburgh, Cincinnati, Lexington, Louisville, and St. Louis. A great deal of descriptive material is included on sanitation, water supply, wharf construction, street lighting, and street maintenance.

Wakstein, Allen M., ed. *The Urbanization of America: An Historical Anthology.* See chapter on "Planning, Engineering, and Administration."

Wallace, Christopher M. "Water Out of the Desert." *Southwestern Studies,* VI (1969), 1-48. Case study of the development of El Paso's water supply, particularly in the 1950s and 1960s.

Ward, Michael. "The Peoria Waterworks." *Historic Illinois,* 3 (Dec. 1980), 8-9, 13. Interesting sketch of pumping stations and well houses built from 1890 to 1913.

Waring, George E. *Report on the Social Statistics of Cities.* 2 vols. See chapter on "Planning, Engineering, and Administration."

"Water News of Past Fifty Years." *Water Works Engineering,* LXXX (Dec. 21, 1927), 1789–90. Problems that confronted waterworks engineers in years gone by.

"Water Supply of Louisville, Kentucky." *Municipal Engineering,* XLV (Dec. 1913), 515-19. Brief history of the city's water supply improvements, particularly in regard to purification.

"Water Supply of San Francisco." *Fire and Water,* XXIII (March 12, 1898), 83-84. Useful source on the development of San Francisco's water supply prior to Hetch Hetchy.

Waters, Frank. *The Colorado.* See chapter on "Irrigation."

Warner, Sam B., Jr. "Public Health Reform and the Depression of 1873-1878." *Bulletin of the History of Medicine.* See chapter on "Sewers and Wastewater Treatment."

Wegmann, Edward. *The Water Supply of the City of New York, 1658-1895.* New York: John Wiley & Sons, 1896. xi + 316 pp. Illustrations, maps, charts, tables, diagrams, appendices, and index. A precursor for what is now regarded as the field of "public history." Wegmann, one of the greatest early authorities on dam design, used a historical format to present his report on the construction of New York's New Croton water supply system. The book's opening chapters trace the development of New York's water supply from the seventeenth century to the 1880s. They illustrate that the "welfare and growth of a community are intimately connected with its water-supply." Subsequent chapters give full details of the decade-long construction of the New Croton system. The book is embellished with more than 150 illustrations.

Weidner, Charles H. *Water for a City: A History of New York City's Problem from the Beginning to the Delaware River System.* New Brunswick: Rutgers University Press, 1974. xi + 399 pp. Illustrations, notes, and index. One of the few book-length case studies of an urban water supply system. Weidner explores the political, economic, and technological aspects of the topic in a thorough and competent manner.

Wertenbaker, Thomas J. *Norfolk: Historic Southern Port.* See chapter on "Sewers and Wastewater Treatment."

Wheeler, Kenneth W. *To Wear a City's Crown: The Beginnings of Urban Growth in Texas, 1836-1865.* Cambridge: Harvard University Press, 1968. xii + 222 pp. Illustrations, maps, notes, bibliography, and index. Although a generally sound discussion of Texas urbanization, the book contains only a smattering of information on water supplies, refuse control, street paving, and public buildings.

Whipple, George C. "History of Water Purification." *Proceedings of the American Society of Civil Engineers,* XLVII (Dec. 1921), 654-59. Brief essays on the origins of water filtration and treatment.

Whipple, George Chandler. *State Sanitation: A Review of the Work of the Massachusetts State Board of Health.* See chapter on "Sewers and Wastewater Treatment."

Whipple, George C. *Typhoid Fever: Its Causation, Transmission, and Prevention.* New York: John Wiley & Sons, 1908. xxxvi + 407 pp. Illustrations, charts, tables, graphs, appendices, and index. A classic book that contains a strong chapter on the effect of water filtration in various cities on reducing typhoid epidemics.

Whitaker, J. Russell, and Edward Ackerman. *American Resources: Their Management and Conservation.* See chapter on "Sewers and Wastewater Treatment."

White, Gilbert F. *Strategies of American Water Management.* Ann Arbor: University of Michigan Press, 1970. xiii + 155 pp. Map, tables, graphs, diagrams, notes, bibliography, and index. An excellent analysis of federal and state water programs. White explores the problems associated with single- and multiple-purpose water programs and suggests new planning and development approaches more in harmony with environmental principles.

Whitelaw, John. "Cleveland Water Works." *Report of Proceedings of the Eighth Annual Meeting of the American Water Works Association (1888), 114-28. Thumbnail sketch of the facility's development from 1854 to the 1880s.*

Whitney, Charles Allen. "John Eastwood: Unsung Genius of the Drawing Board." *Montana: The Magazine of Western History,* XIX (Summer 1969), 38-49. Biographical sketch of a noted designer of multiple arched dams in the West.

Wilcox, Delos F. *Municipal Franchises.* See chapter on "Urban Mass Transportation."

Williams, C. Arch. *The Sanitary District of Chicago: History of Its Growth and Development As Shown By Decisions of the Courts and Work of Its Law Department.* See chapter on "Waterways."

Williams, Marilyn Thornton. "New York City's Public Baths: A Case Study in Urban Progressive Reform." *Journal of Urban History.* See chapter on "Public Buildings."

Williams, Marilyn Thornton. "Philanthropy in the Progressive Era: The Public Baths of Baltimore." *Maryland Historical Magazine,* 72 (Spring 1977), 118-31. Excellent discussion of the public baths created in thirty-one American cities.

Williams, Marilyn Thornton. "The Municipal Bath Movement in the United States, 1890-

1915." Doctoral dissertation, New York University, 1972. 240 pp. Competent treatment of the movement from 1890 to 1915 to build public baths that would provide the poor a means of attaining personal cleanliness.

Williams, Ralph Chester. *The United States Public Health Service, 1798-1950.* See chapter on "Sewers and Wastewater Treatment."

Wilson, G. Lloyd; James M. Herring; and Roland B. Eutsler. *Public Utility Industries.* See chapter on "Urban Mass Transportation."

Wilson, Samuel, Jr., ed. *Impressions Respecting New Orleans by Benjamin Boneval Latrobe: Diary & Sketches, 1818-1820.* See chapter on "Public Buildings."

Wilson, Thomas. "Municipal Pumping Stations of Detroit." *Power,* XLI (Feb. 2, 1915), 150-53. Development of the city's major waterworks from 1876 to 1915.

Wolman, Abel. "Contributions of Engineering to Health Advancement." *Transactions of the American Society of Civil Engineers.* See chapter on "Sewers and Wastewater Treatment."

Wolman, Abel. "George Warren Fuller: A Reminiscence." *Essays in Public Works History,* 2 (Sept. 1976), 1-30. Entertaining and penetrating reflections on the career of an outstanding engineer who pioneered many landmark developments in the wastewater and water treatment fields.

Wolman, Abel. "75 Years of Improvement in Water Supply Quality." *Journal of the American Water Works Association,* 48 (Aug. 1956), 905-14. Well-written essay on early water treatment landmarks.

Wolman, Abel; Wellington Donaldson; and L. H. Enslow. "Recent Progress in the Art of Water Treatment." *Water Works and Sewage,* LXXVII (July 1930), 239-43.

Wood, Richard Coke. *The Owens Valley and the Los Angeles Water Controversy: Owens Valley as I Knew It.* Stockton, Calif.: University of the Pacific, 1973. 77 pp. Illustrations, maps, notes, and bibliography. A highly personal, subjective account of the "Little Civil War" between irrigators and the City of Los Angeles for control of Owens Valley Water. The book effectively presents the farmers' side of the story. Furthermore, it contains a good discussion of the construction of the Los Angeles Aqueduct.

Wright, Lawrence. *Clean and Decent: The Fascinating History of the Bathroom & the Water Closet.* See chapter on "Sewers and Wastewater Treatment."

Wurm, Ted. *Hetch Hetchy and Its Dam Railroad.* Berkeley, Calif.: Howell-North Books, 1973. 298 pp. Illustrations, maps, bibliography, and index. The popular history of a unique railroad that served the construction camps for the project that brought water from the Sierras to San Francisco. The volume contains a fine collection of construction photography.

Yard, Robert Sterling. "The Unforgotten Story of Hetch Hetchy." *American Forests.* See chapter on "Parks and Recreation."

Zimmerman, Jane. "The Formative Years of the North Carolina Board of Health, 1877-1893." *North Carolina Historical Review,* XXI (Jan. 1944), 1-34. Gives some attention to the board's concern over the state's sewerage systems, street drainage, and water supply sources.

7

Solid Wastes

The following bibliography consists of books, articles, and dissertations that deal with the history of generating, collecting, and disposing of solid wastes in the United States. The term *solid wastes* refers to the useless, unwanted, or discarded materials resulting from society's normal activities. Wastes may be solids, liquids, or gases. Solid wastes are classed as refuse. Liquid wastes are mainly sewage and industrial wastewaters. Atmospheric wastes consist of particulate matter such as dust, smoke, fumes, and gases.

Although most solid wastes in the United States originate from agricultural or mining activities, refuse collection and disposal systems have been designed primarily for handling wastes generated in urban communities. Solid wastes from urban and industrial sources in the United States totaled more than 360 million tons in the mid-1970s. This amount included 250 million tons of residential, commercial, and institutional wastes and 110 million tons of industrial wastes. In the last half-century, the amount and types of wastes have changed radically. In 1920, Americans individually produced an average of 2.8 pounds of solid waste daily; in 1975, they produced about 6 pounds; and current estimates indicate that the amount could well reach 10 pounds by the mid-1980s. With the increased emphasis on packaging in the post-World War II era, the ratio of paper in municipal solid wastes has risen about 50 percent.

Not all solid wastes are collected and disposed of by public or private collectors. Some wastes are abandoned, dumped, or disposed of at the point of origin; others are hauled away by the producers to dumps, landfills, and incinerators. Yet the handling of solid wastes is estimated to cost nearly $6 billion a year. It is, therefore, one of the most perplexing and costly public works services—and one on which little historical research has been conducted.

Special thanks to Richard Fenton, Deputy Public Works Director, City of Saint Petersburg, Florida, whose generous contribution to the Public Works Historical Society was used to support the preparation of this chapter.

Addams, Jane. *Twenty Years at Hull House: With Autobiographical Notes.* New York: MacMillan Company, 1938. xvii + 462 pp. Illustrations and index. The author describes her tenure as garbage inspector for Chicago's Nineteenth Ward at the turn of the century—one of the many experiences recalled in this volume.

Armstrong, Ellis L.; Michael C. Robinson; and Suellen M. Hoy, co-eds. *History of Public Works in the United States, 1776-1976.* See chapter on "Planning, Engineering, and Administration."

Atkins, Gordon. *Health, Housing, and Poverty in New York City, 1865-1898.* Ann Arbor: Edwards Brothers, 1947. xiii + 342 pp. Illustrations, notes, bibliography, appendices, and index. A fine study of efforts to improve public health conditions in New York after the Civil War. Considerable data is included on the city's water and sewer systems as well as efforts to keep streets clean. An entire chapter is devoted to the street-cleaning program of George E. Waring, Jr.

Baker, M. N. *Municipal Engineering and Sanitation.* See chapter on "Planning, Engineering, and Administration."

Beard, Mary Ritter. *Woman's Work in Municipalities.* New York: D. Appleton and Company, 1916. ix + 344 pp. Index. Describes the work and influence of women in nearly every aspect of civic improvement. Through their clubs and organizations, they were effective in securing cleaner streets, improved garbage disposal methods, public baths and laundries, adequate sewerage, water, and drainage systems, and better parks and playgrounds. Women were also in the forefront of the "City Beautiful" movement, which gave impetus to modern city planning.

Bee, Walter D. "Ten Years' Operation of a Municipal Reduction Plant." *Proceedings of the American Society for Municipal Improvements,* 27 (1920), 10-11. An outline of garbage disposal practices at a Columbus, Ohio plant since 1910.

Bennett, Helen Christine. *American Women in Civic Work.* New York: Dodd, Mead and Company, 1915. ix + 277 pp. Illustrations. Includes one chapter on "Caroline Bartlett Crane," which describes her turn-of-the-century sanitation work in Kalamazoo, Michigan, and in other cities where she was hired as a sanitary consultant.

Bettmann, Otto L. *The Good Old Days—They Were Terrible!* New York: Random House, 1974. xiii + 207 pp. Illustrations and bibliography. Graphics from the files of the Bettmann Archive which demonstrate that the past—particularly in regard to the collection and disposal of waste, the cleaning of streets, and the purification of water—was not always golden.

Blake, John B. *Public Health in the Town of Boston, 1630-1822.* See chapter on "Community Water Supply."

Bosch, Allan Whitworth. "The Salvation Army in Chicago, 1885-1914." Doctoral dissertation, University of Chicago, 1965. iii + 349 pp. Maps, charts, tables, notes, appendices, and bibliography. Includes a short section on recycling campaigns conducted by the Salvation Army in the late 1880s.

Branch, Joseph G. *Heat and Light from Municipal and Other Waste.* See chapter on "Energy."

Bridenbaugh, Carl. *Cities in Revolt: Urban Life in America, 1743-1776.* See chapter on "Planning, Engineering, and Administration."

Bridenbaugh, Carl. *Cities in the Wilderness: The First Century of Urban Life in America, 1625-1742.* See chapter on "Planning, Engineering, and Administration."

Brieger, Gert H. "Sanitary Reform in New York City: Stephen Smith and the Passage of the Metropolitan Health Bill." *Bulletin of the History of Medicine,* 40 (Sept.-Oct. 1966), 407-29. A description of Stephen Smith's—physician, editor, and council member of the New York Sanitary Association (1859)—fight for passage of the Metropolitan Health Bill (1866). It created a health department for the New York metropolitan area and is viewed as "a major triumph in the history of public health" and sanitary reform.

Brown, Alan S. "Caroline Bartlett Crane and Urban Reform." *Michigan History,* LVI (Winter 1972), 287-301. A fine article on Crane's career as a municipal housekeeper and sanitarian.

Bruttini, Arturo. *Uses of Waste Materials: The Collection of Waste Materials and Their Uses for Human and Animal Food in Fertilizers and* *in Certain Industries, 1914-1922.* London: P. S. King & Son, 1923. xx + 367 pp. Illustrations, diagrams, tables, notes, and indexes. A detailed explanation of how by-products of industry, offals, residues of all kinds, and raw materials were used by various countries during and immediately following World War I in the preparation of food for humans or livestock and in the manufacture of fertilizers. The monograph contains technical as well as descriptive material.

Bureau of the Census (Department of Commerce and Labor). *Statistics of Cities Having a Population of 8,000 to 25,000: 1903.* See chapter on "Roads, Streets, and Highways."

Bureau of the Census (Department of Commerce and Labor). *Statistics of Cities Having a Population of 30,000: 1904.* See chapter on "Roads, Streets, and Highways."

Cassedy, James H. "Hygeia: A Mid-Victorian Dream of a City of Health." *Journal of the History of Medicine and Allied Sciences.* See chapter on "Sewers and Wastewater Treatment."

Cassedy, James H. "The Flamboyant Colonel Waring: An Anti-Contagonist Holds the American Stage in the Age of Pasteur and Koch." *Bulletin of the History of Medicine,* 36 (March-April 1962), 163-76. George E. Waring, Jr., is described as an energetic and inventive engineer, with a penchant for showmanship, who raised sanitary engineering to the dignity of a profession. He is faulted, however, for failing to see the shortcomings of anti-contagionism and to realize that sanitation alone could not end the yellow fever problem in Cuba.

Chapin, Charles V. *Municipal Sanitation in the United States.* Providence, R.I.: Snow & Farnham, 1901. viii + 970 pp. Tables, notes, appendices, and index. Classic public health text that includes lengthy discussions of refuse disposal, sewers, and water purification.

Civic Club of Allegheny County, Pittsburgh, Pennsylvania. *Fifty Years of Civic History, 1895-1945.* Pittsburgh: Civic Club of Allegheny County, 1945. 61 pp. Index. A brief chronology of the club's accomplishments—from the passage of garbage disposal ordinances to the construction of public comfort stations.

Cohn, Morris M., and Dwight F. Metzler. *The Pollution Fighters: A History of Environmental Engineering in New York State.* See chapter on "Sewers and Wastewater Treatment."

Cook, Ann; Marilyn Gittell; and Herb Mack, eds. *City Life, 1865-1900: Views of Urban America.* New York: Praeger Publishers, 1973. xiii + 292 pp. Illustrations. Good collection of largely nineteenth-century photographs and documents depicting urban problems such as waste accumulation, traffic congestion, and the lack of parks.

Dawson, Russell Leonard. "The Economics of Regional Planning for Solid Waste Management." Doctoral dissertation, University of California, Berkeley, 1970. 288 pp. Provides an historical overview of the development of solid waste problems and efforts by communities to resolve them.

Dial, Timothy. "Refuse Disposal and Public Health in Atlanta During the Progressive Era: A Continuing Crisis." *Atlanta Historical Bulletin,* 17 (Fall/Winter 1972), 31-39. The author shows how the delay in providing an adequate waste disposal facility not only cost Atlanta money but also contributed to its poor public health record.

Duffy, John. *A History of Public Health in New York City, 1625-1866.* New York: Russell Sage Foundation, 1968. xiv + 619 pp. Map, notes, appendices, bibliography, and index. A definitive analysis of the foundations on which New York's public health institutions rest. Several chapters address in a most thorough fashion crucial public works topics—street sanitation, the advent of sanitary engineering, sewerage and drainage, and market regulations—and their impact on the health and welfare of a community.

Duffy, John. *A History of Public Health in New York City, 1866-1966.* New York: Russell Sage Foundation, 1974. xxi + 690 pp. Illustrations, notes, appendices, bibliographical essay, and index. An excellent institutional history of the city's various public health agencies and programs. The contributions of public works facilities and services to improving the quality of life receive cursory coverage.

Feinstein, Estelle F. *Stamford in the Gilded Age: The Political Life of a Connecticut Town, 1868-1893.* See chapter on "Planning, Engineering, and Administration."

Fenton, Richard. "Current Trends in Municipal Solid Waste Disposal in New York City." *Resource Recovery and Conservation,* 1 (1975), 167-76. After summarizing the history of refuse disposal and resource recovery in New York City from the 1890s, the author discusses current trends in the city's refuse disposal practices.

Fenton, Richard. *Outline History of the Department of Sanitation.* New York: City of New York Department of Sanitation, 1954. 20 pp. On the history of New York City's sanitation department from 1881 to 1952. This narrowly circulated chronology highlights significant changes in the department's "thinking, equipment, and procedures."

Fisher, Edwin A. "Engineering and Public Works in the City of Rochester During the Past Century." *Centennial History of Rochester, New York.* See chapter on "Planning, Engineering, and Administration."

Fuller, George W. "The Place of Sanitary Engineering in Public Health Activities." *American Journal of Public Health.* See chapter on "Sewers and Wastewater Treatment."

Geisheker, Bernard J. "Progress is the Key." *American City,* 71 (Dec. 1956), 82-84. Briefly reviews Milwaukee's forty-six-year history of incineration.

Gerhard, William Paul. *The Disposal of Household Wastes.* New York: D. Van Nostrand, 1890. 195 pp. Appendices. Offers a great deal of insight into nineteenth-century methods for solid wastes and sewage disposal.

Greeley, Samuel A. "Municipal Facilities for Public Health." *Civil Engineering.* See chapter on "Sewers and Wastewater Treatment."

Greeley, Samuel A. "Street Cleaning and the Collection and Disposal of Refuse." *Proceedings of the American Society of Civil Engineers,* LIII (Sept. 1927), 1618-27. A general and brief review of the handling of wastes by municipalities during the previous 150 years by a respected sanitary engineer.

Griffith, Ernest S. *A History of American City Government: The Conspicuous Failure, 1870-1900.* See chapter on "Planning, Engineering, and Administration."

Griffith, Ernest S. *A History of American City Government: The Progressive Years and Their Aftermath, 1900-1920.* See chapter on "Planning, Engineering, and Administration."

Harkins, Michael J. "Public Health Nuisances in Omaha, 1870-1900." *Nebraska History.* See chapter on "Sewers and Wastewater Treatment."

Hering, Rudolph, and Samuel A. Greeley. *Collection and Disposal of Municipal Refuse.* New York: McGraw-Hill, 1921. xii + 653 pp. Illustrations, charts, graphs, diagrams, and index. A classic study of collection and disposal practices primarily in the United States during a ten-year period (1910-1920) by two prominent sanitary engineers. Following a brief historical introduction, the authors describe and recommend "the best known methods and works."

Hersey, H. S. "Incinerators—Municipal, Industrial, and Domestic." *Transactions of the American Society of Mechanical Engineers,* 59 (1937), 267-78. The author reviews briefly the historical development of incinerator plants and discusses design trends in the United States and abroad. The greater part of the article is devoted to the incineration of municipal wastes.

Horton, John P. "The Street-Cleaning Revolution." 2 parts. *American City,* 78 (March and April 1963), March: 106-08; April: 104-06. Traces the development of street-cleaning brushes and their impact on urban sanitation.

Hoy, Suellen M. "People in Public Works: Caroline Bartlett Crane." *APWA Reporter,* 45 (June 1978), 4-5. Biographical sketch highlighting the contributions of one woman in improving sanitary practices in numerous American cities, particularly Kalamazoo, Michigan, in the late nineteenth century.

Hoy, Suellen M. "People in Public Works: Jean Vincenz." *APWA Reporter,* 47 (Sept. 1980), 6-7. A biographical sketch which underscores Vincenz's creative work with sanitary landfills.

Hoy, Suellen M. "People in Public Works: Mary McDowell." *APWA Reporter,* 46 (Sept. 1979), 4-5. A biographical account that describes how Chicago's "Garbage Lady" brought about improved collection and disposal practices at the turn of the century.

Hoy, Suellen M., and Michael C. Robinson.

Recovering the Past: A Handbook of Community Recycling Programs, 1890-1945. Chicago: Public Works Historical Society, 1979. 24 pp. Illustrations and bibliography. An examination of late nineteenth- and twentieth-century public programs for recycling municipal wastes. This booklet can provide assistance to communities evaluating the feasibility of adopting source separation and recovery programs.

Johnson, Worth. "41 Years of Refuse Collection in Long Beach." *Western City,* XXVIII (May 1962), 34-35. Brief historical overview of solid waste collection in the city accompanied by photos of early collection vehicles.

Kelly, Katie. *Garbage: The History and Future of Garbage in America.* New York: Saturday Review Press, 1973. 232 pp. Index. Highly entertaining and impressionistic story of solid waste collection and disposal in the New York City area.

Klein, Maury, and Harvey A. Kantor. *Prisoners of Progress: American Industrial Cities, 1850-1920.* New York: Macmillan Publishing Company, 1976. xii + 459 pp. Illustrations, tables, notes, bibliography, and index. On the effect of industrialization and urbanization on American society. There are brief discussions of street cleaning (Waring's practices in New York City), sewage disposal, sources of power (electricity), public water supplies, and park development.

Kliewer, Waldo O. "The Foundations of Billings, Montana." *Pacific Northwest Quarterly.* See chapter on "Planning, Engineering, and Administration."

Koller, Theodor. *The Utilization of Waste Products: A Treatise on the Rational Utilization, Recovery, and Treatment of Waste Products of All Kinds.* London: Scott, Greenwood, & Son, 1915. viii + 327 pp. Diagrams, tables, notes and index. An early, practical guide that describes the why, when, and how of using waste materials. First published in German in 1902, the author warns that it is "only by utilizing to the full every product which is handled that prosperity for all may be assured."

Larsen, Lawrence H. "Nineteenth-Century Street Sanitation: A Study of Filth and Frustration." *Wisconsin Magazine of History,* 52 (Spring 1969), 239-47. After chronicling the filthy condition of streets in several American cities, the author contends that "advances in street cleaning did not loom as a major accomplishment of Americans in the nineteenth century," despite technological improvements, growing awareness of the health hazard, and increased public spending. Instead it was the automobile that prompted the most significant advancements.

Larsen, Lawrence H. *The Urban West at the End of the Frontier.* Lawrence: Regents Press of Kansas, 1978. xiii + 173 pp. Tables, notes, bibliographical essay, and index. An analytical study of the western urban experience. There are several important chapters: "Improving the Environment"; "Sanitation Practices"; and "The Application of Technology."

Lincicome, Michelle. "Sewage, Garbage and Rats." *Illinois History,* 27 (April 1974), 162-63.

Linton, Ron M. *Terracide: America's Destruction of Her Living Environment.* See chapter on "Sewers and Wastewater Treatment."

MacColl, E. Kimbark. *The Shaping of a City: Business and Politics in Portland, Oregon, 1885-1915.* See chapter on "Waterways."

McDowell, Mary. "City Waste" in Caroline Hill, comp. *Mary McDowell and Municipal Housekeeping: A Symposium.* Chicago: n.p., 1938. 1-10. Chicago's "Garbage Lady" recounts her municipal housekeeping experiences and accomplishments from 1900 to 1927.

McFarland, Jeanne Miller. "California Municipal Solid Waste Management: A Case Study in Public Enterprise." Doctoral dissertation, University of California, Berkeley, 1972.

McKelvey, Blake. *Rochester: An Emerging Metropolis, 1925-1961.* See chapter on "Roads, Streets, and Highways."

McKelvey, Blake. *Rochester on the Genesee: The Growth of a City.* See chapter on "Parks and Recreation."

McKelvey, Blake. *Rochester: The Flower City, 1855-1890.* See chapter on "Sewers and Wastewater Treatment."

McKelvey, Blake. *Rochester: The Quest for Quality, 1890-1925.* See chapter on "Urban Mass Transportation."

McKelvey, Blake. *Rochester: The Water Power City, 1812-1854.* See chapter on "Waterways."

Massachusetts. Sanitary Commission. *Report of a General Plan for the Promotion of Public and Personal Health.* See chapter on "Sewers and Wastewater Treatment."

Melosi, Martin V. *Garbage in the Cities: Refuse, Reform, and the Environment.* College Station: Texas A & M Univerity Press, 1981. 344 pp. Illustrations, notes, bibliography, and index. A landmark in the field, the book treats environmental, economic, political, technological, social, and intergovernmental themes largely in the period between 1880 and 1920.

Melosi, Martin V. "'Out of Sight, Out of Mind': The Environment and Disposal of Municipal Refuse, 1860-1920." *Historian,* 35 (Aug. 1973), 621-40. This article describes, in general, solid waste problems (especially disposal) of the late nineteenth and early twentieth centuries and how various groups acted to ameliorate the worst conditions. It gives particular attention to the work of New York City's Street Cleaning Commissioner George E. Waring, Jr.

Melosi, Martin V., ed. *Pollution and Reform in American Cities, 1870-1930.* Austin: University of Texas Press, 1980. xiii + 212 pp. Charts, tables, graphs, notes, and bibliographical essay. An examination of "the environmental impact of industrialization on urban growth during the nineteenth and early twentieth centuries." The following chapters will be of special interest to scholars of public works history: "Environmental Crisis in the City: The Relationship between Industrialization and Urban Pollution" by Martin V. Melosi; "Triumph and Failure: The American Response to the Urban Water Supply Problem, 1860-1923" by Stuart Galishoff; "The Development and Impact of Urban Wastewater Technology: Changing Concepts of Water Quality Control, 1850-1930" by Joel A. Tarr, James McCurley, and Terry F. Yosie; "Refuse Pollution and Municipal Reform: The Waste Problem in America, 1880-1917" by Melosi; "Pollution and Political Reform in Urban America: The Role of Municipal Engineers, 1840-1920" by Stanley K. Schultz and Clay McShane; and "'Municipal Housekeeping': The Role of Women in Improving Urban Sanitation Practices, 1880-1917" by Suellen M. Hoy. The bibliographical essay is especially useful.

Melosi, Martin V. "Pragmatic Environmentalist: Sanitary Engineer George E. Waring, Jr." *Essays in Public Works History,* 4 (April 1977), 1-30. Reviews the career of the prominent nineteenth-century sanitary engineer, Colonel George E. Waring, Jr., and illustrates how he fostered a public consciousness of the problems of pollution through improved collection and disposal practices in New York City. There is also a section on Waring's drainage and sewerage engineering. Appendix I is a reprint of Waring's "The Disposal of a City's Waste" (1865); Appendix II is Waring's "New York, A.D., 1997: A Prophecy" (1899).

Melosi, Martin V. "Urban Pollution: Historical Perspective Needed." *Environmental Review,* III (Spring 1979), 37-44. A bibliographical essay pointing out ways in which the study of urban pollution provides opportunities for examining important environmental issues.

Morris, Margaret Francine, ed. *Essays on the Gilded Age.* Austin: University of Texas Press, 1973. 108 pp. Notes. Of special importance is H. Wayne Morgan's "America's First Environmental Challenge, 1865-1920." Morgan traces the roots of modern ecological problems in the wake of accelerating industrialization. He describes the causes and extent of some of the early pollutants of the land (refuse), air (smoke), and water (sewage) but demonstrates that "the effort to conserve America's natural resources was a major public concern at the turn of the century."

Morse, Wm. F. *The Collection and Disposal of Municipal Waste.* New York: Municipal Journal and Engineer, 1908. xvii + 462 pp. Illustrations, drawings, tables, and index. A short historical sketch of collection and disposal practices in North American communities from the mid-1880s followed by one of the earliest and most comprehensive manuals on the subject.

Morse, William F. "The Practical Questions Concerned in the Collection and Disposal of Municipal Waste." *Journal of the Association of Engineering Societies,* XLV (Sept. 1910), 73-102. Traces the development of various methods of collecting and disposing of waste since the late nineteenth century.

Mumford, Lewis. *The City in History: Its Origins, Its Transformations, and Its Prospects.* New York: Harcourt, Brace & World, 1961. xii + 657 pp. Illustrations, bibliography, and index. The majority of the book deals with the ancient city. The author finds in it, particularly Greece, "essential activities and values" which he believes should become "a primary condition for the further development of the city in our time." Such topics as waste disposal, water supply, and road and building construction are discussed in several sections.

New York-New Jersey Metropolitan Chapter of the American Public Works Association. *Public Works in Metropolitan New York-New Jersey.* See chapter on "Planning, Engineering, and Administration."

Olton, Charles S. "Philadelphia's First Environmental Crisis." *Pennsylvania Magazine of History and Biography,* XCVIII (Jan. 1974), 90-100. Very explicit description of sewage and solid waste problems in eighteenth-century Philadelphia and the measures implemented to control these nuisances.

Peterson, Arthur Everett, and George William Edwards. *New York as an Eighteenth Century Municipality.* 2 vols. New York: Columbia University Press, 1917. Vol. I: xxii + 199 pp.; Vol. II: 205 pp. Notes. One of the few treatments of seventeenth- and eighteenth-century urban public works. Considerable material is included on street construction, repair, and lighting; refuse disposal; public wharves; and ferries.

Pomerantz, Sidney I. *New York: An American City, 1783-1803.* See chapter on "Community Water Supply."

Ravenel, Mazyck P., ed. *A Half Century of Public Health: Jubilee Historical Volume of the American Public Health Association.* See chapter on "Sewers and Wastewater Treatment."

Richmann, William A. *The Sweep of Time.* Elgin, Ill.: Elgin Sweeper Company, 1962. 63 pp. Illustrations. An interesting essay on street sanitation in the United States at the turn of the century. Separate chapters are devoted to Waring's practices in New York City, "other systems and methods," and finally Elgin's solution to early twentieth-century street-cleaning problems.

Savas, E. S., ed. *The Organization and Efficiency of Solid Waste Collection.* Lexington, Mass.: Lexington Books, 1977. xix + 285 pp. Figures, tables, notes, appendices, and index. Includes Christopher Niemczewski's chapter on "The History of Solid Waste Management" from 3500 B. C. to the twentieth century. He shows how the handling of solid wastes became more complex with the growth of urban centers.

Schultz, Stanley K., and Clay McShane. "To Engineer the Metropolis: Sewers, Sanitation, and City Planning in Late-Nineteenth-Century America." *Journal of American History.* See chapter on "Planning, Engineering, and Administration."

Shaw, Albert. *Life of Colonel George E. Waring, Jr.: The Greatest Apostle of Cleanliness.* New York: Patriotic League, 1899. 49 pp. Illustrations and appendices. A brief testimonial to New York City's most famous street-cleaning commissioner. The author, editor of *American Review of Reviews* and an ardent progressive, greatly admired Waring's effectiveness and industry. In the preface, he writes: "Colonel Waring's work for the protection of human life and physical and moral health, through cleaning the cities, has been so successful and so vast that he stands out as the great Hercules of modern times."

Shaw, Peter Lawrence. "Public Service Delivery System Overload and Clientele Impact: An Examination of the New York City Department of Refuse Collection, 1959-1970." Doctoral dissertation, New York City University, 1970.

Skelton, Luther William III. "Planning as an Educative Process: The Development of Solid Waste Policy in the St. Louis Area." Doctoral dissertation, University of Missouri, Columbia, 1975. 202 pp. The study concentrates on the development of a solid waste policy for the St. Louis area which includes seven counties in Missouri and Illinois.

Skolnik, Richard. "George Edwin Waring, Jr.: A Model for Reformers." *New York Historical Society Quarterly,* LII (Oct. 1968), 354-78. A study of Waring's tenure as New York City's street cleaning commissioner. Besides depicting Waring as a dynamic administrator with exceptional executive abilities who demonstrated that reform prescriptions were valuable as "an effective alternative to machine methods," the author emphasizes the connections between the reform impulse and sanitation improvements.

Stetler, Gilbert A. "The Birth of a Frontier Boom Town: Cheyenne 1867." *Annals of Wyoming.* See chapter on "Community Water Supply."

Stewart, George R. *Not So Rich As You Think.* Boston: Houghton Mifflin Company, 1968. vi + 248 pp. Illustrations and index. A series of essays on the serious problem of waste disposal—refuse and sewage—in an affluent society. The author's "horror story" is the way Americans have continuously and "cheaply polluted their environment—earth, air, and water—until there remained no decency of life." There are individual chapters on sewage, factory effluents, garbage, junk, litter, agricultural and mineral refuse, and atomic wastes among others.

Still, Bayrd. "Milwaukee, 1870-1900: The Emergence of a Metropolis." *Wisconsin Magazine of History,* XXIII (Dec. 1939), 138-62. Briefly touches upon the city's solid waste collection, street paving and lighting, and sewage disposal systems.

Still, Bayrd. *Milwaukee: The History of a City.* See chapter on "Sewers and Wastewater Treatment."

Sutherland, Douglas. *Fifty Years on the Civic Front.* Chicago: Civic Federation, 1943. 98 pp. Chronology. A thumbnail sketch of the activities of Chicago's Civic Federation since 1893. The chronology at the end outlines the evolution of a citizen movement. There are sections on "Cleaning the City Streets," "Unification of the Chicago Parks," and "Sanitary District Survey" as well as a great deal of material on other subjects related to the general improvement of municipal government.

Tarr, Joel A. "From City to Farm: Urban Wastes and the American Farmer." *Agricultural History.* See chapter on "Sewers and Wastewater Treatment."

Tarr, Joel A. "Urban Pollution—Many Long Years Ago." *American Heritage,* XXII (Oct. 1971), 65-69, 106. This illustrated article explains that the old gray mare was not the ecological marvel in American cities that horse lovers like to believe.

Tindall, William. *Origin and Government of the District of Columbia.* See chapter on "Planning, Engineering, and Administration."

Tolman, William Howe. *Municipal Reform in the United States.* See chapter on "Planning, Engineering, and Administration."

Van Tassell, Alfred J., ed. *Our Environment: The Outlook for 1980.* See chapter on "Community Water Supply."

Very, E. D. "Some Notes on the Development of Street Cleaning Methods." *Engineering and Contracting,* XLII (Oct. 21, 1914), 394-96. Discusses Waring's practices in New York City in the 1890s as well as more recent experiments in cleaning with machines.

Waring, George E., Jr. *A Report on the Final Disposition of the Wastes of New York.* New York: Martin B. Brown, 1896. 159 pp. Illustrations, tables, appendix, and index. An important report to New York City's mayor by its most prominent street-cleaning commissioner ten months following his appointment. Waring makes a strong argument for the separation of wastes at the source if they are to be disposed of in an effective manner.

Waring, George E., Jr. *Report on the Social Statistics of Cities.* 2 vols. See chapter on "Planning, Engineering, and Administration."

Waring, George E., Jr. *Street Cleaning and the Disposal of a City's Wastes: Methods and Results of the Effect upon Public Health, Public Morals, and Municipal Prosperity.* New York: Doubleday & McClure Co., 1898. ix + 230 pp. Illustrations, tables, diagrams, appendix, and index. Chapter 1 of this volume is a brief history of street-cleaning practices in New York City before Waring's appointment as street-cleaning commissioner. The remainder of the book deals with his efforts to make New York "clean in every part." Special attention is given to practices in European cities as well as to the creation of juvenile street-cleaning leagues.

Wheeler, Kenneth W. *To Wear A City's Crown: The Beginnings of Urban Growth in Texas, 1836-1865.* See chapter on "Community Water Supply."

Williams, Ralph Chester. *The United States Public Health Service, 1798-1950.* See chapter on "Sewers and Wastewater Treatment."

Wilson, Howard E. *Mary McDowell, Neighbor.* Chicago: University of Chicago Press, 1928. xiii + 235 pp. Illustrations and index. A biography of a fascinating woman known alternately as the "Garbage Lady" or the "Duchess of Bubbly Creek." See especially the chapter entitled "The Garbage Lady."

Wisbey, Herbert A., Jr. *Soldiers Without Swords: A History of the Salvation Army in the United States.* New York: MacMillan Company, 1955. ix + 242 pp. Notes, appendices, bibliographical essay, and index. Several pages of this book are devoted to the pioneering recycling campaigns launched by the Salvation Army during the late nineteenth century.

Worrell, Dorothy. *The Women's Municipal League of Boston: A History of Thirty-Five Years of Civic Endeavor.* Boston: Women's Municipal League, 1943. xvi + 224 pp. Chart and tables. Compiled from annual reports and special bulletins and published on the league's thirty-fifth anniversary, this history illustrates the role of women in improving urban sanitary practices and conditions. See in particular the chapters on "Public Improvements and Sanitation," "Streets and Alleys," and "Smoke."

Worster, Donald, ed. *American Environmentalism: The Formative Period, 1860-1915.* See chapter on "Planning, Engineering, and Administration."

Wortman, Marlene Stein. "Domesticating the Nineteenth-Century American City." *Prospects: An Annual of American Cultural Studies,* 3 (1977), 531-72. Reviews the role of women (especially in Chicago) in improving municipal sanitary conditions and in establishing parks and playgrounds. This collection of essays is edited by Jack Salzman.

8

Roads, Streets, and Highways

The young nation that emerged from the War of Independence had a primitive transportation system. The rivers and the sheltered coastal waters provided the principal arteries for travel and commerce. Roads in various stages of development extended from these arteries. A few, near and within the largest cities, were "artificial" roads, ditched and sometimes surfaced with gravel or pounded stones. The remainder were improved only to the extent of having stumps and boulders removed and the worst irregularities leveled. Many were impassable for wheeled vehicles in winter or during the spring thaw. Travelers crossed small streams by fording and large ones by ferrying. Bridges were few, small, and unreliable.

In 1900 there was a national total of about 2.4 million miles of road; but only a few hundred miles had hard-surface paving, and most of these were within cities. By the mid 1970s, the United States had 1.8 million miles of bituminous and portland-cement concrete-surfaced roads, 1.3 million miles of gravel and stone-surfaced roads, and about 900,000 miles of non-surfaced roads.

The books, articles, and dissertations that appear below review in detail the varied efforts and competing interests that contributed to the development of the United States' system of roads, streets, and highways. Many of these sources explain how the advent of the automobile and the growth of road mileage altered American attitudes and values. Also included in this chapter are historical publications on bridges, tunnels, and traffic devices.

Abbott, Carl. "Civic Pride in Chicago, 1844-1860." *Journal of the Illinois State Historical Society*, LXIII (Winter 1970), 399-421. A general discussion of Chicagoans' mid-nineteenth-century pride in their city's commercial growth and prosperity and their determination "to build . . . the finest City of the West." The author concedes, however, that Chicagoans were not proud of their streets or waterworks.

Abbott, Carl. "The Plank Road Enthusiasm in the Antebellum Middle West." *Indiana Magazine of History*, LXVII (June 1971), 95-116. A perceptive article in which the author examines reasons behind the enthusiasm for plank roads in the early 1840s and the realities that accounted for the rapid dissipation of interest by the mid-1850s.

Adams, Kramer. *Covered Bridges of the West: A History and Illustrated Guide, Washington, Oregon, California*. Berkeley, Calif.: Howell-North Books, 1963. 146 pp. Illustrations, maps, tables, appendix, and index. The author contends that Washington, Oregon, and California "can claim more covered spans than the New England states of Rhode Island, Maine, Connecticut, Massachusetts and New Hampshire combined." The history of these western covered bridges is described briefly in the volume's text and illustrated with many photographs; a couple of maps pinpoint their locations.

Aird, Charles Clifton. "The Highway Pattern of Minnesota." Master's thesis, University of Chicago, 1931. viii + 250 pp. Illustrations, maps, charts, notes, and bibliography. A discussion of Minnesota's highway pattern. Some historical data (particularly in the charts) appears in the study.

Albjerb, Victor L. "Internal Improvements without a Policy (1789-1861)." *Indiana Magazine of History*. See chapter on "Waterways."

Allen, C. Frank. "Roads and Road Building." *Journal of the Association of Engineering Societies*, X (May 1891), 223-59. A useful article and discussion on "the proper principles of road building" at the turn of the century. It is only slightly historical in nature.

Allen, Richard Sanders. *Covered Bridges of the Middle Atlantic States*. Brattleboro: Stephen Greene Press, 1959. 120 pp. Illustrations, diagrams, appendices, glossary, bibliography, and index. The first part of the book emphasizes "the great bridges of the past" and their engineering and historical significance (the bridge over the Schuylkill at Philadelphia, for example). The second part of the book is devoted to covered bridges "still standing" in Delaware, Maryland, Pennsylvania, Virginia, West Virginia, and the District of Columbia.

Allen, Richard Sanders. *Covered Bridges of the Northeast*. Brattleboro: Stephen Greene Press, 1957. 121 pp. Illustrations, bibliography, glossary, appendices, and index. Includes excellent sections on bridge engineering and construction in several northeastern states.

Allen, Richard Sanders. *Covered Bridges of the South*. Brattleboro: Stephen Greene Press, 1970. v + 55 pp. Illustrations, diagrams, appendices, glossary, bibliography, and index. A brief survey of covered bridges in North Carolina, South Carolina, Georgia, Alabama, Tennessee, Kentucky, Mississippi, Arkansas, and Texas.

Allen, Turner W. "The Turnpike System in Kentucky: A Review of State Road Policy in the Nineteenth Century." *Filson Club History Quarterly*, XXVIII (July 1954), 239-59. Emphasizes the early use of the toll system in Kentucky to finance new highway construction.

Allhands, J. L. *Tools of the Earth Mover: Yesterday and Today, Preserved in Pictures*. Huntsville, Tex.: Sam Houston College Press, 1951. vii + 362 pp. Illustrations and index. Excellent source of information on the evolution of construction equipment that includes rare illustrations of pre-twentieth-century devices.

Allinson, Edward P., and Boise Penrose. *Philadelphia, 1681-1887: A History of Municipal Development*. See chapter on "Planning, Engineering, and Administration."

Altshuler, Alan. *The City Planning Process: A Political Analysis*. Ithaca: Cornell University Press, 1965. x + 466 pp. Maps, notes, bibliography, and index. A collection of case studies on planning and politics. Of special interest is the chapter on "The Intercity Freeway," one of St. Paul's largest public works projects with sections in and around the city. The time period covered dates from the end of World War II to 1958.

American Association of State Highway Officials. *The First Fifty Years, 1914-1964*. Washington, D. C.: American Association of Highway Officials, 1965. ii + 379 pp. Illustrations, maps, charts, and tables. The story of AASHO's "beginning, purposes, growth, activities and achievement." One chapter is devoted to a review of the early history of American road building.

American Road Builders Association. "History of ARBA, 1902-1977." *American Road Builder*, 54 (March-April 1977), 1-88. A "Diamond Jubilee Edition."

Amick, George E. "Post Roads in Southern Indiana." *Indiana Magazine of History*, XXX (Dec. 1934), 331-34. A brief look at the routes of the old post roads, established by Congress up to 1825.

Ammann, O. H. "Advances in Bridge Construction." *Civil Engineering*, 3 (Aug. 1933), 428-32. Includes specific information on arch, girder, truss, cantilever, and suspension bridges.

Ammann, O. H. "George Washington Bridge:

General Conception and Development." *Proceedings of the American Society of Civil Engineers*, 58 (Aug. 1932), 969-1035. Includes a section on "History, Legislation, and Financing" by the famous bridge builder and chief engineer of the Port of New York Authority.

Andrew, Charles E. "Construction History of San Francisco Bay Bridge." *California Highways and Public Works*, 15 (Feb. 1937), 10-11, 20. Beginning in 1928.

Applegate, Lindsay. "Notes and Reminiscences of Laying Out and Establishing the Old Emigrant Road into Southern Oregon in the Year 1846." *Quarterly of the Oregon Historical Society*, XXII (March 1921), 12-45. Personal reflections on the South Road Expedition.

Archibald, Raymond. "Survey of Timber Highway Bridges." *Transactions of the American Society of Civil Engineers*, CT (1953), 782-88. A general review of advances.

Armstrong, Ellis L.; Michael C. Robinson; and Suellen M. Hoy, eds. *History of Public Works in the United States, 1776-1976.* See chapter on "Planning, Engineering, and Administration."

Arpee, Edward. *Lake Forest, Illinois: History and Reminiscences, 1861-1961*. See chapter on "Community Water Supply."

Artingstall, William. "Chicago River Tunnels—Their History and Method of Reconstruction." *Journal of the Western Society of Engineers*, XVI (Nov. 1911), 869-921. Includes historical data on the Van Buren Street, Washington Street, and La Salle Street tunnels. Extensive drawings complement this article.

Atkins, Gordon. *Health, Housing, and Poverty in New York City, 1865-1898.* See chapter on "Solid Wastes."

Auvil, Myrtle. *Covered Bridges of West Virginia: Past and Present*. Parsons, W. Va.: McClain Printing Company, 1977. 249 pp. Illustrations and index. Published first in 1972, this book is a series of brief sketches, accompanied by photographs, of covered wooden bridges in West Virginia.

Bailey, Walter L. "Historic Buildings of North Dakota: Eastwood Park Bridge—Minot." *North Dakota History*, 42 (Winter 1975), 3. A short history of a cantilever, T-beam type, concrete bridge (1927) built in three spans supported on two piers. It is "the only one of its kind ever known to have been built in North Dakota."

Baker, T. Lindsay. "The Survey of the Santa Fe Trail, 1825-1827." *Great Plains Journal*, 14 (Spring 1975), 211-34. Describes "the first and only measured survey ever to be conducted on the route of the Santa Fe Trail."

Baldridge, Kenneth W. "Nine Years of Achievement: The Civilian Conservation Corps in Utah." Doctoral dissertation. See chapter on "Irrigation."

Baldwin, Kenneth H. *Enchanted Enclosure: The Army Engineers and Yellowstone National Park, A Documentary History*. See chapter on "Parks and Recreation."

Barce, Elmore. "The Old Chicago Trail, and the Old Chicago Road." *Indiana Magazine of History*, XV (March 1919), 1-14. Traces the nearly identical line of the trail and the road from southern parts into Chicago.

Barlow, Mary S. "History of the Barlow Road." *Quarterly of the Oregon Historical Society*, III (March 1902), 71-81. Highlights the road work of Samuel K. Barlow of Kentucky who proposed and executed the first wagon road over the Cascade Mountains. (Taken from *Recollections of Seventy Years by William Barlow*.)

Barnes, Joseph W. "Bridging the Lower Falls." *Rochester History*, XXXVI (Jan. 1974), 1-24. Records the reasons behind the rise and fall of the Carthage (1819) and Genesee Suspension (1856) bridges and their effects on the growth of Carthage and Rochester, New York.

Barnes, Joseph W. "Historic Broad Street Bridge and the Erie Canal Sesquicentennial, 1825-1875." *Rochester History*, XXXVII (July 1975), 1-20. Points out the canal's unique place in Rochester's transportation history and the role of Broad Street Bridge.

Barnes, Joseph W. "The N. Y. Central Elevates Its Tracks Under Municipal Pressure." *Rochester History*, XXXIII (Jan. 1971), 1-24. Discussion of a successful effort by the city during the 1870s to force the New York Central to raise its tracks above grade level.

Barry, Louise. "The Fort Leavenworth-Fort Gibson Military Road and the Founding of Fort Scott." *Kansas Historical Quarterly*, XI (Feb. 1942), 115-29. A description of the establishment of Fort Scott and the importance of the

Western military road in determining its location.

Bartlett, Richard A. "Those Infernal Machines in Yellowstone . . . ." *Montana: The Magazine of Western History*. See chapter on "Parks and Recreation."

Baxter, Sylvester. "Architectural Features of the Boston Parks." *American Architect and Building News*. See chapter on "Parks and Recreation."

Beach, Ursula Smith. "Tennessee's Covered Bridges—Past and Present." *Tennessee Historical Quarterly*, XXVIII (Spring 1969), 3-23. Contains a general introduction and short paragraphs with historical information on individual bridges.

Beaver, Patrick. *A History of Tunnels*. London: Peter Davies, 1972. xi + 155 pp. Illustrations, diagrams, notes, bibliography, and index. A general history of tunneling in which the majority of examples are drawn from outside the United States.

Bebout, John E., and Ronald J. Grele. *Where Cities Meet: The Urbanization of New Jersey*. See chapter on "Urban Mass Transportation."

Beckett, Derrick. *Great Buildings of the World: Bridges*. London: Hamlyn Publishing Group, 1969. 191 pp. Illustrations, bibliography, glossary, and index. Design descriptions of bridges around the world and over time. One chapter is on "Squire Whipple's Truss Bridge."

Belasco, Warren James. *Americans on the Road: From Autocamp to Motel, 1910-1945*. Cambridge: MIT Press, 1979. ix + 212 pp. Illustrations, notes, bibliographical guide, and index. Generally on tourism—"what Americans actually did *with* their cars . . . ." There is one chapter on municipal autocamps (1920-1924).

Bell, A. C. "History and Selection of Street Paving in the City of New Orleans." *Journal of the Association of Engineering Societies*, XXII (Feb. 1899), 45-57. A historical sketch of New Orleans (site and origins) and a review of improvements in street paving.

Bell, James Christy. "Opening a Highway to the Pacific, 1838-1846." Doctoral dissertation, Columbia University, 1921. 211 pp.

Bemis, Samuel Flagg. "Captain John Mullan and the Engineers' Frontier." *Washington Historical Quarterly*, XIV (July 1923), 201-05. Describes the road's national significance at dedication ceremony at Walla Walla, Washington, where Lieutenant John Mullan began the road's construction in 1859.

Bender, Averam B. "Military Transportation in the Southwest, 1848-1860." *New Mexico Historical Review*, XXXII (April 1957), 123-50. On the federal government's role in road building.

Bender, A. B. "Opening Routes across West Texas, 1848-1850." *Southwestern Historical Quarterly*, XXXVII (Oct. 1933), 116-35. Examines the role of army officers and engineers in opening Texas to trade and settlement. They explored the country, surveyed the principal rivers, constructed a network of roads, and established military posts.

Bender, Averam B. *The March of Empire: Frontier Defense in the Southwest, 1848-1860*. See chapter on "Military Installations."

Bender Charles. "Historical Sketch of the Successive Improvements in Suspension Bridges to the Present Time." *Transactions of the American Society of Civil Engineers*, I (1867-1872), 27-43. Traces general improvements in the construction of suspension bridges from 1796 to 1868.

Benesch, A. "The Development of Highways in the State of Illinois Since Its Early Beginning." *Journal of the Western Society of Engineers*, 44 (Feb. 1939), 3-11. Beginning with early nineteenth-century county thoroughfares and showing how closely they were interwoven with the development of Chicago.

Bergendoff, R. N. "Notable Bridges in the United States." *Civil Engineering*, 7 (May 1937), 321-25. Emphasizes outstanding features of some landmarks in bridge development.

Bettmann, Otto L. *The Good Old Days—They Were Terrible!* See chapter on "Solid Wastes."

Bienenfeld, Bernard. "Origin and History of Asphalt." *Municipal Engineering*, XII (May 1897), 271-84. Emphasizes the materials from which asphalt is and has been made.

Billings, Henry. *Bridges*. New York: Viking Press, 1967. 159 pp. Illustrations, diagrams, and index. A popular treatment of "those fascinating structures which span our rivers, chasms, and roads." A special feature of the book is the diagrammatic chapter explaining how bridges do their work.

Billings, Henry. *Construction Ahead*. New York: Viking Press, 1951. 158 pp. Illustrations, maps, charts, diagrams, and table. A popular history of a road in New York's northern Dutchess County—Route 199.

Birk, Russell Charles. "The Historical Markers Program." *Journal of the Illinois State Historical Society*, LXI (Summer 1968), 191-96. A brief history (1935-1968) and an inventory.

Bjork, Kenneth. *Sage in Steel and Concrete: Norwegian Engineers in America*. See chapter on "Planning, Engineering, and Administration."

Black, Archibald. *The Story of Bridges*. New York: Whittlesey House, 1936. xviii + 226 pp. Illustrations and index. An illustrated story "featuring the romance of bridge building and written entirely for the lay reader."

Black, Archibald. *The Story of Tunnels*. New York: Whittlesey House, 1937. xv + 245 pp. Illustrations and index. A popular, illustrated history of tunneling, "written entirely for the non-technical reader." The book includes material on aqueducts, dams, and subways as well as road and highway tunnels.

Blackford, Francis W. "The Development of Roads and Street Pavements." *Journal of the Association of Engineering Societies*, XXII (April 1899), 156-68. From Roman roads to current practices.

Bloodgood, Simeon De Witt. *A Treatise on Roads, Their History, Character, and Utility*. Albany, N. Y.: O. Steele, 1838. vi + 227 pp.

Blow, Ben. *California Highways: A Descriptive Record of Road Development by the State and by Such Counties as Have Paved Highways*. San Francisco: H. S. Crocker Company, 1920. xviii + 308 pp. Illustrations, maps, and index. Tells "what has been done in California as to the development of state and county highway systems." The author, manager of the Good Roads Bureau of the California State Automobile Association, dedicates the book "To the Women of California Who Have Helped More Than Any Other Agency in the Fight for Good Roads."

Bluestone, Daniel M., ed. *Cleveland: An Inventory of Historic Engineering and Industrial Sites*. See chapter on "Community Water Supply."

Boeck, George A. "A Decade of Transportation Fever in Burlington, Iowa, 1845-1855." *Iowa Journal of History*, 56 (April 1958), 129-52. Reviews in particular "the plank road pioneering" of Burlington and the motivation of those responsible to create a grand metropolis. The author argues that the Burlington experience was not an isolated one; this city and others like it were "the first victims and subsequent carriers of the 'internal improvements fever'."

Bolton, Kate. "The Great Awakening of the Night: Lighting America's Streets." *Landscape*, 23 (1979), 41-47. A well-written, concise chronicle of the evolution of street-lighting technology during the early twentieth century.

Boniol, John Dawson, Jr. "The Walton Road." *Tennessee Historical Quarterly*, XXX (Winter 1971), 402-12. Traces the history and describes the significance of a popular route between the present sites of Kingston and Nashville.

Borth, Christy. *Mankind on the Move: The Story of Highways*. Washington, D. C.: Automotive Safety Foundation, 1969. v + 314 pp. Illustrations and index. A popular history of roads "with a wealth of authentic and fascinating detail about the men who built them, the people who used them, and the never-ending interplay between roads and vehicles down through the centuries."

Boughter, I. F. "Internal Improvements in Northwestern Virginia: A Study of State Policy prior to the Civil War." Doctoral dissertation, University of Pittsburgh, 1930. xi + 295 pp. Notes and bibliography. Traces attempts by the state of Virginia to create a comprehensive system of internal improvements which would meet the needs of northwestern Virginia and develop the tidewater section as a major outlet for western trade. The section is devoted to the establishment and initial activities of the state's Board of Public Works.

Bowers, Karl S. "Bridge Rehabilitation Programs." *Traffic Quarterly*, XXXIV (April 1980), 263-70. A short discussion of federal bridge programs prior to the 1978 Highway Bridge Replacement and Rehabilitation Program. Most of the article is, however, devoted to an interpretation of the latter.

Boyd, Mark F. "The First American Road in Florida: Pensacola-St. Augustine Highway, 1824." 2 parts. *Florida Historical Society Quarterly*, XIV (Oct. 1935 and Jan. 1936), Oct.: 73-106; Jan.: 139-92. Largely a collection of documents relating to the survey and construction of the historic highway.

Boyer, W. H., and Irving A. Jelly. "An Early American Suspension Span." *Civil Engineering*, 7 (May 1937), 338-40. A description and brief historical account of the old chain bridge (1826) at Lehigh Gap, Pennsylvania.

Bradenburg, Phyllis and David. *Kentucky's Covered Bridges: Vanishing Kentucky Scenes*. Cincinnati: Harvest Press, 1968. 83 pp. Illustrations and appendix. A photographic record, accompanied by brief descriptions of Kentucky's covered bridges. The appendix is a list of "Covered Bridge Societies."

Bradley, Harold C., and David R. Brower. "Roads in the National Parks." *Sierra Club Bulletin*, 34 (June 1949), 31-54. A discussion of "the standards and purposes of national-park roads" in the past and how they meet present and future requirements. The critical question asked by the authors is "whether national-park roads now on the boards or now being built need to be as 'good' and costly as they are."

Bridenbaugh, Carl. Cities in Revolt: *Urban Life in America, 1743-1776*. See chapter on "Planning, Engineering, and Administration."

Bridenbaugh, Carl. *Cities in the Wilderness: The First Century of Urban Life in America, 1625-1742*. See chapter on "Planning, Engineering, and Administration."

Briggs, John E. "Along the Old Military Road (1839)." *Palimpsest*, II (Feb. 1921), 49-59. From Dubuque to Iowa City.

Brilliant, Ashleigh E. "Social Effects of the Automobile in Southern California during the Nineteen-Twenties." Doctoral dissertation, University of California, Berkeley, 1964. 325 pp.

Brilliant, Ashleigh E. "Some Aspects of Mass Motorization in Southern California, 1919-1929." *Southern California Quarterly*, XLVII (1965), 191-208. A good case study of the 1920s boom in automobile ownership that includes material on the reasons for adoption of traffic controls.

Brindley, John E. "Road Legislation in Iowa." *Applied History*, I (1912), 3-91. One of the studies published in the State Historical Society of Iowa's Applied History series. This essay presents "both the historical and comparative facts" of constructive road legislation and administration. The first section is entitled "Historical Analysis of Road Legislation" and includes discussions of the distribution of power and authority, tendencies toward centralization and decentralization, and economic and engineering aspects of the problem.

Brittain, James E. *A Brief History of Engineering in Georgia and Guide to 76 Historic Engineering Sites*. See chapter on "Planning, Engineering, and Administration."

Browin, Frances Williams. *Big Bridge to Brooklyn: The Roebling Story*. New York: Aladdin Books, 1956. 192 pp. Illustrations. For a young audience.

Brown, Cecil Kenneth. *The State Highway System of North Carolina: Its Evolution and Present Status*. Chapel Hill: University of North Carolina Press, 1931. xi + 260 pp. Chart, notes, and index. The first nine chapters trace the history of public roads in North Carolina from the earliest roads laid out and maintained by local authority to the last of the bond issues for the state highway system in 1927.

Brownell, Blaine A. "A Symbol of Modernity: Attitudes Toward the Automobile in Southern Cities in the 1920s." *American Quarterly*, XXIV (March 1972), 20-44. A perceptive discussion of the cultural and symbolic effect of the automobile on southern life and customs. Portions of the article are devoted to the decline of street railways and the "jitney" phenomenon.

Brownell, Blaine A. "Birmingham, Alabama: New South City in the 1920s." *Journal of Southern History*, XXXVII (Feb. 1972), 21-48. Discusses at some length the city's traffic problems, created by an upsurge in the number of private automobiles, and the plan (subsequently put into effect) devised by Ross W. Harris, a traffic engineer from Madison, Wisconsin. The author only mentions "the poor condition of the city's streets, the inefficiency of municipal garbage collection, and the flooding of some portions of the city during heavy rains because of inadequate sewer drainage."

Brownell, Blaine A. *The Urban Ethos in the South*. See chapter on "Planning, Engineering, and Administration."

Bruce, Mary Hoge. "The Wilderness Road." *Bulletin of the Historical and Philosophical Society of Ohio*, 7 (Oct. 1949), 232-38. On Daniel Boone's efforts to make the road "accessible to travelers."

Bruce, Robert. *The National Road*. Washington, D. C.: National Highways Association, 1916. 96 pp. Illustrations and maps. A thorough history and tracing of the United States' "most historic thoroughfare."

Brush, Charles F. "Development of Electric Street Lighting." *Journal of the Cleveland Engineering Society*, IX (Sept. 1916), 55-57. In Cleveland since 1876.

Brush, Charles F. "Some Reminiscences of Early Electric Lighting." *Journal of the Franklin Institute*, 206 (July 1928), 3-16. Recalls installing public street lighting in Cleveland's Public Square in 1879.

Bryan, Wilhelmus Bogart. *A History of the National Capital: From Its Foundation through the Period of the Adoption of the Organic Act*. See chapter on "Planning, Engineering, and Administration."

Brydon, Norman F. "The Covered Bridges of New Jersey." *New Jersey History*, 85 (1967), 100-22. One-paragraph descriptions of individual bridges which are the result of the author's "attempt to track down, county by county, and town by town, records of all covered bridges, past and present, in New Jersey."

Buckmaster, Jeanne Arwilda. "Internal Improvements in Illinois from 1818 to 1850." Master's thesis. See chapter on "Waterways."

Burcham, Mildred Baker. "Scott's and Applegate's Old South Road." *Oregon Historical Quarterly*, XLI (Dec. 1940), 405-23. On Levi Scott and Jesse Applegate's expedition (1846) to locate a southern route into Oregon.

Burdick, Chas. B. "Old Chicago Roads." *Journal of the Western Society of Engineers*, 43 (June 1938), 118-29. A discussion of Chicago's nineteenth-century roads by a partner of Alvord, Burdick & Howson, Engineers.

Bureau of the Census, Department of Commerce and Labor. *Statistics of Cities Having a Population of 8,000 to 25,000: 1903*. Washington, D. C.: Government Printing Office, 1906. 231 pp. Tables and notes. The statistics in this bulletin (Bulletin 45) for cities with populations of 8,000 to 25,000 correspond to those presented for larger cities in Bulletin 20 and include data on: paved streets; street lighting; street railways; public schools, libraries, and hospitals; street-cleaning; municipal waterworks; sewers; gas and electric plants; and public parks. The introduction to this bulletin also gives a concise statement of the basis of the census classification together with definitions of technical terms.

Bureau of the Census, Department of Commerce and Labor. *Statistics of Cities Having a Population of over 30,000: 1904*. Washington, D. C.: Government Printing Office, 1906. 209 pp. Tables and notes. Bulletin 50 is a continuation of earlier reports on the statistics of various sized cities (see bulletins 20 and 45). As in the other Bureau of the Census publications, there are statistics on nearly every kind of public works facility or service.

Bureau of Public Roads, U. S. Department of Commerce. *Highways and Economic and Social Changes*. Washington, D. C.: Government Printing Office, 1964. viii + 221 pp. Illustrations, maps, charts, tables, graphs, diagrams, notes, and appendices. An analysis of "the results of more than 100 economic impact studies in which State highway developments, universities, and the Bureau of Public Roads have cooperated" since 1961. Only a limited number of reports on these studies were printed. Thus, this volume is intended to provide "a historical record of the research" conducted on the relationship of highway improvement to economic and social change.

Burlingame, Roger. *Engines of Democracy: Inventions and Society in Mature America*. See chapter on "Energy."

Burmeister, W. J. "The Changing Image of the Highway Official." *American Road Builder*, 44 (Feb. 1967), 12-13, 20. Wisconsin's state highway engineer argues that there "has been a remarkable change from the old-time highway official to the modern socially and politically minded administrator of 1967."

Burnham, Daniel H., and Edward H. Bennett. *Plan of Chicago*. See chapter on "Planning, Engineering, and Administration."

Burnham, John Chynoweth. "The Gasoline Tax and the Automobile Revolution." *Mississippi Valley Historical Review*, XLVIII (Dec. 1961), 435-59. Reviews the early development of the gasoline tax (which since 1919 has financed over half of the nation's main highways), its extraordinary growth, and its relationship to the automobile revolution. The author states that this tax "stands as evidence that Americans were willing to pay for the almost infinite expansion of their automobility."

Burns, Lee. "The National Road in Indiana." *Indiana Historical Society Publications*, 7 (1919), 209-37. Explains the reasons for building "the great highway that crosses Central Indiana from east to west" and describes its impact on the state.

Byrne, Edward A. "Brooklyn Bridge—A Half Century of Service." *Civil Engineering*, 3 (June 1933), 299-303. Emphasizes the obstacles that were overcome in promoting and financing the project.

Byrne, J. J., ed. "Engineering in the Forest Service: Six Memoirs." *Forest History*. See chapter on "Parks and Recreation."

Cable, Mary. *The Avenue of the Presidents*. Boston: Houghton Mifflin Company, 1969. xxii + 248 pp. Illustrations, bibliography, and index. A popular history of Pennsylvania Avenue in Washington, D. C.

Caldwell, Dorothy J. "Missouri's Covered Bridges." *Missouri Historical Review*, LXI (Jan. 1967), 229-36. A general description of several of Missouri's remaining covered bridges.

Cameron, A. D., and C. A. B. Halvorson. "Developments in Street Lighting Units (Electric)." *Transactions of the Illuminating Engineering Society*, XV (April 30, 1920), 163-74. Since World War I.

Campbell, Albert H. "Report upon the Pacific Wagon Roads, Constructed Under the Direction of the Hon. Jacob Thompson, Secretary of the Interior, in 1857-'58-'59." *Executive Documents Printed by Order of the House of Representatives during the Second Session of the Thirty-fifth Congress, 1858-'59: In Thirteen Volumes*, 9 (March 1, 1859, Ex. Doc. 108), 3-125. Campbell was the general superintendent of the Pacific Wagon Roads. This is his "report upon the operations of the several wagon road expeditions organized under the provisions of the acts of Congress approved July 22, 1856, February 17, 1857, and March 3, 1857."

Campbell, Ballard. "The Good Roads Movement in Wisconsin, 1890-1911." *Wisconsin Magazine of History*, XLIX (Summer 1966), 273-93. Thoroughly recounts the movement to improve roads in Wisconsin from 1890 to 1911, when state aid became an established policy for future road construction.

Caro, Robert A. *The Power Broker: Robert Moses and the Fall of New York*. See chapter on "Planning, Engineering, and Administration."

Carroll, H. Bailey. *The Texan Santa Fe Trail*. Canyon: Panhandle-Plains Historical Society, 1951. x + 201 pp. Illustrations, maps, notes, appendix, bibliography, and index. A factual, day-by-day account of the 1841 Texan Santa Fe Expedition. The author recaptures many of the experiences of "a group of voyagers who in 1841, in attempting to tie together the new capital of Texas and the ancient one of New Mexico, revealed a surprising amount of the unsettled, unexplored Southwest." Old and new materials are used in an attempt to determine "the route and chronology of the trail."

Carrott, Richard G. *The Egyptian Revival: Its Sources, Monuments, and Meaning, 1808–1858*. See chapter on "Public Buildings."

Carter, A. N. "World's Best Highways through Modern Equipment." *Transactions of the American Society of Civil Engineers*, CT (1953), 293-302. Emphasizes the impact of mechanization on highway development.

Casey, Powell A. "Military Roads in the Florida Parishes of Louisiana." *Louisiana History*, XV (Summer 1974), 229-42. Traces and gives brief history of the military roads between the Mississippi and Pearl rivers and between the 31° parallel and the Bayou Manchac-Amite River.

Cassady, Stephen. *Spanning the Gate*. Mill Valley, Calif.: Squarebooks, 1979. 132 pp. Illustrations and maps. A beautifully illustrated history of San Francisco's Golden Gate Bridge.

Catlin, George B. "Michigan's Early Military Roads." *Michigan History Magazine*, XIII (April 1929), 196-207. An outline of Secretary of War John C. Calhoun's plan (1819) for building military roads and canals in the United States followed by a description of the roads constructed in Michigan.

Catlin, George B. *The Story of Detroit*. See chapter on "Community Water Supply."

"Centennial of Portland Cement." *Building Age*, XLVI (Feb. 1924), 83. Celebrates the centennial of the invention of portland cement by reviewing its history.

Chambers, Smiley N. "Internal Improvements in Indiana: No. II—The National Road." *Indiana Magazine of History*, III (June 1907), 58-83. Part of a paper read before the Indiana Centennial Association on July 4, 1900. The article emphasizes Indiana's need for "a great highway" and the steps taken to obtain it.

Chaney, Raymond C. "Racetrack to Highway: San Diego's Early Automobile Days." *Journal of San Diego History*, XVII (Spring 1971), 28-40. Outstanding article on the city's long-term efforts to become the key western terminus of a transcontinental highway.

Chanute, O. "Address at the Annual Convention at Chattanooga, Tenn., May 22D, 1891." *Transactions of the American Society of Civil Engineers*, XXIV (May 1891), 397-429. Reviews major engineering achievements during the past year, giving special attention to bridges and tunnels. Octave Chanute was president of the American Society of Civil Engineers in 1891.

Chappell, Gordon. *Historic Resource* Study—*East and West Potomac Parks: A History*. See chapter on "Parks and Recreation."

Cheever, L. O. "Covered Bridges in Iowa." *Palimpsest*, LI (Nov. 1970), 452-96. An explanation of how and why covered bridges came to Iowa plus an alphabetical, annotated list of bridges by county.

Chittenden, H. M. "The Government Road System of the Yellowstone National Park." *Proceedings of the International Good Roads Congress*, 21 (Sept. 1901), 72-78. A significant presentation by a prominent corps engineer-officer who explains the government's road policy in Yellowstone.

Clark, James Everett. "The Impact of Transportation Technology on Suburbanization in the Chicago Region, 1830-1920." Doctoral dissertation, Northwestern University, 1977. 158 pp.

Cleveland, Reginald M., and S. T. Williamson. *The Road Is Yours: The Story of the Automobile and the Men Behind It*. New York: Greystone Press, 1951. 304 pp. Illustrations and index. A popular history of the automobile with some discussion of how "the automobile took the nation out of the mud."

Clonts, F. W. "Travel and Transportation in Colonial North Carolina." *North Carolina Historical Review*. See chapter on "Waterways."

Coburn, Raymond W. "The Construction and Maintenance of Bituminous Macadam Roads." *Journal of the Boston Society of Civil Engineers*, X (Sept. 1923), 298-313. Includes two pages on the "History and Types of Bituminous Macadam Roads."

Cochran, Thomas C., ed. *The New American State Papers: Transportation.* Wilmington, Del.: Scholarly Resources Inc., 1972. 741 pp. Map, charts, and tables. The first of seven volumes in the series, this book contains pre-Civil War material (mainly on roads, canals, and internal improvements in general) drawn from three major sources: the original American State Papers, published between 1832 and 1861; the serial volumes of the official documents of the United States Congress printed continuously after 1817; and the Legislative Records Section of the National Archives. Cochran, the general editor, provides a five-page, summary introduction on pre-Civil War transportation development in the United States.

Cohn, David L. *Combustion on Wheels: An Informal History of the Automobile Age*. Boston: Houghton Mifflin Company, 1944. x + 272 pp. Illustrations and index. Contains only a brief discussion of the effect of the automobile on American highways.

Cole, H. E. "The Old Military Road." *Wisconsin Magazine of History*, IX (Sept. 1925), 47-62. Traces and gives the history of the military road from Green Bay to Prairie du Chien.

Committee of the American Wood Preservers' Association. "Treated Wood Block Pavements: Their History in the United States." *Municipal Engineering*, XLVIII (Feb. 1915), 94-100. A summary of advancements, beginning with the first extensive use of modern creosoted wood block in Indianapolis in 1896.

Committee on History and Heritage of American Civil Engineering. *American Wooden Bridges*. New York: American Society of Civil Engineers, 1976. v + 176 pp. Illustrations, diagrams, notes, bibliography, and index. A history of the evolution of America's wooden bridges. The purpose of the book is to "foster a greater public appreciation of the role of the American wooden bridge in America's development, and thus aid in their preservation as landmarks."

"Concrete Pavements—History and Summary of Practice." *Engineering & Contracting*, XXXVIII (July 10, 1912), 44-46. Since 1893.

Condit, Carl W. *American Building: Materials and Techniques from the First Colonial Settlements to the Present*. See chapter on "Public Buildings."

Condit, Carl W. *Chicago, 1910-29: Building, Planning, and Urban Technology*. See chapter on "Planning, Engineering, and Administration."

Condit, Carl W. *Chicago, 1930-1970: Building, Planning, and Urban Technology*. See chapter on "Planning, Engineering, and Administration."

Condit, Carl W. "Sullivan's Skyscrapers as the Expression of Nineteenth Century Technology." *Technology and Culture*, I (Winter 1959), 78-93. The author explains the influence of the Eads and Dixville bridges on work of Louis Sullivan.

Congdon, Herbert Wheaton. *The Covered Bridge: An Old American Landmark Whose Romance, Stability, and Craftsmanship Are Typified by the Structures Remaining in Vermont*. New York: Alfred A. Knopf, 1946. 151 pp. Illustrations, bibliography, and index. A romantic review of Vermont's covered bridges.

Conger, Roger Norman. "The Waco Suspension Bridge." *Texana*, 1 (Summer 1963), 181-224.

Connery, Robert H., and Richard H. Leach. *The Federal Government and Metropolitan Areas*. See chapter on "Planning, Engineering, and Administration."

Conzelman, Joseph H. "History of Bituminous Concrete Pavements in Which Broken Stone or Gravel is Used." *Engineering and Contracting*, XLI (March 25, 1914), 372-74. For streets, beginning in 1840.

Cook, Harry T. *The Borough of the Bronx, 1639-1913: Its Marvelous Development and Historical Surroundings*. New York: Harry T. Cook, 1913. x + 189 pp. Illustrations and index. Includes lengthy chapters on the historical evolution of the borough's bridges and parks.

Corbett, Scott. *Bridges*. New York: Four Winds Press, 1978. 122 pp. Illustrations and index. A highly readable history of bridges from ancient times to the present. The drawings by Richard Rosenblum are stunning. Young readers/researchers will consider this book a treat.

Corbett, William P. "Men, Mud and Mules: The Good Roads Movement in Oklahoma, 1900-1910." *Chronicles of Oklahoma*, LVIII (Summer 1980), 132-49. Describes how local interests worked with federal authorities "to improve highway transportation in rural Oklahoma."

Cottman, George S. "Internal Improvement in Indiana: No. I.—The First Thoroughfares." *Indiana Magazine of History*, III (March 1907), 12-20. An overview of the development of Indiana's earliest trails, traces, and roads.

Couper, William. *Claudius Crozet: Soldier-Scholar-Educator-Engineer (1789-1964)*. Charlottesville, Va.: Historical Publishing Company, 1936. 221 pp. Notes, appendices, and index. Biography of Virginia's state engineer who gave Virginia one of the best road systems in the country and played a major role in establishing and organizing Virginia Military Institute.

Cowdrey, Albert E. *A City for the Nation: The Army Engineers and the Building of Washington, D. C., 1790-1967*. See chapter on "Planning, Engineering, and Administration."

Cox, Richard J. "Professionalism and Civil Engineering in Early America: The Vicissitudes of James Shriver's Career, 1815-1826." *Maryland Historical Magazine*. See chapter on "Planning, Engineering, and Administration."

Cranmer, H. Jerome. *New Jersey in the Automobile Age: A History of Transportation*. Princeton: D. Van Nostrand Company, 1964. xiii + 139 pp. Illustrations, maps, bibliographical essay, and index. A part of the New Jersey Historical Series, this volume presents an overview of the state's transportation development. Special attention is given to the period following World War I.

Creighton, Wilbur Foster. *Building of Nashville*. See chapter on "Public Buildings."

Creighton, Wilbur F., Jr. "Wilbur Fisk Roster, Soldier and Engineer." *Tennessee Historical Quarterly*. See chapter on "Sewers and Wastewater Treatment."

Crittenden, Charles Christopher. "Overland Travel and Transportation in North Carolina, 1763-1789." *North Carolina Historical Review*, VIII (July 1931), 239-57. Discusses the improved (since the proprietary period) but still inadequate transportation facilities in North Carolina during the late eighteenth century.

Crittenden, Charles Christopher. "Transportation and Commerce in North Carolina, 1763-1789." Doctoral dissertation, Yale University, 1930.

Crocker, Francis B. "The History of Electric Lighting." *Electrical World*, XXVII (May 9, 1896), 511-13. Only indirectly refers to street lighting.

Cron, F. W. "Roads for Vicksburg National Military Park." *Civil Engineering*. See chapter on "Parks and Recreation."

Cross, Jack L. "Federal Wagon Road Construction in New Mexico Territory, 1846-1860." Master's thesis, University of Chicago, 1949. vi + 104 pp. Maps, notes, and bibliography. The author sees "wagon roads and railroads as part and parcel of one process." He contends that the explorations, topographical surveys, and wagon road building conducted mostly by army engineers contributed "mightily to later railroad development."

Crow, Jeffrey J. "People in Public Works: Harriet M. Berry." *APWA Reporter*, 44 (Nov. 1977), 4-5. Describes the efforts and dedication of Berry, secretary of North Carolina's Good Roads Association, in galvanizing the state's campaign for improved roads.

Cummins, D. H. "Toll Roads in Southwestern Colorado." *Colorado Magazine*, XXIX (April 1952), 98-104. Demonstrates that "the early history of transportation in southwestern Colorado is the history of the toll road movement."

Curtis, William T. S. "Cabin John Bridge." *Records of the Columbia Historical Society of Washington, D. C.* (1899), 293-307. A brief history of a bridge that spans Cabin John Creek a few miles above the city of Washington.

Dale, William Pratt, II. "The Tombigbee Rooster Bridge." *Alabama Review*, XXV (April 1972), 119-33. A history of the effort to bridge the Tombigbee River near Demopolis, Alabama.

Dallaire, Gene. "The Birth and Growth of History's Most Exciting Building Material [Prestressed Concrete]." *Civil Engineering*. See chapter on "Planning, Engineering, and Administration."

Daniels, George H. *Science in American Society: A Social History*. See chapter on "Waterways."

Danker, Donald. "The Influence of Transportation upon Nebraska Territory." *Nebraska History*. See chapter on "Waterways."

Danko, George Michael. "The Evolution of the Simple Truss Bridge, 1790 to 1850: From Empiricism to Scientific Construction." Doctoral dissertation, University of Pennsylvania, 1979. 263 pp.

Darnell, Victor. "Lenticular Bridges from East Berlin, Connecticut." *IA: The Journal of the Society for Industrial Archeology*, 5 (1979), 19-32. On the lenticular truss patented by William O. Douglas in 1878, which "led to the construction of hundreds of spans of that unique profile in the years from 1878 to the late 1890s." Most of these were built by the East Berlin companies.

Darrow, M. S. "Asphalt Pavements." *Cornell Civil Engineer*, 20 (Oct. 1911), 23-29. A brief history of the technology of asphalt paving.

Davies, J. Vipond. "Progress in the Art of Tunneling." *Engineering News-Record*, 92 (April 17, 1924), 674-79. A review of advances in the art of tunnel construction from the 1870s to the 1920s by a consulting engineer.

Davies, Richard O. *The Age of Asphalt: The Automobile, the Freeway, and the Condition of Metropolitan America*. Philadelphia: J. B. Lippincott Company, 1975. xii + 139 pp. Notes and bibliographical essay. An "intensely personal interpretation" of the evolution of the nation's transportation policies. The book is particularly harsh in its treatment of the policies of the Eisenhower Administration.

Davis, Charles. "A System of National Highways." *Military Engineer*, XX (March-April 1928), 116-19. A description of road building in the United States by the president of the National Highways Association.

Davis, Grant Miller. *The Department of Transportation*. See chapter on "Planning, Engineering, and Administration."

Davison, George S. "A Century and a Half of American Engineering." *Proceedings of the American Society of Civil Engineers*. See chapter on "Planning, Engineering, and Administration."

Dawson, Craig. "Roads for the Rich: Highway Development and the Upper Class of Kansas City, 1923-1936." Bachelor's honors thesis, University of Kansas, 1978.

Dean, Arthur W. "Massachusetts Highways." *Journal of the Boston Society of Civil Engineers*, XVI (Dec. 1929), 493-553. A detailed review of road building in Massachusetts since the turnpike era. The author briefly discusses such subjects as the origins of the Massachusetts Highway Commission and Department of Public Works, early highway financing, evolving use of materials for road construction, etc. The main emphasis is, however, current.

Dearing, Charles L. *American Highway Policy*. Washington, D. C.: Brookings Institution, 1941. xi + 286 pp. Charts, tables, notes, appendices, and index. This study, which is "the outgrowth of inquiries directed to the Brookings Institution by the Commissioner of Public Roads," analyzes and classifies the basic purposes and principal beneficiaries of several types of public roads. Chapter II reviews the "Evolution of Highway Policy in America to 1916."

Dearing, Charles L., and Wilfred Owen. *National Transportation Policy*. See chapter on "Airways and Airports."

Deibler, Dan Grove. *Metal Truss Bridges in Virginia: 1865-1932*. 5 Vols. Charlottesville: Virginia Highway & Transportation Research Council, 1975. Vol. 1: 55 pp.; Vol. 2: iii + 84 pp.; Vol. 3: iii + 68 pp.; Vol. 4: iii + 39 pp.; Vol. 5: iii + 42 pp. Illustrations, maps, graphs, notes, and bibliography. A history of road and bridge building technology in Virginia. The subjects discussed in each volume are: an examination of the development of the truss form and an annotated list of nineteenth- and early twentieth-century bridge companies (1); the Staunton Construction District (2); the Culpeper Construction District (3); the Fredericksburg Construction District (4); and the Richmond Construction District (5).

Demoro, Harre. "The PCC Car—Still a Good Idea." *Mass Transit*, 11 (June 1975), 14-15, 29.

De Nevers, Noel, ed. *Technology and Society*. Reading, Mass.: Addison-Wesley Publishing Company, 1972. ix + 307 pp. Largely a collection of reprints that discuss the history of technological change. Subjects covered include the disposal of wastes in coastal waters and the effect of highways on the environment.

Derry, T. K., and Trevor I. Williams. *A Short History of Technology: From the Earliest Times to A. D. 1900*. See chapter on "Planning, Engineering, and Administration."

Diehl, John A. "Covered Bridges in Ohio." *Bulletin of the Historical and Philosophical Society of Ohio*, 7 (April 1949), 123-25.

Dorsey, Florence. *Road to the Sea: The Story of James B. Eads and the Mississippi River*. New York: Rinehart & Company, 1947. xii + 340 pp. Illustrations, notes, and bibliography. A biography of Eads that includes many aspects of his prominent engineering career. Several chapters are devoted to Eads bridges.

Doss, Richard B. "Andrew Jackson, Road Builder." *Journal of Mississippi History*, XVI (Jan. 1954), 1-21. On Jackson's role in planning and building the famous military highway which bore his name.

Draney, Joseph Rock. "Asphalt—Origin, History, Development—Its Relation to Petroleum." *Americana*, XXXIII (April 1939), 196-221. On the origins and diversified uses of "this remarkably versatile product" by a former president of the Asphalt Association.

Drinker, Henry S. *Tunneling, Explosive Compounds, and Rock Drills*. New York: John Wiley & Sons, 1878. 1031 pp. Illustrations, drawings, tables, diagrams, and index. Richly illustrated classic text on the subject that includes a history of tunneling.

Duane, William. *A View of the Law of Roads, Highways, Bridges and Ferries in Pennsylvania*. Philadelphia: James Kay, Jun. & Brother, 1848. xii + 156 pp. Index. A unique and valuable source on the early history of roads and bridges. The law with respect to state roads, bridges, streets, turnpikes, and ferries is covered.

Duffus, R. L. *The Santa Fe Trail*. New York: Longmans, Green and Company, 1931. xi + 283 pp. Illustrations, maps, bibliography, and index. A popular account of "one of the most heroic and certainly not the least glamorous of all the episodes of the Westward Movement."

Dunbar, Seymour. *A History of Travel in America: Showing the Development of Travel and Transportation from the Crude Methods of the Canoe and the Dog-Sled to the Highly Organized Railway Systems of the Present, Together with a Narrative of the Human Experiences and Changing Social Conditions that Accompanied this Economic Conquest of the Continent*. 4 vols. New York: Greenwood Press, 1968. Vol. I: li + 339 pp.; Vol. II: 340-740; Vol III: 741-1124; and Vol. IV: 1125-1529. Illustrations, maps, notes, tables, appendices, bibliography, and index. As the subtitle indicates, these four volumes describe America's transportation network through the nineteenth century as well as early ideas of people about travel facilities, their efforts to create ever more sophisticated methods of travel, and their experiences while using contemporary conveyances and systems. (First published in 1915 by Bobbs-Merrill.)

Dunham, Norman Leslie. "The Bicycle Era in American History." Doctoral dissertation, Harvard University, 1957.

Durrenberger, Joseph Austin. *Turnpikes: A Study of the Toll Road Movement in the Middle Atlantic States and Maryland*. Cos Cob, Conn.: John E. Edwards, 1968. 188 pp. Notes, bibliography, and index. Published first in 1931, this study examines the decisions pertaining to turnpike construction, operation, and control in New York, New Jersey, Pennsylvania, and Maryland. The author also looks at the effect of canal and railway construction on highway traffic.

Eaton, Thelma. *The Covered Bridges of Illinois*. Ann Arbor: Edwards Brothers, Inc., 1968. x + 190 pp. Illustrations, maps, appendix, bibliography, and index. A record of many of Illinois' highway covered bridges (the appendix lists 137) and a readable compilation of material related to their construction.

Eckel, C. L. "The Development of Simple Types of Bridge Structures in the United States." *Colorado Engineer*, 25 (Nov. 1928), 10-11, 31-32, 34. Emphasis on truss bridges.

Edwards, Llewellyn Nathaniel. *A Record of History and Evolution of Early American Bridges*. Orono, Me.: University Press, 1959. xii + 204 pp. + 54 figures. Illustrations and appendix. A history of bridges from the "pre-colonial period" (prior to 1600) to 1900 by a bridge engineer, who spent most of his career in the employ of the U. S. Bureau of Public Roads.

Edwards, Llewellyn N. "The Evolution of Early American Bridges." *Maine Technology Experiment Station (University of Maine)*, No. 15 (Oct. 1934), 1-30. From seventeenth-century wooden bridges to iron and reinforced concrete bridges of the nineteenth and early twentieth centuries.

Edwards, Llewellyn N. "The Evolution of Early American Bridges." *Transactions of the Newcomen Society (London) for the Study of the History of Engineering and Technology*, 13 (1932-1933), 95-116. An abstract of a paper read at Caxton Hall, Westminster, March 15, 1933, on American bridge development from the colonial period (wooden bridges) to the mid nineteenth century (metal).

Ellenberger, William J. "History of the Street Car Lines of Montgomery County." *Montgomery County Story*, 17 (May 1974), 1-10.

Elliott, T. C. "The Mullan Road: Its Local History and Significance." *Washington Historical Quarterly*, XIV (July 1923), 206-09. Presented at the dedication of a monument at Walla Walla, Washington, where Lieutenant John Mullan began construction of the road in 1859.

Ellis, Harry K. "Bridge-Building in Pennsylvania a Century Ago." *Engineering News-Record*, 97 (Sept. 2, 1926), 378-79. A brief description of the stone and timber bridges built on petition.

Ellis, Harry K. "Sixty-Year-Old Trusses of Cast Iron Still in Service." *Engineering News-Record*, 111 (Nov. 16, 1933), 597-98. A one-page description of two bridges (1870) in Bethlehem, Pennsylvania.

"Engineering in Mecklenburg County, North Carolina." *Engineering News-Record*, 103 (Oct. 10, 1929), 576-79. Overview of road improvements by the county's engineering department during the 1920s.

Eno, F. H. "A Decade of Progress in Highway Research." *Ohio State University Studies: Engineering Series*, No. 20 (March 1930), 1-30. An investigation of improvements in highway construction and maintenance since 1920. The article is technical and emphasizes the effect of soil conditions on pavements.

Esarey, Logan. "Internal Improvements in Early Indiana." *Indiana Historical Society Publications*. See chapter on "Waterways."

Everest, Allan S. "Early Roads and Taverns of the Champlain Valley." *Vermont History*, XXXVII (Autumn 1969), 247-55. Entertaining sketch of road conditions in Vermont from the 1780s to the 1840s.

Farquhar, Francis P. "Exploration of the Sierra Nevada." *California Historical Society Quarterly*. See chapter on "Parks and Recreation."

Farrell, Richard T. "Internal-Improvement Projects in Southwestern Ohio, 1815-1834." *Ohio History*. See chapter on "Waterways."

Fellmeth, Robert C. *Politics of Land: Ralph Nader's Study Group Report on Land Use in California*. See chapter on "Planning, Engineering, and Administration."

Fenzke, Gerhard Alexander. "The California Highway System: Revenues and Expenditures, 1895-1945." Doctoral dissertation, University of California, Santa Barbara, 1978. xvi + 256 pp. Maps, charts, tables, graph, diagram, notes, appendices, and bibliography. Presents a history of California's revenue and expenditure policies and shows "how the state through its fiscal highway policies built a sound highway system."

Finch, J. K. "A Hundred Years of American Civil Engineering, 1852-1952." *Transactions of the American Society of Civil Engineers*. See chapter on "Planning, Engineering, and Administration."

Fischer, LeRoy H., and Robert E. Smith. "Oklahoma and the Parking Meter." *Chronicles of Oklahoma*, XLVII (Summer 1969), 168-208. An interesting and appropriate story of the development of the device for, as the authors note, "the first practical parking meter was invented by Oklahomans, produced by Oklahomans, and sold by Oklahomans."

Fisher, Edwin A. "Engineering and Public Works in the City of Rochester During the Past Century." *Centennial History of Rochester, New York*. See chapter on "Planning, Engineering, and Administration."

Fisher, Jane. *Fabulous Hoosier: A Story of American Achievement*. New York: Robert M. McBride & Company, 1947. vii + 263 pp. Illustrations. A biographical account of Carl J. Fisher, the father of the transcontinental Lincoln Highway, by his wife.

Fisher, W. D. "Good Roads in The West." *Good Roads*, LXVI (Jan. 1924), 9-10. Includes some historical data on roads in South Dakota, Wyoming, and Montana.

Flaxman, Edward. *Great Feats of Modern Engineering*. London: Blackie & Son Limited, 1936. 287 pp. Illustrations, maps, diagrams, and index. United States' engineering feats discussed in this book are mainly bridges and tunnels. There is, however, one chapter on "the Catskill Aqueduct" and one on "Power from Niagara."

Fleming, L. A., and A. R. Standing. "The Road to 'Fortune': The Salt Lake Cutoff." *Utah Historical Quarterly*, 33 (Summer 1965), 248-71. Narrates the location of the cutoff and presents its history.

Fleming, William Foster. "San Antonio: The History of a Military City, 1865-1880." Doctoral dissertation, University of Pennsylvania, 1963. 445 pp. Discusses the city's growth from 1865 to 1880. Some material is included on the construction of streets, sidewalks, and other facilities.

Fletcher, Robert, and J. P. Snow. "A History of the Development of Wooden Bridges." *Transactions of the American Society of Civil Engineers*, 99 (1934), 314-408. A detailed chronology of the development of wooden bridge types from ancient times.

Flink, James J. *America Adopts the Automobile, 1895-1910*. Cambridge: Massachusetts Institute of Technology, 1970. 343 pp. Illustrations, tables, bibliography, and index. A definitive, thorough overview of innovations in the automobile industry during the early twentieth century that transformed American social and economic institutions. The book discusses the early technological evolution of the automobile as well as the governmental response to its adoption. It includes an especially insightful discussion of the impetus the car gave to road development.

Flink, James J. *The Car Culture*. Cambridge: MIT Press, 1975. x + 260 pp. Notes and index. A good summary of the impact of the automobile on American civilization. The book is generally critical of the "automobile revolution" and contains substantive discussions of the evolution of federal and state highway policies.

Fogelson, Robert M. *The Fragmented Metropolis: Los Angeles, 1850-1930*. See chapter on "Community Water Supply."

Folmsbee, Stanley John. "Sectionalism and Internal Improvements in Tennessee, 1796-1845." Doctoral dissertation. See chapter on "Waterways."

Forbes, R. J. *Man the Maker: A History of Technology and Engineering*. See chapter on "Planning, Engineering, and Administration."

Foreman, Grant. *A History of Oklahoma*. Norman: University of Oklahoma Press, 1942. xiv + 384 pp. Illustrations, maps, bibliography, and index. Most of this study deals with Oklahoma's pre-statehood period, especially Indian policy. One excellent chapter discusses early river navigation and roads. Furthermore, scattered throughout the volume are cursory treatments of frontier military posts.

Forness, Norman Olaf. "The Origins and Early History of the United States Department of the Interior." Doctoral dissertation. See chapter on "Public Buildings."

Foster, Harriet McIntyre. "Memories of the National Road." *Indiana Magazine of History*, XIII (March 1917), 60-66. Reminiscences read at the dedication of the marker at the crossing of the National and Michigan roads in Indianapolis.

Foster, Mark S. "The Western Response to Urban Transportation, 1900-1940: A Tale of Three Cities, 1900-1945." *Journal of the West*. See chapter on "Urban Mass Transportation."

Fowle, Frank F. "Early American Timber Bridges." *Journal of the Western Society of Engineers*, 42 (June 1937), 95-102. From their initial use in about 1790 until the Civil War period.

Francisco, Ellsworth. "Newark, N. J., Makes Rapid Progress in Improving Street Lighting." *American City*, 39 (July 1928), 96-98. Outlines history of street lighting in Newark from 1836.

Fraser, Chelsea. *The Story of Engineering in America*. See chapter on "Planning, Engineering, and Administration."

Freeman, Otis W. "Early Wagon Roads in the Inland Empire." *Pacific Northwest Quarterly*, 45 (Oct. 1954), 125-30. Includes information on the following: Colville Road, Mullan Road, Cottonwood Road, Old Territorial Road, Texas Road, Kentucky Trail, Wild Horse Trail, and White Bluffs Road.

Frost, Harwood. *The Art of Roadmaking: Treating of the Various Problems and Operations in the Construction and Maintenance of Roads, Streets, and Pavements*. New York: McGraw-Hill Book Company, 1910. xvii + 544 pp. Illustrations, maps, diagrams, appendices, bibliography, and index. Contains short introductory chapter entitled "Historical Sketch of Road Development."

Fuller, Wayne E. "Good Roads and Rural Free Delivery of Mail." *Mississippi Valley Historical Review*, XLII, (June 1955), 67-83. Describes how the inauguration of rural free delivery of mail in 1896 shaped the farmers' demand for improved roads.

Fuller, Wayne E. *The American Mail: Enlarger of the Common Life*. Chicago: University of Chicago Press, 1972. xi + 378 pp. Bibliographical essay and index. Contains brief discussions of road conditions and improvements in relation to mail delivery.

Fuller, Wayne E. "The Ohio Road Experiment, 1913-1916." *Ohio History*, 74 (Winter 1965), 13-28; 70-71. A well-researched article that recounts the rebuilding (paving) of what the people of Zanesville called the West Pike, a fifty-two-mile link in the National Road, which ran from Cumberland, Maryland, to Illinois.

Galli, Geraldine. "100 Years of Construction News." *Engineering News-Record*. See chapter on "Planning, Engineering, and Administration."

Garland, John M. "The Nonecclesiastical Activities of an English and a North Carolina Parish: A Comparative Study." *North Carolina Historical Review*, L (Jan 1973), 32-57. Contains a brief discussion on how roads were built and maintained in North Carolina and English parishes.

Gayler, Carl. "American Metal Bridges Fifty Years Ago." *Engineering News-Record*, 95 (Sept. 3, 1925), 385-86. Contends that in the 1870s bridge designing practice improved because bridge design was "taken out of the hands of competing bridge companies and turned over to trained engineers."

Geddes, Norman Bel. *Magic Motorways*. New York: Random House, 1940. 297 pp. Illustrations and maps. Some scattered historical material.

Gentry, North Todd. "Plank Roads in Missouri." *Missouri Historical Review*, XXXI (April 1937), 272-87. On mid-nineteenth-century road construction.

Gies, Joseph. *Adventure Underground: The Story of the World's Great Tunnels*. New York: Doubleday & Company, Inc., 1962. 260 pp. Illustrations and bibliography. A popular history of tunnels. Approximately one third of this book deals with United States tunnels and their builders.

Gies, Joseph. *Bridges and Men*. Garden City, N. Y.: Doubleday & Company, 1963. xv + 343 pp. Illustrations, tables, diagrams, appendix, bibliography, and index. A general, well-written history of bridges (not only in the United States) and their builders. A great deal of space is given to the work of James Eads and John Roebling.

Gies, Joseph. *Wonders of the Modern World*. See chapter on "Sewers and Wastewater Treatment."

Gilbert, Gilbert H.; Lucius I. Wightman; and W. L. Saunders. *The Subways and Tunnels of New York: Methods and Costs*. New York: John Wiley & Sons, 1912. xiv + 372 pp. Illustrations, maps, diagrams, appendices, and index. A fact-filled account of New York City's tunnel and subway system, based largely on the records and papers of the engineers and contractors who built it. The system includes one complete subway connecting three boroughs; eight subaqueous tunnels under the East River; six subaqueous tunnels under the Hudson River to the mainland; two subaqueous tunnels under the Harlem River to the Bronx; the belt-line tunnels and the New York subway of the McAdoo system; and the Bergen Hill and crosstown tunnels of the Pennsylvania Railroad. The text is accompanied by numerous illustrations, maps, and diagrams.

Gilchrist, David T., ed. *The Growth of Seaport Cities, 1790-1825: Proceedings of a Conference Sponsored by the Eleutherian Mills-Hagley Foundation, March 17-19, 1966*. See chapter on "Waterways."

Gillmore, Q. A. *A Practical Treatise on Roads, Streets, and Pavements*. New York: D. Van Nostrand, 1885. 258 pp. Illustrations, tables, diagrams, and index. The fifth edition (first published in 1876) of a popular and useful guide to the design, construction, and maintenance of roads, streets, sidewalks, railways, and tramways.

Gilmore, Harlan. *Transportation and the Growth of Cities*. Glencoe, Ill.: Free Press, 1953. vi + 170 pp. Notes, bibliography, and index. An analysis of transportation systems and their effects on the growth of cities. The author suggests that the vitality of cities was dependent on roads, railroads, and waterways that enabled them to control marketing and production over a large geographical area.

Givens, Larry D. "The California Highway Commission and the Truckee River Route." *Nevada Historical Society Quarterly*, XVII (Fall 1974), 153-64. Thorough planning and administrative account of the efforts to build a section of Route 40 across the Sierra Nevada to the Nevada state line. The author provides an excellent sketch on the evolution of the highway commission.

Glaab, Charles N., and A. Theodore Brown. *A History of Urban America*. See chapter on "Community Water Supply."

Glass, Brent D., ed. *North Carolina: An Inventory of Historic Engineering and Industrial Sites*. Washington, D. C.: Historic American Engineering Record, 1975. xv + 109 pp. Illustrations and index. A well-organized inventory that includes sketches of bridges, power plants, and lighthouses.

Glass, Remley J. "Early Transportation and the Plank Road." *Annals of Iowa*, 21 (Jan. 1939), 502-34. Includes some general history of nineteenth-century plank roads.

Glass, Remley J. "Plank Roads in Northeastern Iowa." *Annals of Iowa*, 22 (Jan. 1940), 77-81. A supplement to the author's earlier article (see above).

Goetzmann, William H. *Army Exploration in the American West*. See chapter on "Planning, Engineering, and Administration."

Goode, Rudyard Byron. "The Distribution and Disposition of Highway Funds in Virginia." Doctoral dissertation, University of Virginia, 1954.

Goodrich, Carter. "The Gallatin Plan After One Hundred and Fifty Years." *Proceedings of the American Philosophical Society*. See chapter on "Waterways."

Goodwin, H. Marshall, Jr. "Right-of-Way Controversies in Recent California Highway-Freeway Construction." *Southern California Quarterly*, LVI (Spring 1974), 61-105. Perceptive and thoroughly researched discussion of the opposition of homeowners and businessmen to freeway construction due to the disruptions caused by relocations.

Goodwin, H. Marshall, Jr. "The Arroyo Seco: From Dry Gulch to Freeway." *Southern California Quarterly*, XLVII (March 1965), 73-102. A history of the Pasadena Freeway, connecting downtown Los Angeles with Pasadena, from the first survey in 1895 to when the parkway was dedicated in 1940.

Gordon, Leon M., II. "Effects of the Michigan Road on Northern Indiana, 1830-1860." *Indiana Magazine of History*, XLVI (Dec. 1950), 377-402. Evaluates the Michigan Road's role in the development of the northern part of the state.

Gorman, Mel. "Charles F. Brush and the First Public Electric Street Lighting System in America." *Ohio Historical Quarterly*, 70 (Jan. 1961), 128-41. Reviews Brush's "contribution to urban civilization" in the city of Cleveland. The author, a professor of chemistry at the University of San Francisco, applauds Brush for integrating his system: "dynamo, arc lights, insulation, and carbon rods were conceived as integral parts of a unified whole . . . ."

Gottman, Jean. *Megalopolis: The Urbanized Northeastern Seaboard of the United States*. See chapter on "Planning, Engineering, and Administration."

Gould, George Edwin. *Indiana Covered Bridges Thru the Years*. Indianapolis: Indiana Covered Bridge Society, 1977. 64 pp. Illustrations and bibliography.

Greeley, Samuel A. "Street Cleaning and the Collection and Disposal of Refuse." *Proceedings of the American Society of Civil Engineers*. See chapter on "Solid Wastes."

Green, Constance McLaughlin. *History of Naugatuck, Connecticut*. See chapter on "Sewers and Wastewater Treatment."

Green, Constance McLaughlin. *Holyoke, Massachusetts: A Case Study of the Industrial Revolution in America*. See chapter on "Waterways."

Green, Constance McLaughlin. *Washington: Capital City, 1879-1950*. See chapter on "Community Water Supply."

Green, Constance McLaughlin. *Washington: Village and Capital, 1800-1878*. See chapter on "Urban Mass Transportation."

Green, Lida L. "Markers for Remembrance: The Mormon Trail." *Annals of Iowa*, 40 (Winter, 1970), 190-93. Discusses markers placed by the Civilian Conservations Corps to identify the historic route.

Greenough, W. B. "Developments in Brick Pavement Construction." *American City*, XXII (April 1920), 387-90.

Gregg, Kate L., ed. *The Road to Santa Fe: The Journal and Diaries of George Champlin Sibley and Others Pertaining to the Surveying and Marking of a Road from the Missouri Frontier to the Settlements of New Mexico, 1825-1827*. Albuquerque: University of New Mexico Press, 1952. viii + 280 pp. Illustration, maps, notes, appendix, bibliography, and index. A compilation of the many letters, several diaries, Sibley's journal, and the commission's report concerning the survey of the road to Santa Fe. This "highway between nations" was intended not only to encourage western settlement but to promote trade with northern Mexico. Sibley, who was an Indian agent at Fort Osage, Missouri, when appointed by President John Quincy Adams (March 16, 1825) to the three-man commission responsible for the survey, took the initiative in the commission's work, wrote the history of the project, and made the government report.

Gregory, J. W. *The Story of the Road: From the Beginning down to A. D. 1931*. London: Alexander Maclehose & Company, 1931. xii + 311 pp. Illustrations, maps, notes, and indexes. A history of roads (located mostly outside the United States) by a geology professor at the University of Glasgow. There is one three-page section entitled "The Roads of the United States."

Gross, Howard H. "The Evolution of Street Paving in Chicago." *Municipal Journal and Engineer*, XI (Nov. 1901), 206-07. From wood to brick, asphalt, and granite top macadam.

Grover, A. J. "Street Improvements in the City

of Omaha." *Proceedings of the Nebraska Association of Engineers and Surveyors*, I (1884-1885), 43-50. During the preceding decade.

Gutheim, Frederick, and Wilcomb E. Washburn. *The Federal City: Plans & Realities*. See chapter on "Planning, Engineering, and Administration."

Hafen, LeRoy R. "Raton Pass, an Historic Highway." *Colorado Magazine*, VII (Nov. 1930), 219-21. On an eighteenth-century landmark located on the Colorado-New Mexico boundary south of Trinidad.

Hafen, LeRoy R. "The Coming of the Automobile and Improved Roads to Colorado." *Colorado Magazine*, VIII (Jan. 1931), 1-15. Describes the far-reaching effects of the introduction of the automobile on transportation and road making in Colorado.

Hafen, LeRoy R. *The Overland Mail, 1849-1869: Promoter of Settlement, Precursor of Railroads*. New York: AMS Press, 1969. 361 pp. Illustrations, map, notes, bibliography, and index. First published in 1926, this early history of the postal service documents the importance of postal roads to western settlement and communication. The mail stage is viewed as "the precursor of the railroad."

Hall, Clayton Colman, ed. *Baltimore: Its History and Its People*. See chapter on "Community Water Supply."

Halprin, Lawrence. *Freeways*. New York: Reinhold Publishing Corporation, 1966. 159 pp. Illustrations and index. A photographic survey of freeway design principles in a historical (chronological) setting. A few bridges and tunnels are included.

Hamilton, Peter Joseph. "Early Roads of Alabama." *Transactions of the Alabama Historical Society*, II (1897-1898), 39-56. A historical review of Alabama's Indian trails, trade routes, colonial roads, and early nineteenth-century highways.

Hammon, Neal Owen. "Early Roads into Kentucky." *Register of the Kentucky Historical Society*, 68 (April 1970), 91-131. An encyclopedia of the state's first trails and roads.

Hanes, J. C., and J. M. Morgan, Jr. *The History and Heritage of Civil Engineering in Virginia*. Lexington, Va.: Virginia Section, American Society of Civil Engineers, 1973. 98 pp. Illustrations and appendices. Includes data on ASCE's Virginia Section as well as historical descriptions of the James River Canal, Little River Turnpike, Alexandria and Georgetown Canal, Pentagon Building, Chesapeake Bay Bridge Tunnel, Big Walker Tunnel, and the Shirley Highway.

Hansen, Harry. *Scarsdale: From Colonial Manor to Modern Community*. See chapter on "Community Water Supply."

Hansen, Marcus L. "Phantoms on the Old Road." *Palimpsest*, II (Feb. 1921), 35-48. On the "Old Military Road" (1839) which extended from Dubuque to Iowa City.

Harden, John. *North Carolina Roads and Their Builders*. Raleigh: Superior Stone Company, 1966. iii + 252 pp. Illustrations and index. A continuation of an earlier work on North Carolina's roads by Capus Waynick. This volume contains a brief history of the state's roads, from 1952 to 1965, as well as information on North Carolina's official highway organization and its highway builders and suppliers.

Hardin, Thomas L. "The National Road in Illinois." *Journal of the Illinois State Historical Society*, LX (Spring 1967), 5-22. On Illinois' historic role in the westward extension of the National Road.

Harris, Charles Wayne. "Pathway to the Southwest: Transportation and Communication along the Gila Trail." Doctoral dissertation, Oklahoma State University, 1973. 281 pp.

Harrison, Joseph Hobson, Jr. "The Internal Improvement Issue in the Politics of the Union, 1783-1825." Doctoral dissertation, University of Virginia, 1954. viii + 696 pp. Maps, notes, appendices, and bibliography. Excellent study of early internal improvements that reflects prodigious research and insights. In addition to the political dimensions of the subject, the study contains a host of information on early nineteenth-century engineers and engineering.

Harrison, Ward. "A New Era in Street Illumination." *Journal of the Cleveland Engineering Society*, VII (May 1915), 419-41. On significant developments since the early nineteenth century. The article includes considerable technical data.

Harrison, Ward; O. F. Haas; and Kirk M.

Reid. *Street Lighting Practice*. New York: McGraw-Hill Book Company, 1930. x + 270 pp. Illustrations, maps, charts, tables, graphs, diagrams, appendices, and index. The first chapter (nine pages) reviews the history of street illumination. The remainder of the book discusses problems of an engineering character as well as those of contractual relations, methods of financing, and maintenance provisions.

Hart, Virginia. *The Story of American Roads*. New York: Sloane, 1950. 243 pp. Illustrations and maps.

Hartman, J. Paul. *Civil Engineering Landmarks: State of Florida*. See chapter on "Planning, Engineering, and Administration."

Hartsough, Mildred. "Transportation as a Factor in the Development of the Twin Cities." *Minnesota History*. See chapter on "Waterways."

Hataway, Marsha Perry. "The Development of the Mississippi State Highway System, 1916-1932." *Journal of Mississippi History*, XXVIII (Nov. 1966), 286-303. Records the successes and failures of Mississippi road-building pioneers.

Hatch, Charles E., Jr. "The Great Road: Earliest Highway Used and Developed by the English at Jamestown." *Virginia Magazine of History and Biography*, 57 (Jan. 1949), 14-21. Shows "the close relationship between historical and archeological research" at the Jamestown Archeological Project. The project was set up by the National Park Service in the mid 1930s, and the discovery of the traces of the old road ranks as one of the project's major findings.

Haupt, Herman. *Reminiscences of General Herman Haupt: With Notes and a Personal Sketch by Frank Abial Flower*. Milwaukee: Wright & Joys Company, 1901. 331 pp. Illustrations, appendix, and index. Reminiscences of a nineteenth-century engineer who served as general superintendent (1850-1852) and as chief engineer (1852-1856) on the Pennsylvania Railroad; then in 1856, he accepted an invitation from the state of Massachusetts to work on the Hoosac Tunnel.

Heath, Milton Sydney. *The Role of the State in Economic Development in Georgia to 1860*. See chapter on "Waterways."

Hebden, Norman, and Wilbur S. Smith. *State-City Relationships in Highway Affairs*. New Haven: Yale University Press, 1950. xvi + 230 pp. Illustrations, tables, charts, graphs, notes, and index. The first section of the book is devoted to a discussion of the development of state-city relationships in highway matters. A good portion of the remainder of the study is placed in historical context.

Heilbron, Bertha L., ed. "Territorial Daguerreotypes: Bridging the Mississippi." *Minnesota History*, XXIX (March 1948), 29-35. Jane Gay Fuller's 1855 account of the opening of the suspension bridge at St. Anthony in Minnesota Territory. It appears in a letter to her cousin, Hiram Fuller, a prominent journalist who owned and edited the New York *Mirror*.

Hewes, L. I. "America's Park Highways." *Civil Engineering*. See chapter on "Parks and Recreation."

Hewes, L. I. "Highway Transportation since 1928." *Civil Engineering*, 8 (Sept. 1938), 585-88. Explains how increased highway use (73 percent) in the past decade has influenced highway development.

Higgins, Frances. "The Wilderness Road." *Indiana Magazine of History*, XIII (March 1917), 56-59. Short history of the Kentucky route from Mt. Vernon to Cumberland Gap, sometimes known as "Boone Way" since it is "the same as was marked out by Daniel Boone himself."

Highway Research Board. National Academy of Sciences. *Ideas and Actions: A History of the Highway Research Board 1920–1970.* Washington, D.C.: Highway Research Board, 1970. xi + 243 pp. Illustrations, charts, tables, appendices, and index. A fiftieth-anniversary organizational history.

Hileman, R. G. "An Iowa Road Challenge." *Palimpsest*, XLVI (Feb. 1965), 123-28. On highway problems and developments since 1958.

Hill, C. S. "Half a Century of Road Development." *Engineering News-Record*, 92 (April 17, 1924), 685-86. Brief piece on highway development at the turn of the twentieth century by an associate editor of *Engineering News-Record*. He includes a surprisingly large quantity of factual material.

Hill, Forest G. *Roads, Rails & Waterways: The Army Engineers and Early Transportation*. See chapter on "Waterways."

Hindle, Brooke. *Technology in Early America: Needs and Opportunities for Study*. See chapter on "Planning, Engineering, and Administration."

Hindley, Geoffrey. *A History of Roads*. London: Peter Davies, 1971. ix + 158 pp. Illustrations, maps, bibliography, and index. Traces the general lines of development in the history of the world's overland transport. Only two chapters discuss roads in the United States.

History and Heritage Committee (San Francisco Section/ASCE). *Historic Engineering Landmarks of San Francisco and Northern California*. See chapter on "Public Buildings."

History and Heritage Committee (Los Angeles Section/ASCE). *Historic Civil Engineering Landmarks of Southern California*. See chapter on "Irrigation."

Hoffman, Abraham. "Angeles Crest: The Creation of a Forest Highway System in the San Gabriel Mountains." *Southern California Quarterly*, L (Sept. 1968), 309-45. On road building for sightseeing and recreational purposes in the Angeles National Forest, 1919-1961.

Hogan, Paul J. "Civilian Conservation Corps and the Farm Island Causeway." *South Dakota History*, 8 (Fall 1978), 312-26. Photo essay of a CCC project near Pierre, South Dakota.

Holbrook, Stewart H. *The Old Post Road*. New York: McGraw-Hill Book Company, 1962. iii + 273 pp. Illustrations, map, bibliography, and index. An interesting account of one of America's earliest highways, the Boston Post Road. Designated an official post road (the New York to Boston route) in the late seventeenth century, it took on added significance and sophistication.

Holland, Rupert Sargent. *Big Bridge*. Philadelphia: Macrae-Smith Company, 1934. 266 pp. Illustrations. Written for a wide audience and divided into four parts: "Early Times," "Timber and Stone," "Iron and Steel," and "Big Bridge [George Washington]."

Holmes, Edward H., and John T. Lynch. "Highway Planning in the Past, Present, and Future." *Transactions of the American Society of Civil Engineers*, 124 (1959), 149-63. Brief history of highway research and planning regarding the development of the federal-aid road system.

Holmes, William F. "Turnpikes Across the Peninsula." *Delaware History*, X (April 1962), 71-104. Early nineteenth-century turnpikes across the isthmus between Chesapeake and Delaware bays.

Holt, W. Stull. *The Bureau of Public Roads: Its History, Activities and Organization*. Baltimore: Johns Hopkins Press, 1923. xi + 123 pp. Notes, appendices, bibliography, and index. One of the "Service Monographs" prepared by the Institute for Government Research. The first chapter is a forty-page history of the Department of Agriculture's Bureau of Public Roads.

Holt, W. Stull. *The Office of the Chief of Engineers of the Army: Its Non-Military History, Activities, and Organization*. See chapter on "Planning, Engineering, and Administration."

Hopkins, H. J. *A Span of Bridges: An Illustrated History*. London: David & Charles Limited, 1970. 288 pp. Illustrations, diagrams, bibliography, and index. Prepared by an engineer, this volume emphasizes the theory and practice of bridge building in an historical context.

Horn, C. Lester. "Oregon's Columbia River Highway." *Oregon Historical Quarterly*, LXVI (Sept. 1965), 249-71. Vivid recollection by a participant in the construction of the project, which was completed in 1915.

Horton, John P. "The Street-Cleaning Revolution." *American City*. See chapter on "Solid Wastes."

Horton, Tom. "To Save a Valley." *Historic Preservation*, 32 (July/Aug. 1980), 2-9. How a one-lane bridge in Kanai's Valley "stands between Hawaii as it used to be and the onslaught of tourism and development." A brief history of the Hanalei Bridge is presented.

How, Louis. *James B. Eads*. New York: Houghton, Mifflin and Company, 1900. vi + 120 pp. Illustration. A short biographical account of Eads' professional life by his grandson. He gives particular attention to Eads' training, ironclad gunboats used during the Civil War, famous St. Louis bridge, and Mississippi River jetties.

Hoy, Suellen M. "People in Public Works: Ben Franklin." *APWA Reporter*, 43 (July 1976), 14-15, 27. Describes Franklin's active interest in the improvement of Philadelphia's streets.

Hoy, Suellen M. "People in Public Works: Charles H. Purcell." *APWA Reporter*, 46 (Feb. 1979), 4-5. A biographical sketch of the director of California's Department of Public Works from 1943 to 1951. Purcell's greatest accomplishment was the construction of the San Francisco-Oakland Bay Bridge.

Hoy, Suellen M. "People in Public Works: Jack Sverdrup." *APWA Reporter*, 45 (Nov. 1978), 4-5. A biographical sketch of the founder of the St. Louis-based consulting engineering firm of Sverdrup & Parcel, whose early work was largely bridge design and construction.

Hoy, Suellen M. "People in Public Works: John Loudon McAdam." *APWA Reporter*, 47 (April 1980), 6-7. A biographical sketch which emphasizes McAdam's contributions to improving roads in Great Britain and the United States.

Hoy, Suellen M. "People in Public Works: Washington and Emily Roebling." *APWA Reporter*, 45 (Feb. 1978), 4-5. Highlights Washington Roebling's effort and dedication in completing the bridge (Brooklyn) designed by his father, John. The article also summarizes Emily Roebling's service to the bridge and her husband.

Hoy, Suellen M. "People in Public Works: William Phelps Eno." *APWA Reporter*, 43 (Oct. 1976), 12-13. Reviews the early life and career of "the father of traffic safety," emphasizing the ways he promoted a uniform and workable traffic code.

Hoyt, Franklin. "The Bradshaw Road." *Pacific Historical Review*, XXI (1952), 243-54. On William Bradshaw's road (1862) from Los Angeles to the Colorado River mines.

Hoyt, Hugh Myron, Jr. "The Good Roads Movement in Oregon: 1900-1920." Doctoral dissertation, University of Oregon, 1966. 287 pp.

Hubbard, Theodora Kimball, and Henry Vincent. *Our Cities To-Day and To-Morrow: A Survey of Planning and Zoning Progress in the United States*. See chapter on "Planning, Engineering, and Administration."

Hulbert, Archer Butler. *Boone's Wilderness Road*. Cleveland: Arthur H. Clark Company, 1903. 207 pp. Illustration, maps, and notes. The sixth volume in the "Historic Highways of America" series in which the author describes Daniel Boone's opening of "the longest, blackest, hardest road of pioneer days in America."

Hulbert, Archer Butler. *Braddock's Road and Three Relative Papers*. Cleveland: Arthur H. Clark Company, 1903. 218 pp. Illustrations, maps, and notes. The fourth volume in the "Historic Highways of America" series in which the author describes in detail the building of Braddock's Road in 1755. According to Hulbert, "few roads ever cost so much, ever amounted to so little at first, and then finally played so important a part in the development of any continent."

Hulbert, Archer Butler. *Indian Thoroughfares*. Cleveland: Arthur H. Clark Company, 1902. 152 pp. Illustrations and maps. The second volume in the "Historic Highways of America" series in which the author describes the routes of the more important Indian thoroughfares and suggests the importance of studying them.

Hulbert, Archer Butler. *Military Roads of the Mississippi Basin: The Conquest of the Old Northwest*. Cleveland: Arthur H. Clark Company, 1904. 237 pp. Illustrations, maps, notes, and appendices. The eighth volume in the "Historic Highways of America" series in which the author treats five of the early campaigns in the portion of America known as the Mississippi Basin—Clark's campaigns against Kaskaskia and Vincennes in 1778 and 1779; and Harmar's, St. Clair's, and Wayne's campaigns against the northwestern Indians in 1790, 1791, and 1793-94.

Hulbert, Archer Butler. *Paths of the Mound-Building Indians and Great Game Animals*. Cleveland: Arthur H. Clark Company, 1902. 140 pp. Maps. The first in a multi-volume series of "Historic Highways in America." It describes the routes of the mound-building Indians and the trails of the large game animals, particularly the buffalo. The author contends that they "set the course of landward travel in America on the watersheds of the interior of the continent."

Hulbert, Archer Butler. *Pioneer Roads and Experiences of Travelers (Volume I)*. Cleveland: Arthur H. Clark Company, 1904. 201 pp. Illustrations and notes. The eleventh volume in the "Historic Highways of America" series is devoted to a discussion of the evolution of highways from Indian trails to macadamized roads; the travel experiences of Francis Baily, an eminent British astronomer, on the Pennsylvania Road; the story of Zane's Trace; and Judge James Hall's descriptions of travel in Kentucky.

Hulbert, Archer Butler. *Pioneer Roads and Experiences of Travelers (Volume II)*. Cleveland: Arthur H. Clark Company, 1904. 202 pp. Maps and notes. In the twelfth volume in the "Historic Highways of America" series, the author focuses his attention on two lines of pioneer movement—one through northern Virginia (the Old Northwestern Turnpike) and the other through central New York (the Genesee Road). The final chapter contains the most fascinating passages on pioneer travel in America from Charles Dickens' *American Notes*.

Hulbert, Archer Butler. *Portage Paths: The Keys of the Continent*. Cleveland: Arthur H. Clark Company, 1903. 194 pp. Maps and notes. In the seventh volume in the "Historic Highways of America" series, the author first describes the nature, use, and evolution of the best known portages and then presents a "Catalogue of American Portages" in which he includes extracts from other studies on the same subject.

Hulbert, Archer Butler. *The Cumberland Road*. Cleveland: Arthur H. Clark Company, 1904. 208 pp. Illustrations, maps, notes, and appendices. In this tenth volume in the "Historic Highways of America" series, the author discusses the building, operation, and control of the National Road as well as its most important official function—providing a means for transporting United States mail.

Hulbert, Archer Butler. *The Old Glade (Forbes's) Road (Pennsylvania State Road)*. Cleveland: Arthur H. Clark Company, 1903. 205 pp. Illustrations, maps, and notes. In the fifth volume of the "Historic Highways of America" series, the author tells the story of building a road which, throughout the Revolutionary War, was "the main thoroughfare over which the western forts received ammunition and supplies."

Hulbert, Archer Butler. *The Paths of Inland Commerce: A Chronicle of Trail, Road, and Waterway*. New Haven: Yale University Press, 1921. xi + 211 pp. Illustrations, bibliography, and index. A popular account of the role of transportation in the nation's development.

Hulbert, Archer Butler. *Washington's Road: The First Chapter of the Old French War*. Cleveland: Arthur H. Clark Company, 1903. 215 pp. Illustrations and maps. The third volume in the "Historic Highways of America" series in which the author looks at "Washington and his times . . . from the standpoint of the road he opened across the Alleghanies in 1754."

Hungerford, Edward. *The Story of Public Utilities*. See chapter on "Urban Mass Transportation."

Hunt, Rockwell Dennis, and William Sheffield Ament. *Oxcart to Airplane*. Los Angeles: Powell Publishing Company, 1929. iii + 458 pp. Illustrations, bibliography, and index. An account of transportation developments in California in two parts: Part I, "Hoofs, Wheels, and Wings," by Rockwell D. Hunt; and Part II, "By Sea to California," by William S. Ament. Sections in the first part describe roads and highways, street cars and jitneys, and airways and airports.

Hunter, Robert Fleming. "The Turnpike Movement in Virginia, 1816-1860." Doctoral dissertation, Columbia University, 1957. 378 pp.

Hunter, Robert F. "The Turnpike Movement in Virginia, 1816-1860." *Virginia Magazine of History and Biography*, 69 (July 1961), 278-89. A review of the turnpike movement in Virginia, where "the state gave financial aid to the turnpike companies." In New England, unlike Virginia, the state "left private enterprise to find its own funds."

Hunter, Robert F. "Turnpike Construction in Antebellum Virginia." *Technology and Culture*, IV (Spring 1963), 177-200. In 1816 the Virginia General Assembly created a Fund for Internal Improvement and a Board of Public Works to administer the fund. A year later, the assembly passed the General Turnpike Law to assist the Board of Public Works in its dealing with private turnpike companies. The author examines the sort of highway system produced in this mixed undertaking and looks at the career of Claudius Crozet, the Virginia Board of Public Works' principal engineer.

Huse, Charles Phillips. *The Financial History of Boston From May 1, 1822 to January 31,*

1909. See chapter on "Community Water Supply."

Hutton, William R. *The Washington Bridge over the Harlem River at 181st Street, New York City: A Description of Its Construction*. New York: Leo Von Rosenberg, 1889. 96 pp. + LXIII plates. Illustrations, maps, diagrams, and tables. A classic account of the construction of the Washington Bridge (1886-1889) over the Harlem River by its chief engineer. It is accompanied by sixty-three plates that were prepared from the working drawings.

Hyde, Charles H. *The Lower Peninsula of Michigan: An Inventory of Historic Engineering and Industrial Sites*. See chapter on "Community Water Supply."

"Illinois Society [of Engineers] Celebrates Its 50th Anniversary." *Engineering News-Record*. See chapter on "Planning, Engineering, and Administration."

Imberman, Eli Woodruff. "The Formative Years of Chicago Bridge & Iron Company." 2 vols. Doctoral dissertation, University of Chicago, 1973. Vol I: viii + 263 pp.; Vol. II: 264-623 pp. Illustrations, diagrams, notes, appendices, and bibliography. A thoroughly researched history of the Chicago Bridge & Iron Company that includes several chapters on the advancements in bridge building to 1900, biographical information on Horace E. Horton (the company's founder), and lengthy discussions of the Fort Snelling and Dubuque High bridges.

Inman, Henry. *The Old Santa Fe Trail: The Story of a Great Highway*. New York: Macmillan Company, 1898. xvii + 493 pp. Illustrations, notes, maps, and index. A popular history of the trail by an ex-army officer. The book is dedicated to and contains prefatory remarks by William F. "Buffalo Bill" Cody.

Inman, Henry, and William F. Cody. *The Great Salt Lake Trail*. Topeka: Crane & Company, 1899. xiii + 529 pp. Illustrations, notes, and index. Presents "the story of the Trail in the days long before the building of a railroad was believed to be possible." The trappers, scouts, Indians, Mormons, and gold diggers all receive their due.

Isaac, Paul E. "Municipal Reform in Beaumont, Texas, 1902-1909." *Southwestern Historical Quarterly*. See chapter on "Planning, Engineering, and Administration."

Israel, Paul B. "Spanning the Golden State: A History of the Highway Bridge in California." Master's thesis, University of California at Santa Barbara, 1979.

Jackson, Donald C. "Railroads, Truss Bridges, and the Rise of the Civil Engineer." *Civil Engineering*, 47 (Oct. 1977), 97-101. The author contends that "civil engineers played a leading role in the development of the U. S. railroads, especially in the design and construction of thousands of truss bridges to carry trains over rivers and ravines" and that the failure of many of the bridges designed by steel manufacturers "ultimately gave birth to the independent consulting engineer."

Jackson, W. Turrentine. "Federal Road Building Grants for Early Oregon." *Oregon Historical Quarterly*, L (March 1949), 3-29. As a territory, Oregon received appropriations from Congress for "military roads"; later when Oregon became a state, federal aid to road building "came more often in the form of land grants which in time were transferred to private enterprise by the state." The author contends that the significant aspects of federal road building policy "in the far western territories and states can be observed through developments in Oregon."

Jackson, W. Turrentine. "The Army Engineers as Road Builders in Territorial Iowa." *Iowa Journal of History*, 47 (Jan. 1949), 15-33. Argues that the roads built by army engineers in Iowa were "undoubtedly the best constructed and among the most widely used . . . during the territorial days."

Jackson, W. Turrentine. "The Army Engineers as Road Surveyors and Builders in Kansas and Nebraska, 1854-1858." *Kansas Historical Quarterly*, XVII (1949), 37-59. Shows army engineers as expert, pioneer road builders, even though civilian contractors eventually took over the federal government's road building program in Kansas and Nebraska. According to Congress, the army engineers had been too thorough and too slow.

Jackson, W. Turrentine. *Wagon Roads West: A Study of Federal Road Surveys and Construction in the Trans-Mississippi West, 1846-1869*. New Haven: Yale University Press, 1965. xix + 422 pp. Illustration, maps, notes, bibliography, and index. Originally published in 1952, this edition contains a foreword by historian William H. Goetzmann who states that "the chief significance" of the volume "is to indicate the degree of dependence of the West upon government aid in some form." Jackson emphasizes the political as well as the economic decisions made in Washington "to aid the Western emigrant by building all-important primary roads."

Jacobs, David, and Anthony E. Neville. *Bridges, Canals & Tunnels*. Eau Claire, Wis.: E. M. Hale and Company, 1968. 159 pp. Illustrations, map, diagrams, appendix, and index. Published by the American Heritage Publishing Company in association with the Smithsonian Institution, this book underscores the fact that early bridges, canals, and tunnels helped to create American society rather than "to serve an existing society." The volume is richly illustrated.

Jakeman, Adelbert M. *Old Covered Bridges: The Story of Covered Bridges in General, With a Description of the Remaining Bridges in Massachusetts and Connecticut*. Brattleboro, Vt.: Stephen Day Press, 1935. 107 pp. Illustrations. A romantic account.

Jakkula, A. A. *A History of Suspension Bridges in Bibliographical Form*. College Station, Texas: Agricultural and Mechanical College of Texas, 1941. 564 pp. Indexes. A thorough, annotated bibliography of suspension bridges published by the Public Roads Administration and the Agricultural and Mechanical College of Texas (No. 7 in the Fourth Series, Vol. 12 of the *Bulletin of the Agricultural and Mechanical College of Texas*).

"James B. Eads." *Scientific American Supplement*, XXIII (May 7, 1887), 9447-49. A lengthy, biographical article reviewing various aspects of Eads' career as both bridge builder and inventor. Reprinted from *Popular Science Monthly*.

James, J. G. "50 Years of White Lines." *Roads and Road Construction*, 42 (Dec. 1964), 409-14. On materials and practices used in road marking.

Jameson, Charles Davis. "The Evolution of the Modern Railway Bridge." *Popular Science Monthly*, XXXVI (Feb. 1890), 461-81. A technical explanation, accompanied by drawings, of how the design of railway bridges has evolved.

Jeffrey, Thomas E. "Internal Improvements and Political Parties in Antebellum North Carolina, 1836-1860." *North Carolina Historical Review*. See chapter on "Waterways."

Jelly, Irving A. "Anatomy of an Old Covered Bridge." *Civil Engineering*, 11 (Jan. 1941), 12-14. Discusses in general covered bridges in Pennsylvania and in particular the Portland (Pa.)-Columbia (N. J.) bridge over the Delaware River. This 1869 bridge was once known as the Columbia Delaware Bridge.

Jenkins, James T., Jr. "The Story of Roads." *American Road Builder*, 44 (Sept. 1967), 13-44. In summary form a popular history of roads "from Indian trails to packhorse trails, wagon roads, bicycle paths, automobile roads and . . . superhighways."

Jenkins, James T., Jr. "The Story of Roads—Part I." *American Road Builder*, 34 (May 1957), 4-7. A brief chronicle of road building in the seventeenth and eighteenth centuries.

Jenkins, James T., Jr. "The Story of Roads—Part II." *American Road Builder*, 34 (June 1957), 8-11. A narrative describing "the arduous process of road building since the refinement of animal and Indian trails."

Jenkins, James T., Jr. "The Story of Roads—Part III." *American Road Builder*, 34 (July-Aug. 1957), 16-17, 20-22. On early nineteenth-century defense roads and toll roads.

Jenkins, James T., Jr. "The Story of Roads—Part IV." *American Road Builder*, 34 (Nov. 1957), 10-13. Descriptions of famous western trails: the Oregon Trail, the Santa Fe Trail, the Mormon Trail, and the Pony Express.

Jenkins, James T., Jr. "The Story of Roads—Part V." *American Road Builder*, 35 (April 1958), 8-9. Describes the bridging of the continent by rail to the advent of the motor car.

Jenkins, James T., Jr. "The Story of Roads—Part VI." *American Road Builder*, 35 (July 1958), 8-11. Covers the period between the first automobiles in 1900 through the 1916 Federal Aid Act.

Jenkins, James T., Jr. "The Story of Roads—Part VII." *American Road Builder*, 35 (Sept. 1958), 9-11. Summarizes major highway developments in the 1920s, 1930s, and early 1940s. For example, highways were marked with standardized information and directional signs.

Jenkins, James T., Jr. "The Story of Roads—Part VIII (Conclusion)." *American Road Builder*, 35 (Dec. 1958), 6-8. The concluding essay in the series reviews more recent developments—from the opening of the Alaskan Highway through the 1956 Highway Act.

Jenks, William L. "Fort Gratiot Turnpike." *Michigan History Magazine*, IX (1925), 150-61. Records facts related to the construction of a road from Detroit to Fort Gratiot. Lewis Cass, governor of the Territory of Michigan, was the road's most active promoter.

Jensen, James Maurice. "The Development of the Central Valley Transportation Route in California to 1920." Doctoral dissertation, University of Southern California, 1965. 205 pp.

Johnson, A. N. "Notes on Road Building in Washington's Time." *Journal of the Western Society of Engineers*, XXII (Oct. 1917), 579-82. A brief look at road building at the turn of the nineteenth century.

Johnson, Charles A. "The Development of the Suspension Bridge." *Architectural Forum*, XLIX (Nov. 1928), 721-27. From the late eighteenth century. Numerous photographs accompany the article.

Johnson, Charles B. "On and About the National Road in the Early Fifties." *Transactions of the Illinois State Historical Society* (1922), 59-65. In Illinois.

Johnson, Leland R. *Memphis to Bristol: A Half Century of Highway Construction*. Nashville: Tennessee Road Builders Association, 1978. 235 pp. Illustrations, maps, appendices, bibliography, and index. Commemorates the fiftieth anniversary of the Texas Road Builders Association. One of the few good state histories of road and highway construction.

Johnson, Mary Elizabeth. *Emergency Employment in Onondaga County*. See chapter on "Planning, Engineering, and Administration."

Johnson, Palmer O., and L. Oswald Harvey. *The National Youth Administration*. See chapter on "Public Buildings."

Jonasson, Jonas A. "Local Road Legislation in Early Oregon." *Oregon Historical Quarterly*, XLII (June 1914), 162-75. Reviews the appropriate legislation and describes the growing network of territorial roads in Oregon (1844-1859).

Jones, Herbert G. *The King's Highway from Portland to Kittery: Stagecoach & Tavern Days on the Old Post Road*. Portland, Me.: Longfellow Press, 1953. 228 pp. Illustrations. Written for an audience familiar with the southern part of Maine, the author confesses that he has "endeavored to deal primarily with the unusual and little known facts and the romantic association of localities than to record purely historical events."

Jordan, Philip D. *The National Road*. Indianapolis: Bobbs-Merrill Company, 1948. 442 pp. Illustrations, map, notes, bibliography, and index. A history of the National Road. This account describes "the actual construction of the pike from the first surveys to the final surfacing." It was "not primarily produced for historians, but rather for those thousands of Americans . . . who themselves, as contemporary tourists, wish to know the narrative of the National Road."

Judd, Jacob. "A City's Streets: A Case Study of Brooklyn, 1834-1855." *Journal of Long Island History*, IX (Winter-Spring 1969), 32-43. One of the few case studies of street and sidewalk construcion prior to the Civil War. Judd places major emphasis on the provincial outlook of the community's leaders.

Judd, Jacob. "Brooklyn's Health and Sanitation, 1834-1855." *Journal of Long Island History*. See chapter on "Sewers and Wastewater Treatment."

Kahn, Edgar Myron. "Andrew Smith Hallidie." *California Historical Society Quarterly*, XIX (June 1940), 144-56. Biographical sketch of a nineteenth-century engineer who earned a reputation for his wire suspension bridges and originated cable railway transportation.

Kaloupek, Walter E. "The History and Administration of the Iowa Highway Safety Patrol." *Iowa Journal of History and Politics*, XXXVI (Oct. 1938), 339-86. Describes the need for, creation of, and administration of the Iowa Highway Safety Patrol.

Kanarek, Harold. "The U. S. Army Corps of Engineers and Early Internal Improvements in Maryland." *Maryland Historical Magazine*. See chapter on "Waterways."

Kaplan, Michael D. "The Toll Road Building

Career of Otto Mears, 1881-1887." *Colorado Magazine*, LII (Spring 1975), 153-170. The author shows that Mears' most significant contribution to Colorado's transportation development was "the building of his toll road system and his part in the campaign to convert it to a modern road network."

Kasling, Robert W. "The Highway Pattern of Colorado." Master's thesis, University of Chicago, 1940. vii + 110 pp. Illustrations, maps, graphs, notes, and bibliography. A delineation and interpretation of Colorado's highway pattern. This geography thesis emphasizes the problems accompanying "the survey, construction, and maintenance of highways." Historical data appears throughout the study.

Keith, William G. "Development of the Chicago Street-Lighting System." *Engineering World*, 15 (Dec. 1919), 39-41. Describes progress since 1887 when the first municipal electric light plant was established in the basement of a fire engine house.

Kelley, Ben. *The Pavers and the Paved*. New York: Donald W. Brown, 1971. viii + 183 pp. Notes, sources, and index. Only incidental history in this critique of the federal-aid expressway program. The author is a former public affairs director for the federal road program in the U. S. Department of Transportation.

Kemp, E. L., and J. K. Kemp. *A History of the Weston & Gauley Bridge Turnpike*. N. p.: U. S. Army Corps of Engineers, Huntington District, 1979. 62 pp. Illustrations, maps, appendix, and bibliography. Traces the building of a nineteenth-century Virginia turnpike (1848-1857) and highlights the period's improved road-building techniques.

Kemp, E. L. "An Introduction to the Structural Evaluation of Historic Reinforced Concrete Structures." *Concrete International*. See chapter on "Public Buildings."

Kemper, Charles E. "The Indian Road." *Virginia Magazine of History and Biography*, L (Jan. 1942), 63-65. The author traces the Indian Road from central New York through Pennsylvania, Maryland, and Virginia. The road ended in the Tuscarora towns of North Carolina. (The Tuscaroras were a branch of the Iroquois Indians who settled in North Carolina.)

Kendall, Charles P. "Engineer's Nightmare: Bridging the Colorado at Yuma in 1915." *Journal of Arizona History*, 19 (Autumn 1978), 283-96. A description of the difficulties encountered in building the Yuma bridge, linking Arizona and California.

Kendrick, Baynard. *Florida Trails to Turnpikes, 1914-1964*. Tallahassee: Rose Printing Company, 1964. xv + 297 pp. Illustrations, maps, tables, appendix, glossary, bibliography, and index. A cooperative project of the Florida State Road Board, Asphalt Contractors Association of Florida, Florida Limerock Institute, and Florida Road Builders Association. This volume is a fifty-year history of the State Road Department and Florida road building particularly in the twentieth century.

Kincaid, Robert L. *The Wilderness Road*. Indianapolis: Bobbs-Merrill Company, 1947. 392 pp. Illustrations, maps, notes, bibliographical essay, and index. A meticulous study of the picturesque pathway from the eastern Piedmont to Kentucky by "a man born in the hill country of Georgia."

King, Arthur G. "Origins of Some Cincinnati Streets—A Street in Clifton." *Bulletin of the Historical and Philosophical Society of Ohio*. See chapter on "Military Installations."

Kingsford, W. *History, Structure, and Statistics of Plank Roads in the United States and Canada*. Philadelphia: A. Hart, 1851. 40 pp. Tables and diagrams.

Kirkland, Edward C. *Industry Comes of Age: Business, Labor, and Public Policy, 1860-1897*. See chapter on "Waterways."

Kirkland, Edward Chase. *Men, Cities, and Transportation: A Study in New England History, 1820-1900*. See chapter on "Waterways."

Kliewer, Waldo O. "The Foundations of Billings, Montana." *Pacific Northwest Quarterly*. See chapter on "Planning, Engineering, and Administration."

Knight, Oliver. *Fort Worth: Outpost on the Trinity*. See chapter on "Urban Mass Transportation."

Knowles, Morris. "History of Civil Engineering in Western Pennsylvania." *Proceedings of the Engineers' Society of Western Pennsylvania*. See chapter on "Planning, Engineering, and Administration."

Knowlton, Ezra C. *History of Highway De-*

velopment in Utah. Salt Lake City: Utah State Department of Highways, 1964. xxv + 943 pp. Illustrations, maps, charts, tables, notes, appendices, and index. A comprehensive study of road and highway development in Utah by a long-time employee of the State Road Commission. The emphasis is on the state's role in planning, designing, financing, constructing, operating, and maintaining the road system.

Koke, Richard J. "Milestones along the Old Highways of New York City." *New-York Historical Society Quarterly*, XXXIV (July 1950), 165-234. A study of the milestones (stone markings) which once stood in New York City, especially along the post roads to Albany and to Boston.

Kouwenhoven, John A. "Eads Bridge: The Celebration." *Missouri Historical Society Bulletin*, XXX (April 1974), 159-180. Describes the high and low points of the July 4, 1874 opening-day celebration.

Krenkel, John Henry. "Internal Improvements in Illinois, 1818-1848." Doctoral dissertation. See chapter on "Waterways."

Kropf, W. J. "The Development of Road Drainage As Revealed by the History of Roads." *Good Roads*, LXXIII (Jan. 1930), 12, 14, 16, 18. Features the prominent role of drainage in the development of the modern road.

Kulik, Gary, and Julia C. Bonham. *Rhode Island: An Inventory of Historic Engineering and Industrial Sites*. Washington, D. C.: Historic American Engineering Record, 1978. xvi + 296 pp. Illustrations and index. Useful compilation of sketches of historic bridges, dams, waterworks, power plants, and water transportation facilities.

Kutler, Stanley I. *Privilege and Creative Destruction: The Charles River Bridge Case*. Philadelphia: J. B. Lippincott Company, 1971. viii + 191 pp. Illustration, map, notes, bibliographical essay, and index. Detailed discussion of an important public policy question. The author presents the tale of two bridges—the Charles River Bridge (1786) and an adjacent competing bridge (1828) which unlike the former, was to be toll-free—and evaluates "the role of law and legal institutions in accommodating the process of creative destruction wrought by technological and economic change." In 1837 the United States Supreme Court sustained the state of Massachusetts' action and denied the appeal of the proprietors who had argued that the new bridge destroyed the tolls (the property) of the old structure and "thus constituted the taking of private property for public use without compensation."

Kyle, John H. *The Building of TVA*. See chapter on "Flood Control and Drainage."

Labatut, Jean, and Wheaton J. Lane, eds. *Highways in Our National Life: A Symposium*. Princeton: Princeton University Press, 1950. xvi + 506 pp. Illustrations, tables, graphs, notes, bibliography, and index. An important collection of essays which presents the viewpoints of specialists who understand "both the historical and analytical aspects of the highway." See especially Herbert J. Spinden's "The Indian Trail from the Time of the Mayas to the Colonial Period," Wheaton J. Lane's "The Early Highway in America, to the Coming of the Railroad," Albert C. Rose's "The Highway from the Railroad to the Automobile," and Spencer Miller, Jr.'s "History of the Modern Highway in the United States."

Landis, Charles I. *The First Long Turnpike in the United States*. Lancaster, Penn.: New Era Publishing Company, 1917. 126 pp. Illustrations, maps, appendices, and index. A history of the Philadelphia and Lancaster Turnpike, with an introductory chapter on the King's Highway which preceded the turnpike.

Lane, Oscar, ed. *World Guide to Covered Bridges*. South Peabody, Mass.: National Society for the Preservation of Covered Bridges, Inc., 1972. xi + 192 pp. Illustrations and index. A list of covered bridges in the world, organized first by country and then by regional or political jurisdictions within the country. Once located, information is given on spans, length, year built, and type of bridge.

Lane, Wheaton J. *From Indian Trail to Iron Horse: Travel and Transportation in New Jersey, 1620-1860*. See chapter on "Waterways."

Lane, Wheaton J. "Transportation and Travel in New Jersey, 1620-1860." Doctoral dissertation, Princeton University, 1935.

Lang, P. G., Jr. "Ninety-Four Years of Bridges at Harpers Ferry." *Engineering News-Record*, 107 (Sept. 17, 1931), 446-48. The story of the Potomac River bridges at Harpers Ferry, "from covered timber 'arches' of 1836 to [Wendel]

Bollman iron trusses and on to modern steel structures."

Larned, J. N. *A History of Buffalo: Delineating the Evolution of the City*. See chapter on "Sewers and Wastewater Treatment."

Larsen, Arthur J. "Roads and the Settlement of Minnesota." *Minnesota History*, 21 (Sept. 1940), 225-40. How roads—from wilderness trails to railroads—contributed to the settlement of Minnesota in the mid-nineteenth century.

Larsen, Arthur J. "The Development of the Minnesota Road System." Doctoral dissertation, University of Minnesota, 1927. iv + 540 pp. Illustrations, maps, notes, and bibliography. From pre-territorial Minnesota to the 1920s.

Larsen, Lawrence H. *The Urban West at the End of the Frontier*. See chapter on "Solid Wastes."

Larson, Laurence Marcellus. "A Financial and Administrative History of Milwaukee." *Bulletin of the University of Wisconsin: Economics and Political Science Series*. See chapter on "Planning, Engineering, and Administration."

Larson, T. A. *History of Wyoming*. See chapter on "Irrigation."

Latrobe, Benjamin Henry. *Report of Benj. H. Latrobe, Consulting Engineer, on the Troy and Greenfield Railroad and Hoosac Tunnel*. Boston: Wright & Potter, 1869. 29 pp. A precise description of "the progress and condition" of the Hoosac Tunnel by one of the nineteenth century's most famous public works engineer-administrators.

Lavender, David. *Westward Vision: The Story of the Oregon Trail*. New York: McGraw-Hill Book Company, 1963. 424 pp. Map, notes, bibliography, and index. A history of the trail written for a wide audience.

Lawmill, J. Richard. "The Anthony Wayne Parkway." *Bulletin of the Historical and Philosophical Society of Ohio*. See chapter on "Parks and Recreation."

Leavitt, H. Walter. "Some Interesting Phases of the Development of Transportation in Maine." *Journal of the Maine Association of Engineers*, No. 16, Part II (April 1940), 1-96. An informal presentation of some of the highlights in Maine's transportation development, particularly during the nineteenth century (early roads, canals, and railroads).

Lee, Judson F. "Transportation as a Factor in the Development of Northern Illinois Previous to 1860." Doctoral dissertation, University of Chicago, 1913.

Lee, Judson Fiske. "Transportation—A Factor in the Development of Northern Illinois Previous to 1860." *Journal of the Illinois State Historical Society*, 10 (April 1917), 17-85. A poorly written essay that nevertheless includes some unique material on river and lake commerce, plank roads, and railroads in northern Illinois prior to the Civil War.

Le Gacy, Arthur Evans. "Improvers and Preservers: A History of Oak Park, Illinois, 1833-1940." Doctoral dissertation. See chapter on "Sewers and Wastewater Treatment."

Leissler, Frederick. *Roads and Trails of Olympic National Park*. Seattle: University of Washington Press, 1971. xii + 84 pp. Illustrations and maps.

Lemmon, Sarah McCulloch. "Raleigh—An Example of the 'New South'?" *North Carolina Historical Review*. See chapter on "Community Water Supply."

Lemmon, Sarah McCulloch. "Transportation in the Twentieth Century—A Historical Memoir." *North Carolina Historical Review*, LVI (April 1979), 194-201. Gives a brief description of general road conditions. Most of the article describes transportation vehicles.

Lemon, James T. "Urbanization and the Development of Eighteenth-Century Southeastern Pennsylvania and Adjacent Delaware." See chapter on "Waterways."

Leonard, William R. "Effect of Highway Competition on Railways, 1921-1929." Doctoral dissertation, Cornell University, 1935.

Lepawsky, Albert. *State Planning and Economic Development in the South*. See chapter on "Planning, Engineering, and Administration."

Lesley, Robert W. *History of the Portland Cement Industry in the United States: With Appendices Covering Progress of the Industry by Years and An Outline of the Organization and Activities of the Portland Cement Association*. Chicago: International Trade Press, 1924. xiv + 330 pp. Illustrations, tables, notes, appendices, and index. Beginning in the late eighteenth century, this volume includes information on the discovery of Portland Cement, its varied uses in the United States, pioneer companies, and how the industry developed. The author is the first president of the Portland Cement Association.

Lesley, Robert W. "History of the Portland Cement Industry in the United States." *Journal of the Franklin Institute*, CXLVI (Nov. 1898), 324-48. Since 1850, following construction of the London drainage works.

Lewis, Clifford M. "The Wheeling Suspension Bridge." *West Virginia History*, 33 (April 1972), 203-33. Provides a good history of the bridge and biographical sketch of engineer Charles Ellet, Jr.

Lewis, Gene D. *Charles Ellet, Jr.: The Engineer as Individualist, 1810-1862*. Urbana: University of Illinois Press, 1968. ix + 220 pp. Illustrations, maps, notes, appendix, and index. A biography of a respected nineteenth-century bridge and canal engineer, who "made a valiant effort to resist the growing specialization of engineering."

Lewis, Nelson P. "From Cobblestones to Asphalt and Brick." *Paving and Municipal Engineering*, X (April 1896), 232-40. Describes street improvements, particularly in Brooklyn, and tells how well-paved streets "foster a healthy public spirit and municipal pride." (Lewis was then engineer of street construction and maintenance for the City of Brooklyn.)

Lewis, Nelson P. "Modern City Roadways." *Appletons' Popular Science Monthly*, LVI (March 1900), 524-39. Includes scattered historical data on street paving.

Lillard, Richard G. *Desert Challenge: An Interpretation of Nevada*. See chapter on "Irrigation."

Lincoln Highway Association. *The Lincoln Highway: The Story of a Crusade That Made Transportation History*. New York: Dodd, Mead & Company, 1935. xv + 315 pp. Illustrations, maps, appendices, and index. An official history of the Lincoln Highway Association and its major accomplishments. Special attention is given to the contributions of association officers and to Carl G. Fisher, who conceived and promoted the idea of a transcontinental highway.

Lind, William E. "Thomas H. MacDonald: A Study of the Career of an Engineer and His Influence on Public Roads in the United States, 1919-1953." Master's thesis, American University, 1965.

Lindenthal, Gustav. "Bridge Engineering." *Engineering News-Record*, 92 (April 17, 1924), 652-57. A summary of "the distinctive features in the progress of design and construction of bridges in different countries" since the 1870s.

Lindenthal, Gustav. "Monumental Bridges." *Journal of the Cleveland Engineering Society*, IX (July 1916), 17-27. A review of the world-famous bridges by a renowned bridge engineer. Many illustrations accompany the brief text.

Lohr, Lenox R., ed. *Centennial of Engineering: History and Proceedings of Symposia, 1852-1952*. See chapter on "Planning, Engineering, and Administration."

Long, S. H. *Road from Washington City to Buffalo: Letter from the Secretary of War, Transmitting a Report of Surveys of Proposed Routes of a National Road from the City of Washington to Buffalo, in the State of New York*. Washington: Gales & Seaton, 1827. 39 pp. Tables. A report presented to the speaker of the House of Representatives and read before the House Committee on Roads and Canals (19th Congress, 2nd Session, February 17, 1827) by Major S. H. Long of the Topographical Engineers following his examination of "several routes for a National Road leading from Washington to Buffalo, in the State of New York."

Look Magazine Editors. *The Santa Fe Trail: A Chapter in the Opening of the West*. New York: Random House, 1946. 271 pp. Illustrations. A heavily illustrated history of the Santa Fe Trail. The authors have attempted to see it "as a part of the whole westward movement" and judge its impact on westward expansion.

Loomis, Richard Thomas. "The History of the Building of the Golden Gate Bridge." Doctoral dissertation, Stanford University, 1959. 250 pp.

Lorwin, Lewis L. *Youth Works Programs, Problems and Policies*. See chapter on "Public Buildings."

Lotchin, Roger W. *San Francisco, 1846-1858: From Hamlet to City*. New York: Oxford University Press, 1974. xxviii + 406 pp. Illustrations, maps, notes, and index. A good urban history that contains brief discussions of the city's early streets and water supply systems.

Lupfer, Edward P. "Westward the Course of Empire—Extending a Network of Transportation Over the Country in a Single Century." *Civil Engineering*, 3 (May 1933), 254-58. From trails to railroads and highways. Special attention is given to the Pony Express mail service.

Lupo, Alan; Frank Colcord; and Edmund P. Fowler. *Rites of Way: The Politics of Transportation in Boston and the U. S. City*. Boston: Little, Brown and Company, 1971. viii + 294 pp. Illustrations, appendices, notes, and index. Describes the successful fight for a freeway moratorium in Boston.

Luthy, Jesse Lynn. "Transportation in Colonial Virginia." Master's thesis, American University, 1933.

Lyons, Neva Lowery. "The Highways of the Southern Peninsula of Michigan." Master's thesis, University of Chicago, 1931. ix + 147 pp. Illustrations, maps, tables, notes, and bibliography. Investigates the relationship of the southern peninsula's highway pattern and its use to the natural environment of the region. Historical information is scattered throughout the thesis (Department of Geography).

McAdam, John Loudon. *Remarks on the Present System of Road Making; with observations, Deduced from Practice and Experience, with a View to a Revision of the Existing Laws, and the Introduction of Improvement in the Method of Making, Repairing, and Preserving Roads, and Defending the Road Funds from Misapplication*. London: Longman, Hurst, Rees, Orme, and Brown, 1821. 196 pp. Notes and table. A classic publication by the general surveyor of roads in England's Bristol District. His findings and recommendations would have a significant influence on his American counterparts.

Macaulay, David. *Underground*. See chapter on "Planning, Engineering, and Administration."

Maclear, Anne Bush. *Early New England Towns: A Comparative Study of Their Development*. See chapter on "Planning, Engineering, and Administration."

McClelland, John M. *R. A. Long's Planned City: The story of Longview*. See chapter on "Planning, Engineering, and Administration."

McClintock, Miller. *Street Traffic Control*. New York: McGraw-Hill Book Company, 1925. xi + 233 pp. Illustrations, tables, notes, and index. Analyzes "the causes of existing street traffic difficulties," summarizes "the experiences of the greater American cities," and presents "the conclusions of the foremost practical experts." Only Chapter I, which discusses the origin and growth of street traffic problems, is historical in nature.

McCloskey, Joseph F. "History of Military Road Construction." *Military Engineer*, XLI (Sept.-Oct. 1949), 353-56. From "Early Work in France and England" in the eighteenth century to the "Road Building Equipment" of the early twentieth century in the United States.

MacColl, E. Kimbark. *The Growth of a City: Power and Politics in Portland, Oregon, 1915 to 1950. See chapter on "Planning, Engineering, and Administration."*

McCullough, David. *The Great Bridge*. New York: Simon and Schuster, 1972. 636 pp. Illustrations, notes, appendix, bibliography, and index. An enthralling, fact-filled narrative of the building of the Brooklyn Bridge. The author describes in detail the odds against the bridge's successful completion during its fourteen years of construction; and he brings to life John Roebling, who designed the bridge, his son Washington, who implemented the plan, and Emily Roebling, who nursed her disabled husband and saw that his orders were obeyed.

McCullough, David. "The Treasure from the Carpentry Shop: The Extraordinary Original Drawings of the Brooklyn Bridge." *American Heritage*, 31 (Dec. 1979), 19, 28-29. Describes the unusual collection of drawings (many signed by Washington A. Roebling) discovered by Francis P. Valentine, a young civil engineer working for the City of New York's Department of Transportation, in early 1969.

MacDonald, Thomas H. "How Highway Financing Has Evolved." *Engineering News-Record*, 104 (Jan. 2, 1930), 4-7. An explanation of how roads and highways have been financed, particularly in the late nineteenth and early twentieth centuries.

MacDonald, Thomas H. "Our Present Road System: How It Was Created and How It Grew." *Engineering News-Record*, 102 (Jan. 3, 1929), 4-7. The chief of the U. S. Bureau of

Public Roads reviews highway developments from the "cleared trail" of the seventeenth century to the current system of "3,000,000 miles located and 500,000 miles surfaced."

MacDonald, Thomas H. "The History and Development of Road Building in the United States." *Proceedings of the American Society of Civil Engineers*, LIII (Sept. 1927), 1545-70. From "Colonial Road Building" to "Highway Conditions at the Close of the Second Decade."

MacDonald, Thomas H. "Two Thousand Years of Road Building." *Roads and Streets*, LXVII (June 1927), 245-50. A general review of "three great programs of highway building"—in Rome beginning with Julius Caesar, in France under Napoleon, and in the United States since 1916.

MacGill, Caroline E. *History of Transportation in the United States before 1860*. See chapter on "Waterways."

McGregor, Alexander C. "The Economic Impact of the Mullan Road on Walla Walla, 1860-1883." *Pacific Northwest Quarterly*, 65 (July 1974), 118-29. Shows how the road "proved important as a pack trail to mining and agricultural areas" and provided "the impetus for Walla Walla's sudden rise to prominence as a major center for agricultural activities in the Pacific Northwest."

McKay, John Gordon. "The Development of Highway Legislation Finance and Policies Among the Several States, 1890-1921." Doctoral dissertation, University of Wisconsin, 1971.

McKee, Harley J. "Original Bridges on the National Road in Eastern Ohio." *Ohio History*, 81 (Spring 1972), 131-44. A description of bridges observed "during 1971 while the author was inspecting structures which had been researched by the Historic American Buildings Survey" in the 1930s. Photographs accompany the text.

McKelvey, Blake. "'Canaltown'": A Focus of Historical Tradition." *Rochester History*. See chapter on "Waterways."

McKelvey, Blake. "East Avenue's Turbulent History." *Rochester History*, XXXIII (April and July 1966), 25-48. Reviews the many transformations of "Rochester's most beautiful street."

McKelvey, Blake. *Rochester: An Emerging Metropolis, 1925-1961*. Rochester: Christopher Press, 1961. xvi + 404 pp. Illustrations, map, chart, bibliography, and index. Excellent conclusion to the author's four-volume history of Rochester. Development of the city's public works systems are discussed.

McKelvey, Blake. *Rochester on the Genesee: The Growth of a City*. See chapter on "Parks and Recreation."

McKelvey, Blake. *Rochester: The Flower City, 1855-1890*. See chapter on "Sewers and Wastewater Treatment."

McKelvey, Blake. *Rochester: The Quest for Quality, 1890-1925*. See chapter on "Urban Mass Transportation."

McKelvey, Blake. *Rochester: The Water-Power City, 1812-1854*. See chapter on "Waterways."

McKelvey, Blake. "Snowstorms and Snow Fighting—The Rochester Experience." *Rochester History*, XXVII (Jan. 1965), 1-24. The city's response to heavy snowstorms from horse and buggy days to the 1960s.

McMechen, Edgar Carlisle. *The Moffat Tunnel of Colorado: An Epic of Empire*. 2 vols. Denver: Wahlgreen Publishing Company, 1927. Vol. I: 300 pp.; Vol. II: 280 pp. Illustrations, maps, tables, diagrams, notes, and appendix. A fascinating and compelling story "of the persistence and achievement of an ideal." Buttressed by solid facts, the author chronicles in novel-like fashion the building of the Moffat Tunnel.

McShane, Clay. "American Cities and the Coming of the Automobile, 1870-1910." Doctoral dissertation, University of Wisconsin, Madison, 1975. 344 pp.

McShane, Clay. "Transforming the Use of Urban Space: A Look at the Revolution in Street Pavements, 1880-1924." *Journal of Urban History*, 5 (May 1979), 279-307. Over half of the nation's urban streets were unpaved in 1880; by 1924 municipalities had paved almost all urban streets. McShane explains how and why this happened and discusses the various types of pavements used.

Mahlberg, Blanche Billings. "Edward J. Allen, Pioneer and Roadbuilder." *Pacific Northwest Quarterly*, 44 (Oct. 1953), 157-160. Profile of the builder of the first road across the Cascade Mountains.

Manson, Marsden. "A Brief History of Road Conditions and Legislation in California." *Transactions of the American Society of Civil Engineers*, XLVIII (Aug. 1902), 327-56. From 1894. The paper includes lengthy quotations from the legislation and is followed by a discussion.

March, H. J. "Paving Brick and Brick Pavements." *Journal of the Association of Engineering Societies*, XXIII (Aug. 1899), 91-117. Contains a smattering of historical data on brickmaking and the usefulness of brick for street pavements. Most of the article is technical.

Martin, William Elejius. "Early History of Internal Improvements in Alabama." *Johns Hopkins University Studies in Historical and Political Science*. See chapter on "Waterways."

Mason, Philip Parker. "The League of American Wheelmen and the Good Roads Movement, 1880-1905." Doctoral dissertation, University of Michigan, 1957. 282 pp.

Masters, Frank M. "Toll Bridges During the Past Decade." *Engineering News-Record*, 106 (Feb. 1931), 227-31. Explains the rise and decline of the private toll bridge and the growth of a publicly owned toll bridge plan (using revenue bonds) during the 1920s.

Mather, Stephen T. "Engineering Applied to National Parks."*Proceedings of the American Society of Civil Engineers*. See chapter on "Parks and Recreation."

May, George S. "The Good Roads Movement in Iowa." *Palimpsest*, XXXVI (Jan. 1955), 1-64. From the late nineteenth century to the 1950s. There are separate sections on "The Old Roads," "Good Roads Organizations," "Road Administration," "Getting Out of the Mud," and "Post-War Road Problems."

May, George S. "The Good Roads Movement in Iowa." *Palimpsest*, XLVI (Feb. 1965), 65-128. Outstanding case study that includes a fine collection of illustrations and a particularly strong section on the administration of early state roads.

May, George S. "The King Road Drag in Iowa." *Iowa Journal of History*, 53 (July 1955), 247-72. On D. Ward King's crusade "to spread the good news" of the road drag built of split logs.

Mayer, Harold M. "Transportation and Internal Circulation." *Journal of Geography*. See chapter on "Urban Mass Transportation."

Melnick, Mimi and Robert. "Manhole Covers: Artifacts in the Streets." *California Historical Quarterly*, LV (Winter 1976), 352-63. An interesting article on "a vast unheeded repository of industrial art." Besides pointing out the decorative appeal of many of these covers, the authors discuss the changing functions, designs, and materials from which they are made. The unique illustrations are intriguing.

Melosi, Martin V., ed. *Pollution and Reform in American Cities, 1870-1930*. See chapter on "Solid Wastes."

Melosi, Martin V. "Pragmatic Environmentalist: Sanitary Engineer George E. Waring, Jr." *Essays in Public Works History*. See chapter on "Solid Wastes."

Merchant, Frank. "Colorado's First Highway Commission, 1910-12." 2 parts. *Colorado Magazine*, XXXII (Jan. and April 1955), Jan.: 74-77; April: 146-51. A record of the commission's achievements by the Colorado Department of Highways' information officer.

Merdinger, Charles J. *Civil Engineering through the Ages*. See chapter on "Planning, Engineering, and Administration."

Meyer, Balthasar Meyer. *History of Transportation in the United States Before 1860*. See chapter on "Waterways."

Miars, David H. *A Century of Bridges*. Wilmington, Ohio: Cox Printing Company, 1972. viii + 47 pp. Illustrations and bibliography. Prepared for the Clinton County Historical Society, this booklet records the history of the Champion Bridge Company and the development of industrial manufacturing in Wilmington, Ohio.

"Milestones in U. S. Civil Engineering." *Civil Engineering*. See chapter on "Planning, Engineering, and Administration."

"Milestones in U. S. Public Works: Tacoma's Narrows Bridge." *APWA Reporter*, 42 (April 1975), 14. Explains the reasons for "Galloping Gertie's" collapse.

"Milestones in U. S. Public Works: The Tamiami Trail." *APWA Reporter*, 42 (Aug. 1975), 20-21. Describes construction of Florida's most historic highway, which traverses the Everglades from Miami to the state's west coast.

"Milestones in U. S. Public Works: Bicycle Paths—A New Idea or an Old One?" *APWA Reporter*, 43 (April 1976), 26-27. Explains the popularity of bicycle paths in the late nineteenth century.

Millar, Preston S. "Historical Sketch of Street Lighting." *Transactions of the Illuminating Engineering Society* (April 30, 1920), 185-202. Describes early illuminants. A special section of the article reviews early American practices.

Millar, Preston S. "Notes on Street Lighting in American Cities—1909-1930." *American City*, 43 (Sept. 1930), 139-40.

Miller, Carol Poh. "The Rocky River Bridge: Triumph in Concrete." *IA: The Journal of the Society for Industrial Archeology*, 2 (1976), 47-58. A descriptive article of a unique bridge. Designed by Cuyahoga County (Ohio) Bridge Engineer A. M. Felgate, the Rocky River Bridge was "both the last and the longest long-span concrete arch in the United States to be built with unreinforced ribs."

Miller, Carroll (Mrs.). "The Romance of the Old Pike." *Western Pennsylvania Historical Magazine*, 10 (Jan. 1927), 1-37. A tribute to those who built and traveled the National Road.

Miller, David E. "The Donner Road through the Great Salt Lake Desert." *Pacific Historical Review*, XXVII (Feb. 1958), 39-44. On the wagon road built by the Donner party in 1846, that extended from the present site of Henefer, Utah, to the Salt Lake Valley.

Miller, Keith Linus. "Building Towns on the Southeastern Illinois Frontier, 1810-1830." Doctoral dissertation. See chapter on "Waterways."

Miller, William D. *Memphis during the Progressive Era, 1900-1917*. See chapter on "Sewers and Wastewater Treatment."

Mills, Randall V. "A History of Transportation in the Pacific Northwest." *Oregon Historical Quarterly*. See chapter on "Waterways."

Mitchell, Isabel S. *Roads and Road-Making in Colonial Connecticut*. New Haven: Yale University Press for the Tercentenary Commission of the State of Connecticut, 1933. 32 pp. Map. A discussion of how Connecticut's roads were financed, laid out, and maintained from the 1640s to the 1770s.

Mock, Elizabeth B. *The Architecture of Bridges*. New York: Museum of Modern Art, 1949. 127 pp. Illustrations, diagrams, and glossary. A richly illustrated volume of bridge architecture. It portrays through photographs and paragraph-length captions the best and the worst in stone, wood, metal arch, suspension cable, metal beam, reinforced concrete, and reinforced concrete arch bridges. The book was prepared by the curator of the Museum of Modern Art's Department of Architecture and funded, in large part, by the American Bridge Company.

Moffatt, Walter. "Transportation in Arkansas, 1818-1840." *Arkansas Historical Quarterly*, XV (Autumn 1956), 187-201. Describes in general terms the strenuousness of traveling in Arkansas during this period.

Moir, E. W. "Tunnels and Modern Methods of Tunnelling." *Engineering Magazine*, I (Sept. 1891), 818-30. On the evolution of improved methods in the United States and Europe.

Moline, Norman T. *Mobility and the Small Town, 1900-1930: Transportation Change in Oregon, Illinois*. Chicago: University of Chicago, Department of Geography, 1971. ix + 169 pp. Illustrations, maps, tables, notes, and bibliography. A sound case study of the influence of transportation changes on a small Illinois community. The microcosmic study offers especially strong insights on the effect of the automobile and roads on the pattern of town life and community self-image.

Monzione, Joseph. "People in Public Works: William R. Hutton." *APWA Reporter*. See chapter on "Waterways."

Moore, William H. "History and Purposes of the Good Roads Movement." *Proceedings of the International Good Roads Congress*, 21 (Sept. 1901), 10-14. Since 1892 by the president of the National Good Roads Association.

Moorhead, Max L. *New Mexico's Royal Road: Trade and Travel on the Chihuahua Trail*. Norman: University of Oklahoma Press, 1958. xi + 234 pp. Illustrations, maps, notes, bibliography, and index. A narrative and description of "the origins, development, inner workings, and significance of the commercial, cultural, political, and military traffic on the oldest major highway in what is now the United States."

Moorhead, Max L. "Spanish Transportation in the Southwest, 1540-1846." *New Mexico Historical Review*, XXXII (April 1957), 107-22. Highlights distinctive features of Spanish and Mexican overland transportation in the Southwest.

Moran, Daniel E. "Foundation Development during Fifty Years." *Engineering News-Record*. See chapter on "Planning, Engineering, and Administration."

Morgan, J. Allen. "State Aid to Transportation in North Carolina." *North Carolina Booklet*, X (Jan. 1911), 122-54. To improve public roads and river navigation, from 1776 to 1835.

Morrill, John Barstow, and Paul O. Fischer, eds. *Planning the Region of Chicago*. See chapter on "Planning, Engineering, and Administration."

Morris, Ernest. "A Glimpse of Moffat Tunnel History." *Colorado Magazine*, IV (March 1927), 63-66. A quick look at the obstacles that were overcome in completing the Moffat Tunnel (1913-1927), which brought eastern and western Colorado together.

Moses, Robert. *Public Works: A Dangerous Trade*. See chapter on "Planning, Engineering, and Administration."

Mowbray, A. Q. *Road to Ruin*. Philadelphia: J. B. Lippincott Company, 1969. 240 pp. The author contends that "the United States is swiftly destroying its cities and its wilderness with highways" and fears that before long "the environment will have become utterly hostile to human life."

Mumford, Lewis. "Bridges and Buildings." *New Yorker*, 7 (Nov. 21, 1931), 46-48. Compares the George Washington Bridge ("Now the best around the waters of New York") to the Brooklyn Bridge.

Mumford, Lewis. *From the Ground Up: Observations on Contemporary Architecture, Housing, Highway Building, and Civic Design*. See chapter on "Public Buildings."

Mumford, Lewis. "The Brooklyn Bridge." *American Mercury*, XXIII (Aug. 1931), 447-50. Calls attention to the "aesthetics" of "the most satisfactory object of nineteenth century engineering in America." The article contains biographical data on the Roeblings.

Mumford, Lewis. *The City in History: Its Origins, Its Transformations, and Its Prospects*. See chapter on "Solid Wastes."

Mumford, Lewis. *The Highway and the City*. New York: Harcourt, Brace & World, 1963. viii + 246 pp. A series of essays, first published in the 1950s, dealing with "a wide range of cities, buildings, and monuments." The book's title is taken from the concluding essay in which Mumford criticizes the American people and their Congress for approving a $26-billion highway program in 1957. He states that the American has sacrificed "his life as a whole to the motorcar" and reduced "a one-dimensional transportation system, by motorcar alone, to a calamitous absurdity." The author's theme is much the same in "The Skyway's the Limit." The volume also contains a series of essays on "Historic Philadelphia."

Murray, Keith A. "Building a Wagon Road Through the Northern Cascade Mountains." *Pacific Northwest Quarterly*, 56 (April 1965), 49-56. A record of the financing, surveying, and construction of the old Cascade Wagon Road in northern Washington.

Murray, Robert A. "Trading Posts, Forts and Bridges of the Caspar Area: Unraveling the Tangle on the Upper Platte." *Annals of Wyoming*, 47 (Spring 1975), 5-30. Interesting historical detective work based on primary sources.

Myer, Donald Beekman. *Bridges and the City of Washington*. Washington, D. C.: U. S. Commission of Fine Arts, 1974. viii + 96 pp. Illustrations, maps, notes, glossary, and bibliography. An "historical and visual record" of Washington's bridges: Potomac River, Anacostia River, Rock Creek, and special bridges.

Myers, Denys Peter. *Gaslighting in America: A Guide for Historic Preservation*. See chapter on "Energy."

Nadeau, Remi A. *City Makers: The Men Who Transformed Los Angeles from Village to Metropolis During the First Great Boom, 1868-76*. See chapter on "Waterways."

Nasiatka, Thomas M. *Tunneling Technology: Its Past and Present*. Washington, D. C.: United States Department of the Interior, Bureau of Mines, 1968. 12 pp. Appendix and bibliography. Briefly describes the present state of the art and the technological highlights of tunneling from its inception to the present. The appendix is a chart of "Tunnel Data."

National Automobile Dealers Association. *The History of Transportation*. Midland, Mich.: Northwood Institute, 1967. xvii + 261 pp. Maps, charts, and graphs. Pedestrian overview of the development of canal, highway, and airport facilities.

National Highway Users Conference. *Military Roads: A Brief History of the Construction of Highways by the Military Establishment*. Washington, D. C.: National Highway Users Conference, 1935. 20 pp. Appendix and bibliography. The appendix of this study is a complete list of military roads built in the United States.

Naylor, Bob. "The Building of the Ambassador Bridge." *Chronicle: The Magazine of the Historical Society of Michigan*, 15 (Winter 1980), 4-9. Joseph Bower spanned the Detroit River in five years and created the world's longest international suspension bridge.

Neff, Gene L. "People in Public Works: Pioneer Bridge Builder Wendel Bollman, 1814-1884." *APWA Reporter*, 46 (April 1979), 4-5. A biographical sketch of the individual credited with being the first iron bridge builder in the United States and the inventor (1850) of a truss bridge similar to a suspension bridge.

Nelson, E. C. "Presidential Influence on the Policy of Internal Improvements." *Iowa Journal of History and Politics*. See chapter on "Waterways."

Nelson, George A. "The St. Helens-Hillsborough Territorial Road." *Oregon Historical Quarterly*, LII (June 1951), 101-07. Traces the road's route and describes the people who built it beginning in 1852.

Nelson, Harold L. "Military Roads for War and Peace—1791-1836." *Military Affairs*, XIX (1955), 1-14. Outlines the steps taken in establishing a federal policy of military road building "to fill the nation's military and socio-economic needs."

Nelson, Lee H. *A Century of Oregon Covered Bridges, 1851-1952*. Portland: Oregon Historical Society, 1960. 101-211 pp. Illustrations, notes, and bibliography. A richly illustrated essay on Oregon's covered bridges—"their beginnings, development and decline, together with some mention of the builders and techniques." (The booklet was reprinted from the June 1960 *Oregon Historical Quarterly*.)

Nettels, Curtis. "The Mississippi Valley and the Constitution, 1815-29." *Mississippi Valley Historical Review*. See chapter on "Waterways."

Nevins, Allan, and John A. Krout, eds. *The Greater City: New York, 1898-1948*. New York: Columbia University Press, 1948. vii + 260 pp. Illustrations. A rather breezey, undocumented history written to commemorate the fiftieth anniversary of the consolidation of Manhattan, Brooklyn, the Bronx, Queens, and Richmond into the City of New York. Discussions are included on transportation systems, parks, public buildings, and other public works facilities and services.

New York-New Jersey Metropolitan Chapter of the American Public Works Association. *Public Works in Metropolitan New York-New Jersey*. See chapter on "Planning, Engineering, and Administration."

Noreen, Sarah Pressey. *Public Street Illumination in Washington, D. C.: An Illustrated History*. Washington, D. C.: George Washington University, 1975. viii + 55 pp. Illustrations, notes, appendices, and bibliography. Part of a series of monographs on Washington, D. C. The focus is on the city as a major urban center rather than as the federal capital. The author considers the role of technological advances in shaping urban life as well as the legacy of artifacts in the urban environment. To better understand the role of street lighting in Washington, Noreen reviews the history of public illumination: the technological advances in energy sources, the changing social patterns brought about by increasing use of hours previously dark; and the aesthetic heritage in the design of street-lighting fixtures.

"North Carolina's Roadbuilding: A Romance of Achievement." *Manufacturers Record*, LXXXV (May 22, 1924), 67-68. Reviews and commends the state of North Carolina for the way in which it spent $76 million on good roads from 1921 to 1924. Two articles of interest follow this introductory statement: Frank Page's "North Carolina Invests $76,000,000 in Good Roads" (pp. 69-76); and W. N. Everett's "What North Carolina Has Done and Is Doing" (pp. 77-82).

Noyes, Edward. "A Letter of James B. Eads." *Missouri Historical Society Bulletin*, XXVI (Jan.

1970), 113-18. Eads discusses his plans to use the plenum pneumatic process for sinking the piers of the St Louis bridge in this 1869 letter to Rear Admiral J. A. Dahlgren.

O'Brien, Bob Randolph. "The Roads of Yellowstone, 1870-1915." *Montana: The Magazine of Western History*, 17 (July 1967), 30-39.

O'Brien, Bob Randolph. "The Yellowstone National Park Road System: Past, Present and Future." Doctoral dissertation, University of Washington, 1965. 276 pp.

O'Callaghan, Jerry A. "Klamath Indians and the Oregon Wagon Road Grant, 1864-1938." *Oregon Historical Quarterly*, LIII (March 1952), 23-28. Only briefly describes the wagon road construction that took place on misappropriated Indian land (1864). The article explains the events leading up to 1938 when the Supreme Court awarded the Klamath Indians five million dollars.

O'Dea, William T. *The Social History of Lighting*. London: Routledge and Kegan Paul, 1958. xvi + 254 pp. Illustrations, map, diagrams, and indexes. One section of Chapter IV ("Light for Travel") is devoted to street lighting. However, only a few pages refer to advancements in the United States.

O'Gorman, James F. "Sandy Creek Bridge." *Missouri Historical Society Bulletin*, XV (July 1959), 296-303. Short history of the covered bridge (1872) spanning Sandy Creek, twenty miles south of St. Louis in Jefferson County.

Olmsted, Frederick Law. "The Town-Planning Movement in America." *Annals of the American Academy of Political and Social Science*. See chapter on "Planning, Engineering, and Administration."

O'Neill, Richard W. *High Steel, Hard Rock, and Deep Water: The Exciting World of Construction*. New York: Macmillan Company, 1965. vi + 280 pp. Illustrations, glossary, bibliography, and index. An illustrated, dramatic story of how individuals in the construcion industry work—"from the engineers who plan the jobs to the sandhogs who dig tunnels and the iron drivers who punch home red-hot rivets on high steel." The author describes bridges, dams, tunnels, highways, and skyscrapers, emphasizing the "firsts," "biggests," and "bests."

Orcutt, Philip Dana. "Maine Recreates the First Pile Bridge in America." *Engineering News-Record*, 113 (Nov. 15, 1934), 616-17. Description of a timber trestle bridge at York Village, Maine, that was designed to copy the appearance of the original bridge built on the site in 1761.

Osterweis, Rollin G. *Three Centuries of New Haven, 1638-1938*. See chapter on "Community Water Supply."

Ovaitt, Alton B. "The Movement of a Northern Trail: The Mullan Road, 1859-1869." Doctoral dissertation, University of California, Berkeley, 1948.

Owen, Wilfred. *The Accessible City*. See chapter on "Urban Mass Transportation."

Owen, Wilfred. *The Metropolitan Transportation Problem*. Washington, D. C.: Brookings Institution, 1966. xiii + 266 pp. Map, chart, tables, graphs, notes, appendix, and index. Outstanding analysis of the causes and consequences of urban transportation problems. The author suggests a comprehensive program of reforms that includes greater reliance on public transportation.

Oxley, J. M. "Portland Cement." *Engineering Journal* (Montreal), VIII (Jan. 1925), 3-10. A description of its discovery, early uses, and development.

Page, Frank. "Five Years of State Road Building and Its Results." *Public Roads: A Journal of Highway Research*, 7 (Nov. 1926), 177-84, 189. Demonstrates how road building in North Carolina during the previous five years "has linked . . . trunk-line railroads and . . . waterways into an effective transportation machine."

Page, Logan Waller. "State Aid in Road Building." *Engineering Record*, 62 (Dec. 24, 1910), 741-42. A sketch that includes some historical information.

Page, Logan Waller. "The National Government as a Factor in Highway Development." *Good Roads Magazine*, X (Nov. 1909), 402-04. Describes the minimal role of the federal government in nineteenth-century road building.

Palmer, George Thomas. "Historic Landmarks along the Highways of Illinois." *Transactions of the Illinois State Historical Society*, (1932) 41-62. Traces historic markings along Illinois' roads and highways.

Parish, John C. "The Old Military Road." *Palimpsest*, II (Feb. 1921), 33-34. On an old ridge road (1839) which ran from Dubuque to Iowa City.

Parks, Roger Neal. "Roads of New England, 1790-1840." Doctoral dissertation, Michigan State University, 1966. 283 pp.

Passer, Harold C. *The Electrical Manufacturers, 1875-1900: A Study in Competition, Entrepreneurship, Technical Change, and Economic Growth*. See chapter on "Energy."

Paul, Charles L. "Beaufort, North Carolina: Its Development as a Colonial Town." *North Carolina Historical Review*, XLVII (Oct. 1970), 370-87. Surveys the town's development from 1713 to 1770. The article includes material on roads, streets, and public buildings.

Paxson, Frederic L. "The Highway Movement, 1916-1935." *American Historical Review*, LI (Jan. 1946), 236-53. A discussion of the parentage and evolution of the highway movement which, between two great wars, came alive, "passed through its initial phase, and settled down as other frontiers have settled down into operating institutions." According to Paxson, this "frontier of gas and concrete" bound an area of "continental dimensions into a unit for the first time in history."

Peckham, Howard H. "Mail Service in Indiana Territory." *Indiana Magazine of History*, XLVII (June 1951), 155-64. Emphasizes the need for and subsequent improvement of roads.

Perrigo, Lynn. "Municipal Beginnings at Boulder, Colorado, 1871-1900." *Colorado Magazine*. See chapter on "Community Water Supply."

Peters, Kenneth Earl. "The Good Roads Movement and the Michigan State Highway Department, 1905-1917." Doctoral dissertation, University of Michigan, 1972. 308 pp. One of the best case studies of the Good Roads Movement. The focus of the dissertation is the planning and promotional activity of the state's highway department.

Petersen, William J. "The Old Road—Then and Now." *Palimpsest*, LI (June 1970), 277-80. On individuals (Parish, Briggs, and Hansen) who have written on Iowa's "Old Military Road."

Peterson, Arthur Everett, and George William Edwards. *New York as an Eighteenth Century Municipality*. See chapter on "Solid Wastes."

Peterson, J. L. "History and Development of Precast Concrete in the United States." *Journal of the American Concrete Institute*. See chapter on "Planning, Engineering, and Administration."

Petty, Ben H. "Highways—Then and Now: Mileposts in the Development of Modern Roads." *Roads and Streets*, 84 (Oct. 1941), 60-74. A summary of major developments by a Purdue University professor of highway engineering.

Phelps, Dawson A. "The Natchez Trace in Tennessee History." *Tennessee Historical Quarterly*, XIII (Sept. 1954), 195-203. On the rise (1780-1815) and decline (after 1815) of an historic road.

Phelps, Dawson A. "The Natchez Trace: Indian Trail to Parkway." *Tennessee Historical Quarterly*, XXI (Sept. 1962), 203-18. Reviews the history of a frontier road and tells how it became a parkway (not highway) in the national park system.

Phillips, Ulrich Bonnell. *A History of Transportation in the Eastern Cotton Belt to 1860*. See chapter on "Waterways."

Piehl, Frank J. "Shall We Gather at the River." *Chicago History*, II (Fall-Winter 1973), 196-205. On Chicago's early bridges and the battles between ship owners and captains who "were demanding unobstructed navigation" and citizens and merchants who "were fighting for ferries and bridges."

Pierce, Bessie Louise. *A History of Chicago*. See chapter on "Community Water Supply."

Pillsbury, Richard. "The Urban Street Pattern as a Culture Indicator: Pennsylvania, 1682-1815." *Annals of the Association of American Geographers*, 60 (Sept. 1970), 428-46. Shows that early street patterns were "determined by cultural rather than economic or physical considerations."

"Pioneer Roads across the Alleghanies: Comparisons with the Alaska Highway and the Pioneer Road to Panama." *Military Engineer*, XXXVII (Sept. 1945), 364-68. After studying accounts of "the construction of two of the first military roads built in America: the Braddock's and Forbes's Roads," the author contends that the Alaska Highway and the

Pioneer Road to Panama will in time meet commercial and tourist needs as well as fulfill military objectives.

Platt, Harold Lawrence. "Urban Public Services and Private Enterprise: Aspects of the Legal and Economic History of Houston, Texas, 1865-1905." Doctoral dissertation. See chapter on "Planning, Engineering, and Administration."

Plowden, David. *Bridges: The Spans of North America*. New York: Viking Press, 1974. 328 pp. Illustrations, diagrams, bibliography, and index. A photographic study of North American bridges. The author gives special attention to old and/or historic structures out of a fear that they may be replaced because they are "too old or in other ways inadequate to handle the burdens of modern times." The book is organized by structural material: stone and brick, wood, iron and steel, and concrete.

Plummer, Wilbur C. "The Road Policy of Pennsylvania." Doctoral dissertation, University of Pennsylvania, 1925. 121 pp. Maps, table, notes, and bibliography. An historical examination of "roads and road administration in Pennsylvania from the earliest settlements to the present time."

Pomerantz, Sidney I. *New York: An American City, 1783-1803*. See chapter on "Community Water Supply."

Pommer, Patricia J. "Plank Roads: A Chapter in the Early History of Wisconsin Transportation (1846-1871)." Master's thesis, University of Wisconsin, 1950.

Potter, Issac B. "The Common Roads of Europe and America." *Engineering Magazine*, I (Aug. 1891), 613-26. On the development and improvement of public roads.

Prather, Geneal. "The Construction of the Michigan Road, 1830-1840." *Indiana Magazine of History*, XL (Sept. 1944), 242-79. Describes the financing, surveying, and building of the Michigan Road, which began at Madison on the Ohio River and extended northward by way of Greensburg, Indianapolis, and South Bend to Michigan City.

Prather, Geneal. "The Struggle for the Michigan Road." *Indiana Magazine of History*, XXXIX (March 1943), 1-24. Reviews the problems encountered in building the "most famous of Indiana's state highways."

Preston, Howard L. *Automobile Age Atlanta: The Making of a Southern Metropolis, 1900-1935*. Athens: University of Georgia Press, 1979. Illustrations, maps, tables, notes, bibliographic essay, and index. Outstanding case study of the influence of the automobile on the "process of city building." The book also offers extensive coverage of the decline of street railways due to automobile competition.

Princeton University Art Museum and Department of Civil Engineering. *The Eads Bridge*. Princeton, N. J.: Princeton University, 1975. 84 pp. Illustrations, figures, chronology, table of selected facts, and notes. Catalogue of an exhibition funded by the National Endowment for the Arts and the United States Steel Corporation. The volume contains essays on "Engineering Education and the Art Museum" and on Eads and his bridge. There is also an extract from Eads' first report to the directors of the Illinois and St. Louis Bridge Company in May 1868.

Prosch, Thomas W. "The Military Roads of Washington Territory." *Washington Historical Quarterly*, II (Jan. 1908), 118-26. Praises the plans and good intentions of army engineers but explains why their road-building efforts were not more successful.

Prucha, Francis Paul. *Broadax and Bayonet: The Role of the United States Army in the Development of the Northwest, 1815-1860*. See chapter on "Military Installations."

Public Works Administration. *America Builds: The Record of PWA*. See chapter on "Planning, Engineering, and Administration."

Pusey, Wm. Allen. *The Wilderness Road to Kentucky: Its Location and Features*. New York: George H. Doran Company, 1921. xiii + 145 pp. Illustrations and maps. An attempt to trace the exact location of the Wilderness Road through the use of old surveys, deeds, local maps, and personal examinations of the road.

Quaife, Milo M. *Chicago's Highways Old and New: From Indian Trail to Motor Road*. Chicago: D. F. Keller & Company, 1923. 278 pp. Illustrations, maps, appendix, and index. A splendid reconstruction of the pioneer highways that influenced the development of Chicago prior to the coming of the railroads. Public works historians will enjoy the author's lively accounts of the trials of early road builders. This generally forgotten book is a gem.

Rae, John B. *The American Automobile: A Brief History*. Chicago: University of Chicago Press, 1965. xv + 265 pp. Illustrations, maps, tables, appendix, bibliographical essay, and index. A fine book that incorporates material on the evolution of highway systems.

Rae, John B. "The Evolution of the Motor Bus as a Transport Mode." *High Speed Ground Transportation Journal*, 5 (Summer 1971), 221-35. One of the few good historical articles on this subject.

Rae, John B. *The Road and Car in American Life*. Cambridge: MIT Press, 1971. xiv + 390 pp. Illustrations, tables, graphs, maps, footnotes, bibliography, and index. Perhaps the best single volume on the development of the automobile and roads. The author presents excellent discussions of the evolution of highway policies, the decline of mass transit and railroads, as well as the transformation of demographic and land-use patterns in urban areas.

Ratigan, William. *Highways over Broad Waters: Life and Times of David B. Steinman, Bridgebuilder*. Grand Rapids: Wm. B. Eerdmans Publishing Company, 1959. 359 pp. Illustrations, bibliography, and index. A laudatory biography of one of the twentieth-century's most accomplished engineers and bridge builders. His most famous structure is Michigan's Mackinac Bridge; several chapters in the book are devoted to its design and construction.

Ratliff, Charles E., Jr. "The Centralization of Governmental Expenditures for Education and Highways in North Carolina, 1929-1952." Doctoral dissertation, Duke University, 1954. x + 522 pp. Tables, notes, appendix, and bibliography. Explains how and why "North Carolina became the most centralized state in the country as measured by the proportion of school and road funds supplied by the state."

Reardon, William J. "A Little-Known Tunnel." *Bulletin of the Historical and Philosophical Society of Ohio*, 9 (July 1951), 227-33. On an abandoned tunnel (1855) laid out by Erasmus Gest, son of Joseph Gest, one of Cincinnati's early city engineers.

Reed, Richard William. "Toll Roads in the State Highway System." Doctoral dissertation, Clark University, 1955. 408 pp. Historical discussion of the evolution of toll roads. Most of the dissertation is devoted to the origin and operation of modern toll roads in five states—Pennsylvania, Connecticut, Maine, New Hampshire, and New Jersey.

Reeder, Ray M. "The Mormon Trail: A History of the Salt Lake to Los Angeles Route to 1869." Doctoral dissertation, Brigham Young University, 1966. vi + 426 pp. Maps, notes, appendices, and bibliography. Summarizes developments that took place on the Salt Lake-Los Angeles route prior to 1869, when the completion of the transcontinental railroad revolutionized western transportation.

Reier, Sharon. *The Bridges of New York*. New York: Quadrant Press, Inc., 1977. 160 pp. Illustrations, maps, drawings, tables, glossary, and bibliography. A well-illustrated resource book which contains single chapters on Brooklyn Bridge, Williamsburg Bridge, Queensboro and Manhattan Bridge, Hell Gate Arch Bridge, Harlem River Bridges, George Washington Bridge, Staten Island Bridges, Triborough Bridges, and Verrazano-Narrows Bridge. There is a short, concluding chapter on maintenance.

Remley, David A. *Crooked Road: The Story of the Alaska Highway*. New York: McGraw-Hill Book Company, 1976. xi + 253 pp. Illustrations, map, notes, and index. A very readable but factual account of the building of the Alaska Highway. The author gives special attention to the individuals involved in its planning and construction. He makes good use of transcripts from oral interviews.

Remsberg, Stanley Ray. "United States Administration of Alaska: The Army Phase, 1867-1877: A Study in Federal Governance of an Overseas Possession." Doctoral dissertation, University of Wisconsin, Madison, 1975. 760 pp.

Reps, John W. *Cities of the American West: A History of Frontier Urban Planning*. See chapter on "Planning, Engineering, and Administration."

Reps, John W. *The Making of Urban America: A History of City Planning in the United States*. See chapter on "Planning, Engineering, and Administration."

Rice, Philip Morrison. "Internal Improvements in Virginia: 1775-1860." Doctoral dissertation. See chapter on "Waterways."

Richardson, Elmo R. "Western Politics and New Deal Policies: A Study of T. A. Walters of Idaho." *Pacific Northwest Quarterly*. See chapter on "Flood Control and Drainage."

Riddick, Winston Wade. "The Politics of National Highway Policy, 1953-1966." Doctoral dissertation, Columbia University, 1973. 416 pp.

Ridgeway, Arthur. "The Mission of Colorado Toll Roads." *Colorado Magazine*, IX (Sept. 1932), 161-69. A brief discussion of the purpose of Colorado's toll bridges followed by a five-page listing of "the record of the legislative authorization of toll roads from the very first session of the Territorial Legislature beginning on September 9, 1861."

Ridgway, Robert. *Robert Ridgway*. See chapter on "Planning, Engineering, and Administration."

Ringwalt, J. L. *Development of Transportation Systems*. See chapter on "Waterways."

Ripple, David A. *History of the Interstate System in Indiana*. 4 vols. Lafayette, Ind.: Purdue University and Indiana State Highway Commission, 1976. Vol.I: xxviii + 113 pp.; Vol. II: 114-370 pp.; Vol. III: 371-731 pp.; Vol. IV: 732-892 pp. Maps, tables, figures, notes, bibliography, and appendix. This "Joint Highway Research Project" was prepared by a Purdue University graduate instructor in research (School of Civil Engineering). The report covers the period from the late 1930s through 1972 and describes the development of the national program, the evolution of policies and standards, route history, and the program's cost, funding, and general benefits.

Ritter, Joyce N. "People in Public Works: Thomas H. MacDonald and Charles D. Curtiss." *APWA Reporter*, 46 (Oct. 1979), 4-5, 17. Describes the professional lives as well as the teamwork that existed between these two public officials who had long careers in the Bureau of Public Roads.

Robbins, Mary Caroline. "Village Improvement Societies." *Atlantic Monthly*. See chapter on "Parks and Recreation."

Roberts, Clarence N. "History of the Paving Brick Industry in Missouri." *Missouri Historical Review*, XLVI (July 1952), 357-62. From the late 1880s until the industry was forced to surrender to the concrete interests between 1910 and 1915.

Roberts, Edward Graham. "The Roads of Virginia, 1607-1840." Doctoral dissertation, University of Virginia, 1950. vii + 299 pp. Maps, notes, appendices, and bibliography. Traces the roads of Virginia and outlines the evolution of the administrative system under which the roads were constructed and maintained.

Robinson, Charles Mulford. *Better Binghamton: A Report to the Mercantile-Press Club of Binghamton, N. Y.* See chapter on "Planning, Engineering, and Administration."

Robinson, Charles Mulford. *Modern Civic Art: Or the City Made Beautiful*. New York: G. P. Putnam's Sons, 1903. iv + 381 pp. Index. In the first chapter, the author discusses how the city has changed for the better during the late nineteenth century. He attributes many of the improvements to public works facilities and services. The remainder of the book outlines ways of continuing and promoting the beautification of cities, especially through the use of art in streets and parks.

Robinson, Michael C. "People in Public Works: James B. Eads." *APWA Reporter*, 44 (Oct. 1977), 4-5. A biographical sketch of one of the nineteenth century's most renowned engineers and inventors. The article describes in particular Eads' design and construction work on the famous steel-arched bridge over the Mississippi River at St. Louis.

Robinson, Michael C. "People in Public Works: Othmar H. Ammann." *APWA Reporter*, 47 (June 1980), 4-5. Describes his legacy of monumental and beautiful bridges.

Robinson, Michael C. "People in Public Works: Peter Kiewit, Jr." *APWA Reporter*. See chapter on "Flood Control and Drainage."

Robison, Jon. "Covered Bridges of Madison County." *Annals of Iowa*, 38 (Fall 1966), 413-26.

Rodgers, Cleveland. *Robert Moses: Builder for Democracy*. See chapter on "Planning, Engineering, and Administration."

Rogers, Elizabeth, comp. *A Nation in Motion: Historic American Transportation Sites*. See chapter on "Waterways."

Roller, Duane H. D., ed. *Perspectives in the History of Science and Technology*. Norman: University of Oklahoma Press, 1971. x + 307 pp. Illustrations, notes, and index. A collection of papers presented at a symposium at the University of Oklahoma in 1969. The only essay of interest to public works historians is John B. Rae's "The Car and the Road: Highway Technology and Highway Policy" and the commentaries by Carroll Pursell and Eugene S. Ferguson. The topics included in Rae's article are, however, developed in greater detail in his book, *The Road and the Car in American Life*.

Roper, Daniel C. *The United States Post Office: Its Past Record, Present Condition, and Potential Relation to the New World Era*. New York: Funk & Wagnalls Company, 1917. xvii + 382 pp. Illustrations, appendix, and index. Highlights the "effect of postal service upon social progress." The chapter on "The Network of Post Roads" may be of some interest.

Rose, Albert C. "Historic American Highways." *Annual Report of the Board of Regents of the Smithsonian Institution* (1939), 499-512. From 1539 to 1939. The text is accompanied by thirty-five photographs illustrating high points in road development during four centuries.

Rose, Albert C. *Historic American Roads: From Frontier Trails to Superhighways*. New York: Crown Publishers, 1976. viii + 118 pp. Illustrations, maps, and index. An expanded edition of an earlier, pictorial history of public roads in colonial America and the United States by a Bureau of Public Roads highway engineer. This softcover book contains full-color illustrations by Carl Rakeman, an artist employed by the Bureau of Public Roads in the 1920s.

Rose, Albert C. *Public Roads of the Past*. Washington, D. C.: American Association of State Highway Officials, 1952. 101 pp. Illustrations and bibliography. A series of sketches, first published in *American Highways*, from 1944-1949, by highway engineer and historian of the Bureau of Public Roads. Nearly half of the book is devoted to Roman roads; however, there are chapters on pioneer road builders (Pierre Tresaquet, John Metcalf, Thomas Telford, and John McAdam), right-hand rule of the road, development of surveying instruments, and highways of middle America.

Rose, Mark H. *Interstate Express Highway Politics, 1941-1956*. Lawrence, Kans.: Regents Press of Kansas, 1979. xii + 169 pp. Notes, bibliography, and index. A thorough analysis of the role of various interest groups in fashioning highway policies in the 1940s and 1950s. The author outlines the many conflicting visions of reform and perceptions of growth, examines the intricacies of highway finance in the face of vast economic swings, and describes the political maneuvers and obstacles of the Roosevelt, Truman, and Eisenhower administrations.

Rose, William Ganson. *Cleveland: The Making of a City*. See chapter on "Sewers and Wastewater Treatment."

Rouse, Parke, Jr. *The Great Wagon Road from Philadelphia to the South*. New York: McGraw-Hill Book Company, 1973. xii + 292 pp. Illustrations, map, notes, bibliography, and index. A colorful chronicle (1607-1877) of the principal highway of the eighteenth-century frontier southward from Pennsylvania.

Rudofsky, Bernard. *Streets for People: A Primer for Americans*. Garden City, N. Y.: Doubleday & Company, 1969. 351 pp. Illustrations, notes, and index. A heavily illustrated book which traces "the origins of the American street—if ever so sketchily—to colonial times."

Ruhloff, F. Carl. "Evolution of Modern Construction Machinery." *Civil Engineering*. See chapter on "Planning, Engineering, and Administration."

Russ, William A., Jr. "The Partnership between Public and Private Initiative in the History of Pennsylvania." *Pennsylvania History*, XX (Jan. 1953), 1-21. Concentrates, for the most part, on the partnership in building roads, canals, and railroads.

Ryan, W. D. "The History of Illumination with Special Reference to the Lighting of the Panama-Pacific Exposition and Modern Street Lighting Practice." *Proceedings of the American Society for Municipal Improvements*, 26 (1919), 324-47. Very little history—the emphasis is on modern street-lighting practice.

Salkowski, Albert S. "Reconstructing a Covered Timber Bridge." *Civil Engineering*, 33 (Oct. 1963), 36-39. A technical demonstration of how the Bunker Hill Road Bridge (1880) on Gunpowder Falls in Baltimore County was restored in 1947.

Salt, Harriet. *Mighty Engineering Feats: Clear and Concise Descriptions of Ten of the Greatest American Engineering Feats*. See chapter on "Planning, Engineering, and Administration."

Sandström, Gösta E. *Man the Builder*. New York: McGraw-Hill Book Company, 1970. 280 pp. Illustrations, maps, diagrams, appendix, glossary, bibliography, and index. A history of technology that focuses primarily on "man in his capacity of builder." The structures—roads, bridges, harbors, canals, dams, and tunnels—chosen for inclusion in the book belong to "the great monuments of the past" and relate to "the development of civil engineering in the western world."

Sandström, Gösta E. *Tunnels*. New York: Holt, Rinehart, and Winston, 1963. xii + 427 pp. Illustrations, drawings, glossary, bibliography and index. A technological history of tunnel building—from earliest times to the present, in the United States and abroad. Several pages of the book are devoted to the Hoosac Tunnel, Great Lakes tunnels, and Hudson River tunnels.

Sargent, Paul D. "Central Road Authorities." *Engineering & Contracting*, XL (July 9, 1913), 34-36. Traces the development of a few northeastern state highway laws and shows the transition from local to centralized control of road offices.

Sargent, John H. "Street Pavement—Past, Present and Future." *Journal of the Association of Engineering Societies*, VI (Sept. 1887), 329-40. Short review of early pavement practices by a member of the Civil Engineers' Club of Cleveland. He specifically cites pavement improvements in Cleveland.

Sawyer, Robert W. "Beginnings of McKenzie Highway, 1862." *Oregon Historical Quarterly*, XXXI (Sept. 1930), 261-68. Road built across the Cascade Range in the 1860s.

Schneider, Charles C. "The Evolution of the Practice of American Bridge Building." *Transactions of the American Society of Civil Engineers*, LIV (June 1905), 213-34. Emphasizes the "marvelous progress" made in bridge building in the nineteenth century.

Schneider, Norris F. *The National Road: Main Street of America*. Columbus: Ohio Historical Society, 1975. 40 pp. Illustrations, map, and bibliography. A well-written and nicely illustrated essay that would appeal to a broad audience. First appeared in *Ohio History* in Spring 1974.

Schneider, Norris F. *Y Bridge City: The Story of Zanesville and Muskingum County, Ohio*. Cleveland: World Publishing Company, 1951. 414 pp. Illustrations, maps, and index. A history of Zanesville and the Muskingum Valley. It includes spatterings of information on such public works subjects as roads and highways, bridges, canals, flood-control projects, and public buildings.

Schuyler, Hamilton. *The Roeblings: A Century of Engineers, Bridgebuilders and Industrialists*. Princeton: Princeton University Press, 1931. xx + 424 pp. Illustrations, chart, notes, and index. A highly laudatory biography of three generations of Roeblings (1831-1931) and their contributions to bridge building in the United States.

Schwartz, Gary T. "Urban Freeways and the Interstate System." *Southern California Law Review*, 49 (March 1976), 406-513.

Scott, Leslie M. "Oregon Coast Highway." *Oregon Historical Quarterly*, XXXIII (Sept. 1932), 268-70. A brief history of the highway by the chairman of the Oregon State Highway Commission.

Scott, Mel. *American City Planning Since 1890*. See chapter on "Planning, Engineering, and Administration."

Scott, Quinta, and Howard S. Miller. *The Eads Bridge*. Columbia: University of Missouri Press, 1979. 142 pp. Illustrations, notes, and index. A "Photographic Essay" followed by an "Historical Appraisal" of "a stunning technical and artisic achievement."

Searight, Thomas B. *The Old Pike: A History of the National Road, with Incidents, Accidents, and Anecdotes Thereon*. Uniontown, Pa.: Thomas B. Searight, 1894. 384 pp. Illustrations and appendix. A history of a highway "so largely instrumental in promoting the early growth and development" of the United States by an individual who "was born and reared on the line of the road, and has spent his whole life amid scenes connected with it."

Sessions, Gordon M. *Traffic Devices: Historical Aspects Thereof*. Washingon, D. C.: Institute of Traffic Engineers, 1971. iii + 149 pp. Illustrations, notes, and bibliography. Prepared from the historical material collected by ITE's Committee on Development of Historic Traffic Control Devices. The text contains an unusual amount of interesting information on traffic devices but abounds with quotations from other sources.

Shallat, Todd. "People in Public Works: Joseph Strauss." *APWA Reporter*, 46 (May 1979), 4-5. A biographical sketch of the chief engineer of the Golden Gate Bridge.

Shank, William. *Historic Bridges of Pennsylvania*. York: American Canal & Transportation Center, 1974. 68 pp. Illustrations and bibliography. Contains short biographical sketches of Pennsylvania bridge builders of the 1800s and brief descriptions of various kinds of bridges found in the state.

Sherwood, Esther. "The Highway Pattern of Iowa." Master's thesis, University of Chicago, 1935. ix + 195 pp. Illustrations, maps, tables, notes, and bibliography. Although prepared for the Department of Geography, this thesis contains an entire chapter on the development of Iowa's highway pattern.

Shideler, William Watson. "The Highway Pattern of Ohio." Master's thesis, University of Chicago, 1939. vii + 184 pp. Illustrations, maps, notes, and bibliography. A discussion of Ohio's highway pattern. The entire first chapter is historical in nature; it presents the evolution of the pattern.

Short, C. W., and R. Stanley-Brown. *Public Buildings: A Survey of Architecture of Projects Constructed by Federal and Other Governmental Bodies between the Years 1933 and 1939 with the Assistance of the Public Works Administration*. See chapter on "Public Buildings."

Simmons, David. "Bridge Preservation in Ohio." *Cities & Villages*, XXVI (Aug. 1978), 13-18. An historical overview of the diverse types of nineteenth- and twentieth-century bridges that are the concern of the Ohio Historic Preservation Office. Numerous photographs accompany the article.

Singley, Grover. "Retracing the Military Road from Point Douglas to Superior." *Minnesota History*, 40 (Spring 1967), 233-47. A precise examination of the Minnesota Territory's road system. It came into existence on July 18, 1850 when Congress passed the Minnesota Road Act, authorizing five "Military Roads" and providing for their construction.

Sioussat, St. George Leakin. "Highway Legislation in Maryland and Its Influence on the Economic Development of the State." Doctoral dissertation, Johns Hopkins University, 1899. 85 pp.

Skramstad, Harold K. "The Professional Life of William Rich Hutton, Civil Engineer." Doctoral dissertation. See chapter on "Waterways."

Smith, Catherine Blaskovich. "The Terminus of the Cumberland Road on the Ohio." *West Virginia History*, XIV (April 1953), 193-264. An account of the rivalry between Steubenville, Wellsburg, and Wheeling for the terminus of the Cumberland Road.

Smith, Dana P. "The Old Mottville Bridge." *Michigan History Magazine*, X (July 1926), 401-03. A brief sketch of a covered bridge (1833) at Mottville in the southwest corner of St. Joseph County, Michigan.

Smith, Duane A. *Rocky Mountain Mining Camps: The Urban Frontier*. Bloomington: Indiana University Press, 1967. xii + 304 pp. Illustrations, map, notes, bibliographical essay, and index. A well-researched history that includes a smattering of information on early western roads and sanitary conditions in the mining camps.

Smith, Frances P. "Asphalt in Modern Highway Construction." 2 parts. *Good Roads*, LXVI (April and May 1924), April: 98-100; May: 130-32. Traces the use of asphalt in highway construction since the first sheet asphalt pavement was laid in 1870 in Newark, New Jersey.

Sofronie, Ramiro. "Seven Events in the History of Suspension Bridges." *Noesis*, 4 (1978), 55-59. Describes significant structural changes from 1817 to 1966.

Special Committee on Concrete and Reinforced Concrete (ASCE). "Progress Report of the Special Committee on Concrete and Reinforced Concrete." *Transactions of the American Society of Civil Engineers*, LXXVII (Dec. 1914), 385-437. Section 2 of this report is a three-page historical sketch of the use of concrete (and later reinforced concrete) in the United States from the late eighteenth century.

Speedy, John C., III. "From Mules to Motors:

Development of Maintenance Doctrine for Motor Vehicles by the U. S. Army, 1896-1918." Doctoral dissertation, Duke University, 1977. xiii + 422 pp. Illustrations, map, tables, charts, notes, appendix, and bibliography. A fine study on a topic that deserves greater attention from scholars. The dissertation traces the army's adoption of motor vehicles and frustrating efforts to implement maintenance programs. Fleet managers continue to wrestle with maintenance problems Speedy identifies.

Spielmann, Arthur, and Charles B. Brush. "The Hudson River Tunnel." *Transactions of the American Society of Civil Engineers*, IX (July 1880), 259-77. A technical presentation describing methoas used in constructing the Hudson River Tunnel. Of particular interest is the discussion (pp. 273-77) led by James B. Eads and participated in by E. S. Chesbrough and William R. Hutton.

Sprague, Charles A. "Williamette Highway—The Seventh across the High Cascades." *Oregon Historical Quarterly*, XLI (Sept. 1940), 243-49. Condensation of a gubernatorial address given at the dedication of the Williamette Highway on July 30, 1940.

Stapleton, Darwin H., ed. *The Engineering Drawings of Benjamin Henry Latrobe*. See chapter on "Waterways."

Starling, Robert B. "The Plank Road Movement in North Carolina." 2 parts. *North Carolina Historical Review*, XVI (Jan. and April 1939), Jan.: 1-22; April: 147-73. Discusses the construction and operation of approximately 500 miles of plank roads in North Carolina between 1849 and 1861. The author also recounts the forces that made "the downfall of the plank road system of highways inevitable.

Starr, John T. "The Army Engineers . . . Pioneers in American Transportation." *Highway Magazine*, 49 (May-June 1958), 92-95. Highlights the careers of Joseph G. Totten and Stephen H. Long.

Steelman, Julien R. "Fifty-five Years of Road Building." *American Road Builder*, 34 (July-Aug. 1957), 4-5. "A short run-down on highway activities then [1902] and now" by the president of the American Road Builders Association.

Steinman, D. B. "Bridges and Man's Increased Mobility." *Transactions of the American Society of Civil Engineers*, CT (1953), 767-81. Emphasizes the "indispensable role" of bridges in shrinking distances and facilitating travel.

Steinman, D. B. "Fifty Years of Progress in Bridge Engineering." *Connecticut Society of Civil Engineers*, 48 (1932), 43-59. "A period of unprecedented achievement in bridge engineering," according to the author. He gives special attention to the Eads Bridge, Hell Gate Arch Bridge, Carquinez Strait Bridge, Sixth Street Bridge (Pittsburgh), and the St. Johns Bridge.

Steinman, David B. *The Builders of the Bridge: The Story of John Roebling and His Son*. New York: Harcourt, Brace and Company, 1945. viii + 457 pp. Illustrations, bibliography, and index. A thoroughly researched biography of John Roebling and a detailed account of the building of Brooklyn Bridge. Special attention is given to Roebling's success in spanning the Niagara, the use of caissons in constructing the foundations of Brooklyn Bridge, and Washington Roebling's role in completing his father's work.

Steinman, David B., and John T. Nevill. *Miracle Bridge at Mackinac*. Grand Rapids: Wm. B. Eerdmans Publishing Company, 1957. 208 pp. Illustrations and index. Written for the general reader, the authors have simplified the complicated "while telling the story of how man went about building a bridge that *couldn't* be built." The foreword is by Michigan's governor.

Steinman, David B., and Sara Ruth Watson. *Bridges and Their Builders*. New York: G. P. Putnam's Sons, 1941. xvi + 379 pp. Illustrations. A general, narrative account of bridges and their builders from "the beginnings of history" through the twentieth century. The author's admiration for those who have conquered both physical forces and ignorance by building bridges, even the most primitive, is strikingly evident.

Stelter, Gilbert A. "The Birth of a Frontier Boom Town: Cheyenne 1867." *Annals of Wyoming*. See chapter on "Community Water Supply."

Stephens, John H. *Towers, Bridges, and Other Structures*. New York: Sterling Publishing, 1976. 288 pp. Illustrations and index.

Stern, Joseph S., Jr. "The Suspension Bridge: They Said It Couldn't Be Built." *Bulletin* *of the Cincinnati Historical Society*, 23 (Oct. 1965), 211-28. On the Covington and Cincinnati Suspension Bridge, the longest suspension bridge in the world at the time of its dedication (1867).

Stevens, Harry R. *The Ohio Bridge*. Cincinnati: Ruter Press, 1939. xiii + 213 pp. Illustrations and appendix. A history of the Ohio River bridge between Covington, Kentucky, and Cincinnati, Ohio. There is a sizeable amount of material on engineers Charles Ellet and John Roebling—the former suggested building a suspension bridge across the Ohio; the latter volunteered to do it.

Stevens, John Austin. "Christopher Colles: The First Projector of Inland Navigation in America." *Magazine of American History*. See chapter on "Waterways."

Stevenson, David. *Sketch of the Civil Engineering of North America* . . . . See chapter on "Waterways."

Stewart, George R. *U. S. 40: Cross Section of the United States of America*. Boston: Houghton Mifflin Company, 1953. viii + 311 pp. Illustrations and maps. Popular history and description of the route.

Still, Bayrd. *Milwaukee: The History of a City*. See chapter on "Sewers and Wastewater Treatment."

Still, Bayrd. "Milwaukee, 1870-1900: The Emergence of a Metropolis." *Wisconsin Magazine of History*. See chapter on "Solid Wastes."

Still, Bayrd, ed. *Urban America: A History with Documents*. See chapter on "Planning, Engineering, and Administration."

Stine, Jeffrey K. "People in Public Works: Russell G. Cone." *APWA Reporter*, 47 (Oct. 1980), 4-5. Describes Cone's role (supervisor of on-site construction) in the building of the Golden Gate Bridge and other bridges.

Streeter, Floyd Benjamin. *Prairie Trails & Cow Towns: With Illustrations from Old Prints*. Boston: Chapman & Grimes, 1936. 236 pp. Illustrations, notes, bibliography, and index. A collection of stories and tales about life on wagon and cattle trails rather than a description of the trails themselves.

Stuart, Darwin G. "Coordinated Freeway-Park Developments." *Traffic Quarterly*, XXI (July 1967), 355-78. A serious, historical discussion of the building of controlled-access highways and the development of needed recreational sites by an engineer-planner.

Sullivan, James H. "Paving Progress in Greater Boston." *Journal of the Association of Engineering Societies*, LI (Dec. 1913), 326-50. Denotes improvements in specifications and materials since the early nineteenth century. The article is followed by the transcription of a useful discussion.

Sundquist, James L. *Politics and Policy: The Eisenhower, Kennedy, and Johnson Years*. See chapter on "Parks and Recreation."

Swaim, Benjamin. *The North Carolina Road Law, Now in Force: Containing All the Acts of Assembly, and Decisions of the Supreme Court on the Subject of Roads, Ferries and Bridges* . . . . Asheborough, N. C.: Southern Citizen Office, 1842. From the eighteenth century.

Swanson, Leslie C. *Covered Bridges in Illinois, Iowa and Wisconsin*. Moline, Ill.: Leslie C. Swanson, 1970. 48 pp Illustrations and maps. Thumbnail sketches of covered bridges located in the tri-state area.

Syrett, Harold Coffin. *The City of Brooklyn, 1865-1898*. See chapter on "Urban Mass Transportation."

Talese, Gay. *The Bridge*. New York: Harper and Row, 1964. 140 pp. Illustrations and appendix. Impressionistic, journalistic account of the construction of the Verrazano-Narrows Bridge. The text is accompanied by a superb collection of construction drawings by Lili Rethi.

Talkington, Henry L. "Mullan Road." *Washington Historical Quarterly*, VII (Oct. 1916), 301-06. An account of Lieutenant John Mullan's commission to build a military road through Montana, Idaho, and Washington.

Taylor, George Rogers. *The Transportation Revolution, 1815-1869*. See chapter on "Waterways."

Taylor, Joseph Henry. "Fort Totten Trail." *North Dakota Historical Quarterly*, IV (July 1930), 239-46. Describes the communication link between Fort Totten and Fort Stevenson.

Taylor, Philip Elbert. "The Turnpike Era in

New England." Doctoral dissertation, Yale University, 1934. 391 pp.

ter Braake, Alex L. "Postal History of the James River and Kanawha Turnpike." *West Virginia History*, XXXIII (Oct. 1971), 27-54. Includes general information on road conditions, uses, and maintenance from 1785 to the Civil War.

"The Almanac of Significant Events in Building a Greater America, 1874-1949." *Engineering News-Record*. See chapter on "Planning, Engineering, and Administration."

"The Columbia River Highway in Oregon." *Good Roads*, XI (Jan. 1, 1916), 3-8. A contemporary account that includes an historical introduction, beginning with the first wagon road (1856) built on the Oregon side of the river.

"The Evolution of a Highway." *American Road Builder*, 44 (Jan. 1967), 12-14. A pictorial account of a portion of the National Pike.

"The Iron Link: Port Huron-Sarnia Railway Tunnel." *Michigan History*, LIV (Spring 1970), 62-72. A three-page history of the tunnel connecting Sarnia, Ontario, to Port Huron, Michigan, followed by several pages of photographs.

"The Old National Bridge over the White Water River at Richmond, Ind." *Proceedings of the Purdue Society of Civil Engineering*, 2 (1897), 61-63. A brief history of an 1835 covered bridge.

"The Story of Cement, Concrete, and Reinforced Concrete." *Civil Engineering*, 47 (Nov. 1977), 63-65. On the evolution of these construction materials from the mid-eighteenth century.

Thompson, Carl D. *Public Ownership: A Survey of Public Enterprises, Municipal, State, and Federal in the United States and Elsewhere*. See chapter on "Energy."

Thuesen, H. G. "Reminiscences of the Development of the Parking Meter." *Chronicles of Oklahoma*, XLV (Summer 1967), 112-42. Autobiographical account by the self-proclaimed developer of the first operable parking meter.

Thurston, William N. "Transportation in Florida Before the Civil War." Master's thesis, Florida State University, 1969. 119 pp. Map, notes, and bibliography. Describes development in three modes of transportation—wagon and state roads, rivers, and railroads.

Tilden, Charles J. "New York's First Printed Traffic Regulations Issued Just 25 Years Ago." *American City*, XXXIX (Nov. 1928), 135-36. A brief historical reminder of an important event in New York City's history. The article explains how the city's first set of published regulations, largely the work of William Phelps Eno, formed the basis of subsequent codes.

Tillson, G. W. "Some Recent Improvements in Street Pavements." *Proceedings of the Engineers' Club of Philadelphia*, XXIX (July 1912), 183-97. Compares early street pavements with those of 1910.

Tillson, G. W. *Street Pavements and Paving Material*. New York: John Wiley & Sons, 1912. xvi + 651 pp. Illustrations, drawings, tables, and index. This popular and unique manual on city pavements—"the methods and materials of their construction"—was first published in 1900. The second edition is both revised and enlarged.

Tillson, Geo. W. "The Selection of Street Pavements." *Engineering and Contracting*, XXXVI (Oct. 18, 1911), 403-06. Examines various features—cost, durability, noiselessness, non-slipperiness, and sanitariness—of pavements in use since the 1890s.

Tindall, William. *Origin and Government of the District of Columbia*. See chapter on "Planning, Engineering, and Administration."

Tindall, William. "The Origin of the Parking System of This City." *Records of the Columbia Historical Society of Washington, D. C.*, 4 (1901), 75-99. Reviews the laws and ordinances regulating street parking in Washington, D. C.

Tolman, William Howe. *Municipal Reform in the United States*. See chapter on "Planning, Engineering, and Administration."

Tompkins, D. A. *Road Building and Broad Tires*. Charlotte, N. C.: D. A. Tompkins, 1901. 22 pp. Illustrations. A brief history, fourth edition, of "Mecklenburg's [N. C.] good roads together with some arguments in favor of broad tires for all vehicles." (The author is owner of an engineering and contracting company in Charlotte.)

Trachtenberg, Alan. *Brooklyn Bridge: Fact*

and Symbol. New York: Oxford University Press, 1965. viii + 182 pp. Illustrations, notes, and index. Brooklyn Bridge is seen as a remarkable piece of engineering and a rich cultural symbol. The author explores all aspects of the bridge—first as fact, then as symbol—and uncovers its relationships to economic realities as well as to cultural ideals.

Trachtenberg, Alan. "The Rainbow and the Grid." *American Quarterly*, XVI (Spring 1964), 3-19. An analysis of Thomas Pope's *A Treatise on Bridge Architecture*. The first historical study of bridges to appear in America, Pope's book, the author contends, is "surely an appropriate vehicle for the first recorded plan for what became the New World's greatest bridge [Brooklyn Bridge]." Trachtenberg also reviews other plans and proposals for a "magnificent" bridge across the East River.

Truesdale, Dorothy S. "Historic Main Street Bridge." *Rochester History*, III (April 1941), 1-24. Demonstrates how this nineteenth-century bridge promoted and developed settlement in Rochester.

Tullock, H. S. "The Horse-and-Buggy Days of Bridge Building." *Civil Engineering*, 10 (Sept. 1940), 563-66. Reviews bridge building, particularly in Missouri, from the Civil War to the turn of the century.

Tunnard, Christopher, and Henry Hope Reed. *American Skylines: The Growth and Form of Our Cities and Towns*. See chapter on "Planning, Engineering, and Administration."

Turnbull, Archibald Douglas. *John Stevens: An American Record*. See chapter on "Waterways."

Tyrrell, Henry Grattan. *History of Bridge Engineering*. Chicago: Henry Grattan Tyrrell, 1911. 479 pp. Illustrations, diagrams, and indexes. A general history of bridge engineering by an engineer. The first chapters discuss ancient and medieval bridges; the remaining chapters are organized according to types (stone, wooden, cast iron, suspension, cantilever, concrete, and others) of bridges constructed since 1760.

Upton, Neil. *An Illustrated History of Civil Engineering*. See chapter on "Planning, Engineering, and Administration."

U. S. Department of Commerce. Bureau of the Census. *Historical Statistics of the United States: Colonial Times to 1970*. See chapter on "Planning, Engineering, and Administration."

U. S. Department of Transportation. Federal Highway Administration. *America's Highways 1776-1976: A History of the Federal-Aid Program*. Washington, D. C.: Government Printing Office, 1977. vi + 553 pp. Illustrations, maps, notes, and index. A richly illustrated (color as well as black and white photographs), comprehensive study of a federal public works program. The volume is divided into two parts. Part I is a broad-brush highway history beginning with the pre-Revolutionary War era and ending at the passage of the 1956 Federal-Aid Highway Act. Part II is more technically oriented and includes eleven chapters on administration, planning, research, design, construction, and maintenance. In addition, the development of the interstate highway system is brought up-to-date. Biographical profiles of prominent highway administrators are interspersed throughout the text.

Vanderhill, Burke G. "The Alachua Trail: A Reconstruction." *Florida Historical Quarterly*, LV (April 1977), 423-38. Traces the Indian pathway which led southward from the Altamaha River of Georgia to the Alachua country of Florida.

Van der Zee, Jacob. "The Roads and Highways of Territorial Iowa." *Iowa Journal of History and Politics*, III (April 1905), 175-225. Reviews Iowa's road and highway development in the mid nineteenth century.

Van Metre, T. W. *Transportation in the United States*. Chicago: Foundation Press, Inc., 1939. viii + 403 pp. Maps, tables, bibliography, and index. Designed primarily for use as a textbook in general transportation courses. Part I is entitled "The History of America's Transportation."

Van Trump, James D. "A Trinity of Bridges: The Smithfield Street Bridge Over the Monongahela River at Pittsburgh." *Western Pennsylvania Historical Magazine*, 58 (Oct. 1975), 439-70. A study of the three versions of Pittsburgh's first river bridge erected at Smithfield Street as well as "a consideration of the development of the technology of bridge construction during the nineteenth century."

Vermeule, Cornelius C. "Early Transportation in and about New Jersey." *Proceedings of the New Jersey Historical Society*, IX (April 1924),

106-24. An address before the New Brunswick Historical Club in which the speaker reviews the development of the state's navigation, road, and railroad systems.

Very, E. D. "Some Notes on the Development of Street Cleaning Methods." *Engineering and Contracting*. See chapter on "Solid Wastes."

Vogel, Robert M. "The Engineering Contributions of Wendel Bollman." *Contributions from the Museum of History and Technology*, Papers 34-44 (1966), 77-104. Describes the contributions of a self-taught Baltimore civil engineer who was "the first to evolve a system of bridging in iron to be consistently used on an American railroad."

Vogel, Robert M. "Tunnel Engineering—A Museum Treatment." *Contributions from the Museum of History and Technology*, Papers 34-44 (1966), 201-39. Presents developments in the field of tunneling from 1830 to 1900, based on a series of models constructed for the Smithsonian Institution's Museum of History and Technology.

Waddell, J. A. L. "An Emergency Bridge at Kansas City." *Military Engineer*, XX (Nov.-Dec. 1928), 465-70. Describes how the "Flow Line Bridge" over the Kaw River at Kansas City was designed and built in ten days following the flood of May and June 1903.

Waddell, J. A. L. *Bridge Engineering*. 2 vols. New York: John Wiley & Sons, 1925. Vol. I: lxxv + 1064 + lx pp.; Vol. II: 1065-2176 pp. Illustrations, charts, tables, graphs, diagrams, glossary, and indexes. A monumental study of bridge engineering by one of the profession's most respected bridge builders. The first chapter of Volume I describes the "Evolution of Bridge Engineering."

Waddell, J. A. L. "The Evolution of Art and Science in Our Bridges, A Memoir." *Journal of the Association of Chinese & American Engineers*, XIII (July 1932), 1-16. From 1881, when the author (a respected bridge engineer) "entered the field of bridgework."

Wade, Richard C. *The Urban Frontier: The Rise of Western Cities, 1790-1830*. See chapter on "Community Water Supply."

Wakstein, Allen M., ed. *The Urbanization of America: An Historical Anthology*. See chapter on "Planning, Engineering, and Administration."

Walzer, John Flexer. "Transportation in the Philadelphia Trading Area, 1740-1775." Doctoral dissertation, University of Wisconsin, 1968. 351 pp.

Waring, George E., Jr. *Report on the Social Statistics of Cities*. 2 vols. See chapter on "Planning, Engineering, and Administration."

Waring, George E., Jr. "The Cleaning of a Great City." *McClure's Magazine*. See chapter on "Solid Wastes."

Warne, Clifton. "Some Effects of the Introduction of the Automobile on Highways and Land Values in Nebraska." *Nebraska History*, 38 (March 1957), 43-58. Provides a short history of road development in Nebraska during the first third of the twentieth century.

Warner, Sam Bass, Jr. *The Urban Wilderness: A History of the American City*. See chapter on "Urban Mass Transportation."

Warren, Fred J. "The Development of Bituminous Pavements." *Municipal Journal and Engineer*, XI (Sept. 1901), 108-09. From the 1870s when the first pavements were introduced into the United States.

Warren, George C. "Country Highway and Airport Pavement, 1893-1930." *Proceedings of the Twenty-Seventh Annual Convention of the American Road Builders Association*, January 11-18, 1930. See chapter on "Airways and Airports."

Waters, Thomas F. *A History of the Old Argilla Road in Ipswich, Massachusetts*. Salem, Mass.: Salem Press, 1900. 43 pp.

Watson, Alan D. "Regulation and Administration of Roads and Bridges in Colonial Eastern North Carolina." *North Carolina Historical Review*, XLV (Oct. 1968), 399-417. The author shows that overland travel in North Carolina was "barely possible during the proprietary period and only slightly more tolerable by the Revolution." This situation, he contends, was not due to a lack of legislation. Rather it stemmed, in large part, from "the ever-present disdain for authority" and the physical obstacles (sounds, swamps, marshes) that "were formidable obstructions to effecting a general program of road and bridge administration."

Watson, Alan D. "The Ferry in Colonial North Carolina: A Vital Link in Transportation." *North Carolina Historical Review*. See chapter on "Waterways."

Watson, Harry L. "Squire Oldway and His Friends: Opposition to Internal Improvements in Antebellum North Carolina." *North Carolina Historical Review*. See chapter on "Waterways."

Watson, Sara Ruth. "Some Historic Bridges of the United States." *Engineering Issues*, 101 (July 1975), 383-90. From the old North Bridge (1775) at Concord, Massachusetts, to San Francisco's Golden Gate (1937).

Watson, Wilbur J. "Architectural Principles of Bridge Design." *Civil Engineering*, 8 (March 1938), 181-84. Shows how aesthetic design principles of 2,000 years ago are applicable to most modern structures.

Watson, Wilbur J. *A Decade of Bridges, 1926-1936*. Cleveland: J. H. Jansen, 1937. xv + 125 pp. Illustrations, bibliography, appendices, and geological index. Contains engineering and descriptive data on bridges completed between 1926 and 1936. The author is a professional engineer.

Watson, Wilbur J. *Bridge Architecture: Containing Two-Hundred Illustrations of the Notable Bridges of the World; Ancient and Modern with Descriptive, Historical and Legendary Text*. New York: William Helburn, Inc., 1927. 288 pp. Illustrations, appendices, and index of plates and general text. A large and richly illustrated book of bridges. Many United States' structures are discussed and pictured.

Watson, Wilbur J. and Sara Ruth. *Bridges in History and Legend*. Cleveland: J. H. Jansen, 1937. xvi + 248 pp. Illustrations, notes, bibliography, and index. Rather than a treatise on the art or science of bridge building, this book shows "the significance of the bridge in civilization, in the thoughts of man and in his art." (The bridges discussed are not limited to those located in the United States.) There are separate chapters on toll bridges, covered bridges, and bridge builders.

Waynick, Capus. *North Carolina Roads and Their Builders*. Raleigh: Superior Stone Company, 1952. vii + 308 pp. Illustrations, maps, diagrams, appendix, and index. Presents brief historical sketches of the North Carolina State Highway Commission from 1934-1937.

Weber, Robert David. "Rationalizers and Reformers: Chicago Local Transportation in the Nineteenth Century." Doctoral dissertation, University of Wisconsin, 1971. 432 pp.

Webster, George S., and Samuel Tobias Wagner. "History of the Pennsylvania Subway, Philadelphia and Sewer Construction Connected Therewith." *Transactions of the American Society of Civil Engineers*, XLIV (1900), 1-33. Covers attempts to remove grade railway crossings on Philadelphia streets.

Weigold, Marilyn E. "Pioneering in Parks and Parkways: Westchester County, New York, 1895-1945." *Essays in Public Works History*. See chapter on "Parks and Recreation."

Weitzman, David. "A Conversation with Bridge 3." *Historic Preservation*, 21 (Nov./Dec. 1979), 10-17. A short history of Burger Creek Bridge (1880s) in Mendocino County, California, and an explanation of why it is "in danger of being replaced or altered under a massive federal highway program."

Wells, Donald N. and Merle W. "The Oneida Toll Road Controversy, 1864-1880." *Oregon Historical Quarterly*, LVIII (June 1957), 113-26. Describes an Idaho transportation controversy, initiated by the removal of the Oneida county seat from Soda Springs to Malad on January 5, 1866.

Wells, Rosalie. *Covered Bridges of America*. New York: W. E. Rudge, 1931. 135 pp. Illustrations.

Wertenbaker, Thomas J. *Norfolk: Historic Southern Port*. See chapter on "Sewers and Wastewater Treatment."

Westermaier, F. V. "Recent Developments in Gas Street Lighting." *Transactions of the Illuminating Engineering Society*, XV (April 30, 1920), 175-84. Attributes progress to the use of more efficient lamps, improved fixtures, and better administration by municipalities.

Whatley, Larry. "The Works Progress Administration in Mississippi." *Journal of Mississippi History*. See chapter on "Public Buildings."

Wheeler, Kenneth W. *To Wear a City's Crown: The Beginnings of Urban Growth in Texas, 1836-1865*. See chapter on "Community Water Supply."

Whipple, S. *An Elementary and Practical Treatise on Bridge Building*. New York: D. Van Nostrand, 1872. vi + 317 pp. Drawings and notes. First published in 1847, this enlarged edition of Whipple's original essays on the principles and fundamentals of bridge building remain unequaled.

Whipple, S. *A Work on Bridge Building: Consisting of Two Essays, the One Elementary and General, the Other Giving Original Plans, and Practical Details for Iron and Wooden Bridges*. Utica, N. Y.: H. H. Curtiss, 1847. iv + 120 pp. + X plates. Table and diagrams. A technical treatise by a master bridge builder.

Wilbur Smith and Associates. *Future Highways and Urban Growth*. New Haven: Automobile Manufacturers Association, 1961. xxviii + 376 pp. Illustrations, maps, charts, tables, graphs, notes, appendices, and bibliography. A study of the National System of Interstate and Defense Highways by a prominent transportation consulting firm. It encourages "a continued and accelerated program of express highway construction, particularly in urban areas." There is a brief introduction of an historical nature; most statistics are drawn from the 1950s.

Williams, Archibald. *The Romance of Modern Engineering*. Philadelphia: J. B. Lippincott Company, 1904. 377 pp. Illustrations. Written for a popular audience, the volume contains single chapters on "American Bridges," "Dams and Aqueducts," and "The Harnessing of Niagara."

Williams, Arthur. "The History of Street Lighting in New York City." *American City*, XXXIV (March 1926), 295-96. A quick look at some of the positive effects of street lighting in New York City.

Williams, Charles Alexander. "The History and Operations of the Pennsylvania Turnpike System." Doctoral dissertation, University of Pittsburgh, 1954. 344 pp.

Williams, J. W. "Military Roads of the 1850's in Central West Texas." *West Texas Historical Association Yearbook*, XVIII (Oct. 1942), 77-91. A short history of the military roads surrounding Abilene.

Williams, J. W. "The Butterfield Overland Mail Road across Texas." *Southwestern Historical Quarterly*, LXI (July 1957), 1-19. Relying on the use of surveyors' notes and "the simple arithmetic of distance," the author attempts "to establish more definitely the route of an interesting old trail" that crossed Texas just before the Civil War.

Williams, J. Waynam, Jr. "James B. Eads and His St. Louis Bridge." *Civil Engineering*, 47 (Oct. 1977), 102-06. After looking at the plans, the experts said the nation's first major steel bridge across the Mississippi at St. Louis would not stand up—would not "carry its own weight." The author of this article shows how Eads proved them wrong.

Willoughby, William R. "Early American Interest in Waterway Connections Between the East and West." *Indiana Magazine of History*. See chapter on "Waterways."

Wilson, Ben Hur. "Plank Road Fever." *Palimpsest*, 15 (Sept. 1934), 289-318. A history of plank roads in Iowa.

Wilson, Ben Hur. "Steel Spans a River." *Palimpsest*, XXVIII (June 1947), 207-17. On the first steel bridge in the United States, the famous "Hay Bridge" of the Chicago and Alton Railroad, spanning the Missouri River near the village of Glasgow, Missouri.

Wilson, John R., and Morris M. Townley. *Street Improvements by Cities and Towns in the State of Indiana: Containing the Statutes, with Comments thereon, and Forms*. Indianapolis: W. B. Burford, Printer, 1905. 124 pp.

Wilson, John Russell. "The Old National Road in Pennsylvania." *Good Roads*, XI (Feb. 5, 1916), 69-71. Traces the road (1818) and describes how it was constructed, financed, and maintained.

Winpenny, Thomas R. "The Nefarious Philadelphia Plan and Urban America: A Reconsideration." *Pennsylvania Magazine of History and Biography*. See chapter on "Planning, Engineering, and Administration."

Winther, Oscar Osburn. "Early Commercial Importance of the Mullan Road." *Oregon Historical Quarterly*, XLVI (March 1945), 22-35. Demonstrates the Mullan Road's commercial and military importance to the early history of the Far West in general and Montana in particular.

Winther, Oscar Osburn. "Inland Transportation and Communication in Washington, 1844-1859." *Pacific Northwest Quarterly*, XXX (Oct. 1939), 371-86. Early territorial attempts at road building.

Winther, Oscar Osburn. "The Place of Transportation in the Early History of the Pacific Northwest." *Pacific Historical Review*, XI (Dec. 1942), 383-96. Broad survey of the influence of trails, roads, and waterways on the political, economic, and social history of the Pacific Northwest.

Winther, Oscar Osburn. "The Roads and Transportation of Territorial Oregon." *Oregon Historical Quarterly*, XLI (March 1940), 40-52. Highlights transportation improvements in territorial Oregon from 1849 to 1859.

Winther, Oscar Osburn. "The Southern Overland Mail and Stagecoach Line, 1857-1861." *New Mexico Historical Review*, XXXII (April 1957), 81-106. Describes a pioneer experiment in overland passenger and mail service in the Southwest on the eve of the Civil War.

Winther, Oscar Osburn. *The Transportation Frontier: Trans-Mississippi West, 1865-1900*. New York: Holt, Rinehart and Winston, 1964. xvi + 224 pp. Illustrations, maps, charts, notes, bibliographical essay, and index. A definitive study that analyzes how available transportation routes shaped westward migration. It is the first and finest serious study of all aspects of western transportation from the advent of overland freighting to the automobile era. Winther stresses more than most historians the role of water transportation in the settlement of the Far West.

Wixom, Charles W. *Pictorial History of Roadbuilding*. Washington, D. C.: American Road Builders' Association, 1975. 207 pp. Illustrations, appendix, and bibliography. A well-illustrated chronicle of road building in the United States. In this instance, the text accompanies the photographs which were selected from collections of many federal as well as state agencies.

Wood, Frederic J. *The Turnpikes of New England and Evolution of the Same through England, Virginia, and Maryland*. Boston: Marshall Jones Company, 1919. xvii + 461 pp. Illustrations, maps, bibliography, and index. A thorough examination of the engineering, economic, and archeological aspects of the earliest turnpikes and toll bridges in Massachusetts, Maine, New Hampshire, Vermont, Rhode Island, and Connecticut. There are also separate chapters on the Lancaster Turnpike, the Cumberland Road, and the Maysville Pike. The author is a professional engineer.

Wood, Walter K. "Henry Edmundson, the Alleghany Turnpike, and 'Fotheringay' Plantation: Planting and Trading in Montgomery County, Virginia, 1805-1847." *Virginia Magazine of History and Biography*, 83 (July 1975), 304-20. Emphasizes Edmundson's entrepreneurial spirit vis-a-vis the Alleghany Turnpike, strategically located to accommodate local and western migration traffic.

Wood, Walter Kirk. "The Allegheny Turnpike and Internal Improvements, 1800-1850." Master's thesis, Virginia Polytechnic Institute, 1969.

Woodward, C. M. *A History of the St. Louis Bridge; Containing a Full Account of Every Step in Its Construction and Erection, and Including the Theory of the Ribbed Arch and the Tests of Materials*. St. Louis: G. I. Jones and Company, 1881. xx + 391 pp. + XLVI plates. Illustrations, map, graphs, diagrams, tables, and index. A remarkably full account (and a very large book) of the building of the St. Louis Bridge seven years after its completion. The author, "an eye-witness of many of the important operations attending the construction of the Bridge," was Thayer professor of mathematics and applied mechanics at Washington University. The volume is a classic in its own right.

Woodworth, R. B. "Tunnels, Particularly Subaqueous." *Official Proceedings of the Railway Club of Pittsburgh*, IX (Dec. 22, 1909), 56-118. Begins with a two-page historical introduction and includes a smattering of historical data throughout the remainder of the article.

Wright, Dana. "Military Trails in North Dakota: Fort Abercrombie to Fort Ransom with Notes on the History of Fort Ransom." *North Dakota Historical Quarterly*, 17 (Oct. 1950), 241-52. A short history of a high-water trail and a fort that, because of its location on a huge hill, was a "known landmark."

Wright, Dana. "Military Trails in North Dakota: Fort Abercrombie to Fort Wadsworth, 1864." *North Dakota Historical Quarterly*, 18 (April-July 1951), 157-70. Brief history of a little known trail in southeastern North Dakota.

Wright, Dana. "Military Trails in North Dakota: Fort Ransom to Fort Totten." *North Dakota History*, 16 (Oct. 1949), 203-10. On a trail first used by army soldiers between August 12 and 17, 1863.

Wright, Dana. "Military Trails in North Dakota: The Fort Totten-Abercrombie Trail." *North*

Dakota History, 13 (Jan.-April 1946), 80-96. Traces the trail between Fort Totten and Fort Abercrombie.

Wright, Dana. "Military Trails in North Dakota: The Fort Totten-Abercrombie Trail from the Sibley Crossing to the Red River." *North Dakota History*, 13 (July 1946), 103-11. A precise account of one of the oldest crossings in North Dakota.

Wright, Dana. "The Black Hills Trail: Fort Abraham Lincoln to the South Dakota Line." *North Dakota History*, 25 (Jan. 1958), 14-20. Presents the history of "80 miles more or less from the location of old Fort Abraham Lincoln to the present South Dakota state line, in the vicinity of Morristown, South Dakota."

Wright, Dana. "The Sibley Trail in North Dakota." *North Dakota Historical Quarterly*, I (April 1927), 30-45. The first of several parts on North Dakota's Sibley Trail, named after Henry Hastings Sibley who led a military expedition "to punish the hostile bands of Sioux who had taken part in the Indian uprising of 1862 in Minnesota."

Wright, Dana. "The Sibley Trail in North Dakota: Chapter II. In Ransom County." *North Dakota Historical Quarterly*, I (July 1927), 4-13. A continuation of the first part that appeared in the April 1927 issue (see above).

Wright, Dana. "The Sibley Trail: Chapter III. In Barnes County." *North Dakota Historical Quarterly*, II (Jan. 1928), 120-28. A continuation of parts I and II (see above).

Wrone, David R. "Illinois Pulls Out of the Mud." *Journal of the Illinois State Historical Society*, LVIII (Spring 1965), 54-76. On the strategies and accomplishments of the state's good roads movement (1900-1930).

Yost, Edna. *Modern American Engineers*. See chapter on "Planning, Engineering, and Administration."

Young, Edward M. *The Great Bridge: The Verrazano-Narrows Bridge*. New York: Ariel/Farrar, Straus & Giroux, 1965. 103 pp. Illustrations. Outstanding drawings of the bridge's construction accompany the popular text..

Young, Hugh E. "The Value of Planned City Development: A Record of 24 Years of Progress Under the Chicago Plan." *Civil Engineering*. See chapter on "Planning, Engineering, and Administration."

Young, Jeffie. "The Development of Transportation in Missouri to 1860." Master's thesis, University of Chicago, 1922. iii + 72 pp. Notes and bibliography. Reviews the various stages of transportation development "in that portion of the Louisiana Purchase which in 1820 became the state of Missouri from 1800 to 1860."

Young, Jeremiah Simeon. "A Political and Constitutional Study of the Cumberland Road." Doctoral dissertation, University of Chicago, 1902. 107 pp. Map, notes, and bibliography. This dissertation traces "the origin, construction, administration and surrender of the Cumberland road" which the author sees as "the central thread running through the subject of internal improvements" until 1856.

Zangrando, Joanna Schneider. "Monumental Bridge Design in Washington, D. C. as a Reflection of American Culture, 1886-1932." Doctoral dissertation, George Washington University, 1974. 583 pp.

Zucker, Paul. *American Bridges and Dams*. New York: Greystone Press, 1941. 16 pp. + 48 plates. Illustrations, diagrams, and bibliography. Demonstrates the "artistic appearance and beauty of American bridges and dams."

Zueblin, Charles. *American Municipal Progress: Chapters in Municipal Sociology*. See chapter on "Planning, Engineering, and Administration."

9

Urban Mass Transportation

The availability of urban mass transportation systems has been a determining factor in shaping the character and pattern of American cities. The first omnibuses and horsecars extended the distances traveled to work by city dwellers, a phenomenon that was accelerated by the introduction of electric trolleys, interurbans, subways, and elevated rail networks. In the nineteenth century, public transit systems helped to transform the urban environment from a mixed condition into highly segregated working, shopping, and living areas. Central business districts became ringed by industrial and residential areas. This process was given even greater impetus by the widespread adoption of the automobile and motor bus, which expanded the growth of bedroom suburban communities.

The following citations illustrate that this complex, multidimensional subject has received attention from scholars in many disciplines. Although there is a profusion of "buff" books in this field, their inclusion has been purposefully limited. Most of the books, articles, and dissertations focus on changes in public transportation technology since the mid-nineteenth century and how they affected the quality, character, and shape of urban areas. There is a heavy emphasis on the relationship between transit development and residential, commercial, and industrial patterns; changes in population densities, housing, ridership habits, and the journey to work, as well as suburbanization and the geographical distribution of social classes. Mass transit systems have also been profoundly influenced by government policies with respect to ownership, regulation, taxation, and the eventual development of street and highway systems for its principal antagonist—the private automobile. Various aspects of transit administration and financing are also treated.

Collectively, these sources trace the birth, triumph, decline, and recent renaissance of urban public transportation. The automobile still reigns supreme, but there are indications that public transportation is making a strong comeback. Ridership on urban mass transportation systems has registered significant increases since 1974. Furthermore, rising fuel cost and other factors are forcing communities to place greater reliance on this important servant of the community. The recent surge of scholarly interest in this subject is an indication of its significance in urban planning and administration.

Adams, John S. "Residential Structure of Midwestern Cities." *Annals of the Association of American Geographers*, 60 (March 1970), 37-61. A highly technical, complex article that discusses the spatial dynamics of urban development. The author describes a growth model that presents the interrelationships between transportation technology, construction cycles, and urban residential patterns.

Anderson, Edward A. *PCC Cars of Boston, 1937-1967*. Cambridge: Boston Street Railway Association, 1968. 52 pp. Illustrations and maps. A nostalgic and heavily illustrated overview of Boston surface transit lines.

Armstrong, Ellis L.; Michael C. Robinson; and Suellen M. Hoy, eds. *History of Public Works in the United States, 1776-1976*. See chapter on "Planning, Engineering, and Administration."

Arnold, Bion J.; H. B. Fleming; and George Weston. "Phases in the Development of the Street Railways of Chicago." *Journal of the Western Society of Engineers*, XIV (Oct. 1909), 625-47. Series of flatulent banquet speeches.

Aronson, Dennis. "The Pomona Street Railways in the Southern California Boom of the 1880s." *Southern California Quarterly*, XLVII (Sept. 1965), 245-67. A competent history of five lines that operated in Pomona, California, in the 1880s and 1890s. The article skillfully illustrates the relationships between street railway development and real estate speculation.

Bailey, Margaret Burton. "The Boston Elevated Railway: A Case Study of a Public Corporation." Master's thesis, University of Chicago, 1938. iii + 123 pp. Tables, notes, appendix, and bibliography. An excellent analysis that traces the origins of the Boston Elevated Railway as a private company and its subsequent history as a public corporation. Subjects such as internal administration and the role of pressure groups are included.

Baker, M. N. *Municipal Engineering and Sanitation*. See chapter on "Planning, Engineering, and Administration."

"Baltimore Recalls Pioneer Road." *Electric Railway Journal*, 66 (Aug. 15, 1925), 244-45. Celebration of the fortieth anniversary of an electric line that began operating in 1885.

Barger, Harold. *The Transportation Industries, 1889-1946: A Study of Output, Employment, and Productivity*. New York: National Bureau of Economic Research, Inc., 1951. xvi + 288 pp. Tables, charts, notes, appendices, and index. Discusses the growth of major transportation industries with respect to volume, employment, and productivity. The book focuses on steam railroads, electric railroads, pipelines, waterways, and airlines. The statistical compilations are especially valuable to students of transportation history.

Barnard, John H. "How the Trolley Cars Came to Asheville, N. C." *AERA*, XXI (Aug. 1930), 490-94. Recollections of a pioneer in the development of electric traction.

Barnes, Joseph. "The N. Y. Central Elevates Its Tracks under Municipal Pressure." *Rochester History*. See chapter on "Roads, Streets and Highways.

Barrett, Paul Frances. "Mass Transit, the Automobile, and Public Policy in Chicago, 1900-1930." Doctoral dissertation, University of Illinois at Chicago Circle, 1976. 722 pp. Maps, tables, notes, appendices, and bibliography. This dissertation discusses policies adopted by the City of Chicago that helped to make mass transportation less attractive while increasing the usefulness of the private automobile. The author contends that negative public attitudes toward mass transit companies fostered the growth of facilities that favored the automobile.

Barrett, Paul. "Public Policy and Private Choice: Mass Transit and the Automobile in Chicago between the Wars." *Business History Review*, XLIX (Winter 1975), 473-97. A brilliant analysis of the influence of popular and official attitudes on technological change. The author concludes that "public policy, grounded in the conception of urban transit as a private business and of the automobile as a public good, played a critical role in the decline of public transportation and the triumph of the automobile in Chicago." The quality of Chicago's mass transit suffered due to negative regulation, short-term franchises, heavy taxation, and general suspicion of municipal ownerships.

Barth, Gunther. *Instant Cities: Urbanization and the Rise of San Francisco and Denver*. New York: Oxford University Press, 1975. xix + 310 pp. Notes and index. Little of this well-written book deals with public works subjects. However, Chapter VIII, "Technology Stimulates Transition," contains discussions of the effects of railroads and street railways on the urban structure of Denver and San Francisco.

Bean, Walton. *Boss Reuf's San Francisco: The Story of the Union Labor Party, Big Business, and the Graft Prosecution*. See chapter on "Community Water Supply."

Bebout, John E., and Ronald J. Grele. *Where Cities Meet: The Urbanization of New Jersey*. Princeton: D. Van Nostrand Company, 1964. xiii + 127 pp. Illustrations, maps, bibliographical essay, and index. Chapter 5 of this book, "The Spreading City," incorporates information on rapid transit systems, bridges, roads, and water systems. The publication is Volume 22 of "The New Jersey Historical Series."

Bemis, Edward W., ed. *Municipal Monopolies*. New York: Thomas Y. Crowell and Company, 1899. ix + 691 pp. Tables, graphs, and index. An essential source for historians and students of public versus private ownership and regulation of public utilities. The collection of essays by individual authors covers community water supply, municipal lighting, street railways, and gas utilities. The book generally supports public ownership of these services.

Black, Archibald. *The Story of Tunnels*. See chapter on "Roads, Streets, and Highways."

Blackburn, Glen A. "Interurban Railroads of Indiana." *Indiana Magazine of History*, XX (Sept. 1924; Dec. 1924), 221-79; 400-63. A rather uninspired catalog of Indiana interurbans.

Bridenbaugh, Carl. *Cities in Revolt: Urban Life in America*, 1743-1776. See chapter on "Planning, Engineering, and Administration."

Bridenbaugh, Carl. *Cities in the Wilderness: The First Century of Urban Life in America, 1625-1742*. See chapter on "Planning, Engineering, and Administration."

Briggs, G. M. "Around the Car Barn Table." *National Safety News*, 14 (Nov. 1926), 19-21. Nostalgic reflections on the convenience and safety of horse cars.

Brownell, Blaine A. "A Symbol of Modernity: Attitudes Toward the Automobile in Southern Cities in the 1920s." *American Quarterly*. See chapter on Roads, Streets, and Highways."

Brownell, Blaine A. "The Notorious Jitney and the Urban Transportation Crisis in Birmingham in the 1920s." *Alabama Review*, XXV (April 1972), 105-18.

Bryant, George T. "The Gripman Wore a Sheepskin Coat: A Memoir on Local Chicago Transportation at the Turn of the Century." *Chicago History* (Spring 1970), 47-56. Personal memoir of horsecars, cablecars, trolleys, and the El.

Bureau of the Census (Department of Commerce and Labor). *Statistics of Cities Having a Population of 8,000 to 25,000: 1903*. See chapter on "Roads, Streets and Highways."

Bureau of the Census (Department of Commerce and Labor). *Statistics of Cities Having a Population of 30,000: 1904*. See chapter on "Roads, Streets, and Highways."

Callow, Alexander B., Jr., ed. *American Urban History*. New York: Oxford University Press, 1973. xiv + 684 pp. Map, tables, graphs, and bibliography. Joel Tarr's "From City to Suburb: The Moral Influence of Transportation Technology" is the only section in this reader that deals directly with an urban public works topic. Tarr's essay discusses the influence of mass transit technology on suburbanization. The volume was first published in 1968.

Carman, Harry James. *The Street Surface Railway Franchises of New York City*. New York: Columbia University, 1919. 259 pp. Maps, notes, bibliography, and index. A factual survey of the franchise history of street railways on Manhattan Island. The author opposes municipal ownership of the network and advocates more effective regulation.

Carson, Robert B. *What Ever Happened to the Trolley?* Washington, D. C.: University Press of America, 1978. vii + 117 pp. Illustrations, map, charts, tables, notes, and bibliography. One of the better historical surveys of the rise and decline of street railways from 1859 to the 1940s. The author recommends the re-introduction of trolleys to meet city transportation needs.

Catlin, George B. *The Story of Detroit*. See chapter on "Community Water Supply."

Chandler, Allison. "The Horse-Car Interurban from Cottonwood Falls to Strong City." *Kansas Historical Quarterly*, XXIV (Winter 1958), 385-98. Discussion of a transit line between Cottonwood Falls and Strong City, Kansas.

Chandler, Allison. "The Westmoreland Interurban Railway." *Kansas Historical Quarterly*, XXVIII (Autumn 1962), 301-09. Routine summary of an interurban that operated in northeastern Kansas.

Cheape, Charles W. *Moving the Masses: Urban Public Transit in New York, Boston, and Philadelphia, 1880-1912*. Cambridge: Harvard University Press, 1980. x + 285 pp. Maps, charts, notes, bibliographical essay and index. Perhaps the most significant study in the history of mass transportation published in the past decade. The author's research and analysis is prodigious. Cheape delineates the basic characteristics of transit firms; describes the economic, technological, political, and social environment in which they were created; and outlines the interaction between private enterprise and government during the period.

Clark, James Everett. "The Impact of Transportation Technology on Suburbanization in the Chicago Region, 1830-1920." Doctoral dissertation. See chapter on "Roads, Streets, and Highways."

Clark, William J. "A Decade of Electric Railway Development." *Electrical World*, XXX (Sept. 18, 1897), 335. Thumbnail sketch of early electric street railways in New York State.

Clarke, T. Wood. *Utica for a Century and a Half*. See chapter on "Community Water Supply."

Condit, Carl W. *Chicago, 1910-29: Building, Planning, and Urban Technology*. See chapter on "Planning, Engineering, and Administration."

Condit, Carl W. "The Pioneer Stage of Railroad Electrification." *Transactions of the American Philosophical Society*, 67 (Nov. 1977), 3-45. Prodigiously researched, definitive study of the early evolution of railroad and street railway electrification technology.

Condit, Carl W. *The Port of New York: A History of the Rail and Terminal System from the Beginnings to Pennsylvania Station*. Chicago: University of Chicago Press, 1980. xvii + 456 pp. Illustrations, maps, tables, diagrams, notes, bibliography, and index. A brilliant, multidimensional discussion of "the railroad as a technological entity of major urbanistic importance." The book analyzes the genesis, growth, and capacity of the rail and terminal system that serves the city. Although the scope of the treatment of rapid transit is relatively limited, information is included on this subject.

Condit, Carl W. *The Railroad and the City: A Technological and Urbanistic History of Cincinnati*. Columbus: Ohio State University Press, 1977. xiv + 335 pp. Illustrations, notes, bibliography, appendices, and index. Outstanding study of the influences of rail technology on the structure of Cincinnati.

Conklin, Groff. *All About Subways*. New York: Julian Messner, 1938. 212 pp. Illustrations. A heavily illustrated primer on subway design and construction.

Cook, Ann; Marilyn Gittell; and Herb Mack, eds. *City Life, 1865-1900: Views of Urban America*. See chapter on "Solid Wastes."

Cooke, Morris Llewellyn, ed. *Public Utility Regulation*. See chapter on "Energy."

Cowdrey, Albert E. *A City for the Nation: The Army Engineers and the Building of Washington, D. C., 1790-1967*. See chapter on "Planning, Engineering, and Administration."

Cox, Harold E. "'Daily Except Sunday': Blue Laws and the Operation of Philadelphia Horsecars." *Business History Review*, XXXIX (Summer 1965), 228-42. The uncertainties of predicting and mitigating social reactions to technological innovation are amusingly demonstrated in this study.

Cox, H. E. "Jim Crow in the City of Brotherly Love: The Segregation of Philadelphia Horse Cars." *Negro History Bulletin*, XXVI (Dec. 1962), 119-23. An interesting discussion of attempts to desegregate street railways in Philadelphia during the mid 1860s. Blacks were given full access to public transportation in 1867 by state law.

Crump, Spencer. *Ride the Big Red Cars: How Trolleys Helped Build Southern California*. Los Angeles: Trans-Anglo Books, 1965. 238 pp. Illustrations, maps, notes, and appendix. One of the best case studies of street railway and interurban growth and decline. The author discusses the influence of the automobile and bus as a cause of the demise of electric railways in southern California.

Cudahy, Brian J. *Rails under the Mighty Hudson: The Story of the Hudson Tubes, the*

Pennsylvania Tunnels, and Manhattan Transfer. Brattleboro, Vt.: Stephen Greene Press, 1975. 79 pp. Illustrations, maps, notes, and appendices. A well-written—although brief—account of the building of those structures cited in the title and their impact on the New York-New Jersey metropolitan area. The author concludes with an epilogue entitled "An Ode to Penn Station."

Cudahy, Brian J. *Under the Sidewalks of New York: The Story of the Greatest Subway System in the World*. Brattleboro, Vt.: Stephen Greene Press, 1979. 176 pp. Illustrations, maps, notes, chronology, appendices, and index. Well-written and thorough popular history of New York City's subway system.

Davis, Grant Miller. *The Department of Transportation*. See chapter on "Planning, Engineering, and Administration."

Davis, James Leslie. *The Elevated System and the Growth of Northern Chicago*. Evanston: Department of Geography, Northwestern University, 1965. xvi + 180 pp. Illustrations, maps, tables, notes, bibliography, and appendices. An exceptionally thorough study of the impact of the Chicago elevated system upon the development of settlement and land-value patterns in northern Chicago.

DeCamp, Roderick Kyle. "The Chicago Transit Authority: A Study in Responsibility." Doctoral dissertation, University of Chicago, 1978.

Dewees, Donald N. "The Decline of American Street Railways." *Traffic Quarterly*, 24 (Oct. 1970), 563-81. Perhaps the best survey of the reasons for the decline of street railways after World War I. The author's sophisticated analysis challenges the concept that declining ridership due to automobile competition made rapid transit unprofitable. The car changed "the environment in which the street railways operated so that their costs rose rapidly relative to alternative means of travel." The motor bus became a vehicle better suited to the more diffuse and changing passenger demands.

Doig, Jameson W. "The Politics of Metropolitan Transportation: A Study of the New York-New Jersey Metropolitan Rapid Transit Commission." Doctoral dissertation, Princeton University, 1961. 532 pp.

Dolan, Eleanor. "The Effect of Rapid Transit on Land Value and Building Construction in Boston, Cambridge, and Arlington, 1900-1930." Doctoral dissertation, Radcliff College, 1935. 61 pp.

Donaho, John Albert. "The Chicago Subway: A Pattern for the Federal-Municipal Relationship." Master's thesis, University of Chicago, 1943. v + 131 pp. Notes, appendices, and bibliography. One of the few case studies of a Public Works Administration project. The thesis contains unique material on the interrelationships of the federal and city governments in building the subway.

Drummond, James O. "Transportation and the Shaping of the Physical Environment in an Urban Place, Newark, 1820-1900." Doctoral dissertation, New York University, 1979. 330 pp.

Dumke, Glenn S. "Early Interurban Transportation in the Los Angeles Area." *The Quarterly, Historical Society of Southern California*, XXII (Dec. 1940), 131-49. Comprehensive overview of the development of public transportation in Los Angeles to about 1915.

Dyer, Frank Lewis; Thomas Commerford Martin; and William Henry Meadowcroft. *Edison: His Life and Inventions*, 2 vols. New York: Harper & Brothers Publishers, 1929. Vol. I: viii + 472 pp.; Vol. II: vi + 473-1036 pp. Illustrations, appendices, and index. A commemorative bibliography of Edison that includes chapters on his first central power station and work in the field of electric traction.

Easton, Alexander. *A Practical Treatise on Street or Horse-Power Railways*. Philadelphia: Crissy & Markley, Printers, 1859. vi + 149 pp. Illustrations. A classic treatise on the early development of horsecars and omnibuses. It is an excellent source of information on street-railway technology and administration.

Farrell, Michael R. *Who Made All Our Streetcars Go? The Story of Rail Transit in Baltimore*. Baltimore: NRHS Publications, 1973. 319 pp. Illustrations, maps, glossary, bibliography, and index. A solid case study that is superior to most transit "buff" books.

Fellmann, Jerome D. "Pre-Building Growth Patterns of Chicago." *Annals of the Association of American Geographers*, 47 (March 1957), 59-82. The influence of transit networks on the evolution of subdivisions is perceptively analyzed in this article.

"Fifty Years Ago—And Today." *Electric Traction*, XXVII (Sept. 1931), 413-15. Weak sketch of the transition from horse-to-electric-powered traction.

Finster, Jerome, ed. *The National Archives and Urban Research*. Athens: Ohio University Press, 1974. xii + 164 pp. Tables, notes, bibliographies, and index. The book is a collection of papers presented at the Conference on the National Archives and Urban Research held June 18-19, 1970. Glen E. Holt's contribution, "Urban Mass Transit History: Where We Have Been and Where We Are Going," is an excellent bibliographical essay. Public works historians may also wish to consult Leonard Rapport, "Urban Transportation Records in the National Archives."

Fischer, Joel. "Urban Transportation: Home Rule and the Independent Subway System in New York City, 1917-1925." Doctoral dissertation, St. John's University, 1978. 395 pp.

Fisher, Edwin A. "Engineering and Public Works in the City of Rochester during the Past Centuy." *Centennial History of Rochester, New York*. See chapter on "Planning, Engineering, and Administration."

Fogelson, Robert M. *The Fragmented Metropolis: Los Angeles, 1850-1930*. See chapter on "Community Water Supply."

Foster, Abram John. "The Coming of the Electrical Age to the United States." Doctoral dissertation. See chapter on "Energy."

Foster, Mark S. "City Planners and Urban Transportation: The American Response, 1900-1940." *Journal of Urban History*, 5 (May 1979), 365-96. Outstanding analysis of urban transportation planning. The author concludes that "it is nearly inconceivable how the predominant place of the electric trolley could have remained unchallenged or how urban planners could have enabled cities to avoid mid-century transportation chaos."

Foster, Mark S. "The Model-T, the Hard Sell, and Los Angeles's Urban Growth: The Decentralization of Los Angeles during the 1920s." *Pacific Historical Review*, LXIV (Nov. 1975), 459-84. An outstanding discussion of the influence of transportation planning and technology on the urbanization process. Foster conclusively demonstrates that Los Angeles' decentralized pattern was the result of decisions by city planners that encouraged adoption of the automobile at the expense of public transportation. The city's population doubled during a decade when the automobile won widespread public acceptance. Consequently, Los Angeles became the prototype of the decentralized "midtwentieth-century metropolis."

Foster, Mark S. "The Western Response to Urban Transportation, 1900-1940: A Tale of Three Cities, 1900-1945." *Journal of the West*, 18 (July 1979), 31-39. Examines mass transit policy and city planners' contributions in Denver, Los Angeles, and Seattle. The author argues that western urban planners sanctioned the inevitable pre-World War II, horizontal sprawl; and, more importantly, they rationalized it as a positive social good.

Freund, Peter Frederick. "Labor Relations in the New York City Rapid Transit Industry, 1945-1960." Doctoral dissertation, New York University, 1964. 227 pp.

Galli, Geraldine. "100 Years of Construction News." *Engineering News-Record*. See chapter on "Planning, Engineering, and Administration."

Gilchrist, David T., ed. *The Growth of Seaport Cities, 1790-1825: Proceedings of a Conference Sponsored by the Eleutherian Mills-Hagley Foundation, March 17-19, 1966*. See chapter on "Waterways."

Glaab, Charles N., and Theodore A. Brown. *A History of Urban America*. See chapter on "Community Water Supply."

Goeddertz, Henry. "Early Public Transportation in Denver." *Colorado Magazine*, XXVI (April 1949), 125-27. Weak article on Denver's first street railways.

Goheen, Peter G. *Victorian Toronto, 1850-1900: Pattern and Process of Growth*. Chicago: University of Chicago, Department of Geography, 1970. xiii + 278 pp. Illustrations, maps, tables, notes, bibliography, appendices, and index. One of the best case studies of the processes of late nineteenth-century urbanization. The author's discussion of how the street railways shaped the geographical distribution of social classes is especially noteworthy.

Grant, H. Roger. "Arkansas's Paper Interurbans." *Arkansas Historical Quarterly*, XXXIX (Spring 1980), 53-63. Explains why interurban projects were stillborn in Arkansas.

Grant, H. Roger. "The Excelsior Springs Route: Life and Death of a Missouri Interurban." *Missouri Historical Review,* LXV (Oct. 1970), 37-50. The rise and decline of an interurban transit line between Kansas City and St. Joseph, Missouri.

Grant, H. Roger. "Wyoming's Electric Railway Project." *Annals of Wyoming,* 52 (Spring 1980), 16-21.

Grant, Howard. *Notes from the Underground.* San Francisco: Reid & Tarics Associates, 1976. viii + 71 pp. Illustrations, maps, bibliography, and index. A highly laudatory "architect's view" of the BART public transportation system.

Green, Constance McLaughlin. *History of Naugatuck, Connecticut.* See chapter on "Sewers and Wastewater Treatment."

Green, Constance McLaughlin. *Washington: Village and Capital, 1800-1878.* Princeton: Princeton University Press, 1962. xix + 445 pp. Illustrations, notes, bibliographical essay, and index. An outstanding history by one of the nation's finest historians. The book contains thoughtful analyses of the development of the city's public works. During the post-Civil War era, a public works construction program was launched that transformed Washington's livableness and appearance.

Green, Constance McLaughlin. *Washington Capital City, 1879-1950.* See chapter on "Community Water Supply."

Griffith, Ernest S. *A History of American City Government: The Conspicuous Failure, 1870-1900.* See chapter on "Planning, Engineering, and Administration."

Griffith, Ernest S. *A History of American City Government: The Progressive Years and Their Aftermath, 1900-1920.* See chapter on "Planning, Engineering, and Administration."

Grosser, Hugo S. "The Movement for Municipal Ownership in Chicago." *Annals of the American Academy of Political and Social Science,* XXVII (Jan.-June 1906), 72-90. Shows that the movement for municipal ownership in Chicago "is as old, almost as the city itself." The author discusses the concept in general and then in relation to the street railway lines.

Hager, Louis P., ed. *History of the West End Street Railway.* Boston: Louis P. Hager, 1892. 296 pp. Illustrations. A history of street railways in Boston designed to promote public acceptance of electrification. The book contains an interesting chapter on transit in foreign countries.

Haley, Robert Murkland. "The American Electric Railway Interurban: An Epoch in Transportation Development." Doctoral dissertation, Northwestern University, 1936. ii + 209 pp. Maps, charts, tables, notes, appendices, and bibliography. Deals principally with the evolution of interurbans in Indiana, but it also includes strong chapters on the general evolution of the industry.

Hall, Clayton Colman, ed. *Baltimore: Its History and Its People.* See chapter on "Community Water Supply."

Hanna, John H. "Evolution of Community Transportation." *Electric Railway Journal,* 75 (Sept. 15, 1931), 497-502. A buff overview by a transit owner.

Hansen, Harry. *Scarsdale: From Colonial Manor to Modern Community.* See chapter on "Community Water Supply."

Harlan, Homer. "Charles Tyson Yerkes and the Chicago Transportation System." Doctoral dissertation, University of Chicago, 1975. vi + 311 pp. Notes and bibliography. An insightful analysis of the street-railway magnate who was responsible for the coordination or construction of over 60 percent of the city's transit lines. Yerkes is viewed much more favorably by Harlan than by many other historians.

Hatch, James. "The Development of the Electric Railway." *Journal of the Western Society of Engineers,* XIII (Aug. 1908), 489-513. Poorly organized summary of some landmarks of early electric railway history.

Heidorn, Robert D. "Urban Mass Transportation with Special Emphasis on Downstate Illinois Cities: A Study in the Formation of Public Policy." Doctoral dissertation, University of Illinois, Champaign-Urbana, 1963. 196 pp.

Heilman, Ralph E. *Chicago Traction: A Study of the Efforts of the Public to Secure Good Service.* Princeton: Princeton University Press, 1908. xi + 131 pp. Notes and appendices. A valuable source of information on the early growth of Chicago's street-railway system. The author discusses the fiscal abuses of company owners and the lack of adequate service; he suggests that the system should be brought under municipal ownership.

Hilton, George W. "Denver's Cable Railways." *Colorado Magazine,* XLIV (Winter 1967), 35-52. An analysis of Denver's experience with the cable car. The author finds it an "unfavorable" one "because of the city's adamancy on requiring continuance of the City Cable Railway lines long after cable traction ceased to be economical.

Hilton, George W. *The Cable Car in America: A New Treatise upon Cable or Rope Traction as Applied to the Working of Street and Other Railways.* Berkeley, Calif.: Howell-North Books, 1971. 484 pp. Illustrations, maps, bibliography, and index. The handsome, heavily illustrated work is an exemplary survey of this broad topic. The first half, that chronicles the technological evolution of the cable car, is followed by capsule histories of individual transit systems.

Hilton, George W. "The Decline of Railroad Commutation." *Business History Review,* XXVI (Summer 1962), 171-87. A survey of the economic factors that caused the decline of the railroad commuter business.

Hilton, George W. "Rail Transit and the Pattern of Modern Cities: The California Case." *Traffic Quarterly,* XXI (July 1967), 379-93. Demonstrates the relationship between geographical patterns and urban transportation technology in Los Angeles and California.

Hilton, George W., and John F. Due. *The Electric Interurban Railways in America.* Stanford: Stanford University Press, 1960. 463 pp. Illustrations, maps, notes, bibliography, and index. A comprehensive treatment of the rise and decline of the interurbans. The first half of the book—which covers technology, government regulation, finance, and the industry's demise—is followed by state-by-state summaries of individual interurban systems.

Hoffecker, Carol E. *Wilmington, Delaware: Portrait of an Industrial City, 1830-1910.* See chapter on "Sewers and Wastewater Treatment."

Holli, Melvin G. *Reform in Detroit: Hazen S. Pingree and Urban Politics.* New York: Oxford University Press, 1969. xvii + 269 pp. Notes, bibliographical essay, and index. An outstanding biography of the reformer who served as mayor of Detroit from 1890 to 1897. The author illustrates how the public transit question turned Pingree into a social reformer and an advocate of municipal ownership of some public services.

Hornung, Clarence P. *Wheels Across America: A Pictorial Cavalcade Illustrating the Early Development of Vehicular Transportation.* New York: A.S Barnes & Co., 1959. 341 pp. Illustrations. This popular, heavily illustrated volume contains a chapter on the early development of street-railway systems. The illustrations are unique and effectively used.

Hoyt, Homer. *One Hundred Years of Land Values in Chicago: The Relationship of the Growth of Chicago to the Rise of its Land Values, 1830-1933.* Chicago: University of Chicago Press, 1933. xxxii + 519 pp. Maps, tables, charts, footnotes, bibliography, appendices, and index. A pioneering, though somewhat turgid, study of the relationship of land values to urban growth. The book offers especially sound analyses of the role railroads and streetcar systems played in determining land use patterns.

Hubbard, Theodora Kimball, and Henry Vincent. *Our Cities To-Day and To-Morrow: A Survey of Planning and Zoning Progress in the United States.* See chapter on "Planning, Engineering, and Administration."

Hungerford, Edward. *The Story of Public Utilities.* New York: G.P. Putnam's Sons, 1928. xiv + 384 pp. Illustrations and index. A popular history of public and private utilities that seeks to give "a picture of the origin, the development, the general organization and the practical workings of the utilities which serve our cities and our country." The comprehensive book includes chapters on the development of canals, street railways, city lighting, electrical production, streets, bridges, water supply, sewerage, parks, and utility regulation.

Hunt, Rockwell Dennis, and William Sheffield Ament. *Oxcart to Airplane.* See chapter on "Roads, Streets, and Highways.

Huse, Charles Phillips. *The Financial History of Boston from May 1, 1822 to January 31, 1909.* See chapter on "Community Water Supply."

Hutchins, Jere C. *Jere C. Hutchins: A Personal Story.* Detroit: n.p., 1938. xii + 372 pp. Illustrations, appendix, and index. An interesting autobiography of a street railway magnate. Most of the book chronicles the crusade of reform politicians against his Detroit United

Railway, which was eventually purchased and operated by the city. It offers an unusual perspective on municipal ownership campaigns during the Progressive era.

Huth, Tom. "Chicago's El Rattles on—and Outlasts Its Critics." *Historic Preservation,* 32 (Jan.-Feb. 1980), 2-9. Traces preservationist efforts to save the El and suggests ways to upgrade the public facility.

Interborough Rapid Transit. *The New York Subway: Its Construction and Equipment.* New York: Arno Press, 1969. 154 pp. Illustrations, maps, and diagrams. A well-written popular history of the system that deals extensively with its facilities and rolling stock. The volume was first published in 1904.

Jackson, A. T. "Austin's Streetcar Era." *Southwestern Historical Quarterly,* LVIII (Oct. 1954), 235-48. Survey of the city's surface lines from 1875 to 1940.

Jackson, Kenneth T., and Stanley K. Schultz, eds. *Cities in American History.* New York: Alfred A. Knopf, 1972. xi + 506 pp. Maps, tables, notes, and bibliographical essay. A fine collection of reprinted and original scholarly works. Glen E. Holt's "The Changing Perception of Urban Pathology: An Essay on the Development of Mass Transit in the United States" offers an excellent overview of the evolution of public transportation to 1920. It illustrates that the unresponsiveness of transit owners to public complaints hastened adoption of the automobile.

James, William Alfred. "The History of Urban Transportation in Pittsburgh and Allegheny County with Emphasis upon the Major Technological Developments." Masters thesis, University of Pittsburgh, 1947. Maps, notes, and bibliography. An outstanding case study of the growth of mass transit institutions and technology. The coverage of street railway technology is especially thorough.

Johnson, James D., comp. *A Century of Chicago Streetcars, 1858-1958.* Wheaton, Ill.: Traction Orange Company, 1964. 144 pp. Illustrations and maps. Largely a photo album.

Johnson, Joseph French. "The Recent History of Municipal Ownership in the United States." *Municipal Affairs.* See chapter on "Community Water Supply."

Johnson, Scott R. "The Trolley Car as a Social Factor: Springfield, Massachusetts." *Historical Journal of Western Massachusetts,* I (Fall 1972), 5-17. Pedestrian case study of the influence of the trolley on the town's social and economic growth.

Jones, William C., et al. *Mile-High Trolleys: A Nostalgic Look at Denver in the Era of the Streetcars.* Denver: National Railway Historical Society, 1975. 128 pp. Illustrations and maps.

Kaempffert, Waldemar. "New York's First Subway." *Scientific American,* CVL (Feb. 24, 1912), 176-77. Intriguing article of an experimental pneumatic subway built in 1869.

Kahn, Edgar Myron. "Andrew Smith Hallidie." *California Historical Society Quarterly.* See chapter on "Roads, Streets, and Highways."

Kahn, Edgar M. *Cable Car Days in San Francisco.* Stanford University: Stanford University Press, 1940. xv + 124 pp. Illustrations, maps, appendix, and bibliography. A substantive, popular account of the growth of San Francisco's street railways.

Kennedy, Charles J. "Commuter Services in the Boston Area, 1835-1860." *Business History Review,* 36 (Summer 1976), 153-70. A landmark article that discusses the influence of railroads on commuter travel and suburbanization in the 1840s and 1850s. Kennedy convincingly argues that the early railroads "assured the development of the American suburb" and "stimulated the construction of Boston's horse-drawn street-railways."

Kheel, Theodore W., and J. K. Turcott. *Transit and Arbitration: A Decade of Decisions and the Path to Transit Peace.* Englewood Cliffs, N.J.: Prentice-Hall, 1960. vi + 602 pp. Illustrations and indexes. The first chapter of this book is a well-researched history of "Transit Labor in New York, 1745-1959." The material on eighteenth-century ox-carts is especially unique.

King, LeRoy O., Jr. *100 Years of Capital Traction: The Story of Streetcars in the Nation's Capital.* Dallas: Leroy O. King, Jr., 1972. xii + 329 pp. Illustrations, maps, charts, notes, appendices, bibliography, and index. A beautifully illustrated and comprehensive buff transit book.

Kirkland, Edward C. *Industry Comes of Age:*

Business, Labor, and Public Policy, 1860-1897. See chapter on "Waterways."

Knight, Oliver. *Fort Worth: Outpost on the Trinity*. Norman: University of Oklahoma Press, 1953. xiii + 302 pp. Illustrations, maps, notes, appendices, bibliography, and index. Breezy historical survey that includes material on the city's street, water, and transit systems.

Krim, Arthur J. "The Innovation and Diffusion of the Street Railway in North America." Masters thesis, University of Chicago, 1967. vii + 145 pp. Illustrations, maps, charts, tables, notes, appendix, and bibliography. A competent investigation that includes a statistical profile of street railway development from 1830 to 1920. The author contends that the diffusion of street railways was governed by the age and size of cities rather than spatial characteristics. The thesis contains an incisive chapter on the technological development of the street railway.

Kulski, Julian Eugene. *Land of Urban Promise: Continuing the Great Tradition: A Search for Significant Urban Space in the Urbanized Northeast*. See chapter on "Planning, Engineering, and Administration."

Lamare, Judith Louise. "Urban Mass Transportation Politics in the Los Angeles Area: A Case Study in Metropolitan Policy-Making. Doctoral dissertation, University of California, Los Angeles, 1973. 311 pp.

Larned, J. N. *A History of Buffalo: Delineating the Evolution of the City*. See chapter on "Sewers and Wastewater Treatment."

Lemmon, Sarah McCulloch. "Raleigh—An Example of the New South?" *North Carolina Historical Review*. See chapter on "Community Water Supply."

Lenderink, A. Rodney. "The Electric Interurban Railway in Kalamazoo County." *Michigan History*, XLIII (March 1959), 43-93. An exhaustive, if not tedious, interurban case study.

Lind, Alan R. *Chicago Surface Lines: An Illustrated History*. Park Forest, Ill.: Transport History Press, 1974. 416 pp. Illustrations, maps, and appendix. One of the better popular histories intended for transit buffs.

Lipman, Andrew Davis. "The Rochester Subway: Experiment in Municipal Rapid Transit." *Rochester History*, XXXVI (April 1974), 1-2 . An excellent transit case study.

Lowry, Goodrich. *Streetcar Man: Tom Lowry and the Twin City Rapid Transit Company*. Minneapolis: Lerner Publishing Company, 1979. xiv + 176 pp. Illustrations, maps, appendices, bibliography, and index. A rather dull, superficial biography of the builder of the Twin Cities' street railway system by his grandson. The book includes a chapter on Lowry's successful campaign to defeat a movement for public ownership of the transit network at the turn of the century.

Macaulay, David. *Underground*. See chapter on "Planning, Engineering, and Administration."

McCloy, J. W. "They Do Strange Things on the Bowery." *AERA*, XXI (Oct. 1930), 604-11. Interesting account of public reaction to the first horse-drawn street railway in New York City, 1832.

MacColl, E. Kimbark. *The Growth of a City: Power and Politics in Portland, Oregon, 1915 to 1950*. See chapter on "Planning, Engineering, and Administration."

MacColl, E. Kimbark. *The Shaping of a City: Business and Politics in Portland, 1885-1915*. See chapter on "Waterways."

McDonald, Forest. "Street Cars and Politics in Milwaukee, 1896-1910." 2 parts. *Wisconsin Magazine of History*, 39 (Spring and Summer 1956), Spring: 166-70; Summer: 253-57, 271-73. Excellent article on feuds between the Milwaukee Electric Railway and Light Company and various city politicians. McDonald suggests that much of the agitation was politically motivated and that the company was innocent of many of the accusations leveled against it.

McDonald, William Smith. "The Union Traction Company of Indiana." Doctoral dissertation, Ball State University, 1969. 167 pp.

McKay, John P. *Tramways and Trolleys: The Rise of Urban Mass Transportation in Europe*. Princeton: Princeton University Press, 1976. xvi + 266 pp. Illustrations, tables, notes, bibliography, and index. A statistical and historical investigation of the European electric tramway industry between 1890 and 1910, which focuses primarily on France, Germany, and Great Britain. Comparisons with similar developments in the United States are offered throughout the book.

McKelvey, Blake. *Rochester: An Emerging*

Metropolis, 1925-1961. See chapter on "Roads, Streets, and Highways."

McKelvey, Blake. *Rochester on the Genesee: The Growth of a City.* See chapter on "Parks and Recreation."

McKelvey, Blake. *Rochester: The Flower City, 1855-1890.* See chapter on "Sewers and Wastewater Treatment."

McKelvey, Blake. *Rochester: The Quest for Quality, 1890-1925.* Cambridge: Harvard University Press, 1956. xiv + 432 pp. Illustrations, bibliography, and index. Includes public works activities within the context of dynamic urban advances and intense campaigns for civic reforms.

McKelvey, Blake. *The Urbanization of America, 1860-1915.* See chapter on "Community Water Supply."

MacLaren, Malcolm. *The Rise of the Electrical Industry during the Nineteenth Century.* See chapter on "Energy."

MacMurray, George J. "50 Years of Transit." *Bus Transportation,* 30 (Feb. 1951), 46-49. Superficial overview of mass transit history.

McNeill, Clarence Ernest. "The Financial History of the Municipal Subways of New York City." Doctoral dissertation, Yale University, 1928.

McShane, Clay. *Technology and Reform: Street Railways and the Growth of Milwaukee, 1887-1900.* Madison: State Historical Society of Wisconsin, 1974. ix + 187 pp. Maps, tables, notes, bibliographical essay, and index. A competent case study of street railway development in this midwestern city. Following an opening chapter on technological evolution, the author deals with the public's attitude toward this innovation, the interests served by the trolley, and efforts by reformers to regulate public transportation. McShane also demonstrates the close relationship between transit and real estate interests.

McWhorter, A. D. "Development of the Street Railway Car Body." AERA, XVIII (Sept. 1927), 185-91. Valuable, condensed study of the evolution of the streetcar body.

Mallach, Stanley. "The Origins of the Decline of Urban Mass Transportation in the United States, 1890-1930." *Urbanism Past & Present,* 8 (Summer 1979), 1-17. By far the best short work on the causes and consequences of street railway expansion and decline. Its excellent bibliography is a useful source for researchers and teachers.

Massouh, Michael. "Innovations in Street Railways before Electric Traction: Tom L. Johnson's Contributions." *Technology and Culture,* 18 (April 1977), 202-17. The article describes the transit innovations attributed to Tom L. Johnson, Cleveland street-railway magnate. Johnson is credited with introducing the farebox, the single-fare transfer system, and the shallow-conduit cable-traction system. The author suggests that Johnson was more innovative than other traction businessmen.

Mayer, Harold Melvin. "The Railway Pattern of Metropolitan Chicago." Doctoral dissertation, University of Chicago, 1943. viii + 168 pp. Illustrations, maps, table, notes, and bibliography. A descriptive overview of Chicago's railway network that includes the effects of the routes on the city's industrial and residential patterns. The author recommends greater comprehensive planning so that the "railways which nurtured Chicago in its infancy, will then be able to serve it equally well in its maturity."

Mayer, Harold M. "Transportation and Internal Circulation." *Journal of Geography,* XLVIII (Oct. 1969), 390-405. One of the better essays on the influence of rapid transit and the automobile in shaping the form of cities.

Mayer, Harold M., and Richard C. Wade. *Chicago: Growth of a Metropolis.* Chicago and London: University of Chicago Press, 1969. ix + 510 pp. Illustrations, maps, bibliography, and index. Public works generally receive only cursory coverage in this heavily illustrated history of Chicago. The volume, however, includes good discussions of the city's rapid transit systems.

Meier, August, and Elliott Rudwick. "The Boycott Movement Against Jim Crow Streetcars in the South, 1900-1906." *Journal of American History,* LV (March 1969), 756-75. Explains the surge of boycotts that occurred in the South at the turn of the century in response to the passage of numerous Jim Crow streetcar laws. "The remarkable thing," the authors note, "is not that the boycotts failed, but that they happened in so many places and lasted as long as they often did."

Middleton, William D. *The Interurban Era.*

Milwaukee: Kalmbach Publishing Company, 1961. 431 pp. Illustrations, drawings, and bibliography. Records "something of the colorful era of the interurbans." It is largely pictorial and includes a list and description of "Electric Railway Museums in the United States and Canada."

Middleton, William D. *The Time of the Trolley.* Milwaukee: Kalmbach Publishing Company, 1967. 435 pp. Illustrations and index. A heavily illustrated, popular, nostalgic treatment of the trolley's evolution. The book emphasizes technological development as well as the history of specific urban street railway systems.

Milch, Robert J. "Birth of a Subway." *American History Illustrated,* I (Dec. 1966), 19-27. On New York City's first subway which opened in October 1904.

"Milestones in U.S. Public Works: PATH Rail Rapid Transit System." *APWA Reporter,* 42 (June 1975), 18-19. The history of the Port Authority Trans-Hudson (PATH) Rail Rapid Transit System, formerly the Hudson and Manhattan Railroad, which provides service via under-river tunnels between stations in New Jersey and New York City.

Miller, John Anderson. *"Fares, Please": From Horse-Cars to Streamliners.* New York and London: D. Appleton-Century Company, 1941. xvii + 204 pp. Illustrations, bibliography, and index. A classic popular history of urban mass transportation. The book identifies historical landmarks of this field, including technological developments and specific community transit systems.

Miller, William D. *Memphis during the Progressive Era, 1900-1917.* See chapter on "Sewers and Wastewater Treatment."

Miller, Zane L. *"Boss Cox's Cincinnati: Urban Politics in the Progressive Era.* New York: Oxford University Press, 1968. xv + 301 pp. Maps, tables, notes, and index. A well-balanced and finely crafted political history that offers insights into the development of Cincinnati's rapid transit, water, sewer, and park systems.

Mills, Randall V. "Early Electric Interurbans in Oregon. I. Forming the Portland Railway, Light and Power System." *Oregon Historical Quarterly,* XLIV (March 1943), 82-104. Comprehensive discussion of the growth and decline of electric transit in the Portland metropolitan area.

Mills, Randall V. Early Electric Interurbans in Oregon. II. The Oregon Electric and Southern Pacific Systems." *Oregon Historical Quarterly,* XLIV (Dec. 1943), 386-410. A good case study of electric railway competition.

Mohl, Raymond A. "The Industrial City." *Environment,* 18 (June 1976), 28-38. Includes a short section on the influence of public transportation on urban development.

Monroe, Robert Grier. "The Gas, Electric Light, Water and Street Railway Services in New York City." *Annals of the American Academy of Political and Social Science.* See chapter on "Community Water Supply."

Myers, Gustavus. "History of Public Franchises in New York City." *Municipal Affairs,* IV (March 1900), 71-206. Principally deals with the evolution of street railway franchises.

Myers, Rex. "Trolleys of the Treasure State." *Montana: The Magazine of Western History,* XXII (April 1972), 34-47. Good overview of the growth and decline of trolleys in Bozeman, Helena, and other Montana cities.

Nadeau, Remi A. *City Makers: The Men Who Transformed Los Angeles* from Village to Metropolis during the First Great Boom, 1868-76. See chapter on "Waterways."

Nevins, Allan, and John A. Krout., eds. *The Greater City: New York, 1898-1948.* See chapter on "Roads, Streets, and Highways."

New York-New Jersey Metropolitan Chapter of the American Public Works Association. *Public Works in Metropolitan New York-New Jersey.* See chapter on "Planning, Engineering, and Administration."

Norton, Samuel Wilbur. *Chicago Traction: A History Legislative and Political.* Chicago: n.p., 1907. 240 pp. Illustrations and notes. A plea for municipal ownership that includes a political and legal history of mass transit in Chicago.

O'Geran, Graeme. *A History of the Detroit Street Railways.* Detroit: Conover Press, 1931. xvii + 459 pp. Illustrations, maps, tables, charts, notes, appendix, bibliography, and index. One of the best histories of mass transit development within an urban area. The author chronicles all phases of municipal public transportation from the horsecar to the motor bus. The long battle between public officials and private interests over control of the system is also discussed. By 1930 Detroit had the world's largest street railway network under public ownership.

Oihus, Colleen A. "Street Railways in Grand Forks, North Dakota: 1887-1935." *North Dakota History,* 44 (Spring 1977), 12-21. Presents Grand Forks' street railway history as a reflection of the national street railway era.

Olmsted, Roger R. "The First Cable Car." *American West,* II (Fall 1965), 14-17. Thumbnail discussion of the 1873 Clay Street Railway Company with the original drawing A. S. Hallidie made of the system.

Owen, Wilfred. *The Accessible City.* Washington, D.C.: Brookings Institution, 1972. x + 150 pp. Illustrations, tables, notes, appendix, bibliography, and index. Perhaps the most thoughtful polemic against the degradation of urban life caused by automobiles and the roads they travel on. Owen seeks a solution in the adoption of better city planning and greater development of mass transit systems.

Owen, Wilfred. *The Metropolitan Transportation Problem.* See chapter on "Roads, Streets, and Highways."

Owen, Wilfred. *Cities in the Motor Age.* New York: Viking Press, 1959. xiv + 176 pp. Illustrations, appendices, and index. A plea for urban planning that places strong emphasis on greater use of mass transit to improve the quality of city life. The book contains some historical information on the role of transportation systems in shaping land use patterns.

Passer, Harold C. *The Electrical Manufacturers, 1875-1900: A Study in Competition, Entrepreneurship, Technical Change, and Economic Growth.* See chapter on "Energy."

Pendergrass, Lee Forrest. "Urban Reform and Voluntary Association: A Case Study of the Seattle Municipal League, 1910-1929." Doctoral dissertation, University of Washington, 1972. 143 pp. Table, notes, and bibliography. A look at reform politics in Seattle through a study of the city's municipal league during its first decade. Major battles were waged over the municipal ownership of street railways and utilities.

Perentesis, John Louis. "The Formulation of a Rapid Transit Plan for the Detroit Metropolitan Area, 1953-1958." Doctoral dissertation, University of Michigan, 1960. 339 pp.

Phillips, E. Bryant. "Early Street Railways in Council Bluffs." *Iowa Journal of History,* 48 (April 1950), 121-32. A well-researched descriptive history of street railways in Council Bluffs, Iowa, from 1859 to about 1900.

Phillips, E. Bryant. "Horse Car Days and Ways in Nebraska." *Nebraska History,* XXIX (March 1948), 16-32. Describes the advantages and disadvantages of horse cars.

Phillips, E. Bryant. "Interurban Projects In and Around Omaha." *Nebraska History,* XXX (Sept. 1949), 257-85. A continuation of a previous article (see above). The author shows that "more actual interurban operation occurred in Lincoln than in Omaha."

Phillips, E. Bryant. "Interurban Projects in Nebraska." *Nebraska History.* XXX (June 1949), 163-82. On interurban projects in and around Lincoln.

Piehl, Frank J. "Our Forgotten Streetcar Tunnels." *Chicago History,* IV, (Fall 1975), 130-38. Popular overview of the subject.

Pierce, Bessie Louise. *A History of Chicago.* See chapter on "Community Water Supply."

Platt, Harold Lawrence. "Urban Public Services and Private Enterprise: Aspects of the Legal and Economic History of Houston, Texas, 1865-1905." Doctoral dissertation. See chapter on "Planning, Engineering, and Administration."

Post, Robert C. "The Fair Fare Fight: An Episode in Los Angeles History." *Southern California Quarterly,* LII (Sept. 1970), 275-98. Outstanding case study of a public controversy in the mid 1920s that explores various dimensions of attempts to gain municipal ownership of the city's transit system.

Pred, Allan R. *The Spatial Dynamics of U.S. Urban-Industrial Growth, 1800-1914: Interpretive and Theoretical Essays.* Cambridge: M.I.T. Press, 1966. x + 225 pp. Maps, tables, notes, and index. Several of the book's chapters discuss how canals and transit systems influenced the urban growth process.

Preston, Howard L. *Automobile Age Atlanta: The Making of a Southern Metropolis, 1900-1935.* See chapter on "Roads, Streets, and Highways."

Purdy, Harry Leslie. "The Cost of Municipal Operations of the Seattle Street Railway."

University of Washington Publications in the Social Sciences, VIII (1929-1939), 1-28. A good case study of the deteriorating financial position of street railways following World War I. The author defends the management of this municipally owned system and concludes that political interference, automobile competition, and heavy capital payments were responsible for operational difficulties.

Radway, Raymond F. *All Time Catalogue of Interurban and Street Railway Books and Bulletins.* n.p.: n.p., 1971. Illustrations. A state-by-state buff bibliography.

Rae, John B. "The Evolution of the Motor Bus as a Transport Mode." *High Speed Ground Transportation Journal,* 5 (Summer 1971), 221-35. The best source of information on the development of the motor bus. The article traces its technological evolution and the reasons why the bus replaced the trolley car as the principal means of public transportation. In the conclusion, Rae suggests reforms that would prompt commuters to leave their cars at home and travel by bus.

Rae, John B. "Transportation Technology and the Problem of the City." *Traffic Quarterly,* 22 (July 1968), 229-314. Discussion of the relationships of transportation to urban growth and problems created by over-reliance on the automobile.

Reeves, William Fullerton. "Rapid Transit Elevated Lines in New York City." *New York Historical Society Quarterly Bulletin,* XVIII, XIX (Jan. 1935; April 1935), Jan: 59-82; April: 3-17.

Reeves, William Fullerton. *The First Elevated Railroads in Manhattan and the Bronx of the City of New York: The Story of Their Development and Progress.* New York: New York Historical Society, 1936. i + 137 pp. Illustrations and index. A descriptive, rather shallow history of elevated railway development in New York City from the Civil War to the turn of the century. However, the book's sixty-four illustrations on elevated construction and operation are a unique historical resource.

Reifschneider, Felix E. *Interurbans of the Empire State.* Orlando, Fla.: By author, 1949. v + 47 pp. Illustrations, maps, and index. This small publication describes in brief historical sketches all of New York's interurban lines and a few rapid transit lines.

Reifschneider, Felix E. *Trolley Lines of the Empire State: (City and Suburban).* Orlando, Fla.: By author, 1950. ii + 57 pp. Illustrations and index. A description of New York's "small and medium size city systems and suburban lines."

Rhoda, Richard. "Urban Transport and the Expansion of Cincinnati, 1858-1920." *Cincinnati Historical Society Bulletin,* 35 (Summer 1977), 131-43. Good case study of the relationships between public transportation and urban expansion.

Ridgway, Robert. *Robert Ridgway.* See chapter on "Planning, Engineering, and Administration."

Roberts, Sidney I. "Portrait of a Robber Baron: Charles T. Yerkes." *Business History Review,* XXXV (Autumn 1961), 345-71. An entertaining and well-written account of the corruption and financial legerdemain of Chicago's traction king. The article suggests that Yerkes' flamboyant transgressions and contempt for public opinion ignited a reform movement that led to his downfall.

Rose, William Ganson. *Cleveland: The Making of a City.* See chapter on "Sewers and Wastewater Treatment."

Ross, D. Reid, and C. W. Weister. "The Relationship between Urban Growth and Transportation Development in the Cincinnati-Northern Kentucky Area." *Bulletin of the Historical and Philosophical Society of Ohio,* 21 (April 1963), 112-32. Good discussion of how roads, navigation, and mass transportation influenced the region's development.

Rowsome, Frank, Jr. *Trolley Car Treasury: A Century of Streetcars—Horsecars, Cable Cars, Interurbans, and Trolleys.* New York: McGraw-Hill Book Company, 1956. vii + 200 pp. Illustrations. A delight for transit buffs. The illustrations and narrative cover the landmarks of street railway technology.

Saltzman, Arthur. "Para-Transit: Taking the Mass Out of Mass Transit." *Technology Review,* 75 (July/Aug. 1973), 46-53. This article focuses on dial-a-ride and similar para-transit modes. It offers an entertaining overview of the "jitney" phenomenon that swept the country in 1914 and 1915. The author suggests that there are similarities between these two demand-responsive public transportation sytems.

Saylor, Larry J. "Street Railroads in Columbus, Ohio, 1862-1920." *Old Northwest,* 1 (Sept. 1975), 291-315. A fine and thoughtful history of public transportation in this midwestern city.

Schmidt, Emerson P. *Industrial Relations in Urban Transportation.* Minneapolis: University of Minnesota Press, 1937. xii + 264 pp. Notes, bibliography, and index. Most of this fine book is devoted to the labor aspects of urban public transportation, but major historical sections discuss technology, finances, regulations, and public ownership.

Schmidt, Royal J. "The *Chicago Daily News* and Traction Politics, 1876-1920." *Journal of the Illinois State Historical Society,* LXIV (Autumn 1971), 312-26. Illustrates editorial attitude of the paper towards this municipal reform issue.

Segal, Morley. "James Rolph, Jr. and the Early Days of the San Francisco Municipal Railway." *California Historical Society Quarterly,* XLIII (March 1964), 3-18. Efforts of San Francisco's mayor to create the first publicly owned street railway line.

Smerk, George M. "The Streetcar: Shaper of American Cities." *Traffic Quarterly,* 21 (Oct. 1967), 569-84. Perhaps the best short statement of the influence of street railways on urban and suburban growth patterns. Smerk offers a lucid and insightful commentary on the dynamics of this process.

Smerk, George M. *Urban Mass Transportation: A Dozen Years of Federal Policy.* Bloomington: Indiana University Press, 1974. xvi + 388 pp. Tables, graphs, notes, bibliography, and index. The definitive book on the evolution of the federal mass transportation program.

Smith, Henry Bradford, and Blake McKelvey. "Rochester's Turbulent Transit History." *Rochester History,* XXX (July 1968), 1-24. Points up the important roles "played by successive transit facilities—horsecars, trolleys, and buses—in Rochester's history."

Solomon, Richard J., and Arthur Saltzman. *History of Transit and Innovative Systems.* Cambridge: M.I.T. Urban Systems Laboratory, 1971. vi + 70 pp. Tables, charts, graphs, footnotes, and bibliography. A concise, well-written summary of trends in the transit industry from the early 1900s to the present. It focuses on changes in government policies, ridership habits, and mass transit administration that caused the industry to decline after World War I. The authors advocate the wide use of "Dial-A-Ride" systems to meet contemporary needs.

Speirs, F. W. "The Street Railway System of Philadelphia." *Johns Hopkins University Studies in Historical and Political Science,* XV (1897), 95-209. An excellent study of early Philadelphia street railway history that also offers a broad-based institutional overview. The author discusses the evolution of monopolistic control, attempts at public ownership and regulation, and the influence of transit corporations in state and municipal government. The article includes a discussion of racial discrimination on streetcars as well as labor relations, subjects rarely addressed by transit historians.

Speirs, Frederic W. *The Street Railway System of Philadelphia: Its History and Present Condition.* Baltimore: Johns Hopkins Press, 1897. Notes, bibliography, appendix, and index. A comprehensive history that covers public regulation, municipal ownership, and employee relations.

Spengler, Edwin H. "Land Values in New York in Relation to Transit Facilities." Doctoral dissertation, Columbia University, 1930. 179 pp. Maps, appendices, bibliography, and index. The study was written in response to proposals to fund transit improvements in New York through special assessments on property benefited by the improvement. Through an analysis of public transportation and property values in New York from 1905 to 1927, the author demonstrates that new transit facilities do not necessarily raise adjacent property values. The study challenges assumptions regarding mass transportation and land values still adhered to by many scholars.

Sprague, Frank J. "Early History of the Trolley." *AERA,* XIX (May 1928), 301-03. Reflections by the builder of the first successful overhead trolley system.

Sprague, Frank J. "Growth of Electric Railways." *Proceedings of the American Electric Railway Association: 1916* (Oct. 10-12, 1916), 273-317. From 1834 to 1916. It includes information on experiments, inventions, and the actual operations of various railways.

Sprague, Harriet. *Frank J. Sprague and the Edison Myth.* New York: William-Frederick Press, 1947. 24 pp. Notes. An effort to gain greater recognition for Sprague as a pioneer in the fields of electrical transmission and street railways.

Still, Bayrd. *Milwaukee: The History of a City.* See chapter on "Sewers and Wastewater Treatment."

Syrett, Harold Coffin. *The City of Brooklyn, 1865-1898.* New York: Columbia University Press, 1944. 293 pp. Notes, bibliography, and index. Although the emphasis of the book is political and administrative, one chapter discusses the development of street railways, construction of Prospect Park, and the building of the Brooklyn Bridge.

Tarr, Joel Arthur. *A Study in Boss Politics: William Lorimer of Chicago.* See chapter on "Waterways."

Tarr, Joel A., ed. *Retrospective Technology Assessment—1976.* See chapter on "Sewers and Wastewater Treatment."

Tarr, Joel A. "Transportation Innovation and Changing Spatial Patterns in Pittsburgh, 1850-1934." *Essays in Public Works History,* 6 (April 1978), 1-64. A landmark case study on the influence of transportation system on land use and travel in the Pittsburgh area. The section on public transit illustrates how "a series of transportation innovations radically changed residential, commercial, and industrial patterns within the Pittsburgh region." A subsequent section on the impact of the automobile in Allegheny County from 1910-1934 examines changes in population, housing, mode-to-work, and journey-to-work.

Tarr, Joel A. "Transportation Planning in 1875: The American Society of Civil Engineers and Their Plan for Rapid Transit in New York City." *High Speed Ground Transportation Journal,* 7 (Summer 1973), 265-88. Concerned with an early example of urban transit planning. The article discusses a proposal for an elevated transit system in New York City. The report had a large impact on the deliberations of the New York Rapid Transit Commission which authorized construction of the lines.

Tarr, Joel A. "Urban Transportation: History and Planning." *APWA Reporter,* 44 (Dec. 1977), 14-16. Describes how history can be useful "to transportation planners in designing urban models and in anticipating future demographic and economic impacts of new systems."

Taylor, George Roberts. "The Beginnings of Mass Transportation in Urban America." 2 parts. *Smithsonian Journal of History,* 1 (Summer 1966; Fall 1966), 35-50; 31-54. The best study of the development of urban mass transportation prior to the Civil War. The analysis focuses primarily on Boston, New York, and Philadelphia.

Thelen, David P. *The New Citizenship: Origins of Progressivism in Wisconsin, 1885-1900.* Columbia: University of Missouri Press, 1972. 340 pp. Notes, bibliography, and index. One of the few studies that acknowledges the central role of public works in Progressive reform. The author traces efforts to gain public control of electrical, water, sewer, and waste collection services. Chapter 12, "Politics, Reform, and Streetcars in Milwaukee," is an important contribution to understanding the interrelatedness of politics and mass transit development.

Thompson, Carl D. *Public Ownership: A Survey of Public Enterprises, Municipal, State, and Federal, in the United States and Elsewhere.* See chapter on "Energy."

Tindall, William. "Beginnings of Street Railways in the National Capital." *Records of the Columbia Historical Society,* 21 (1918), 24-86. Good summary of the legal, financial, operational, and technological aspects of public transportation in Washington, D.C., 1830-1900.

Turbeville, Daniel E. III. *The Electric Railway Era in Northwest Washington, 1890-1920.* Western Washington University: Center for Pacific Studies, 1979. xi + 199 pp. Illustrations, maps, tables, graphs, appendices, and bibliography. A well-researched transit study based on the records of some forty companies. It is also a welcome addition to the growing volume of literature on the economic history and historical geography of the Pacific Northwest.

U.S. Department of Commerce. Bureau of the Census. *Historical Statistics of the United States: Colonial Times to 1970.* See chapter on "Planning, Engineering, and Administration."

Vance, James E., Jr. *Geography and Urban Evolution in the San Francisco Bay Area.* Berkeley: University of California Institute of

Governmental Studies, 1964. v + 89 pp. Maps, tables, and notes. Excellent historical overview of spatial dynamics that offers an especially strong discussion of the area's public transportation systems.

Wade, Richard C. "America's Cities are (Mostly) Better Than Ever." *American Heritage,* 30 (Feb.-March 1979), 4-13. The author contends that "the present city, for all its problems, is cleaner, less crowded, safer, and more livable than its turn-of-the-century counterpart." Although many social problems still exist, improvements such as mass transportation and other public works systems have made the city a better place to live.

Wagner, Richard M., and Roy J. Wright. *Cincinnati Streetcars: No. 5—1895-1911.* Cincinnati: Wagner Car Company, 1971. 178-248 pp. Illustrations and maps. A chronological year-by-year account, heavily illustrated history of Cincinnati's street railway system. Portions of the *Street Railway Journal* are reprinted.

Wakstein, Allen M., ed. *The Urbanization of America: An Historical Anthology.* See chapter on "Planning, Engineering, and Administration."

Walker, James Blaine. *Fifty Years of Rapid Transit, 1864-1917.* New York: Law Printing Company, 1918. 291 pp. Illustrations. A classic study of rapid transit's development in New York City. The progressive author focuses on the sordid side of the topic, especially the financial skulduggery and political corruption of company owners.

Walmsley, Mildred M. "The Bygone Electric Interurban Railway System." *Professional Geographer,* XVII (May 1965), 1-6. Thin overview of the rise and decline of interurbans.

Ward, David. "A Comparative Historical Geography of Streetcar Suburbs in Boston, Massachusetts, and Leeds, England: 1850-1920." *Annals of the Association of American Geographers,* 54 (Dec. 1964), 477-89. An excellent example of comparative geographical and historical analysis. The author concludes that different conditions of urban growth in Leeds and Boston between 1870 and 1920 greatly affected the contrasting development of mass transit, government control over building, the extent and appearance of streetcar suburbs, and popular confidence in the possibility of suburban life. The adoption of street railway systems in the United States was more rapid because of a faster population growth rate and fewer controls on land development.

Warner, Sam B., Jr. *Streetcar Suburbs: The Process of Growth in Boston, 1870-1900.* Cambridge: Harvard University Press and MIT Press, 1962. xxi + 208 pp. Illustrations, maps, charts, notes, bibliography, appendices, and index. A definitive, landmark study of the effect of transit systems on the evolution of the urban form. The author offers penetrating insights on the social effects of suburbanization. It is a seminal study that inspired other scholars to explore the processes of metropolitan expansion.

Warner, Sam Bass, Jr. *The Private City: Philadelphia in Three Periods of Its Growth.* Philadelphia: University of Pennsylvania Press, 1968. xii + 236 pp. Tables, notes, appendices, and index. One of the most important books on urban history published in the last fifteen years. Warner contends that "twentieth century urban America presents a picture of endlessly repeated failures." He also suggests that the inability to create an effective urban habitat is directly related to the "enduring tradition of privatism in a changing world." Warner discusses three eras of Philadelphia's history: 1770-1780, 1830-1860, and 1920-1930. Although the emphasis is on demographic and social change, the book contains perceptive insights into the influence of mass transportation on land use and suburbanization.

Warner, Sam Bass, Jr. *The Urban Wilderness: A History of the American City.* New York: Harper and Row, 1972. xx + 303 pp. Illustrations, notes, bibliography, and index. A brilliant, interdisciplinary history of the American urban environment. Considerable material is included on city planning and the influence of transit and road systems on land use.

Weber, Harry P. *Outline History of Chicago Traction.* Chicago: n.p., 1937. xlvii + 452 pp. Maps, tables, appendices, and index. A convoluted hodgepodge of narrative and documents on the evolution of Chicago's mass transit network. The book's lack of coherent organization makes it difficult to use.

Weber, Robert David. "Rationalizers and Reformers: Chicago Local Transportation in the Nineteenth Century." Doctoral dissertation, University of Michigan, 1971. 432 pp. Notes and bibliography. One of the best historical analyses of the institutional development of an urban transit system. The author exhaustively covers the evolution of transit technology, politics, corporate institutions, legal aspects, and attempts by reformers to rationalize mass transit through public ownership. Few histories of urban transportation are as insightful and multi-dimensional as this study.

Wertenbaker, Thomas J. *Norfolk: Historic Southern Port.* See chapter on "Sewers and Wastewater Treatment."

White, John H., Jr. "By Steam Car to Mt. Lookout: The Columbia and Cincinnati Street Railroad." *Bulletin of the Cincinnati Historical Society,* 25 (April 1967), 93-107. Solid case study of a steam commuter line.

White, John H., Jr. "Cincinnati & Westwood Railroad Co." *Bulletin of the Historical and Philosophical Society of Ohio,* XV (April 1957), 131-40.

White, John H., Jr. "Public Transport in Washington before the Great Consolidation of 1902." *Records of the Columbia Historical Society of Washington, D.C.* (1966-1968), 216-30. Outstanding article on the street railway systems that served the nation's capital during the nineteenth century.

White, John H., Jr. "The Cincinnati Inclined Plane Railway Company: The Mount Auburn Incline and the Lookout House." *Cincinnati Historical Society Bulletin,* 27 (Spring 1969), 7-23. Deeply researched article on a historic public transportation system.

White, John H., Jr. "The College Hill Narrow Gauge." *Bulletin of the Historical and Philosophical Society of Ohio,* 18 (Oct. 1960), 227-39.

White, John H., Jr. "The Mt. Adams & Eden Park Railway, 'The Kerper Road.'" *Bulletin of the Historical and Philosophical Society of Ohio,* 17 (Oct. 1959), 243-76. Excellent case study of a unique cable railway that operated from the 1870s to the 1890s in Cincinnati, Ohio.

Whittemore, L. H. *The Man Who Ran the Subways: The Story of Mike Quill.* New York: Holt, Rinehart and Winston, 1968. xii + 308 pp. Illustrations, bibliography, and index. A lively biography of the stormy career of this labor leader. Quill's tenure as head of New York City's Transit Workers Union was marked by monumental battles with city officials.

Wilcox, Delos F. *Municipal Franchises.* 2 vols. Chicago: University of Chicago Press, 1910, 1911. Vol. I.: xix + 710 pp.; Vol. II.: xxi + 885 pp. Notes, appendix, bibliography, and indexes. A definitive, classic study of the special privileges private monopolies enjoyed in American cities during the early 1900s. Volume II is largely devoted to street railway and other public transportation systems. Other subjects covered in the two books include franchises for water supply, sewers, electricity, and natural gas.

Willson, Beckles. *The Story of Rapid Transit.* New York: D. Appleton and Company, 1903. 204 pp. Illustrations and index. A popular history of all forms of transportation that includes rather insipid chapters on street railways and steam navigation.

Wilson, G. Lloyd; James M. Herring; and Roland B. Eutsler. *Public Utility Industries.* New York: McGraw-Hill Book Company, 1936. xiv + 412 pp. Charts, tables, graphs, notes, and index. Discusses the economic, legal, and sociological characteristics of various public services. Chapters are included on electricity generation, water supply, and urban rapid transit.

Wright, Wade H. *History of the Georgia Power Company, 1855-1956.* See chapter on "Energy."

Zingler, Leonard Marion. "Financial History of the Chicago Street Railways." Doctoral dissertation, University of Illinois, 1931. xiv + 269 pp. Maps, charts, tables, graphs, appendices, and bibliography. Good survey of the economic, organizational, and legal history of Chicago street railway companies.

Zueblin, Charles. *American Municipal Progress: Chapters in Municipal Sociology.* See chapter on "Planning, Engineering, and Administration."

Zunz, Olivier. "Technology and Society in an Urban Environment: The Case of the Third Avenue Elevated Railway." *Journal of Interdisciplinary History,* III (Summer 1972), 89-102.

10

Airways and Airports

Air carriers were first used to fly mail in the United States on May 15, 1918, when United States Army pilots carried letters from New York City to Washington, D.C. By August 1918 the Post Office Department had assumed the army's mail-carrying duties, and by 1920 it operated an airmail service from coast to coast. However, in 1925 the Air Mail Act authorized the postmaster general to award contracts to private carriers, and these contracts marked the beginning of organized air transportation in the United States.

Since the 1920s, Americans have become increasingly dependent on air transportation. Even though it is only a little more than fifty years old, air transport has superseded every other means of transportation, except the private automobile, in terms of passenger miles traveled. Air transportation is not only the fastest but one of the most comfortable ways to travel over long distances; and, until recently, it was considered the most economical.

Airports and related aviation activities play a vital role in the nation's economy. Besides aiding air travelers, airports provide jobs through the use of local services for air cargo, aircraft maintenance, food catering, and ground transportation in and around the airport. Regular purchases of fuel, supplies, and equipment from local distributors inject further income into local communities; while airport retail shops, hotels, and restaurants "recycle" money among community members.

Good airports are always an attraction to business firms requiring air cargo and passenger service. Statistics indicate that companies seeking to relocate or to open branch offices consider airport accessibility in the area a prime requisite for site selection. Thus, land located near airports usually increases in value as the local economy begins to benefit from the presence of an airport. For example, land in proximity to Chicago's O'Hare International Airport, which sold for no more than $800 an acre in the 1950s, had a 1975 market value of $100,000 an acre. Near Phoenix's Sky Harbor Airport, commercial land value rose from $26,000 per acre in 1961 to a record high of $130,000 per acre in 1974.

Wedded to the concepts of fast communication, easy access, and widespread distribution, the United States has become a nation of airplanes and airports. Without them, American society could hardly exist as it does. Yet, as dependent as Americans have become on air transportation, historians have neglected to examine fully its impact on American life. Listed below are the comparatively few historical books, articles, and dissertations that relate to airport and airways development in the United States.

Adams, Harry T. "The Cliff Maus Airport." *American Aviation Historical Society Journal,* 14 (Summer 1969), 85-94. Reviews the flying career of W.C. Maus and records the early (pre-World War II) history of the Corpus Christi airport.

Allen, Roy. *Great Airports of the World.* London: Ian Allen, 1968. 184 pp. Illustrations and diagrams. Descriptions of major world airports in an historical context. The United States airports included are: Chicago's O'Hare; Los Angeles' International; New York's John F. Kennedy International, LaGuardia, and Newark; and Washington's Dulles International.

Armstrong, Ellis L.; Michael C. Robinson; and Suellen M. Hoy, eds. *History of Public Works in the United States, 1776-1976.* See chapter on "Planning, Engineering, and Administration."

Bigelow, A. A. "Airport Growth in 1930-1931." *Airway Age,* 12 (Jan. 1931), 72-74. The author explains why "the over-development in the rest of the industry has not been experienced in the airport field."

Bilstein, Roger Eugene. "Prelude to the Air Age: Civil Aviation in the U.S., 1919-1929." Doctoral dissertation, Ohio State University, 1965. 176 pp.

Bilstein, Roger E. "Technology and Commerce: Aviation in the Conduct of American Business, 1918-29." *Technology and Culture,* 10 (July 1969), 392-411. Includes one section on United States' airmail service.

Blankenship, Edward G. *The Airport: Architecture—Urban Integration—Ecological Problems.* New York: Praeger Publishers, 1974. 159 pp. Illustrations, maps, charts, diagrams, and index. A narrowly focused study of airport terminals and their effectiveness as passenger-handling facilities. Design examples are taken from the 1930s to the present as well as from various parts of the world. Most of the drawings and photographs are of airport terminals in the United States. The text is in English and German.

Boone, Andrew R. "Campaigning for an Airport." *Aviation,* XXIV (Feb. 6, 1928), 310-13. A brief account of how a group of enthusiastic San Diego citizens succeeded in obtaining a $650,000 airport bond issue, beginning in 1924.

Breniman, William A. *The Airway Pioneer.* n.p.: Society of Airway Pioneers, 1971. 72 pp. Illustrations. Tells the story of the airway radio service from 1920 to 1970.

Brown, Jerold E. "Where Eagles Roost: A History of Army Airfields before World War II." Doctoral dissertation, Duke University, 1977. ix + 330 pp. Illustrations, maps, tables, notes, and bibliography. An examination of the principle factors that influenced the development of army flying fields, ground installations, and air bases in an attempt "to determine what implications the experiences of early aviation planners have for present and future planners."

Burkhardt, Robert. *The Federal Aviation Administration.* New York: Frederick A. Praeger, 1967. x + 249 pp. Illustrations, charts, appendices, bibliography, and index. There are single chapters on such topics as air traffic control, air safety problems, airports and airport aids, and airports in the nation's capital. The author, a reporter, has relied heavily on his own "contemporaneous notes" and previously published news reports as well as material housed within the agency.

Burlage, George Edward. "Federalism's Expanding Dimensions: A Case Study of Decision-Making of the Dallas-Fort Worth Regional Airport." Master's thesis, North Texas State University, 1969. Examines the federal government's role in persuading the cities of Dallas and Forth Worth to cooperate in the establishment of a regional airport that would serve both cities.

Champie, Ellmore A. *The Federal Turnaround on Aid to Airports, 1926-38.* Washington, D.C.: Department of Transportation, Federal Aviation Administration, 1973. 25 pp. Table and notes. Examines the course of events that persuaded Congress, some twelve years after passage of the 1926 Air Commerce Act, that "civil airports fulfilled a broader function than merely serving their own communities and constituted, therefore, an area of Federal interest."

Cohen, Stanley. "Dallas/Fort Worth to Open World's Largest Airport This Month." *Consulting Engineer,* XLI (Sept. 1973), 72-81. Includes a short history.

Condit, Carl W. *Chicago, 1930-1970: Building, Planning, and Urban Technology.* See chapter on "Planning, Engineering, and Administration."

Connery, Robert H., and Richard H. Leach. *The Federal Government and Metropolitan Areas.* See chapter on "Planning, Engineering, and Administration."

Coyler, D. B. "The Air Mail Service." *Journal of the Western Society of Engineers,* XXXII (June 1927), 161-64. A brief history of its growth since 1919. There are bits and pieces of information on early airfields.

Cullinan, Gerald. *The Post Office Department.* New York: Frederick A. Praeger, 1968. xvi + 272 pp. Illustrations, appendices, bibliography, and index. Contains a brief discussion of airmail service between World War I and II.

Damon, Ralph S. *"TWA": Nearly Three Decades in the Air.* New York: Newcomen Society in North America, 1952. 32 pp. Contains brief descriptions of early airfields and airmail service.

Davies, R. E. G. *Airlines of the United States since 1914.* London: Putnam, 1972. xiii + 745 pp. Illustrations, maps, tables, appendices, bibliography, and index. Except for sections in the first chapters on early airways and airmail service, this volume recounts stages in the United States' advancement to a position of world leadership in commercial air transport.

Davies, R. E. G. *A History of the World's Airlines.* London: Oxford University Press, 1964. xxxi + 591 pp. Illustrations, maps, charts, tables, graphs, and index. The standard reference for students of air transport history. The amount of material directly related to the development of United States' airports is minimal.

Davis, Grant Miller. *The Department of Transportation.* See chapter on "Planning, Engineering, and Administration."

Dearing, Charles L., and Wilfred Owen. *National Transportation Policy.* Washington, D.C.: Brookings Institution, 1949. xiv + 459 pp. Tables, notes, appendices, and index. Includes a still useful overview of federal promotion of transportation facilities and services. The following subjects are covered: airways and airports, water transportation, and highway transportation.

d'Orcy, Ladislas. "The Dawn of Commercial Aviation: Why We Have Trailed Behind Europe and How We Hope to Catch Up in the Near Future." *Scientific American,* CXXIII (Nov. 27, 1920), 546, 555, 557. An overview of commercial aviation following World War I. The author laments the fact that the United States trails European countries but predicts rapid advancement.

Doherty, Richard Paul. "The Origin and Development of Chicago O'Hare International Airport." Doctoral dissertation, Ball State University, 1970. 446 pp. Comprehensive history that explores the facility's background and subsequent use. Considerable insight is offered on federal-municipal relations in the development of airports.

Duke, Donald. *Airports and Airways: Cost, Operation and Maintenance.* New York: Ronald Press, 1977. xii + 178 pp. Illustrations, maps, graphs, tables, appendices, and index. Classic text on the design, planning, and operation of airports as well as aids to navigation.

Eastman, James N., Jr. "Location and Growth of Tinker Air Force Base and Oklahoma City Air Material Area." *Chronicles of Oklahoma,* L (Autumn 1972), 326-46. Insightful discussion of how community leaders convinced the federal government to build the facilities near Oklahoma City.

Elliott, Arlene. "The Rise of Aeronautics in California, 1849-1940." *Southern California Quarterly,* LII (March 1970), 1-32. An examination of the factors that made California "into the aviation center of the United States." A ten-page chronology of California aviation (1869-1929) is appended.

Federal Aviation Agency. *Historical Fact Book: A Chronology, 1926-1963.* Washington, D.C.: U.S. Government Printing Office, 1966. Maps, charts, and bibliography. Contains basic historical data on the federal government's role in the development of civil aviation.

Federal Aviation Administration. *The Airport—Its Influence on the Community Economy.* Washington, D.C.: U.S. Government Printing Office, 1967. v + 79 pp. Illustrations, maps, charts, and bibliography. Identifies the economic benefits that have accrued to representative communities—Hereford, Texas; Sumter, South Carolina; Hayward, California; Frederick, Maryland; and Fairmont, Minnesota—from "the development of airports built primarily for use by general aviation with financial assistance under the Federal-aid Airport Program." Each case study looks at the city/region's early development and shows how it changed.

Fellmeth, Robert C. *Politics of Land: Ralph Nader's Study Group Report on Land Use in California.* See chapter on "Planning, Engineering, and Administration."

Fisher, Edwin A. "Engineering and Public Works in the City of Rochester during the Past Century." *Centennial History of Rochester, New York.* See chapter on "Planning, Engineering, and Administration."

Foulois, Benjamin D., and C. V. Glines. *From the Wright Brothers to the Astronauts: The Memoirs of Major General Benjamin D. Foulois.* New York: McGraw-Hill Book Company, 1968. xiii + 306 pp. Illustrations and index. Reminiscences of an Air Corps chief (1931). In one chapter, he recalls the problems the Air Force confronted when President Franklin D. Roosevelt cancelled airmail contracts with independent operators in February 1934.

Fowle, Frank F. "Octave Chanute: Pioneer Glider and Father of the Science of Aviation." *Indiana Magazine of History,* XXXII (Sept. 1936), 226-30. Brief biographical sketch of Chanute in an address given at Gary, Indiana—the site of Chanute's experiments with gliders in 1896 and 1897.

Frank, Carrolyle M. "Who Governed Middletown? Community Power in Muncie, Indiana, in the 1930s." *Indiana Magazine of History.* See chapter on "Planning, Engineering, and Administration."

Friedman, Paul D. "Birth of an Airport: From Mines Field to Los Angeles International—L.A. Celebrates the 50th Anniversary of Its Airport." *American Aviation Historical Society Journal,* 23 (Winter 1978), 285-95. A brief history of LAX prepared in anticipation of its fiftieth birthday.

Friedman, Paul David. "Fear of Flying: The Development of Los Angeles International Airport and the Rise of Public Protest Over Jet Aircraft Noise." Master's thesis, University of California, Santa Barbara, 1978. xiii + 231 pp. Illustrations, maps, tables, diagrams, notes, and bibliography. A history of the airport, emphasizing its fluctuating relationship with the surrounding community over the question of noise.

Galli, Geraldine. "100 Years of Construction News." *Engineering News-Record.* See chapter on "Planning, Engineering, and Administration."

Gilbert, Glen A. *Air Traffic Control.* Chicago: Ziff-Davis Publishing Company, 1945. xiv + 274 pp. Illustrations, maps, charts, tables, diagrams, and index. An early text on "the existing systems" of air traffic control with a thirty-two-page introductory chapter on the "Development of Air Traffic Control."

Grief, Martin. *The Airport Book: From Landing Field to Modern Terminal.* New York: Mayflower Books, 1979. 192 pp. Illustrations, diagrams, and index. Graphically illustrates the development of the airport from the first canvas seaplane hangars to today's highly sophisticated air terminals. Over 200 photographs are included; they are accompanied by a brief text.

Hansen, Chuck. "Hamilton Air Force Base, 1931-1950: A Pictorial Tribute." *American Aviation Historical Society Journal,* 24 (Winter 1979), 269-72. An illustrated chronicle of the last operational Air Force base near San Francisco Bay. The base was the site of numerous wartime departures for the Pacific theater and the western terminus of many homecoming flights at the war's end.

Harmel, Falk. "A History of Army Aviation." *Popular Aviation,* 3 (Dec. 1928), 17-27, 114-15. From 1909.

Hartman, J. Paul. *Civil Engineering Landmarks: State of Florida.* See chapter on "Planning, Engineering, and Administration."

Hinckley, Robert H., et al. "Civil Aviation: The Story of the CAA." *Flying and Popular Aviation,*

XXX (Feb. 1942), 35–66. Since its creation in 1938.

Horgan, James Joseph. "City of Flight: The History of Aviation in Saint Louis." Doctoral dissertation, Saint Louis University, 1965. 607 pp. Discusses the development of the Saint Louis Airport, but mostly deals with the evolution of aircraft.

Howard, George P., ed. *Airport Economic Planning.* Cambridge: MIT Press, 1974. xiv + 638 pp. Charts, tables, graphs, and notes. An attempt "to bring together in a systematic manner both published and unpublished work relevant to the extensive scope of airport economics and finance." Since the volume contains papers and articles by experts in the field, it is a useful source for anyone conducting research on airport development. As John Wiley, former director of aviation for the Port Authority of New York and New Jersey, points out in the foreword: "A work of this nature preserves for the future the lessons learned and steps taken to prepare for the big changes of the past."

Hubbard, Henry V.; Miller McClintock; and Frank B. Williams. *Airports: Their Location, Administration, and Legal Basis.* Cambridge: Harvard University Press, 1930. xvi + 190 pp. Illustrations, charts, diagrams, notes, appendices, and index. An attempt by the authors to help local communities arrive at "reasoned and reasonable decisions" regarding airport development and administration. Small amounts of historical information are scattered throughout the volume.

Hunt, Rockwell Dennis, and William Sheffield Ament. *Oxcart to Airplane.* See chapter on "Roads, Streets, and Highways."

Ingle, John P. *Aviation's Earliest Years in Jacksonville, 1878-1935.* Jacksonville: Jacksonville Historical Society, 1977. x + 94 pp. Illustrations, bibliography, and indexes.

Jackson, William E., ed. *The Federal Airways System.* Washington, D.C.: Institute of Electrical and Electronic Engineers, 1970. vii + 458 pp. Illustrations, maps, diagrams, bibliography, and index. Incidental history with chapters on such subjects as airports, facility ground aids, and air traffic control.

Jordon, William A. *Airline Regulation in America: Effects and Imperfections.* Baltimore: Johns Hopkins Press, 1970. xvi + 352 pp. Tables, diagrams, notes, appendices, bibliography, and index. On the economic effects of airline regulation. There is only a minimal amount of material on airport construction, operations, and services.

Kelley, Charles J., Jr. *The Sky's the Limit: The History of the Airlines.* New York: Coward-McCann, 1963. 317 pp. Illustrations, notes, bibliography, and index. A history of commercial aviation with portions of the book devoted to early airways and airports, federal regulation, and technological advances.

Kent, Ralph J., Jr. *Safe, Separated, and Soaring: A History of Federal Civil Aviation Policy, 1961-1972.* Washington, D.C.: U.S. Department of Transportation, Federal Aviation Administration, 1980. vii + 422 pp. Illustrations, notes, bibliographical essay, and index. The fourth and concluding volume covering the history of the Federal Aviation Administration and its predecessor agencies.

Kirchherr, Eugene Carl. "Airport Land Use in Chicago Metropolitan Area: A Study of the Historical Developments, Characteristics, and Special Problems of a Land Use Type Within a Metropolitan Area." Doctoral dissertation, Northwestern University, 1959.

Kirchherr, Eugene C. "Aviation and Airport Land Use in the Chicago Region, 1910-1941." *Bulletin of the Illinois Geographical Society,* 16 (Dec. 1974), 32-47. An analysis of the origins and emerging pattern of land use around airports, commercial or fixed-base, in the Chicago region.

Komons, Nick A. *Bonfires to Beacons: Federal Civil Aviation Policy under the Air Commerce Act, 1926-1938.* Washington, D.C.: U.S. Department of Transportation, Federal Aviation Administration, 1978. vii + 454 pp. Illustrations, bibliographical comment and notes, and index. From "The Chaos of Laissez Faire in the Air" to the 1938 Civil Aeronautics Act. The book emphasizes the partnership of business and the federal government in developing the airplane's potential.

Kramer, Kevin L. "The Burke Airport Issue: A Case Study in Policy and Citizen Opposition." Master's thesis, Johns Hopkins University, 1975. Deals with the successful opposition of local citizens to the development by the federal government of an international airport at Burke, Virginia.

Lane, D. R. "Recent Developments of Municipal Airports in the West." *American City,* XXXVII (July 1927), 1-5. Overview of western airport development (Portland, San Diego, Oakland, San Francisco) during previous year.

Lepawsky, Albert. *State Planning and Economic Development in the South.* See chapter on "Planning, Engineering, and Administration."

Lewis, W. Davis, and Wesley Phillips Newton. *Delta: The History of an Airline.* Athens: University of Georgia Press, 1979. xiii + 503 pp. Illustrations, maps, notes, appendices, bibliography, and index. The first history of an American commercial airline to be written by professional historians. Thorough and scholarly in nature, it can be read with pleasure by a nonacademic audience. There are scattered pieces of information on such subjects as airmail routes, airline regulation, air safety, Atlanta's air terminal, and Hartsfield International Airport.

Lipsner, Benjamin B. *The Airmail: Jennies to Jets.* New York: Wilcox & Follett Company, 1951. xii + 306 pp. Illustrations, tables, appendices, and index. The first superintendent of the Division of Aerial Mail Service, United States Post Office Department, describes "the embryonic efforts in the development of the government postal airmail service."

Long, G. Allison. "Huffman Prairie." *American Aviation Historical Society Journal,* 25 (Summer 1980), 107-11. An account of the Wright Brothers flying field (1904-1905) on Huffman Prairie, now a part of the Wright-Patterson air force base complex.

Lorwin, Lewis L. *Youth Works Programs: Problems and Policies.* See chapter on "Public Buildings."

Matt, Paul R. "Cicero Flying Field." *Historical Aviation Album,* XI and XII (n.d.), 57-68; 127-40. Detailed history of the first flying fields in Chicago (Cicero and Ashburn) from 1911 through 1916. The article includes extensive biographical information on personalities associated with activities at these fields.

Milch, Jerome E. "Feasible and Prudent Alternatives: Airport Development in the Age of Public Protest." *Public Policy,* 24 (Winter 1976), 81-109. An analysis of airport development since 1960 and an explanation of the source of organized opposition to it.

Milch, Jerome. "Inverted Pyramids: The Use and Misuse of Aviation Forecasting." *Social Studies of Science,* 6 (Feb. 1976), 5-32. Describes the relationship of long-range forecasting to airport planning and summarizes the Federal Aviation Administration's role as "a primary source of national air travel forecasts for the United States" since the 1960s.

Milner, William R. "Development of Aviation and Air Facilities in Nebraska." *Nebraska History,* XXVI (Oct.-Dec. 1945), 221-25. A brief review since World War I.

Moffett, William A. "Twenty Years of Naval Aviation." *Popular Aviation,* 3 (Dec. 1928), 28-34, 113-14. From 1908.

Morgan, Allen E. "Naval Reserve Aviation Base, Long Beach, 1929-1942." 2 parts. *American Aviation Historical Society Journal,* 16 and 17 (Winter 1971; Spring 1972), 280-95; 30-35. Part 1 is an account of "The Early Years"; Part 2 looks at "Major Training Base Buildup to W.W. II."

Morrill, John Barstow, and Paul O. Fischer, eds. *Planning the Region of Chicago.* See chapter on "Planning, Engineering, and Administration."

Murphy, William B. "Beginnings of Hickman Field." *American Aviation Historical Society Journal,* 10 (Winter 1965), 288-90. Describes plans for and building of the large military air base in Hawaii.

National Automobile Dealers Association. *The History of Transportation.* See chapter on "Roads, Streets, and Highways."

Nelkin, Dorothy. *Jetport: The Boston Airport Controversy.* New Brunswick, N.J.: Transaction Books, 1974. vi + 197 pp. Maps, tables, notes, and index. Analyzes the dynamics of technological controversy through "the details of a particular conflict concerning airport development—a plan to extend Logan International Airport in Boston, Massachusetts." Most chapters in this useful book deal with policies and problems of airport development in general; but it also contains specific sections on the history of Logan International.

New York-New Jersey Metropolitan Chapter of the American Public Works Associa-

tion. *Public Works in Metropolitan New York-New Jersey.* See chapter on "Planning, Engineering, and Administration."

Nye, Willis L. "The First San Francisco Airport." *American Aviation Historical Society Journal,* 5 (Spring 1960), 71-72. A very brief history of the airport in "The Mail Sack" column of the journal.

Office of Science and Technology. *Alleviation of Jet Aircraft Noise near Airports: A Report of the Jet Aircraft Noise Panel.* Washington, D.C.: U.S. Government Printing Office, 1966. iii + 167 pp. Illustrations, charts, tables, graphs, and notes. Contains only a smattering of historical data on airport development and federal aviation regulations.

Ogburn, William Fielding. *The Social Effects of Aviation.* Boston: Houghton Mifflin Company, 1946. vi + 755 pp. Illustrations, tables, notes, bibliography, and index.

Olmsted, Marle. "Langley Field 1917-1945." *American Aviation Historical Society Journal,* 10 (Spring 1965), 3-12. An illustrated history which also describes the various aircraft that flew into the field prior to 1944.

Palmer, A. D., comp. and ed. *Buffalo Airport, 1926-1976.* Buffalo: Niagara Frontier Transportation Authority, 1976. 104 pp. Illustrations. Heavily illustrated, popular history of the facility and the aircraft it served.

Paradis, Adrian A. *Two Hundred Million Miles A Day.* Philadelphia: Chilton Book Company, 1969. x + 213 pp. Illustrations, appendices, and index. Although this book is primarily about the evolution of commercial aviation in the United States, there are two chapters, "The Air Mail" and "The Airport Crisis," that would be useful to anyone conducting research on airport development. The author is a former employee of American Airlines.

Petersen, William J. "Iowa City Municipal Airport." *Palimpsest,* XI (Sept. 1930), 404-14. One of the few publications that records the early history of a municipal airport.

Platt, Myles M. "The Wayne County Airport: An Evolution in Public Policy." Doctoral dissertation, University of Michigan, 1962. 256 pp.

Puffer, Claude E. *Air Transportation.* Philadelphia: Blakiston Company, 1941. xxiv + 675 pp. Tables, notes, appendices, bibliography, and index. An analysis of federal legislation and administration vis-à-vis the air transportation industry since 1925. There are brief discussions of airport and airway construction and operations and longer sections devoted to airmail acts and services.

Rae, John B. *Climb to Greatness: The American Aircraft Industry, 1920-1960.* Cambridge: MIT Press, 1968. xiii + 280 pp. Illustrations, tables, notes, appendices, bibliography, and index. Although there is little information directly related to the history of airport facilities, the author shows how the aircraft industry "has depended for its existence on one major customer, the United States government." Of particular interest may be the section on "Politics and the Air Mail."

Ray, Thomas W. "First Year of Naval Aviation." *American Aviation Historical Society Journal,* 12 (Fall 1967), 198-214. Explains how and why the navy initiated an aviation program in 1910.

Redford, Emmette S. *Congress Passes the Federal Aviation Act of 1958.* University: University of Alabama Press, 1951. 35 pp. Notes. Describes the background, drafting, and passage of the 1958 Aviation Act. The emphasis is on the legislative process. The booklet was published for the Inter-University Case Program as an aid "to the teaching and practice of public administration and policy formation."

Redford, Emmette S. *The Regulatory Process: With Illustrations from Commercial Aviation.* Austin: University of Texas Press, 1969. x + 336 pp. Tables, notes, bibliography, and index. A collection of interpretative essays and case narratives, almost all of which were previously published as separate pieces. There are single chapters on the 1938 Civil Aeronautics Act and the Air Transport Association as well as more general ones on government regulation.

Rhode, Bill. "The Lost Airports." *American Aviation Historical Society Journal,* 3 (July-Sept. 1958), 137-47. An introductory statement followed by an annotated list of "all the old flying fields in the Greater New York and Philadelphia Metropolitan areas."

Richmond, Samuel B. *Regulation and Competition in Air Transportation.* New York: Columbia University Press, 1961. ix + 309 pp. Tables, notes, appendices, and index. The first chapter contains an early history of airline economic regulation prior to the 1938 Civil

Aeronautics Act. The remaining chapters discuss developments in the creation and control of competition in the air transportation industry from 1938 to 1960. There is no historical information on particular airport facilities or operations.

Robinson, Douglas H. "Old Ithaca Airport, 1914-1965." *American Aviation Historical Society Journal,* 15 (Spring 1970), 14-18. Describes the commercial and public uses of the Ithaca field.

Rochester, Stuart I. *Takeoff at Mid-Century: Federal Civil Aviation Policy in the Eisenhower Years, 1953-1961.* Washington, D.C.: U.S. Department of Transportation, Federal Aviation Administration, 1976. ix + 351 pp. Illustrations, tables, charts, bibliographical comment and notes, and index. Describes how and why the Eisenhower Administration "decided to abandon the 20-year-old Civil Aeronautics Act for a Federal civil aviation charter [1958] more responsive to the special demands of the emerging jet age." This volume is the first in a four-volume series dealing with the Federal Aviation Administration and its predecessor agencies.

Rogers, Elizabeth, comp. *A Nation in Motion: Historic American Transportation Sites.* See chapter on "Waterways."

Rosenburg, Roy. *History of Inglewood: Narrative and Biographical.* Inglewood, Calif.: Arthur H. Cawston, 1938. 215 pp. Illustrations and index. Contains an historical sketch of Mines Field Airport (1927). This history also includes descriptions of the city's water system and utilities.

Rutledge, Thomas W. "Early U.S. Aerial Mail Service at Heller Field." *American Aviation Historical Society Journal,* 17 (Winter 1972), 269-72. Author's reminiscences of U.S. Air Mail Service operations at Heller Field near Newark, New Jersey, from 1919 to 1921.

Scamehorn, Howard L. *Balloons to Jets.* Chicago: Henry Regnery Company, 1957. xiv + 271 pp. Illustrations and index. A history of aeronautics in Illinois, 1855-1955. There are important chapters on airmail (1911-1927), military aeronautics (1916-1955), and airports (1919-1955).

Scamehorn, Howard Lee. "The Formative Period of Aviation in Illinois, 1890-1919." Doctoral dissertation, University of Illinois, 1956. 254 pp.

Schaufler, Frank H. "U.S. Airmail 60 Years Young." *American Aviation Historical Society Journal,* 23 (Fall 1978), 196-203. A salute to airmail pioneers. The article recounts the events of May 15, 1918, when a small team of Army Signal Corps pilots inaugurated the world's first regularly scheduled airmail service.

Scott, Stanley H., and Levi H. Davis. *A Giant in Texas: A History of the Dallas-Fort Worth Regional Airport Controversy, 1911-1974.* Quanah, Texas: Nortex Press, 1974. v + 128 pp. Illustrations, notes, and bibliography. One of the few historical accounts of the building of a major airport. The book has a generous supply of photographs and includes "Comments" from the mayors of Dallas and Fort Worth and the chairman of the Regional Airport Board.

Scullin, George. *International Airport: The Story of Kennedy Airport and U.S. Commercial Aviation.* Boston: Little, Brown and Company, 1968. 319 pp. Illustrations and index. A general history of the planning and building of the John F. Kennedy International Airport and a discussion of its impact on commercial aviation.

Short, C. W., and R. Stanley-Brown. *Public Buildings: A Survey of Architecture of Projects Constructed by Federal and Other Governmental Bodies between the Years 1933 and 1939 with the Assistance of the Public Works Administration.* See chapter on "Public Buildings."

Shrader, Welman A. *Fifty Years of Flight: A Chronicle of the Aviation Industry in America, 1903-1953.* Cleveland: Eaton Manufacturing Company, 1953. 178 pp. Illustrations and index. A chronology that includes some data on airports and airways. The emphasis is on aircraft.

Smith, Henry Ladd. *Airways: The History of Commercial Aviation in the United States.* New York: Alfred A. Knopf, 1942. vi + 430 + xv pp. Illustrations, notes, appendices, bibliography, and index. A popular description of the background and development of commercial aviation. Early chapters review the role of government in building the air transportation system.

Smith, Vi. *From Jennies to Jets: The Aviation History of Orange County.* Fullerton, Calif.: Sultana Press, 1974. xvii + 226 pp. Illustrations and index. Includes a chapter on the history of Orange County Airport.

Smith, Wallace. "The Framingham Airport." *American Aviation Historical Society Journal,* 14 (Spring 1969), 16-20. Discusses the erratic development plans for the never-to-be-municipal airport in Framingham, Massachusetts.

Solberg, Carl. *Conquest of the Skies: A History of Commercial Aviation in America.* Boston: Little, Brown and Company, 1979. vi + 441 pp. Illustrations, bibliography, and index. Includes general information on airport "beginnings," traffic control at airports, airport terminals, and federal aid to airports. The author gives a good amount of attention to the role of the U.S. Army and Post Office Department in furthering airway and airport development.

Stanton, Charles I. "Federal Airways Modernization Program." *Air Commerce Bulletin,* 9 (Sept. 15, 1937), 45-56. Discussion of airways modernization and improvement program preceded by a brief summary of previous initiatives.

Sterling, Hubbard. "Chagrin Sinks into History, or Death of an Airport." *American Aviation Historical Society Journal,* 25 (Summer 1980), 158-59. A short account of the closing of Chagrin Falls, Ohio, airport after fifty years of operations, with a few abbreviated items on scattered events at the airport during its operational history.

Stevenson, Gordon McKay, Jr. *The Politics of Airport Noise.* Belmont, Calif.: Duxbury Press, 1972. ix + 148 pp. Notes, graphs, and index. Good discussion of the regulatory and technical efforts to control airport noise.

Stratford, Alan H. *Airports and the Environment: A Study of Air Transport Development and its Impact upon the Social and Economic Well-being of the Community.* New York: St. Martin's Press, 1974. xiii + 158 pp. Illustrations, charts, tables, graphs, bibliography, and index. A report on "the present status of airports within the community" worldwide. The author identifies key factors—noise, pollution, traffic—which have caused conflict with the environment and discusses "the corrective forces which have been put to work." Few, if any, examples are taken from the period before the 1960s.

Stroud, John. *The World's Airports.* London: Bodley Head, 1973. 128 pp. Illustrations and index. Traces the airport story "from its earliest days." It includes brief histories and descriptions of 495 airports in 117 countries. There is one chapter on "New York and the USA" and another largely descriptive chapter on the Dallas/Fort Worth Regional Airport. There are numerous illustrations.

Swisher, Jacob A. "Air Mail in the Twenties." *Palimpsest,* XXVI (Jan. 1945), 12-20. Recalls some improvements (especially in night flights) in airmail transportation during the 1920s.

Tarr, Joel A., ed. *Retrospective Technology Assessment—1976.* See chapter on "Sewers and Wastewater Treatment."

Thayer, Frederick C., Jr. *Air Transport Policy and National Security: A Political, Economic, and Military Analysis.* Chapel Hill: University of North Carolina Press, 1965. xxiii + 352 pp. Tables, notes, bibliography, and index. A critical analysis of "the interrelationships of the political, military, and economic aspects of both military airlift policy and commercial air transport policy" beginning in the 1920s.

The Airport and Its Neighbors: The Report of the President's Airport Commission. Washington, D.C.: U.S. Government Printing Office, 1952. x + 116 pp. Illustrations, charts, graphs, diagrams, appendices, and bibliography. Recommendations to the President (Harry S. Truman) "to alleviate certain immediate problems inherent in the present location and use of airports and . . . to insure sound and orderly development of a national system of airports, to safeguard the welfare of the communities and to meet the needs of air commerce and the national defense."

"The Development and Operation of Cleveland Airport." *Airway Age,* IX (Aug. 1928), 14-17. Since 1924.

Turnbull, Archibald D., and Clifford L. Lord. *History of United States Naval Aviation.* New Haven: Yale University Press, 1949. xiii + 345 pp. Illustrations, bibliography, and index. A chronicle of the main events influencing the development of naval aviation from the late 1890s through World War II. The authors (Turnbull, deputy director of Naval Records and History; and Lord, former head of the Naval Aviation History Unit) give only limited attention to the navy's airways and airports. Instead they emphasize the complementary roles of naval sea and air power.

Tweney, George H. "Air Transportation and the American West." *Montana: The Magazine of Western History,* XIX (Autumn 1968), 68-77. Contains information on the development of airmail routes and their significance to western cities.

Tyler, Poyntz, ed. *Airways of America.* New York: H.W. Wilson Company, 1958. 189 pp. Bibliography. A collection of articles from various sources, most of which deal with the airplane as "the predominant means of public transportation in the United States." Only a few of the essays are set within an historical framework.

U.S. Army Corps of Engineers. *A Selected Bibliography on Airport Design and Construction, January 1930-July 1940.* Washington, D.C.: Office of the Chief of Engineers, 1940. 37 pp. Provides access to a host of literature on the planning, design, and construction of airports in the 1930s.

U.S. Department of Commerce. *Bureau of the Census. Historical Statistics of the United States: Colonial Times to 1970.* See chapter on "Planning, Engineering, and Administration."

U.S. Department of Transportation. *Establishment of New Major Public Airports in the United States.* Washington, D.C.: Federal Aviation Administration, 1977. 136 pp. Bibliography.

Ward, Earl F. "Airway Traffic Control." *Air Commerce Bulletin,* 9 (Oct. 15, 1937), 73-77. An overview of the control of air traffic from the enactment of the 1926 Air Commerce Act.

Warner, Edward P. "Development of Transportation by Air." *Scientific Monthly,* XVIII (April 1924), 383-93. The author discusses air transport development in the United States and abroad and laments the fact that America "continues too long to lag behind the other nations of the world in the exploitation by private enterprise of the commercial possibilities of aircraft." The author also looks at the evolution of airmail routes and government aid to air transportation.

Warner, Edward Pearson. *The Early History of Air Transportation.* Northfield, Vt.: Norwich University, 1938. v + 74 pp. Biographical notes. An essay on the history of air transport (1870-1930) in which the author attempts "to reconstruct the atmosphere of significant periods, and to suggest the historic implications, and the influence on the future, of the more significant events."

Warren, George C. "Country Highway and Airport Pavement, 1893-1930." *Proceedings of the Twenty-Seventh Annual Convention of the American Road Builders Association, January 11-18, 1930,* pp. 265-68. Explains the gradual conversion to bituminous macadam.

Warren, George C. "History of Country Highway and Airport Pavement." *Good Roads.* See chapter on "Roads, Streets, and Highways."

Wenneman, Jos. H. *Municipal Airports.* Cleveland: Flying Review Publishing Company, 1931. xxvii + 879 pp. Illustrations, maps, tables, diagrams, appendix, and index. An unusually helpful resource on the development of municipal airports. Besides individual sections on the history of aviation, airmail service, and international conferences, the author has included the text of federal acts and regulations, digests of state aviation laws and enabling acts, and ordinances of the principal cities having airports on main airways.

Whatley, Larry. "The Works Progress Administration in Mississippi." *Journal of Mississippi History.* See chapter on "Public Buildings."

Wheat, George Seay, ed. *Municipal Landing Fields and Air Ports.* New York: G. P. Putnam's Sons, 1920. xiv + 96 pp. Illustrations, maps, drawings, and appendix. Excellent overview of the status of airway and airport development in 1920.

Whitnah, Donald R. *Safer Skyways: Federal Control of Aviation, 1926-1966.* Ames, Iowa State University Press, 1966. xii + 417 pp. Illustrations, notes, appendix, glossary, bibliography, and index. An examination of the federal control of aviation in the United States since 1926. The primary purpose of governmental regulation, according to the author, is "making the airways safer for all forms of aircraft and passengers."

Wilson, Eugene E. *Air Power for Peace.* New York: McGraw-Hill Book Company, 1945. Graphs and bibliography. On the development of air power and policy in the United States' armed services.

Wilson, Eugene E. *Kitty Hawk to Sputnik to Polaris: A Contemporary Account of the Struggle over Military and Commercial Air Policy in the United States.* Barre, Mass.: Eugene

E. Wilson, 1960. xviii + 231 pp. Bibliography and index. A general discussion of the evolution of air policy in the United States, accompanied by a reappraisal of Western air-nuclear policy. The book contains no information on the development of airport facilities or services.

Wilson, John R. M. *Turbulence Aloft: The Civil Aeronautics Administration Amid Wars and Rumors of Wars, 1938-1953.* Washington, D.C.: U.S. Department of Transportation, Federal Aviation Administration, 1979. ix + 346 pp. Illustrations, charts, bibliographical comment and notes, glossary, and index. On the CAA and why it "never quite fulfilled its original promise."

Wood, John Walter. *Airports: Some Elements of Design and Future Development.* New York: Coward-McCann, 1940. xv + 364 pp. Illustrations, maps, diagrams, notes, appendices, bibliography, and index. A useful reference book on airports throughout the world. There are historical sketches of nineteen United States airports.

Works Progress Administration. *America Spreads Her Wings.* Washington, D.C.: Works Progress Administration, 1937. 34 pp. Illustrations, maps, and tables. Describes the WPA's airports and airways program.

Wright, Monte Duane. *Most Probable Position: A History of Aerial Navigation to 1941.* Lawrence: University Press of Kansas, 1972. xi + 280 pp. Illustrations, maps, diagrams, notes, bibliography, appendices, and index. Offers a great deal of material on pre-World War II aids to navigation.

11

Public Buildings

Throughout American history, public buildings have served as symbolic expressions of the institutions, culture, and ideals of the nation. The structures that house government offices, offer cultural inspiration, and provide entertainment account for nearly half of the nonresidential building construction in the United States. Many public buildings such as capitols, courthouses, and city halls are sources of community identity. Because of their symbolic importance and their monumentality, aesthetic considerations have always been a paramount concern.

In the past, designs for American public buildings were inspired by classical ideals, and derivations of Greek and Roman architectural precepts were reflected in most government-built structures. In the twentieth century, more functional styles emerged. The emphasis on utilitarianism has been accompanied by technological and engineering advancements that have made buildings self-contained environmental systems. As a result, the services of well-trained building managers, engineers, and custodial personnel are required to maintain these complex public works.

The following bibliography concentrates primarily on histories of local, state, and federal buildings. Historical material on monuments and memorials can be found in the chapter on "Parks and Recreation." Books, articles, and dissertations on architectural schools and styles, as well as autobiographies and biographies of architects, have not been listed unless they contain substantive discussions of public buildings.

"A History of the Grand Central Terminals in New York." *Architecture and Building,* XLV (April 1913), 137-40. Beginning with the first terminal at 42nd Street begun in 1869 and completed in 1871.

Abbott, N. C. "That Cass County Court House—An Informal History." *Nebraska History,* XXIX (Dec. 1948), 339-50. Describes the building's unique architectural style and relates its history.

Alderfer, William K. "How Illinois Preservationists Finally Saved the Old Capitol." *Journal of the Illinois State Historical Society,* LXI (Winter 1968), 431-42. On the "sporadic efforts (1898-1961) to preserve the Sangamon County Courthouse and restore the appearance it had when it was the Illinois State Capitol (1841-1876)."

Alexander, Robert L. "Maximilian Godefroy in Virginia: A French Interlude in Richmond's Architecture." *Virginia Magazine of History and Biography*, 69 (Oct. 1961), 416-33. A study of French engineer Maximilian Godefroy's work (1816) in Virginia: Capital Square, the courthouse, and city hall.

Allinson, Edward P., and Boise Penrose. *Philadelphia, 1681-1887: A History of Municipal Development.* See chapter on "Planning, Engineering, and Administration."

Ames, Winslow. "The Vermont State House." *Journal of the Society of Architectural Historians*, XXIII (Dec. 1964), 193-99. Describes "a small drama of professional standing which is connected with one of the nicest of small state capitols" in Montpelier between 1857-1860.

Andrews, Wayne. *Architecture, Ambition and Americans.* New York: Harper & Brothers, 1955. xxv + 315 pp. Illustrations, diagrams, bibliography, and index. First published in 1947, the volume is a general history of American architecture. It begins with the colonies and concludes with "The Chicago Story, 1883-1955." The author tells "the story of the outstanding buildings, the men who designed them and the people for whom they were built."

Armstrong, Ellis L.; Michael C. Robinson; and Suellen M. Hoy, eds. *History of Public Works in the United States, 1776-1976.* See chapter on "Planning, Engineering, and Administration."

Arpee, Edward. *Lake Forest Illinois: History and Reminiscences, 1861-1961.* See chapter on "Community Water Supply."

Arthur, Stanley. *A History of the U.S. Custom House, New Orleans.* New Orleans: Survey of Federal Archives, 1940. iii + 62 pp. Illustrations, maps, tables, and bibliography.

Austin, Deanna. "Springfield's Union Station: Depot Recalls Early Days of Railroad Travel." *Historic Illinois*, 3 (Aug. 1980), 4, 14. A historical sketch of one of the city's landmarks (1898).

Baker, Paul R. *Richard Morris Hunt.* See chapter on "Parks and Recreation."

Banham, Reyner. *The Architecture of the Well-Tempered Environment.* London: Architectural Press, 1973. 295 pp. Illustrations, diagrams, notes, and index. First published in 1969, this general history of architecture was prepared under a grant from the Graham Foundation of Chicago. Most of the author's examples are of privately owned buildings.

Bannister, Turpin C. "The Genealogy of the Dome of the United States Capitol." *Journal of the Society of Architectural Historians*, VII (Jan.-June 1948), 1-31. Good collection of source material on the evolution of this important architectural masterpiece.

Barnes, Joseph W. "Rochester's City Halls." *Rochester History*, XL (April 1978), 1-24. On the various buildings used as city halls (beginning in 1817).

Bauer, Anne. "The Charlestown State Prison." *Historical Journal of Western Massachusetts*, II (Fall 1973), 22-29. Brief account of the prison built in 1805.

Baxter, Sylvester. "Architectural Features of the Boston Parks." *American Architect and Building News.* See chapter on "Parks and Recreation."

Beekman, Fenwick. "The Origin of 'Bellevue' Hospital: As Shown in the New York City Health Committee Minutes—during the Yellow Fever Epidemics of 1793-1795." *New-York Historical Society Quarterly*, XXXVII (July 1953), 205-27. On how the hospital sporadically served yellow fever victims until 1811 when the city fathers acted to set up a permanent establishment.

Beeson, Leola Selman. "The Old State Capitol in Milledgeville and Its Cost." *Georgia Historical Quarterly*, XXXIV (Sept. 1950), 195-202. On the building's construction (1805) and cost ($79,976.40).

Belisle, D. W. *History of Independence Hall: From the Earliest Period to the Present Time.* Philadelphia: James Challen & Son, 1859. 396 pp. Illustrations. Includes biographical sketches of the signers of the Declaration of Independence.

Black, W. M. *The United States Public Works.* See chapter on "Flood Control and Drainage."

Bobinski, George S. *Carnegie Libraries: Their History and Impact on American Public Library Development.* Chicago: American Library Association, 1969. xiv + 256 pp. Illustrations, tables, appendices, bibliography, and index. Examines the influence of Carnegie philanthropy upon the history of United States public libraries. See especially the chapters on "Obtaining a Library Building" and "Carnegie Library Architecture."

Bostwick, Arthur E. *The American Public Library.* New York: D. Appleton and Company, 1929. xiv + 471 pp. Illustrations, appendices, and index. First published in 1910, this fourth edition discusses the development of the public library in the United States. Two chapters, "Library Buildings" and "County Libraries," may be useful.

Bower, Robert K. "Frontier Stone: The Story of Iowa's Old Capitol." *Palimpsest,* 57 (July/Aug. 1976), 98-121. A history of Iowa's mid-nineteenth-century capitol building.

Brainard, Newton C. "The Old State House." *Connecticut Historical Society Bulletin,* 22 (Jan. 1957), 19-22. A description of the Senate Chamber's furniture (based on a recent discovery of the original bills). No architectural or structural information is given on the building itself.

Brantley, William H. *Three Capitals: A Book About the first Three Capitals of Alabama.* Boston: Merrymount Press, 1947. xiv + 265 pp. Illustrations, maps, notes, appendix, and index.

Briggs, John Ely. "A Penitentiary for Iowa." *Palimpsest,* XX (Dec. 1939), 400-10. Records the problems involved in building Iowa's penitentiary (1840) at Fort Madison.

Brooks, George R. "The Old Post Office." *Missouri Historical Society Bulletin,* XX (July 1964), 307-09. Brief history of one of five federal buildings designed and built between 1868 and 1885 by Alfred B. Mullett, supervising architect of the United States Treasury.

Brown, Elizabeth Gaspar. "Two Courthouses on Main Street, Waukesha County, Wisconsin, 1846-1959." *American Journal of Legal History,* XV (Jan. 1971), 3-37. Records the experience in the financing, construction, furnishing, and maintenance of two Main Street courthouse buildings in southeastern Wisconsin.

Brown, Glenn. *History of the United States Capitol.* 2 vols. Washington, D.C.: Government Printing Office, Vol. I: 1900; Vol. II: 1903. Vol. I: xxi + 113 pp. + 136 plates + v; Vol. II: xi + 115-255 pp. + 137-322 plates. Illustrations, tables, diagrams, bibliography, and indexes. A large and thoroughly researched history, accompanied by numerous "plates giving reproductions of old drawings and prints, as well as photographs of the existing building." Special attention is given to the work of William Thornton, Benjamin Henry Latrobe, Charles Bulfinch, Robert Mills, Thomas U. Walter, M.C. Meigs, Edward Clark, Frederick Law Olmsted, and Thomas Wisedell.

Brown, Glenn, comp. *Papers Relating to the Improvement of the City of Washington, District of Columbia.* Washington: Government Printing Office, 1901. 91 pp. Illustrations and maps. A collection of papers on government buildings, landscapes, monuments, and statutes. There is an introduction by Charles Moore, clerk of the Senate Committee on the District of Columbia.

Brown, Glenn. "The American Institute of Architects—Its Policies and Achievements." *American Architect,* CXXIX (Jan. 5, 1926), 29-36. Since 1837.

Bruegmann, Robert. "Holabird & Roche and Holabird & Root: The First Two Generations." *Chicago History,* IX (Fall 1980), 131-65. Describes H&R's role in making Chicago "America's most architectural city." The article, which is well illustrated, includes a section on "Public Buildings."

Brumbaugh, Thomas B.; Martha I. Strayhorn; and Gary G. Gore, eds. *Architecture of Middle Tennessee: The Historic American Buildings Survey.* Nashville: Vanderbilt University Press, 1974. xvii + 170 pp. Illustrations, diagrams, and notes. A cooperative project of Vanderbilt University Press and the Historic American Buildings Survey, the book is "a celebration of the architecture of Middle Tennessee from its beginnings to 1920."

Brumbaugh, Thomas B. "The Architecture of Nashville's Union Station." *Tennessee Historical Quarterly,* XXVII (Spring 1968), 3-13. Contains biographical data on its architect-engineer, Richard Montfort, and describes the problems encountered in financing and constructing this "unique and inspired creation."

Bryan, Wilhelmus Bogart. *A History of the National Capitol: From Its Foundation through the Period of the Adoption of the Organic Act.* See chapter on "Planning, Engineering, and Administration."

Bryant, Keith, Jr. "The Railway Station as a Symbol of Urbanization in the South, 1890-1920." *South Atlantic Quarterly,* 75 (Autumn

1976), 499-509. Sees the massive passenger railway station as "a symbol of corporate prosperity, urban expansion, and anticipated economic growth" in the South during the three decades after 1890.

Bryant, Keith L., Jr. "Urban Railroad Station Architecture in the Pacific Northwest." *Journal of the West,* XVII (Oct. 1978), 12-20. Shows how the railroad station, along with the skyscraper, emerged as one of the "most important architectural achievements of the period from 1890 to 1920."

Bryant, Keith L., Jr. "Cathedrals, Castles, and Roman Baths: Railway Station Architecture in the Urban South." *Journal of Urban History,* 2 (Feb. 1976), 195-230. Describes many of the "large, technologically sound, and architecturally significant railway stations" acquired by Southern cities and towns from 1890 to 1920. The author contends that these structures suggest "the absence of a 'lag' in the physical maturation of southern urban centers."

Bulfinch, Ellen Susan. *The Life and Letters of Charles Bulfinch, Architect.* Boston: Houghton Mifflin Company, 1896.

Burchard, John, and Albert Bush-Brown. *The Architecture of America: A Social and Cultural History.* Boston: Little, Brown and Company, 1961. xi + 595 pp. Illustrations, notes, bibliography, and index. A general, scholarly history of architecture. Commissioned by the American Institute of Architects, the book emphasizes "the impact of our changing society on the profession and the resulting architecture." The authors give equal coverage to private and public buildings.

Bureau of the Census (Department of Commerce and Labor). *Statistics of Cities Having a Population of 8,000 to 25,000: 1903.* See chapter on "Roads, Streets, and Highways."

Bureau of the Census (Department of Commerce and Labor). *Statistics of Cities Having a Population of over 30,000: 1904.* See chapter on "Roads, Streets, and Highways."

Burg, David F. *Chicago's White City of 1893.* Louisville: University Press of Kentucky, 1976. xvi + 382 pp. Illustrations, map, notes, and index. An evaluation of the cultural impact of the World's Columbian Exposition, otherwise known as the Chicago World's Fair of 1893. Of special interest is the chapter on "Exhibits, Pastimes & Pleasures" which describes the White City's main exhibit—the buildings.

Burns, Henry, Jr. *Origin and Development of Jails in America.* Carbondale, Ill.: n.p., 34 pp. Notes. Provides cursory treatment of the subject.

Burns, Lee. "Early Architects and Builders of Indiana: With an Account of Some of Their More Important Work." *Indiana Historical Society Publications,* 11 (1937), 179-215. Identifies some of Indiana's most famous buildings and builders. Although a good portion of the article is devoted to architectural styles and private residences, several pages describe public buildings in Corydon, the seat of government in 1816, and in Indianapolis, Fort Wayne, Vincennes, Covington, and Madison.

Burton, Frank. "A Concise History of Building Codes from the Earliest Days." *Engineering and Contracting,* LXVIII (Feb. 1929), 81-85. Contains some material on early building ordinances in Philadelphia and Detroit. Most of the article is concerned with ancient building legislation.

Butler, Alexander R. "A 'Wilderness Rejoicing': The New Capitol of Michigan, 1871-79." *Michigan History,* XXXVIII (Sept. 1954), 273-84. On the construction and architecture of Michigan's state capitol in Lansing.

Cady, John Hutchins. *The Civic and Architectural Development of Providence, 1636-1950.* Providence: The Book Shop, 1957. xvii + 320 pp. Illustrations, maps, notes, index. Contains a serious evaluation of Providence architecture as well as a description of the city's physical growth and development. The author is an historian employed by the Providence Preservation Society.

Caemmerer, H. P. *Washington: The National Capital.* See chapter on "Planning, Engineering, and Administration."

Campbell, Robert C. "A History of Public School Building Finance in New Jersey, 1871-1961." Doctoral dissertation, Pennsylvania State University, 1963. 234 pp.

Campioli, Mario E. "The Proposed Extension of the West Central Front of the Capitol." *Records of the Columbia Historical Society of Washington, D.C.* (1969-1970), 212-36. An address delivered before the Columbia Historical Society on December 10, 1969. The speaker reviews the general history of the United States Capitol and describes specific improvements proposed for its west central front.

Caro, Robert A. *The Power Broker: Robert Moses and the Fall of New York.* See chapter on "Planning, Engineering, and Administration."

Carroll, Virginia R. "The Galena Market House, Oldest in the Midwest." *Journal of the Illinois State Historical Society,* XLV (Spring 1952), 51-54. A brief history of a building (1846) used to sell goods and produce and to hold public meetings.

Carrott, Richard G. *The Egyptian Revival: Its Sources, Monuments, and Meaning, 1808-1858.* Berkeley: University of California Press, 1978. xxi + 221 pp. Illustrations, notes, bibliographical essay, and index. Contains a notable amount of material on American prisons. Special attention is given to the New York Halls of Justice and House of Detention. There is also information on bridges, waterworks, monuments, and courthouses.

Carter, Edward C., II. "Benjamin Henry Latrobe and Public Works: Professionalism, Private Interest, and Public Policy in the Age of Jefferson." *Essays in Public Works History.* See chapter on "Planning, Engineering, and Administration."

Carter, Edward C., II, ed. *The Papers of Benjamin Henry Latrobe: The Virginia Journals of Benjamin Henry Latrobe, 1795-1798.* 2 vols. New Haven: Yale University Press, 1977. Vol. I: lxxx + 293 pp.; Vol. II: xii + 295-575 pp. Illustrations, maps, chronology, biographical appendix, and index. Records general observations on Virginia society, politics, topography, and fauna. Volume I begins with Latrobe's "Journal of the Voyage from London, England, to Norfolk, Virginia, in 1795/96"; Volume II concludes with "An Essay on Landscape . . . Richmond and Philadelphia, 1798-1799." Of some interest might be Latrobe's account of his first major American commission, the Virginia State Penitentiary; of more interest will be Carter's introductory essay entitled "Benjamin Henry Latrobe: Architect and Engineer (1764-1820)." Included are details about the canals, buildings, and other public works he designed.

Chalfant, Randolph W. "Calvert Station: Its Structure and Significance." *Maryland Historical Magazine,* 74 (March 1979), 11-22. Presents the history of Baltimore's "first modern building" and "a prototype of the planned, multi-purpose terminal" (1850).

Chapman, Edward H. *Cleveland: Village to Metropolis, A Case Study of Problems of Urban Development in Nineteenth-century America.* See chapter on "Planning, Engineering, and Administration."

Chicago Municipal Reference Library. *Chicago Architecture: A Selected Bibliography of Materials in the Chicago Municipal Library.* Chicago: Municipal Reference Library, 1979. 9 pp. A partially annotated bibliography of thirty-seven sources.

Chinn, Armstrong. "History of Chicago Passenger Stations: Grand Central Station Group." *Journal of the Western Society of Engineers,* 42 (April 1937), 81-82. A brief historical sketch from 1867 by the chief engineer of the Alton Railroad Company.

Clark, Appleton P., Jr. "Origin of the Building Regulations." *Records of the Columbia Historical Society of Washington,* D.C., 4 (1901), 166-72. A description and brief explanation of "the terms and conditions for regulating the materials and manner of the buildings and improvements on the lots of the City of Washington (1791)."

Cleland, Ethel. "New Facts About the Corydon State House." *Indiana Magazine of History,* IX (March 1913), 14-19. Outlines the early history of the old state house at Corydon, Indiana.

Cohan, Zara. "A Comprehensive History of the State House of New Jersey and Recommendations for Its Continuation as a Historic Site." Master's thesis, Newark State College, 1969.

Cole, John Y. "The Main Building of the Library of Congress: A Chronology, 1871-1965." *The Quarterly Journal of the Library of Congress,* XXIX (Oct. 1972).

Cole, Maurice F. *Michigan's Courthouses: Old and New.* Royal Oak, Mich.: Author, 1974. iii + 167 pp. Illustrations. A pictorial account of eighty-three county courthouses. Brief narrative descriptions accompany the photographs.

Coleman, Christopher B. "Restoration of the

Capitol at Corydon." *Indiana Magazine of History*, XXX (Sept. 1934), 255-58. On Indiana's first statehouse (c. 1812).

Coleman, Laurence Vail. *Museum Buildings*. 2 vols. Washington, D.C.: American Association of Museums, 1950s. Illustrations, appendix, and indexes. A general study for museum planners and builders by the director of the American Association of Museums.

Coleman, Laurence Vail. *The Museum in America: A Critical Study*. 3 vols. Washington, D.C.: American Association of Museums, 1939. Vol. I: viii + 218 pp.; Vol. II: xiii + 221-428 pp.; Vol. III: xvii + 431-730 pp. Illustrations, appendices, and index. A successful attempt by the author "to see museums as a whole—the institution in different patterns, the work it does, the people who give it life—all in the matrix of society." Whole chapters are devoted to "public museums," "museums and the state," "museums and the nation," and "museum buildings." Volume III contains a series of appendices, "constituting a record for the end of 1938," which list various kinds of museums, their geographical location, date of opening, cost of building, etc.

Columbo, Elda. "The Heart of the Chicago Public Library: The Central Building." *Illinois Libraries*, 54 (April 1972), 275-78. Since its opening in the 1890s.

Condit, Carl W. *American Building: Materials and Techniques from the First Colonial Settlements to the Present*. Chicago: University of Chicago Press, 1968. xiv + 329 pp. Illustrations, list of "Important Dates," bibliography, and index. A pioneering study on "the anatomy and physiology—rather than the cosmetics—of American building." The author gives his attention primarily to construction materials and techniques; his main focus is on "what holds the building together." This book is particularly rich in material on bridges and dams as well as on buildings.

Condit, Carl W. *American Building Art: The Nineteenth Century*. New York: Oxford University Press, 1960. xvii + 371 pp. Illustrations, diagrams, notes, bibliography, and index. A comprehensive history of building techniques as they developed into the structural basis of modern building. The author has arranged his material so that the fundamental narrative of need, invention, and practical application constitutes the text proper. A large number of substantive notes appear at the end of the book. The twentieth century is covered in a subsequent volume.

Condit, Carl W. *American Building Art: The Twentieth Century*. New York: Oxford University Press, 1961. xviii + 427 pp. Illustrations, notes, bibliography, and index. This well-illustrated volume continues the story of building techniques and structural art begun in *American Building Art: The Nineteenth Century*. Extending to the present time, the volume relates "how Ameican architects and engineers have utilized the profound changes in technology and in American society to produce meaningful structures."

Condit, Carl W. *Chicago, 1910-29: Building, Planning, and Urban Technology*. See chapter on "Planning, Engineering, and Administration."

Condit, Carl W. "Cincinnati Passenger Stations before 1930: A Technological and Urbanistic Survey." *Railroad History*, 132 (Spring 1975), 5-36. A fascinating look at railroad terminal facilities in Cincinnati in the nineteenth and early twentieth centuries. The author describes both the architecture and the purposes of each station.

Condit, Carl W. "Sullivan's Skyscrapers as the Expression of Nineteenth Century Technology." *Technology and Culture*. See chapter on "Roads, Streets, and Highways."

Condit, Carl W. *The Chicago School of Architecture: A History of Commercial and Public Building in the Chicago Area, 1875-1925*. Chicago: University of Chicago Press, 1966. xviii + 238 pp. Illustrations, diagrams, notes, bibliography, and index. First published in 1964, this book is an outgrowth of *The Rise of the Skyscraper* (1952). Condit has added material on the technical and formal background of the Chicago school of architecture and "on the structural details of the buildings themselves, on the genesis of the major buildings, the social, economic, and intellectual history of the city, and contemporary attitudes toward the work of the school."

Cooley, Everett L. "Utah's Capitols." *Utah Historical Quarterly*, XXVII (July 1959), 259-73. Presents a history, description, and photographs of successive capitol buildings.

Cooley, Laura C. "The Los Angeles Public Library." *The Quarterly, Historical Society of*

Southern California, XXII (March 1941), 5-23. History of the facility from 1844 to the 1930s that focuses on the people who directed it.

Coursey, Clark. *Courthouses of Texas.* Brownwood, Tex.: Banner Printing Co., 1962.

Cowdrey, Albert E. *A City for the Nation: The Army Engineers and the Building of Washington, D.C.: 1790-1967. See chapter on "Planning, Engineering, and Administration."*

Craig, Lois. "The Boston City Hall and Its Antecedents." *Journal of the American Institute of Architects*, 69 (Sept. 1980), 46-53. Examines the evolution of city halls, particularly their uses and symbolism.

Craig, Lois, and the Staff of the Federal Architecture Project. *The Federal Presence: Architecture, Politics, and Symbols in United States Government Building.* Cambridge: MIT Press, 1978. xvii + 580 pp. Illustrations, drawings, table, bibliography, and index. A well-structured and comprehensive survey of federal public architecture and land use. The evolution of federal public buildings is securely placed within the context of the debates and design politics of each architectural era. The text's 900 photographs and drawings make it a major pictorial resource. The volume also contains a thorough bibliography. Public works historians, urban planners, and buildings and grounds practitioners will value the quantity of material gathered into a single volume.

Cramer, C. H. *Open Shelves and Open Minds: A History of the Cleveland Public Library.* Cleveland: Press of Case Western Reserve University, 1972. x + 279 pp. Illustrations, notes, and index. Covers the first century of the library (1869-1969).

Crane, Paul and Sophie. "Historic Jails of Tennessee." *Tennessee Historical Quarterly*, XXXIX (Spring 1980), 3-10. Photos accompanied by some descriptive narrative.

Crawford, Lewis F. "The Liberty Memorial Building." *North Dakota Historical Quarterly*, I (Oct. 1926), 44-48. A brief history of the Bismarck building that "since occupancy has housed the Supreme Court, the Adjutant General, the State Historical Society, and the Library Commission, with their various departments."

Crawford, William. *Report of William Crawford, Esq., on the Penitentiaries of the United States, addressed to His Majesty's Principal Secretary of State for the Home Department.* London: House of Commons, 1834. 229 pp. Illustrations, diagrams, tables, notes, and appendix. A report on visits to penitentiaries in fifteen states "to ascertain the practicability and expediency of applying the respective systems on which they are governed, or any parts thereof, to the prisons" of Great Britain. Crawford describes the physical features of the penitentiaries as well as the numbers of prisoners detained there, their offenses, and their rehabilitation programs.

Creighton, Wilbur Foster. *Building of Nashville.* Nashville: Wilbur F. Creighton, 1969. v + 205 pp. Illustrations and index. Poorly written, amateurish history of public construction in Nashville. Subjects covered include the state capitol, bridges, water supply, and navigation.

Creighton, Wilbur F., Jr. Wilbur Fisk Foster, Soldier and Engineer." *Tennessee Historical Quarterly.* See chapter on "Sewers and Wastewater Treatment."

Cronin, John F. "The Elsinore Tower." *Bulletin of the Historical and Philosophical Society of Ohio*, 9 (Jan. 1951), 46-49. On the formidable building astride the entrance to a Cincinnati park.

Crosby, Jack T., Sr. *The State Capitol of Michigan.* Lansing, Mich.: Historical Society of Greater Lansing, 1968. 23 pp. Illustrations. An address (June 6, 1968) by the president of the Historical Society of Greater Lansing.

Crutchfield, James A. "Pioneer Architecture in Tennessee." *Tennessee Historical Quarterly*, XXXV (Summer 1976), 162-74. Describes the role of the stockade, the blockhouse, and the log cabin in taming the wilderness for settlement.

Cullinan, Gerald. *The Post Office Department.* Washington, D.C.: Praeger Library of U.S. Government Departments and Agencies, 1968.

Cullinan, Nicholas C. "History of the Seattle General Postoffice." *Washington Historical Quarterly*, XVII (July 1926), 211-17. Largely an administrative history since 1853.

Cummings, Abbott Lowell. "The Ohio State Capitol Competition." *Journal of the Society of*

Architectural Historians, XII (May 1953), 14-18. In 1838.

Cummings, Hubertis. "Pennsylvania's State Houses and Capitols." *Pennsylvania History,* XX (Oct. 1953), 409-16. Presents in brief form, "the story of Pennsylvania's various state capitols" from 1729.

Cummings, Hubertis. "Stephen Hills and the Building of Pennsylvania's First Capitol." *Pennsylvania History,* XX (Oct. 1953), 417-37. On carpenter and builder Hills' unique role in constructing Pennsylvania's first capitol.

Cunningham, H. F. "The Old City Hall, Washington, D.C." *Architectural Record,* XXVII (March 1915), 268-72. A brief sketch of a building begun in 1820, completed in 1849, and converted into a courthouse in 1871.

Dahl, Curtis. "Mr. Smith's American Acropolis." *American Heritage,* VII (June 1956), 38-43; 104-05. On Franklin W. Smith's plan (1900) "to transform Washington, D.C., into a capital of such beauty and cultural advantage that never again would an American be tempted to go abroad for artistic or intellectual reasons."

Dain, Phyllis. *The New York Public Library: A History of Its Founding and Early Years.* New York: New York Public Library, 1972. xix + 466 pp. Notes, bibliography, and index.

Daniel, Hawthorne. *Public Libraries for Everyone: The Growth and Development of Library Services in the United States, Especially since the Passage of the Library Services Act.* Garden City, N.Y.: Doubleday & Company, 1961. 192 pp. Appendix and index. An overview of library developments generally with particular emphasis on various regions of the country after 1956.

Daniel, Jean Houston, and Daniel Price. *Executive Mansions and Capitols of America.* New York: G.P. Putnam's Sons, 1969. 290 pp. Illustrations, appendix, bibliography, and index. Heavily illustrated profiles of state executive mansions and capitol buildings.

Davies, Jane B. "A.J. Davis' Projects for a Patent Office Building, 1832-1834." *Journal of the Society of Architectural Historians,* XXIV (Oct. 1965), 229-51. On the origin of the design of a building that was "a major influence on the development of Washington's classical style."

Dean, William. "A History of the Capitol Buildings of Minnesota with an Account of the Struggles for Their Location." *Minnesota Historical Society Collections,* XII (1905-1908), 1-42.

Dekle, Clayton B. "The Tennessee State Capitol." *Tennessee Historical Quarterly,* XXV (Fall 1966), 213-38. An account confined largely to the Capitol's construction and restoration.

Denson, Wilbur Thurman. "A History of the Chicago Auditorium." Doctoral dissertation, University of Wisconsin, Madison, 1974. 347 pp.

Department of Public Works, City of New York. *The Renascence of City Hall.* New York: City of New York, 1956. 95 pp. Illustrations and maps. A series of articles on New York's city hall with an introduction by American historian Allan Nevins. The second section, "City Hall in Retrospect," as well as separate articles in other sections on "The Rehabilitation of City Hall" and "Municipal Government, Then and Now" are especially informative.

Downey, Martha Jane. "The Vandalia Statehouse: From Frontier Capitol to State Historic Site." *Historic Illinois,* 2 (Feb. 1980), 1-2. A short history of a building that served as the Illinois Capitol during Vandalia's brief reign as the state's second capital city (beginning in 1820).

Draper, Joan Elaine. "The San Francisco Civic Center: Architecture, Planning and Politics." Doctoral dissertation, University of California, Berkeley, 1979. 529 pp. Shows that San Franciscans saw the construction of these buildings (1912+) as more than a slum clearance project or an abstract beautification scheme. They supported the construction plan because it was "an important political issue and part of a broader municipal reform program." The Civic Center is a prime example of American Beaux-Arts design.

Droege, John A. *Passenger Terminals and Trains.* New York: McGraw-Hill Book Company, 1916. vii + 410 pp. Illustrations, maps, and index. Excellent descriptive overview of terminal architecture and the services the facilities provide.

Drumm, Stella, and Charles van Ravensway. "The Old Court House." *Glimpses of the Past,* VII (Jan.-June 1940), 3-41. A history of a court building constructed in stages from 1839 to 1862.

Duryee, Sacket L. *A Historical Summary of the Work of the Corps of Engineers in Washington, D.C. and Vicinity, 1852-1952.* See chapter on "Planning, Engineering, and Administration."

Early, James. *Romanticism and American Architecture.* New York: A. S. Barnes and Co., 1965. 171 pp. Illustrations, notes, and index. On nineteenth-century architecture. Of particular interest is the introduction on "Jefferson's Capitol and the Older Classicism."

Eberhard, Ernest. "Fifty Years of Agitation for Better Design of Government Buildings and Government Employment of Private Architects." *American Architect,* CXXXIX (June 1931), 24-25, 80-88.

Ericsson, Henry, and Lewis E. Myers. *Sixty Years a Builder: The Autobiography of Henry Ericsson.* Chicago: A. Kroch and Son, Publishers, 1942. ix + 388 pp. Illustrations and index. An autobiography of a prominent, Swedish-born contractor who became Chicago's building commissioner in 1911.

Esbin, Martha. "Old Capitol Library: Its History, Contents, and Restoration." *Annals of Iowa,* 42 (Winter 1975), 523-40. On the library's collections and administration since 1838 and its restoration in 1973.

Fant, Christie Zimmerman. *The State House of South Carolina.* Columbia: R. L. Bryan, 1970. 118 pp. Illustrations.

Feinstein, Estelle F. *Stamford in the Gilded Age: The Political Life of a Connecticut Town, 1868-1893.* See chapter on "Planning, Engineering, and Administration."

Fitch, James Marston. *American Building: The Environmental Forces That Shape It.* Cambridge, Mass.: Riverside Press, 1972.

Fitch, James Marston. *American Building: The Historical Forces That Shaped It.* New York: Schocken Books, 1973. ix + 350 pp. Illustrations, notes, and index. First published in 1947, this book was revised and enlarged in 1966 and published in paperback in 1973. It is a chronological treatment of the developments in American building, both public and private, from 1620 to 1965. While neither comprehensive or exhaustive, it is an informed and readable survey of one of America's largest production fields.

Fitch, James Marston. *Architecture and the Esthetics of Plenty.* See chapter on "Planning, Engineering, and Administration."

Fleming, Robins. "Building Regulations in the United States." *Civil Engineering,* 8 (Nov. 1938), 730-32. A general review of the development of building codes, particularly their purposes and sponsors.

Forrester, Allen, comp. *The City Hall, Baltimore: History of Construction and Dedication.* Baltimore: Mayor and City Council, 1877. vi + 141 pp. Illustrations.

Forness, Norman Olaf. "The Origins and Early History of the United States Department of the Interior." Doctoral dissertation, Pennsylvania State University, 1964. 253 pp. Notes, appendix, and bibliography. Largely administrative history of the department from 1849 to 1860. It deals sparingly with land grants for internal improvements, management of public buildings in Washington, D.C., and construction of wagon roads in the West.

Fortenbaugh, Robert. *Nine Capitals of the U.S.* York, Penn.: Maple Press Company, 1973. Reprint of a 1948 edition.

Frankfurter, Felix. "History in Brick and Stone and Mortar." *Journal of the American Institute of Architects,* XV (Feb. 1951), 64-70. An informal presentation before the National Council for the Preservation of Historic Sites and Buildings (Oct. 1950).

Fray, I. T. *They Built the Capitol.* Richmond: Garrett and Massie 1940. xvi + 324 pp. Illustrations, diagrams, chronology, bibliography, and index. A heavily illustrated history of the nation's Capitol. The author emphasizes the work of individuals (engineers, architects, sculptors, etc.) who had a part in constructing this famous building.

Fraser, Chelesa. *The Story of Engineering in America.* See chapter on "Planning, Engineering, and Administration."

Freeman, L. Willard. "Mayo General Hospital." *Journal of the Illinois State Historical Society,* XLIV (Spring 1951), 26-31. Chronicles the brief history (1943-1946) of an army hospital in Galesburg, Illinois.

Gale, Frederick C. *The History of the Capitol Building and Governor's Mansion, State of Nevada.* Carson City: n.p., 1968. 35 pp. Illustrations.

Galli, Geraldine. "100 Years of Construction News." *Engineering News-Record.* See chapter on "Planning, Engineering, and Administration."

Garvan, Anthony N. B. *Architecture and Town Planning in Colonial Connecticut.* New Haven: Yale University Press, 1951. xiv + 166 pp. Illustrations, maps, charts, graphs, diagrams, notes, bibliographical essay, and index. A thought-provoking investigation of "the relationship between domestic architecture and the demography and national origins of colonial Connecticut." The author demonstrates, in particular, that colonial house design cannot be understood independently of land ownership and town planning. There is an interesting chapter on Connecticut's public buildings.

Gatling, Eva Ingersoll. "John Berry of Hillsboro, North Carolina." *Journal of the Society of Architectural Historians,* X (March 1951), 18-22. Briefly describes the Orange County Courthouse, probably Berry's most outstanding work.

Gatton, John Spaulding. "'Only for Great Attractions': Louisville's Amphitheatre Auditorium. *Register of the Kentucky Historical Society,* 78 (Winter 1980), 27-38.

Giedion, Sigfried. *Space, Time and Architecture: The Growth of a New Tradition.* See chapter on "Planning, Engineering, and Administration."

Gies, Joseph. *Wonders of the Modern World.* See chapter on "Sewers and Wastewater Treatment."

Gilchrist, Agnes Addison. *William Strickland: Architect and Engineer, 1788-1854.* Philadelphia: University of Pennsylvania Press, 1950. xvii + 145 pp. + 50 plates. Illustrations, appendices, and index. The first three chapters are devoted to summary discussions of Strickland's life, character, and style. The first section of the appendices contains a separate account of each building designed by Strickland—a bibliography, brief history, and a description which generally includes comment on style, plan, materials, cost, and outstanding features.

Gilheany, Rosary S. "Early Newark Hospitals." *Proceedings of the New Jersey Historical Society,* LXXXIII (Jan. 1965), 10-23. Brief historical sketches of Newark's first military and civilian hospitals.

Gillette, Howard, Jr. "Philadelphia's City Hall: Monument to a New Political Machine." *Pennsylvania Magazine of History and Biography,* XCVII (April 1973), 233-49. Illustrates the origins of the historic structure in urban machine politics.

Glaab, Charles N., and A. Theodore Brown. *A History of Urban America.* See chapter on "Community Water Supply."

Goeldner, Paul Kenneth. "Temples of Justice: Nineteenth-Century County Courthouses in the Midwest and Texas." Doctoral dissertation, Columbia University, 1970.

Goode, George Brown, ed. *The Smithsonian Institution, 1846-1896: The History of its First Half Century.* City of Washington: Smithsonian Institution, 1897. x + 856 pp. Illustrations, notes, appendix, and index. Of particular interest is the one chapter on "The Smithsonian Building and Grounds" by the book's editor.

Goode, James M. *Capital Losses: A Cultural History of Washington's Destroyed Buildings.* Washington, D.C.: Smithsonian Institution Press, 1979.

Goode, James M. "Vanished Washington and Its 'Capital Losses.'" *Smithsonian,* 10 (Dec. 1979), 58-66. On Washington, D.C., buildings that have been destroyed since the nineteenth century.

Gordon, Winifred and Douglas. "The Dome of the Annapolis State House." *Maryland Historical Magazine,* 67 (Fall 1972), 294-97. A discussion of conflicting information on the source of the design of the state house dome.

Goss, Peter L. "The Architectural History of Utah." *Utah Historical Quarterly,* 43 (Summer 1975), 208-39. Mostly a discussion of styles.

Grant, Roger H. "The Country Railroad Station in the West." *Journal of the West,* XVII (Oct. 1978), 28-40. Describes this building's vital role as "the conduit through which people and goods traveled." The text is complemented by numerous photographs and drawings.

Grant, U. S., 3rd. "The National Capital: Reminiscences of Sixty-Five Years." *Records of the Columbia Historical Society of Washington, D.C.* (1957-1959), 1-15. Reflections on the physical change that had taken place in Washington, D.C., since 1894. The author was formerly director of the district's Office of Public Buildings and Grounds.

Greeley, W. R. "Our 48 State Capitol Buildings." *American City,* XL (May 1929), 123-30. Contains photographs of and the construction dates and architects' names of forty-eight state capitol buildings.

Green, Constance McLaughlin. *Washington: Village and Capitol, 1800-1878.* See chapter on "Urban Mass Transportation."

Greene, William Robert. "Early Development of the Illinois State Penitentiary System." *Journal of the Illinois State Historical Society,* LXX (Aug. 1977), 185-95. Although the major emphasis is on the prisoners' treatment, there is a discussion of the facilities in which they were housed.

Greer, Joubert Lee. "The Building of the Texas State Capitol, 1882-1888." Master's thesis, University of Texas, 1932.

Guiness, Desmond, and Julius Trousdale Sadler, Jr. *Mr. Jefferson, Architect.* New York: Viking Press, 1973. 177 pp. Illustrations and map. Largely photographs, accompanied by some text, of buildings designed by Jefferson. The public buildings are found principally in Richmond and Washington.

Gurney, Gene. *The Library of Congress: A Picture Story of the World's Largest Library.* New York: Crown Publishers, 1966. 128 pp. Illustrations. The first chapter is a short history of the library. The photographs, more than the text, describe the building's design and construction.

Gutheim, Frederick. *One Hundred Years of Architecture in America, 1857-1957: Celebrating the Centennial of the American Institute of Architects.* New York: Reinhold Publishing Corporation, 1957. 96 pp. Illustrations. Except for a two-page foreword by the author, the volume is largely photographs.

Gutheim, Frederick, and Wilcomb E. Washburn. *The Federal City: Plans & Realities.* See chapter on "Planning, Engineering, and Administration."

Hales, George P. *Los Angeles City Hall.* Los Angeles: Board of Public Works, 1928. xi + 63 pp. Illustrations.

Hall, Charles L. "The Kansas Courthouses by George P. Washburn, Architect." *Journal of the West,* XVII (Jan. 1978), 74-80. An examination of the thirteen courthouses Washburn designed for Kansas counties.

Hamlin, A. D. F. "Twenty-Five Years of American Architecture." *Architectural Record,* XL (July 1916), 3-18. A review of American architecture—"more sophisticated," "more mature," and "more self-conscious"—from 1891 to 1916. The author contends that the most noticeable features of American architecture during this period "have been the development of steel skeleton construction and the influence of several great exhibitions, especially of that at Chicago in 1893."

Hamlin, Talbot. *Benjamin Henry Latrobe.* New York: Oxford University Press, 1955. xxxvi + 633 pp. Illustrations, diagrams, notes, appendix, bibliography, and index. A major biography of the father of American professional architecture and the leading public works engineer of his generation. The author, an architectural historian, emphasizes the architectural side of Latrobe's life and career. However, Hamlin does present single chapters on his subject's work for the United States government (1798-1812) and rebuilding of the Capitol (1815-1817) as well as large sections on the Philadelphia and New Orleans waterworks. Hamlin concludes with a chapter entitled "Latrobe as Engineer."

Hammond, Alonzo J. "Development of Railroad Passenger Terminals." *Civil Engineering,* I (Oct. 1931), 1176-81. Discusses the various kinds of terminals (especially large ones such as those in New York and Chicago) that have been built, how they were financed, and their relationship to the cities in which they are located.

Hansen, Harry. *Scarsdale: From Colonial Manor to Modern Community.* See chapter on "Community Water Supply."

Hardin, Bayless E. "The Capitols of Kentucky." *Register of the Kentucky State Historical Society,* 43 (July 1945), 173-200. Good historical overview of the state's various capitol buildings.

Harper, Herbert L. "The Antebellum Courthouses of Tennessee." *Tennessee Historical Quarterly,* XXX (Spring 1971), 3-25. Contains brief historical sketches of seven pre-Civil War courthouses and the counties of which they are the seats of government.

Harris, Michael H., and Donald G. Davis, Jr., comps. *American Library History: A Bibliography*. Austin: University of Texas Press, 1978. xix + 260 pp. Indexes.

Harris, Neil. "The Gilded Age Revisited: Boston and the Museum Movement." *American Quarterly*, XIV (Winter 1962), 545-66. Explains how the Boston institution, one of the first public museums chartered in America, was a model for many later foundations.

Hartman, Edwin P. *Adventures in Research: A History of the Ames Research Center, 1940-1965*. Washington, D.C.: National Aeronautics and Space Administration, 1970. xx + 555 pp. Illustrations, bibliography, appendices, and index.

Hartman, J. Paul. *Civil Engineering Landmarks: State of Florida*. See chapter on "Planning, Engineering, and Administration."

Hazelton, George C., Jr. *The National Capitol: Its Architecture, Art, and History*. New York: J.F. Taylor & Company, 1914. 301 pp. Illustrations, appendix, and index. First published in 1897, the author presents the history of the Capitol, its architecture and art, through historical events and individual biography.

Hecht, Arthur. "The Takoma Park Public Library." *Records of the Columbia Historical Society of Washington, D.C.* (1966-1968), 318-35. History of the first public library branch in the District of Columbia.

Held, Ray F. *Public Libraries in California, 1849-1878*. Berkeley: University of California Press, 1963. ix + 193 pp. Notes, bibliographic note, appendices, and index. An interpretive study of the public library movement in one state.

Henderson, Jerry. "Nashville's Ryman Auditorium." *Tennessee Historical Quarterly*, XXVIII (Winter 1968), 305-28. Records the history of the auditorium from 1889 to 1920, when it fulfilled requirements for the religious, educational, political, and musical needs of Nashville. Very little of the article is concerned with the physical structure.

Hermanson, David R. "Indiana County Courthouse of the Nineteenth Century." *Ball State University Faculty Lecture Series*, 1967-68 (1968), pp. 13-37.

Hillman, F. W. "History of the Chicago Passenger Stations: North Western Stations." *Journal of the Western Society of Engineers*, 42 (June 1937), 127-32. A brief historical sketch from 1847 by the assistant engineer of maintenance of the Chicago & Northwestern Railroad Company.

Hines, Thomas S. *Burnham of Chicago: Architect and Planner*. New York: Oxford University Press, 1974. xxiii + 445 pp. Illustrations, diagrams, notes, appendices, bibliographical essay, and index. A thoroughly researched and comprehensive biography of an individual (1846-1912) who earned an international reputation as an architect, planner, organizer, and cultural leader.

Hines, Thomas S. "The Paradox of 'Progressive' Architecture: Urban Planning and Public Building in Tom Johnson's Cleveland." *American Quarterly*, XXV (Oct. 1973), 426-28. On the inconsistencies in the architectural development of Johnson's Cleveland (1901-1909).

Historic American Buildings Survey. *Documenting a Legacy: 40 Years of the Historic American Buildings Survey*. Washington, D.C.: Library of Congress, 269-94 pp. Illustrations. A reprint from the *Quarterly Journal of the Library of Congress*.

Historic American Buildings Survey. *Historic American Buildings Survey. Catalog Supplement of the Measured Drawings and Photographs of the Survey in the Library of Congress, Comprising Additions Since March 1, 1941*. Washington, D.C.: National Park Service, 1959. 182 pp. Illustrations and drawings. Listed in alphabetical order by states.

Historic American Buildings Survey. *New Haven Architecture: Selections from the Historic American Buildings Survey*. Washington, D.C.: United States Department of the Interior, National Park Service. v + 160 pp. Illustrations, maps, and diagrams. Includes physical descriptions and historical accounts of eleven buildings (the New Haven city hall and courthouse are among them) "representing a cross section of styles, uses, and dates of what remains of New Haven's early architecture. . . ."

Historic American Buildings Survey. *Wisconsin Architecture: A Catalog of Buildings Represented in the Library of Congress, with Illustrations from Measured Drawings*. Washington, D.C.: United States Department of the Interior, National Park Service, 1965. 80 pp.

Illustrations, diagrams, maps, and bibliography. A research of historically and architecturally important buildings in Wisconsin, keyed to the Historic American Buildings Survey's archive in the Library of Congress.

Historic American Engineering Record. *Rehabilitation: Fairmount Waterworks, 1978: Conservation and Recreation in a National Historic Landmark.* See chapter on "Community Water Supply."

"Historic Buildings of North Dakota: Alfred Dickey Free Library—Jamestown." *North Dakota History,* 40 (Summer 1973), 3. A brief history of a public structure (1918) that shows the influence of the Chicago School of Architecture.

"Historic Buildings of North Dakota: Dickey County Courthouse—Ellendale." *North Dakota History,* 41 (Winter 1974), 3. An historical sketch of a courthouse (1912) that "exemplifies the early twentieth century shift toward public buildings of a less massive and less imposing appearance."

"Historic Buildings of North Dakota: McFarland Hall—Valley City." *North Dakota History,* 40 (Winter 1973), 3. A short history of "Old Main" (1892) on the campus of Valley City State College.

"Historic Buildings of North Dakota: State Capitol—Bismarck." *North Dakota History,* 43 (Spring 1976), 4. A short history of North Dakota's state capitol (1934).

"Historic Buildings of North Dakota: The Administration Building at NDSU, Fargo." *North Dakota History,* 39 (Spring 1972), 3. A brief history of the oldest existing structure (1892) on the campus of North Dakota State University of Fargo.

"Historic Buildings of North Dakota: The Liberty Memorial Building, Bismarck." *North Dakota History,* 39 (Winter 1972), 5. A short description of the oldest of the six buildings (1924) occupying the state capitol grounds.

"Historic Buildings of North Dakota: Wells County Courthouse—Fessenden." *North Dakota History,* 39 (Fall 1972), 3. An historical sketch of "an excellent example of the massive and imposing public buildings favored in the late nineteenth century." The courthouse opened on January 1, 1896.

History and Heritage Committee, Los Angeles Section of the American Society of Civil Engineers. *Civil Engineering Landmarks of Southern California.* See chapter on "Irrigation."

History and Heritage Committee, San Francisco Section of the American Society of Civil Engineers. *Historic Civil Engineering Landmarks of San Francisco and Northern California.* San Francisco: Pacific Gas and Electric Company, 1977. 52 pp. Illustrations and map. Short, informative sketches of pioneering public works structures in San Francisco and northern California. Although many public buildings are represented, the booklet also contains material on bridges, tunnels, and community water supplies.

"History of the San Francisco Public Library." *Municipal Record,* XVIII (Nov. 19, 1925), 403-04. A spotty account. See also a short article that follows: "Library Rebuilt since 1906" (p. 409).

Hitchcock, Henry-Russell, and William Seale. *Temples of Democracy: The State Capitols of the USA.* New York: Harcourt Brace Jovanovich, 1976. xii + 339 pp. Illustrations, notes, bibliography, and index. A richly illustrated and well-documented history of state capitols. The research for this book was sponsored by the Victorian Society in America and funded by the National Endowment for the Humanities.

Hoffman, Donald. *The Architecture of John Wellborn Root.* Baltimore: Johns Hopkins University Press, 1973. xvix + 263 pp. Illustrations, notes, bibliography, and index. Evaluates the work of Root, who "led the way in the art of the high office building." Of interest is the chapter on "The World's Columbian Exposition" as well as those sections on nineteenth-century railroad stations.

Holcomb, Richmond C. *A Century with Norfolk Naval Hospital, 1830-1930.* Portsmouth, Va.: Printcraft Publishing Company, 1930. 543 pp. Illustrations, diagrams, tables, index. A history of the nation's oldest naval hospital (1830s) and the United States Navy's Medical Department by a captain in the Medical Corps. The author makes an effort to explain the effects of specific medical advances on navy practices.

Holleman, Thomas J., and James P. Gallagher. *Smith, Hinckman & Grylls: 125 Years of*

Architecture and Engineering, 1853-1978. Detroit: Wayne State University Press, 1978. 239 pp. Illustrations, notes, appendices, bibliography, and index.

Holmes, M. Patricia. "The St. Louis Union Station." *Missouri Historical Society Bulletin,* XXVII (July 1971), 248-58. A history of the building's construction, alterations, and renovations and a discussion of its architectural richness.

Holmes, Nicholas H., Jr. "Capitols of the State of Alabama." *Alabama Review,* 32 (July 1979), 163-72.

Holt, Glen E. "Will Chicago's Itinerant City Hall Be Moved Once More?" *Chicago History,* VI (Fall 1977), 155-66. Reviews the history of the structure (1848), explaining why it has become one of the city's "most stable institutions in the course of the past century."

Holt, W. Stull. *The Office of the Chief of Engineers of the Army: Its Non-Military History, Activities, and Organization.* See chapter on "Planning, Engineering, and Administration."

Hosmer, Charles B., Jr. *Presence of the Past: A History of the Preservation Movement in the United States before Williamsburg.* New York: G.P. Putman's Sons, 1965. 386 pp. Illustrations, notes, bibliography, and index. A unique historical survey of the efforts and aspirations of the people who began to save buildings (public and private) of the American past. The author concludes his narrative in 1926.

Hughel, C. G. "History of Chicago Passenger Stations: Dearborn Street Station Group." *Journal of the Western Society of Engineers,* 42 (April 1937), 78-81. A brief historical sketch from 1879 by the chief draftsman of the Chicago & Western Indiana Railroad Company.

Hunsberger, George S. "The Architectural Career of George Hadfield." *Records of the Columbia Historical Society of Washington, D.C.,* (1951-1952), 46-65. A biographical sketch of a British architect (1764-1826) who worked on the Capitol Building before Benjamin Henry Latrobe.

Hunter, L. L. "Vision and Work: The Supervising Architect's Contribution to Magnificent Washington." *Records of the Columbia Historical Society of Washington, D.C.* (1957-1959), 69-81. Provides a historical sketch of the Office of the Supervising Architect in the United States Public Buildings Service.

Hunter, Robert John. *The Origin of the Philadelphia General Hospital, Blockley Division.* n.p.: Philadelphia, 1955. 40 pp. Illustrations and bibliography.

Huxtable, Ada Louise. *Classic New York: Georgian Gentility to Greek Elegance.* Garden City, N.Y.: Doubleday & Company, xvi + 142 pp. Illustrations, notes, glossary, bibliography, and index. An attempt "to document the architecture of the city . . . through a survey of its successive styles and ways of building. "One chapter is devoted to "Tasteful Temples: Public Monuments and Prestige Buildings."

Huxtable, Ada Louise. *Will They Ever Finish Bruckner Boulevard?* New York: Macmillan Company, 1970. xix + 268 pp. Illustrations and index. Thought-provoking selections from Huxtable's work as a critic for the New York *Times* during the 1960s. The book's first part, "The Urban Scene," contains commentaries primarily on structures and events in New York City. Her scope broadens in the second part, "Architecture," to include examples from other places when discussing the "Decline and Fall of Public Building," "The State of the Art," and "Preservation."

Ickes, Harold L. *The Historic American Building Survey.* Washington, D.C.: Government Printing Office, 1936. iii + 15 pp. A brief review of the Historic American Buildings Survey's work from 1933.

Irwin, Jack C. "Dallas County Courthouse: Texas Historical Architecture." *Texas Architect,* 18 (April 1968), 25-27.

Jacobs, James B. "Stateville: A Natural History of a Maximum Security Prison." 2 vols. Doctoral dissertation, University of Chicago, 1975. Vol. I: vi + 147 pp.; Vol. II: 148-563 pp. Tables, notes, appendices, and bibliography. A sociological study of an Illinois penitentiary. The first volume reviews the institution's history but little attention is given to the structure itself.

Jacobus, Melancthon W. "The City Hall and Market House in Hartford." *Connecticut Historical Society Bulletin,* 35 (Jan. 1970), 1-6. Description of the planning and construction of the buildings in the 1820s and 1830s.

Jensen, Merrill, ed. *Regionalism in America.* Madison: University of Wisconsin Press, 1951.

xvi + 425 pp. Notes and bibliographical essays. A fine collection of essays on all aspects of regionalism. The following are particularly noteworthy: Rexford Newcomb, "Regionalism in American Architecture"; Gordon R. Clapp, "The Tennessee Valley Authority"; and Elmer Starch, "The Great Plains-Missouri Valley Region."

Johannesen, Eric. "Simeon Porter: Ohio Architect." *Ohio History,* 74 (Summer 1964), 169-90. Reviews the career of an individual "who achieved the distinction of having done some of the most notable post-colonial and Greek Revival work in northern Ohio" and who created "a body of equally notable Victorian eclectic work." Besides private residences and churches, the article describes many of Porter's school (high school, college, and university) buildings.

Johnson, Frederick. "The Civilian Conservation Corps: Public Works or Panacea?" *Public Works,* III (Oct. 1980), 80-81, 117. Personal reflections on CCC work (1934) in Whitewater State Park in southeastern Minnesota.

Johnson, Palmer O., and Oswald L. Harvey. *The National Youth Administration.* Washington, D.C.: U.S. Advisory Committee on Education, 1938. x + 120 pp. Chart, tables, notes, appendices, and index. A good overview of the administration and projects undertaken by the National Youth Administration. Some 120 "outstanding projects" are listed that include remodeling and construction of public buildings, highway beautification, and development of parks and recreational areas.

Johnston, Frances Benjamin, and Thomas Tileston Waterman. *The Early Architecture of North Carolina: A Pictorial Survey.* Chapel Hill: University of North Carolina Press, 1947. xxiii + 290 pp. Illustrations, maps, diagrams, and index. A thorough look at many of North Carolina's "colonial" buildings. A variety of public structures are included.

Johnston, Norman. *The Human Cage: A Brief History of Prison Architecture.* New York: Walker and Company, 1973. 68 pp. Illustrations, diagrams, and notes. General but well-illustrated history of correctional architecture in the world, especially in the United States, during the past four centuries. The volume was prepared for the Institute of Corrections of the American Foundation with funds granted by the Law Enforcement Assistance Administration. The author concludes that "the history of prison architecture stands as a discouraging testament of our sometimes intentional, sometimes accidental degradation of our fellow man."

Jones, Granville L. "The History of the Founding of the Eastern State Hospital of Virginia." *American Journal of Psychiatry,* 110 (March 1954), 644-50. On the oldest state mental hospital (1773) in the country. Robert Smith of Philadelphia designed the building (it is briefly described).

Jones, Robert Allen. "Cass Gilbert: Midwestern Architect in New York." Doctoral dissertation, Case Western Reserve University, 1976. Contains useful information on the New York City Custom House.

Jordy, William H. *American Buildings and Their Architects: Progressive and Academic Ideals at the Turn of the Twentieth Century.* Garden City, N.Y.: Doubleday & Company, 1972.

Katz, Herbert and Marjorie. *Museums, U.S.A.: A History and Guide.* Garden City, N.Y.: Doubleday & Company, 1965. x + 395 pp. Illustrations, appendix, bibliographical essay, and index. A history of the museum in America from the eighteenth century. A great deal of attention is given to museum programs and exhibits; the physical structures are discussed only incidentally.

Kaufman, Edgar, and Ben Raeburn, eds. *Frank Lloyd Wright: Writings and Buildings.* New York: Horizon Press, 1960. 346 pp. Illustrations and diagrams. A collection of portions of Wright's most telling writings with explanatory introductions by the editors. Many of the selections are taken from Wright's *An Autobiography, A Testament, Architectural Forum,* and *Architectural Record.* The volume ends with a list of "Wright's Executed Works" arranged geographically.

Keller, William E. "Newspaper Notes on Early Capitols." *Journal of the Illinois State Historical Society,* LXI (Winter 1968), 457-62. Newspaper descriptions of building conditions in the first four of Illinois' six capitols—one in Kaskaskia and three in Vandalia.

Kemp, E. L. "An Introduction to the Structural Evaluation of Historic Reinforced Concrete Structures." *Concrete International,* 1 (Oct. 1979), 88-95. An overview of the early development, use, and value of reinforced concrete. The author also presents ways of evaluating "the strength and serviceabiity of historic reinforced concrete structures."

Kennan, Clara B. "Arkansas's Old State House." *Arkansas Historical Quarterly,* IX (Spring 1950), 33-42. Constructed in the 1830s.

Keyes, Margaret N. "Old Capitol Restored." *Palimpsest,* 57 (July/Aug. 1976), 122-28. Describes the task of restoring Iowa's Old Capitol—"a challenge of research, of organization, and of building."

Keyes, Margaret N. "'The Gallery Will Be Reserved for Ladies.'" *Annals of Iowa,* 42 (Summer 1973), 1-16. On Iowa's first State Capitol (1842) and current efforts to restore it.

Kidney, Walter C. *Historic Buildings of Ohio.* Pittsburgh: Ober Park Associates, Inc., 1972. v + 130 pp. Illustrations, note on sources, and index. A selection (public and commercial buildings as well as private residences) from the records of the Historic American Buildings Survey.

Kidney, Walter C. *The Architecture of Choice: Eclecticism in America, 1880-1930.* New York: George Braziller, 1974. viii + 178 pp. Illustrations, notes, and index. Traces the history of Eclecticism. Of special interest is the chapter on "The Grandeur of State"—on the architecture of various federal, state, county, and municipal government buildings.

Kimball, Fiske. *American Architecture.* Indianapolis: Bobbs-Merrill Company, 1928. 262 pp. Illustrations, notes, and index. An enthusiastic defense of American architecture. Various public buildings are described as the author highlights "great deeds . . . done along the way."

Kimball, Fiske. "Jefferson and the Public Buildings of Virginia: I. Williamsburg, 1770-1776; II. Richmond, 1779-1780." *Huntington Library Quarterly,* XII (Feb. and May 1949), Feb.: 115-20; May: 303-10. Excellent analysis and overview of Jefferson's architectural contributions to his state.

Kimball, Fiske. "The Genesis of the White House." *Century Magazine,* 95 (Feb. 1918), 523-28. A review of "the earliest ideas" regarding the White House's design. The article emphasizes Thomas Jefferson's influence.

Kimball, Fiske, and Bennett Wells. "The Competition for the Federal Buildings, 1792-1793." *Journal of the American Institute of Architects,* VII (Jan., Feb., March, July, and Dec. 1919). Jan.: 8-12; Feb.: 98-102; March: 202-10; July: 355-61; and Dec.: 521-28. On the first significant architectural competition (for the National Capitol and the President's House) in the United States.

Kimball, Fiske. "Thomas Jefferson and the First Monument of the Classical Revival in America." Doctoral dissertation, University of Michigan, n.d. Illustrations and notes. On the Virginia State Capitol (1789) in Richmond. Reprinted from the American Institute of Architects' *Journal;* no dates are given.

Kirker, Harold. *The Architecture of Charles Bulfinch.* Cambridge: Harvard University Press, 1969. xxiii + 398 pp. Illustrations, diagrams, notes, appendices, bibliography, and index. A critical reappraisal of the works of Bulfinch, the first native American architect. Of special interest are the sections on monuments and memorials, courthouses, state houses, jails, and penitentiaries.

Kirker, Harold and James. *Bulfinch's Boston, 1787-1817.* New York: Oxford University Press, 1964. ix + 305 pp. Illustrations, map, notes, and index. The story of Bulfinch's involvement in Boston affairs—politics, society, reform, education, town improvements, town planning, and architecture.

Kite, Elizabeth S. *L'Enfant and Washington: 1791-1792.* Baltimore: Johns Hopkins University Press, 1929.

Knutson, Robert. "The White City: The World's Columbian Exposition of 1893." Doctoral dissertation, Columbia University, 1956. Excellent source on the design and construction of the exposition's exhibits.

Koeper, H. F. *Historic St. Paul Buildings: A Report of the Historic Sites Committee.* St. Paul: St. Paul City Planning Board, 1964. 116 pp. Illustrations.

Kurjack, Dennis C. "The 'President's House' in Philadelphia." *Pennsylvania History,* XX (Oct. 1953), 380-94. On the residence built to accommodate President George Washington and his successors—an executive mansion in what was hoped to be the permanent capital of the United States.

Laist, Theodore. "Two Early Mississippi Valley State Capitols." *Western Architect,* XXXV (May 1926), 53-58. In Arkansas and Mississippi. The short histories are accompanied by exquisite drawings and photographs.

Lancaster, Clay. "New York City Hall Stair Rotunda Reconsidered." *Journal of the Society of Architectural Historians,* XXIX (March 1970), 33-39. Presents a brief history of the building as well as the unusually beautiful staircase.

Langsam, Walter E. "The New York Capitol, 1863-1876." Master's thesis, Yale University, 1968.

Latrobe, John H. B. "Construction of the Public Buildings in Washington." *Maryland Historical Magazine,* IV (Sept. 1909), 221-28. The author offers some insight into the work of his distinguished father.

Leeming, Joseph. *The White House in Picture and Story.* New York: George W. Stewart Publishers, Inc., 1973.

Leigh, Robert D. *The Public Library in the United States.* New York: Columbia University Press, 1950. ix + 272 pp. Notes, appendix, and index. Contains almost no information on physical facilities but does discuss financial support and operations.

"Letters to Jefferson Relative to the Virginia Capitol." *William and Mary Quarterly,* 5 (April 1925), 95-98. Two letters, dated March 20 and October 18, 1785, from James Buchanan and Wm. Hay "In Behalf of the Directors."

Lewis, O. F. *The Development of American Prisons and Prison Customs, 1776-1845.* Montclair, N.J.: Patterson Smith, 1967. Reprint of 1922 edition.

Lingelbach, William E. "Philadelphia and the Conservation of the National Heritage." *Pennsylvania History,* XX (Oct. 1953), 339-56. On the conservation and redevelopment of Independence Hall and surrounding public buildings.

Looker, Henry B. "The Office of Surveyor of the District of Columbia." *Records of the Columbia Historical Society of Washington, D.C.* (1899), 208-16. Describes, by interpreting each legislative act, the responsibilities of the Office of Surveyor of the District of Columbia.

Lorwin, Lewis L. *Youth Works Programs: Problems and Policies.* Washington, D.C.: American Council on Education, 1941. xi + 195 pp. Tables, notes, appendices, and index. A discussion and overview of public youth work programs launched during the New Deal—Civilian Conservation Corps, Works Projects Administration, and National Youth Administration. Young people were involved in the construction of public buildings, roads, streets, dams, parks, airports, and other facilities.

Luciano, Michael J. "A Study of the Origin and Development of the General Services Administration as Related to Its Present Operational Role, Direction, and Influence." Doctoral dissertation, New York University, 1968.

McCallum, Ian Robert Moore. *Architecture, U.S.A.* New York: Reinhold Publishing Corporation, 1959. 216 pp. Illustrations, diagrams, and bibliography.

McCready, Eric Scott. "The Nebraska State Capitol: Its Design, Background and Influence." *Nebraska History,* 55 (Fall 1974), 325-461. A thorough study of the architecture of the Nebraska State Capitol and its related sculptural and mosaic programs. The author includes a ten-page bibliography of books, catalogues, and pamphlets.

McKee, Harley J. "Building for the State of New York, 1790-1890." 12 parts. *Empire State Architect,* XVI and XVII (Jan.-Feb. 1956 through Nov.-Dec. 1957), one-to-two pages in each issue. A series begun in an attempt to interest contemporary architects and builders in the "experiences of their predecessors in doing work for the State." Some of the topics covered are: Government House, state offices, Capitol Park, New State Hall, New Capitol, and State Education Building.

McKee, Harley J. "Glimpses of Architecture in Michigan." *Michigan History,* L (March 1966), 1-27. Contains one section on public buildings and includes information on the following: State Capitol in Lansing, the City Hall in Grand Rapids, Eaton County and Ionia County courthouses, Capitol Hill School in Marshall, a part of the Kalamazoo State Hospital group, and City Hall in Detroit.

McKee, Harley J., comp. *Recording Historic Buildings.* Washington, D.C.: U.S. Government Printing Office, 1970. xi + 165 pp. Illustrations, diagrams, bibliography, and index. States "the principles and standards for recording historic architecture" developed by the

Historic American Buildings Survey during the previous thirty years.

McKee, Harley J., comp. "Records of Buildings in the State of Michigan." *Michigan History,* L (March 1966), 28-49. A list of entries, made in 1965, which updates and expands the entries of the Historic American Buildings Survey's 1941 *Catalog* and 1959 *Supplement*.

McKell, Charles R. "The Utah State Hospital: A Study in the Care of the Mentally Ill." *Utah Historical Quarterly,* XXIII (Oct. 1955), 297-327. Gives some attention to the construction and maintenance of the facility.

McKelvey, Blake. "A History of Penal and Correctional Institutions in the Rochester Area." *Rochester History,* XXXIV (Jan. 1972), 1-24. Largely on theory and practice.

McLanathan, Richard B. K. "Bulfinch's Drawings for the Main State House." *Journal of the Society of Architectural Historians,* XIV (May 1955), 12-17. A description of drawings found in 1942.

McLaughlin, Charles C. "The Capitol in Peril? The West Front Controversy from Walter to Stewart." *Records of the Columbia Historical Society of Washington, D.C.* (1969-1970), 237-65.

McNabb, W. R. "History of the Knoxville City Hall." *Tennessee Historical Quarterly,* XXXI (Fall 1972), 256-60. On a unique Greek revival structure, constructed in 1848 as the main building of the Tennessee School for the Deaf and purchased by the city in 1922.

Maddox, Dawn. "Historic Buildings of North Dakota: Mayville Public Library-Mayville." *North Dakota History,* 43 (Fall 1976), 3. A short history of a public library which was the gift of two Pennsylvania natives who in 1878 introduced bonanza wheat farming on their holdings near Mayville.

Mahoney, Nell Savage. "William Strickland and the Building of Tennessee's Capitol, 1845-1854." *Tennessee Historical Quarterly,* IV (June 1945), 98-153. A history of "the erection of Tennessee's capitol," designed and built by Philadelphia architect Strickland.

Mahoney, Nell Savage. "William Strickland's Introduction to Nashville, 1845." *Tennessee Historical Quarterly,* IX (March 1950), 46-63. Describes the architect's first visit to Nashville "on business connected with the proposed Capitol of the State of Tennessee."

Markowitz, Arnold L. *Historic Preservation: A Guide to Information Sources.* Detroit: Gale Research Company, 1980. xv + 279 pp. Appendix and indexes. A survey of historic preservation literature, "intended to be of use to students of historic preservation, to practitioners of the various professions and occupations concerned with historic preservation, and to members of organizations concerned with historic preservation, from local groups to government organizations." The volume includes chapters on "General Reference Works," "Historical and Current Overviews," and "Interpretation of History through Buildings, Objects, and Sites."

Meeks, Carroll L. V. *The Railroad Station: An Architectural History.* New Haven: Yale University Press, 1956. xxvi + 203 pp. Illustrations, tables, diagrams, notes, appendix, bibliographical essay, and index. Primarily a study of Western world architecture since 1800 as revealed by the passenger railroad station. Although not all the stations described in the book were built with public money, many were. According to the author, the station was "an essential part of the new system of transportation; it reflected the impact of the technology and mobility of the masses." Material for the volume was drawn from both Europe and the United States.

Mehaffey, Joseph C. "Early History of the White House." *Military Engineer,* XX (May-June 1928), 201-06. Describes the original construction and three major repair operations in 1814, 1902, and 1927.

"Meticulous Mr. Meigs." *American History Illustrated,* XV (Nov. 1980), 34-37. A brief description of Montgomery C. Meigs' part in constructing the Capitol dome in Washington, D.C.

"Milestones in U.S. Civil Engineering." *Civil Engineeing.* See chapter on "Planning, Engineering, and Administration."

"Milestones in U.S. Public Works: Penn Square—Three Centuries of Public Works." *APWA Reporter,* 43 (Feb. 1976), 20-21. A description of the site of Philadelphia's first waterworks and monumental city hall. Short histories of both of these structures are also included.

"Milestones in U.S. Public Works: Tower on the Plains—the Nebraska State Capitol." *APWA Reporter,* 42 (Dec. 1975), 22. A descriptive sketch of a structure "that marked a distinct break with the neoclassical tradition that had previously dominated public building design."

Miller, Keith Linus. "Building Towns on the Southeastern Illinois Frontier." Doctoral dissertation. See chapter on "Waterways."

Miller, Nory. "The Statehouse Remodeling, a Costly Snafu." *Inland Architect,* 19 (April 1975), 8-12. Gives short history of the Illinois State Capitol.

Miner, H. Craig. "The Capitol Workmen: Labor Policy on a Public Project." *Capitol Studies,* 3 (Fall 1975), 45-52. An examination of the federal government's response to labor difficulties connected with the construction of the wings of the United States Capitol Building (erected between 1851 and the end of the decade.)

Miner, H. Craig. "The United States Government Building at the Centennial Exhibition, 1874-77." *Prologue: The Journal of the National Archives,* 4 (Winter 1972), 202-18.

Moore, Charles. *Daniel H. Burnham: Architect, Planner of Cities.* See chapter on "Planning, Engineering, and Administration."

Moore, Evelyn R. "The Cahokia Courthouse: Most Traveled Historic Site in Illinois." *Historic Illinois,* 3 (Aug. 1980), 1-3. A historical sketch of the oldest courthouse in Illinois. Torn down and rebuilt three times, the building has been a private home, courthouse, saloon, concession, and exhibit.

Moorhead, Max L. "Rebuilding the Presidio of Santa Fe, 1789-1791." *New Mexico Historical Review,* XLIX (April 1974), 123-42. The author emphasizes the problems encountered and shows how they were "typical of those attending public works projects in colonial New Mexico."

Moran, Daniel E. "Foundation Development during Fifty Years." *Engineering News-Record.* See chapter on "Planning, Engineering, and Administration."

Morrison, Hugh. *Early American Architecture: From the First Colonial Settlements to the National Period.* New York: Oxford University Press, 1966. xiv + 619 pp. Illustrations, diagrams, notes, suggested readings, and index. A comprehensive volume (first printed in 1952) of "architecture in the American Colonies from St. Augustine in 1565 to San Francisco in 1848." Only a small part of the book deals with the architecture of public buildings. But one chapter, for example, contains information on "Georgian Public Buildings in New England;" and some sections describe schools, meeting houses, wharfs, etc.

Moses, Robert. *Public Works: A Dangerous Trade.* See chapter on "Planning, Engineering, and Administration."

Mottier, C. H. "History of Chicago Passenger Stations: Central Station Group." *Journal of the Western Society of Engineers,* 42 (Oct. 1937), 250-57. An historical sketch from 1855 (South Water Street Station) by an engineering assistant of the Illinois Central.

Mumford, Lewis. *From the Ground Up: Observations on Contemporary Architecture, Housing, Highway Building, and Civic Design.* New York: Harcourt, Brace and Company, 1956. viii + 243 pp. Thought-provoking essays, first published in 1947, on contemporary building and highway planning in New York City. These reviews, which appeared initially in the *New Yorker,* raise and confront issues that are universal.

Mumford, Lewis. *Roots of Contemporary American Architecture: A Series of Thirty-Seven Essays Dating from the Mid-Nineteenth Century to the Present.* New York: Reinhold Publishing Corporation, 1952. vii + 454 pp. Index. A collection of essays that "helped form modern architecture in the United States during the last century." Note especially the first selection entitled "A Backward Glance" by Mumford.

Mumford, Lewis. *Sticks and Stones: A Study of American Architecture and Civilization.* New York: Boni and Liveright, 1924. 247 pp. Bibliography. One of the great seminal works on the history of American architecture. The forces which shaped architectural forms are lucidly described. The author concludes the study with a plea for intelligent city planning.

Mumford, Lewis. *The City in History: Its Origins, Its Transformations, and Its Prospects.* See chapter on "Solid Wastes."

Mumford, Lewis. *The Highway and the City.*

See chapter on "Roads, Streets, and Highways."

Murray, John Allen. "The Fourth Genius." *National Historical Magazine,* LXXIV (Jan. 1940), 4-9. Sketch of the nation's Capitol Building.

Myers, Denys Peter, comp. *Maine Catalog: Historic American Buildings Survey.* Portland: Maine State Museum, 1974. vii + 254 pp. Illustrations, maps, diagrams, notes, bibliography, and index. A list of measured drawings, photographs, and written documentation pertaining to Maine's historic architecture. The book is organized chronologically and contains more material on private than public buildings.

Nairn, Ian. *The American Landscape: A Critical View.* New York: Random House, 1965. 152 pp. Illustrations. Financed by the Rockefeller Foundation, this book "tries to show in the simplest way . . . what happens to objects when they are set down together in the environment." There is an historical context to this heavily illustrated volume.

National Society of Colonial Dames of America. *Three Centuries of Custom Houses.* Washington, D.C.: National Society of the Colonial Dames of America, 1972. xviii + 355 pp. Illustrations and bibliography.

National Trust for Historic Preservation. *A Courthouse Conservation Handbook.* Washington, D.C.: Preservation Press, 1976. 75 pp. Illustrations, appendices, and bibliography. Of significance is the chapter on the "Architectural History of the American Courthouse."

Neil, J. Meredith. "Administrators, Architects, and Campus Development: Washington State University, 1890-1905." *Journal of the Society of Architectural Historians,* XXIX (May 1970), 144-55. Describes the building of a college campus and its relationship to the development of architecture in the Pacific Northwest.

Neil, J. Meredith. "The Architecture of C.W. Dickey in Hawaii." *Hawaiian Journal of History,* IX (1975), 101-13. A short article and catalogue of Dickey's completed work (public and private). The author contends that no one has "a more central place in Hawaii's architectural history" than Dickey.

Nervi, Pier Luigi. *Aesthetics and Technology in Building.* Cambridge: Harvard University Press, 1965. xiii + 201 pp. Illustrations, diagrams, and index. Architecture seen as a synthesis of technology and art. The first chapter, "From the Past to the Present," reviews the transformation in building methods and styles.

Nevins, Allan, and John A. Krout, eds. *The Greater City: New York, 1898-1948.* See chapter on "Roads, Streets, and Highways."

Nevins, Frank J. "History of Chicago Passenger Stations: LaSalle Street Station Group." *Journal of the Western Society of Engineers,* 42 (June 1937), 124-27. A short historical sketch from 1851 by a valuation engineer of the Rock Island Lines.

"New York Navy Yard, Brooklyn." *Scientific American,* LXXXI (March 3, 1900), 138-39. Includes a short history of the facility and a description of its buildings.

New York-New Jersey Metropolitan Chapter of the American Public Works Association. *Public Works in Metropolitan New York-New Jersey.* See chapter on "Planning, Engineering, and Administration."

Newcomb, Rexford. *Architecture of the Old Northwest Territory: A Study of Early Architecture in Ohio, Indiana, Illinois, Michigan, Wisconsin, & Part of Minnesota.* Chicago: University of Chicago Press, 1950. xvii + 176 pp. + XCVI plates. Illustrations, maps, diagrams, notes, and index. A fine synthesis of architectural art—both private and public—in the old Northwest.

Newcomb, Rexford. *The Old Mission Churches and Historic Houses of California.* Philadelphia: J.B. Lippincott Company, 1925. xvii + 379 pp. Illustrations, maps, diagrams, notes, appendix, and index. A beautifully illustrated chronicle of early mission architecture in California. Some information is included on Spanish irrigation practices.

Nolen, John, ed. *City Planning: A Series of Papers Presenting the Essential Elements of a City Plan.* See chapter on "Planning, Engineering, and Administration."

North, Arthur T. "The American Public Building: The Popular Misconception of Its Purpose, and Its Consequent Lack of Usefulness." *Architectural Forum,* XLIX (Aug. 1928), 291-97. On the evolving uses of America's public buildings.

Norton, Paul F. "Latrobe's Ceiling for the Hall of Representatives." *Journal of the Society of*

Architectural Historians, X (May 1951), 5-10. Describes the exchange between Latrobe and Jefferson over construction of the ceiling.

Norton, Paul F. "Latrobe, Jefferson and the National Capitol." Doctoral dissertation, Princeton University, 1952. ix + 362 pp. + 68 plates. Illustrations, notes, and bibliography. This study emphasizes "the use of a new design for a Capitol building to meet the needs of a unique legislative system, to show the Capitol's influence on later architecture, and to describe . . . the history of its construction and the changes in its style while Thomas Jefferson was President and Benjamin Henry Latrobe was the architect."

"Notes on the Building of Oklahoma's State Capitol." *Chronicles of Oklahoma,* L (Autumn 1972), 374-76. Details on the awarding of the construction contract for the building.

O'Donnell, Thomas Edward. "Recording the Early Architecture of Illinois in the Historic American Buildings Survey." *Transactions of the Illinois State Historical Society* (1934), 185-213. Describes some of Illinois' early architecture and explains the work of the Historic American Buildings Survey before it became a permanent, federal institution.

Oehlerts, D. E. "The Development of American Public Library Architecture from 1850 to 1940." Doctoral dissertation, Indiana University, 1975.

O'Kelley, Doramae. "Late Nineteenth-Century Courthouse Architecture in Northwestern Ohio." *Ohio History,* 88 (Summer 1979), 311-26. On the significance of the county courthouse as evidenced by its architecture. The article contains more pages of photographs than text.

Olmsted, Roger, and T. H. Watkins. *Here Today: San Francisco's Architectural Heritage.* San Francisco: Chronicle Books, 1968. xi + 334 pp. Illustrations, appendix, glossary, and index. This study, sponsored by the Junior League of San Francisco, highlights residential and commercial buildings. It does, however, contain biographical sketches of architects "who have made especially important, individual contributions to the history of West Bay architecture."

Olson, A. B. "History of Chicago Passenger Stations: Union Station Group." *Journal of the Western Society of Engineers,* 42 (Oct. 1937), 258-61. A short historical sketch from 1880 by a valuation attorney for the Chicago Union Station Company.

O'Neill, John P., ed. *Historic American Buildings Survey: Catalog of the Measured Drawings and Photographs of the Survey in the Library of Congress, January 1, 1938.* Washington, D.C.: U.S. Department of the Interior, National Park Service, 1938. vi + 284 pp. Illustrations, diagrams, appendix, and index. A list (organized alphabetically by state) of the material created by the Historic American Buildings Survey and held by the Library of Congress. There are no descriptions of the buildings themselves in this book.

Osborn, Frederic J. *Green-Belt Cities.* See chapter on "Planning, Engineering, and Administration."

Owen, Robert Dale. *Hints on Public Architecture, Containing, among Other Illustrations, Views and Plans of the Smithsonian Institution: Together with an Appendix Relative to Building Materials.* New York: George P. Putnam, 1849. xvii + 119 pp. Illustrations, diagrams, tables, notes, and appendix. A brief treatise on "the purity of style" in public architecture by the chairman of the Building Committee of the Smithsonian Institution.

Padover, Saul K. *Thomas Jefferson and the National Capital.* Washington, D.C.: Government Printing Office, 1946. xxxvi + 522 pp. Illustrations, maps, tables, and bibliography.

Pare, Richard, ed. *Court House: A Photographic Document.* New York: Horizon Press, 1978. Illustrations, bibliography, and index. A fine pictorial and narrative guide to the history of American courthouses.

Paul, Charles L. "Beaufort, North Carolina: Its Development as a Colonial Town." *North Carolina Historical Review.* See chapter on "Roads, Streets, and Highways."

Payne, Richard W. "A History of Utah's Territorial Capitol Building at Fillmore, 1857-1869." Master's thesis, Brigham Young University, 1971.

Peck, Ralph B. "History of Building Foundations in Chicago." *Bulletins and Other Publications of the Engineering Experiment Station, University of Illinois,* XLI (1948), 1-64. A case study, 1871-1915, which "epitomizes the development of foundation engineering throughout the world." Chapter VI on "The Public Buildings, 1871-1894" contains sections on the Federal Building, City Hall, and County Building.

Peterson, Charles E., ed. *Building Early America: Contributions toward the History of a Great Industry.* Radnor, Pa.: Chilton Book Company, 1976. xvi + 407 pp. Illustrations, diagrams, notes, and index. Proceedings of a symposium held in Philadelphia (March 27-29, 1974) to celebrate the 250th birthday of the Carpenter's Company of the City and County of Philadephia. The purpose of the symposium and the book is to recognize "the builder's part in the history of the new nation." The essays on topics such as roofing, central heating, and early nineteenth-century lighting are of special interest.

Peterson, Charles E., ed. "Early Architects of Independence Hall." *Journal of the Society of Architectural Historians,* XI (Oct. 1952), 23-26. On Edmund Woolley, Robert Mills, and John Haviland.

Pevsner, Nikolaus. *A History of Building Types: The A. W. Mellon Lectures in the Fine Arts, 1970.* Princeton: Princeton University Press for the Trustees of the National Gallery of Art, 1976. 352 pp. Illustrations, notes, bibliography, and index. An "outline history of building types." Of special interest are the chapters on national monuments, government buildings (four separate chapters), libraries, museums, prisons, railway stations, and market halls. The emphasis is on nineteenth-century structures, many of which are located outside the United States.

Phelps, Henry P. *History and Description of the Capitol at Albany: With Picture of the Completed Portion.* Albany: By the author, 1880. 15 pp. Illustration. Gives a good but brief history of the New York capitol. This booklet is an excerpt from what was to appear later in "Albany Hand-Book for 1881."

Philadelphia Society for Alleviating the Miseries of Public Prisons. *A View and Description of the Eastern Penitentiary of Pennsylvania.* Philadelphia: C.G. Childs, 1830. 8 pp. Illustration and diagram. A physical description of a model prison built by the state of Pennsylvania in the belief that "this immense and expensive structure" would contribute "to the amelioration and protection of her populace."

Phippen, Walter G. "From Charter Street to the Lookout: The Salem Hospital—A Brief History." *Essex Institute Historical Collections,* CII (April 1966), 89-162. Largely an administrative history by one of Salem (Mass.) hospital's most prominent physicians.

Pickard, John. *Report of the* [*Missouri*] *Capitol Decoration Commission, 1917-1928.* Columbia: State of Missouri, Capitol Decoration Commission, 1928. 151 pp. Illustrations and index. Gives a short, descriptive history of the state capitol and explains at length how money from the Capitol Tax Fund was used to furnish and decorate the building.

Pickens, Buford. "Mr. Jefferson as Revolutionary Architect." *Journal of the Society of Architectural Historians,* XXXIV (Dec. 1975), 257-79. Argues that Fiske Kimball's interpretation of Jefferson as "the patron saint" of "turn-of-the-century, reactionary heroes in the triumph of 'the American classic'" is incorrect. In the process, the author describes several of the public buildings designed by Jefferson.

Pierson, William H., Jr. *American Buildings and Their Architects.* Garden City, N.Y.: Doubleday, 1970-1972. 4 vols. Illustrations, plans, and biographical references.

Place, Charles A. *Charles Bulfinch, Architect and Citizen.* Boston: Houghton Mifflin Company, 1925. xiv + 294 pp. Illustrations and maps.

Pomerantz, Sidney I. *New York, an American City, 1783-1803: A Study of Urban Life.* See chapter on "Community Water Supply."

Potter, Merle. "The North Dakota Capital Fight." *North Dakota Historical Quarterly,* VII (Oct. 1932), 25-36. The story of Bismarck's efforts to keep the capital.

Price, Edward T. "The Central Courthouse Square in the American County Seat." *Geographical Review,* 58 (Jan. 1968), 29-60.

Public Works Administration. *America Builds: The Record of TVA.* See chapter on "Planning, Engineering, and Administration."

Radoff, Morris L. *Buildings of the State of Maryland at Annapolis.* Annapolis: Hall of Records Commission, State of Maryland, 1954. xi + 140 pp. Illustrations, notes, appendix, and index. A "documentary account of the life of public buildings" erected by the state of Maryland since 1695.

Radoff, Morris L. *The County Courthouses and Records of Maryland: Part One—The Courthouses.* Annapolis: Hall of Records Commission, State of Maryland, 1960. xiv + 175 pp. Illustrations, notes, and index. Presents historical descriptions of Maryland's county courthouses. There is a second volume, "Part Two," which is a catalogue of the records held in these courthouses.

Radoff, Morris Leon. *The State House at Annapolis.* Annapolis: Hall of Records Commission, State of Maryland, 1972. xiii + 128 pp. Illustrations.

Randall, Frank A. *History of the Development of Building Construction in Chicago.* Urbana: University of Illinois Press, 1949. xvi + 388 pp. Illustrations, map, appendix, and indexes. A general survey (1830-1948) by an experienced structural engineer. Encyclopedic in nature, the volume contains innumerable facts on the history of structures, foundation engineering and construction methods, builders, and planners in separately labeled paragraphs.

Rath, Frederick L., and Merrilyn Rodgers O'Connell. *A Bibliography on Historical Organization Practices: Historic Preservation.* Nashville, Tenn.: American Association for State and Local History, 1975. ix + 141 pp. Appendix and index. An excellent guide to sources for planners, public works practitioners, preservationists, and conservationists. The bibliography is annotated and includes chapters on "Historic Preservation in Perspective," "Preservation Law," "Urban Development and Redevelopment," "Preservation Research and Planning," and "Preservation Action."

Rathjen, Frederick W. "The Texas State House: A Study of the Building of the Texas Capitol Based on Reports of the Capitol Building Commissioners." *Southwestern Historical Quarterly,* 60 (April 1957), 433-62.

Read, Charles F. "The Old State House, and Its Predecessor the First Town House." *Proceedings of the Bostonian Society* (Jan. 14, 1908), 32-50. A short history of two public buildings—the first was constructed in 1658 and destroyed by fire in 1711; the second was completed in 1713.

Regenery, Dorothy F. *An Enduring Heritage: Historic Buildings of the San Francisco Peninsula.* Stanford: Stanford University Press, viii + 124 pp. Illustrations, bibliography, and index.

Reinders, Robert C. *End of an Era: New Orleans, 1850-1860.* New Orleans: Pelican Publishing Company, 1964. xiv + 254 pp. Illustrations, maps, notes, and index. Includes chapters on the city's architecture and wharf as well as brief discussions of its water and sewer systems.

Reps, John W. *Cities of the American West: A History of Frontier Urban Planning.* See chapter on "Planning, Engineering, and Administration."

Reps, John W. *The Making of Urban America: A History of City Planning in the United States.* See chapter on "Planning, Engineering, and Administration."

Reechie, Nancy Ann. "Ohio Courthouses: An Analysis of Representative Nineteenth-Century Architectural Styles." Master's thesis, University of Virginia, 1976.

Richmond, Robert W. "Kansas Builds a Capitol." *Kansas Historical Quarterly,* XXXVIII (Autumn 1972), 249-67. From 1866, when the legislature appropriated funds "for the creation of a State House," until 1903, when the state paid its final voucher. The article describes construction plans, finances, and operations as well as the politics involved in completing the project. Numerous fine illustrations accompany the text.

Richmond, Robert W. "The First Capitol of Kansas." *Kansas Historical Quarterly,* XXI (Spring 1955), 321-25. On the "large stone warehouse" built in Pawnee in 1855.

Riley, Edward M. "Philadelphia, the Nation's Capital, 1790-1800." *Pennsylvania History,* XX (Oct. 1953), 357-79. Recounts attempt to retain its status as the nation's capital through a grand building program.

Riley, Edward M. "The Colonial Courthouses of York County, Virginia." *William and Mary College Quarterly,* 22 (Oct. 1942), 299-414. Presents a brief history of the four courthouses and their associated buildings erected on one lot in Yorktown since 1697. Much of the information for this article came from historical research and from an archeological investigation conducted by the National Park Service in 1941.

Ring, Daniel F. "The Cleveland Public Library

and the WPA: A Study in Creative Partnership. *Ohio History,* 84 (Summer 1975), 158-64. Discusses at length the bibliography and fine arts projects funded by the Works Progress Administration. The article refers only to the $67,500 from the Public Works Administration to aid in financing the construction of new library buildings.

Risley, Mary. *House of Healing: The Story of the Hospital.* Garden City, N.Y.: Doubleday & Company, 1961. 288 pp. Illustrations and index. A general narrative on the development of hospitals in the world. There is one chapter on "Hospitals in the U.S.A."

Rissler, Howard F. "The State Capitol, 1837-1876." *Journal of the Illinois State Historical Society,* LXI (Winter 1968), 397-430. Presents a brief history and highlights Abraham Lincoln's role in the building's construction.

Roberts, O. M. "The Capitols of Texas." *Quarterly of the Texas State Historical Association,* 11 (Oct. 1898), 117-23. Only pieces of information on the capitol buildings.

Robertson, James I., Jr. "Old Capitol: Eminence to Infamy." *Maryland Historical Magazine,* 65 (Winter 1970), 394-412. On the sixty-year life of the Old Capitol. It first served as the nations' capitol (until 1819); it was then used as a school, a fashionable hotel, and finally a prison.

Robinson, Charles Mulford. *The Improvement of Towns and Cities: Or the Practical Basis of Civic Aesthetics.* See chapter on "Planning, Engineering, and Administration."

Robinson, Erik. "Henry Ford and the Postville Courthouse." *Historic Illinois,* 3 (Oct. 1980), 1-3, 13-15. A short history of the courthouse and an explanation of how Ford's purchase reflects preservation ideas of the 1920s.

Robinson, John Beverley. "The School Buildings of New York." *Architectural Record,* VII (Jan.-March 1889), 359-84. Descriptions and illustrations of some of New York City's old school buildings.

Robinson, Michael C. "People in Public Works: Benjamin Henry Latrobe." *APWA Reporter,* 47 (Dec. 1980), 4-6. A brief biographical sketch emphasizing Latrobe's architectural and engineering genius.

Robinson, Michael C. "People in Public Works: Robert Mills." *APWA Reporter,* 45 (March 1978), 4-5. A biographical sketch of the state engineer and architect of South Carolina who later became federal architect and engineer of the United States. The Washington Monument was Mills' most important work.

Robinson, Willard B. "Military Architecture at Mobile Bay." *Journal of the Society of Architectural Historians,* XXX (May 1971), 119-39. Gives special attention to Fort Conde, Fort Charlotte, Fort Morgan, and Fort Gaines.

Robinson, Willard B. "The Public Square as a Determinant of Courthouse Form in Texas." *Southwestern Historical Quarterly,* LXXV (Jan. 1972), 339-72. A thought-provoking article on the influence of the square in determining the form of Texas courthouses. Numerous photographs accompany the text.

Roderick, Terry. "History of the Old Colony House at Newport: As Recorded by Early and Modern Writers." *Bulletin of the Newport Historical Society,* 63 (Oct. 1927), 1-36. From the early eighteenth century.

Roper, Daniel C. *The United States Post Office: Its Past Record, Present Condition, and Potential Relation to the New World Era.* New York: Funk & Wagnalls, 1917.

Rosenberger, Homer T. "Thomas Ustick Walter and the Completion of the United States Capitol." *Records of the Columbia Historical Society of Washington, D.C.* (1948-1950), 273-322. A lengthy article describing Walter's work (1851-1865) as architect of the Capitol Extension.

Rosenthal, Alfred. *Venture into Space: Early Years of the Goddard Space Flight Center.* Washington, D.C.: National Aeronautics and Space Administration, 1968, xvi + 354 pp. Illustrations, tables, charts, bibliography, appendices, and index.

Roth, Leland M. *A Concise History of American Architecture.* New York: Harper and Row, 1979. xxvi + 399 pp. Illustrations, chronology, glossary, bibliography, and index. Good text that covers conceptual imagery, style, building technology, and town planning theory.

Ruchelman, Leonard I. *The World Trade Center: Politics and Policies of Skyscraper Development.* Syracuse: Syracuse University, 1977. ix + 176 pp. Illustrations, tables, notes, appendices, and index. Underscores the panoply of factors involved in planning the construction of high-rise public buildings. By focusing on the World Trade Center (construction began in 1966) in New York City, the author provides a trenchant case study of how decision-making—proposing, planning, modifying, and implementing a large building project—affects or is responsive to fundamental societal concerns.

Rudd, J. William, comp. *Historic American Buildings Survey: Chicago and Nearby Illinois Areas.* Park Forest, Ill.: Prairie School Press, 1966. iv + 52 pp. Illustrations and indexes. A list which includes records of 307 historic buildings, "represented by 243 measured drawings, 600 photographs, 612 data pages, and 216 inventory forms."

Rush, Richard. "To California with Love." *Progressive Architecture* (Nov. 1979), 88-93. On the restoration of the California State Capitol. The first page presents a short history of the structure.

Ryan, William, and Desmond Guiness. *The White House: An Architectural History.* New York: McGraw-Hill Book Company, 1980. x + 196 pp. Illustrations, diagrams, notes, bibliography, and index. A lavishly illustrated look at the most famous residence in the United States. The volume vividly describes the design, construction, and present condition of the executive mansion.

Salley, Alexander S. *The State House of South Carolina, 1751-1936.* Columbia, S.C.: Cary Printing Company, 1937. 39 pp. Illustrations.

Sawyer, Philip. "The Design of Public Buildings." *Architectural Forum,* LV (Sept. 1931), 257-64. Describes general trends since the early nineteenth century.

Saylor, Henry H. *The AIA's First Hundred Years.* Washington, D.C.: American Association of Architects, 1957.

Schneider, Norris F. *Y Bridge City: The Story of Zanesville and Muskingum County Ohio.* See chapter on "Roads, Streets, and Highways."

Schuyler, Montgomery. "The New Custom House at New York." *Architectural Record,* XX (July 1906), 1-14. Compares it to the old custom house on Wall Street.

Schwartz, Alvin. *Museum: The Story of America's Treasure Houses.* New York: E.P. Dutton & Co., Inc., 1967. 256 pp. Illustrations, notes, and index. Describes in general the history and practices of art, history, natural history, and science and industry museums. There is information on how they are financed but little on the physical facilities.

Schwartz, Nancy B., comp. *District of Columbia Catalog, 1974.* Charlottesville: University Press of Virginia, 1974. xliii + 193 pp. Illustrations, diagrams, appendices, and index. A guide to the Historic American Buildings Survey's documentary records for over 350 buildings—standing or demolished—in the District of Columbia. The catalog contains a brief description and gives the exact street location for all of the listed buildings.

Schwartz, Sally. "The Old State House: A Study of its Origins and Construction." *Delaware History,* XVII (Spring-Summer 1977), 179-90. A history of a public building in Dover, Delaware, which was originally planned to be the Kent County courthouse.

Scully, Arthur, Jr. *James Dakin, Architect: His Career in New York and the South.* Baton Rouge: Louisiana State University Press, 1973. xiv + 208 pp. Illustrations, notes, bibliography, and index. A biographical study of one of the major American architects of the early nineteenth century. The author gives special attention to Dakin's work in New Orleans, Mobile, and Baton Rouge.

Scully, Vincent. *American Architecture and Urbanism.* New York: Praeger Publishers, 1975. 275 pp. Illustrations, bibliography, and index. A "critical essay" on the history of architecture in which individual buildings are examined as part of an urban environment. The author agrees that "there is no difference between architecture and city planning." The book was first published in 1969.

Sener, William. "Thomas U. Walter and His Works." *Americana,* XXXIII (April 1939), 151-79. A biographical sketch of a prominent nineteenth-century architect who, as architect of the United States (1851), planned and executed extension of the Capitol Buildings. His first important commission as architect (1832) was for the Philadelphia County Prison.

Sexton, R. W., ed. *American Public Buildings of Today: City Halls—Court Houses—Municipal Buildings—Fire Stations—Libraries—Museums—Park Buildings.* New

York: Architectural Book Publishing Company, 1931. ii + 209 pp. Illustrations and floor plan drawings. A collection of essays, set within an historical framework, on the following subjects: the design of municipal buildings and their influence in setting standards in architectural art; architectural lighting of public buildings; museum trends; library planning; and buildings in public parks.

Shambaugh, Benj. F. "The Founding of Iowa City." *Palimpsest,* XX (May 1939), 137-76. See especially "Surveying the Capital Site," "A Plan for the Capitol," and "John F. Rague: Architect."

Shank, Wesley I. *The Iowa Catalog: Historic American Buildings Survey*. Iowa City: University of Iowa Press, 1979. xiii + 158 pp. Illustrations, map, diagrams, notes, bibliographical essay, appendix, and index. A list of buildings in Iowa recorded by the Historic American Buildings Survey (HABS) from 1933 to 1977. Each entry in the book gives a concise physical description and historical account and lists the number of HABS records for the structure. A fine essay on "Historic Architecture in Iowa" precedes the catalog proper.

Shannon, M.A.S. "Charles Bulfinch, the First American Architect." *Architecture,* LII (Dec. 1925), 431-36. A biographical sketch which highlights Bulfinch's public architecture in Massachusetts (state capitol building) and Boston.

Sheridan, Genevieve Rose. "The Art and Architecture of the Library of Congress." Doctoral dissertation, George Washington University, 1977. 226 pp.

Short, C. W., and R. Stanley-Brown. *Public Buildings: A Survey of Architecture of Projects Constructed by Federal and Other Governmental Bodies between the Years 1933 and 1939 with the Assistance of the Public Works Administration.* Washington, D.C.: Government Printing Office, 1939. xxiii + 697 pp. Illustrations, tables, diagrams, and index. An absolute "must" for anyone conducting research on the work of the Public Works Administration (PWA). This volume presents photographs, drawings, and detailed descriptions of "the best examples of the different types of buildings and other structures" constructed by PWA during the 1930s. They include local government buildings, auditoriums and armories, libraries, schools, college and university buildings, hospitals and penal institutions, warehouses and docks, sewage disposal plants, recreational buildings, waterworks, light and power plants, airfields and hangars, dams, bridges and highways, army and navy posts, post offices, and public housing. The information in this book is based on a report made for President Franklin D. Roosevelt in May 1939. The authors were members of the "Committee on Architectural Surveys" which prepared the report.

Skramstad, Harold K. "The Engineer as Architect in Washington: The Contribution of Montgomery Meigs." *Records of the Columbia Historical Society of Washington, D.C.* (1969-1970), 266-84. An excellent article describing and reflecting on Meigs' contributions to the physical development of the nation's capital. There are detailed summaries of his work on the Washington Aqueduct, the National Museum Building, and the Pension Building.

Slauson, Allan B., ed. *A History of the City of Washington: Its Men and Institutions.* Washington, D.C.: Washington Post Co., 1903. 481 pp. Illustrations and index. Contains individual chapters on the White House, Capitol, Washington's libraries, and parks.

Smalley, E. V. "The White House." *Century Magazine,* XXVII (April 1884), 803-15. A descriptive essay, accompanied by sketches, of one of the United States' most recognized buildings. The White House's history is presented in a popular manner.

Smith, Darrell Hevenor. *The Office of the Supervising Architect of the Treasury: Its History, Activities, and Organization.* Baltimore: John Hopkins Press, 1923. xii + 138 pp. Tables, notes, appendices, bibliography, and index. The first chapter reviews the agency's history, beginning in the early nineteenth century when the office was charged "with the construction and maintenance of public buildings under the jurisdiction of the Treasury Department."

Snow, Cordelia Thomas. "A Brief History of the Palace of the Governors & a Preliminary Report on the 1974 Excavation." *El Palacio,* 80 (Fall 1974), 6-22. On a national historic landmark located in Santa Fe and often said to be the oldest public building in the United States.

Steelman, John R. "The White House." *Records of the Columbia Historical Society of Washington, D.C. (1948-1950)*, 205-13. A short history by the assistant to the President of the United States.

Stillman, Damie. "New York City Hall: Competition and Execution." *Journal of the Society of Architectural Historians,* XXIII (Oct. 1964), 129-42. Beginning in February 1802. The article describes this public building as "a beautiful structure, sensitively designed and finely detailed," and the circumstances surrounding its execution as "indicative of the architectural climate in the new United States."

Sturgis, Russell. "The New Library of Congress: A Study in Decorative Architecture." *Architectural Record,* VII (Jan.-March 1898), 295-332. A detailed description of the plans for the building and the completed structure from 1888. There are numerous drawings and illustrations.

Susskind, Charles. *Understanding Technology.* See chapter on "Planning, Engineering, and Administration."

Tallmadge, Thomas E. "A Once Famous Competition, Now Forgotten." *Illinois Society of Architects Monthly Bulletin,* 24 (Aug.-Sept. 1939), 6-7. On the competition to rebuild Chicago's Courthouse after the 1871 fire.

Tatum, George B. *Penn's Great Town: 250 Years of Philadelphia Architecture Illustrated in Prints and Drawings.* Philadelphia: University of Pennsylvania Press, 1961. 352 pp. Illustrations, notes to illustrations, bibliography, and index. A richly illustrated history of "Philadelphia buildings and the men who built them."

Thayer, R. H., comp. *History, Organization, and Functions of the Office of the Supervising Architect of the Treasury Department. . . .* Washington, D.C.: U.S. Government Printing Office, 1886. 54 pp.

"The Almanac of Significant Events in Building a Greater America, 1874-1949." *Engineering News-Record.* See chapter on "Planning, Engineering, and Administration."

"The Most Magnificent City Hall in the World." *Municipal Journal and Engineer,* XI (July 1901), 1-4. Describes the thirty-year construction period and the nearly completed city hall of Philadelphia.

"The Razing and Reconstruction of the Old State Capitol: A Brief Record in Pictures." *Journal of the Illinois State Historical Society,* LXI (WInter 1968), 443-52. Gives a brief history of the building and illustrates major stages in its razing and reconstruction since January 1966.

"The Work of Messrs. Carère & Hastings." *Architectural Record,* XXVII (Jan. 1970), 1-120. Includes brief descriptions and illustrations of several public buildings—Paterson (N.J.) City Hall, New York Public Library, Senate Office Building, Brooklyn Bridge Terminal, etc.

Thom, DeCourcy W. "The Old Senate Chamber." *Maryland Historical Magazine,* XXV (Dec. 1930), 365-84. In the Maryland State House (1772).

Thompson, Neil B. *Minnesota's State Capitol: The Art and Politics of a Public Building.* St. Paul: Minnesota Historical Society, 1974. 100 pp. Illustrations, notes, appendix, and index. Brilliant case study of the design and political aspects of public architecture.

Torres, Louis. "Federal Hall Revisited." *Journal of the Society of Architectural Historians,* XXIX (Dec. 1970), 327-38. A precise history and description of New York City's Federal Hall, "one of the finest examples of architecture of the Federal Period."

Torres, Louis. "John Frazee and the New York Custom House." *Journal of the Society of Architectural Historians,* XXIII (Oct. 1964), 143-50. Describes Frazee's work following his appointment, at a critical time, to the position of "Architect and Superintendent" (1835).

Tower, Edward M. "American Architectural Heritage." *Military Engineer,* 68 (May-June 1976), 207-09.

Treon, John A. "Politics and Concrete: The Building of the Arkansas State Capitol, 1899-1917." *Arkansas Historical Quarterly,* XXXI (Summer 1972), 99-133. Shows how "the erection of Arkansas's Capitol Building caused the downfall of a score of politicians, resulted in the imprisonment of a state senator, damaged the reputation of a nationally-prominent architect, and brought economic ruin to a building contractor." The article is followed by an appendix prepared by George R. Mann, the architect of the Arkansas State Capitol Building from 1899 to 1909.

Tubesing, Richard L. *Architectural Preservation in the United States, 1965-1974: A Bibliography of Federal, State and Local Government*

Publications. Monticello, Ill.: Council of Planning Librarians, 1975. 93 pp. There are four main sections: "Architectural Preservation," "Historic Sites Registers," "Historic Structures" (many are public buildings), and "Preservation Legislation." The bibliography is not annotated.

Tunnard, Christopher, and Henry Hope Reed. *American Skylines: The Growth and Form of Our Cities and Towns.* See chapter on "Planning, Engineering, and Administration."

U.S. Commission of Fine Arts and the Historic American Buildings Survey. *Georgetown Architecture—The Waterfront.* Washington, D.C.: U.S. Department of the Interior, National Park Service, 1968. iii + 297 pp. Illustrations, map, diagrams, and appendix. Documents buildings on Georgetown's waterfront.

U.S. Congress. House of Representatives. *Documentary History of the Construction and Development of the United States Capitol Building and Grounds. Report No. 646, 58th Congress, 2d Session.* Washington, D.C.: Government Printing Office, 1904. iv + 1312 pp. Illustrations, maps, and index. A collection of official documents including statutes, reports, debates, and correspondence, relating to the history of the building and development of the Capitol.

U.S. Department of the Treasury. *A History of Public Buildings under the Control of the Treasury Department.* Washington: Government Printing Office, 1901. 648 pp. Illustrations and index. A useful and comprehensive collection of historical sketches of various public buildings (exclusive of marine hospitals and quarantine stations) operated by the Treasury Department. The sketches are arranged alphabetically by states and cities. Most of the buildings described are courthouses, custom houses, and post offices.

U.S. Department of the Treasury. *Supervising Architect's Office.* *Annual Report of the Supervising Architect of the Treasury.* Washington, D.C.: U.S. Government Printing Office, 1866-1939.

U.S. General Services Administration. *Agriculture Administration Building.* Washington, D.C.: U.S. Government Printing Office, 1964. Number 2 in the Historical Building Study series.

U.S. General Services Administration. *Executive Office Building.* Washington, D.C.: U.S. Government Printing Office, 1972. Number 3 in the Historical Building Study series.

U.S. General Services Administration. *Galveston Custom House.* Washington, D.C.: U.S. Government Printing Office, 1973. Number 4 in the Historical Building Study series.

U.S. General Services Administration. *Pension Building.* Washington, D.C.: U.S. Government Printing Service, 1964. Number 1 in the Historical Building Study series.

Van Neste, W. Lane, and Virgil E. Baugh, comps. *Preliminary Inventory of the Records of the Public Buildings Service.* Washington, D.C.: U.S. General Services Administration, National Archives and Records Service, 1958.

Virginia Historic Landmarks Commission and Historic American Buildings Survey. *Virginia Catalog: A List of Measured Drawings, Photographs, and Written Documents in the Survey.* Charlottesville: University Press of Virginia, 1976. xii + 461 pp. Illustrations, maps, and diagrams. Lists records on more than 3,800 structures (both public and private) in Virginia. The book is divided into the catalog proper (over 900 entries) and the inventory (about 2,900 entries). Buildings listed in the catalog tend to be more completely recorded and documented than those in the inventory.

Vyzralek, Frank E.; H. Roger Grant; and Charles Bohi. "North Dakota's Railroad Depots: Standardization on the Soo Line." *North Dakota History,* 42 (Winter 1975), 4-26. A study of the North Dakota depot building used by the Soo Line and its precedessor. Like many western roads, the Soo Line developed a simple classification system for its most popular standardized station plans, based largely on size.

Waddell, Gene. "Robert Mills's Fireproof Building." *South Carolina Historical Magazine,* 80 (April 1979), 105-35. Completed in 1825-1826 in Charleston, South Carolina. A thorough discussion of Mills' plan and finished structure, accompanied by numerous drawings and illustrations.

Wade, Michael Glen. "David Reichard Williams: Avant-Garde Architect and Community Planner, 1890-1962." Doctoral dissertation, University of Southwestern Louisiana, 1978. ix

+ 440 pp. Illustrations, diagrams, notes, and bibliography. Describes Williams' "positive influence" on government architecture during the 1930s and 1940s. In Washington he served as chief of the Federal Emergency Relief Administration's Community Building Program and then as director of the Division of Work Projects in the National Youth Administration; during the war, he supervised the building of defense housing for the federal works agency.

Warner, John De Witt. "Civic Centers." *Municipal Affairs,* VI (March 1902), 1-23. A sketchy look at the benefits that have accrued to cities in ancient and modern times that have built civic centers.

Watson, Alan D. "County Fiscal Policy in Colonial North Carolina." *North Carolina Historical Review,* LV (July 1978), 284-305. Reviews the fiscal affairs of county government in colonial North Carolina and shows that public buildings—courthouses; jails plus pillories, stocks, and whipping posts; and warehouses—absorbed "a large proportion of county disbursements."

Webb, Todd, and Willard B. Robinson. *Texas Public Buildings of the Nineteenth Century.* Austin: University of Texas Press for the Amon Carter Museum of Western Art, 1974. xiv + 290 pp. Illustrations, notes, glossary, bibliography, and index. The result of a survey of Texas' historic buildings conducted by the school of architecture at the University of Texas at Austin.

Weber, Gustavus A., and Laurence F. Schmeckebier. *The Veterans' Administration: Its History, Activities, and Organization.* Washington, D.C.: Brookings Institution, 1934. xi + 490 pp. Tables, notes, appendices, bibliography, and index. Records the agency's history and contains a good deal of information on the homes and hospitals for which the administration is responsible.

Weigley, Russell F. "Captain Meigs and the Artists of the Capitol: Federal Patronage of Art in the 1850s." *Records of the Columbia Historical Society of Washington, D.C.* (1969-1970), 285-305. From 1853 when Meigs was appointed supervising engineer of the United States Capitol.

Weigley, Russell Frank. "M. C. Meigs: Builder of the Capitol and Lincoln's Quartermaster General: A Biography." Doctoral dissertation, University of Pennsylvania, 1956. Deals principally with Meigs' role as the designer of the Capitol and his work as quartermaster general during the Civil War.

Welch, June Rayfield, and J. Larry Nance. *The Texas Courthouse.* Dallas: GLA Press, 1971. iii + 342 pp. Illustrations and bibliography.

Whatley, Larry. "The Works Progress Administration in Mississippi." *Journal of Mississippi History,* XXX (Feb. 1968), 35-50. Deals primarily with the political and press reaction to the program. However, it does summarize WPA activities with respect to public buildings, roads and streets, parks, sewer systems, and airports.

Wheeler, Joseph L., and Alfred Githens. *The American Public Library Building: Its Planning and Design with Special Reference to its Administration and Service.* New York: Charles Scribner's Sons, 1941. 484 pp. Illustrations and index. Only the first chapter discusses the evolution of the library as a public facility.

Wheeler, Kenneth W. *To Wear a City's Crown: The Beginnings of Urban Growth in Texas, 1836-1865.* See chapter on "Community Water Supply."

Whiffen, Marcus. "The Early County Courthouses of Virginia." *Journal of the Society of Architectural Historians,* XVIII (March 1959), 2-10.

Whiffen, Marcus. *The Public Buildings of Williamsburg: Colonial Capital of Virginia.* Williamsburg: Colonial Williamsburg, 1958. xvi + 269 pp. Illustrations, diagrams, notes, bibliography, and index. A history of the public buildings of the colonial period at Williamsburg—"an attempt to tell how and why and through whom those buildings came to be what they were, to relate them to the architecture of contemporary England, and to show how they influenced the architecture of the rest of Virginia."

Whitaker, Charles Harris, and Harley Burr Alexander. *The Architectural Sculpture of the State Capitol at Lincoln, Nebraska. . . .* New York: Press of the American Institute of Architects, 1926. 16 pp. + 45 plates.

Whitaker, Charles Harris. "Our Stupid and Blundering National Policy of Providing Public Buildings." *AIA Journal,* 2 parts (Feb. and March 1916).

White, Theo. B. *Paul Phillips Cret: Architect and Teacher.* Philadelphia: Art Alliance Press, 1973. 94 pp. Illustrations, notes, bibliography, and index. Biography of the French-born architect who taught at the University of Pennsylvania, designed the Federal Reserve Board Building in Washington, D.C., and had a large influence on American building design.

Whitehall, Walter Muir. *Boston: A Topographical History.* See chapter on "Roads, Streets, and Highways."

Whitehall, Walter Muir. *Boston Public Library: A Centennial History.* Cambridge: Harvard University Press, 1956. x + 274 pp. Illustrations, tables, sources, appendix, and index. An institutional history of a pioneer library (1854).

Whitworth, Henry P., ed. *Carolina Architecture and Allied Arts: A Pictorial Review of Carolina's Representative Architecture.* Miami: Frederick Findeisen, 1939. 60 + 32A pp. Illustrations. Includes photographs and descriptive captions (particularly of construction materials and those who provided them) of some public buildings. The book was prepared mainly for architects and contractors.

Wilde, Edward S. "The New York City Hall." *Century Magazine,* XXVII (April 1884), 865-71. A detailed description (with sketches) of the city hall, based on the papers and reports of its architect, John McComb.

Williams, Marilyn Thornton. "New York City's Public Baths: A Case Study in Urban Progressive Reform." *Journal of Urban History,* 7 (Nov. 1980), 49-81. On New York City's public bath movement as an illustration of "yet another facet in urban progressivism"—environmental improvement.

Williams, Ralph Chester. *The United States Public Health Service, 1798-1950.* See chapter on "Sewers and Wastewater Treatment."

Wilson, Ben Hur. "The First Courthouse." *Palimpsest,* XX (Oct. 1939), 325-39. Describes the effort that went into building the Mount Pleasant courthouse (1840), "a handsome building at one time, and a matter of county pride."

Wilson, J. Appleton. "Restoration of the Senate Chamber." *Maryland Historical Magazine,* XXII (March 1927), 54-62. Beginning in 1876 (in Annapolis).

Wilson, Samuel, Jr., ed. *Impressions Respecting New Orleans by Benjamin Henry Boneval Latrobe: Diary & Sketches, 1818-1820.* New York: Columbia University Press, 1951. xxiv + 196 pp. Illustrations, maps, notes, appendices, and index. A beautifully illustrated monograph with an informative introduction on Latrobe's public works and architectural career. In the introduction, the editor gives special attention to Latrobe's work in New Orleans (pp. xiv-xxi contain a brief history of the city's waterworks). Throughout these published recollections, Latrobe comments on New Orleans' public buildings; one section is, in fact, entitled "Mode of Building in New Orleans; Public Buildings. . . ."

Wodehouse, Lawrence. "Alfred B. Mullett and His French Style Government Buildings." *Journal of the Society of Architectural Historians,* XXXI (March 1972), 22-37. A biographical sketch of Mullett (1834-1890) and an analysis of his work, particularly as supervising architect to the Treasury Department (1866-1874).

Wodehouse, Lawrence. *American Architects from the Civil War to the First World War.* Detroit: Gale Research Company, 1976. xii + 343 pp.

Wodehouse, Lawrence. *American Architects from the First World War to the Present.* Detroit: Gale Research Company, 1977. xiii + 305 pp.

Wodehouse, Lawrence. "Ammi Burnham Young, 1798-1874." *Journal of the Society of Architectural Historians,* XXV (Dec. 1966).

Wodehouse, Lawrence. "Frank Pierce Milburn (1868-1926), a Major Southern Architect." *North Carolina Historical Review,* L (July 1973), 289-303. A biographical sketch of Milburn's life and work. He designed many state capitol buildings, courthouses, schools, railway stations, etc. in states south of Washington, D.C.

Wodehouse, Lawrence. "John McArthur, Jr. (1823-1890)." *Journal of the Society of Architectural Historians,* XXVIII (Dec. 1969), 271-83. Describes several of McArthur's public buildings in Philadelphia in an attempt "to place Arthur and his designs in the context of other architects and their buildings of the 1860s, '70s, and '80s . . . ."

Wodehouse, Lawrence. "The Custom House, Galveston, Texas, 1857-1861, by Ammi Burnham Young." *Journal of the Society of Architectural Historians,* XXV (March 1966), 64-67.

Wood, Ernest. "A Radical Settles Down in Raleigh, N.C." *AIA Journal,* 69 (Sept. 1980), 54-61. Describes the architecture and symbolism of the Nowicki pavillion, located on the North Carolina State Fairgrounds, and gives a brief history of the structure.

Wood, Richard G. "The Marine Hospital at Napoleon." *Arkansas Historical Quarterly,* XIV (Spring 1955), 38-42. On Army Officer Stephen Harriman Long and the construction of a hospital for merchant seamen at Napoleon, Arkansas (1848).

Woodford, Frank B. *Parnassus on Main Street: A History of the Detroit Public Library.* Detroit: Wayne State University Press, 1965. 487 pp. Illustrations, notes, and appendices. Describes the library's (1865) role in enriching the cultural and intellectual life of Detroit's citizens.

Works Progress Administration. *Inventory: An Appraisal of the Results of the Works Progress Administration.* Washington, D.C.: Works Progress Administration, 1938. 100 pp. Illustrations. Overview of WPA activities including the construction of public buildings and other works.

Writer's Program, Works Project Administration, State of North Carolina. *Raleigh: Capital of North Carolina.* Raleigh: Sesquicentennial Commission, 1942. x + 170 pp. Illustrations, map, chronology, and index. A general history of the city with short historical sketches of numerous public buildings. One section of the narrative presents a history of "The State House."

Young, Edgar B. *Lincoln Center: The Building of an Institution.* New York: New York University Press, 1980. xvi + 334 pp. Illustrations, notes, chronology, and index. Demonstrates how the private and public sectors can be partners in the creation of a magnificent cultural institution.

Zorn, Walter Lewis. *The Capitols of the United States of America.* Monroe, Mich.: By the author, 1955. v + 176 pp. Illustrations and index. Photographs, with enough text "to make the pictures intelligible," of the nation's state capitols.

Zueblin, Charles. *American Municipal Progress: Chapters in Municipal Sociology.* See chapter on "Planning, Engineering, and Administration."

12

Parks and Recreation

The history of parks in the United States is a dynamic story, characterized in large part by long struggles and eventual triumphs that have created a cornucopia of leisure opportunities. Early park initiatives in America can be traced to the colonists who first used open, public lands for grazing but later converted some of them into recreational places. By the late eighteenth and early nineteenth centuries, plazas, commons, squares, and village greens could be found in many of the larger cities. Since good park design was generally lacking, and few open spaces existed in congested urban areas, cemeteries frequently became popular park settings. Two nineteenth-century events—the creation of Central Park in the heart of New York City in 1856 and the establishment of Yellowstone National Park by the federal government in 1872—had considerable influence on the United States' park movement and contributed significantly to its subsequent growth and strength.

In 1976, when the nation celebrated its bicentennial, more than 2,700 municipalities had programs involving 805,000 acres of parks and recreational areas within their boundaries. Counties had also developed extensive programs, particularly in the East. State park and recreational organizations administered 3,550 parks, totaling 8.9 million acres in scenic areas, recreational forests, and sites of historical significance. The federal government's involvement in establishing and managing more than 300 separate park programs further demonstrated the national importance and magnitude of parks and recreational areas.

The following books, articles, and dissertations offer information and insight into the development of local, state, and federal efforts to improve the quality of life and the general well-being of Americans by providing them with public parks and recreational facilities. Historical material on monuments is also included.

Abbot, Arthur P. *The Greatest Park in the World, Palisades Interstate Park: Its Purposes, History and Achievements*. New York: Historian Publishing Company, 1914. 64 pp. Illustrations and maps. On New York-New Jersey's Palisades Interstate Park.

Abbott, Carl. "The Active Force: Enos A. Mills and the National Park Movement." *Colorado Magazine*, 56 (Winter/Spring 1979), 56-73. Examines the career of a Colorado "naturalist, businessman, and campaigner for national parks" during the first decades of the twentieth century. Abbott highlights Mills accomplishments in the conservation field but shows how these achievements were "marred by conflicting aims and an aggressive self-importance."

Adams, Ansel. *There We Inherit: The Parklands of America*. San Francisco: Sierra Club, 1962. 103 pp. Illustrations and notes. A tribute in photographs to the nation's parks.

Agee, James K. "Issues and Impacts of Redwood National Park Expansion. *Environmental Management,* 4 (1980), 407–23. Describes especially the movement to expand the park (1968–1978).

Alberts, Robert C. *The Shaping of the Point: Pittsburgh's Renaissance Park.* Pittsburgh: University of Pittsburgh Press, 1980. xvi + 247 pp. Illustrations, notes, bibliographical essay, and index. Centers on the design and construction of a thirty-six-acre park at the Point, where two rivers meet to form the Ohio. According to the author, the park was "where civic leaders, politicians, city planners, architects, landscape designers, traffic engineers, academic historians, and several motivated interest groups fought for their theories, their aesthetic principles, and their claimed rights."

Albright, Horace M. "Harding, Coolidge, and the Lady Who Lost Her Dress." *American West*, VI (Sept. 1969), 24-32. The former superintendent of Yellowstone National Park (1919-1929) recalls famous visitors to the park as well as administrative problems during the 1920s.

Albright, Horace M. "Harlan Page Kelsey." *National Parks Magazine*, 33 (Feb. 1959), 12-13. A sketch of Kelsey's career, emphasizing his promotion of national parks in New England, North Carolina, Tennessee, and Virginia.

Albright, Horace M. "John D. Rockefeller, Jr." *National Parks Magazine*, 35 (April 1961). Describes Rockefeller's philanthropy to national parks.

Albright, Horace M., and Frank J. Taylor. *'Oh, Ranger!' A Book about the National Parks*. New York: Dodd, Mead & Company, 1941. xiv + 272 pp. Illustrations and index. Includes a chapter on the history of the national parks by the director (Albright) of the National Park Service from 1929 to 1933.

Albright, Horace M. *Origins of the National Park Service Administration of Historic Sites*. Philadelphia: Eastern National Park and Monument Association, 1971. 24 pp.

Albright, Horace Marden. "The Great and Near-Great in Yellowstone." *Montana: The Magazine of Western History*, XXII (Summer 1972), 80-89. Recollections of noteworthy park visitors and particular administrative problems from 1913 to 1929.

American Society of Landscape Architects. "Minute on the Life and Services of Charles Mulford Robinson, Associate Member." *Landscape Architecture*. See chapter on "Planning, Engineering, and Administration."

Armstrong, Chester H., comp. *History of the Oregon State Parks, 1917-1963*. Salem: Oregon State Highway Department, Parks Division, 1965. x + 268 pp. Illustrations, maps, and tables. A general history of the state parks movement with individual sketches of Oregon's state parks.

Armstrong, Ellis L.; Michael C. Robinson; and Suellen M. Hoy, eds. *History of Public Works in the United States, 1776-1976*. See chapter on "Planning, Engineering, and Administration."

Athearn, Robert G. *High County Empire: The High Plains and Rockies*. New York: McGraw-Hill, 1960. viii + 360 pp. Illustrations, maps, notes, and bibliography. Chapter 12 contains some historical information on the National Park Service and its effect on the upper Missouri River region.

Augspurger, Marie M. *Yellowstone National Park: Historical and Descriptive*. Middletown, Ohio: Naegele-Auer Printing Co., 1948. xxxi + 247 pp. Illustrations, bibliography, and index. A popular history of Yellowstone National Park by one, who at an early age, was impressed by its majesty and grandeur.

Bade, William Frederic. *The Life and Letters of John Muir*. 2 vols. Cambridge: Riverside Press, 1924. Vol. I: ix + 399 pp.; Vol. II: iv + 454 pp. Illustrations, notes, and index. A biography and selected writings of Muir (1838-1914), the California wilderness preservationist and founder of the Sierra Club.

Bain, Kenneth R.; Rob Phillips; and Paul D. Travis. "Benson Park: Shawnee Citizens at Leisure in the Early Twentieth Century." *Chronicles of Oklahoma*, LVII (Summer 1979), 164-70. A brief historical sketch, with several photographs, of a park that no longer exists. It was once the property of the Interurban Railway Company that operated the Shawnee streetcars.

Baker, M. N. *Municipal Engineering and Sanitation*. See chapter on "Planning, Engineering, and Administration."

Baker, Paul R. *Richard Morris Hunt*. Cambridge: MIT Press, 1980. xvi + 588 pp. Illustrations, notes, appendix, bibliography, and index. A biography of an individual who was known as the dean of American architects in the latter part of the nineteenth century. Hunt's work was varied; he designed buildings for private, commercial, and public purposes. Several of the monuments and memorials he designed "helped forward the renewed unifying nationalism which followed the Civil War and Reconstruction." Whole chapters are devoted to "The Central Park Gateways," "Monuments and Memorials," "Public Work in the Early Nineties," and "The Chicago Fair."

Baldridge, Kenneth W. "Nine Years of Achievement: The Civilian Conservation Corps in Utah." Doctoral dissertation. See chapter on "Irrigation."

Baldwin, Kenneth H. *Enchanted Enclosure: The Army Engineers and Yellowstone National Park, A Documentary History*. Washington, D. C.: Office of the Chief of Engineers, U. S. Army, 1976. xiii + 111 pp. Illustrations, maps, and notes. A collection of the original reports "which tell the story . . . of the dedicated service of the Engineers to the cause of conservation." Corps engineers were among the first to explore the park area and were responsible for designing, building, and maintaining its roads.

Bartlett, Richard A. "From Imagination to Reality: Thomas Moran and the Yellowstone." *Prospects: An Annual of American Cultural Studies*, 3 (1977), 111-24. A description of painter Moran's Yellowstone work and an explanation of how "his treatment of its beauties reflects the American image of the scenic West in the period 1865-1900." This collection of essays is edited by Jack Salzman.

Bartlett, Richard A. *Nature's Yellowstone*. Albuquerque: University of New Mexico Press, 1974. xiii + 250 pp. Illustrations, map, notes, bibliography, and index. On the natural history of the Yellowstone area before 1872 and its establishment as a national park.

Bartlett, Richard A. "Those Infernal Machines in Yellowstone. . . ." *Montana: The Magazine of Western History*, XX (Summer 1970), 16-29. Describes the successful campaign to open Wyoming's Yellowstone National Park to automobiles in 1915 and its effect on traffic regulations and road maintenance.

Bartlett, Richard A. "Will Anyone Come Here for Pleasure?" *American West*, VI (Sept. 1969), 10-16. Presents the early history of Yellowstone National Park, emphasizing tourism and the 1883 visit of President Chester A. Arthur.

Bauer, Clyde Max. *Yellowstone—Its Underworld: Geology and Historical Anecdotes of Our Oldest National Park*. Albuquerque: University of New Mexico Press, 1948. x + 122 pp. Illustrations, maps, and bibliography. Some history of the park area since 1830 is included.

Baxter, Sylvester. "Architectural Features of the Boston Parks." 3 parts. *American Architect and Building News*, LXI (July 16, Aug. 13, Sept. 10, 1898), July: 19-20; Aug.: 51-52; Sept.: 83-84. Reviews and comments on bridges, gates, terraces, stairways, landings, fountains, statues, monuments, and buildings for shelter, refreshments, and administration in Boston's parks.

Beal, Merrill D. "A History of Yellowstone National Park." Doctoral dissertation, Washington State University, 1946. 341 pp.

Beal, Merrill D. *The Story of Man in Yellowstone*. Caldwell, Idaho: Caxton Printers, Ltd., 1949. 320 pp. Illustrations, maps, notes, appendices, bibliography, and index. A history of Yellowstone National Park with single chapters on the creation of the park, general administration, and the National Park Service. The volume emphasizes efforts to preserve the park's scenic beauty and wilderness. (The Yellowstone Library and Museum Association published revised editions in 1956 and 1960.)

Beard, Mary Ritter. *Woman's Work in Municipalities*. See chapter on "Solid Wastes."

Beasley, Betty A. "A Comparative Study of the Expansion of Park Facilities, Equipment, and Activities of the Dallas Park and Recreation Departments." Master's thesis, North Texas State College, 1950.

Bender, Thomas. "The 'Rural' Cemetery Movement: Urban Travail and the Appeal of

Nature." *New England Quarterly*, XLVII (June 1974), 196-211. Shows that mid-nineteenth-century cemeteries were used "more as pleasure grounds than as places for burial" and that they were "designed as counterbalances to the city."

Bigelow, Martha Mitchell. "Isle Royale National Park Movement or a Study in Frustrations." *Michigan History*, 41 (March 1957), 35-44. The effort (1921-1946) to create Isle Royale National Park in Michigan.

Bing, Richard. "George Washington's Monument." *Constructor*, LVIII (Dec. 1976), 18-25. Good historical summary of the construction of the Washington Monument accompanied by a choice selection of illustrations.

Blakelock, Chester R. "Four of Our State Parks." *Long Island Forum*, 12 (June 1949), 113-16. On the following state parks since 1924: Montauk Point, Hither Hills, Wildwood, and Sunken Meadow.

Blakelock, Chester R. "The Story of Bethpage State Park." *Long Island Forum*, 14 (March 1951), 43-44, 53-54. Located on Long Island, New York, since 1931.

Blatnik, John A. "Voyageurs—The Wilderness Park." *National Parks & Conservation Magazine*, 48 (Sept. 1974), 4-7. Includes some historical information on Voyageurs National Park, in Minnesota.

Blodgett, Geoffrey. "Frederick Law Olmsted: Landscape Architecture as Conservative Reform." *Journal of American History*, LXII (March 1976), 869-89. The author carefully examines Olmsted's view of society and the purpose of his parks. Openly elitist, he believed a park was a work of art whose primary benefits were "mainly visual and physic." He was, therefore, frequently unhappy with the public's failure to see the value of "highly contemplative" recreation as well as its plans for and use of Central Park.

Blohm, Ernest V. "Albert E. Sleeper State Park." *Michigan Conservation*, 23 (Sept.-Oct. 1953), 27-29. On the forests and lumber industry around Caseville, Michigan, and the establishment of a state park (1830-1953).

Board of Commissioners, Rochester, New York. *Report of the Board of Park Commissioners of the City of Rochester, N. Y., 1888 to 1898*. Rochester: Union and Advertiser Press, 1898. 109 pp. Illustrations and tables. Summarizes "the doings of the Park Board from the time of its organization" until 1898.

Boardman, Samuel H. "Oregon State Park System: A Brief History." *Oregon Historical Quarterly*, 55 (Sept. 1954), 179-233. Boardman, Oregon's state parks superintendent from 1929 to 1951, describes and gives the history of fifteen parks in the system.

Bonney, Orrin H. and Lorraine. *Battle Drums and Geysers: The Life and Journals of Lt. Gustavus Cheyney Doane, Soldier and Explorer of the Yellowstone and Snake River Regions*. Chicago: Swallow Press, 1970. xxv + 622 pp. Illustrations, maps, notes, appendices, bibliography, and index. A lengthy biography of the individual who led the small cavalry that accompanied General Henry D. Washburn's early expedition of Yellowstone. The "heart of the book deals with Doane's journal account of the famous 1870 expedition."

Bonney, Orrin H. and Lorraine. "Lieutenant G. C. Doane: His Yellowstone Exploration Journal." *Journal of the West*, IX (April 1970), 222-39. On the Washburn-Langford expedition which explored the Yellowstone region in 1870.

Bowers, Maynard O. *Through the Years in Glacier National Park: An Administrative History*. West Glacier, Mont.: Glacier Natural History Association, 1960. v + 111 pp. Illustrations, map, notes, and bibliography. Includes some history of the area.

Bradley, Harold C., and David R. Brower. "Roads in the National Parks." *Sierra Club Bulletin*. See chapter on "Roads, Streets, and Highways."

Bradley, Seth B. "The Origin of the Denver Mountain Parks System." *Colorado Magazine*, IX (Jan. 1932), 26-29. A summary of the beginnings of the Mountain Parks system (1910) by a Denver citizen.

Brayer, Herbert Oliver, ed. "Exploring the Yellowstone with Hayden, 1872: Diary of Sidford Hamp." *Annals of Wyoming*, 14 (Oct. 1942), 253-98. On an expedition which led to the creation of Yellowstone National Park.

Brockman, C. Frank. *Recreational Use of Wild Lands*. New York: McGraw-Hill Book Company, 1959. xii + 346 pp. Illustrations, maps, tables, bibliography, and index. A textbook that discusses the background, importance, values, and fundamental requirements of the recreational management of wild lands. One chapter is devoted to historical highlights of the recreational use of wild lands in state and national parks in relation to the conservation movement in the United States.

Brodeur, David D. "Evolution of the New England Town Common, 1630-1966." *Professional Geographer*, XIX (Nov. 1967), 313-19. The author shows that most "commons were not first conceived of as parks" but "actually derive from the original lot of the *first parish meetinghouse*."

Brower, J. V. *Itasca State Park: An Illustrated History*. St. Paul: Minnesota Historical Society, 1904. xxiii + 285 pp. Illustrations, maps, and index. Volume II in the Minnesota Historical Collections.

Brown, Glenn, comp. *Papers Relating to the Improvement of the City of Washington, District of Columbia*. See chapter on "Public Buildings."

Brown, James W. "The Administration of Law in Yellowstone National Park." *Wyoming Law Journal*, 14 (Fall 1959), 9-16. On the federal government's sole jurisdiction over the administration of justice in the park since 1872.

Brown, William H., ed. *History of Warren County, New York*. Glen Falls, N. Y.: Board of Supervisors of Warren County, 1963. 302 pp. Illustrations and maps. Includes a chapter on the Adirondack State Park.

Buchholtz, C. W. "No Trail Too Steep: The Dream and Reality of Recreation in Our Western National Parks." *Journal of the West*, XVII (July 1978), 95-108. A general review of the development of the western national park system and an examination of the changing concepts regarding the appropriate recreational use of these parks.

Buchholtz, Curtis W. "The Historical Dichotomy of Use and Preservation in Glacier National Park." Master's thesis, University of Montana, 1969.

Buchholtz, C. W. "The National Park as a Playground." *Journal of Sports History*, 5 (Winter 1978), 21-36. Describes the role of National Park Service officials and the influence of the automobile in determining methods of park visitation and in promoting recreational uses of national parks.

Buchholtz, Curtis W. "W. R. Logan and Glacier National Park." *Montana: The Magazine of Western History*, XIX (Summer 1969), 2-17.

Buck, Paul Herman. "The Evolution of the National Park System of the United States." Master's thesis, Ohio State University, 1922. 133 pp. Notes, appendices, and index. A concise history beginning with the establishment of Yellowstone National Park in 1872 and continuing to the early 1920s. The concluding chapter describes the "Functions of the National Park System."

Bureau of the Census (Department of Commerce and Labor). *Statistics of Cities Having a Population of 8,000 to 25,000: 1903*. See chapter on "Roads, Streets, and Highways."

Bureau of the Census (Department of Commerce and Labor). *Statistics of Cities Having a Population of 30,000: 1904*. See chapter on "Roads, Streets, and Highways."

Burnham, Daniel H., and Edward H. Bennett. *Plan of Chicago*. See chapter on "Planning, Engineering, and Administration."

Butcher, Devereux. "Do Our Historic Areas Deserve the Dignity of a Separate Bureau?" *National Parks Magazine*, 30 (Oct.-Dec. 1956), 152-57. Describes the National Park Service's historic preservation work since 1916.

Butcher, Devereux. *Exploring Our National Parks and Monuments*. New York: Oxford University Press, 1957. 106 pp. Illustrations, maps, and bibliography. Includes historical descriptions of the nation's parks and monuments, but emphasizes the National Park Service's administrative policies toward them. (Houghton Mifflin has published revised and enlarged editions.)

Butcher, Devereux. "National Parks Association." *Journal of Forestry*, 44 (March 1946), 184-85. On the history and activities of this organization, founded in 1919, to promote the national park concept.

Byrne, J. J., ed. "Engineering in the Forest Service: Six Memoirs." *Forest History*, 14 (Jan. 1971), 6-17. Of special interest are: Henry M. Shank, "Mapping the West"; L. H. LaFauer,

"Engineering and the Depression"; Jack Hamblet, "Chrome Mines Road Project."

Caemmerer, H. P. *Washington: The National Capital*. See chapter on "Planning, Engineering, and Administration."

Cameron, Jenks. *The National Park Service: Its History, Activities and Organization*. New York: D. Appleton and Company, 1922. xii + 172 pp. Map, appendices, bibliography, and index. A service monograph (No. 11) of the Institute for Government Research, this study is a history and analysis of the park service and the national park system. Special attention is also given to national monuments.

Campbell, Bernard T. "Shiloh National Military Park." *Tennessee Historical Quarterly*, XXI (March 1962), 3-18. A short history of the battlefield and a lengthier description of "the movement to have the Shiloh battlefield set aside as a National Military Park."

Campbell, Carlos Clinton. *Birth of a National Park in the Great Smoky Mountains: An Unprecedented Crusade Which Created, As Gift of the People, the Nation's Most Popular Park*. Knoxville: University of Tennessee Press, 1960. xii + 155 pp. Illustrations, maps, tables, and notes. Describes the work of the Great Smoky Mountains Conservation Association, establishment of the Great Smoky Mountains National Park in North Carolina and Tennessee (1934), and its subsequent development. (A new edition was issued in 1970.)

Caro, Robert A. *The Power Broker: Robert Moses and the Fall of New York*. See chapter on "Planning, Engineering, and Administration."

Carrott, Richard G. *The Egyptian Revival: Its Sources, Monuments, and Meaning, 1808–1858*. See chapter on "Public Buildings."

Cary, John. "Park Planning and Historic Resources: The Upper Delaware Valley." *Pennsylvania History*, XXXII (April 1965), 113-29. Inventory of historic sites to justify creation of a national recreation area in the upper Delaware Valley.

Cate, Donald F. "Recreation and the U.S. Forest Service: A Study of Organizational Response to Changing Demands." Doctoral dissertation, Stanford University, 1963. xi + 650 pp. Illustrations, maps, tables, notes, appendices, and bibliography. Contains some history of the recreational use of national forests.

Catlin, George B. *The Story of Detroit*. See chapter on "Community Water Supply."

Chadwick, George F. *The Park and the Town: Public Landscape in the 19th and 20th Centuries*. New York: Frederick A. Praeger Publishers, 1966. 388 pp. Illustrations, maps, diagrams, notes, bibliography, and index. A well-researched examination of the Victorian's main contribution to urban life—the public park. Only a very small portion of the book is devoted to parks in the United States.

Chandler, Robert. "Robert W. Sawyer: 'He Thought in Terms of Forever.' " *American Forests*, 65 (Dec. 1959), 16-17, 44, 46-49. On a Bend, Oregon, newspaper editor and his leadership role in the state parks movement.

Chappell, Gordon. *Historic Resource Study–East and West Potomac Parks: A History*. Denver: United States Department of the Interior, National Park Service, 1973. iii + 186 pp. Notes and appendices. A general history of the reclamation, development, and use of Potomac Park. The first chapter reviews "Commerce on the Potomac, 1790-1870"; a later chapter discusses "New Bridges in Potomac Park, 1941-1971."

Chittenden, H. M. "The Government Road System of the Yellowstone National Park." *Proceedings of the International Good Roads Congress*. See chapter on "Roads, Streets, and Highways."

Chittenden, Hiram Martin. *The Yellowstone National Park: Historical and Descriptive*. Cincinnati: Robert Clarke Company, 1905. x + 355 pp. Illustrations, maps, appendix, and index. A popular guide to Yellowstone National Park. This revised and enlarged edition (first printed in 1895) contains a full account of the park's early history as well as informative chapters on topography, geology, roadways, fauna and flora, and administration. (There have been subsequent editions and revisions—1915, 1924, 1933, and 1949—to bring the volume up to date.)

Chittenden, Hiram Martin. *The Yellowstone National Park*. Norman: University of Oklahoma Press, 1964. xxi + 208 pp. Illustrations, maps, notes, appendix, bibliography, and index. Edited with an introduction by Richard A. Bartlett. This volume includes the historical sketch of the 1895 (first) edition and a biographical sketch of the author.

Christensen, Thomas P. "The State Parks of Iowa." *Iowa Journal of History and Politics*, XXVI (July 1928), 331-414. Describes Iowa's movement for the conservation of scenery and forests for public parks. Detailed accounts of individual park areas are included.

Civic Club of Allegheny County, Pittsburgh, Pennsylvania. *Fifty Years of Civic History, 1895-1945*. See chapter on "Solid Wastes."

Clarke, T. Wood. *Utica for a Century and a Half*. See chapter on "Community Water Supply."

Clary, David A. *The place where Hell bubbled up: A History of the First National Park*. Washington, D. C.: National Park Service, 1972. 68 pp. Illustrations and map. A richly illustrated history of Wyoming's Yellowstone National Park.

Clary, Raymond H. *The Making of Golden Gate Park, The Early Years: 1865–1906*. San Francisco: California Living Books—San Francisco Examiner Division of the Hearst Corporation, 1980. xiv + 192 pp. Illustrations, bibliography, and index. A history (beginning in 1868) of a park that "ranks among the finest of the many wonders of San Francisco." The first chapter recalls "The Birth of American Parks."

Clawson, Marion. "The Crisis in Outdoor Recreation." *American Forests*, 65 (March 1959), 22-31, 40-41. Contains some history of outdoor recreation in national parks during the twentieth century.

Clements, Kendrick A. "Politics and the Park: San Francisco's Fight for Hetch Hetchy, 1908-1913." *Pacific Historical Review*, XLVIII (May 1979), 185-215. The author focuses his attention on San Francisco's side in the Hetch-Hetchy controversy and shows that "the city's victory was to a great extent the result of a skillfully planned and executed campaign and that the issues in the controversy were more complicated and ambiguous than historians have heretofore realized."

Clepper, Henry. *Origins of American Conservation*. See chapter on "Flood Control and Drainage."

Clepper, Henry. "The Birth of the C. C. C." *American Forests*, 79 (March 1973), 8-11. On the origins of the Civilian Conservation Corps and the roles of Franklin D. Roosevelt and Ovid Butler.

Cleveland, H. W. S. *Landscape Architecture As Applied to the Wants of the West*. Pittsburgh: University of Pittsburgh Press, 1965. xxv + 59 pp. Notes. The author (Horace William Shaler—1814-1900), whose work centered in the Midwest, belonged to that remarkable generation of landscape architects which produced Frederick Law Olmsted and Charles Eliot. First published in 1873, this book contains a fine introductory essay by Roy Lubove and a useful chapter by Cleveland on "City Parks—Lessons of the Central Park. . . ."

Cleveland, H. W. S. *The Public Grounds of Chicago: How to Give Them Character and Expression*. Chicago: Charles D. Lakey, Publisher, 1869. 20 pp. An interesting report by a professional landscape gardener, who recommends improvements for Chicago's parks by describing the actions and accomplishments of New York, Philadelphia, Baltimore, Brooklyn, and Boston.

Cohen, Stan. *The Tree Army: A Pictorial History of the Civilian Conservation Corps, 1933-1942*. Missoula, Mont.: Pictorial Histories Publishing Company, 1980. 160 pp. Illustrations, maps, appendix, and bibliography. Shows through photographs "how the enrollees lived and worked."

Coleman, Bevley R. "A History of State Parks in Tennessee." Doctoral dissertation, George Peabody College for Teachers, 1963. v + 424 pp. Notes and bibliography. A thorough study of Tennessee's park system, with an introductory chapter on the "History and Philosophy of Public Parks in the United States." Demonstrates the large role of the Tennessee Valley Authority in developing the state park system.

Collier, Malcolm. "Jens Jensen and Columbus Park." *Chicago History*, IV (Winter 1975), 225-34. The story of Jensen's rise from street sweeper to superintendent of West Parks and an internationally known conservationist and landscaper. Special attention is given to his role in the development of Columbus Park.

Condit, Carl W. *Chicago, 1910-29: Building, Planning, and Urban Technology*. See chapter on "Planning, Engineering, and Administration."

Connecticut State Park and Forest Commission. *Connecticut State Parks: A Report on Their Growth, Cost, and Use, 1914-1931*. Hartford: Connecticut State Park and Forest Commission, 1932. 23 pp. General survey.

Connery, Robert H., and Richard H. Leach. *The Federal Government and Metropolitan Areas*. See chapter on "Planning, Engineering, and Administration."

Cook, Ann; Marilyn Gittell; and Herb Mack, eds. *City Life, 1865-1900: Views of America*. See chapter on "Solid Wastes."

Cook, Harry T. *The Borough of the Bronx, 1639-1913: Its Marvelous Development and Historical Surroundings*. See chapter on "Roads, Street, and Highways."

Cooling, B. Franklin. "Fort Donelson National Military Park." *Tennessee Historical Quarterly*, XXIII (Sept. 1964), 203-20. Records the history and describes the conversion of Fort Donelson into a national park.

Cotterill, Roland. "The Parks, Playgrounds and Boulevards of Seattle: How Five Million Dollars Has Been Raised and Spent in Five Years—A Park Commission with Broad Powers." *American City*, VII (July-Dec. 1912), 204-07. The author describes how the city of Seattle went about providing "a park or playground within a half-mile of every home in the city."

Cox, Thomas R. "Conservation by Subterfuge: Robert W. Sawyer and the Birth of the Oregon State Parks." *Pacific Northwest Quarterly*, 64 (Jan. 1973), 21-29. Underscores the role of Sawyer and other members of the Oregon State Highway Commission in developing the state's parks during the 1920s.

Cox, Thomas R. "Weldon Heyburn, Lake Chatcolet, and the Evolving Concept of Public Parks." *Idaho Yesterdays*, 24 (Summer 1980), 2-15. A history of Idaho's first state park, which reflects America's changing understanding of the nature and use of public parks.

Cramton, Louis C. *Early History of Yellowstone National Park and Its Relation to National Park Policies*. Washington, D. C.: U. S. Government Printing Office, 1932. iii + 148 pp. Bibliography and appendices. A history—presented largely through legislative documents—of Yellowstone's early exploration, the March 1, 1872 act authorizing it, and the enduring struggle for its proper administration, protection, and development.

Cranz, Galen. "Models for Park Usage: Ideology and the Development of Chicago's Public Parks." Doctoral dissertation, University of Chicago, 1971. xi + 365 pp. Illustrations, tables, notes, appendix, and bibliography. Discusses "the conditions which led to the sharp changes in how parks were conceived of and planned" in Chicago from 1869 to 1971.

Crawford, Andrew Wright. "The Development of Parks Systems in American Cities." *Annals of the American Academy of Political and Social Science*, XXV (March 1905), 218-34. Considers the development of urban parks as "the most promising feature of American civic life during the last decade." The author discusses park planning in a large number of United States cities.

Creighton, Thomas H. *The Architecture of Monuments: The Franklin Delano Roosevelt Memorial Competition*. New York: Reinhold Publishing Corporation, 1962. 192 pp. Illustrations and index. On the work of the Franklin D. Roosevelt Memorial Commission (1955) and the results of the competition (1961) it sponsored.

Curtis, Gregory G. "Connecticut Historic Riverway: A Case Study of Acceptance and Rejection of a National Recreation Area." Doctoral dissertation, University of Connecticut, 1974. vi + 185 pp. Maps, notes, appendix, and bibliography. Explains why—in the context of intergovernmental relations—a federal proposal, initiated in Congress in 1965, to establish a National Recreation Area on the Connecticut River did not succeed.

Darling, F. Fraser, and Noel D. Eichhorn. *man & nature in the National Parks: Reflections on Policy*. Washington, D. C.: Conservation Foundation, 1969. 86 pp. Illustrations. First issued in 1960, this book examines the impact of man—tourism and visitor use—on national parks. Incidental history.

Denis, J. W. "The Nashville City Cemetery." *Tennessee Historical Quarterly*, II (March 1943), 30-42. On Nashville's most historic burial ground, opened in 1822.

Dickinson, Joel Ray. "The Creation of Redwood National Park: A Case Study in the Politics of Conservation." Doctoral dissertation,

University of Missouri at Columbia, 1974. 729 pp.

Dobie, John Gilmore. *The Itasca Story*. Minneapolis: Ross & Haines, 1959. ix + 202 pp. Illustrations, maps, tables, and bibliography. An Itasca State Park in Minnesota since 1803.

Dodds, Gordon B. "Conservation & Reclamation in the Trans-Mississippi West: A Critical Bibliography." *Arizona and the West*. See chapter on "Irrigation."

Dodds, Gordon B. *Hiram Martin Chittenden: His Public Career*. See chapter on "Flood Control and Drainage."

Dodds, Gordon B. "The Historiography of American Conservation: Past and Prospects. *Pacific Northwest Quarterly*. See chapter on "Irrigation."

Doell, Chas. E., and Gerald B. Fitzgerald. *A Brief History of Parks and Recreation in the United States*. Chicago: Athletic Institute, 1954. viii + 129 pp. Notes and bibliography. A general history of the park and recreation movements in the United States by a park and recreation administrator and a recreation educator.

Donaldson, Alfred Lee. *A History of the Adirondacks*. 2 vols. New York: Century Company, 1921. Vol. I: 298 pp.; Vol. II: 299-363 pp. Illustrations, maps, charts, and bibliography. A comprehensive history of New York's Adirondack Mountains.

Dorr, George Bucknam. *Acadia National Park: Its Origins and Background*. Bangor, Maine: Burr Printing Company, 1942. Early history of national park in Maine.

Dorr, George Bucknam. *Acadia National Park: Its Growth and Development . . . Book II*. Bangor, Maine: Burr Printing Company, 1946. 46 pp. Illustrations. Chiefly reminiscences by the author, a park promoter.

Douglas, William O. *A Wilderness Bill of Rights*. Boston: Little, Brown and Company, 1965. iii + 192 pp. Illustrations, appendix, and index. A strong plea for the creation of inviolate wilderness areas by a U. S. Supreme Court justice. The book outlines many environmental problems and contains historical treatments of federal park policies.

Eaton, Leonard K. *Landscape Artist in America: The Life and Work of Jens Jensen*. Chicago: University of Chicago Press, 1964. xi + 240 pp. Illustrations, diagrams, notes, and bibliographical essay. A biography of an individual who viewed landscape architecture as an art and whose landscapes, mostly in the Midwest, are "among the finest works of American Art." The second section of the book is devoted to Jensen's "public work"—parks.

Eliot, Charles. *Charles Eliot: Landscape Architect*. Cambridge: Riverside Press, 1902. xxiv + 770 pp. Illustrations, maps, appendices, and index. A detailed review of Eliot's early life, training, and professional career. This book is indispensable for any study of the development of urban parks.

Everhart, William C. *The National Park Service*. New York: Praeger Publishers, 1972. xii + 276 pp. Illustrations, map, chart, appendices, bibliography, and index. A history of the National Park Service by a veteran park service interpreter. Published to coincide with the hundredth anniversary of the establishment of Yellowstone National Park, this study contrasts the early stages of the park movement and the narrowly defined mission of the National Park Service with its broadened, environmental responsibilities of the 1970s.

Fabos, Julius Gy., Gordon T. Milde, and V. Michael Weinmayr. *Frederick Law Olmsted, Sr.: Founder of Landscape Architecture in America*. Amherst: University of Massachusetts Press, 1968. 114 pp. Illustrations and maps.

Fadely, Marian E. "Isabelle's Story." *American Forests*, 61 (April 1955), 37, 51-52. On a National Park Service information officer and editor (1916-1950s) whose writings promoted the national parks concept.

Fagerlund, Gunnar O. *Olympic National Park, Washington*. Washington, D. C.: U. S. National Park Service, 1954. 67 pp. Illustrations, map, and bibliography. Contains some history of the park.

Fahl, Ronald J., comp. *North American Forest and Conservation History: A Bibliography*. Santa Barbara, Calif.: American Bibliographical Center—Clio Press, 1977. 408 pp. Index. An extensive bibliography of secondary, published sources on the history of North American forests, including parks, and management, and the conservation of natural resources in general.

Farquhar, Francis P. "Colonel George W. Stewart, Founder of Sequoia National Park." *Sierra Club Bulletin*, 17 (1932), 49-52. On a Visalia newspaperman who vigorously promoted establishment of the California park.

Farquhar, Francis P. "Exploration of the Sierra Nevada." *California Historical Quarterly*, IV (March 1925), 2-58. Trace the course of "the exploration of the Sierra Nevada of California from the time when it first became known to white men to the present day." The narrative highlights attempts to locate transportation routes, to create national parks, and to establish a national forest reserve; it also includes short sections on individual explorers and surveyors.

Farquhar, Francis P. *History of the Sierra Nevada*. Berkeley: University of California Press, 1965. xiv + 245 pp. Illustrations, maps, bibliography, and index. On the national parks and forests of the California range, emphasizing events related to their discovery and efforts to preserve their natural beauty.

Farquhar, Francis P. "Legislative History of Sequoia and Kings Canyon National Parks." *Sierra Club Bulletin,* 26 (Feb. 1941), 42-58. From 1880.

Farquhar, Francis P. "Stephen T. Mather: 1867-1930." *Sierra Club Bulletin*, 16 (1931), 55-59. On the National Park Service's first director (1917-1928).

Farquhar, Francis P. "Walker's Discovery of Yosemite." *Sierra Club Bulletin*, 27 (Aug. 1942), 35-49. On Joseph Reddeford Walker's expedition and the discovery of Yosemite Valley (1833).

Farquhar, Francis P. *Yosemite, the Big Trees and the High Sierra: A Selective Bibliography*. Berkeley: University of California Press, 1948. xii + 104 pp. Illustrations. Annotated guide to literature on the history of the Sierra Nevada and its national parks.

Fein, Albert. *Frederick Law Olmsted and the American Environmental Tradition*. New York: George Braziller, 1972. xi + 180 pp. Illustrations, maps, notes, bibliography, and index. This biography shows Olmsted's strong influence on the parks (and recreation) and environmental movements.

Fein, Albert, ed. *Landscape into Cityscape: Frederick Law Olmsted's Plans for a Greater New York City*. See chapter on "Planning, Engineering, and Administration."

Feinstein, Estelle F. *Stamford in the Gilded Age: The Political Life of a Connecticut Town, 1868-1893*. See chapter on "Planning, Engineering, and Administration."

Fendall, Gary K. "Historical Aspects of the Willamette River Park System." Master's thesis, Oregon College of Education, 1968.

Finfer, Lawrence A. "Leisure as Social Work in the Urban Community: The Progressive Recreation Movement, 1890-1920." Doctoral dissertation, Michigan State University, 1974. 326 pp. An excellent source on the movement to create playgrounds and recreational centers during the Progressive era.

Fischer, LeRoy H. "The Honey Springs National Battlefield Park Movement." *Chronicles of Oklahoma*, XLVII (Spring 1969), 515-30. Presents a brief history of the site of the Civil War Battle of Honey Springs, describes the efforts of other states to develop similar kinds of sites as national battlefield parks, and advocates Honey Springs' conversion into a national park.

Fisher, Edwin A. "Engineering and Public Works in the City of Rochester During the Past Century." *Centennial History of Rochester, New York*. See chapter on "Planning, Engineering, and Administration."

Ford, George B. "The Park System of Kansas City, Mo." *Architectural Record*, XL (Dec. 1916), 499-504. A brief review of "the most extensive park system in the country for a city of its size." The author acknowledges that landscape architect George F. Kessler and "an intelligent and far-seeing Park Board" are responsible for the plan's success.

Fosdick, Raymond B. *John D. Rockefeller, Jr.: A Portrait*. New York: Harper & Row, 1956. ix + 477 pp. Illustrations. Describes Rockefeller's active interest in the nation's parks. He donated millions of dollars to preserve and enlarge them and to improve their administration.

Foster, Laura. "Honeymoon in Hetch Hetchy." *American West*, VIII (May 1971), 10-15. Based on the personal experience (1914) of Robert and Dorothy Duryea. The Hetch Hetchy Valley was dammed to provide a water supply for San Francisco. It has been the focal point of a major controversy between "preservationist conservationists" and "utilitarian conservationists."

Foy, Bernard L., comp. *A Bibliography for the TVA Program*. See chapter on "Flood Control and Drainage."

Frantz, Joe B. "The Meaning of Yellowstone: A Commentary." *Montana: The Magazine of Western History*, XXII (Summer 1972), 5-11. Describes the growth of the national park concept and the problems increasing tourism created for the National Park Service. Some history of the Wyoming area is included.

Frederick, Robert Allen. "Colonel Richard Lieber, Conservationist and Park Builder: The Indiana Years." Doctoral dissertation, Indiana University, 1960. 468 pp. On the director of the Indiana Department of Conservation (1919-1933) and a leader in the state's park movement.

French, Stanley. "The Cemetery as Cultural Institution: The Establishment of Mount Auburn and the 'Rural Cemetery' Movement." *American Quarterly*, XXVI (March 1974), 37-59. On Boston's Mount Auburn (1831), a "garden" cemetery.

Fridley, Russell W. "Yellowstone to Voyageurs: The Evolution of an Idea." *Minnesota History*, 43 (Summer 1972), 70-71. Brief statement on the national park concept with special reference to Voyageurs National Park in Minnesota.

Frye, Mary Virginia. "The Historical Development of Municipal Parks in the United States: Concepts and Their Application." Doctoral dissertation, University of Illinois, 1964. 304 pp.

Futrell, J. William. "Parks to the People: New Directions for the National Park System." *Emory Law Journal*, 25 (Spring 1976), 255-316. Some historical material is included in this examination of "current conflicts in federal park and outdoor recreation planning." The Chattahoochee River corridor in Atlanta is the article's focal point.

Gallagher, H. M. Pierce. *Robert Mills: Architect of the Washington Monument, 1781-1855*. New York: Columbia University Press, 1935. xxv + 233 pp. Illustrations, diagrams, notes, appendices, bibliography, and index. A biography of one of the United States' first native-born public work professionals. Before becoming federal architect and engineer in 1836, he served for many years on South Carolina's Board of Public Works. As this biography attests, the Washington Monument was Mills' most important work. Half of the volume contains copies of essays and letters written by Mills.

Galusha, Hugh D., Jr. "Yellowstone Years." *Montana: The Magazine of Western History*, IX (July 1959), 2-21. Describes the work of Yellowstone National Park's official photographers, House of Haynes, since 1881.

Gammertsfelder, Joseph W. "A Study of Glacier National Park." Master's thesis, Ohio University, 1947.

Gatewood, Willard B., Jr. "Conservation and Politics in the South, 1899-1906." *Georgia Review*, XVI (Spring 1962), 30-42. On the movement for creation of a national park in Georgia, North Carolina, and the southern Appalachians of Tennessee.

Gatewood, Willard Badgette, Jr. "North Carolina's Role in the Establishment of the Great Smoky Mountains National Park." *North Carolina Historical Review*, XXXVII (April 1960), 165-84. A thorough account of North Carolina's forty years (1899-1940) of crusading to establish the Great Smoky Mountains National Park.

Gilmour, Robert S., and John A. McCauley. "Environmental Preservation and Politics: The Significance of 'Everglades Jet Port.' " *Political Science Quarterly*, 90 (Winter 1975-76), 719-38. Describes how two governmental actions regarding the construction of a massive jet airport facility in the early 1970s "spared Everglades National Park yet another powerful human threat to its existence."

Glaab, Charles N. *The American City: A Documentary History*. See chapter on "Energy."

Glaab, Charles N., and A. Theodore Brown. *A History of Urban America*. See chapter on "Community Water Supply."

Glendin, Frances. "A Talk with Horace Albright." *Sierra*, 64 (Sept./Oct. 1979), 30-37. An interesting and informative interview with a founding father of the National Park Service.

Glendin, Frances. "A Talk with William Whalen." *Sierra*, 64 (Sept./Oct. 1979), 38-44. A general discussion of the park service's development and current recreational and environmental issues with the agency's director.

Goddard, Mabel. *The Public Parks of Freeport, Illinois: Their First Century, 1849-1949*. Freeport: Wagner Printing Company, 1948. xi + 102 pp. Illustrations and bibliography. A popular account of the origin and development of the city's park system. The volume was sponsored by the park commissioner and former president of the park board.

Goplen, Arnold O. "The Historical Significance of Fort Lincoln State Park." *North Dakota History*, 13 (Oct. 1946), 151-221. The early history of one of North Dakota's most historic sites. Within its boundaries are the Ruins of the Mandan Slant Indian Village and the Fort Abraham Lincoln Cavalry and Infantry posts.

Gower, Calvin W. "The CCC Indian Division: Aid for Depressed Americans, 1833-1942." *Minnesota History*, 43 (Spring 1972), 3-13. Particularly in Minnesota.

Gower, Calvin W. "The Civilian Conservation Corps and American Education: Threat to Local Control?" *History of Education Quarterly*, 7 (Spring 1967).

Gower, Calvin W. "The CCC, the Forest Service, and Politics in Maine, 1933-1936." *New England Social Studies Bulletin*, 30 (Spring 1973), 15-21.

Graham, Frank, Jr. *Man's Dominion: The Story of Conservation in America*. See chapter on "Planning, Engineering, and Administration."

Graham, Frank, Jr. *The Adirondack Park: A Political History*. New York: Alfred A. Knopf, 1978. xiii + 314 pp. Illustrations, map, notes, and index. Describes "the ideas, controversies, agreements, legislation, and administration that affected the Adirondack Park from the earliest times . . . ." This book was funded by a grant from the New York State Heritage Trust to the National Audubon Society.

Gray, David E., comp. *Reflections on the Recreation and Park Movement*. Dubuque, Ia.: W. C. Brown, 1973. ix + 370 pp. Illustrations.

Gray, John S. "Trails of a Trailblazer: P. W. Norris and Yellowstone." *Montana: The Magazine of Western History*, XXII (Summer 1972), 54-63. Biographical sketch of Philetus W. Norris, Yellowstone National Park superintendent from 1877 to 1882.

Green, Charles Sylvester, comp. *Conservation and Development in North Carolina*. Raleigh: North Carolina Department of Conservation and Development, 1953. 372 pp. Some of the conference papers on state parks and forests are historical.

Green, Constance McLaughlin. *History of Naugatuck, Connecticut*. See chapter on "Sewers and Wastewater Treatment."

Green, Constance McLaughlin. *Washington: Capital City, 1879-1950*. See chapter on "Community Water Supply."

Green, Constance McLaughlin. *Washington: Village and Capital, 1800-1878*. See chapter on "Urban Mass Transportation."

Griffith, Ernest S. *A History of American City Government: The Conspicuous Failure, 1870-1900*. See chapter on "Planning, Engineering, and Administration."

Griffith, Ernest S. *A History of American City Government: The Progressive Years and Their Aftermath, 1900-1920*. See chapter on "Planning, Engineering, and Administration."

Groves, Helen H. and Harold M. "The City Beautiful: The Madison Park and Pleasure Drive Association, 1892-1938." *Wisconsin Magazine of History*, 40 (Spring 1975) 197-206. Discusses the influence of this voluntary citizen group on the development of the city's parks and other beautification projects.

Gustafson, A. F., et al. *Conservation in the United States*. Ithaca: Comstock Publishing Company, 1939. xi + 445 pp. Illustrations, maps, tables, diagrams, bibliography, and index. A series of essays on the problems of managing natural resources. Included are discussions of national and state parks, soil conservation, municipal water supply, and irrigation. The book represents a comprehensive statement of New Deal conservation philosophies and policies.

Gutheim, Frederick. "Who Designed the Washington Monument?" *Journal of the American Institute of Architects*, XV (March 1951), 136-42. The answer: the spirit of the age.

Gutheim, Frederick, and Wilcomb E. Washburn. *The Federal City: Plans & Reali-*

ties. See chapter on "Planning, Engineering, and Administration."

Haas, Garland A. "Parks and Recreation in the Seattle Metropolitan Area: A Study in Policy Development and Administration." Doctoral dissertation, University of Washington, 1958. vii + 345 pp. Maps, charts, tables, graphs, notes, appendix, and bibliography. An analysis and evaluation of the political organization, practices, and public policies of the various state and local agencies having responsibilities for the operation of parks and recreational facilities in the Seattle Metropolitan area.

Haines, Aubrey L. "Lost in the Yellowstone: An Epic of Survival in the Wilderness." *Montana: The Magazine of Western History*, XXII (Summer 1972), 31-41. Describes the search for Truman C. Everts, who was lost from the Washburn-Doane exploration party in 1870. The publicity given this search brought support for the movement to establish Yellowstone National Park.

Haines, Aubrey L. *The Yellowstone Story: A History of Our First National Park.* 2 vols. Yellowstone National Park: Yellowstone Library and Museum Association in cooperation with Colorado Associated University Press, 1977. Vol. I: xv + 385 pp.; Vol. II: xvii + 543 pp. Illustrations, maps, charts, notes, appendices, bibliography, and indexes. A spirited history of Yellowstone by an individual who knows the park well (1946-1959, park engineer; 1959-1969, park historian). Volume II contains complete appendices of biographical, legislative, and statistical information.

Haines, Aubrey L. *Yellowstone National Park: Its Exploration and Establishment*. Washington, D. C.: National Park Service, 1974. xxiii + 218 pp. Illustrations, maps, notes, appendix, bibliography, and index. On the park's early history.

Hall, Clayton Colman, ed. *Baltimore: Its History and Its People*. See chapter on "Community Water Supply."

Halprin, Lawrence. *Cities*. Cambridge: MIT Press, 1973. 240 pp. Illustrations, diagrams, and index. Some historical information is included in this well-illustrated book on the development of open spaces in cities. Subjects covered include parks, street furniture, fountains, paving stones, and urban forestry.

Halsey, Elizabeth. *The Development of Public Recreation in Metropolitan Chicago*. Chicago: Chicago Recreation Commission, 1940. xii + 334 pp. Maps, charts, tables, notes, appendix, bibliography, and index. A study of public recreation development in Chicago and the region surrounding it. A large portion of the book is devoted to the history of Chicago's parks, playgrounds, water fronts, etc.; other parts deal with the administration of public recreation as well as current problems and possible solutions.

Hampton, H. Duane. "Conservation and Cavalry: A Study of the Role of the United States Army in the Development of a National Park System, 1886-1917," Doctoral dissertation, University of Colorado, 1965. 403 pp.

Hampton, H. Duane. *How the U. S. Cavalry Saved our National Parks*. Bloomington: Indiana University Press, 1971. iii + 246 pp. Illustrations, map, notes, bibliography, and index. Summarizes the U. S. Army's management of Yellowstone National Park from 1886 to 1918. The author gives some attention to Yosemite, General Grant, and Sequoia national parks.

Hampton, H. Duane. "Knut Forsberg: The Ironic Story of His Rejected Plan for Yellowstone." *Landscape Architecture*, 68 (May 1978), 222-27. Shows that the plan of this nineteenth-century Swedish architect was "superior to the unplanned development of the past century."

Hampton, H. Duane. "The Army and the National Parks." *Forest History*, 10 (Oct. 1966), 2-17. On Yellowstone National Park under the army's administration (1886-1916).

Hampton, H. Duane. "The Army and the National Parks." *Montana: The Magazine of Western History*, XXII (Summer 1972), 64-79. Describes the army's administration of Yellowstone from 1886 to 1916 and includes a reference to the region's history since 1870.

Hampton, H. Duane, ed. "With Grinnell in North Park." *Colorado Magazine*, XLVIII (Summer 1971), 273-98. George Bird Grinnell's account of a visit to North Park, Colorado, in 1879. The editor's introduction contains a biographical sketch of Grinnell, scientist and western national park enthusiast.

Hanmer, Lee F. *Public Recreation: A Study of*

Parks, Playgrounds and Other Outdoor Recreation Facilities. New York: Committee on Regional Plan of New York and Its Environs, 1928. 256 pp. Illustrations, maps, tables, notes, appendix, bibliography, and index. This study attempts to define the recreation needs of the New York region and determine how they can be met. General historical information on the area's parks and park facilities is scattered throughout the volume.

Hansen, Harry. *Scarsdale: From Colonial Manor to Modern Community*. See chapter on "Community Water Supply."

Hanson, James Austin. "The Civilian Conservation Corps in the Northern Rocky Mountains." Doctoral dissertation, University of Wyoming, 1973. 404 pp. A solid descriptive history of the corps' activities.

Hartzog, George B. "Over the Years with the National Park Service." *National Parks Magazine*, 43 (May 1969), 13-14, 19-20. Since 1916.

Harvey, Frederick L. *History of the Washington National Monument and the Washington National Monument Society*. Washington, D. C.: U. S. Government Printing Office, 1903. 362 pp. Illustrations.

Hatch, Charles E., Jr. "The Great Road: Earliest Highway Used and Developed by the English at Jamestown." *Virginia Magazine of History and Biography*. See chapter on "Roads, Streets, and Highways."

Hauberg, John H. "The New Black Hawk State Park." *Journal of the Illinois State Historical Society*, XX (July 1927), 265-81. Presents the history of the site before it became an Illinois state park in June 1927.

Haupt, Richard E., et al. "The Changing Face of Fountain Square." *Bulletin of the Cincinnati Historical Society*, 27 (Fall 1969), 239-57. On Henry Probasco's gift to the city of Cincinnati, the "Genius of Water" Fountain (1872). Many illustrations accompany the short text.

Hay, William M. "History of State Parks." *Tennessee Conservationist* (March/April 1947), 3, 10, In Tennessee from the mid 1930s.

Hazard, Patrick D. and the editors. "George Washington's Monument." *American Heritage*, XX (Dec. 1968), 68-73. Emphasizes the financial difficulties encountered in erecting this memorial.

Heald, Weldon F. "The Yellowstone Story: Genesis of the National Park Idea." *Utah Historical Quarterly*, 28 (April 1960), 99-110. A history of the area from 1807 to 1872. The author argues that creation of the first national park in 1872 established "the idea that the federal government is responsible for protecting American scenery in its natural state for the benefit and enjoyment of all the people."

Henderson, G. L. *Yellowstone National Park: Past, Present, and Future*. Washington, D. C.: Gibson Brothers, 1891.

Hendrickson, Kenneth E., Jr. "The Civilian Conservation Corps in Pennsylvania: A Case Study of a New Deal Relief Agency in Operation." *Pennsylvania Magazine of History and Biography*, C (Jan. 1976), 66-96. An assessment of the administrative history of the CCC in Pennsylvania.

Hewes, L. I. "America's Park Highways." *Civil Engineering*, 2 (Sept. 1932), 537-40. The deputy chief engineer of the U. S. Bureau of Public Roads describes the bureau's roadbuilding work in national parks since 1924.

Hoffman, Abraham. "Angeles Crest: The Creation of a Forest Highway System in the San Gabriel Mountains." *Southern California Quarterly*. See chapter on "Roads, Streets, and Highways."

Holland, F. Ross. *Rocky Mountain National Park: Historical Background Data*. Denver: National Park Service, 1971. 163 pp. Illustrations, map, appendix, and bibliography. Good example of public history designed to furnish background information for master planning.

Holland, Kenneth, and Frank Ernest Hill. *Youth in the CCC*. Washington, D. C.: American Council on Education, 1942. xv + 263 pp. Illustrations, tables, and appendix. A laudatory overview of projects undertaken by members of the Civilian Conservation Corps.

Holland, Reid A. "Life in Oklahoma's Civilian Conservation Corps." *Chronicles of Oklahoma*, 48 (Summer 1970), 224-34.

Holland, Reid. "The Civilian Conservation Corps in the City: Tulsa and Oklahoma City in the 1930s." *Chronicles of Oklahoma*, LIII (Fall 1975), 367-75. Highlights the CCC's work in urban parks.

Holleran, L. G. "Development of Parks and Parkways in Westchester County, New York." *Journal of the Boston Society of Civil Engineers*, XVI (Sept. 1929), 381-91. The deputy chief engineer of the Westchester County Park Commission describes improvements in the county park system during the 1920s.

Holmes, Frank R. "Palisades Interstate Park, New Jersey." *Americana*, 17 (April 1923), 186-91. A short history of a state (New York/ New Jersey) park along the Hudson River.

Holmes, Michael S. "The New Deal and Georgia's Black Youth." *Journal of Southern History*, XXXVIII (Aug. 1972), 443-60. On the Civilian Conservation Corps in Georgia.

Holt, Glen E. "Private Plans for Public Spaces: The Origins of Chicago's Park System, 1850-1875." *Chicago History*, VIII (Fall 1979), 173-84. Demonstrates that Chicago's parks were "created through the efforts of business and civic leaders, physicians, lawyers, and real estate developers who responded to a need that public officials were unwilling or unable to satisfy."

Holt, W. Stull. *The Office of the Chief of Engineers of the Army: Its Non-Military History, Activities, and Organization.* See chapter on "Planning, Engineering, and Administration."

Howard, William G. "Forests and Parks of the Empire State [New York]." *American Forests*, 38 (March 1932), 165-68. Since 1885.

Hoy, Suellen M. "Governor Samuel M. Ralston and Indiana's Centennial Celebration." *Indiana Magazine of History*, LXXI (Sept. 1975), 245-66. Reveals that a significant consequence of Indiana's anniversary celebration was the emergence of a system of state parks.

Hoy, Suellen M. "People in Public Works: Robert Moses." *APWA Reporter*, 43 (June 1976), 22-23. A brief summary of Moses' multifaceted public works career. His special interest in the development of park and parkway systems is highlighted.

Hoyt, Ray. *'We Can Take it': A Short Story of the C. C. C.* New York: American Book Company, 1935. 128 pp. Illustrations. Includes an account of the beginnings of the Civilian Conservation Corps.

Hubbard, Theodora Kimball. "H. W. S. Cleveland: An American Pioneer in Landscape Architecture and City Planning." *Landscape Architecture*, XX (Jan. 1930), 92-111. Gives particular attention to his work in Minneapolis.

Hubbard, Theodora Kimball, and Henry Vincent. *Our Cities To-Day and To-Morrow: A Survey of Planning and Zoning Progress in the United States*. See chapter on "Planning, Engineering, and Administration."

Hudson, Dale A. "Sierra Club v. Department of Interior: The Fight to Preserve the Redwood National Park." *Ecology Law Quarterly*, 7 (no. 3, 1979), 781-859. A legal and historical examination of attempts to expand Redwood National Park (1970s).

Humphreys, Hubert. "In a Sense Experimental: The Civilian Conservation Corps in Louisiana." 2 parts. *Louisiana History*, 5 and 6, (Fall 1964 and Winter 1965), Fall: 345-67; Winter: 27-52. Reviews effective CCC programs, emphasizing those in flood control, soil conservation, erosion control, and general education.

Hungerford, Edward. *The Story of Public Utilities*. See chapter on "Urban Mass Transportation."

Huse, Charles Phillips. *The Financial History of Boston from May 1, 1822 to January 31, 1909*. See chapter on "Community Water Supply."

Huth, Hans. *Nature and the American: Three Centuries of Changing Attitudes*. Berkeley: University of California Press, 1957. xvii + 250 pp. Illustrations, notes, bibliography, and index. A pioneering study in which the author presents "the basic developments which led to the conservation movement" in the United States. Huth discusses the city park movement, summer vacations and travel, romantic painters, national parks, and other topics related to outdoor recreation and conservation.

Huth, Hans. "Yosemite: The Story of an Idea." *Sierra Club Bulletin*, 33 (March 1948), 47-78. The author argues that "Yosemite, not Yellowstone, was the first park of national importance" and urges historians and others to abandon "the common assumption that the national park idea was born at a campfire in Yellowstone in 1870."

Ingersoll, William T. "Loads of Change: Four Parks in Alaska." *Journal of the West*, VII (April 1968), 178-92. A brief history of Mount McKinley National Park, and Glacier Bay, Katmai, and Sitka national monuments.

Isaac, Paul E. "Municipal Reform in Beaumont, Texas, 1902-1909." *Southwestern Historical Quarterly*. See chapter on "Planning, Engineering, and Administration."

Ise, John. *Our National Park Policy: A Critical History*. Baltimore: Johns Hopkins University Press, 1961. xiii + 701 pp. Maps, notes, and index. This comprehensive analysis of the evolution of the national park system and policy and directed primarily to scenic and archeological parks and monuments and secondarily to forest and grazing lands. Historical and recreational areas receive only limited treatment. It contains a history of each park and of each National Park Service administration since 1916. The study was funded by Resources for the Future.

Jackson, Frances. "Military Use of Haleakala National Park." *Hawaiian Journal of History*, VI (1972), 129-41. Describes the conflicts between the National Park Service and the military over use of Hawaii National Park during and following World War II.

Jackson, William Turrentine. "The Cook-Folsom Exploration of the Upper Yellowstone, 1869." *Pacific Northwest Quarterly*, 32 (July 1941), 307-22. Describes the usefulness of this expedition to the area that would become Yellowstone National Park.

Jackson, William Turrentine. "The Creation of Yellowstone National Park." *Mississippi Valley Historical Review*, XXIX (Sept. 1942), 187-206. Reviews the political struggle and citizen movement in Montana from the 1860s to 1872. The author shows that they were factors that led to the park's creation.

Jackson, William Turrentine. "The Early Exploration and Founding of Yellowstone National Park." Doctoral dissertation, University of Texas, 1940. xx + 299 pp. Illustrations, maps, notes, and bibliography. An early history of Yellowstone which demonstrates how the exploration of the park region "symbolized the development of the Trans-Mississippi West and particularly the Rocky Mountain region."

Jackson, W. Turrentine. "The Washburn-Doane Expedition into the Upper Yellowstone, 1870." *Pacific Historical Review*, X (June 1941), 189-208. Shows how interest in the expedition led to creation of the first national park in the United States.

James, Harlean, ed. *American Planning and Civic Annual*. Washington, D. C.: American Planning and Civic Association, 1937. x + 404 pp. Illustrations, notes, and index. Contains papers read at a number of planning conferences during 1937. Of interest to historians are the following essays: "The National Parks Service, 1917-1937," by Horace M. Albright and "State Park Development under the Civilian Conservation Corps Program" by Robert Fechner.

James, Harlean. *Romance of the National Parks*. New York: Arno Press, 1972. xiv + 240 pp. Illustrations and map. Contains some history of the national parks movement.

James, James Alton. "The Beginning of a State Park System for Illinois." *Transactions of the Illinois State Historical Society*, 1936, 53-62. Includes information on the historical background of Starved Rock and early state park legislation.

Jameson, John Robert, Sr. "Big Bend National Park of Texas: A Brief History of the Formative Years, 1930-1952." Doctoral dissertation, University of Toledo, 1974. v + 208 pp. Maps, notes, appendices, and bibliography. In presenting the history of this park—a product of the Depression—the author gives special attention to "the publicity and fund raising campaigns, land acquisition, visitor and employee experiences in the 'last frontier,' development plans for the park, and the idea of an international park on the Rio Grande."

Jarrett, Henry, Ed. *Perspectives on Conservation*. See chapter on "Planning, Engineering, and Administration."

Jebsen, Harry; Robert M. Newton; and Patricia R. Hogan. *Centennial History of the Dallas, Texas, Park System, 1876-1976*. Lubbock: Texas Tech Department of Park Administration, Landscape Architecture and Horticulture, 1976. xxiv + 959 pp. Illustrations, maps, notes, bibliography, and index. An exhaustive case study that should be an inspiration to others working in this field. No horticultural, political, or institutional aspect is left out.

Jenkins, Hal. *A Valley Renewed: The History of the Muskingum Watershed Conservancy District*. See chapter on "Flood Control and Drainage."

Joffe, Joseph. "John W. Meldrum: The Grand Old Man of Yellowstone National Park." 2

parts. *Annals of Wyoming*, 13 (Jan. 1941), 5-47; (April 1941), 105-40. On the park's commissioner (1894-1935).

Johnson, Charles W. "The Army and the Civilian Conservation Corps, 1933-42." *Prologue*, 4 (Fall 1972), 139-56.

Johnson, Charles W. "The Army, the Negro and the Civilian Conservation Corps: 1933-1942." *Military Affairs*, 36 (Oct. 1972), 82-88.

Johnson, Charles W. "The Civilian Conservation Corps: The Role of the Army." Doctoral dissertation, University of Michigan, 1968. 246 pp. From 1933 to 1942.

Johnson, Frederick. "The Civilian Conservation Corps: Public Works or Panacea?" *Public Works*, III (Oct. 1980), 80-81, 117. Personal reflections on CCC work (1934) in Whitewater State Park in southeastern Minnesota.

Johnson, Mary Elizabeth. *Emergency Employment in Onondaga County*. See chapter on "Planning, Engineering, and Administration."

Johnson, Palmer O., and Oswald L. Harvey. *The National Youth Administration*. See chapter on "Public Buildings."

Johnson, Paul C. "Turn of The Wheel: The Motor Car vs. Yosemite." *California Historical Quarterly*, LI (Fall 1972), 205-12. On federal regulations governing admission and use of automobiles in Yosemite National Park (1914).

Johnston, Johanna. *Frederick Law Olmsted: Partner with Nature*. New York: Dodd, Mead & Company, 1975. 125 pp. Illustrations, bibliography, and index.

Jones, Holway R. *John Muir and the Sierra Club: The Battle for Yosemite*. San Francisco: Sierra Club, 1965. xvii + 207 pp. Illustrations, appendices, bibliography, and index. Written by "a devotee of Muir and the Sierra Club," this monograph recounts the events surrounding the creation of the Sierra Club (1892) by John Muir. Nearly half of the book is devoted to the club's involvement in the Hetch Hetchy Valley controversy. Although the author regards the lost battle as a great tragedy, he contends that it firmly established "the importance and influence of the Sierra Club in conservation matters."

Jones, Holway R. "Mysterious Origin of the Yosemite Park Bill." *Sierra Club Bulletin*, 48 (Dec. 1963), 69-79. On the 1890 act which established Yosemite National Park.

Judd, Barbara. "Edward M. Bigelow: Creator of Pittsburgh's Arcadian Parks." *Western Pennsylvania Historical Magazine*, 58 (Jan. 1975), 53-68. An examination of Bigelow's (Pittsburgh's director of public works from 1888 to 1906) concentrated efforts to develop a system of public parks which "would give Pittsburgh the esthetic dimension it lacked as an industrial city" and "would serve as effective and benevolent instruments of social control."

Kaufman, Edgar, Jr., ed. *The Rise of an American Architecture*. New York: Praeger Publishers, 1970. x + 241 pp. Illustrations, maps, diagrams, notes, appendices, bibliography, and index. A collection of essays on "the contribution of nineteenth-century America to the history of architecture and city planning." The most interesting essay is Albert Fein's "The American City: The Ideal and the Real." He discusses the park complex as a result of "the interaction of religious-social need, English model, and individual genius."

Kauffmann, Erle. "The Great Yellowstone Adventure." *American Forests and Forest Life*, 35 (Aug. 1929), 457-61. Describes explorations leading to the creation of Yellowstone National Park.

Kearns, Kevin Corrigan. "The History of the Acquisition, Development, and Restoration of Forest Park, 1870-1910." Doctoral dissertation, St. Louis University, 1966. 216 pp.

Keller, Jane Eblen. *Adirondack Wilderness: A Story of Man and Nature*. Syracuse: Syracuse University Press, 1980. xix + 241 pp.

Kelsey, F. W. *The First County Park System: A Complete History of the Inception and Development of Essex County Parks of New Jersey*. New York: J. S. Ogilvie Publishing Company, 1905.

Keyes, Nelson Beecher. *America's National Parks: A Photographic Encyclopedia of Our Magnificent Natural Wonderlands*. Garden City, N. Y.: Doubleday, 1957.

Kieley, James F. "William Henry Jackson: Yellowstone's Pioneer Photographer." *National Parks & Conservation Magazine*, 46 (July 1972), 11-17. From 1871 to the 1930s.

Kilgore, Bruce M. and L. S. "Forty Years Defending Parks: A History of the National Park Association." *National Parks Magazine,* 33 (May 1959), 13-15. Since its founding in 1919.

Kingery, Robert. "The State Parks and Illinois History." *Transactions of the Illinois State Historical Society* (1936), 63-68. Reviews the various problems of administering Illinois' state parks and includes numerous photographs of "typical state parks and memorials."

Kirk, Ruth. *Exploring Crater Lake Country*. Seattle: University of Washington Press, 1975. 96 pp. Illustrations, maps, and index. Prepared in cooperation with the Crater Lake Natural History Association. Some general historical information is included.

Kirk, Ruth. *Exploring Mount Rainier*. Seattle: University of Washington Press, 1968. v + 104 pp. Illustrations and maps. Only a smattering of history.

Kirk, Ruth. *Exploring the Olympic Peninsula*. Seattle: University of Washington Press, 1967. 128 pp. Illustrations and maps. Contains a short historical chapter. It was first published in 1964.

Kirk, Ruth. *Exploring Yellowstone*. Seattle: University of Washington Press, 1972. vi + 120 pp. Illustrations, maps, and index. Prepared in cooperation with the Yellowstone Library and Museum Association. There is one section on the park's history.

Kirk, Ruth. *Washington State: National Parks, Historic Sites, Recreation Areas, and Natural Landmarks*. Seattle: Unviersity of Washington Press, 1974. 64 pp. Illustrations, maps, appendix, and index. Makes particular historical references to Olympic, Mount Rainier, and North Cascades national parks.

Kirk, Ruth. *Yellowstone: The First National Park*. New York: Atheneum Publishers, 1974. 98 pp. Illustrations. Prepared for a popular audience.

Kirker, Harold. *The Architecture of Charles Bulfinch*. See chapter on "Public Buildings."

Kittredge, Frank A. "Preserving a Valuable Heritage." *Civil Engineering*, 2 (Sept. 1932), 533-37. The chief engineer of the National Park Service describes public works improvements (trails and roads, buildings, sewage plants, flood control, water supply, etc.) in the nation's parks during the previous seven years.

Klein, Maury, and Harvey A. Kantor. *Prisoners of Progress: American Industrial Cities, 1850-1920*. See chapter on "Solid Wastes."

Koch, P. "Discovery of the Yellowstone National Park: A Chapter of Early Exploration in the Rocky Mountains." *Magazine of American History*, XI (June 1884), 497-512. Emphasizes the park's natural beauty as seen by Indian traders and trappers, prospectors, and government explorers and surveyors.

Kogan, Bernard P. "Chicago's Pier." *Chicago History*, V (Spring 1976), 28-38. A skillful historical piece on the development, decline, and rebirth of a multiple-purpose waterfront facility—Navy Pier.

Knapp, Richard F. "Play for America: The National Recreation Association, 1906-1950." Doctoral dissertation, Duke University, 1971. x + 252 pp. Notes and bibliography. Shows how this association was "the major continuing institutional influence on the development of municipal public recreation in the United States" for half a century.

Kranz, Marvin Wolf. "Pioneering in Conservation: A History of the Conservation Movement in New York State, 1865-1903." Doctoral dissertation, Syracuse University, 1961. 634 pp.

Kuppens, Francis X. "On the Origin of the Yellowstone National Park." *Jesuit Bulletin*, 41 (Oct. 1962), 6-7, 14.

Lacy, Leslie Alexander. *The Soil Soldiers: The Civilian Conservation Corps in the Great Depression*. Radnor, Pa.: Chilton Book Company, 1976. ix + 293 pp. Illustrations and index. A popular, though insightful, overview of the corps' activities and administration with respect to flood control, recreation, irrigation, and other endeavors.

Lambert, Darwin. "Patterns in National Park Association History." *National Parks Magazine*, 43 (May 1969), 4-8. Since 1919.

Lancaster, R. Kent. "Green Mount: The Introduction of the Rural Cemetery into Baltimore." *Maryland Historical Magazine*, LXXIV (March 1979), 62-79.

Landy, Jacob. "The Washington Monument Project in New York." *Journal of the Society of Architectural Historians*, XXVIII (Dec. 1969), 291-97. From 1833 to 1856, when "the first permanent public monument to Washington was unveiled" in New York City.

Lane, James B. *"City of the Century": A History of Gary, Indiana*. Bloomington: Indiana University Press, 1978. xiv + 339 pp. Illustrations, map, notes, bibliography, and index. Includes some material on the development of the city's park system.

Langford, Nathaniel Pitt. *The Discovery of Yellowstone Park: Journal of the Washburn Expedition to the Yellowstone and Firehole Rivers in the Year 1870*. Lincoln: University of Nebraska Press, 1972. lxi + 125 pp. Illustrations, maps, table, notes, appendix, and index. First issued in 1905. The introduction tells of the movement to establish Yellowstone National Park.

Larned, J. N. *A History of Buffalo: Delineating the Evolution of the City*. See chapter on "Sewers and Wastewater Treatment."

Larson, A. Karl. "Zion National Park with Some Reminiscences Fifty Years Later." *Utah Historical Quarterly*, 37 (Fall 1969), 408-25. A brief historical account completed by memories of the park's dedication (1920).

Lawmill, J. Richard. "The Anthony Wayne Parkway." *Bulletin of the Historical and Philosophical Society of Ohio*, 9 (Jan. 1951), 40-45. Describes the activities of the Anthony Wayne Parkway Board (1947)—to develop recreational and historic sites and to provide easy access to them by means of connecting highways.

Leavitt, Charles Wellford. "A Half Century of Landscape Architecture." *American Architect*, CXXIX (Jan. 5, 1926), 61-64. Since the late nineteenth century.

Lee, Ronald F. *Family Tree of the National Park System: A Chart with Accompanying Text Designed to Illustrate the Growth of the National Park System, 1872-1972*. Philadelphia: Eastern National Park & Monument Association, 1972. 99 pp. Tables and index. An attempt to explain how the National Park System grew from a single, original public reservation—Yellowstone National Park—to embrace almost 300 natural, historical, recreational, and cultural properties situated throughout the United States, its territories, and island possessions. A family tree chart accompanies the text.

Lee, Ronald F. *Public Use of the National Park System, 1872-2000*. Washington D. C.: National Park Service, 1968. 93 pp. Bibliography. Contains some history of national park policy.

Lemmon, Sarah McCulloch. "Raleigh—An Example of the 'New South'?" *North Carolina Historical Review*. See chapter on "Community Water Supply."

Lepawsky, Albert. *State Planning and Economic Development in the South*. See chapter on "Planning, Engineering, and Administration."

LeRoy, Bruce, ed. *H. M. Chittenden: A Western Epic*. See chapter on "Flood Control and Drainage."

Leunes, Barbara Laverne Blythe. "The Conservation Philosophy of Stewart L. Udall, 1961-1968." Doctoral dissertation, Texas A&M University, 1977. ix + 215 pp. Notes and bibliography. Competent overview of Udall's term as secretary of the U. S. Department of the Interior. Emphasis is placed on "his ideas of aesthetic and utilitarian conservation and on the evolution of these ideas which allowed him to give philosophical expression to ecological conservation."

Lewis, Eugene. *Public Entrepreneurship: Toward a Theory of Bureaucratic Political Power—The Organizational Lives of Hyman Rickover, J. Edgar Hoover, and Robert Moses*. Bloomington: Indiana University Press, 1980. x + 274 pp. Charts, notes, and index. An attempt to understand "the bureacratic presence in modern American political life" by analyzing "the organizational lives" of three powerful individuals. Although some seventy pages recount the career of Robert Moses, the author's treatment is almost entirely dependent on Robert A. Caro's *The Power Broker*.

Lieber, Emma. *Richard Lieber, by His Wife, Emma*. Indianapolis: Privately printed, 1947. 170 pp. Illustrations. On the director of the Indiana Department of Conservation (1919-1933) and National Park Service consultant.

Lincoln, Robert P. "Hot Springs National Park." *Fur-Fish-Game*, 89 (July 1949), 3-6, 23. In Arkansas, since 1804.

Lindsay, Diana. ""The Creation of the Anzo Borrego Desert State Park." *Journal of San Diego History*, 19 (Fall 1973), 14-26.

Little, John J. "Island Wilderness: A History of Isle Royale National Park." Doctoral dissertation, University of Toledo, 1978. vii + 243 pp. Map, notes, and bibliography. A study of "the effort to establish and administer Lake Superior's most prominent island within the national park system." The author shows how distance and isolation "hampered efficient administration and popular acceptance" and how sporadic swings between a desire for preservation and development created obstacles in determining the park's use.

Livingood, James W. "Chickamauga and Chattanooga National Military Park." *Tennessee Historical Quarterly*, XXIII (March 1964), 3-23. Records the history of several scattered areas in Tennessee and Georgia—the most important and largest unit is the Chickamauga Battlefield, the site of the park headquarters.

Lorwin, Lewis L. *Youth Works Programs: Problems and Policies*. See chapter on "Public Buildings."

Lowry, Alexander, and Deanne Earnshaw. *Castle Rock: West of Skyline*. Los Altos, Calif.: Sempervirens Fund, 1973. 32 pp. Illustrations. Outlines the movement to establish Castle Rock State Park in the Santa Cruz Mountains.

Lubove, Roy. *Twentieth-Century Pittsburgh: Government, Business, and Environmental Change*. See chapter on "Planning, Engineering, and Administration."

Luckett, William W. "Cumberland Gap National Historical Park." *Tennessee Historical Quarterly*, XXIII (Dec. 1964), 303-20. Relates Cumberland Gap's early history and explains why (its "richness in history along with the scenic beauty of the mountain") and how it was made into a national park.

Lutney, Robert S. "Katmai National Monument." *National Parks Magazine*, 30 (Jan.-March 1956), 7-15, 36-37. Describes the volcanic eruption of Mount Katmai in 1912 and the creation of a national monument in 1918.

McCall, Joseph R. and Virginia N. *Outdoor Recreation: Forest, Park and Wilderness*. Beverly Hills: Benziger Bruce & Glencoe, 1977. ix + 358 pp. Illustrations, appendices, and index. Classroom text that includes a historical sketch on parks and recreation in the United States.

McCarthy, George Michael. "Colorado Confronts the Conservation Impulse, 1891-1907." Doctoral dissertation, University of Denver, 1969. 538 pp.

McCarthy, Michael P. "Politics and the Parks: Chicago Businessmen and the Recreation Movement." *Journal of the Illinois State Historical Society*, LXV (Summer 1972), 158-72. Shows that the Chicago system of parks and playgrounds owes much of its success at the turn of the century to prominent businessmen.

McCloskey, Michael. "The Last Battle of the Redwoods." *American West*, VI (Sept. 1969), 55-64. On the efforts to create Redwood National Park in California (1918-1968).

McCloskey, Michael. "Wilderness Movement at the Crossroads, 1945-1970." *Pacific Historical Review*, XLI (Aug. 1972), 346-61. A paper by the executive director of the Sierra Club that adds measurably to an understanding of the post-World War II wilderness movement.

McClurg, Virginia. "The Making of Mesa Verde Into a National Park." *Colorado Magazine*, VII (Nov. 1930), 216-19. From the late nineteenth century.

MacColl, E. Kimbark. *The Growth of a City: Power and Politics in Portland, Oregon, 1915 to 1950*. See chapter on "Planning, Engineering, and Administration."

McConnell, Grant. "The Conservation Movement—Past and Present." *Western Political Quarterly*. See chapter on "Irrigation."

Macdonald, Stuart H. "Evaluation of Recreational Reuse of Abandoned Railroad Rights-of-Way." Master's thesis, Utah State University, 1979. vi + 187 pp. Tables, appendices, and bibliography. An examination of the issues involved in the recreational reuse of abandoned railroad rights-of-way. Chapter II is an "Historical Overview."

McEntee, James J. *Now They Are Men: The Story of the CCC*. Washington, D. C.: National Home Library Foundation, 1940, 69 pp. A general history of the Civilian Conservation Corps since 1933.

McFarland, J. Horace. "Thirty Years of Conservation and Planning." *Planning Problems of City, Region, State and Nation: Presented at the Twenty-Sixth National Conference on City Planning . . . .* (October 22 to 24, 1934), 146-48. Describes briefly the American Civic Association's involvement in the movement to preserve Niagara Falls and other parks and waterfronts.

McGroarty, John Steven. *Los Angeles: From the Mountains to the Sea*. See chapter on "Waterways."

McIntyre, Robert Norman. "A Brief Administrative History of Mount Rainier National Park, 1899-1952." Master's thesis, University of Washington, 1952.

McKelvey, Blake. "An Historical View of Rochester's Parks and Playgrounds." *Rochester History*, XI (Jan. 1949), 1-24. Examines "historically and descriptively the sixty-one-year old Rochester park system."

McKelvey, Blake. *Rochester: An Emerging Metropolis, 1925-1961*. See chapter on "Roads, Streets, and Highways."

McKelvey, Blake. *Rochester on the Genesee: The Growth of a City*. Syracuse: Syracuse University Press, 1973. xiii + 292 pp. Illustrations, maps, and index. One of the best urban biographies. Most public works facilities and services receive some attention.

McKelvey, Blake. *Rochester: The Flower City, 1855-1890*. See chapter on "Sewers and Wastewater Treatment."

McKelvey, Blake. *Rochester: The Quest for Quality, 1890-1925*. See chapter on "Urban Mass Transportation."

McKelvey, Blake. *Rochester: The Water Power City, 1812-1854*. See chapter on "Waterways."

McLaughlin, Charles Capen, ed., and Charles E. Beveridge, assoc. ed. *The Papers of Frederick Law Olmsted: Volume I–The Formative Years, 1822-1852*. Baltimore: Johns Hopkins University Press, 1977. xx + 423 pp. Illustrations, maps, notes, appendices, and indexes. Contains, in fully annotated form, the best of Olmsted's letters, unpublished writings, and newspaper and periodical articles during this thirty-year period. McLaughlin has written an insightful introductory chapter on Olmsted's life and work—"done at a time when the landscape architect and the sanitary engineer combined forces to plan for our cities."

McMurty, Grady Shannon. "The Redwood National Park: A Case Study of Legislative Compromise." Master's thesis, Syracuse University, 1972.

Manning, Thomas G. *Government in Science: The U. S. Geological Survey, 1867-1894*. See chapter on "Planning, Engineering, and Administration."

Mantor, Lyle. "Fort Kearney and the Westward Movement," *Nebraska History*. See chapter on "Military Installations."

Manucy, Albert C., ed. *The History of Castillo de San Marcos & Fort Matanzas from Contemporary Narratives and Letters*. Washington, D. C.: National Park Service, 1943. vi + 38 pp. Illustrations and bibliography.

Martin, Roscoe C., ed. *TVA: The First Twenty Years, a Staff Report*. See chapter on "Flood Control and Drainage."

Martinson, Arthur D. "Mount Rainier National Park: First Years." *Forest History*, 10 (Oct. 1966), 26-33. On administrative and development problems in the park from 1899 to 1915.

Martinson, Arthur David. "Mountain in the Sky: A History of Mount Rainier National Park." Doctoral dissertation, Washington State University, 1966. 182 pp.

Martinson, Arthur D. "The Story of a Mountain: A Pictorial History of Mount Rainier National Park." *American West*, VIII (March 1971), 34-41. Largely on the movement leading to its establishment as a national park (1899).

Mather, Stephen T. "Engineering Applied to National Parks." *Proceedings of the American Society of Civil Engineers*, 54 (Dec. 1928), 2673-84. The National Park Service's director focuses his remarks on the development of road systems (past and present) in the nation's parks.

Mattes, Merrill J. "Behind the Legend of the Colter's Hell: The Early Exploration of Yellowstone National Park." *Mississippi Valley Historical Review*, XXXVI (Sept. 1949), 251-82. Attempts to set the record straight on the early explorations of Yellowstone (prior to 1869).

Matthews, Albert. "The Word 'Park' in the United States." *Publications of the Colonial Society of Massachusetts*, VIII (April 1904), 373-99. Includes references to Yellowstone and Yosemite when discussing some early history of the national parks concept and movement.

Mauk, Charlotte E. *Yosemite and the Sierra Nevada . . . Selections from the Works of John Muir*. Boston: Houghton Mifflin Company, 1948. xix + 132 pp. Illustrations. Descriptions and observations of Muir.

Melbo, Irving Robert. *Our Country's National*

Parks. 2 vols. Indianapolis: Bobbs-Merrill, 1941. Illustrations and maps. Includes a description and brief history of each park.

Merriam, Lawrence C., Jr. "The National Park System: Growth and Outlook." *National Parks & Conservation Magazine*, 46 (Dec. 1972), 4-12. Some general history since 1872.

Meyer, Roy W. "Forestville: The Making of a State Park." *Minnesota History*, 44 (Fall 1974), 82-95. On the state park movement in Minnesota and the creation of Forestville State Park (1963).

Michaud, Howard H. "Conservation of Recreational and Scenic Resources." *Proceedings of the Indiana Academy of Science*, 66 (1957), 268–74. On state parks and recreational areas in Indiana since 1915.

Miles, John G. "The Redwood Park Question." *Forest History*, 11 (April 1967), 6-11, 31. Includes some information on the movement to establish the national park.

"Milestones in U. S. Public Works: Jones Beach State Park." *APWA Reporter*, 43 (Jan. 1976), 23. A short history of the most famous of Long Island state parks.

Miller, J. Jefferson II. "The Designs for the Washington Monument in Baltimore." *Journal of the Society of Architectural Historians*, XXIII (March 1964), 19-28. On the design competition beginning in 1813. The article gives special attention to Robert Mills' winning design, selected in May 1814.

Miller, Thomas W. "The Genesis and Programs of the Nevada State Park System." *Planning and Civic Comment*, 24 (June 1958), 47-49. Since 1923.

Miller, William D. *Memphis during the Progressive Era, 1900-1917*. See chapter on "Sewers and Wastewater Treatment."

Miller, Zane L. *Boss Cox's Cincinnati: Urban Politics in the Progressive Era*. See chapter on "Urban Mass Transportation."

Mills, Enos A. *Early Estes Park*. Estes Park, Colo.: Mrs. E. A. Mills, 1959. xx + 52 pp. Illustrations, map, and diagrams. Includes a biographical sketch of the author (1870-1922) by his wife. The booklet was first printed in 1911.

Mills, Enos A. *The Rocky Mountain National Park*. Boston: Houghton Mifflin, 1932. xxiii + 239 pp. By the Colorado conservationist and park enthusiast who was influential in establishing Rocky Mountain National Park. The volume was first published in 1924.

Mills, Enos A. *Your National Parks*. Boston: Houghton Mifflin, 1917. xxi + 431 pp. Illustrations, bibliography, appendices, and index. Essentially historical descriptions of American and Canadian parks and monuments.

Mitchell, John G. "The Bitter Struggle for a National Park." *American Heritage*, XXI (April 1970), 97-108. On the movement to establish Everglades National Park in Florida.

Montes, Gregory E. "San Diego's City Park, 1868-1902: An Early Debate on Environment and Profit." *Journal of San Diego History*, 23 (Spring 1977), 40-59.

Morgan, Arthur E. *The Miami Conservancy District*. See chapter on "Flood Control and Drainage."

Morrill, John Barstow, and Paul O. Fischer, eds. *Planning the Region of Chicago*. See chapter on "Planning, Engineering, and Administration."

Moses, Robert. *A Tribute to Governor Smith*. New York: Simon and Schuster, 1962. 63 pp. Illustrations. A fascinating tribute by one of the twentieth-century's most prominent public works administrators. Researchers can obtain useful insights into the characters of both men through a reading of this small book.

Moses, Robert. *Public Works: A Dangerous Trade*. See chapter on "Planning, Engineering, and Administration."

Muir, John. *Our National Parks*. Boston: Houghton, Mifflin Company, 1901. 382 pp. Illustrations, map, tables, appendix, and index. The author describes "the beauty, grandeur, and all-embracing usefulness of our wild mountain forest reservations and parks"—especially Yellowstone, Yosemite, Sequoia, and General Grant National parks.

Muir, John. "The Creation of Yosemite National Park." *Sierra Club Bulletin*, 29 (Oct. 1944), 49-60.

Muir, John. *The Yosemite*. New York: Century Company, 1912. 284 pp. Illustrations. Relates some history of Yosemite National Park."

Muller, Herman J. "The Civilian Conservations Corps, 1933-1942." *Historical Bulletin*,

28 (March 1950), 55-60. On CCC's work in the nation's parks and forests.

Musselman, Lloyd Keith. "Rocky Mountain National Park, 1915-1965: An Administrative History." Doctoral dissertation, University of Denver, 1969. 363 pp.

Nairn, Ian. *The American Landscape: A Critical View*. See chapter on "Public Buildings."

Nash, Roderick. "John Muir, William Kent, and the Conservation Schism." *Pacific Historical Review*, XXXVI (Nov. 1967), 423-33. On California congressman Kent and his political battles with Muir and others who attempted to prevent the construction of Hetch Hetchy Dam in Yosemite National Park.

Nash, Roderick, ed. *The American Environment: Readings in the History of Conservation*. See chapter on "Planning, Engineering, and Administration."

Nash, Roderick. "The American Invention of National Parks." *American Quarterly*, XXII (Fall 1970), 726-35. Describes the nineteenth-century origins of national parks in the United States and their influence "around the world."

Nash, Roderick. *Wilderness and the American Mind*. New Haven: Yale University Press, 1967. ix + 256 pp. Notes, bibliographical essay, and index. Traces the transformation in American attitudes toward wilderness areas from "a moral and physical wasteland fit only for conquest and fructification" to appreciation and concern. The book contains excellent chapters on the Hetch Hetchy controversy as well as the careers of John Muir and Aldo Leopold, prophets of what Nash describes as the "wilderness cult." It is clearly written and well researched. (A revised and enlarged edition was published in 1973.)

National Park Service, United States Department of the Interior. *A Study of the Park and Recreation Problem of the United States*. Washington, D. C.: U. S. Government Printing Office, 1941. xi + 279 pp. Illustrations, maps, charts, tables, and index. Presents an overall picture of recreational needs and cites ways that public park systems (national, state, county, metropolitan, and municipal) can meet them. Information of an historical nature is scattered; however, there is one section on the "History of State Park Legislation."

Neal, Edward Charles. "A Comparative Survey of Educational and Experiential Backgrounds of Past and Present Professional Recreators of the Dallas Park and Recreation Department." Master's thesis, North Texas State University, 1973.

Nelson, Beatrice Ward. *State Recreation: Parks, Forests and Game Preserves*. Washington, D. C.: National Conference on State Parks, Inc., 1928. xi + 436 pp. Illustrations and tables. An early reference book on state parks and other recreational areas. The first chapter is "A History of State Recreational Areas."

Nevins, Allan, and John A. Krout, eds. *The Greater City: New York, 1898-1948*. See chapter on "Roads, Streets, and Highways."

New York-New Jersey Metropolitan Chapter of the American Public Works Association. *Public Works in Metropolitan New York-New Jersey*. See chapter on "Planning, Engineering, and Administration."

Newhall, Nancy; Osborn Fairfield; and Horace M. Albright. *A Contribution to the Heritage of Every American: The Conservation Activities of John D. Rockefeller, Jr.* New York: Alfred A. Knopf, 1957. 179 pp. Shows how the national park system benefitted from Rockefeller's philanthropy.

Noble, Iris. *Frederick Law Olmsted: Park Designs*. New York: Julian Messner, 1974. 191 pp. Bibliography and index. A popular biography of the nineteenth-century park and city planner.

Ober, Michael J. "The CCC Experience in Glacier National Park." *Montana: The Magazine of Western History*, XXVI (July 1976), 30-39. Describes the work and contributions of the 1,278 recruits in the Civilian Conservation Corps to be assigned to Glacier Park.

Oberholtzer, Ernest C. "The Chronicle of the Olmsteds." *Living Wilderness*, 64 (Spring 1958), 1-4. On the contributions of Frederick Law Olmsted, Sr.; John Charles Olmsted (nephew and stepson); and Frederick Law Olmsted, Jr. to landscape architecture.

O'Brien, Bob Randolph. "The Roads of Yellowstone, 1870-1915." *Montana: The Magazine of Western History*. See chapter on "Roads, Streets, and Highways."

O'Brien, Bob Randolph. "The Yellowstone National Park Road System: Past, Present and Future." Doctoral dissertation. See chapter on "Roads, Streets, and Highways."

Olmsted, F. L. "Public Parks and the Enlargement of Towns." *Journal of Social Science*, III (1871), 1-36. The prominent landscape architect advocates the systematic development and maintenance of public parks. He outlines their benefits to the public health and well being of communities. (First published as a book in 1870.)

Olmsted, Frederick Law. "The Landscape Architecture of the World's Columbian Exposition." *Inland Architect and News Record*, XXI (Aug. 1893), 18-21. On site selection and subsequent preparations in Chicago's Jackson Park.

Olmsted, Frederick Law. "The Town-Planning Movement in America." *Annals of the American Academy of Political and Social Science*. See chapter on "Planning, Engineering, and Administration."

Olmsted, Frederick Law. "The Yosemite Valley and the Mariposa Big Trees: A Preliminary Report (1865)." *Landscape Architecture*, 43 (Oct. 1952), 12-25. A reprint of Yosemite State Park Commissioner Olmsted's report to the California legislature with an introduction by Laura Wood Roper.

Olmsted, Frederick Law, Jr., and Theodora Kimball, eds. *Forty Years of Landscape Architecture: Central Park*. Cambridge: MIT Press, 1973. xviii + 575 pp. Illustrations, maps, notes, appendices, and bibliography. This edition is reproduced from volume 2 of *Frederick Law Olmsted, Landscape Architect, 1822-1903: Forty Years of Landscape Architecture; Being the Professional Papers of Frederick Law Olmsted, Senior* (1928). It includes a series of papers dealing with the conception, design, construction, and management of Central Park.

Olmsted, Frederick Law, Jr., and Theodora Kimball, eds. *Frederick Law Olmsted: Landscape Architect, 1822-1903*. New York: Benjamin Bloom, 1970. xiii + 575 pp. Illustrations, map, notes, appendices, and bibliography. Two volumes in one of the professional papers of Frederick Law Olmsted. The first volume is devoted to the background of his professional career; the second deals with his professional undertaking, New York's Central Park. These papers were published intitially in 1922.

O'Neill, Eugene James. "Parks and Forest Conservation in New York 1850-1920." Doctoral dissertation, Columbia University, 1963. 231 pp.

Orr, James. *Urban Parks and Open Space: A Bibliography*. Monticello, Ill.: Vance Bibliographies, 1978. 20 pp. A short list of "recent literature dealing with urban parks and open space." Some entries are annotated; very few are historical.

Osborn, Frederic J. *Green-Belt Cities*. See chapter on "Planning, Engineering, and Administration."

Osborn, Marian Lorena. "The Development of Recreation in the South Park System of Chicago." Master's thesis, University of Chicago, 1928. iii + 124 pp. Notes and appendices. Traces the development of the South Park system (1869-1903) and emphasizes how the recreational facilities have grown and broadened (1904-1928).

O'Shaughnessy, M. M. *Hetch Hetchy: Its Origin and History*. See chapter on "Community Water Supply."

Outdoor Recreation Resources Review Commission. *Outdoor Recreation Literature: A Survey*. Washington, D. C.: U. S. Government Printing Office, 1962. ix + 137 pp. Appendices. Includes an essay on the "Historical Development of Outdoor Recreation" by Arthur Hawthorne Carhart and a "Chronology of Significant Events in the History of Outdoor Recreation."

Palisades Interstate Park Commission. *Palisades Interstate Park Commission, 1900-1960*. Bear Mountain, N.Y.: Palisades Interstate Park Commission, 1960. 106 pp. Illustrations, maps, diagrams, and tables. A history of the interstate.

Parkins, A. E., and J. R. Whitaker. *Our Natural Resources and Their Conservation*. See chapter on "Flood Control and Drainage."

Parman, Donald L. "The Indian and the Civilian Conservation Corps." *Pacific Historical Review*, XL (Feb. 1971), 39-56. Work in parks and forests during the 1930s.

Parman, Donald Lee. "The Indian Civilian Conservation Corps." Doctoral dissertation, University of Oklahoma, 1967. 267 pp.

Parsons, Mabel, ed. *Memories of Samuel Parsons: Landscape Architect of the Department of Public Parks, New York*. New York: Knickerbocker Press, 1926. xlix + 150 pp. Illustrations. In large part, Parsons' "personal reminiscences of Central Park recording his long association of close to thirty years in its service." Parsons also describes his training, relationship with Calvert Vaux, and other aspects of his career.

Paulsen, David F. *Natural Resources in the Governmental Process: A Bibliography Selected and Annotated*. Tucson: University of Arizona Press, 1970. 99 pp. Index. A rather limited selection of sources on subjects such as parks and recreation, soil conservation, river basin development and other aspects of water resources.

Peacock, Blanche G. "Reelfoot Lake State Park." *Tennessee Historical Quarterly*, XXXII (Fall 1973), 205-32. On the origin of the lake (1811-1812 earthquakes) and the development of the park site.

Pearson, Grant H. *A History of Mount McKinley National Park, Alaska*. Washington, D. C.: National Park Service, 1953. iii + 91 pp. Illustrations, notes, and bibliography. By the park superintendent.

Peplow, Edward H., Jr. "A Tribute to the National Park Service: 1919—Grand Canyon National Park—1969." *Arizona Highways*, 45 (March 1969), 17-19.

Perrigo, Lynn I. "Municipal Beginnings at Boulder, Colorado, 1871-1900." *Colorado Magazine*. See chapter on "Roads, Streets, and Highways."

Petersen, Peter L. "A Park for the Panhandle: The Acquisition and Development of Palo Duro Canyon State Park." *Panhandle-Plains Historical Review*, 51 (1978), 145-78. On the various efforts to preserve the canyon near Amarillo, Texas, which led to the creation of a state park in 1934.

Peterson, Jon A. "The Impact of Sanitary Reform upon American Urban Planning." *Journal of Social History*. See chapter on "Planning, Engineering, and Administration."

Phelps, Dawson A. "The Natchez Trace: Indian Trail to Parkway." *Tennessee Historical Quarterly*. See chapter on "Roads, Streets, and Highways."

Pierce, Bessie Louise. *A History of Chicago*. See chapter on "Community Water Supply."

Pisani, Donald J. "Lost Parkland: Lumbering and Park Proposals in the Tahoe-Truckee Basin." *Journal of Forest History*, 21 (Jan. 1977), 4-17. On the nineteenth-century Tahoe lumber boom and its legacy as well as an explanation of why Lake Tahoe never became a national park.

Place, Howard and Marian T. *The Story of Crater Lake National Park*. Caldwell, Idaho: Caxton Printers, 1974. 84 pp. Illustrations and maps. A history from the region's discovery in 1852 to the park's establishment in 1902.

Place, Marian T. "Cavalcade to Hell." *American Heritage*, V (Spring 1954), 40-43, 56-57. On the 1870 Washburn expedition which led to the creation of Yellowstone National Park.

Pollock, George Freeman. *Skyland: The Heart of the Shenandoah National Park*. n. p., 1960. xv + 238 pp. Illustrations and notes. Describes the author's role in the creation of Shenandoah National Park in Virginia. (The book's editor is Stuart E. Brown, Jr.)

Pomerantz, Sidney I. *New York: An American City, 1783-1803*. See chapter on "Community Water Supply."

Potter, Barrett George. "The Civilian Conservation Corps in New York State: Its Social and Political Impact (1933-1942)." Doctoral dissertation, State University of New York at Buffalo, 1973. 278 pp.

Potts, Merlin K. "Rocky Mountain National Park." *Colorado Magazine*, XLII (Summer 1967), 216-23. Tribute to the park on its fiftieth anniversary and the work of Enos A. Mills.

Public Works Administration. *America Builds: The Record of PWA*. See chapter on "Planning, Engineering, and Administration."

Raftery, John H. "Historical Sketch of Yellowstone National Park." *Annals of Wyoming*, 15 (April 1943), 101-32. Includes history of early explorations and detailed descriptions of the the park.

Rakestraw, Lawrence. "Conservation Historiography: An Assessment." *Pacific Historical Review*, XLI (Aug. 1972), 271-88. A discussion of major themes in the historiography of conservation. No effort is made to comprehensively summarize scholarship in this field. Most citations cover park and forestry topics.

Ranney, Victoria Post. *Olmsted in Chicago*. Chicago: The Open Lands Project, 1972. 40 pp. Illustrations, notes, and sources. Describes Olmsted's contribution to "Chicago's great heritage in its parks."

Rawick, George P. "The New Deal and Youth: The Civilian Conservation Corps, the National Youth Administration, and the American Youth Congress." Doctoral dissertation, University of Wisconsin, 1957. 416 pp.

Reeves, Thomas C. "President Arthur in Yellowstone National Park." *Montana: The Magazine of Western History*, XIX (Summer 1969), 18-29. The visit brought added support for the park's preservation (1883).

Reid, Russell. "Fort Lincoln State Park." *North Dakota Historical Quarterly*, 8 (Jan. 1941), 101-13. The early history of "one of the more important state park areas" of North Dakota. The author states that the completed park "has made accessible to the public an area of exceptional historical, archeological, and recreational importance."

Reid, Russell. "The North Dakota State Park System." *North Dakota Historical Quarterly*, 8 (Oct. 1940), 63-78. A general history of the state park system by its superintendent. He contends that "the development of North Dakota state parks and historic sites really commenced with the establishment of the first CCC park camp assigned to the state."

Reid, Russell. "The De Mores Historic Site." *North Dakota Historical Quarterly*, 8 (July 1941), 268-83. Recounts the history of the De Mores site at Medora, highlighting the fascinating life and career of its previous owner, the Marquis de Mores, a French nobleman.

Reiger, John F. *American Sportsmen and the Origins of Conservation*. New York: Winchester Press, 1975. 352 pp. Illustrations. A general history of the conservation movement which gives particular attention to efforts to protect Yellowstone National Park.

Reps, John W. *Cities of the American West: A History of Frontier Urban Planning.* See chapter on "Planning, Engineering, and Administration."

Reps, John W. *Monumental Washington: The Planning and Development of the Capital Center*. See chapter on "Planning, Engineering, and Administration."

Reps, John W. *The Making of Urban America: A History of City Planning in the United States*. See chapter on "Planning, Engineering, and Administration.

Richardson, Elmo R. *Dams, Parks, & Politics: Resource Development & Preservation in the Truman-Eisenhower Era*. See chapter on "Irrigation."

Richardson, Elmo R. "Federal Park Policy in Utah: The Escalante National Monument Controversy of 1935-1940." *Utah Historical Quarterly*, 33 (Spring 1965), 109-33. Discusses in detail the controversy surrounding the proposed Escalante National Monument plan for the development of a scenic and recreational area in southeastern Utah.

Richardson, Elmo R. "Olympic National Park: Twenty Years of Controversy." *Forest History*, 12 (April 1968), 6-15. Examines the positions of the competing interests in the park's development (1933-1953).

Richardson, Elmo R. "The Civilian Conservation Corps and the Origins of the New Mexico State Park System." *Natural Resources Journal*, 6 (April 1966), 248-67. On the CCC's contributory role.

Richardson, Elmo R. *The Politics of Conservation: Crusades and Controversies, 1897-1913*. See chapter on "Waterways."

Richardson, Elmo R. "Was There Politics in the Civilian Conservation Corps?" *Forest History*, 16 (July 1972), 12-21. Finds Republican allegations of CCC involvement in politics unfounded.

Righter, Robert W. "The Brief, Hectic Life of Jackson Hole National Monument." *American West*, XIII (Nov./Dec. 1976), 30-33, 57-63. Describes the battle to bring Wyoming's Jackson Hole into the national park system.

Righter, Robert W. *The National Parks in the American West.* St. Louis: Forum Press, 1979. 16 pp. Illustration, map, and bibliography. An historical essay describing "the development of a varied park system, uniquely American, but having a worldwide impact." There are separate sections on "Yellowstone National Park," "John Muir and the Sierra Club," "National Monuments," and "Establishing the National Park Service."

Riley, Stephen T. "Charles Francis Adams (1835-1915), Conservationist." *Proceedings of the Massachusetts Historical Society, 1978*,

90 (1979). Describe Adams' role in the preservation of parks and scenery in Massachusetts.

Robbins, Mary Caroline. "Park-Making as a National Art." *Atlantic Monthly,* LXXIX (1897), 86-98. Through a review of the development of American park systems, the author explains that the planning and cultivation of parks is "the most important artistic work which has been done in the United States."

Robbins, Mary C. "The Park Systems of Minneapolis and St. Paul, Minnesota." *Garden and Forest*, X (April 28, 1897), 162-64. Describes the origins and early growth of the Minneapolis and St. Paul park systems (1880s and 1890s).

Robbins, Mary Caroline. "Village Improvement Societies." *Atlantic Monthly*, LXXIX (1897), 212-22. Reviews the early work of a number of village improvement societies, particularly in New England.

Robbins, Roy M. *Our Landed Heritage: The Public Domain, 1776-1970*. See chapter on "Irrigation."

"Robert Mills and the Washington Monument in Baltimore." *Maryland Historical Magazine*, XXXIV (June 1939), 144-60. In-depth treatment of Mills' design.

Robinson, Charles Mulford. *Modern Civic Art: Or the City Made Beautiful*. See chapter on "Roads, Streets, and Highways."

Robinson, Charles Mulford. *Report on a Park System for Council Bluffs, Iowa*. Council Bluffs: Monarch Printing Company, 1914. 24 pp. The author outlines the deficiencies he observed in the city's park systems, describes the kind of system Council Bluffs ought to have, and lists six general principles which should govern the commissioners' selection of park lands.

Rogers, Cleveland. *Robert Moses: Builder for Democracy*. See chapter on "Planning, Engineering, and Administration."

Rogers, Edmund B. "Notes on the Establishment of Mesa Verde National Park." *Colorado Magazine*, XXIX (Jan. 1952), 10-17. A brief history from 1886 to 1913.

Roloff, Clifford E. "The Mount Olympus National Monument." *Washington Historical Quarterly,* 25 (1934), 214-28. Describes the discovery of Olympic Peninsula and the creation of the national monument (1909), later Olympic National Park.

Roper, Laura Wood. *FLO: A Biography of Frederick Law Olmsted*. Baltimore: Johns Hopkins University Press, 1973. xvii + 555 pp. Illustrations, maps, diagrams, notes, appendices, and index. A biography of "America's great pioneer landscape architect" (1822-1903). The author finds him "dedicated passionately and intelligently . . . to conserving the beautiful and healthy and to remedying the ugly and harmful in the American scene a full hundred years before the environment . . . became a matter of popular concern."

Rose, William Ganson. *Cleveland: The Making of a City*. See chapter on "Sewers and Wastewater Treatment."

Rothenberg, Harvey. "A History of the Dallas, Texas Park and Recreation Department from 1850-1970." Master's thesis, North Texas State University, 1973.

Runte, Alfred. "Beyond the Spectacular: The Niagara Falls Preservation Campaign." *New-York Historical Society Quarterly*, LVII (Jan. 1973), 30-50. On the efforts of Charles Eliot Norton and Frederick Law Olmsted and others to preserve Niagara Falls against commercial interests (1869-1885).

Runte, Alfred. *National Parks: The American Experience*. Lincoln: University of Nebraska Press, 1979. xiv + 240 pp. Illustrations, map, notes, bibliographical essay, and index. An interpretative history of "the *idea* of national parks." Specific people, events, and legislation are treated only as they relate to the national park idea.

Runte, Alfred. "Pragmatic Alliance: Western Railroads and the National Parks." *National Parks & Conservation Magazine*, 48 (April 1974), 14-21. How the railroad companies publicized national parks and capitalized on the tourist trade.

Runte, Alfred. "The National Park Idea: Origins and Paradox of the American Experience." *Journal of Forest History*, 21 (April 1977), 64-75. A thoughtful analysis of the forces that contributed to and worked against the national park idea.

Runte, Alfred. " 'Worthless' Lands—Our National Parks." *American West*, X (May 1973), 4-11. Contains some history of the nation's parks. The author examines the idea that these lands were once thought worthless—of little value except for recreational purposes.

Runte, Alfred. "Yellowstone: It's Useless, So Why Not a Park?" *National Parks & Conservation Magazine*, 46 (March 1972), 5-7. On the establishment of Yellowstone National Park.

Russell, Carl P. "A History of the National Park Service." *National Parks Magazine*, 33 (May 1959), 6-11. Prior to and since its creation in 1916.

Russell, Carl P. "Early Years in Yosemite." *California Historical Society Quarterly*, V (Dec. 1926), 238-41. Contains several pages of the unique reminiscences of Stephen F. Grover, one of a party of eight prospectors who made their way into Yosemite Valley in 1852.

Russell, Carl Parcher. *One Hundred Years in Yosemite: The Story of a Great Park and Its Friends*. Yosemite National Park: Yosemite Natural History Association, 1957. 195 pp. Illustrations, chronology, table, and notes. A popular history of the nation's first public park by a National Park Service employee. It emphasizes the accomplishments of "old-timers who took the first steps in creating the reservations."

Russell, Don. "Illinois Monuments on Civil War Battlefields." *Transactions of the Illinois State Historical Society* (1943), 1-37. Documents Illinois' battlefield monuments and memorials which now decorate many of the state's parks.

Salmond, John A. "The Civilian Conservation Corps and the Negro." *Journal of American History*, LII (June 1965), 75-88. The author blames Franklin D. Roosevelt and Robert Fechner, CCC director, for not providing for fuller participation by Negroes in the CCC.

Salmond, John A. *The Civilian Conservation Corps, 1933-1942: A New Deal Case Study*. Durham, N.C.: Duke University Press, 1967. vi + 240 pp. Notes, bibliography, and index. An administrative and political history of the CCC which examines its work in specific parks and forests in the United States.

Sargent, Shirley. *John Muir in Yosemite*. Yosemite: Flying Speer Press, 1971. 48 pp. Illustrations and index. On Muir's attachment to Yosemite National Park in California (1868-1914).

Sargent, Shirley. "Pictures from Yosemite's Past: Galen Clark's Photograph Album." *California Historial Society Quarterly*, XLV (March 1966), 31-40.

Sargent, Shirley. "Wellllllcome to Camp Curry." *California History Quarterly*, LIII (Summer 1974), 131-38. On the Curry Company, tour guides, and innkeepers in Yosemite National Park since 1899.

Sargent, Shirley. "When War Comes to Yosemite." *American West*, XII (March 1975), 40-47. On park administration and visitors (mostly military personnel) to Yosemite during World War II.

Saylor, David L. *Jackson Hole, Wyoming: In the Shadow of the Tetons*. Norman: University of Oklahoma Press, 1970. 268 pp. Illustrations, notes, maps, bibliography, and index. Describes the movement to establish Grand Teton National Park and protection of Jackson Hole.

Schnarff, Robert. *The Yellowstone and Grand Teton National Parks*. New York: David McKay and Company, 1966. vi + 209 pp. Contains some history of the national parks in Wyoming.

Schmitt, Peter J. *Back to Nature: The Arcadian Myth in Urban America*. New York: Oxford University Press, 1969. xxiii + 230 pp. Notes and index. A good study of the "arcadian myth" and efforts by urbanites to escape the rigors of city life. The author suggests that the movement for creation of national and state parks was part of this phenomenon.

Schrepfer, Susan R. "Conflict in Preservation: The Sierra Club, Save-the-Redwoods League, and Redwood National Park." *Journal of Forest History*, 24 (April 1980), 60-77. On the battle to establish the Redwood National Park in the 1960s.

Schuyler, David Paul. "Public Landscapes and American Urban Culture, 1800-1870: Rural Cemeteries, City Parks, and Suburbs." Doctoral dissertation, Columbia University, 1979.

Scott, Ferris Huntington. *The Yosemite Story*. Santa Ana, Calif.: Western Resort Publications, 1954. 64 pp. Illustrations, maps, diagrams, and tables. On Yosemite Valley and national park since 1833.

Scoyen, E. T. "Policies and Objectives of the National Park Service." *Journal of Forestry*, 44 (Sept. 1946), 641-46. A brief history of the national parks, the National Park Service, and the laws creating them.

Segrest, J. L. "Resume of Alabama State Park

History." *Alabama Historical Quarterly*, 10 (1948), 77-80. Since 1927.

Selmeier, Lewis L. "First Camera on the Yellowstone a Century Ago." *Montana: The Magazine of Western History*, XX (Summer 1972), 42-53. Explains how the photographs taken during the Hayden expedition's tour of Yellowstone (1871) were circulated in Congress to win support for the park's creation.

Shankland, Robert. *Steve Mather of the National Parks*. New York: Alfred A. Knopf, 1970. xii + 370 + xxiii pp. Illustrations, map, appendix, bibliography, and index. Mather, the first director of the National Park Service, served from 1916 to 1929. In this third edition (published first in 1951 and reprinted in 1954), the author includes five chapters on the park system's administration by Mather's successors.

Sherfy, Marcella M. "The National Park Service and the First World War." *Journal of Forest History*, 22 (Oct. 1978), 203-05. On the survival of the newly created National Park Service (1916) during World War I—thanks to the "magnetism, skill, and determination" of Stephen T. Mather and Horace M. Albright, director and assistant director respectively.

Shoemaker, Florence J. "The Pioneers of Estes Park." *Colorado Magazine*, XXIV (Jan. 1947), 15-23. Relates the early history of an area which later became part of Colorado's Rocky Mountain National Park (1860s-1890s).

Short, C. W., and R. Stanley-Brown. *Public Buildings: A Survey of Architecture of Projects Constructed by Federal and Other Governmental Bodies between the Years 1933 and 1939 with the Assistance of the Public Works Administration*. See chapter on "Public Buildings."

Silver, David M., ed. "Richard Lieber and Indiana's Forest Heritage." *Indiana Magazine of History*, LXVII (March 1971), 45-55. A biographical sketch of Lieber precedes his report, as chairman of the Committee on Indiana State Centennial Memorial (1916), on the acquisition of Turkey Run which later became a state park.

Simmons, Dennis Elwood. "The Creation of Shenandoah National Park and the Skyline Drive, 1924-1936." Doctoral dissertation, University of Virginia, 1978. vi + 213 pp. Maps, notes, and bibliography. Explains who was responsible for creating the park, "the first major national park east of the Mississippi authorized by Congress," for what reasons, and with what results.

Simon, Andreas, ed. *Chicago, the Garden City: Its Magnificent Parks, Boulevards and Cemeteries*. Chicago: Franz Gindele Printing Company, 1893. 237 pp. Illustrations, map, and index. An early testimonial to the "admirable and extensive Park System of the 'Fair' City." The book contains brief histories of many of Chicago's parks and cemeteries.

Simon, Donald E. "The Public Park Movement in Brooklyn, 1824-1873." Doctoral dissertation, New York University, 1972. 257 pp.

Simutis, Leonard Joseph. "Frederick Law Olmsted's Later Years: Landscape Architecture and the Spirit of Place." Doctoral dissertation, University of Minnesota, 1971. 250 pp.

Slauson, Allan B., ed. *A History of the City of Washington: Its Men and Institutions*. See chapter on "Public Buildings."

Smith, Charles Dennis. "The Appalachian National Park Movement, 1885-1901." *North Carolina Historical Review*, XXXVII (Jan. 1960), 38-65. Recounts the activities of a band of Asheville citizens and their supporters to create a national park in western North Carolina.

Smith, Frank E. *The Politics of Conservation*. See chapter on "Irrigation."

Smith, Guy-Harold. *Conservation of Natural Resources*. See chapter on "Irrigation."

Smith, Robert Patrick. "Illusions and Reality in the Press and Other Contemporary Sources: Urban Recreation in Brooklyn, 1890-1898." Doctoral dissertation, Indiana University, 1973. vii + 282 pp. Map, notes, and bibliography. An in-depth look at Brooklyn's recreational patterns in the last decade of the nineteenth century. These findings are compared to "the media's distortion and exaggeration" of these patterns.

Somers, Dale A. *The Rise of Sports in New Orleans, 1850-1900*. Baton Rouge: Louisiana State University Press, 1972. xv + 320 pp. Notes, bibliography, and index. Only two pages are devoted to the effect of sports on municipal parks and other recreational facilities.

Stevenson, Elizabeth. *Park Maker: A Life of*

Frederick Law Olmsted. New York: MacMillan Publishing Co., 1977. xxv + 484 pp. Illustrations, notes, bibliography, and index. A meticulously researched biography of an early conservationist and preservationist. The chapter entitled "The Boss of Central Park" is particularly noteworthy.

Stewart, Ian Robert. "Central Park 1851-1871: Urbanization and Environmental Planning in New York City." Doctoral dissertation, Cornell University, 1973. 379 pp. The two decades examined in this study span the park's conception, advocacy, political acceptance, construction, and national emulation.

Stewart, Ian R. "New Mexico's State Monuments: One Means of Preserving the Historic Environment of a Multicultural Region." *El Palacio*, 78 (June 1972), 13-31. Includes brief histories of the following state monuments: Coronado, Jemez, Quarai, Abo, El Palacio, Folsom, and Fort Sumner. There is a lengthy bibliography on "Cultural Preservation."

Stewart, Ian R., comp. *Nineteenth-Century American Public Landscape Design: Exchange Bibliography No. 68*. Monticello, Ill.: Council of Planning Librarians, 1969. 20 pp. Not annotated.

Stewart, Ian R. "Politics and the Park: The Fight for Central Park." *New-York Historical Society Quarterly*, LXI (July/Oct. 1977), 124-55. How New York City's "largest and most accessible recreational resource" was acquired . . . . "it was not an easy matter."

Still, Bayrd. *Milwaukee: The History of a City*. See chapter on "Sewers and Wastewater Treatment."

Still, Bayrd, ed. *Urban America: A History with Documents*. See chapter on "Planning, Engineering, and Administration."

Story, Isabelle F. *The National Park Story in Pictures*. Washington, D. C.: Government Printing Office, 1957. 88 pp. Illustrations and map. Since the 1870s.

Stratton, Owen, and Phillip Sirotkin. *The Echo Park Controversy*. University, Ala.: Inter-University Case Program, 1959. xii + 100 pp. Illustrations, maps, and notes. Describes the successful efforts of environmentalists to preserve the Dinosaur National Monument from inundation by a reservoir (1940s-1950s). This volume is number 46 in the "Cases in Public Administration and Policy Formation" series.

Strong, Douglas Hillman. "A History of Sequoia National Park." Doctoral dissertation, Syracuse University, 1964. 350 pp. On the origins of the California park.

Strong, Douglas H. "Sequoia National Park: Discovery and Exploration." *Western Explorer*, 4 (Sept. 1966), 9-27. Presents the history of the Sierra Nevada region before its establishment as a national park (1890).

Strong, Douglas H. "The History of Sequoia National Park, 1876-1926." *Southern California Quarterly*, XLVIII (June, Sept., and Dec. 1966), June: 137-67; Sept.: 265-88; Dec.: 369-99. Describes the movement to establish this California park and efforts to preserve and enlarge it.

Strong, Douglas. "The Man Who 'Owned' Grand Canyon." *American West*, VI (Sept. 1969), 33-40. On the battles of Ralph Cameron, Arizona businessman and U. S. senator, who attempted to monopolize tourist facilities and other developments at Grand Canyon National Park.

Stuart, Darwin G. "Coordinated Freeway-Park Developments." *Traffic Quarterly*. See chapter on "Roads, Streets, and Highways."

Stupka, Arthur. *Great Smoky Mountains National Park, North Carolina and Tennessee*. Washington, D. C.: National Park Service, 1960. 79 pp. Illustrations, map, and bibliography. Some history of the park since 1923 is included.

Sundquist, James L. *Politics and Policy: The Eisenhower, Kennedy, and Johnson Years*. Washington, D. C.: Brookings Institution, 1968. xi + 560 pp. Tables, notes, and index. Chapter 8, "For All, a Better Outdoor Environment," analyzes administrative and legislative efforts to improve national parks and to provide for outdoor recreation and highway beautification.

Sutherland, Douglas. *Fifty Years on the Civic Front*. See chapter on "Solid Wastes."

Sutton, Ann and Myron. *Guarding the Treasured Lands: The Story of the National Park Service*. Philadelphia: J. B. Lippincott, 1965. 160 pp. Illustrations. A general history.

Sutton, Ann and Myron. "The Man from Yosemite." *National Parks Magazine*, 28

(July-Sept. 1954), 102-05, 131-32, 140. On Harold Child Bryant's career as National Park superintendent (1908-1954).

Sutton, Ann and Myron. *The Wilderness World of the Grand Canyon: 'Leave It as It Is.'* Philadelphia: J. B. Lippincott, 1971. xii + 241 pp. Illustrations, maps, appendices, bibliography, and index. Includes some history of Grand Canyon National Park in Arizona.

Sutton, Ann and Myron. *Yellowstone: A Century of the Wilderness Idea*. New York: Macmillan and Yellowstone Library and Museum Association, 1972. 219 pp. Illustrations, bibliography, and index. Includes some general historical information on the national park.

Sutton, S. B., ed. *Civilizing American Cities: A Selection of Frederick Law Olmsted's Writings on City Landscapes*. Cambridge: MIT Press, 1971. v + 310 pp. Illustrations, maps, notes, and index. A collection of Olmsted's general writings on urban society, landscapes, and city design as well as his commentaries on plans for five North American cities—San Francisco, Buffalo, Chicago, Montreal, and Boston. The last chapter contains Olmsted's reports on the university community of Berkeley and the planned community of Riverside, Illinois.

Swain, Donald C. *Federal Conservation Policy, 1921-1933*. See chapter on "Irrigation."

Swain, Donald C. "Harold Ickes, Horace Albright, and the Hundred Days: A Study in Conservation Administration." *Pacific Historical Review*, XXXIV (Nov. 1965), 455-65. An insightful article on the role of Albright, director of the National Park Service, in shaping New Deal conservation policies. Albright, who resigned in August 1933, was able to establish an excellent rapport with Harold Ickes, rancorous secretary of the Department of the Interior.

Swain, Donald C. "The Founding of the National Park Service." *American West*, VI (Sept. 1969), 6-9. On the movement leading to passage of the 1916 National Park Service Act.

Swain, Donald C. "The National Park Service and the New Deal, 1933-1940." *Pacific Historical Review*, XLI (Aug. 1972), 312-32. The author concludes that during the New Deal the National Park Service expanded rapidly and took on "large new functions in recreational planning and development, historic preservation, and public works."

Swain, Donald C. "The Passage of the National Park Service Act of 1916." *Wisconsin Magazine of History*, L (Autumn 1966), 4-17. Comprehensive discussion of the meaning of the act, which "stands as one of the landmarks in the history of conservation in the United States."

Swain, Donald C. *Wilderness Defender: Horace M. Albright and Conservation*. Chicago: University of Chicago Press, 1970. xii + 347 pp. Illustrations, notes, bibliography, and index. This bibliography may also be considered a history of the National Park Service. Albright was assistant to National Park Service director Stephen T. Mather, (1916-1919), superintendent of Yellowstone National Park (1919-1929), and director of the National Park Service (1929-1933).

Swisher, J. A. "Historical and Memorial Parks." *Palimpsest*, XII (June 1931), 201-18. A survey of eleven of Iowa's historic and memorial parks.

Syrett, Harold Coffin. *The City of Brooklyn, 1865-1898*. See chapter on "Urban Mass Transportation."

Tatum, George B. "The origins of Fairmount Park." *Antiques*, LXXXII (Nov. 1962), 502-07. Discusses the nineteenth-century origins of Philadelphia's Fairmount Park and describes the city's architecturally fine waterworks located there.

Tebeau, Charlton W. *Man in the Everglades: 2,000 Years of Human History in the Everglades National Park*. Coral Gables, Fla.: Everglades, Natural History Association and University of Miami Press, 1968. 192 pp.

Thompson, Carl D. *Public Ownership: A Survey of Public Enterprises, Municipal, State, and Federal, in the United States and Elsewhere*. See chapter on "Energy."

Thompson, Huston. "The NPA and Stephen Mather." *National Parks Magazine*, 33 (May 1959), 12. On Mather's role in establishing the National Parks Association.

Thompson, Priscilla M. "Creation of the Wilmington Park System Before 1896." *Delaware History*, XVIII (Fall-Winter 1978), 75-94. An excellent case study of the evolution of an urban park system.

Tilden, Freeman. "Richer of Being: The Century Since Yellowstone." *National Parks & Con-*

servation Magazine, 46 (Jan. 1972), 4-9. Reflections on the parks movement since 1872.

Tilden, Freeman. *The National Parks.* New York: Alfred A. Knopf, 1968. xviii + 562 pp. + xix pp. Illustrations, map, and index. A revised and enlarged edition of a 1951 publication, this heavily illustrated volume was designed to help its readers "appreciate the National Park System and the benefits the parks can bring to the people of America, and of the world." The 1951 edition included only natural areas in the park system; the 1968 edition treats historical and recreational sites as well.

Tilden, Freeman. "The National Park Concept." *National Parks Magazine*, 33 (May 1959), 2-5. On the establishment of Yellowstone National Park and Yosemite National Park (as a state park).

Tilden, Freeman. *The State Parks: Their Meaning in American Life*. New York: Alfred A. Knopf, 1962. xvi + 496 + xi pp. Illustrations, maps, appendices, and index. A comprehensive guide to state parks directed toward legislators, conservation organizations, schools, and the general public. It includes a brief history of the state park movement as well as descriptions and incidental references to the history of particular parks in the Northeast, South, Midwest, and West.

Tindall, William. *Origin and Government of the District of Columbia*. See chapter on "Planning, Engineering, and Administration."

Tobey, G. B. *A History of Landscape Architecture: The Relationship of People to Environment*. New York: American Elsevier Publishing Company, 1973. xiv + 305 pp. Illustrations, diagrams, notes, appendices, bibliography, and index. A broad view of man's relationship to nature and his impact on "the surface features of the world" from 4000 B. C. to the present. The last third of the book deals with the United States in general and in particular. There are, for example, single chapters on the "Beautiful and Picturesque" in the United States, 1800-1850, as well as ones on Frederick Law Olmsted and the City Beautiful movement. Although this study may on occasion be of some value to public works and/or environmental researchers, the contents are too encompassing, the writing too poor, and the index too general for the volume to be of real use.

Tolman, William Howe. *Municipal Reform in the United States*. See chapter on "Planning, Engineering, and Administration."

Torrey, Raymond H. "John Boyd Thacher State Park." *Scenic and Historic America*, 4 (1935), 3-28. General history of a New York park.

Trachtenberg, Marvin. *The Statue of Liberty*. New York: Penguin Books, 1977. 224 pp. Illustrations, table, notes, and index. A good book which features "*Liberty*'s origins, patronage, and public; symbolism, colossal scale, and spectacular setting." See especially the chapters on "The Site" and "Construction."

Trager, Martelle W. *National Parks of the Northwest*. New York: Dodd, Mead, 1939. 216 pp. Illustrations. Some historical data is included.

Trotter, John E. "State Park System in Illinois." Doctoral dissertation, University of Chicago, 1962.

Tunnard, Christopher. *The Modern American City*. See chapter on "Planning, Engineering, and Administration."

Tweed, William. "Sequoia National Park Concessions, 1898-1926." *Pacific Historian*, 16 (Spring 1972), 36-60. Contains an account of the park's origins.

U. S. Department of Commerce. Bureau of the Census. *Historical Statistics of the United States: Colonial Times to 1970*. See chapter on "Planning, Engineering, and Administration."

U. S. Geological Survey. *Ferdinand Vandiveen Hayden and the Founding of the Yellowstone National Park*. Washington, D. C.: U. S. Geological Survey, 1976. 28 pp. Illustrations.

U. S. National Park Service. *A Bibliography of National Parks and Monuments West of the Mississippi River*. Washington, D. C.: Western Museum Laboratories of the National Park Service, Works Progress Administration, and the Civilian Conservation Corps, 1941.

Udall, Stewart L. *The Quiet Crisis*. New York: Holt, Rinehart and Winston, 1963. xiii + 209 pp. Illustrations, notes, and index. A polemic by the secretary of the U. S. Department of the Interior against the degradation of the environment caused by industrialization and exploitation of natural resources. The book traces the evolution of conservation philosophy, laws, and policies through the lives of such people as George Perkins Marsh, Carl Schurz, John Wesley Powell, John Muir, Gifford Pinchot, and Frederick Law Olmsted. It is perhaps the most concise statement of the conservationist's point of view during the Kennedy Administration.

Vance, Linda D. "May Mann Jennings and Royal Palm State Park." *Florida Historical Quarterly*, LV (July 1976), 1-17. On her long-term involvement in preserving and improving Royal Palm State Park in the Everglades.

Van Doren, Carlton S. *America's Park and Recreation Heritage: A Chronology*. Washington, D. C.: U. S. Department of the Interior, 1975. 37 pp. Charts and bibliography. Through brief chronologies in text and chart form, the author presents "the principal governmental and institutional events that have molded present human and physical resources to serve our mobile, leisure-oriented society." This volume is not a comprehensive history of the origins and development of the recreation and parks movement in the United States.

Van Dusen, George. "Politics of 'Partnership': The Eisenhower Administration and Conservation, 1952-1960." Doctoral dissertation. See chapter on "Energy."

Verburg, Edwin Arnold. "The U. S. Army Corps of Engineers' Recreation Development Program: A Comparative Perspective of Equity Related to Policies and Program Outcomes." Doctoral dissertation, George Washington University, 1975. 303 pp.

Vinci, John. "Graceland: The Nineteenth-Century Garden Cemetery." *Chicago History*, VI (Summer 1977), 86-98. Presents a sketchy history of the cemetery (its papers were destroyed in the Great Chicago Fire) and describes "Some of Graceland's Noted Occupants."

Vitz, Carl. "A Brief History of Lytle Square, 1789-1964." *Bulletin of the Cincinnati Historical Society*, 22 (April 1964), 110-22. A historical sketch of the Queen City's one-time social and cultural center.

Voss, J. Ellis. "Summer Resort: An Ecological Analysis of a Satellite Community." Doctoral dissertation, University of Pennsylvania, 1941. xi + 152 pp. Tables, notes, appendices, and bibliography. An interesting study of the growth of Ocean City, New Jersey, as a resort community.

Waring, George E., Jr. *Report on the Social Statistics of Cities*. 2 vols. See chapter on "Planning, Engineering, and Administration."

Watkins, T. H. "Pilgrim's Pride." *American West*, VI (Sept. 1969), 49-54. On the Grand Canyon in Arizona from the 1870s.

Weber, Daniel Barr. "John Muir: The Function of Wilderness in an Industrial Society." Doctoral dissertation, University of Minnesota, 1964. 285 pp.

Weigold, Marilyn E. "Pioneering in Parks and Parkways: Westchester County, New York, 1895-1945." *Essays in Public Works History*, 9 (Feb. 1980), 1-43. On Westchester County's success in developing an impressive system of parks and parkways.

Whatley, Larry. "The Works Progress Administration in Mississippi." *Journal of Mississippi History*. See chapter on "Public Buildings."

Whipple, Gurth. *A History of Half a Century of the Management of the Natural Resources of the Empire State, 1885-1935*. Albany: New York State Conservation Department, 1935. 199 pp. Illustrations, tables, and bibliography. The cover bears the title of *Fifty Years of Conservation in New York State, 1885-1935*. The book emphasizes conservation programs in state parks and forests.

White, Dana F., and Victor A. Kramer, eds. *Olmsted South: Old South Critic/New South Planner*. Westport, Conn.: Greenwood Press, 1979. Illustrations, maps, notes, and index. Excellent collection of essays on Olmsted that illustrate his efforts to initiate the development of parks in Atlanta and other southern cities.

Widder, Keith R. *Mackinac National Park, 1875-1895*. Lansing, Mich.: Mackinac Island State Park Commission, 1975. 48 pp. Illustrations and bibliography.

William A. Behnke Associates. *Cleveland Parks and Recreation Study*. Cleveland: William A. Behnke Associates, 1976. v + 197 pp. Maps, charts, tables, diagrams, appendix, and bibliography. A study "to identify and recommend the most appropriate means of satisfying the park and recreation needs of Cleveland." The first chapter is entitled "Historical Background" and includes sections on "Parkland Acquisition," "Chronological History," and "Public Policy Regarding Parks."

Wilson, William H. *The City Beautiful Movement in Kansas City*. See chapter on "Planning, Engineering, and Administration."

Winkley, John W. *John Muir: A Concise Biography of the Great Naturalist*. Martinez, Calif.: Contra Costa County Historical Society of California, 1959. 141 pp. Illustrations. A biography which highlights Muir's efforts to protect the natural beauty of the Pacific Coast states.

Wirth, Conrad L. *Parks, Politics, and the People*. Norman: University of Oklahoma Press, 1980. xvi + 397 pp. Illustrations, charts, and index. An account of the author's "thirty-six year of experience in planning and administering national parks and other recreational areas . . . ." (The author retired in 1964).

Wisdom, Lloyd Charles. "Community Planning as an Outgrowth of the Park Movement: Frederick Law Olmsted and Urban Design." Master's thesis, University of Washington, 1971.

Wolfe, Linnie Marsh. *Son of the Wilderness: The Life of John Muir*. New York: Alfred A. Knopf, 1947. xviii + 364 + xvi pp. Illustrations, notes, bibliography, and index. The standard biography of Muir (1838-1914), founder of the Sierra Club.

Womack, Bob. "Stone's River National Military Park." *Tennessee Historical Quarterly*, XXI (Dec. 1962), 303-17. Describes the history of the Stone's River Battlefield and how it became a national park.

Wood, Jack. "Jacob Babler: His Contribution to the State Park Movement in Missouri," *Missouri Historical Society Bulletin*, XV (July 1959), 285-95. Includes some history of the state park system while reviewing the work of Babler (1870-1945), who established and endowed the Dr. Edmund A. Babler Memorial State Park near St. Louis, 1934-1938.

Woodbury, Angus M. "A History of Southern Utah and Its National Parks." *Utah Historical Quarterly*, 12 (July-Oct. 1944), 111-209. A lengthy article beginning with "The Indian Heritage" and concluding with "Modern Development of Zion, Bryce and North Rim [1930]."

Woods, James. "The Legend and the Legacy of Franklin D. Roosevelt and the Civilian Conservation Corps (CCC)." Doctoral dissertation, Syracuse University, 1964. 453 pp. On FDR's personal interest in the CCC.

Worster, Donald, ed. *American Environmentalism: The Formative Period, 1860-1915*. See chapter on "Planning, Engineering, and Administration."

Wortman, Marlene Stein. "Domesticating the Nineteenth-Century American City." *Prospects: An Annual of American Cultural Studies*. See chapter on "Solid Wastes."

Wurman, Richard Saul; Alan Levy; and Joel Katz. *The Nature of Recreation: A Handbook in Honor of Frederick Law Olmsted, Using Examples from His Work*. Cambridge: MIT Press, 1972. 76 pp. Illustrations, maps, diagrams, and appendix. A general discussion of recreational needs that includes a brief biography of Olmsted and selections from his writings.

Yard, Robert Sterling. "Organizing the National Parks." *American Forests and Forest Life*, 35 (Aug. 1929), 462-63, 516. On the movement to create a National Park Service.

Yard, Robert Sterling. *Our Federal Lands: A Romance of American Development*. New York: Charles Scribner's Sons, 1928. xvi + 360 pp. Illustrations, map, tables, and index. Includes chapters on national parks, monuments, and forests.

Yard, Robert Sterling. *The Book of the National Parks*. New York: Charles Scribner's Son, 1919. xvi + 436 pp. Illustrations, maps, tables, and index. Descriptive history of national parks and monuments.

Yard, Robert Sterling. *The National Parks Portfolio*. Washington, D. C.: Government Printing Office, 1931. 274 pp. Illustrations and map. Historical references to national parks and monuments are scattered. The volume was published initially in 1916.

Yard, Robert Sterling. "The Unforgotten Story of Hetch Hetchy." *American Forests*, 40 (Dec. 1934), 566-69. On the complicated controversy over the Hetch Hetchy Valley and reservoir in Yosemite National Park (1890-1910.)

Yeager, Dorr G. *National Parks in California*. Menlo Park, Calif.: Lane Publishing Company, 1959. 96 pp. Illustrations and maps. Presents some historical data on Lassen Volcanic,

Kings Canyon, Sequoia, and Yosemite national parks and includes an appendix on national monuments in California.

Young, Hugh E. "The Value of Planned City Development: A Record of 24 Years of Progress Under the Chicago Plan." *Civil Engineering*. See chapter on "Planning, Engineering, and Administration."

Zaitzevsky, Cynthia. "The Olmsted Firm and the Structures of the Boston Park System." *Journal of the Society of Architectural Historians*, XXXII (May 1973), 167-74. Features three documents which "reveal much about the process of the design" of several park structures. The article also describes the role of Frederick Law Olmsted, Sr., "vis-à-vis the consulting or city architects involved. . . ."

Zueblin, Charles. *American Municipal Progress: Chapters in Municipal Sociology*. See chapter on "Planning, Engineering, and Administration."

13

Energy

Energy production and distribution have long been a public sector activity. City-owned companies provided some of the first electricity for street lighting and public use. A large part of the nation's vast hydroelectric potential was developed by state and federal agencies, as well as by publicly owned utilities. However, energy development has been a pluralistic phenomenon involving sharp policy battles with respect to whether public or private entities should produce and market electricity. Furthermore, the past decade has witnessed concern over dwindling supplies, the development of new energy sources and technologies, and the balancing of energy production with the maintenance of a healthful and attractive environment.

The following bibliography is limited to public energy production and distribution. It does not cover fossil fuels, pipelines, gas utilities, and other aspects that fall within the domain of private enterprise. The following annotated sources collectively survey the early development of municipal utilities; public-versus-private battles over generation and transmission; the origin and growth of the Rural Electrification Administration, Tennessee Valley Authority, and other federal power programs; and the development of atomic energy. In addition, the technological, organizational, managerial, political, and economic aspects of the subject are discussed.

"A Sketch of the History of the Gas Supply of New York." *Journal of Gas Lighting, Water Supply, & Sanitary Improvement*, LXXVI (Oct. 2, 1900), 828-29.

Adams, Edward Dean. *Niagara Power: History of the Niagara Falls Power Company, 1886-1918*. Niagara Falls: Niagara Falls Power Company, 1927. xxii + 455 pp. Illustrations and index. Despite the poor quality of its narrative and organization, this volume incorporates considerable source material on central station electrical generation.

Alperin, Lynn M. *Custodians of the Coast: History of the United States Army Engineers at Galveston*. See chapter on "Waterways."

Anderson, William. "The Regulation of Gas and Electric Light Companies in Massachusetts." Doctoral dissertation, Harvard University, 1917.

Andrews, William Ressman. "One Hundred Years of Gas Lighting: An Account of the Early Days of this Art, Which First Stood on Solid Ground in 1820." *Scientific American*, CXXIII (Nov. 27, 1920), 544. The author presents his case: 1920 is the centenary of gas lighting; 1820 "was the dividing line between the experimental stage of gas lighting and the period of demonstrated practicability."

Arent, Leonora. *Electric Franchises in New York City*. New York: Columbia University, 1919. 184 pp. Notes and bibliography. Short histories of utility companies are included in this diatribe against municipal ownership. The book contains particularly good material on municipal taxation of utility firms.

Armstrong, Ellis L; Michael C. Robinson; and Suellen M. Hoy, eds. *History of Public Works in the United States, 1776-1976*. See chapter on "Planning, Engineering, and Administration."

Aston, Rollah E. "Boulder Dam and the Public Utilities." Master's thesis. See chapter on "Irrigation."

Atherton, Lewis. *Main Street on the Middle Border*. Bloomington: Indiana University Press, 1954. xix + 423 pp. Illustrations, notes, appendices, and index. A discussion of the early development of municipal electric utilities is incorporated in this brilliant book.

Axelrod, Alan. "A Century of Light: The Development of Iowa's Electric Utilities." *Palimpsest*, 60 (Sept./Oct. 1979), 130-55. Beginning in the early 1880s. The article is nicely illustrated.

Bader, Louis. "Gas Illumination in New York City, 1823-1863." Doctoral dissertation, New York University, 1970.

Bauer, John, and Peter Costello. *Public Organization of Electric Power: Conditions, Policies, and Program*. New York: Harper & Brothers, 1949. xvi + 263 pp. Tables, appendix, bibliography, and index. An analysis of public versus privately owned power systems. The authors conclude that comprehensive public control "will be decisively in the public interest for expanding production and better living."

Bauer, John, and Nathaniel Gold. *The Electric Power Industry: Development, Organization, and Public Policies*. New York: Harper & Brothers Publishers, 1939. xii + 347 pp. Tables, notes, bibliography, and index. An outstanding source on the growth of private and public electrical utilities. The book addresses technology, organization, management, and regulation.

Baumhoff, Richard G. *The Dammed Missouri Valley: One Sixth of Our Nation*. See chapter on "Flood Control and Drainage."

Beard, Daniel P. "United States Environmental Legislation and Energy Resources: A Review." *Geographical Review*, LXV (April 1975), 229-42. A comprehensive and thoughtful discussion of the influence of environmental legislation on fuel consumption. Some challenging questions are raised regarding the relationships between environmental quality and energy supply.

Bemis, Edward W., ed. *Municipal Monopolies*. See chapter on "Urban Mass Transportation."

Bemis, Edward W. "Some Recent Municipal Gas History." *Forum*, XXV (March 1898), 72-82. Comments on the lease of "the Philadelphia gas-works, for thirty years, to a private company . . . after fifty-six years of public ownership."

Benincasa, Frederick Albert. "The Tennessee Valley Authority from 1933 to 1961." Doctoral dissertation. See chapter on "Flood Control and Drainage."

Bennett, James D. "Roosevelt, Willkie, and the TVA." *Tennessee Historical Quarterly*, XXVIII (Winter 1969), 388-96. Discussion of an important public versus private power controversy.

Bennett, James David, II. "Struggle for Power: The Relationship Between the Tennessee Valley Authority and the Private Power Industry, 1933-1939." Doctoral dissertation, Vanderbilt University, 1969. ii + 324 pp. Notes and bibliography. Perceptive study of the founding and expansion of TVA's power system.

Bessey, Roy F. "The Political Issues of the Hells Canyon Controversy." *Western Political Quarterly*, 9 (Sept. 1956), 676-90. Clash of private versus public interest regarding the construction of dams and power stations in Hells Canyon.

Blackford, Mansel G. "Reform Politics in Seattle during the Progressive Era, 1902-1916." *Pacific Northwest Quarterly*, 59 (Oct. 1968), 177-85. Illustrates how public ownership of utilities was a central Progressive issue.

Blee, C. E. "Development of the Tennessee River Waterway." *Transactions of the Ameri-*

can Society of Civil Engineers. See chapter on "Waterways."

Bolton, Kate. "The Great Awakening of the Night: Lighting America's Streets." *Landscape*. See chapter on "Roads, Streets, and Highways."

Bonbright, James C. *Public Utilities and the National Power Policies*. New York: Columbia University Press, 1940. vii + 82 pp. Bibliography and index. An excellent, often overlooked source on the evolution of public utilities in the 1920s and 1930s. The book includes chapters on the rise of holding companies in the 1920s, the power policies of the Roosevelt Administration, and rural electrification.

Boslaugh, Paul E. "The Great North Platte Dam, Power and Irrigation Project." *Nebraska History*. See chapter on "Irrigation."

Bowman, James S. "Multipurpose River Developments." *Transactions of the American Society of Civil Engineers*. See chapter on "Waterways."

Branch, Joseph G. *Heat and Light from Municipal and Other Waste*. St. Louis: Wm. H. O'Brien Printing and Publishing Co., 1906. vii + 305 pp. Illustrations, tables, and diagrams. This study presaged modern attempts to recover energy by burning municipal refuse. It lists pioneering efforts to implement this practice in the United States and Great Britain. The book also provides an excellent overview of turn-of-the-century incineration technology.

Brittain, James E. *A Brief History of Engineering in Georgia and Guide to 76 Historic Engineering Sites*. See chapter on "Planning, Engineering, and Administration."

Brown, D. Clayton. *Electricity for Rural America: The Fight for the REA*. Westport, Conn.: Greenwood Press, 1980. xvi + 178 pp. Tables, notes, bibliography, and index. By far the best book on the origin, founding, and development of the Rural Electrification Administration.

Brown, D. Clayton. "Hen Eggs to Kilowatts: Arkansas Rural Electrification." *Red River Valley Historical Review*, III (Winter 1978), 119-25. Good case study of cooperation between REA and the Arkansas Power and Light Company, a private utility.

Brown, D. Clayton. *Rivers, Rockets and Readiness: Army Engineers in the Sunbelt: A History of the Fort Worth District, U. S. Army Corps of Engineers, 1950-1975*. See chapter on "Flood Control and Drainage."

Brown, Deward Clayton. "Rural Electrification in the South, 1920-1955." Doctoral dissertation, University of California, Los Angeles, 1970. 334 pp.

Brown, D. Clayton. "Sam Rayburn and the Development of Public Power in the Southwest." *Southwestern Historical Quarterly*, LXXII (Oct. 1974), 140-54. Good case study of the creation of the Southwestern Power Administration.

Brown, Leahmae. "The Development of National Policy with Respect to Water Resources." Doctoral dissertation. See chapter on "Waterways."

Brush, Charles F. "Development of Electric Street Lighting." *Journal of the Cleveland Engineering Society*. See chapter on "Roads, Streets, and Highways."

Bureau of the Census (Department of Commerce and Labor). *Statistics of Cities Having a Population of 30,000: 1904*. See chapter on "Roads, Streets, and Highways."

Bureau of the Census (Department of Commerce and Labor). *Statistics of Cities Having a Population of 8,000 to 25,000: 1903*. See chapter on "Roads, Streets, and Highways."

Burke, Robert E. *Olson's New Deal for California*. Berkeley: University of California Press, 1953. v + 279 pp. Illustration, notes, bibliography, and index. A study of the Democratic state administration of Culbert L. Olson (1938-1942). Of particular interest is the chapter on "The Fight for Public Power." Olson failed in his attempts to secure public ownership of utilities.

Burlingame, Roger. *Engines of Democracy: Inventions and Society in Mature America*. New York: Charles Scribner's Sons, 1940. xviii + 606 pp. Illustrations, maps, notes, bibliography, and index. A pioneering, though somewhat superficial, survey of American technological civilization. Topics such as power, water supply, and roads are discussed.

Busch, Frank J. "History of Montana Rural Electric Cooperatives, 1936-1971." Doctoral dissertation, University of Montana, 1975.

Carmody, John. "Rural Electrification in the United States." *Annals of the American Academy of Political and Social Science*, CCI (Jan. 1939), 82-88.

Catren, Robert. "A History of the Generation, Transmission and Distribution of Electrical Energy in Southern California." Doctoral dissertation, University of California, 1951.

Chevrier, Lionel. *The St. Lawrence Seaway*. See chapter on "Waterways."

Childs, Marquis. *The Farmer Takes a Hand: The Electric Power Revolution in Rural America*. Garden City, N. Y.: Doubleday & Company, 1952. 256 pp. Illustrations. A thorough and highly laudatory account of the origin and growth of the Rural Electrification Administration.

Christie, Jean. "Giant Power: A Progressive Proposal of the Nineteen-Twenties." *Pennsylvania Magazine of History and Biography*, XCVI (Oct. 1972), 480-507. Soundly researched and well-written article on efforts by Morris L. Cooke, George Norris, and other Progressives to promote public power during the 1920s.

Christie, Jean. "Morris Llewellyn Cooke: Progressive Engineer." Doctoral dissertation, Columbia University, 1963.

Christie, Jean. "The Mississippi Valley Committee. Conservation and Planning in the Early New Deal." *Historian*. See chapter on "Planning, Engineering, and Administration."

Clapp, Gordon R. *The TVA: An Approach to the Development of a Region*. See chapter on "Flood Control."

Clarke, T. Wood. *Utica for a Century and a Half*. See chapter on "Community Water Supply."

Clay, Floyd M. *A History of the Little Rock District, U. S. Army Corps of Engineers, 1881-1979*. See chapter on "Flood Control and Drainage."

Cleaveland, Frederic Neill. "Federal Reclamation Policy and Administration: A Case Study in the Development of Natural Resources." Doctoral dissertation. See chapter on "Irrigation."

Coate, Charles E. "Water, Power, and Politics in the Central Valley Project, 1933-1967." Doctoral dissertation, University of California, Berkeley, 1969. 242 pp. A comprehensive history of this key reclamation project. Project features are described as well as stormy public versus private power battles.

Coldwell, O. B. "Beginnings of Electric Power in Oregon." *Oregon Historical Quarterly*, XXXI (March 1930), 25-36. Brief summary of early electric lighting in Portland and other cities.

Coldwell, O. B. "Early Days of Electricity in Portland." *Oregon Historical Quarterly*, XLII (Dec. 1941), 279-94. System built in the 1880s.

Compton, Arthur Holly. *Atomic Quest: A Personal Narrative*. New York: Oxford University Press, 1956. xix + 370 pp. Illustrations, notes, and index. Autobiographical account of a participant in the Manhattan Project.

Consolidated Gas Electric Light and Power Company of Baltimore. *American Gas Centenary, 1816-1916*. Baltimore: Baltimore Gas and Electric News, 1916. A centennial history of the use of natural gas in Baltimore. The principal value of the volume is its rare illustrations.

Cooke, Morris Llewellyn, ed. *Public Utility Regulation*. New York: Ronald Press Company, 1924. ix + 310 pp. Tables, notes, and index. A classic collection of essays on the need for and implementation of regulation of electricity, water, gas, electric railway, and other public services.

Cooke, Morris Llewellyn. *Snapping Cords: Comments on the Changing Attitude of American Cities Toward the Utility Problem*. n. p.: Privately Printed, 1915. 42 pp. Tables and notes. A classic treatise on the need for greater public ownership and/or regulation of public utilities. Cooke became a leading advocate of public power and was appointed the first administrator of the Rural Electrification Administration during the New Deal.

Cooke, Morris Llewellyn. "The Early Days of the Rural Electrification Idea: 1914-1936." *American Political Science Review*, XLII (June 1948), 431-47. A summary of the critical events that led to passage of the Rural Electrification Administration Act in 1936 by the agency's administrator. Cooke highlights the contributions of Gifford Pinchot, George W. Norris, and Franklin D. Roosevelt.

Cooper, Erwin. *Aqueduct Empire: A Guide to Water in California, Its Turbulent History and Its*

Management Today. See chapter on "Irrigation."

Cortelyou, George B. "The Gas Industry." *American Gas Association Monthly*, 15 (Feb. 1933), 41-48. A tribute to the gas industry's centennial. It includes discussions of the cities that used gas for lighting in the early nineteenth century.

Coyle, Davis Cushman. *Conservation: An American Story of Conflict and Accomplishment*. See chapter on "Flood Control and Drainage."

Cunnea, Patricia Edgeworth. "Water Resources Policy Formation in the Appropriations Process: Congress and the Bureau of Reclamation." Doctoral dissertation. See chapter on "Irrigation."

Dale, Alfred George. "Nuclear Power Development in the United States to 1960: A New Pattern in Innovation and Technological Change." Doctoral dissertation, University of Texas, Austin, 1961.

Darling, Arthur B., ed. *The Public Papers of Francis G. Newlands*. 2 vols. Boston: Houghton-Mifflin Company, 1932. Vol. I: xi + 434 pp.; Vol. II: xi + 426 pp. Illustrations, notes, and index. A fine collection of speeches, reports, articles, testimony, and letters by the Nevada senator who championed various conservationist causes in the late nineteenth and early twentieth centuries. Newlands was a proponent of the 1902 Reclamation Act, supported waterway and flood control improvements, and was the Senate's leading spokesman for public development of hydroelectric power.

Davison, George S. "A Century and a Half of American Engineering." *Proceedings of the American Society of Civil Engineers*. See chapter on "Planning, Engineering, and Administration."

Davisson, William I. "Public Utilities in a Frontier City: The Early History of the Tacoma Light and Water Company." *Pacific Northwest Quarterly*. See chapter on "Community Water Supply."

Davisson, William Ira. "The Impact of Electric Power on the Economic Development of the Pacific Northwest." Doctoral dissertation, Cornell University, 1961.

Dawson, Frank G. *Nuclear Power: Development and Management of a Technology*. Seattle: University of Washington Press, 1976. xii + 320 pp. Notes, tables, appendices, bibliography, and index. Comprehensive historical treatment of the peaceful and military uses of atomic energy. Technology and federal policies are the major focus of the study.

De Roos, Robert. *The Thirsty Land: The Story of the Central Valley Project*. See chapter on "Irrigation."

Derry, T. K., and Trevor I. Williams. *A Short History of Technology: From the Earliest Times to A. D. 1900*. See chapter on "Planning, Engineering, and Administration."

Dick, Wesley Arden. "Visions of Abundance: The Public Power Crusade in the Pacific Northwest in the Era of J. D. Ross and the New Deal." Doctoral dissertation, University of Washington, 1973. 425 pp. Notes and bibliography. A solid study of this regional public power movement that discusses its leading actors, social goals, political strategies, and relationship with the federal government.

Dierdorff, John. *How Edison's Lamp Helped Light the West: The Story of the Pacific Power & Light Company and Its Pioneer Forebears*. Portland: Pacific Power & Light Company, 1971. 313 pp. Illustrations and index. A sound electrical utility history that includes useful information on the public versus private power controversy of the 1930s and 1940s.

Dobney, Frederick J. *River Engineers on the Middle Mississippi: A History of the St. Louis District, U. S. Army Corps of Engineers*. See chapter on "Waterways."

Doerksen, Harvey Ray. "The Columbia Interstate Compact: Politics of Water Resources in the Pacific Northwest." Doctoral dissertation, Washington State University, 1974.

Doran, William A. "Early Hydroelectric Power in Tennessee." *Tennessee Historical Quarterly*, XXVII (Spring 1968), 72-82. Discusses small private hydroelectric developments that predated Muscle Shoals and TVA.

Droze, Wilmon H. "TVA and the Ordinary Farmer." *Agricultural History*, 53 (Jan. 1979), 188-202.

Dyer, Frank Lewis; Thomas Commerford Martin; and William Henry Meadowcroft. *Edison: His Life and Inventions*. See chapter on "Urban Mass Transportation."

East, Dennis II. "Water Power and Forestry in Wisconsin: Issues of Conservation, 1890-1915." Doctoral dissertation, University of Wisconsin, 1971.

Eaton, A. C. "The New England Power Company Davis Bridge Development." *Journal of the Boston Society of Civil Engineers*, XII (Jan. 1925), 1-48. Includes a discussion on the evolution of the New England Power System.

Ebel, Alice L. "Municipal Ownership of Electrical Power in Bloomington, Illinois: A Case Study in the Formation of Public Policy." Doctoral dissertation, University of Illinois, Urbana-Champaign, 1960. 535 pp.

"Electricity in the Modern Building." *American Architect*. See chapter on "Public Buildings."

Evans, Paul E. "The Magnificent Obsession of TVA." *Civil Engineering*. See chapter on "Flood Control and Drainage."

Finer, Herman. *The T. V. A.: Lessons for International Application*. See chapter on "Flood Control and Drainage."

Firth, Robert E. "Power on the Plains: A Business History of the Development and Operation of Public Power in Nebraska." Doctoral dissertation, University of Nebraska, 1960.

Firth, Robert E. *Public Power in Nebraska: A Report on State Ownership*. Lincoln: University of Nebraska Press, 1962. xi + 355 pp. Maps, charts, tables, notes, bibliography, and index. An excellent historical analysis of the only state served entirely by an electric power system owned and operated by its citizens. The author portrays why public power became a monopoly in Nebraska—drought, depression, a tradition of municipal ownership, the advent of PWA, federal antitrust legislation, and the movement for rural electrification.

Fisher, Edwin A. "Engineering and Public Works in the City of Rochester During the Past Century." *Centennial History of Rochester, New York*. See chapter on "Planning, Engineering, and Administration."

Finch, J. K. "A Hundred Years of American Civil Engineering, 1852-1952." *Transactions of the American Society of Civil Engineers*. See chapter on "Planning, Engineering, and Administration."

Flaxman, Edward. *Great Feats of Modern Engineering*. See chapter on "Roads, Streets, and Highways."

Fleming, A. P. M. "Industrial and Engineering Achievements." *Civil Engineering*, 3 (Aug. 1933), 423-25. On steam, water, and electrical power.

Foster, Abram John. "The Coming of the Electrical Age to the United States." Doctoral dissertation, University of Pittsburgh, 1952. 379 pp. Notes and bibliography. Surveys the early development of the electrical industry in the United States. Discussions are included on the development of street lighting, central-station generation, long-distance transmission, and street railways.

Foy, Bernard L., comp. *A Bibliography for the TVA Program*. See chapter on "Flood Control and Drainage."

Funigiello, Philip J. *Toward a National Power Policy: The New Deal and the Electric Utility Industry, 1933-1941*. Pittsburgh, University of Pittsburgh Press, 1973. xvii + 296 pp. Notes, bibliography, and index. A significant study of the New Deal's power program. "It relates the early background of specific legislative items and events to the theme of a national power policy." The author suggests that the Roosevelt administration "emphasized resource planning less and less in decision-making after 1935." One chapter is devoted to "Morris L. Cooke and the Origins of the REA."

Francisco, Ellsworth. "Newark, N. J., Makes Rapid Progress in Improving Street Lighting." *American City*. See chapter on "Roads, Streets, and Highways."

Frank, Bernard, and Anthony Netboy. *Water, Land, and People*. See chapter on "Flood Control and Drainage."

Galli, Geraldine. "100 Years of Construction News." *Engineering News-Record*. See chapter on "Planning, Engineering, and Administration."

Galloway, J. D. "Hydro-Electric Power: An Achievement of the Past Half-Century." *Engineering News-Record*, 92 (April 17, 1924), 687-90. A rather sketchy review of the evolution of hydroelectric generation and transmission to the early 1920s. The article focuses on advancements in the fields of mechanical, civil, and electrical engineering.

Gillmore, Vance. *And Work Was Made*

Less . . . : A Brief History of Texas Electric Service Company. Fort Worth: Texas Electric Service Company, 1976. xii + 219 pp. Illustrations and index. A solid utility history. The book illustrates how the company evolved from an electric street railway system into an integrated regional network.

Glaeser, Martin G. *Public Utilities in American Capitalism*. New York: Macmillan Company, 1957. xiii + 624 pp. Charts, tables, appendices, and index. A standard source on the economics, planning, and administrative aspects of public utility regulation. Case studies are included on the growth of regional publicly owned water and power systems for the Los Angeles area, Columbia River Basin, St. Lawrence Seaway and Power Project, and Tennessee Valley Authority.

Glass, Brent D., ed. *North Carolina: An Inventory of Historic Engineering and Industrial Sites*. See chapter on "Roads, Streets, and Highways."

Golze, Alfred R. *Reclamation in the United States*. See chapter on "Irrigation."

Gould, Jacob Martin. *Output and Productivity in the Electric and Gas Utilities, 1899-1942*. New York: National Bureau of Economic Research, 1946. xii + 189 pp. Charts, tables, notes, appendices, and index. Excellent source for statistical information on the development of the electrical and gas industries.

Green, Constance McLaughlin. *Holyoke, Massachusetts: A Case Study of the Industrial Revolution in America*. See chapter on "Waterways."

Green, Michael Knight. "A History of the Public Rural Electrification Movement in Washington to 1942." Doctoral dissertation, University of Idaho, 1968.

Griffith, Ernest S. *A History of American City Government: The Conspicuous Failure, 1870-1900*. See chapter on "Planning, Engineering, and Administration."

Griffith, Ernest S. *A History of American City Government: The Progressive Years and Their Aftermath, 1900-1920*. See chapter on "Planning, Engineering, and Administration."

Groueff, Stephane. *Manhattan Project: The Untold Story of the Making of the Atomic Bomb*. Boston: Little, Brown and Company, 1967. xii + 372 pp. Illustrations, bibliography, and index. Lengthy discussions of the construction of facilities at Oak Ridge, Tennessee, and Hanford, Washington, are included in this largely undocumented account of the Manhattan Project.

Groves, Leslie R. *Now It Can Be Told: The Story of the Manhattan Project*. New York: Harper & Brothers, 1962. xiv + 464 pp. Illustrations, chart, notes, appendices, and index. A lively account of the Manhattan Project by the army general who directed its development from 1942 to 1946.

Harding, S. T. "Background of California Water and Power Problems." *California Law Review*, 38 (Oct. 1950), 547-71.

Harper, John L., and J. A. Johnson. "Hydroelectric Development at Niagara Falls." *Journal of the American Institute of Electrical Engineers*, XL (July 1921), 561-76. Good technical history of power development at the Niagara Falls site.

Harrison, Ward. "A New Era in Street Illumination." *Journal of the Cleveland Engineering Society*. See chapter on "Roads, Streets, and Highways."

Hart, Henry C. *The Dark Missouri*. See chapter on "Flood Control and Drainage."

Havemeyer, Loomis, ed., et al. *Conservation of Our Natural Resources*. See chapter on "Irrigation."

Hearst, James. "Farm Life When the Power Changed." *Palimpsest*, 60 (Sept./Oct. 1979), 156-61. Personal memories of how farm life changed with the advent of electricity.

Hellman, Richard. "Government Competition in the Electric Utility Industry of the United States: Case Studies of Origins and Results." Doctoral dissertation, Columbia University, 1967.

Hewlett, Richard G., and Francis Duncan. *Atomic Shield, 1947-1952: A History of the United States Atomic Energy Commission*. Washington, D. C.: U. S. Atomic Energy Commission, 1972. xviii + 718 pp. Illustrations, maps, diagrams, notes, appendices, bibliographies, and indexes. Excellent treatment of the agency's early years.

Hewlett, Richard G., and Oscar E. Anderson. *The New World, 1939-1946: A History of* *the United States Atomic Energy Commission*. Washington, D. C.: U. S. Atomic Energy Commission, 1962. xv + 766 pp. Illustrations, maps, diagrams, notes, appendices, bibliographies, and indexes. A comprehensive, deeply researched, and well-written account of the agency's founding and background.

Hindle, Brooke. *Technology in Early America: Needs and Opportunities for Study*. See chapter on "Planning, Engineering, and Administration."

Hodge, Clarence Lewis. *The Tennessee Valley Authority: A National Experiment in Regionalism*. See chapter on "Flood Control and Drainage."

Hoffecker, Carol E. *Wilmington, Delaware: Portrait of an Industrial City, 1830-1910*. See chapter on "Sewers and Wastewater Treatment."

Holbrook, Stewart H. *The Columbia*. See chapter on "Waterways."

Houghton, N. D. "Problems in Public Power Administration in the Southwest—Some Arizona Applications." *Western Political Quarterly*, IV (March 1951), 116-29. A critical analysis of public power generation by an official of a large private utility firm.

Howard, W. V. *Authority in TVA Land*. See chapter on "Flood Control and Drainage."

Hubbard, Preston J. *Origins of the TVA: The Muscle Shoals Controversy, 1920-1932*. See chapter on "Flood Control and Drainage."

Hubbard, Preston J. "The Muscle Shoals Controversy, 1920-1932: Public Policy in the Making." Doctoral dissertation, Vanderbilt University, 1955. ii + 556 pp. Notes and bibliography. Excellent analysis of the successful effort led by Senator George W. Norris to thwart Henry Ford's bid to assume control of the federal hydroelectric facilities at Muscle Shoals.

Huber, Walter L. "An Engineering Century in California." *Transactions of the American Society of Civil Engineers*. See chapter on "Planning, Engineering, and Administration."

Hughes, Thomas Park. "Technology and Public Policy: The Failure of Giant Power." *Proceedings of the IEEE*, 64 (Sept. 1976), 1361-71.

Hughes, Thomas P. "The Electrification of America: The System Builders." *Technology and Culture*, 20 (Jan. 1979), 124-61. Comprehensive and well researched article on the contributions to electrification made by Thomas Edison, Samuel Insull, and S. Z. Mitchell.

Hungerford, Edward. *The Story of Public Utilities*. See chapter on "Urban Mass Transportation."

Hyde, Charles H. *The Lower Peninsula of Michigan: An Inventory of Historic Engineering and Industrial Sites*. See chapter on "Community Water Supply."

Ickes, Harold L. *The Secret Diary of Harold L. Ickes: The First Thousand Days, 1933-1936*. See chapter on "Planning, Engineering, and Administration."

Jarrett, Henry, ed. *Perspectives on Conservation*. See chapter on "Planning, Engineering, and Administration."

Johnson, Joseph French. "The Recent History of Municipal Ownership in the United States." *Municipal Affairs*. See chapter on "Community Water Supply."

Johnson, Leland R. *Engineers on the Twin Rivers: A History of the Nashville District Corps of Engineers United States Army*. See chapter on "Waterways."

Jones, Payson. *A Power History of the Consolidated Edison System, 1878-1900*. New York: Consolidated Edison Company, 1940. 384 pp. Appendix and index. A dull and superficial book that discusses the first central power station and other landmarks of Edison's career.

Kaiser, William Martin. "Interest Groups and the St. Lawrence Deep Waterway." Master's thesis. See chapter on "Waterways."

Kahrl, William L., ed. *The California Water Atlas*. See chapter on "Irrigation."

Kane, Lucile M. *The Waterfall that Built a City: The Falls of St. Anthony in Minneapolis*. St. Paul: Minnesota Historical Society, 1966. xiv + 224 pp. Illustrations, maps, notes, and index. Well-researched study of the only major waterfall on the Mississippi River. It chronicles the waterfall's changing role from a water-power source for industries to a hydroelectric site.

Kathka, David Arlin. "The Bureau of Reclamation in the Truman Administration: Personnel, Politics, and Policy." Doctoral dissertation. See chapter on "Irrigation."

Kerwin, Jerome G. *Federal Water-Power Legislation*. New York: Columbia University Press, 1926. 396 pp. Tables, notes, appendices, and index. Remains the best source on water power legislation in the early twentieth century. Kerwin carefully records the efforts of conservationists to maintain public control of hydroelectric resources and discusses the congressional battles that led to passage of the 1920 Water Power Act.

King, Clyde Lyndon, ed. *The Regulation of Municipal Utilities*. New York: D. Appleton and Company, 1912. ix + 404 pp. Tables, notes, bibliography, and index. A collection of essays that explore the relative merits of municipal ownership of public utilities versus adequate regulation. Several case studies of state and municipal utility commissions are included.

King, Judson. *The Conservation Fight: From Theodore Roosevelt to the Tennessee Valley Authority*. See chapter on "Flood Control and Drainage."

King, Thomson. *Consolidated of Baltimore, 1816-1950: A History of Consolidated Gas, Electric Light, and Power Company of Baltimore*. Baltimore: Consolidated Gas, Electric Light, and Power Company of Baltimore, 1950. vi + 335 pp. Illustrations, map, chart, bibliography, and index. A good, undocumented history of the first gas company in America and subsequent development of electricity. The author traces the events and personalities of some fifty companies that consolidated to form the single utility.

Klein, Maury, and Harvey A. Kantor. *Prisoners of Progress: American Industrial Cities, 1850-1920*. See chapter on "Solid Wastes."

Kleinsorge, Paul L. *The Boulder Canyon Project: Historical and Economic Aspects*. See chapter on "Irrigation."

Knapp, A. Blair. *Water Power in New York State*. Syracuse: School of Citizenship and Public Affairs, Syracuse University, 1930. 51 pp. Appendices and bibliography. A very useful survey of the political, legislative, and regulatory aspects of water power in New York from 1895 to 1930. The concluding section surveys the water power policies of other states.

Knight, Oliver. "Correcting Nature's Error: The Colorado-Big Thompson Project." *Agricultural History*. See chapter on "Irrigation."

Koller, Theodor. *The Utilization of Waste Products: A Treatise on the National Utilization, Recovery, and Treatment of Waste Products of All Kinds*. See chapter on "Solid Wastes."

Kresky, Edward M. "The New York State Role in the Development of Power from the St. Lawrence River." Doctoral dissertation, New York University, 1960. 458 pp.

Kyle, John H. *The Building of TVA*. See chapter on "Flood Control and Drainage."

Lang, Daniel. *From Hiroshima to the Moon: Chronicles of Life in the Atomic Age*. New York: Simon and Schuster, 1959. xii + 496 pp. Index. A lively journalistic account of the Manhattan Project and post-World War II developments in the atomic energy field.

Larned, A. T., and M. G. Salzman. "Evolution of the Modern Hydroelectric Power Plant." *Transactions of the American Society of Civil Engineers*, CT (1953), 536-55. Features many of the technological developments of "the modern hydroelectric power plant as applied to American practice."

Larned, J. N. *A History of Buffalo: Delineating the Evolution of the City*. See chapter on "Sewers and Wastewater Treatment."

Laurent, Francis W., comp. *A Compilation of the More Important Congressional Acts, Treaties, Presidential Messages, Judicial Decisions and Official Reports and Documents Having To Do with the Control, Conservation, and Utilization of Water Resources*. See chapter on "Flood Control and Drainage."

Layton, Edwin T., Jr. "Scientific Technology, 1945-1900: The Hydraulic Turbine and the Origins of American Industrial Research." *Technology and Culture*, 20 (Jan. 1979), 64-89. Excellent article on the evolution of the turbine.

Lee, Lawrence B. "100 Years of Reclamation Historiography." *Pacific Historical Review*. See chapter on "Irrigation."

Lepawsky, Albert. "Water Resources and American Federalism." *American Science Review*. See chapter on "Waterways."

Leuba, Clarence J. *A Road to Creativity: Arthur Morgan–Engineer, Educator, Adminis-*

trator. See chapter on "Flood Control and Drainage."

Leuchtenburg, William Edward. *Flood Control Politics: The Connecticut River Valley Problem, 1927-1950*. See chapter on "Flood Control and Drainage."

Leuchtenburg, William E. "Roosevelt, Norris and the 'Seven Little TVAs.' " *Journal of Politics*. See chapter on "Flood Control and Drainage."

Lilienthal, David E. *The Journals of David E. Lilienthal: The Atomic Energy Years, 1945-1950*. New York: Harper & Row, 1964. x + 666 pp. Illustrations, appendices, and index. A private and personal record of the author's years as first chairman of the U. S. Atomic Energy Commission.

Lilienthal, David E. *The Journals of David Lilienthal: Volume I: The TVA Years, 1939-1945*. See chapter on "Flood Control and Drainage."

Lilienthal, David E. *TVA: Democracy on the March*. See chapter on "Flood Control and Drainage."

Lincoln, Edmund Earle. "The Results of Municipal Electric Lighting in Massachusetts." Doctoral dissertation, Harvard University, 1917.

Lohr, Lenix R., ed. *Centennial of Engineering: History and Proceedings of Symposia, 1852-1952*. See chapter on "Planning, Engineering, and Administration."

Lowitt, Richard. "A Neglected Aspect of a Progressive Movement: George W. Norris and Public Control of Hydroelectric Power, 1913-1919." *Historian*, XXVII (May 1965), 350-65. Explores the development of Norris' defense and promotion of public power.

Lowitt, Richard. *George W. Norris: The Persistence of a Progressive, 1913-1933*. See chapter on "Irrigation."

Luther, E. Hardy. "Early Development in High Voltage Transmission." *Michigan History*, LI (Summer 1967), 93-115. A well-researched summary of early electrical generation and transmission in the state of Michigan from about 1880 to 1920.

Lyon, Leslie D. "Charlotte's Electrical Plants." *Michigan History*, XLII (June 1958), 188-96. Indicates the technical problems of pioneering public utilities.

Lyons, Barrow. *Tomorrow's Birthright: A Political and Economic Interpretation of Our Natural Resources*. See chapter on "Irrigation."

Mabee, Carleton. *The Seaway Story*. See Chapter on "Waterways."

MacColl, E. Kimbark. *The Growth of a City: Power and Politics in Portland, Oregon, 1915 to 1950*. See chapter on "Planning, Engineering, and Administration."

McCraw, Thomas K. *Morgan vs. Lilienthal: The Feud within the TVA*. See chapter on "Flood Control and Drainage."

McCraw, Thomas K. *TVA and the Power Fight, 1933-1939*. Philadelphia: J. B. Lippincott, 1971. xi + 201 pp. Notes, bibliography, and index. The definitive study of the efforts by private utility companies to block the Tennessee Valley Authority's huge power program. The contest is viewed largely in terms of a personal battle between David Lilienthal, TVA's chairman, and Wendell Willkie who represented the private power interests. The author notes paradoxically that TVA's ringing victory for public power was never duplicated elsewhere.

McCraw, Thomas Kincaid. "TVA and the Power Fight, 1933-1939." Doctoral dissertation, University of Wisconsin, 1970. 362 pp.

McDonald, Forrest. *Let There Be Light: The Electric Utility Industry in Wisconsin, 1881-1955*. Madison: American History Research Center, 1957. x + 404 pp. Illustrations, maps, charts, notes, and index. By far the best study of the evolution of the public and private power industries in a given state.

McDonald, Forrest. "Samuel Insull and the Movement for State Utility Regulatory Commissions." *Business History Review*, XXXII (1958), 241-54. A good discussion of Insull's strategy to combat public ownership of gas and electric utilities during the first two decades of the twentieth century. The author concludes that Insull built his empire with vision and political skill and should be credited for advocating public regulation.

McGeary, M. Nelson. *Gifford Pinchot: Forester-Politician*. See chapter on "Planning, Engineering, and Administration."

McKelvey, Blake. *Rochester: The Flower City, 1855-1890*. Cambridge: Harvard University Press, 1949. xviii + 409 pp. Illustrations, map, charts, notes, and index. A section of the chapter on "New Industrial Growth" deals with public utilities.

McKelvey, Blake. *Rochester: The Quest for Quality, 1890-1925*. Cambridge: Harvard University Press, 1956. xiv + 432 pp. Illustrations, bibliography, and index. Of special interest are the sections on "Utilities in Transition" and "The Utility Empires."

McKinley, Charles. "The Valley Authority and Its Alternatives." *American Political Science Review*. See chapter on "Flood Control and Drainage."

McKinley, Charles. *Uncle Sam in the Pacific Northwest: Federal Management of Natural Resources in the Columbia River Valley*. See chapter on "Irrigation."

MacLaren, Malcolm. *The Rise of the Electrical Industry during the Nineteenth Century*. Princeton: Princeton University Press, 1943. xi + 225 pp. Illustrations, notes, and index. A review of the early discoveries and developments which led to the creation of the great electrical industries. The book is particularly strong in its discussion of pioneer direct- and alternating-current generation systems. Material on the growth of electric street railways is included.

Magnusson, C. Edward. "Hydro-Electric Power in Washington." *Washington Historical Quarterly*, XIX (April 1928), 90-98. Highlights major developments and explains importance to the state.

Mahar, Franklyn Daniel. "Douglas McKay and the Issues of Power Development in Oregon, 1953-1956." Doctoral dissertation, University of Oregon, 1968.

Mahar, Franklyn D. "The Politics of Power: The Oregon Test for Partnership." *Pacific Northwest Quarterly*, 65 (Jan. 1974), 29-37. Perspectives on hydroelectric power policies and their implications for the conservation movement.

Martin, Roscoe, C., ed. *TVA: The First Twenty Years, a Staff Report*. See chapter on "Flood Control and Drainage."

Merritt, Raymond H. *Creativity, Conflict & Controversy: A History of the St. Paul District, U.S. Army Corps of Engineers*. See chapter on "Waterways."

Miller, William D. *Memphis during the Progressive Era, 1900-1917*. See chapter on "Sewers and Wastewater Treatment."

Mills, Gary B. *Of Men & Rivers: The Story of the Vicksburg District.* See chapters on "Flood Control and Drainage."

Moeller, Beverley Bowen. *Phil Swing and Boulder Dam*. See chapter on "Irrigation."

Monroe, Robert Grier. "The Gas, Electric Light, Water and Street Railway Services in New York City." *Annals of the American Academy of Political and Social Science*. See chapter on "Community Water Supply."

Moreell, Ben. *Our Nation's Water Resources–Policies and Politics*. See chapter on "Flood Control and Drainage."

Morgan, Arthur E. *The Making of the TVA*. See chapter on "Flood Control and Drainage."

Morgan Murray. *The Dam*. See chapter on "Irrigation."

Morse, Roy W. "People in Public Works: William Chester Morse." *APWA Reporter*. See chapter on "Planning, Engineering, and Administration."

Moses, Robert. *Public Works: A Dangerous Trade*. See chapter on "Planning, Engineering, and Administration."

Moulton, Harold G.; Charles S. Morgan; and Adah L. Lee. *The St. Lawrence Navigation and Power Project*. Washington, D. C.: Brookings Institution, 1929. xvi + 675 pp. Maps, tables, notes, appendices, and index. A good background source on this international power and navigation project that was not built until after World War II.

Muller, Frederick William. *Public Rural Electrification*. Washington, D. C.: American Council on Public Affairs, 1944. viii + 181 pp. Tables. A tribute to the Rural Electrification Administration and farmer-owned cooperatives.

Murray, William S. *Government Owned and Controlled Compared with Privately Owned and Regulated Electric Utilities in Canada and the United States*. New York: National Electric Light Association, 1922.

Myers, Denys Peter. *Gaslighting in America: A Guide for Historic Preservation*. Washington, D. C.: U. S. Department of the Interior, Heritage Conservation and Recreation Service, 1978.

279 pp. Illustrations, notes, appendix, bibliography, and index. Discusses the types and styles of gas fixtures that were used in buildings and on the streets during the late nineteenth and early twentieth centuries.

Nass, David L. "Public Policy and Public Works: Niagara Falls Redevelopment as a Case Study." *Essays in Public Works History*, 7 (Feb. 1979), 1-46. Excellent case study of the public versus private sector battles to control Niagara power. The essay focuses on the political and legislative aspects of the subject.

Nass, David Lewis. "Public Power and Politics in New York State, 1918-1958." Doctoral dissertation, Syracuse University, 1970.

Newell, Frederick Haynes. *Water Resources: Present and Future Uses*. See chapter on "Irrigation."

Nixon, Edgar B., ed. *Franklin D. Roosevelt and Conservation, 1911-1945*. See chapter on "Planning, Engineering, and Administration."

Nord, David. "The Experts Versus the Experts: Conflicting Philosophies of Municipal Utility Regulation in the Progressive Era." *Wisconsin Magazine of History*, 58 (Spring 1978), 219-36. Insightful and well-researched article on contending utility philosophies: state regulation or municipal ownership.

Noreen, Sarah Pressey. *Public Street Illumination in Washington, D. C.: An Illustrated History*. See chapter on "Roads, Streets, and Highways."

Norris, George W. *Fighting Liberal: The Autobiography of George W. Norris*. See chapter on "Flood Control and Drainage."

Olson, McKinley. *Unacceptable Risk: The Nuclear Power Controversy*. New York: Bantam, 1976.

Orrok, George A. "The Central Station in One Man's Lifetime." *Combustion*, 10 (Sept. 1938), 34-36. Includes interesting statistical information on improvements in the efficiency of central stations.

Parkins, A. E., and J. R. Whitaker. *Our Natural Resources and Their Conservation*. See chapter on "Flood Control and Drainage."

Parkman, Aubrey. *Army Engineers in New England: The Military and Civil Work of the Corps of Engineers in New England, 1775-1975*. See chapter on "Waterways."

Passer, Harold C. *The Electrical Manufacturers, 1875-1900: A Study in Competition, Entrepreneurship, Technical Change, and Economic Growth*. Cambridge: Harvard University Press, 1953. xviii + 412 pp. Illustrations, tables, diagrams, notes, bibliography, and index. The book focuses on four major dimensions of the electrical industry's early growth: entrepreneurship, competition, technical change, and economic growth. A great deal of material is offered on the early development of electrical street lighting and pioneers of the trolley industry. Much of the study deals with the formation of the General Electric and Westinghouse corporations.

Pendergrass, Bonnie Baack. "Public Power, Politics, and Technology in the Eisenhower and Kennedy Years: The Hanford Dual-Purpose Reactor Controversy, 1956-1962." Doctoral dissertation, University of Washington, 1974. iii + 213 pp. Notes, appendices, and bibliography. A good case study of a landmark energy controversy. The author skillfully puts her subject within the context of regional public-private power conflicts and national debates over energy policies in the 1950s and 1960s.

Pendergrass, Lee Forrest. "Urban Reform and Voluntary Association: A Case Study of the Seattle Municipal League, 1910-1929." Doctoral dissertation. See chapter on "Urban Mass Transportation."

Person, Harlow S. "The Rural Electrification Administration in Perspective." *Agricultural History*, XXIV (April 1950), 70-89.

Piccard, Paul J. "Scientists and Public Policy: Los Alamos, August-November, 1945." *Western Political Quarterly*, XVIII (June 1965), 251-62.

Pinchot, Gifford. *Breaking New Ground*. See chapter on "Irrigation."

Platt, Harold Lawrence. "Urban Public Services and Private Enterprise: Aspects of the Legal and Economic History of Houston, Texas, 1865-1905." Doctoral dissertation. See chapter on "Planning, Engineering, and Administration."

Polakov, Walter N. *The Power Age: Its Quest and Challenge*. New York: Covici-Friede Publishers, 1933. 247 pp. Charts, diagrams, notes, and tables. An attempt to demonstrate that Americans "have broken with the Machine

Age once and for all" and have entered "the Power Age." The author explains "how the manifold applications of electrical energy" have increased the nation's productive capacity.

Polk, Tom C. "Appleton, Wisconsin, Celebrates Golden Jubilee of the World's First Hydraulic-Electric Plant." *HELA Bulletin*, XIX (Oct. 1932), 583.

Public Works Administration. *America Builds: The Record of PWA*. See chapter on "Planning, Engineering, and Administration."

Pursell, Carroll W., Jr. "Government and Technology in the Great Depression." *Technology and Culture*, 20 (Jan. 1979), 162-74. Solid analysis of government policies and the impact of technology on society, particularly electrification made possible by TVA, REA, and other programs.

Ransmeier, Joseph Sirera. *The Tennessee Valley Authority: A Case Study in the Economics of Multiple Purpose Stream Planning*. See chapter on "Flood Control and Drainage."

Richardson, Elmo R. *Dams, Parks, & Politics: Resource Development & Preservation in the Truman-Eisenhower Era*. See chapter on "Energy."

Richardson, Elmo R. *The Politics of Conservation: Crusades and Controversies, 1897-1913*. See chapter on "Waterways."

Ridgeway, Marian E. *The Missouri Basin's Pick-Sloan Plan: A Case Study in Congressional Policy Determination*. See chapter on "Flood Control and Drainage."

Riley, Jack. *Carolina Power & Light Company, 1908-1958*. Raleigh, N. C.: 1958. xvi + 354 pp. Illustrations, appendices, bibliography, and index. A good corporate biography that discusses the growth of private and some public electric utilities in North and South Carolina.

Robinson, George O., Jr. *The Oak Ridge Story: The Saga of a People Who Share in History*. Kingsport, Tenn.: Southern Publishers, 1950. 181 pp. Illustrations and index. A journalistic account of the facilities built in Tennessee as part of the Manhattan Project.

Robinson, Michael C. *Water for the West: The Bureau of Reclamation, 1902-1977*. See chapter on "Irrigation."

Rose, Mark H., and John G. Clark. "Light, Heat, and Power: Energy Choices in Kansas City, Wichita, and Denver, 1900-1935." *Journal of Urban History*, 5 (May 1979), 340-64. An ambitious, broad-based, pioneering study of energy adoption and use. The authors trace the growth of gas and electric utilities from small businesses to large consolidated firms. The article also discusses the evolution of energy technology, the social and cultural causes of increased energy demand, and the resultant reshaping of "indoor and outside environments." It is a source of inspiration and ideas for further work in this field.

Rosenberg, Roy. *History of Inglewood: Narrative and Biographical*. See chapter on "Airways and Airports."

Ross, John Ray. " 'Pork Barrels' and the General Welfare: Problems in Conservation, 1900-1920." Doctoral dissertation. See chapter on "Flood Control and Drainage."

Salvage, B. "Overhead Lines or Underground Cables: The Problem of Electrical Power Transmission." *Endeavour*, XXXIV (Jan. 1975), 3-8. Outlines the history of both overhead lines and underground cables and discusses their technical and economic aspects. The article focuses on British electrical transmission, but American examples are included.

Schmid, A. Allan. "Water and the Law in Wisconsin." *Wisconsin Magazine of History*. See chapter on "Waterways."

Schurr, Sam H., and Bruce C. Netschert. *Energy in the American Economy, 1850-1975: An Economic Study of Its History and Prospects*. Baltimore: John Hopkins Press, 1960. xxii + 774 pp. Maps, charts, tables, graphs, notes, appendices, and index. Pioneering study of the influence of energy consumption on the population, gross national product, and other factors. A major chapter is included on hydropower development.

Seckler, David, ed. *California Water: A Study in Resource Management*. See chapter on "Irrigation."

Selznick, Philip. *TVA and the Grass Roots*. Berkeley: University of California Press, 1949.

Settle, William A., Jr. *The Dawning, a New Day for the Southwest: A History of the Tulsa District, Corps of Engineers, 1939-1971*. See chapter on "Waterways."

Sheible, Albert. "Electric Street Lighting." *Electricity*, XVI (April 5, 1899), 196-97. Thin historical overview of the development of street lighting in the United States and Europe.

Short, C. W., and R. Stanley-Brown. *Public Buildings: A Survey of Architecture of Projects Constructed by Federal and Other Governmental Bodies between the Years 1933 and 1939 with the Assistance of the Public Works Association*. See chapter on "Public Buildings."

Smith, Courtland L. *The Salt River Project: A Case Study in Cultural Adaptation to an Urbanizing Community*. See chapter on "Irrigation."

Smith, Frank E., ed. *Conservation in the United States, a Documentary History: Land and Water, 1900-1970*. See chapter on "Irrigation."

Smith, Guy-Harold. *Conservation of Natural Resources*. See chapter on "irrigation."

Springer, Vera. *Power and the Pacific Northwest: A History of the Bonneville Power Administration*. Portland, Oregon: U. S. Department of the Interior, Bonneville Power Administration, 1976. v + 180 pp. Illustrations, maps, bibliography, and index. Effectively illustrated and well-written history of the federal agency that markets electricity in the Pacific Northwest. The author weaves together a variety of social, political, economic, and environmental themes to provide a coherent context for the agency's institutional evolution.

Stauter, Mark Cordell. "The Rural Electrification Administration, 1935-1945: A New Deal Case Study." Doctoral dissertation, Duke University, 1973.

Steffens, Henry John. "James Prescott Joule and the Development of the Principle of the Conservation of Energy." Doctoral dissertation, Cornell University, 1968.

Stevens, Don Lorenza. *A Bibliography of Municipal Utility Regulation and Municipal Ownership*. Cambridge: Harvard University Press, 1918. viii + 410 pp. Index. Includes a strong section on the "History of Utilities and Regulation."

Stewart, James H. "The Financial History of the Kentucky Utilities Company." Doctoral dissertation, University of Kentucky, 1951.

Stifler, Susan Reed. *The Beginnings of a Century of Steam and Water Heating*. Westfield, Mass.: H. B. Smith Co., 1960. 163 pp. Illustrations, notes, bibliographies, and index. This rare book offers an introduction to a subject virtually untouched by historians. Sources cited in this history of the H. B. Smith Company provide further information on the central heating of buildings.

Stobaugh, Robert B., and Daniel Yergin, eds. *Energy Future: Report of the Energy Project at the Harvard Business School*. New York: Random House, 1979.

Stotz, Louis, and Alexander Jamison. *History of the Gas Industry*. New York: Stettiner Brothers, 1938. 534 pp. Illustrations and maps. An amateurish, superficial history of the industry from the early nineteenth century.

Strout, Alan Mayne. "Technological Change and United States Energy Consumption, 1939-1954." Doctoral dissertation, University of Chicago, 1967.

Sundborg, George. *Hail Columbia: The Thirty-Year Struggle for Grand Coulee Dam*. See chapter on "Irrigation."

Sutton, Imre. "Geographical Aspects of Construction Planning: Hoover Dam Revisited." *Journal of the West*. See chapter on "Irrigation."

Swain, Donald C. *Federal Conservation Policy, 1921-1933*. See chapter on "Irrigation."

Swain, Donald C. "The Bureau of Reclamation and the New Deal, 1933-1940." *Pacific Northwest Quarterly*. See chapter on "Irrigation."

Swain, Philip W. "15 Years . . ." *Power*, 79 (Mid-Dec., 1935), 686-91. Development of power plants from 1920 to 1935.

Symposium: *Sources for History of the Thirties*. Fort Worth: Federal Records Center, 1975. 118 pp. Includes an article by D. Clayton Brown on "The Rural Electrification Administration," which is a comprehensive review of sources on this topic.

Tangerman, E. J. "The Story of Power." *Power*, LXXVIII (June 1934), 281-308. Sketch of electrical power generation.

Tarr, Joel A., ed. *Retrospective Technology Assessment–1976*. See chapter on "Sewers and Wastewater Treatment."

Teaford, Jon C. "The State and Industrial Development: Public Power Development in The Old Northwest." *Old Northwest*, 1 (March 1975), 11-34. Illustrates the efforts of states and municipalities during the nineteenth century to provide sources of water power for mills and factories. The article suggests that more research should be undertaken on state efforts to promote industrial resources.

Terral, Rufus. *The Missouri Valley: Land of Drouth, Flood, and Promise*. See chapter on "Irrigation."

Terrell, John Upton. *War for the Colorado River*. See chapter on "Irrigation."

"The North Carolina Fuel Administration." *North Carolina Historical Review*, 1 (April 1924), 138-75. This account—describing the creation, organization, and work of the North Carolina Fuel Administration from 1916-1918—and the documents forming the appendix are part of the agency's records deposited in the state's archives.

Thelen, David P. *The New Citizenship: Origins of Progressivism in Wisconsin, 1885-1900*. See chapter on "Urban Mass Transportation."

Thompson, Carl D. *Public Ownership: A Survey of Public Enterprises, Municipal, State, and Federal, in the United States and Elsewhere*. New York: Thomas Y. Crowell Company, 1925. xviii + 445 pp. Illustrations, maps, charts, tables, notes, bibliography, and index. A paean to public ownership of facilities and utilities supported by the Public Ownership League of America. Examples are cited from virtually every federal, state, and municipal public works field. Particular emphasis is placed on electrical generation and distribution.

Tininenko, Robert D. "Middle Snake River Development: The Controversy Over Hells Canyon, 1947-1955." Master's thesis, Washington State University, 1967. Dams and public versus private hydroelectric policy in the canyon dividing Oregon and Idaho.

Twentieth Century Fund. Power Committee. *Electric Power and Government Policy: A Survey of the Relations Between the Government and the Electric Power Industry*. New York: Twentieth Century Fund, 1948. Maps, tables, and index. A comprehensive survey of the relations between all levels of government and the electric power industry. Despite its heavy private interest bias, the book offers an exhaustive overview of the electrical utility system after World War II.

Twentieth Century Fund. Power Committee. *The Power Industry and the Power Interest: A Summary of the Results of a Survey of the Relations Between the Government and the Electric Power Industry*. New York: Twentieth Century Fund, 1944. xiv + 261 pp. An analysis of the nation's electrical needs conducted in the early 1940s. The book generally identifies the drawbacks of federal power and advocates more effective regulation of private utilities.

U. S. Department of Commerce. *Bureau of the Census. Historical Statistics of the United States: Colonial Times to 1970*. See chapter on "Planning, Engineering, and Administration."

Uhl, W. F. "Water Power over a Century." *Transactions of the American Society of Civil Engineers*. See chapter on "Waterways."

Van Derzee, G. W. "Pioneering the Electrical Age." *Wisconsin Magazine of History*, 41 (Spring 1958), 210-14. Discussion of the world's first hydroelectric central station in Appleton, Wisconsin.

Van Dusen, George. "Politics of 'Partnership': The Eisenhower Administration and Conservation, 1952-1960." Doctoral dissertation, Loyola University, 1974. iii + 308 pp. Notes and bibliography. An outstanding dissertation on conservation policies in the 1950s, especially from the standpoint of attempts by conservative groups to abandon New Deal programs. The study offers particularly strong discussions of energy policies and efforts to thwart Bureau of Reclamation water and power projects.

Van Tassel, Alfred J., ed. *Our Environment: The Outlook for 1980*. See chapter on "Community Water Supply."

Van Valen, Nelson S. "Power Politics: The Struggle for Municipal Ownership of Electric Utilities in Los Angeles, 1905-1937." Doctoral dissertation, Claremont Graduate School, 1963. iv + 398 pp. Notes and bibliography. A brilliant dissertation that should receive recognition as a pathbreaking study of public ownership of electrical utilities. The author explores the political and economic motives of public power champions and examines the tactics they used to fight the private companies.

Vennard, Edwin. *Government in the Power Business*. New York: McGraw-Hill Book Company. xi + 352 pp. Maps, charts, tables, graphs, notes, and index. The case against public power presented by the managing director of the Edison Electric Institute.

Voeltz, Herman C. "Genesis and Development of a Regional Power Agency in the Pacific Northwest, 1933-43." *Pacific Northwest Quarterly*, 53 (April 1962), 65-76. Exhaustive article on unsuccessful attempts to create a Columbia Valley Authority modeled on TVA. It also discusses the first decade of the Bonneville Power Administration, which was created in 1937.

Wahrenbrock, Howard E. "Can We Afford *Not* to Develop the High Tower Windmill Now?" *Public Utilities Fortnightly*, 104 (Sept. 27, 1979), 42-47. Excellent article on a joint Federal Power Commission-Department of the Interior wind power project that was thwarted during the Eisenhower Administration.

Wainwright, Nicholas B. *History of the Philadelphia Electric Company, 1881-1961*. Philadelphia: Nicholas B. Wainwright, 1961. xii + 416 pp. Illustrations, maps, graphs, and index. One of the most comprehensive electrical utility histories. It contains interesting material on the private versus public power fights of the 1930s.

Waltrip, John Richard. "Public Power During the Truman Administration." Doctoral dissertation, University of Missouri, Columbia, 1965.

Warne, William E. *The Bureau of Reclamation*. See chapter on "Irrigation."

Wass, Philmore Burlon. "The New Hampshire Electric Cooperative: Its History and Influence on Rural Living, 1935-1950." Doctoral dissertation, Columbia University, 1951.

Waters, Frank. *The Colorado*. See chapter on "Irrigation."

Wengert, Norman. "Antecedents of TVA: The Legislative History of Muscle Shoals." *Agricultural History*. See chapter on "Flood Control and Drainage."

Whitaker, J. Russell, and Edward A. Ackerman. *American Resources: Their Management and Conservation*. See chapter on "Sewers and Wastewater Treatment."

White, Gilbert F. "A Perspective of River Basin Development." *Journal of Law and Contemporary Problems*. See chapter on "Flood Control and Drainage."

White, Raymond Elliott. "Private Electric Utility Executives: Thoughts on Public Ownership, 1881-1960." Doctoral dissertation, University of Texas, Austin, 1969.

Whitman, Willson. *David Lilienthal: Public Servant in a Power Age*. See chapter on "Flood Control and Drainage."

Wiersema, Harry. "Progress of TVA Power Program." *Civil Engineering*, 12 (Feb. 1942), 77-80. The author reviews TVA's power development since 1933.

Wilcox, Delos F. *Municipal Franchises*. See chapter on "Urban Mass Transportation."

Wildavsky, Aaron. *Dixon-Yates: A Study in Power Politics*. New Haven: Yale University Press, 1962. xx + 351 pp. Notes, bibliography, and index. A well-researched, objective account of an important power controversy that occurred during the early 1950s. The author does a remarkable job of assessing the institutional response of the key contending parties—the Tennessee Valley Authority, Atomic Energy Commission, City of Memphis, and Congress.

Wilkes, James David. "Power and Pedagogy: The National Electric Light Association and Public Education, 1919-1928." Doctoral dissertation, University of Tennessee, 1973. vii + 333 pp. Notes and bibliography. The cooperation between the private utility industry and the educational community during the 1920s is explored in this dissertation. The utilities used the schools to promulgate its opposition to the growth of federal power programs.

Williams, Albert N. *The Water and the Power: Development of the Five Great Rivers of the West*. See chapter on "Irrigation."

Williams, Archibald. *The Romance of Modern Engineering.* See chapter on "Roads, Streets, and Highways."

Williams, C. Arch. *The Sanitary District of Chicago: History of Its Growth and Development As Shown By Decisions of the Courts and Work of Its Law Department*. See chapters on "Waterways."

Wilson, G. Lloyd; James M. Herring; and

Roland B. Eutsler. *Public Utility Industries*. See chapter on "Urban Mass Transportation."

Wright, Wade H. *History of the Georgia Power Company, 1855-1956*. Atlanta: Georgia Power Company, 1957. xii + 386 pp. Illustrations, appendix, and index. Excellent treatment of a major power company that evolved from Atlanta-based gas, street railway, and public utilities.

Wyer, Samuel S. *Niagara Falls: Its Power Possibilities and Preservation*. Washington, D. C.: Smithsonian Institution, 1925. vi + 30 pp. Illustrations, maps, table, notes, and chart. Presented within a historical framework but concerned chiefly with the economic aspects of electric power development and the preservation of Niagara Falls' scenic beauty.

14

Military Installations

Public works are a vital part of the United States military establishment. During the past two centuries, the armed forces have required structures and facilities to house personnel and provide logistical and maintenance support for ground forces, ships, and aircraft. Army arsenals, forts, cantonments, and hospitals have armed, sheltered, and provided training facilities for generations of American troops. Navy shore facilities have evolved from simple wharfs and storehouses into multifaceted complexes consisting of marine bases, supply depots, and research centers. In addition, the Air Force maintains a worldwide network of bases that include training, maintenance, and support facilities that keep sophisticated air combat weapons flying.

The following annotated citations are weighted heavily toward the history of nineteenth-century forts. The profession's interest in western expansion has resulted in a vast literature on this subject. Despite many noteworthy exceptions, there is a relative paucity of books, articles, and dissertations on twentieth-century military construction.

Adams, Mary. "Jefferson's Military Policy with Special Reference to the Frontier, 1805-1809." Doctoral dissertation, University of Virginia, 1958. 331 pp.

Agnew, Ramon Bradford. "Fort Gibson: Terminal on the Trail of Tears." Doctoral dissertation, University of Oklahoma, 1976.

Allen, Richard S. "American Coastal Forts: The Golden Years." *Periodical*, 5 (Summer 1973), 2-7.

Aleshire, Ruth Corty. "Warsaw and Fort Edwards on the Mississippi." *Transactions of the Illinois State Historical Society*, 37 (1930), 200-09. Largely on the development of Warsaw in Hancock County.

Alexander, Thomas G. "Brief Histories of Three Federal Military Installations in Utah: Kearns Army Air Base, Hurricane Mesa, and Green River Test Complex." *Utah Historical Quarterly*, 34 (Spring 1966), 121-37. Describes the installations' effect on the history of Utah.

Alexander, Thomas G., and Leonard J. Arrington. "Camp in the Sagebrush: Camp Floyd, Utah, 1858-1861." *Utah Historical Quarterly*, 34 (Winter 1966), 3-21. Notes the economic, cultural, and social impact of the post on the people of Utah.

Alexander, Thomas G., and Leonard J. Arrington. "The Utah Military Frontier, 1872-1912: Forts Cameron, Thornburgh, and Duchesne." *Utah Historical Quarterly*, 32 (Fall 1964), 330-54. A short history of each fort: Cameron, 1872-1883; Thornburgh, 1881-1884; and Duchesne, 1886-1912.

Alexander, Thomas G., and Leonard J. Arrington. "Utah's First Line of Defense: The Utah National Guard and Camp W. G. Williams, 1926-1965." *Utah Historical Quarterly*, 33 (Summer 1965), 141-56. A short history of the Utah National Guard with some description of the construction, expansion, and more modern facilities at Camp Williams.

Alperin, Lynn M. *Custodians of the Coast: History of the United States Army Engineers at Galveston*. See chapter on "Waterways."

Anderson, Harry H. "A History of the Cheyenne River Indian Agency and Its Military Post, Fort Bennett, 1868-1891." *South Dakota Report and Historical Collections*, XXVIII (1956), 390-551. Provides extensive data on the fort's construction.

Anderson, Thomas M. "Army Posts, Barracks and Quarters." *Journal of the Military Service Institution of the United States*, 2 (1882), 421-47.

Anderson, Thomas M. "Vancouver Barracks—Past and Present." 2 parts. *Journal of the Military Service Institution of the United States*, XXXV (July-Aug.; Sept.-Oct. 1904); July-Aug.: 69-78; Sept.-Oct.; 267-79. A history of an army post located in the state of Washington's Clarke County, less than a hundred miles from the mouth of the Columbia River.

Andrews, Roger. *Old Fort Mackinac on the Hill of History*. Menominee, Mich.: Herald-Leader Press, 1938. 189 pp. Illustrations. A pedestrian, popular history.

Armstrong, Ellis L.; Michael C. Robinson; and Suellen M. Hoy, eds. *History of Public Works in the United States, 1776-1976*. See chapter on "Planning, Engineering, and Administration."

Arrington, Leonard J., and Archer L. Durham. "Anchors Aweigh in Utah: The U. S. Naval Supply Depot at Clearfield, 1942-1962." *Utah Historical Quarterly*, 31 (Spring 1963), 109-26. A history of one of three inland naval supply depots in the United States.

Arrington, Leonard J., and Anthony T. Cluff. *Federally-Financed Industrial Plants Constructed in Utah During World War II*. Logan, Utah: Utah State University Press, 1969. iv + 72 pp. Tables, notes, and appendix. History of how the federal government supported industrial expansion in Utah during World War II.

Arrington, Leonard J., and Thomas G. Alexander, "Sentinels on the Desert: The Dugway Proving Ground (1942-1963) and Deseret Chemical Depot (1942-1955)." *Utah Historical Quarterly*, 32 (Winter 1964), 32-43. Describes the development of two sites selected by the War Department early in World War II when it began to expand its capacity for chemical warfare defense.

Arrington, Leonard J., and Thomas G. Alexander. "Supply Hub of the West: Defense Depot Ogden, 1941-1964." *Utah Historical Quarterly*, 32 (Spring 1964), 99-121. A history of the depot and a summary of its importance to the Utah economy.

Arrington, Leonard J., and Thomas G. Alexander. "The U. S. Army Overlooks Salt Lake Valley: Fort Douglas, 1862-1965." *Utah Historical Quarterly*, 33 (Fall 1965), 326-50. Presents Fort Douglas "as a monument to the non-Mormon contribution to Utah's [economic] development."

Arrington, Leonard J.; Thomas G. Alexander; and Eugene H. Erb, Jr. "Utah's Biggest Business: Odgen Air Material Area at Hill Air Force Base, 1938-1965." *Utah Historical Quarterly*, 33 (Winter 1965), 9-33. A brief presentation of OOAMA's history and a discussion of its economic impact on the state.

Arrington, Leonard J., and Thomas G. Alexander. "World's Largest Military Reserve: Wendover Air Force Base, 1941-63." *Utah Historical Quarterly*, 31 (Fall 1963), 324-35. A history of the base; one section is devoted to "Selection and Construction."

Arthur, Robert. "Early Coast Fortifications." *Military Engineer*, 53 (July-Aug. 1961), 279-81.

Arthur, Robert. *History of Fort Monroe*. Fort Monroe, Va.: Coast Artillery School, 1930. xii + 290 pp. Illustrations, maps, and bibliography.

Ashcraft, Allan C. "Fort Provo, Texas, in 1861." *Texas Military History*, 3 (Winter 1963), 243-47.

Athearn, Rober G. *Forts of the Upper Missouri*. Englewood Cliffs, N. J.: Prentice-Hall, 1967. xi + 339 pp. Illustrations, map, notes, bibliographical essay, and index. Well-written history of forts in the Missouri River Basin during the 1850s and 1860s.

Ayers, J. R. "Naval Drydock Construction." *Transactions of the American Society of Civil*

Engineers, CT (1953), 1192-1204. Describes general advancements from stone to concrete—to keep pace with the larger ships.

Azoy, Anastasio Carlos Mariano. *Three Centuries Under Three Flags*. New York: Headquarters First Army, 1951. 110 pp. Illustrations and index. Pedestrian history of the important installation in New York Harbor.

Babson, Jane F. "The Architecture of Early Illinois Forts." *Journal of the Illinois State Historical Society*, LXI (Spring 1968), 9-40. Excellent study of the architecture of colonial French and British forts.

Baird, W. David. "Fort Smith and the Red Man." *Arkansas Historical Quarterly*, 30 (Winter 1971), 337-48.

Bald, F. Clever. "Fort Miami." *Quarterly Bulletin of the Historical Society of Northwestern Ohio*, 15 (July 1943), 127-38. A documentary outline of the history of Old Fort Miami.

Barrett, Lenora. "Transportation, Supplies, and Quarters for the West Texas Frontier Under the Federal Military System, 1848-1861." *West Texas Historical Association Year Book*, V (June 1929), 87-99. Offers sketchy material on the legislative history of fort and arsenal construction.

Barry, J. Neilson. "Early Oregon Country Forts, A Chronological List." *Oregon Historical Quarterly*, XLVI (June 1945), 101-11. A listing with bibliography.

Barry, Louise. "The Fort Leavenworth-Fort Gibson Military Road and the Founding of Fort Scott." *Kansas Historical Quarterly*. See chapter on "Roads, Streets, and Highways."

Barry, Richard Schriver. "Fort Macon: Its History." *North Carolina Historical Review*, XXVII (April 1950), 163-77. Brief history of a fort located in Beaufort, North Carolina, that is now a state park.

Baumer, William H., Jr. *West Point: Moulder of Men*. New York: D. Appleton-Century Company, 1942. xv + 264 pp. Illustrations and bibliography.

Beach, James H. "Old Fort Hays." *Kansas State Historical Society Collections,* XI (1909-1910), 571-81. A sentimental account of the fort's establishment and abandonment.

Bearss, Edwin C. *Fort Point: Historic Data Section*. Denver: National Park Service, 1973. xxvii + 375 pp. Illustrations, maps, diagrams, and index. A good analysis and summary of the evolution of this historic fort in San Francisco Bay.

Bearss, Edwin C. "In Quest of Peace on the Indian Border: The Establishment of Fort Smith." *Arkansas Historical Quarterly*, 23 (Summer 1964), 123-53.

Beardslee, Clarence G. "Development of Army Camp Planning." *Civil Engineering*, 12 (Sept. 1942), 489-92. Highlights the progress made in developing standards for military establishments during the previous 165 years.

Beckham, Stephen Dow. "Lonely Outpost: The Army's Fort Umpqua." *Oregon Historical Quarterly*, 70 (Sept. 1969), 233-57.

Beckner, Raymond M. *Old Forts of Southern Colorado*. Pueblo, Colo.: O'Brien Printing, 1975. 60 pp. Illustrations. Sketches of some seventeen historic forts.

Beer, Henry Putney. "The Army and the Oregon Trail to 1846." *Pacific Northwest Quarterly*, XXVIII (Oct. 1937), 339-62. On army explorations, expeditions, and post construction on "the line to Oregon" from 1804 to 1849.

Bender A. B. "Military Posts in the Southwest, 1848-1860." *New Mexico Historical Review*, XVI (April 1941), 125-47. Good survey of forts built in present-day Oklahoma, Texas, Colorado, New Mexico, and Arizona.

Bender, A. B. "Opening Routes across West Texas, 1848-1850." *Southwestern Historical Quarterly*. See chapter on "Roads, Streets, and Highways."

Bender, Averam B. *The March of Empire: Frontier Defense in the Southwest, 1848-1860*. Lawrence: University of Kansas Press, 1952. x + 323 pp. Illustrations, notes, bibliography, and index. A comprehensive history of the United States' pre-Civil War policy of trans-Mississippi defense. The book treats road building, stream surveys, and post construction in addition to military operations.

Billias, George A. "Beverly's Seacoast Defenses During the Revolutionary War." *Essex Institute Historical Collections*, XCIV (April 1958), 119-31. One of the most prominent ports on the eastern seaboard during the beginning of the Revolutionary War.

Black, W. M. *The United States Public Works*. See chapter on "Flood Control and Drainage."

Blades, Thomas E., and John W. Wike. "Fort Missoula." *Military Affairs*, 13 (Spring 1949), 29-36.

Bolton, Herbert D. "The Mission as a Frontier Institution in the Spanish American Colonies." *American Historical Review*, XXIII (Oct. 1917), 42-61. Classic study of the use of missions to colonize the Spanish frontier. It includes a great deal of descriptive material on their military role.

Bossom, Alfred C. "The Restoration of Fort Ticonderoga." *Architecture*, LII (Aug. 1925), 275-79.

Boydstun, Q. B. "Fort Gibson Barracks, Powder Magazine, and Bake Oven." *Chronicles of Oklahoma*, L (Autumn 1972), 289-96. Good description of the facilities that are being restored.

Boydstun, Q. B. "The Restoration of Old Fort Gibson." *Chronicles of Oklahoma*, LVIII (Summer 1980), 176-91. Describes the restoration effort but also presents a history of the fort (1824), located on a park in the town of Fort Gibson, Muskogee County, Oklahoma.

Bradford, S. Sydney. "Fort McHenry: 1814: The Outworks in 1814." *Maryland Historical Magazine*, 54 (June 1959), 188-209. A good description of the installations.

Braly, Earl Burk. "Fort Belknap of the Texas Frontier." *West Texas Historical Association Year Book*, XXIX (Oct. 1954), 83-114. One of the key outposts on the Texas frontier from 1851 to 1867.

Brandes, Ray. "A Guide to the History of U. S. Army Installations in Arizona, 1849-1866." *Arizona and the West*, 1 (Spring 1959), 43-65. Contains a short introduction, a list of Arizona's army installations, a general bibliography, and a brief history of fifteen camps and forts of major importance.

Brandes, Ray. *Frontier Military Posts of Arizona*. Globe, Ariz.: Dale Stuart King, 1960. xviii + 94 pp. Illustrations, maps, notes, and bibliography. An insipid, heavily illustrated encyclopedia of frontier posts in Arizona.

Brandes, T. Donald. *Military Posts of Colorado*. Fort Collins, Colo.: Old Army Press, 1973. 77 pp. Illustrations, maps, diagrams, and bibliography. A heavily illustrated, popular encyclopedia of fort development in this western state. The descriptions of the physical facilities are brief and lack substance.

Briggs, John Ely. "The Second Fort Des Moines," *Palimpsest*, XXIV (May 1943), 161-72. History of the founding of the fort in 1843.

Brodie, Bernard, and M. Fawn. *From Crossbow to H-Bomb*. Bloomington: Indiana University Press, 1973. 320 pp. Illustrations, bibliography, and index. A general history of the application of science to war. Sections of the book are devoted to such topics as military engineering, seventeenth-century fortifications, naval warfare and its transformation, the impact of the airplane, and nuclear developments. First published in 1962, this is a revised edition.

Brown, D. Clayton. *Rivers, Rockets, and Readiness: Army Engineers in the Sunbelt: A History of the Fort Worth District, U. S. Army Corps of Engineers, 1950-1975*. See chapter on "Flood Control and Drainage."

Brown, Dee. *Fort Phil Kearny: An American Saga*. New York: G. P. Putnam's Sons, 1962. 251 pp. Map, notes, appendix, bibliography, and index. Very little descriptive information on the construction of the fort is provided in this volume.

Brown, Jerold E. "Where Eagles Roost: A History of Army Airfields before World War II." Doctoral dissertation. See chapter on "Airways and Airports."

Buechler, John. "Fort Ethan Allen: A Post on the Northern Frontier." *Vermont History*, XXXV (Jan. 1967), 3-18. A well-written fort history largely based on primary sources.

Caldwell, Norman W. "Cantonment Wilkinsonville." *Mid-America*, 31 (Jan. 1949), 3-28.

Caldwell, Norman W. "Fort Massac: Since 1805." *Journal of the Illinois State Historical Society*, XLIV (Spring 1951), 47-60.

Caldwell, Norman W. "Fort Massac: The American Frontier Post, 1778-1805." *Journal of the Illinois State Historical Society*, XLIII (Winter 1950), 265-81. A sketchy fort history.

Campbell, Bernard T. "Shiloh National Military Park." *Tennessee Historical Quarterly*. See chapter on "Parks and Recreation."

Cannon, Miles. "Fort Hall on the Saptin River." *Washington Historical Quarterly*, VII (July

1916), 217-32. Explains how it became "one of the most important stations on the famous Oregon Trail."

Carriker, Robert C. *Fort Supply, Indian Territory: Frontier Outpost on the Plains*. Norman: University of Oklahoma Press, 1970. xv + 241 pp. Illustrations, maps, notes, bibliography, and index. Solid history based on primary sources that includes information on the fort's structures and social life.

Carriker, Robert Charles. "Fort Supply, Indian Territory: Frontier Outpost on the Southern Plains, 1868-1894." Doctoral dissertation, University of Oklahoma, 1967.

Chapman, John. "Fort Concho." *Southwest Review*, XXV (April 1940), 258-86. Includes good photographs of the fort taken in the 1880s.

Chapman, John. "Fort Griffin." *Southwest Review*, XXVII (Summer 1942), 426-45. West Texas fort built following the Civil War.

Chapman, John. "Old Fort Richardson." *Southwest Review*, XXXVIII (Winter 1953), 62-69. Describes picket and adobe buildings constructed in the late 1860s.

Chapel, William L. "Camp Rucker: Outpost in Apacheria." *Journal of Arizona History*, 14 (Summer 1973), 95-112. Weak history of an Arizona post.

Chappell, Gordon S. "The Fortifications of Old Fort Laramie." *Annals of Wyoming*, 34 (Oct. 1962), 145-62. The construction of this nineteenth-century fort, especially its lack of defensive structures, "provides a general picture of the western frontier military post."

Christian, Garna Loy. "Sword and Plowshare: The Symbiotic Development of Fort Bliss and El Paso, Texas, 1849-1918." Doctoral dissertation, Texas Tech University, 1977. 547 pp.

Church, William Conant. "John Ericsson, The Engineer." *Scribner's Magazine*, VII (Feb. 1890), 169-85. Emphasizes his early life in Sweden, his engineering training in the Swedish army, and the application of his abilities and inventions to naval construction.

Clark, Dan Elbert. "Early Forts on the Upper Mississippi." *Proceedings of the Mississippi Valley Historical Association*, IV (1910-1911), 91-101. Sketches of pre-Revolutionary War forts.

Clark, Dan Elbert. "Frontier Defense in Iowa, 1850-1865." *Iowa Journal of History and Politics*, XVI (July 1918), 315-86. A largely military history of Iowa forts in the pre-bellum era. Discussions of the facilities are rather thin.

Cohrs, Timothy. "Fort Selden, New Mexico." *El Palacio*, 79 (March 1974), 13-39. A history and description of life at the fort (1865-1887) established on the bank of the Rio Grande eighteen miles north of Las Cruces "to protect the settlers of Mesilla Valley to the south and to guard citizens and livestock crossing the Jornada."

Colby, Carroll B. *Historic American Forts: From Frontier Stockade to Coastal Fortress*. New York: Coward-McCann, 1963. 47 pp. Illustrations.

Coll, Blanche D.; Jean E. Keith; and Herbert H. Rosenthal. *The Corps of Engineers: Troops and Equipment*. Washington, D. C.: Office of Military History, U. S. Department of the Army, 1958. xvii + 622 pp. Illustrations, charts, tables, notes, bibliographical essay, glossary, and index. A fine contribution to the "United States Army in World War II" series. The book covers a multitude of tactical and logistical activities: building and renovating barracks and office buildings, constructing and repairing airfields, improving roads and bridges, and operating pipelines. Emphasis is also given to the corps' organization and administration, advances in machinery, and improvements in mapping.

Connery, Robert H., and Richard H. Leach. *The Federal Government and Metropolitan Areas*. See chapter on "Planning, Engineering, and Administration."

Cook, Fred S. "A Nostalgic Look at Texas' Fort Stockton." *Desert Magazine*, 39 (Aug. 1976), 10-13.

Cooling, B. Franklin. "Fort Donelson National Military Park." *Tennessee Historical Quarterly*. See chapter on "Parks and Recreation."

Cooling, Benjamin Franklin. *Symbol, Sword and Shield: Defending Washington during the Civil War.* Hamden, Conn.: Shoestring Press, 1975.

Corbusier, William T. "Camp Shendan, Nebraska." *Nebraska History*, 42 (March 1961), 29-53.

Covington, James W. "Life at Fort Brooke,

1824-1836." *Florida Historical Quarterly*, XXXVI (April 1958), 319-30. Discussions are included of the barracks and other facilities.

Cowell, Ray Theodore. "History of Fort Townsend." *Washington Historical Quarterly*, XVI (Oct. 1925), 284-89. Established in 1856 to quell Indian disturbances on Puget Sound. The fort was destroyed by fire in 1894.

Cowell, Ray T. "Fort Lawton." *Washington Historical Quarterly*, XIX (Jan. 1928), 31-36. On the fortification built to protect Puget Sound in the late nineteenth century.

Cox, Jess. "Fort Bayard." *New Mexico Magazine*, XLII (April 1964), 6-8. Hundred-year-old fort in southwestern New Mexico that is now the site of a major VA hospital.

Crane, John, and James F. Kieley. *West Point: The Key to America*. New York: McGraw Hill Book Company, 1947. xiii + 290 pp. Illustrations, chronology, and maps.

Crimmins, M. L. "Fort Fillmore." *New Mexico Historical Review*, VI (Oct. 1931), 327-33. Adobe fort built thirty-eight miles west of El Paso in the 1850s.

Crimmins, M. L. "Fort McKavett, Texas." *Southwestern Historical Quarterly*, 38 (July 1934), 28-39.

Cullum, Geo. W. "Defenses of Narragansett Bay, Rhode Island—Historical Sketch." *Magazine of American History*, XI (June 1884), 465-96. Overview of coastal fortifications.

Culverwell, Albert. "Stronghold in the Yakima Country: Fort Simcoe and the Indian War, 1856-59." *Pacific Northwest Quarterly*, 46 (April 1955), 46-51.

Culverwell, Albert. *Stronghold in the Yakima County: The Story of Fort Simcoe, 1856-59*. Olympia, Wash.: State Parks and Recreation Commission, 1956. 20 pp. Illustrations, notes, maps, and bibliography.

Cunningham, A. C. "The Development of the Norfolk Navy Yard." *United States Naval Institute Proceedings*, 36 (March 1910), 221-37. History of the yard from pre-Revolutionary days. It is accompanied by a map and drawings.

Currey, J. Seymour. *The Story of Old Fort Dearborn*. Chicago: A. C. McClurg & Company, 1912. ix + 174 pp. Illustrations. The fort's facilities are incidental to this undocumented, popular book.

"Dakota Military Posts." *South Dakota Historical Collections*, VIII (1916), 77-99. Includes plans and photographs of the facilities.

Davis, Helen W.; Edward M. Hatch; and David G. Wright. "Alexander Parris: Innovator in Naval Facility Architecture." *IA: The Journal of the Society for Industrial Archeology*, 2 (1976), 3-22. Excellent analysis and overview of the naval facilities Parris built, which included ropewalks, dry docks, and hospitals.

Davis, Virgil S. *A History of the Mobile District, 1815 to 1971*. Mobile: Mobile District, South Atlantic Division, Corps of Engineers, 1975. iv + 109 pp. Illustrations, maps, notes, and appendix. Provides extensive coverage of the corps' activities including coastal defenses, river and harbor improvements, military construction, and aerospace projects.

Davisson, Lori. "Arizona's White River—A Working Watercourse." *Journal of Arizona History*. See chapter on "Irrigation."

Davisson, Lori. "Fifty Years at Fort Apache." *Journal of Arizona History*, 17 (Autumn 1976), 301-20. Deals extensively with the fort's buildings and living conditions.

Day, Daniel S. "Fort Sedgwick." *Colorado Magazine,* 42 (Winter 1965), 17-35.

De La Croix, Horst. *Military Considerations in City Planning: Fortifications*. New York: George Braziller, 1972. 128 pp. Illustrations, notes, glossary, bibliography, and index. Good analysis of the influence of fortifications on the structure of urban forms.

Denton, Edgar, III. "The Formative Years of the United States Military Academy, 1775-1833." Doctoral dissertation, Syracuse University, 1964. 307 pp.

Dillard, Walter Scott. "The United States Military Academy, 1865-1900: The Uncertain Years." Doctoral dissertation, University of Washington, 1972. 418 pp.

Dougherty, Dolorita Marie. "A History of Fort Union (North Dakota), 1829-1867." Doctoral dissertation, St. Louis University, 1957.

Dunn, Adrian R. "A History of Old Fort Berthold." *North Dakota History*, 30 (Fall 1963), 157-240. Exhaustive treatment of the fort's military history.

Dunn, Adrian R. *A History of Old Fort Berth-*

old. Bismarck: North Dakota State Historical Society, 1964.

Dupuy, Richard E. *Sylvanus Thayar: Father of Technology in the United States*. West Point: Association of Graduates, West Point, 1958. 24 pp. Illustrations.

Dupuy, R. Ernest. *The Story of West Point, 1802-1943*. Washington, D. C.: Infantry Journal, 1943. 282 pp.

Durand, W. F. "Robert Henry Thurston." *Annual Report of the Board of Regents of the Smithsonian Institution* (1903), 843-49. A biographical sketch of a nineteenth-century navy engineer (1839-1903) who subsequently became a professor of mechanical engineering at Stevens Institute and then Cornell University.

"Early Coast Fortification." *Coast Artillery Journal*, 70 (Feb. 1929), 134-44. Largely a listing of fortifications built prior to 1820.

Edwards, Paul M. "Fort Wadsworth and the Friendly Santee Sioux, 1864-1892." *South Dakota Report and Historical Collections*, XXXI, 74-156. Includes illustrations and descriptions of the fort's facilities.

Egan, Ferol. "The Building of Fort Churchill: Blueprint for a Military Fiasco, 1860." *American West*, IX (March 1972), 4-9. Competent summary of a historic Nevada fort. It contains interesting material on the problems of constructing forts in desert country.

Eller, W. H. "Old Fort Atkinson." *Transactions and Reports of the Nebraska State Historical Society*, IV (1892), 18-29. Dull and superficial essay that includes a plot of the fort.

Ellison, Robert S. *Fort Bridger, Wyoming: A Brief History*. Casper, Wyo.: Historical Landmark Commission of Wyoming, 1938. 81 pp. Illustrations, map, and appendix. Pedestrian account of the famous fort's history.

Emery, B. Frank. "Fort Saginaw." *Michigan History Magazine*, 30 (July-Sept. 1946), 476-503.

Emmett, Chris. *Fort Union and the Winning of the Southwest*. Norman: University of Oklahoma Press, 1965. xvi + 436 pp. Illustrations, maps, notes, appendix, bibliography, and index. A good history of this New Mexico fort that was founded in 1851 and abandoned in 1891. Very little narrative is devoted to the fort's physical features, but several good drawings and photographs are included.

Faulk, Odie B.; Kenny A. Franks; and Paul F. Lambert, eds. *Early Military Forts and Posts in Oklahoma*. Oklahoma City: Oklahoma Historical Society, 1978. vii + 134 pp. Illustrations, maps, and index. An uneven collection of ten essays on various Oklahoma forts and posts.

Fayrot, H. Mortimer. "Colonial Forts of Louisiana." *Louisiana Historical Quarterly*, 26 (July 1943), 722-54. A well-written overview of pre-1800 Louisiana colonial forts that offers considerable material on the facilities' design and construction.

Fine, Lenore, and Jesse A. Remington. *The Corps of Engineers: Construction in the United States*. Washington, D. C.: United States Department of the Army, 1972. xviii + 747 pp. Illustrations, maps, charts, tables, appendix, bibliography, and index. Exhaustive history of the largest construction program undertaken in the nation's history. The book, in addition to discussing the corps' contributions, describes the work of the Quartermaster Corps from which the engineers inherited responsibility for military construction in 1940 and 1941.

Fisher, James. "Fort Wilkins." *Michigan History Magazine*, 29 (April-June), 155-65.

Fleming, William Foster. "San Antonio: The History of a Military City, 1865-1880." Doctoral dissertation, University of Pennsylvania, 1963. 445 pp.

Foreman, Grant. *A History of Oklahoma*. See chapter on "Roads, Streets, and Highways."

Foremen, Grant. *Advancing the Frontier, 1830-1860*. Norman: University of Oklahoma Press, 1933. 363 pp. Illustrations, maps, notes, bibliography, and index. A well-researched history of six forts constructed in present-day Oklahoma as a consequence of government Indian relocation policies. Excellent material is included on the design, operation, and maintenance of the forts.

Foreman, Grant. *Fort Gibson: A Brief History*. Norman: University of Oklahoma Press, 1943.

Foreman, Grant. "The Centennial of Fort Gibson." *Chronicles of Oklahoma*, II (June 1924), 119-28.

Foreman, Sidney. *West Point: A History of the United States Military Academy*. New York: Columbia University Press, 1950. 255 pp. Illustrations, notes, bibliography, and index.

"Fort Atkinson, Iowa." *Annals of Iowa*, IV (July 1900), 448-53. Largely a collection of official correspondence.

Foster, James Monroe, Jr. "Fort Bascom, New Mexico." *New Mexico Historical Review*, 35 (Jan. 1960), 30-62.

Frantz, Joe B. "The Significance of Frontier Forts to Texas." *Southwestern Historical Quarterly*, LXXIV (Oct. 1970), 204-23. Principally a photo album of nineteenth-century Texas forts.

Frazer, Robert W. "Army Agriculture in New Mexico, 1852-53." *New Mexico Historical Review*. See chapter on "Irrigation."

Frazer, Robert W. *Forts of the West: Military Forts and Presidios and Posts Commonly Called Forts West of the Mississippi River to 1898*. Norman: University of Oklahoma Press, 1972. xxxvii + 246 pp. Illustrations, map, diagram, notes, appendix, bibliography, and index. A state-by-state catalog of nineteenth-century forts. The location and role in western history are given for each fort. The author's introduction is an excellent overview of fort development.

Frazer, Robert W. *Mansfield on the Condition of the Western Forts.* Norman: University of Oklahoma Press, 1963. xxi + 254 pp. Drawings, notes, bibliography, and index. Well-edited account of an inspection of military posts in the Oregon country and the territory acquired at the close of the Mexican War.

Frazier, Arthur H. "The Military Frontier: Fort Dearborn." *Chicago History*, IX (Summer 1980), 80-85. Includes early drawings and photographs of the fort.

Freedom, Gary Stuart. "U. S. Military Forts of the Northern Great Plains, 1866-1891: An Historical Geography." Doctoral dissertation, University of Tennessee, 1976.

Friggens, Thomas. "Fort Wilkins: Army Life on the Frontier." *Michigan History*, 61 (Fall 1977), 220-50.

Friggens, Thomas G. "History Comes Alive at Fort Wilkins." *Chronicle: The Magazine of the Historical Society of Michigan*, 15 (Fall 1979), 12-15, 20-24. Includes some sketchy historical information on the fort.

Gallaher, Ruth A. "Fort Des Moines in Iowa History." *Iowa and War*, 22 (April 1919), 1-36. Includes some descriptive construction information.

Garfield, Marvin H. "The Military Post as a Factor in the Frontier Defense of Kansas, 1865-1869." *Kansas Historical Quarterly*, 1 (Nov. 1931), 50-62. A dull fort-building chronicle.

Giffen, Helen S. "Camp Independence—An Owens Valley Outpost." *Historical Society of Southern California Quarterly*, XXIV (Dec. 1942), 128-42.

Giffen, Helen S., and Arthur Woodward. *The Story of El Tejon*. Los Angeles: Dawson's Book Shop, 1942. ix + 146 pp. Illustrations and notes. Dull history of a fort in the South San Joaquin Valley.

Godson, William F. *The History of West Point, 1852-1902*. Philadelphia: n. p., 1934. 108 pp.

Goldberg, Alfred, ed. *A History of the United States Air Force, 1907-1957*. Princeton, N. J.: D. Van Nostrand Company, 1957. ix + 277 pp. Illustrations, bibliography, and index. A collection of chapters related to the establishment and development of the Department of the Air Force and the United States Air Force (USAF). This book was prepared by "staff and command historians," most of whom were located in the USAF Historical Division; the volume marks USAF's tenth anniversary.

Gowans, Frederick Ross. "A History of Fort Bridger from 1841-1858." Doctoral dissertation, Brigham Young University, 1972. vii + 316 pp. Illustrations, maps, notes, appendix, and bibliography. A competent history of a key fort on the Oregon Trail.

Gowans, Fred R. "Some New Notes on Two Old Forts." *Annals of Wyoming*, 46 (Fall 1974), 217-52. Two brief articles on "The Fort on Willow Creek" and "Fort Bridger: Claims and Counter Claims."

Graham, Roy Eugene. "Federal Fort Architecture in Texas during the Nineteenth Century." *Southwestern Historical Quarterly*, LXXIV (Oct. 1970), 165-88. Outstanding comparative analysis of the evolution of federal fort architecture. The article is deeply researched and contains a host of excellent illustrations.

Graham, Louis E. "Fort McIntosh." *Western Pennsylvania Historical Magazine*, 15 (May

1932), 93-119. Fort built on the Ohio River in 1778 near present-day Pittsburgh.

Grange, Roger T., Jr. "Fort Robinson, Outpost on the Plains." *Nebraska History* (Sept. 1958), 191-240. Offers a short section entitled "Building Fort Robinson."

Grant, Bruce. *American Forts, Yesterday and Today*. New York: Dutton, 1965. 381 pp. Illustrations, maps, and bibliography.

Grant, Joseph H. "Old Fort Snelling." *Quartermaster Review*, 13 (March-April 1934), 21-22, 71-72.

Green, James Albert. "Life at Ft. Meigs in 1813 and 1840." *Bulletin of the Historical and Philosophical Society of Ohio*, 7 (Jan. 1949), 3-9.

Green, Sherman. *History of the Seattle District, 1896-1968*. See chapter on "Waterways."

Gregg, Andy. *Drums of Yesterday: The Forts of New Mexico*. Santa Fe: The Press of the Territorian, 1968. 40 pp. Illustrations and map. A sketchy encyclopedia.

Gregg, Kate L. "Building of the First American Fort West of the Mississippi." *Missouri Historical Review*, XXX (July 1936), 345-64. Discussion of the founding of Fort Bellefontaine near the confluence of the Missouri and Mississippi rivers.

Gregg, Kate L. "The History of Fort Osage." *Missouri Historical Review*, 34 (July 1940), 439-88.

Gregory, L. E. "The Corps of Engineers, U. S. N." *Military Engineer*, XVII (Jan.-Feb. 1925), 50-64. Relates the history, organization, and duties of the Navy's Bureau of Yards and Docks, the institution that "links the Navy to the land."

Griffin, Eugene. *Our Sea-Coast Defenses*. New York: G. P. Putnam's Sons, 1885. 62 pp. Map and appendix.

Griswold, Gillett. "Old Fort Sill: The First Seven Years." *Chronicles of Oklahoma*, XXXVI (Spring 1958), 2-14. A good summary of the installation's physical features is included in the article.

Guest, Florian Frances. "Municipal Institutions in Spanish California, 1769-1821." Doctoral dissertation, University of Southern California, 1961. Includes some material on the role of the presidios in the settlement of Spanish California.

Guie, H. Dean. *Bugles in the Valley: Garnett's Fort Simcoe*. Yakima: n. p., 1956.

Gurney, Gene. *The Pentagon*. New York: Crown Publishers, 1964. 146 pp. Illustrations. Popular description of the world's largest office building.

Guthman, William H. *March to Massacre: A History of the First Seven Years of the United States Army*. New York: McGraw Hill Book Company, 1970. xii + 275 pp. Illustrations, maps, bibliography, and index.

Hafen, LeRoy R., and Francis Marion Young. *Fort Laramie and the Pageant of the West, 1834-1890*. Glendale Calif.: Arthur H. Clark Company, 1938. 429 pp. Illustrations, map, diagrams, notes, appendices, and index. A largely military history of the fort. The evolution of the facilities is traced through diagrams and photos.

Hafen, LeRoy R. "Fort St. Vrain." *Colorado Magazine*, XXIX (Oct. 1952), 241-55.

Hagen, Olaf T. "Platte Bridge Station and Fort Caspar." *Annals of Wyoming*, 27 (April 1955), 3-18.

Hagwood, Joseph H., Jr. *Commitment to Excellence: A History of the Sacramento District, U. S. Army Corps of Engineers, 1929-1973*. See chapter on "Flood Control and Drainage."

Haley, J. Evetts. *Fort Concho and the Texas Frontier*. San Angelo, Tex.: San Angelo Standard-Times, 1952. xi + 352 pp. Illustrations, maps, notes, and index. A history of a relatively obscure Texas fort. One chapter is devoted to siting and construction.

Hammer, Kenneth M. "Railroads and the Frontier: Garrisons of Dakota Territory." *North Dakota History*, 46 (Summer 1979), 24-34.

Hammond, John Martin. *Quaint and Historic Forts of North America*. Philadelphia: J. B. Lippincott Company, 1915. xiv + 309 pp. Illustrations and index. A popular, pedestrian history of some thirty American forts.

Handy, Mary Olivia. *History of Fort Sam Houston*. San Antonio: Naylor Company, 1951. xx + 111 pp. Illustrations, notes, bibliography, and index. The book contains a well-researched section that thoroughly discusses the planning, construction, and use of the fort's facilities.

Hanft, Marshall. *The Cape Forts: Guardians of the Columbia*. Portland: Oregon Historical Society, 1973. 64 pp. Illustrations. Largely a photo album.

Hansen, Chuck. "Hamilton Air Force Base, 1931-1950: A Pictorial Tribute." *American Aviation Historical Society Journal*. See chapter on "Airways and Airports."

Hansen, Marcus L. *Old Fort Snelling, 1819-1858*. Iowa City: State Historical Society of Iowa, 1918. xi + 270 pp. Illustration, notes, and index. Chapter 5 of this book, "A Soldiers' World," is an excellent description of the fort's barracks, quarters, storehouses, and other buildings.

Hardeman, Nicholas P. "Brick Stronghold of the Border: Fort Assinniboine, 1879-1911." *Montana, the Magazine of Western History*, 29 (April 1979), 54-67.

Harris, F. R. "Evolution of Tremie-Placed Concrete Dry Docks." *Civil Engineering*. See chapter on "Waterways."

Hart, Herbert M. *Old Forts of the Far West*. Seattle: Superior Publishing Company, 1965. 192 pp. Illustrations, maps, diagrams, bibliography, and index. An enclyclopedia of historic forts in Colorado, Arizona, New Mexico, Utah, Nevada, and California.

Hart, Herbert M. *Old Forts of the Northwest*. Seattle: Superior Publishing, 1963. 192 pp. Illustrations, map, and bibliography.

Hart, Herbert M. *Old Forts of the Southwest*. Seattle: Superior Publishing Company, 1964.

Hart, Herbert M. *Pioneer Forts of the West*. Seattle: Superior Publishing Company, 1967. 192 pp. Illustrations, diagrams, bibliography, and index. An effectively illustrated catalog.

Hartman, J. Paul. *Civil Engineering Landmarks: State of Florida*. See chapter on "Planning, Engineering, and Administration."

Haskett, James N. "The Final Chapter in the Story of the First Fort Smith." *Arkansas Historical Quarterly*, 25 (Autumn 1966), 214-28.

Hatcher, John H. "Fort Phantom Hill." *Texas Military History*, 3 (Fall 1963), 154-64.

Hedren, Paul L. "On Duty at Fort Ridgely, Minnesota, 1853-1867." *South Dakota History*, 7 (Spring 1977), 168-92.

Heilbron, Bertha L., ed. "Territorial Daguerrotypes: Fort Snelling and Minnesota Territory." *Minnesota History*, XXIX (Dec. 1948), 316-20. A letter by civil engineer, George F. Fuller, who in 1853 assisted Lieutenant James W. Obert in making a topographical survey of the Fort Snelling vicinity.

Hinds, James R. "Potomac River Defenses: The First Twenty Years." *Periodical*, 3 (Fall 1973), 2-17. Good overview of facilities built from 1794 to about 1815.

Hinds, James R., and Edmund Fitzgerald. "Fortifications in the Field and on the Frontier." *Periodical*, 9 (Spring 1977), 41-49.

Hinds, James R., and Edmund Fitzgerald. "Introduction to Fortification: Musket Period." *Periodical*, 8 (Fall 1976), 24-28.

Hoekman, Steven. "The History of Fort Sully." *South Dakota Collections and Report*, XXVI (1952), 222-77. Good history of the fort established in 1863 on the Missouri River in present Hughes County, South Dakota.

Holt, John R. *Historic Fort Snelling*. Fort Snelling, Minn.: John R. Holt, 1938. 39 pp. Illustrations and maps.

Holtz, Milton E. "Old Fort Kearny—1846-1848: Symbol of a Changing Frontier." *Montana: The Magazine of Western History*, XXII (Oct. 1972), 44-55. Illustrates the evolution of the fort into an important townsite, Nebraska City, Nebraska.

Horowitz, Louis J., and Boyden Sparkes. *The Towers of New York: The Memoirs of a Master Builder*. New York: Simon and Schuster, 1937. xiv + 277 pp. Illustrations and index. The autobiography of a Polish immigrant who became president of one of the nation's largest construction firms, Thompson-Starrett. Horowitz, who made possible such New York landmarks as the Woolworth and Equitable buildings, discusses their relationship to the surrounding environment. He also describes his company's involvement in the building of military installations during World War I.

Hopper, W. L. "The Birth and Death of an Army Fort." *Military History of Texas and the Southwest*, 10 (1972), 273-77.

Howard, Helen Addison. "Unique History of Fort Tejon." *Journal of the West*, 18 (Jan. 1979), 41-51.

Hoy, Suellen M. "People in Public Works:

Admiral Ben Moreell." *APWA Reporter*, 44 (March 1977), 8-9. Features the prominent career of the founder of the Seabees, builders who could fight.

Hunt, Elvid. *History of Fort Leavenworth, 1827-1927*. Fort Leavenworth: General Service Schools Press, 1926. xii + 298 pp. Illustrations, maps, charts, tables, appendices, bibliography, and index. A solid factual history that includes considerable information on the fort's facilities during various periods of its history.

Hurt, R. Douglas. "Fort Wallace, Kansas, 1865-1882: A Frontier Post During the Indian Wars." *Red River Valley Historical Review*, 1 (Spring 1974), 132-45.

Hurt, R. Douglas. "The Construction and Development of Fort Wallace, Kansas, 1865-1882." *Kansas Historical Quarterly*, 43 (Spring 1977), 44-55.

Hussey, John A. "Fort Casey—Garrison for Puget Sound." *Pacific Northwest Quarterly*, 57 (April 1956), 33-43. An outstanding fort history based largely on government archives.

Hussey, John A. *The History of Fort Vancouver and Its Physical Structure*. Portland: Washington State Historical Society, 1958. xx + 256 pp. + LIV plates. Illustrations, maps, notes, bibliography, and index. More than half of this outstanding book is devoted to the history of the fort's physical structure.

Huston, John Wilson. "Fort Pitt, 1758-1772." Doctoral dissertation, University of Pittsburgh, 1957.

Ivers, Larry E. *Colonial Forts of South Carolina, 1670-1775*. Columbia, S. C.: University of South Carolina Press, 1970. 77 pp. Illustrations and bibliography. A dull encyclopedia.

Jackson, Donald. "A Critic Views Iowa's First Military Post." *Iowa Journal of History*, 58 (Jan. 1960), 31-36. Account of living conditions at Fort Madison in 1811.

Jackson, Donald. "Old Fort Madison, 1808-1913." *Palimpsest*, 39 (Jan. 1958), 1-64.

Jackson, Frances. "Military Use of Haleakala National Park." *Hawaiian Journal of History*. See chapter on "Parks and Recreation."

Jacobs, W. A., and Lyman L. Woodman. *The Alaska District, United States Army Corps of Engineers, 1946-1974*. Elmendorf Air Force Base: n. p., 1976. viii + 145 pp. Illustrations and maps. Records the corps, military construction program, navigation and flood control work, as well as major emergency operations.

Jenkins, William H. "Alabama Forts, 1700-1838." *Alabama Review*, XII (July 1959), 163-80.

Johnson, Judith. "Navy Public Works—1776-1976." *Military Engineer*, 68 (May-June 1976), 186-93.

Johnson, Leland R. *Engineers on the Twin Rivers: A History of the Nashville District Corps of Engineers United States Army*. See chapter on "Waterways."

Johnson, Leland R. *Men, Mountains, and Rivers: An Illustrated History of the Huntington District, U.S. Army Corps of Engineers, 1754-1974*. See chapter on "Waterways."

Johnson, Leland R. *The Headwaters District: A History of the Pittsburgh District, U.S. Army Corps of Engineers*. See chapter on "Waterways."

Johnson, Loren. "Reconstructing Old Fort Snelling." *Minnesota History*, 42 (Fall 1970), 82-98. Discusses the history of the fort and outlines efforts to restore it to the way it looked during the period 1824-1848.

Johnson, Sally A. "Cantonment, Missouri, 1819-1820." *Nebraska History*, 37 (June 1956), 121-33. Fort built on the Missouri River that later became Fort Atkinson.

Johnson, Sally A. "The Sixth's Elysian Fields: Fort Atkinson on the Council Bluffs." *Nebraska History*, 40 (March 1959), 1-38. Key post that guarded the western military frontier in the 1820s.

Jones, Evan. *Citadel in the Wilderness: The Story of Fort Snelling and the Old Northwest Frontier*. New York: Coward-McCann, 1966.

Judd, Walter F. *Palaces and Forts of the Hawaiian Kingdom: From Thatch to American Florentine*. Palo Alto: Pacific Books, 1975. 176 pp. Illustrations, maps, diagrams, notes, bibliography, and index. Good overview of the forts' architecture.

Julian, Allen P. "Fort Pulaski." *Civil War Times Illustrated*, 9 (May 1970), 8-19. Fort that guarded the approach to Savannah, Georgia.

Kalisch, Philip A., and Beatrice J. "Indian

Territory Forts: Charnel Houses of the Frontier, 1839-1865." *Chronicles of Oklahoma*, L (Spring 1972), 65-81. Stresses unhealthy conditions at frontier forts from 1839 to 1855.

Kanarek, Harold. "People in Public Works: William P. Craighill." *APWA Reporter*, 44 (Aug. 1977), 10-11. Reviews Craighill's work as Baltimore's district engineer and emphasizes the Corps of Engineers' navigation improvements on the Atlantic Coast for which he was responsible.

Kanarek, Harold K. *The Mid-Atlantic Engineers: A History of the Baltimore District, U.S. Army Corps of Engineers, 1774-1974*. See chapter on "Waterways."

Kayser, David. "Fort Tulerosa: 1872-1874." *El Palacio*, 79 (Sept. 1973), 24-27. Outlines (beginnings, location, buildings, troops, abandonment, and aftermath) the brief history of this New Mexican fort.

Kellogg, Louise Phelps. "Old Fort Howard." *Wisconsin Magazine of History*, XVIII (Dec. 1934), 125-40. A poorly researched fort history.

Kelly, Lawrence C. "Where Was Fort Canby?" *New Mexico Historical Review*, 42 (Jan. 1967), 49-62.

Kendall, Jane R. "History of Fort Francis E. Warren." *Annals of Wyoming*, 18 (Jan. 1946), 3-66. Describes the first and successive posts as well as miscellaneous buildings. The most interesting and potentially useful section is "Part II: The Water Rights of Fort Warren."

Kenny, Judith Keyes. "The Founding of Camp Watson." *Oregon Historical Quarterly*, LVII (March 1957), 1-16. Key eastern Oregon fort during the 1860s.

Kimball, James P. "Fort Buford." *North Dakota Historical Quarterly*, IV (Jan. 1930), 73-77.

King, Arthur G. "Origins of Some Cincinnati Streets—A Street in Clifton." *Bulletin of the Historical and Philosophical Society of Ohio*, 10 (April 1952), 143-56. On Fort Washington and surrounding military roads and trails.

Kirchner, D. P. "American Harbor Defense Forts." *United States Naval Institute Proceedings*, 84 (Aug. 1958), 92-98.

Kircus, Peggy Dickey. "Fort David A. Russell: A Study of Its History from 1867 to 1890; With a Brief Summary of Events from 1890 to the Present." 2 parts. *Annals of Wyoming*, 40 and 41 (Oct. 1968; April 1969), Oct. 1968: 161-92; April 1969: 83-111. Emphasizes the fort's role in "almost every important engagement with the Indians in this area," as a troop supply camp during the Spanish-American War, and as a demobilization center afterwards.

Kitchens, James H., III. *A History of the Huntsville Division, U. S. Army Corps of Engineers, 1967-1976*. Huntsville, Ala.: Huntsville Division, U. S. Army Corps of Engineers, 1978. xvii + 180 pp. Illustrations, maps, notes, appendix, bibliography, and index. Traces the changing missions of the division from the development of missile systems to the construction of postal facilities, test facilities for NASA, and design of a nationwide munitions production program.

Klawonn, Marion J. *Cradle of the Corps: A History of the New York District, U. S. Army Corps of Engineers, 1775-1975*. See chapter on "Waterways."

Knopf, Richard C.; Raymond S. Baby; and Dwight L. Smith. "The Rediscovery of Fort Washington." *Bulletin of the Historical and Philosophical Society of Ohio*, 11 (Jan. 1953), 3-12.

Koury, Michael J. *Military Posts of Montana*. Bellevue, Neb.: The Old Army Press, 1970. 96 pp. Illustrations, map, and diagrams. An uninspired and poorly written collection.

Kraus, Joe. "Old Forts of Northern Arizona." *Desert Magazine*, 38 (Oct. 1975), 6-9.

Kuth, Priscilla. " 'Picturesque' Frontier: The Army's Fort Dalles." *Oregon Historical Quarterly*, LXVII; LXVIII (Dec. 1966; March 1967), Dec. 1966: 293-347; March 1967: 5-52. Well-written article that contains excellent descriptions of blockhouses and other buildings.

Larrabee, Edward C. M. "New Jersey and the Fortified Frontier System of the 1750s." Doctoral dissertation, Columbia University, 1970. 385 pp.

Lavender, David. *Bent's Fort*. Garden City, N. Y.: Doubleday & Company, 1954. 450 pp. Notes, bibliography, and index. Public works aspects receive scant attention in this lively written fort history.

Layton, Stanford J. "Fort Rawlins, Utah: A

Question of Mission and Means." *Utah Historical Quarterly*, 42 (Winter 1974), 68-83.

Lewis, Emanuel Raymond. *Seacoast Fortifications of the United States: An Introductory History*. Washington, D. C.: Smithsonian Institution Press, 1970. xiv + 145 pp. Illustrations, maps, diagrams, notes, appendices, bibliography, and index. A well-illustrated descriptive overview of the evolution of American seacoast fortifications. The excellent book reflects extensive research in primary historical sources.

Lewis, Kenneth E. "Archeological Investigations at Fort Towson, Choctaw County, Oklahoma, 1971." *Chronicles of Oklahoma*, L (Autumn 1972), 270-88. Includes historical sketch of the fort established in 1824.

Lindsey, David. "The Founding of Chicago." *American History Illustrated*, VIII (Dec. 1973), 24-33. Describes the construction of Fort Dearborn.

Littlefield, Daniel F., Jr., and Lonnie E. Underhill. "Fort Coffee and Frontier Affairs, 1834-1838." *Chronicles of Oklahoma*, LIV (Fall 1976), 314-38. Post established near Fort Smith, Arkansas, in the 1830s.

Littlefield, Daniel F., and Lonnie E. Underhill. "Fort Wayne and Border Violence, 1840-1847." *Arkansas Historical Quarterly*, 36 (Spring 1977), 3-30.

Littlefield, Daniel F., and Lonnie E. Underhill. "Fort Wayne and the Arkansas Frontier, 1838-1840." *Arkansas Historical Quarterly*, 35 (Winter 1976), 334-59.

Livingood, James W. "Chickamauga and Chattanooga National Military Park.." *Tennessee Historical Quarterly*. See chapter on "Parks and Recreation."

Lockwood, Frank C. "Early Military Posts in Arizona." *Arizona Historical Review*, 2 (Jan. 1930), 91-97. Dull listing of Arizona posts in the 1860s and 1870s.

Lupton, David W. "Fort Platte, Wyoming, 1841-1845: Rival of Fort Laramie." *Annals of Wyoming*, 49 (Spring 1977), 83-108.

McDermott, John Dishon. "Fort Laramie's Iron Bridge." *Annals of Wyoming*. See chapter on "Roads, Streets, and Highways."

McKusick, Marshall. "Fort Des Moines (1834-1837): An Archeological Test." *Annals of Iowa*, 42 (Winter 1975), 513-22. Gives a brief history of the fort and explains recent archeological tests and findings.

McNitt, Frank. "Fort Sumner: A Study in Origins." *New Mexico Historical Review*, 45 (April 1970), 101-17.

McNitt, Frank. "Old Fort Wingate: The Inspection Reports." *El Palacio*, 78 (June 1972), 30-36. A short history of this New Mexican fort (1862). The article includes a drawing of the fort's original plan and gives specifications for materials required at the time the fort was established.

Madden, R. B. "The American Society of Naval Engineers." *General Electric Review*. See chapter on "Planning, Engineering, and Administration."

Mahan, Bruce E. "Old Fort Crawford and the Frontier." Doctoral dissertation, State University of Iowa, 1926. xv + 349 pp. Illustrations, map, notes, and index. A good account of one of the more important pre-Civil War forts in the Upper Mississippi Valley.

Mantor, Lyle. "Fort Kearny and the Westward Movement." *Nebraska History*, XXIX (Sept. 1948), 175-207. Traces its history from military post to state park.

Mantor, Lyle Edwin. "The History of Fort Kearny." Doctoral dissertation, State University of Iowa, 1934. 293 pp. Notes, appendices, and bibliography. A solid history of a key military post on the Oregon Trail. The fort's facilities during different eras of its history are thoroughly covered.

Manucy, Albert C., ed. *The History of Castillo de San Marcos & Fort Matanazas from Contemporary Narratives and Letters*. See chapter on "Parks and Recreation."

Marshall, Mortimer M., Jr. "From Barracks to Dormitories." *Military Engineer*, LXVI (Nov.-Dec. 1974), 343-46. Changes in the housing of enlisted personnel since the 1950s.

Mattes, Merrill J. "A History of Old Fort Mitchell." *Nebraska History*, XXIV (April-June 1943), 71-83. Short-lived fort on the Oregon Trail.

Mattes, Merrill J. "Fort Laramie, Guardian of the Oregon Trail." *Annals of Wyoming*, 17 (Jan. 1945), 3-20. A commemorative essay on a fort that in 1849 was transformed "from a sleepy decadent trading post of the American Fur Company to a bustling garrison of the United States Army."

Mattes, Merrill J. "Revival at Old Fort Randall." *Military Engineer*, XLIV (March-April 1952), 88-93. Presents a brief history of this South Dakota fort (1856).

Mattison, Ray H. "Fort Rice—North Dakota's First Missouri River Military Post." *North Dakota History*, 20 (April 1953), 87-108. Includes a section on the fort's physical structures.

Mattison, Ray H. "Old Fort Stevenson." *North Dakota History*, 18 (April-July 1951), 53-92.

Mattison, Ray H. "The Army Post on the Northern Plains, 1865-1886." *Nebraska History*, 35 (March 1954), 17-43.

Mattison, Ray H. "The Military Frontier on the Upper Missouri." *Nebraska History*, 37 (Sept. 1956), 159-82.

Mayer, Harold M. "The Launching of Chicago: The Situation and The Site." *Chicago History*, IX (Summer 1980), 68-79. The founding of Fort Dearborn.

Mayes, William B., Jr. "Did Morphy Blunder: The Closing of Fort Hays, Kansas." *Journal of the West*, 15 (July 1976), 38-48.

Mentzer, Raymond A., Jr. "Camp Baker/Fort Logan: Microcosm of the Frontier Military Experience." *Montana: The Magazine of Western History*, 27 (April 1977), 34-43.

"Milestones in U. S. Public Works: A Salute to the Washington Navy Yard." *APWA Reporter*, 42 (Oct. 1975), 20-21. Describes the Washington Navy Yard as "an outstanding example of the country's early naval public works facilities."

Millis, Wade. "Fort Wayne, Detroit." *Michigan History Magazine*, XX (Winter 1936), 21-49. Describes the general plan of this fort built following the war of 1812.

Milner, P. M. "Fort Macomb." *Publications of the Louisiana Historical Society*, VII (1913-14), 143-52.

Montgomery, Frank C. (Mrs.). "Fort Wallace and Its Relation to the Frontier." *Kansas State Historical Society Collections*, XVII (1926-1928), 189-283. On "the last and most western military post of any permanency in Kansas." Established in 1865, it was first called "Camp Pond Creek."

Moorhead, Max L. *The Presidio: Bastion of the Spanish Borderlands*. Norman: University of Oklahoma Press, 1975. xiii + 288 pp. Illustrations, maps, notes, and bibliography. Deeply researched and well-written account of the influence of presidios on Spanish civilization in the Southwest. Good descriptions of the forts' design and construction are included.

Morgan, Allen E. "Naval Reserve Aviation Base, Long Beach, 1929-1942." *American Aviation Historical Society Journal*. See chapter on "Airways and Airports."

Morgan, James Dudley. *Historic Fort Washington*. Washington, D. C.: n. p., 1904. 19 pp. Illustrations. Largely a collection of correspondence.

Markham, E. M. "Past, Present and Future of Fort Humphreys." *Military Engineer*, XXI (March-April 1929), 125-28. Well-written sketch of the fort located on the Potomac River near Mount Vernon.

Morrison, Charles. "Frontier Forts in the South Branch Valley." *West Virginia History*, XXXVI (Jan. 1975), 131-39. Good compilation of eighteenth-century forts.

Morrison, James Lunsford, Jr. "The United States Military Academy, 1833-1866: Years of Progress and Turmoil." Doctoral dissertation, Columbia University, 1970. 377 pp.

Morrison, William Brown. *Military Posts and Camps in Oklahoma*. Oklahoma City: Harlow Publishing Corporation, 1936. x + 180 pp. Illustrations, notes, bibliography, and index. A fairly good survey of Oklahoma forts. Descriptive information is provided on barracks and other facilities.

Mueller, Richard E. "Jefferson Barracks: The Early Years." *Missouri Historical Review*, 67 (Oct. 1972), 7-30.

Mullin, Cora Phebe. "The Founding of Fort Hartsuff." *Nebraska History Magazine*, XII (April-June 1931), 129-40. Includes a good collection of photos and maps.

Mullin, John R. "Fortifications in America: Application in the New World." *Periodical*, 6 (Spring 1974), 10-18.

Mullin, John R. "Fortifications in America: Invention and Reality." *Periodical*, 6 (Fall 1974), 23-36.

Murphy, Lawrence R. "Cantonment Burgwin, New Mexico, 1852-1860." *Arizona and the West*, 15 (Spring 1973), 5-26.

Murphy, William B. "Beginnings of Hickman Field." *American Aviation Historical Society Journal*. See chapter on "Airways and Airports."

Murray, Robert A. "Cantonment Reno/Fort McKinney No. 1—New Views of an Old Wyoming Army Post." *Annals of Wyoming*, 48 (Fall 1976), 275-79.

Murray, Robert A. "Fort Fred Steele: Desert Outpost on the Union Pacific." *Annals of Wyoming*, 44 (Fall 1972), 139-206. Shows how its history is "closely interwoven with the story of the Union Pacific Railroad" in Wyoming.

Murray, Robert A. *Military Posts in the Powder River Country of Wyoming, 1865-1894*. Lincoln: University of Nebraska Press, 1968. xii + 189 pp. Illustrations, maps, diagrams, notes, appendices, bibliography, and index. A perceptive history of Fort Reno, Fort Philip Kearny, and others in the Powder River Country. The book sets forth the geographical context in which the forts functioned, summarizes their structural history, and discusses the major military operations that occurred near them.

Murray, Robert A. "Trading Posts, Forts and Bridges of the Casper Area—Unraveling the Tangle on the Upper Platte." *Annals of Wyoming*, 47 (Spring 1975), 4-30.

Myers, Lee. "Fort Webster on the Mimbres River." *New Mexico Historical Review*, XLI (Jan. 1966), 47-57. Pedestrian fort history.

Myers, Lee. "Military Establishments in Southwestern New Mexico: Stepping Stones to Settlement." *New Mexico Historical Review*, XLIII (Jan. 1968), 5-48.

Nankivell, John H. "Fort Crawford, Colorado, 1880-1890." *Colorado Magazine*, XI (Jan. 1934), 54-64. Offers good descriptions of the facilities at this short-lived fort.

Nankivell, John H. "Fort Garland, Colorado." *Colorado Magazine*, XVI (Jan. 1939), 13-29. Good description of a fort built on the West slope of the Rocky Mountains in southern Colorado.

Nelson, Harold L. "Military Roads for War and Peace—1791-1836." *Military Affairs*. See chapter on "Roads, Streets, and Highways.

Ney, Virgil. "Daily Life at Fort Atkinson—on the Missouri—1820-27." *Military Review*, 57 (Jan. 1977), 36-48.

Ney, Virgil. "Prairie Generals and Colonels at Cantonment Missouri and Fort Atkinson." *Nebraska History*, 56 (Spring 1975), 51-76.

Nichols, Roger L. "The Founding of Fort Atkinson." *Annals of Iowa*, 37 (Spring 1965), 589-97.

Nichols, Roger L., ed. *The Missouri Expedition, 1818-1820: The Journal of Surgeon John Gale with Related Documents*. Norman: University of Oklahoma Press, 1969. xxvii + 145 pp. Illustrations, maps, notes, appendix, bibliography, and index. An excellent journal of the first major expedition up the Missouri River after Lewis and Clark. It presents a stark and unpleasant description of life at army posts during the early nineteenth century.

Norris, Walter B. *Annapolis: Its Colonial and Naval Story*. New York: Thomas Y. Crowell, 1925. xiv + 323 pp. Illustrations, appendices, and index.

Nothstein, Ira Oliver. "Rock Island and the Rock Island Arsenal." *Journal of the Illinois State Historical Society*, XXXIII (Sept. 1940), 304-40. Undocumented and poorly written history of the arsenal.

Nye, W. S. *Carbine and Lance: The Story of Old Fort Sill*. Norman: University of Oklahoma Press, 1937. xviii + 441 pp. Illustrations, maps, notes, appendices, glossary, and index. Includes some sketchy material on construction of facilities at the post during various phases of its history.

Olphant, J. Orin. "Old Fort Colville." 2 parts. *Washington Historical Quarterly*, XVI (Jan. 1925; April 1925), Jan.: 29-48; April: 83-101. Fort built in 1825 that was the most important interior trading post of the Hudson's Bay Company.

Oliva, Leo E. "Fort Atkinson on the Santa Fe Trail, 1850-1854." *Kansas Historical Quarterly*, 40 (Summer 1974), 212-33.

Olmsted, Merle. "Langley Field 1917-1945." *American Aviation Historical Society Journal*. See chapter on "Airways and Airports."

Onstad, Preston E. "The Fort on the Luckiamute: A Resurvey of Fort Hoskins." *Oregon Historical Quarterly*, 65 (June 1964), 173-96.

Ott, Eloise R. "Fort King: A Brief History." *Florida Historical Quarterly*, XLVI (July 1967), 29-38. History of a fort established in 1827 at present-day Ocala, Florida.

Palmer, Dave R. "Fortress West Point: 19th Century Concept in an 18th Century War." *Military Engineer*, 68 (May-June 1976), 171-74.

Parker, William Thorton. *Annals of Old Fort Cummings, New Mexico, 1867-8*. Northhampton, Mass.: William Thorton Parker, 1916. 56 pp. Illustrations. A pedestrian personal memoir that includes a short physical description of the facility.

Parkman, Aubrey. *Army Engineers in New England: The Military and Civil Work of the Corps of Engineers in New England, 1775-1975*. See chapter on "Waterways."

Pedersen, Lyman Clarence, Jr. "History of Fort Douglas, Utah." Doctoral dissertation, Brigham Young University, 1967. xiv + 461 pp. Illustrations, maps, notes, appendices, and bibliography. Little discussion of physical facilities is included in this history of the fort that overlooks Salt Lake City.

Pierson, Lloyd. "A Short History of Camp Verde, Arizona, to 1890." *El Palacio*, 64 (Nov.-Dec. 1957), 323-39.

Ploger, Robert R. *Vietnam Studies: U. S. Army Engineers, 1965-1970*. Washington, D. C.: Department of the Army, 1974. xiii + 240 pp. Illustrations, maps, charts, tables, appendices, glossary, and index. A thorough, well-written overview of military construction in Vietnam during the rapid build-up of American forces after 1965. In addition to military bases, the Army Corps of Engineers constructed airfields, roads, bridges, and port facilities.

Prance, Lois, and James R. Irwin. "History of Fort Wayne." *Michigan History Magazine*, XXX (Jan.-March 1946), 5-40. Montgomery C. Meigs superintended the construction of this fort in the mid 1840s.

Price, Anna. "French Outpost on the Mississippi: The Three Lives of Fort de Chartres." *Historic Illinois*, 3 (June 1980), 1-4. From 1718 to 1772.

Pride, W. F. *The History of Fort Riley*. n.p.: n. p., 1926. 339 pp. Illustrations and maps. A comprehensive fort history. The author does a good job of tracing the evolution of the fort's layout and buildings.

Prucha, Francis Paul. *A Bibliographical Guide to the History of Indian-White Relations in the United States*. Chicago and London: University of Chicago Press, 1977. x + 454 pp. Appendices and index. An exemplary finding aid that includes a comprehensive section on "United States Military Posts."

Prucha, Francis Paul. *A Guide to the Military Posts of the United States, 1789-1895*. Madison: State Historical Society of Wisconsin, 1964. xiii + 178 pp. Illustrations, maps, appendices, and bibliography. A useful and comprehensive catalog.

Prucha, Francis Paul. *Broadax and Bayonet: The Role of the United States Army in the Development of the Northwest, 1815-1860*. Madison: State Historical Society of Wisconsin, 1953. xv + 263 pp. Illustrations, notes, bibliography, and index. One of the few histories of the nonmilitary services of frontier soldiers. Excellent discussions are included of the evoluion of fort facilities and the impetus military roads gave to settlement.

Prucha, F. Paul. "Fort Ripley: The Post and the Military Reservation." *Minnesota History*, XXVIII (Sept. 1947), 205-24. A good history of the fort founded on the Mississippi River in 1849 and abandoned in 1877. Excellent drawings of the post are included.

Prucha, F. Paul. "The Settler and the Army in Frontier Minnesota." *Minnesota History*, XXIX (Sept. 1948), 231-46. On general settler dissatisfaction with the permanent army posts built on the Mississippi and Minnesota rivers to provide protection against the Indians.

Ranson, Edward. "The Endicott Board of 1885-86 and the Coast Defenses." *Military Affairs*, XXXI (Summer 1967), 74-84. Well-researched study of the board's activities.

Reed, Bill. "Fort McDowell—The 'Most Unhappy Post.' " *Journal of Arizona History*, 17 (Autumn 1976), 321-40. Life at a frontier post near present-day Phoenix.

Reed, Rowena A. "The Endicott Board—Vision and Reality." *Periodical*, II (Summer 1979), 3-17.

Richmond, Henry R., III. *The History of the*

Portland District, Corps of Engineers, 1871-1969. See chapter on "Waterways."

Richmond, Robert W. "Developments Along the Overland Trail from the Missouri River to Fort Laramie, Before 1854." *Nebraska History*, XXXIII (Sept. 1952, and Dec. 1952), Sept.: 154-79; Dec.: 237-48. Good descriptions of facilities built along the route.

Riker, Dorothy, comp. *The Hoosier Training Ground: A History of Army and Navy Training Centers, Camps, Forts, Depots, and Other Military Installations Within the State Boundaries During World War II*. Bloomington: Indiana War History Commission, 1952. xiv + 381 pp. Illustrations, map, notes, chronology, and index. Exhaustive history of Indiana's role in the training of soldiers and sailors during World War II. Considerable material is included on the installations that were established.

Riley, Edward M. "Historic Fort Moultrie in Charleston Harbor." *South Carolina Historical and Genealogical Magazine*, LI (1950), 63-74. Good overview of the fort's evolution from the 1770s to the early 1900s.

Risch, Erna. *Quartermaster Support of the Army: A History of the Corps, 1775-1939*. Washington, D. C.: Quartermaster Historian's Office, 1962. xvii + 796 pp. Illustrations, maps, charts, notes, bibliography, and index. Although this excellent history concentrates on the supply mission of the Quartermaster Corps, scattered throughout the book are discussions of its role in fort construction and transportation.

Rister, Carl. "Fort Griffin." *West Texas Historical Association Year Book*, I (June 1925), 15-24. Includes a list of Texas frontier forts built in the 1850s and 1860s and later abandoned.

Rister, Carl Coke. *Fort Griffin on the Texas Frontier*. Norman: University of Oklahoma Press, 1956. xv + 216 pp. Illustrations, notes, and index. Excellent military history that unfortunately includes little discussion of the fort's physical structure.

Rister, Carl Coke. *The Southwestern Frontier, 1865-1881*. Cleveland: Arthur H. Clark Company, 1928. 336 pp. Illustrations, maps, notes, bibliography, and index. Includes some material on life at frontier posts as well as descriptions of officers quarters and other facilities.

Roberts, Robert B. *New York's Forts in the Revolution*. Cranbury, N. J.: Associated University Presses, 1980. 521 pp. Illustrations, maps, notes, glossary, bibliography, and index. An inventory with capsule histories.

Robinson, Willard B. *American Forts: Architectural Form and Function*. Urbana: University of Illinois Press for the Amon Carter Museum of Western Art, Fort Worth, 1977. xiii + 229 pp. Illustrations, maps, diagrams, notes, appendix, glossary, bibliography, and index. Beautifully illustrated history of the evolution of fort design and construction.

Robinson, Willard B. "Fort Adams—American Example of French Military Architecture." *Rhode Island History*, 34 (Aug. 1975), 76-96. Excellent fort history. Fort Adams was involved in the largest fort restoration ever undertaken in the United States.

Robinson, Willard B. "Maritime Frontier Engineering: The Defense of New Orleans." *Louisiana History*, XVIII (Winter 1977), 5-62. Excellent case study of fort construction and other maritime defenses.

Robinson, Willard B. "Military Architecture at Mobile Bay." *Journal of the Society of Architectural Historians*. See chapter on "Public Buildings."

Robinson, Willard B. "North American Martello Towers." *Society of Architectural Historians Journal*, 33 (May 1974), 158-64.

Robrock, David R. "A History of Fort Fetterman, Wyoming, 1867-1882." *Annals of Wyoming*, 48 (Spring 1976), 5-76.

Rogers, Fred B. "Early Military Posts of Del Norte County." *California Historical Society Quarterly*, XXVI (March 1947), 1-11. Brief sketches of mid-nineteenth-century California forts.

Rogers, Fred B. "Early Military Posts of Mendocino County, California." *California Historical Society Quarterly*, XXVII (1948), 215-28. A weak descriptive history.

Ruth, Kent. *Great Day in the West: Forts, Posts, and Rendezvous Beyond the Mississippi*. Norman: University of Oklahoma Press, 1963. xv + 308 pp. Illustrations, maps, and index. Presents each of 147 important frontier sites "at the period in its history when it was playing an important role in the development of the West."

Ryan, Carl Willard. "Modern Scott: A History of Scott Air Force Base, Illinois." Doctoral dissertation, St. Louis University, 1969.

Ryan, Garry David. "Camp Walbach, Nebraska Territory, 1858-1859." *Annals of Wyoming*, 35 (April 1963), 5-20.

Sacks, Benjamin. "The Origins of Fort Buchanan, Myth and Fact." *Arizona and the West*, VII (Autumn 1965), 207-26.

Sage, Walter N. "The Place of Fort Vancouver in the History of the Northwest." *Pacific Northwest Quarterly*, 39 (April 1948), 83-102. An important British outpost on the Columbia River from 1825 to 1846.

Sanger, Donald Bridgman. *The Story of Old Fort Bliss*. El Paso: n. p., 1933. 26 pp. Bibliography.

Schene, Michael G. "Fort Foster: A Second Seminole War Fort." *Florida Historical Quarterly*, 54 (Jan. 1976), 319-39.

Schilling, Frank A. "Military Posts of the Old Frontier: Arizona—New Mexico." *Historical Society of Southern California Quarterly*, 42 (June 1960), 133-49.

Schubert, Frank Nicholas. "Fort Robinson, Nebraska: The History of a Military Community, 1874-1916." Doctoral dissertation, University of Toledo, 1977. One of the best fort histories written in the past decade. Schubert's research and analysis chart the fort's evolution and its influence on the society and economy of nearby communities.

Scobee, Barry. *Old Fort Davis*. San Antonio: Naylor Company, 1947.

Scott, Kenneth. "The Sandy Hook Lighthouse." *American Neptune*, XXV (April 1965), 123-27. On its construction (1764) and how it increased the safety of navigation to and from the Port of New York.

Short C. W., and R. Stanley-Brown. *Public Buildings: A Survey of Architecture of Projects Constructed by Federal and Other Governmental Bodies between the Years 1933 and 1939 with the Assistance of the Public Works Administration*. See chapter on "Public Buildings."

Sleight, Eleanor Friend. "Fort Defiance." *El Palacio*, 60 (Jan. 1953), 3-11.

Smith, Carlton Bruce. "The United States War Department, 1815-1842." Doctoral dissertation, University of Virginia, 1967. iv + 235 pp. Notes and bibliography.

Smith, G. Hubert. "A Frontier in Peacetime." *Minnesota History*, 45 (Fall 1976), 116-28.

Smith, Merritt Roe. "George Washington and the Establishment of the Harpers Ferry Armory." *Virginia Magazine of History and Biography*, 81 (Oct. 1973), 415-36. Perceptive analysis of why the armory was created at Harpers Ferry.

Smith, Merritt Roe. *Harpers Ferry Armory and the New Technology: The Challenge of Change*. Ithaca: Cornell University Press, 1977. 363 pp. Notes, Illustrations, bibliography, and index. History of the armory from 1798 to 1861 that illustrates the influence of mechanized production on organization, management, and worker morale.

Snow, Edward Rowe. *Historic Fort Warren*. Boston: Yankee Publishing Company, 1941. 87 pp. Illustrations and map. Virtually useless descriptive history of the facility in Boston Harbor.

Snowbarger, Willis E. "The Development of Pearl Harbor." Doctoral dissertation, University of California, Berkeley, 1951.

Snyder, Frank E., and Brian H. Guss. *The District: A History of the Philadelphia District, U. S. Army Corps of Engineers, 1886-1971*. See chapter on "Waterways."

Spear, Elsa. *Fort Phil Kearny, Dakota Territory, 1866-1868*. Sheridan, Wyo.: Quick Printing Company, 1939.

Stanley, Arthur J., Jr. "Fort Leavenworth: Dowager Queen of Frontier Posts." *Kansas Historical Quarterly*, XLII (Spring 1976), 1-23. Heavily illustrated study of the fort's role as a frontier post, military headquarters, and communications center.

Stanley, F., psued. [Stanley Francis Louis Crocchiola.] *Fort Union (New Mexico)*. n.p.: 1953. xii + 305 pp. Illustrations and bibliography. Popular history of a fort that once existed in northern New Mexico.

Stanley, F. *Fort Bascom: Comanche-Kiowa Barrier*. Pampa, Tex.: Pampa Print Shop, 1961. v + 224 pp. Notes and bibliography.

Stanley, F. *Fort Craig*. Pampa, Tex.: Pampa Print Shop, 1963. ii + 204 pp. Index.

Starr, S. Frederick. "Prehistoric Miami Fort." *Bulletin of the Historical and Philosophical Society of Ohio*, 21 (Jan. 1963), 14-21.

Starr, Stephen Z. "Camp Dennison, 1861-1865." *Bulletin of the Historical and Philosophical Society of Ohio*, 19 (July 1961), 166-90.

Stevenson, David. *Sketch of the Civil Engineering of North America. . . .* See chapter on "Waterways."

Stewart, Ronald L. "Fort Sumner: An Adobe Post on the Pecos." *El Palacio*, 77 (Fall 1971), 12-16.

Strate, David Kay. *Sentinel to the Cimarron: The Frontier Experience of Fort Dodge, Kansas*. Dodge City: Cultural Heritage and Arts Center, 1970. 147 pp. Illustrations, maps, notes, bibliography, and index.

Strate, David Kay. "Sentinel to the Cimarron: The Frontier Experience of Fort Dodge, Kansas." Doctoral dissertation, Oklahoma State University, 1969.

Swett, Morris. *Fort Sill, A History*. Fort Sill, Okla.: 1921. 61 pp. Illustrations. Pedestrian history of the fort near Lawton, Oklahoma.

Tanner, George C. "History of Fort Ripley, 1849 to 1859, based on the Diary of Rev. Solon W. Manney, D. D., Chaplain of This Post from 1851 to 1859." *Collections of the Minnesota Historical Society*, X (Part I: 1900-1905), 179-202. Includes a short description of the fort's location and facilities. The remainder is on weather, schools, life at the fort, mission work, etc.

Taylor, Morris F. "Fort Stevens, Fort Reynolds, and the Defense of Southern Colorado." *Colorado Magazine*, 49 (Spring 1972), 143-62.

Temple, Frank M. "Federal Military Defense of the Trans-Pecos Region, 1850-1880." *West Texas Historical Association Year Book*, XXX (Oct. 1954), 40-60. An adequate historical overview.

Texas Legislative Council. *Historic Forts and Missions in Texas–Restoration and Preservation*. Austin: Texas Legislative Council, 1966. x + 111 pp. Appendix.

The Centennial of the United States Military Academy at West Point, New York, 1802-1902. 2 vols. Washington, D.C.: Government Printing Office, 1904. Vol. I: ix + 922 pp.; Vol. II: iii + 433 pp. Illustrations and bibliographies.

Thomases, Jerome. "Fort Bridger: A Western Community." *Military Affairs*, V (1941), 177-88. Contains little on the fort's facilities.

Thomson, William D. "History of Fort Pembina, 1870-1895." *North Dakota History*, 36 (Winter 1969), 4-39. Includes a good description of the fort's construction on the Red River in Dakota Territory.

Toler, Grace Cabot. "Old Fort Wilkenson." *National Historical Magazine*, LXXIV (July-Aug. 1940), 46-47, 72-73.

Tompkins, Sally Kress. "HABS Survey for Fort Sheridan, Illinois." *11593*, 4 (Oct. 1979), 10-14. A discussion of thirty-one historic fort buildings. The survey resulted in a collection of data on historic resources essential for adequate planning and permanent archival documentation of the facilities.

Toulouse, Joseph H. and James R. *Pioneer Posts of Texas*. San Antonio: Naylor Company, 1936. xv + 167 pp. Illustrations, maps, and figures. One of the few early fort histories that gives adequate attention to facilities, layout, and support services such as water supply and sanitation. Descriptions are given of structures such as barracks, officers' quarters, guardhouses, hospitals, bakeries, stables, and schoolhouses.

Tousey, Thomas Grant. *Military History of Carlisle and Carlisle Barracks*. Richmond, Va.: Diety Press, 1939. xvi + 447 pp. Illustrations and diagrams.

Turhollow, Anthony F. *A History of the Los Angeles District, U. S. Army Corps of Engineers, 1898-1965*. See chapter on "Waterways."

Tweet, Roald. *A History of the Rock Island District, Corps of Engineers*. See chapter on "Waterways."

U. S. Army. Engineer School. Museum. *Geneses of the Corps of Engineers: Including Portraits and Profiles of Its Forty Chiefs*. Fort Belvoir, Va.: Engineer Museum, 1953. 55 pp. Illustrations.

U. S. Army. Engineer School. *Pamphlet on the Evolution of the Art of Fortification*. Washington, D.C.: Government Printing Office, 1919. 107 pp.

U. S. Navy. Bureau of Yards and Docks. *Building the Navy's Bases in World War II: History of the Bureau of Yards and Docks, and the Civil Engineer Corps, 1940-1946*. 2 vols. Washington, D. C.: Government Printing Office, 1947. Vol. I: xvi + 447 pp.; Vol. II: xii + 522 pp. Excellent project case studies accompanied by appropriate illustrations.

U. S. Surgeon-General's Office. *A Report on the Hygiene of the United States Army*. Washington, D. C.: Government Printing Office, 1875. lix + 567 pp. Illustrations.

Unrau, William E. "The Story of Fort Larned." *Kansas Historical Quarterly*, XXXIII (1957), 257-80. Excellent descriptive history of a fortification in present-day western Kansas that provided protection for the Santa Fe Trail. The article includes comprehensive discussions of the post's facilities.

Utley, Robert M. "Fort Union and the Santa Fe Trail." *New Mexico Historical Review*, XXXVI (Jan. 1961), 36-48. Military post built in 1851 near present Clayton, New Mexico.

Utley, Robert M. "The Past and Future of Old Fort Bowie." *Arizoniana*, 5 (Winter 1964), 55-60.

Utley, Robert M. "The Presence of the Past: Fort Bowie." *American West*, 16 (March-April 1979), 14-15, 55.

Van Der Zee, Jacob. "Forts in the Iowa Country." *Iowa Journal of History and Politics*, XII (April 1914), 163-204. A sketchy encyclopedia.

Van der Zee, Jacob. "Old Fort Madison: Early Wars on the Eastern Border of the Iowa Country." *Iowa and War*, 7 (Jan. 1918), 1-40.

Van Hoften, Ellen. *History of the Pacific Ocean Division, Corps of Engineers, 1957-1967*. Honolulu: n. p., 1972. vii + 111 pp. Illustrations, maps, notes, bibliography, and appendices.

Wade, Arthur Pearson. "Artillerists and Engineers: The Beginnings of American Seacoast Fortifications, 1794-1815." Doctoral dissertation, Kansas State University, 1977.

Wade, Arthur P. "Mount Dearborn: The National Armory at Rocky Mount, South Carolina, 1802-1829." *South Carolina Historical Magazine*, 81 (July 1980), 207-31. A solid history of the facility.

Waitman, Leonard B. *Horse Soldiers Forts of the Mojave Desert*. Bloomington, Calif.: San Bernardino County Museum Association, 1968. 56 pp. Illustrations.

Waitman, Leonard. "The History of Camp Cody: The Early History of a Desert Water Hole." *Historical Society of Southern California Quarterly*, XXXVI (March 1954), 49-91.

Walsh, Richard. "Fort McHenry: 1814: The Star Fort." *Maryland Historical Magazine*, 54 (Sept. 1959), 296-309. Well-illustrated history of the Baltimore fort built from 1794 to 1803.

Walton, George. *Sentinel of the Plains: Fort Leavenworth and the American West*. Englewood Cliffs, N. J.: Prentice-Hall, 1973. xii + 210 pp. Illustrations, maps, notes, appendices, bibliography, and index. A solid fort history that concentrates on the nineteenth century.

Watts, Florence G. "Fort Knox: Frontier Outpost on the Wabash, 1787-1816." *Indiana Magazine of History*, LXII (March 1966), 51-78. Excellent history of the fort near Vincennes, Indiana. The study is based on primary resources.

Welty, Raymond L. "The Army Fort of the Frontier (1869-1870)." *North Dakota Historical Quarterly*, II (April 1928), 155-67. Includes interesting material on the siting and construction of early forts.

Wertenberger, Mildred. "Fort Totten, Dakota Territory, 1867." *North Dakota History*, 34 (Spring 1967), 125-46.

Wesley, Edgar Bruce. *Guarding the Frontier: A Study of Frontier Defense from 1815 to 1825*. Minneapolis: University of Minnesota Press, 1935. xiv + 217 pp. Maps, notes, appendices, bibliography, and index. A good discussion of military policies, but little information is included on the facilities.

Wesley, Edgar Bruce. "Life at Fort Atkinson." *Nebraska History*, XXX (Dec. 1949), 348-58. Fort near present-day Omaha occupied from 1819 to 1827. It held the largest garrison of any post in the United States during this period.

Wesley, Edgar B. "The Beginnings of Coast Fortification." *Coast Artillery Journal*, 67 (Oct. 1927), 281-90. A useful overview.

Whisenhunt, Donald W. "Fort Richardson: Outpost on the Texas Frontier." *Southwestern Studies*, V (1968), 1-46. Includes excellent discussions of the fort's buildings and the social lives of officers and enlisted men.

Whiting, J. S., and Richard J. *Forts of the State of California*. Longview, Wash.: Daily News Press, 1960. xxiv + 90 pp. Illustrations and maps. A brief compilation of "descriptions and data relating to the name, origin, and existence of military and semi-military establishments in the State of California."

Williams, Ames W. "The Old Fortifications of New York Harbor." *Military Collector and Histories*, 14 (Summer 1970), 37-45.

Williams, Edward G. "A Note on Fort Pitt and the Revolution on the Western Frontier." *Western Pennsylvania Historical Magazine*, 60 (July 1977), 265-76.

Williams, Edward G. "Fort Pitt and the Revolution on the Western Frontier." *Western Pennsylvania Historical Magazine*, 59 (Jan., April, July, Oct. 1976), Jan.: 1-37; April: 129-52; July: 251-87; Oct.: 379-444.

Wilson, Frazer Ells. *Fort Jefferson: The Frontier Post of the Upper Miami Valley*. Lancaster, Pa.: Intelligence Printing Company, 1950. 36 pp. Illustrations. Role of the fort in the frontier history of the Miami Valley of the Old Northwest.

Wilson, W. Emerson. *Fort Delaware*. Newark: University of Delaware Press, 1957. 32 pp. Illustrations.

Woehrmann, Paul. *At the Headwaters of the Maumee: A History of the Forts of Fort Wayne*. Indianapolis: Indiana Historical Society, 1971.

Woehrmann, Paul John. "Fort Wayne, Indiana Territory, 1794-1819: A Study of a Frontier Post." Doctoral dissertation, Kent State University, 1967.

Womack, Bob. "Stone's River National Military Park." *Tennessee Historical Quarterly*. See chapter on "Parks and Recreation."

Wood, Asa A. "Fort Benton's Part in the Development of the West." *Washington Historical Quarterly*, XX (July 1929), 213-22. Served as "the distributing point for a territory which extended from Wyoming far into the British possessions on the north and west beyond the summit of the Rockies."

Wood, Richard G. "Stephen Harriman Long at Belle Point." *Arkansas Historical Quarterly*, XIII (Winter 1954), 338-40. On the establishment of a military post, Fort Smith, on the Arkansas River in 1817.

Wright, Dana. "Military Trails in North Dakota: Fort Abercrombie to Fort Ranson, With Notes on the History of Fort Ransom." *North Dakota Historical Quarterly*. See chapter on "Roads, Streets, and Highways."

Wright, Muriel H. "A History of Fort Cobb." *Chronicles of Oklahoma,* XXXIV (Spring 1956), 53-71. Most of the article deals with the military activities supported by the fort, which was established in 1859.

Young, Rogers W. "The Construction of Fort Pulaski." *Georgia Historical Quarterly*, XX (March 1936), 41-51. Massive red brick fortification built at the mouth of the Savannah River shortly before the Civil War.

Ziebarth, Marilyn, and Alan Ominsky. *Fort Snelling: Anchor Post of the Northwest*. Minneapolis: Minnesota Historical Society, 1970. 35 pp. Illustrations and maps. Part of the "Minnesota Historic Sites Pamphlet Series." It presents the fort's history and describes the reconstruction and restoration efforts begun in 1966.

Index